AF899969

Palgrave Studies in Economic History

Series Editor
Kent Deng
London School of Economics
London, UK

Palgrave Studies in Economic History is designed to illuminate and enrich our understanding of economies and economic phenomena of the past. The series covers a vast range of topics including financial history, labour history, development economics, commercialisation, urbanisation, industrialisation, modernisation, globalisation, and changes in world economic orders.

More information about this series at
http://www.palgrave.com/gp/series/14632

Mustafa K. Mujeri • Neaz Mujeri

Bangladesh at Fifty

Moving beyond Development Traps

palgrave
macmillan

Mustafa K. Mujeri
Institute for Inclusive Finance &
Development (InM)
Dhaka, Bangladesh

Neaz Mujeri
Centre for Research Initiatives (CRI)
Dhaka, Bangladesh

ISSN 2662-6497 ISSN 2662-6500 (electronic)
Palgrave Studies in Economic History
ISBN 978-3-030-56790-3 ISBN 978-3-030-56791-0 (eBook)
https://doi.org/10.1007/978-3-030-56791-0

© The Editor(s) (if applicable) and The Author(s), under exclusive licence to Springer Nature Switzerland AG 2020
This work is subject to copyright. All rights are solely and exclusively licensed by the Publisher, whether the whole or part of the material is concerned, specifically the rights of translation, reprinting, reuse of illustrations, recitation, broadcasting, reproduction on microfilms or in any other physical way, and transmission or information storage and retrieval, electronic adaptation, computer software, or by similar or dissimilar methodology now known or hereafter developed.
The use of general descriptive names, registered names, trademarks, service marks, etc. in this publication does not imply, even in the absence of a specific statement, that such names are exempt from the relevant protective laws and regulations and therefore free for general use.
The publisher, the authors and the editors are safe to assume that the advice and information in this book are believed to be true and accurate at the date of publication. Neither the publisher nor the authors or the editors give a warranty, expressed or implied, with respect to the material contained herein or for any errors or omissions that may have been made. The publisher remains neutral with regard to jurisdictional claims in published maps and institutional affiliations.

Cover illustration: Neil Cooper / Alamy Stock Photo

This Palgrave Macmillan imprint is published by the registered company Springer Nature Switzerland AG.
The registered company address is: Gewerbestrasse 11, 6330 Cham, Switzerland

For Zinnatoon Nadira and Hasib, Moonzeba, Aliyah and Rayhan who have always been our source of inspiration and joy

Preface

Bangladesh is celebrating its fifty years of independence in 2021, following a nine-month long liberation war with the Pakistani army in 1971. During the war, there was extensive destruction and damage to the economy and all types of establishments and infrastructures in both rural and urban areas across the country. During the period, the economic viability of Bangladesh as a nation was in question. In sharp contrast to the initial pessimism, Bangladesh has achieved much in development over the last fifty years. The acceleration in development over the last three decades has generated significant optimism about Bangladesh's growth potential. The country is much ahead today, relative to the rest of the world, than it was during its independence in 1971. In fact, the country stands at a new threshold, with greater triumphs and achievements in many aspects of social and economic life.

This book examines the unfolding of Bangladesh's development drama over the past fifty years. The drama is full of development surprises and extraordinary resilience of the people in the face of frequent natural disasters and man-made calamities. In reality, the country has moved beyond the multiple development traps that it faced during its fifty-year journey to create one of the world's happiest development stories. Bangladesh achieved an inflection point within a short time. Rising from the ashes, the country has now emerged as one of Asia's most remarkable phoenixes and has become one of Asia's amazing and unexpected success stories of recent years.

The book further explores the diverse experience of Bangladesh's development over the last fifty years and comes up with systematic explanations of its success in socioeconomic development, and assesses future trends. The book asserts that explaining Bangladesh's development is not for the simpleminded; any single mono-causal explanation for Bangladesh's development is bound to fall down in the face of reality.

As with all large-scale historical changes, there are many factors and no definite answers can emerge. Still, the book argues that Bangladesh's economic transformation over the last fifty years has largely been driven by social changes, initiated by women empowerment. A large number of micro-level success stories of innovative, low-cost solutions, such as social development-intensive microfinance programmes targeted towards women empowerment and social mobilisation both by the government and the NGOs; women labour-intensive, export-based garments industry; and the boost to earnings and human capital provided by labour migration and inward remittances that has made significant strides towards educating girls and giving women a greater voice, both within the households and in the public sphere.

The book argues that the decades of the 1970s and 1980s—having slow economic growth and adverse macroeconomic fundamentals—may appear as 'lost decades' in Bangladesh's growth history in terms of traditional development yardsticks. On the contrary, the book asserts that these two decades had played important roles in Bangladesh's development through creating the initial condition state at the micro-level by initiating socioeconomic transformation at the grassroots level by both the governmental and nongovernmental efforts. These created the essential building blocks for developing critical linkages between micro- and macro-levels which were the unique features of Bangladesh's development model that ignited the rapid transformation of the later years. The structural and policy reforms, both economy-wide and sector-specific, carried out since the mid-1980s, prepared the macro-economy to effectively respond to the micro-signals for change and adopt appropriate transformations. These micro–macro transmissions and their role in overall development are seldom acknowledged in the traditional development literature.

While the controversy about the effectiveness of microfinance in poverty reduction in Bangladesh is deep, an adequate assessment of the capacity of microfinance to reduce poverty needs to employ an economy-wide framework. Although microfinance can provide some short-term relief from poverty, it is probably not a long-term solution for poverty, especially in situations where the poor households own small amounts of land or other productive assets. A more important aspect of microfinance is its role in increasing the status of women and their bargaining power in the family as most micro-loans are given to women. The overall picture in Bangladesh society is more positive, where many women have been empowered and became successful microentrepreneurs through using microcredit as their stepping stone.

Bangladesh's agricultural modernisation model characterises the sequencing of chemicalisation and mechanisation. The successful case of land-saving technological change occurred after independence with the Green Revolution through an intensifying of input-based production characterised by the use of high-yielding and fertiliser-efficient new varieties of seed (rice and wheat). The policymakers in Bangladesh initiated this variety of agricultural transformation to increase food production and reduce poverty since the 1970s. Mechanisation has come with higher capital intensity later on, as chemicalisation has enabled the farmers to adopt practices that increased both the application and efficiency in the use of chemical fertilisers and other modern inputs required to produce higher levels of output per unit of land. The pattern of industrialisation, on the other hand, has been closely linked with urbanisation resulting from a host of factors. Bangladesh's urban growth dynamics was thus profoundly influenced by the key or strategic industry sectors (including the ready-made garments). The developments have been more akin to the 'production cities' paradigm in contrast with the 'consumption cities' approach.

We would like to express our deep gratitude to many of our teachers, friends and relatives from whom we have benefited through discussions and exchanges over the years. In particular, we would like to remember Professor Mosharraf Hossain, the eminent economist, professor, scholar who always inspired us whenever we met him; and Professor Sanat Kumar Saha who is a role model for us and always guides our thinking process.

We are grateful to Dr Qazi Kholiquzzaman Ahmed, Chairman of the Institute for Inclusive Finance and Development (InM) and the Palli-Karma Sahayak Foundation (PKSF) for his encouragement and support to complete the study. We also express our gratitude to Sifat-E-Azam, Farhana Nargis, Ifrat Jahan, Sadia Afreen Proma, and J. Joha for providing valuable assistance with research and graphics. Finally, we would like to thank Ruth Jenner and Lavanya Devgun of Palgrave Macmillan for commissioning the manuscript and for their help and encouragement throughout the process of finalising the book. We would also like to acknowledge the very helpful editorial and other comments and excellent support given by Palgrave Macmillan.

Finally, the largest part of the credit for writing this book goes to our parents, brothers and sisters, and other family members; especially to Zinnatoon Nadira; without her valuable encouragement and support, especially through shouldering all responsibilities of the family in the absence of which we could not have written the book. We should also mention the encouragement and support provided by Hasib and Moonzeba as well as Aliyah and Rayhan who, despite their busy activities and different professions, helped us in numerous ways to nurture many of our thoughts and ideas.

Dhaka, Bangladesh

Mustafa K. Mujeri
Neaz Mujeri

Contents

1 Introduction 1

2 General Growth Performance 35

3 Poverty and Inequality 115

4 Human and Social Development 171

5 Creating Opportunities 243

6 Creating Jobs 297

7 Social and Climate Change Vulnerability 377

8 Institutions for Development 445

9 Financial-Real Sector Nexus 493

10 Future Perspectives 535

Index 563

Abbreviations

ACC	Anti-Corruption Commission
ADB	Asian Development Bank
BBS	Bangladesh Bureau of Statistics
BDHS	Bangladesh Demographic and Health Survey
BDP	Bangladesh Delta Plan
BDT	Bangladesh Taka
BGMEA	Bangladesh Garments Manufacturers and Exporters Association
BOESL	Bangladesh Overseas Employment and Services Limited
BSSF	Basic Social Security Floor
BTEB	Bangladesh Technical Education Board
CAR	Capital Adequacy Ratio
CBN	Cost-of-Basic-Needs
CBO	Community Based Organisation
CC	Community Clinic
CCT	Conditional Cash Transfer
CEA	Country Environmental Analysis
CEDAW	Convention on the Elimination of all forms of Discrimination Against Women
CMSEs	Cottage, Micro and Small Enterprises
CSO	Civil Society Organisation
CSR	Corporate Social Responsibility
DFS	Digital Financial Services
DP	Development Partner
DRM	Domestic Revenue Mobilisation
ECD	Early Childhood Development
EDL	Essential Drug List
EEF	Extended Fund Facility

EFA	Education for All
ESAF	Enhanced Structural Adjustment Facility
ESD	Essential Service Delivery
FFE	Food for Education
FGD	Focus Group Discussion
GAP	Good Agricultural Practices
GDP	Gross Domestic Product
GDS	Gross Domestic Savings
GFCF	Gross Fixed Capital Formation
GMP	Good Manufacturing Practices
GNI	Gross National Income
GVC	Gross Value Chain
HCI	Human Capital Index
HDI	Human Development Index
HDR	Human Development Report
HIES	Household Income and Expenditure Survey
HNP	Health Nutrition and Population
HSC	Higher Secondary Certificate
ICT	Information and Communication Technology
ILO	International Labour Office
IMF	International Monetary Fund
InM	Institute for Inclusive Finance and Development
IPCC	Intergovernmental Panel on Climate Change
ISIC	International Standard Industrial Classification
IT	Information Technology
L/C	Letter of Credit
LDC	Least Developed Country
LGED	Local Government Engineering Department
LGI	Local Government Institution
LMIC	Lower Middle Income Country
LNOB	Leave No One Behind
MCEs	Micro and Cottage Enterprises
MCP	Master Crafts Person
MDGs	Millennium Development Goals
MFIs	Micro Finance Institutions
MIC	Middle Income Country
MNO	Mobile Network Operator
MOHFW	Ministry of Health and Family Welfare
MoWCA	Ministry of Women and Children Affairs
MPI	Multidimensional Poverty Index
MRA	Microcredit Regulatory Authority
MSMEs	Micro, Small and Medium Enterprises

NBFIs	Non-Bank Financial Institutions
NCTB	National Curriculum and Textbook Board
NEC	National Economic Council
NEET	Not in Education, Employment or Training
NEMAP	National Environmental Management Action Plan
NFE	Non-Formal Education
NGOs	Non-Government Organisations
NPLs	Non-Performing Loans
ODA	Official Development Assistance
OECD	Organisation for Economic Cooperation and Development
OPHI	Oxford Poverty and Human Development Initiative
OPP	Out-of-Pocket Payments
ORS	Oral Rehydration Saline
PCBs	Private Commercial Banks
PFDS	Public Food Grains Distribution System
PFP	Policy Framework Paper
PKSF	Palli-Karma Sahayak Foundation
PPP	Purchasing Power Parity
PRGF	Poverty Reduction and Growth Facility
PVOs	Private Voluntary Organisations
R&D	Research and Development
RCT	Randomised Control Trial
RMGs	Readymade Garments
RTI	Right to Information
SCBs	State-Owned Commercial Banks
SDGs	Sustainable Development Goals
SEC	Securities and Exchange Commission
SEZs	Special Economic Zones
SNA	System of National Accounts
SPF	Social Protection Floor
SSC	Secondary School Certificate
STEP	Skills Towards Employment and Productivity
SWAp	Sector-wide Approach
TAI	Technology Achievement Index
TFP	Total Factor Productivity
TFR	Total Fertility Rate
TNC	Transnational Corporation
TVET	Technical and Vocational Education and Training
UCEP	Underprivileged Children's Education Programme
UISCs	Upazila Information and Service Centres
UNDP	United Nations Development Programme

UNESCAP	United Nations Economic and Social Commission for Asia and the Pacific
UNICEF	United Nations Children Fund
UNRO	United Nations Relief Operation
UP	Upazila Parishad
WDI	World Development Indicators
WEF	World Economic Forum
WGI	Worldwide Governance Indicator
WHO	World Health Organisation
WIPO	World Intellectual Property Organisation

List of Figures

Fig. 2.1	GDP growth rate. GDP growth has accelerated over the long run	36
Fig. 2.2	GDP per capita growth rate. Per capita GDP growth has accelerated as well	37
Fig. 2.3	10-year moving average of real GDP growth	37
Fig. 3.1	Population age structure in Bangladesh, 1911–2011. (Source: BBS, *Population and Housing Census 2011, National Report, Vol. 1, Analytical Report*, Bangladesh Bureau of Statistics, Statistics and Informatics Division, Ministry of Planning, Government of the People's Republic of Bangladesh, Dhaka)	116
Fig. 3.2	Poverty and extreme poverty in the 2000s. (Source: HIES, various years)	122
Fig. 3.3	International poverty headcount, Bangladesh (2011 1.90 PPP). (Source: World Bank (2019))	124
Fig. 3.4	Income poverty in South Asian countries, 2013. (Source: Based on World Bank, PavcalNet)	126
Fig. 3.5	Multidimensional poverty in South Asia. (Source: Based on data from OPHI)	127
Fig. 3.6	Gini coefficient of income distribution in Bangladesh, 1963–2016. (Source: HIES, different years)	131
Fig. 3.7	Palma ratio in Bangladesh, 1963–2016. (Source: Authors' calculation using HIES data. Note: Due to data limitations, the Palma ratio has been constructed using total household income rather than gross national income (GNI))	133
Fig. 3.8	Annualised per capita consumption growth. (Source: World Bank (2019))	136

Fig. 3.9 Share of Deciles in Total Household Income at National Level, 1963–2016 159
Fig. 3.10 Income Share (Urban), 1963–2016 160
Fig. 3.11 Income Share (Rural), 1963–2016 160
Fig. 6.1 Population in Bangladesh (medium variant, in million), 1950–2050. Source: *World Development Indicators 2015*, World Bank 352
Fig. 6.2 Dependency ratio in Bangladesh, 1950–2050. Note: Total dependency ratio is the ratio of population 0–14 and 65+ per 100 population 15–64; child dependency ratio is the ratio of population 0–14 per 100 population 15–64; old-age dependency ratio is the ratio of population 65+ per 100 population 15–64. Source: World Development Indicators 2015, World Bank 354
Fig. 6.3 Working Age Population in Bangladesh, 1950–2050. Note: Population age 15–64 in million. Source: World Development Indicators 2015, World Bank 355

List of Tables

Table 1.1	Financial performance of microfinance sector, June 2018	13
Table 1.2	Long-term trend of key development indicators in major South Asian countries	22
Table 1.3	Growth performance of major South Asian countries	24
Table 1.4	Structural Transformation in South Asia	24
Table 1.5	Investment rate, trade ratio and remittance inflows in South Asia	25
Table 1.6	Status of tertiary education in selected South Asian countries	28
Table 2.1	Gross regional product of East and West Pakistan, 1950–1970	39
Table 2.2	Disparity in public expenditure between East and West Pakistan, 1951–1970	40
Table 2.3	GDP and its components of Bangladesh	42
Table 2.4	Bangladesh's GDP growth rate at constant prices	44
Table 2.5	Bangladesh GDP and GDP per capita, 1960–2017 (Selected years)	44
Table 2.6	Distribution by uses of GDP at current prices, percentages	45
Table 2.7	Distribution of GDP by industrial origin at constant 2006 prices, percentages	48
Table 2.8	GNI per capita and gross domestic savings in selected developing countries (per cent of GDP)	51
Table 2.9	Average and marginal savings in Bangladesh (at 2006 constant prices)	52
Table 2.10	Changes in occupational structure and sectoral contribution to GDP, 1996–2010	65
Table 2.11	Macroeconomic indicators in different phases of growth	71

Table 2.12	Select macroeconomic indicators during different policy regimes	79
Table 2.13	Estimates of TFP growth in Bangladesh	84
Table 3.1	Poverty headcount rates in Bangladesh	121
Table 3.2	Changes in multidimensional poverty in Bangladesh	124
Table 3.3	Changes in poverty in South Asian countries	128
Table 3.4	Income share (per cent) accruing to different quintiles in Bangladesh	128
Table 3.5	Selected social indicators for poorest and richest quintiles in Bangladesh	134
Table 3.6	Poverty trends in Bangladesh, 2000–2016	136
Table 3.7	Rural and urban poverty in Bangladesh, 2000–2016	138
Table 3.8	Uneven poverty reduction across divisions in Bangladesh	138
Table 3.9	Improvement in non-monetary dimensions of well-being	139
Table 3.10	Income share by Deciles and Palma ratio in Bangladesh	160
Table 3.11	Growth in real per capita household income (average and bottom 40 per cent)	161
Table 3.12	Specific policies for more equitable development in Bangladesh	162
Table 4.1	Education system in Bangladesh	179
Table 4.2	Adult and youth literacy rates in Bangladesh	180
Table 4.3	Expansion of primary education in Bangladesh	181
Table 4.4	Selected indicators of primary schooling in Bangladesh	182
Table 4.5	Selected indicators of secondary schooling in Bangladesh	183
Table 4.6	Gross enrolment ratio in tertiary education in Bangladesh	184
Table 4.7	Gross enrolment disparity by poverty status, 2016	185
Table 4.8	Public and private expenditures in education	189
Table 4.9	Public expenditure by level of education	189
Table 4.10	Distribution of beds in public health facilities	201
Table 4.11	Growth of medical facilities and personnel	203
Table 4.12	Health expenditure in Bangladesh	207
Table 4.13	Household OPP as percentage of total health expenditure in SAARC countries	208
Table 4.14	Household consumption and out-of-pocket healthcare expenditure by quintiles	209
Table 4.15	Trends in mortality and life expectancy in Bangladesh	210
Table 4.16	Infant and under-5 mortality rates in Bangladesh	211
Table 4.17	Neo-natal mortality and probability of dying at age 5–14 in Bangladesh	211
Table 4.18	Child malnutrition in Bangladesh	212
Table 4.19	Recent estimates of child malnutrition in Bangladesh	213

Table 4.20	Gender disparity in child mortality	215
Table 4.21	Gender disparity in nutritional status of children	217
Table 4.22	Maternal mortality ratio in Bangladesh	218
Table 4.23	Rich-poor differential in children's nutritional status	220
Table 4.24	Inequity in child mortality and morbidity	221
Table 4.25	Rich-poor differential in women's nutritional status	222
Table 5.1	Dimensions and indicators of TAI	254
Table 5.2	Addressing employment and labour market impact of economic downturns	274
Table 5.3	Total cost of employment and labour market policies within a social floor	276
Table 5.4	Potential Sources of Development Financing for Bangladesh	291
Table 6.1	Selected demographic trends, Bangladesh	299
Table 6.2	Labour force in Bangladesh, 1974–2017 (in million)	303
Table 6.3	Labour force participation rate in Bangladesh	304
Table 6.4	Employed and unemployed labour force in Bangladesh, 1984–2017	305
Table 6.5	Employment status of employed population	306
Table 6.6	Employed population by broad sectors	307
Table 6.7	Employed labour and level of education	309
Table 6.8	Unemployed population in Bangladesh	311
Table 6.9	Distribution of working hours of labour force in Bangladesh, 2000	313
Table 6.10	Gender wage gap in Bangladesh, 2007	320
Table 6.11	Labour market status of youth population	331
Table 6.12	The STEP framework: Integrated programmes across workers' life cycles	358
Table 6.13	Educational status of Bangladesh's labour force, 2010 (in per cent of respective total)	361
Table 6.14	Labour market needs and opportunities for Bangladeshi workers in selected countries	368
Table 7.1	Major cyclones along coastal Bangladesh	388
Table 7.2	Growth of multicity agglomerations, South Asia	399
Table 7.3	Urbanisation in Bangladesh, 1951–2018	400
Table 7.4	Urban finance in Bangladesh (in million BDT)	416
Table 8.1	Major provisions of land related policies and acts in Bangladesh	457
Table 8.2	Land tenure forms in Bangladesh	458
Table 8.3	Changes in tenancy and related indicators in Bangladesh agriculture	459

Table 8.4	Bangladesh performance in worldwide governance indicators	472
Table 8.5	Present structure of local government in Bangladesh	481
Table 9.1	Outreach of banks in Bangladesh, 2015–2016	497
Table 9.2	Microfinance sector in Bangladesh, 2015	499
Table 9.3	Access to financial services from different markets, 2014–2015	500
Table 9.4	Banking sector indicators in Bangladesh	519
Table 10.1	SDGs implementation: Bangladesh and South Asia	556

CHAPTER 1

Introduction

1.1 The Beginning: A War Ravaged Economy

Bangladesh comprises of the huge delta at the confluence of the Ganges and Brahmaputra River systems in South Asia. The region was a loosely incorporated outpost of various empires centred on the Gangetic plain for much of the first millennium A.D. Muslim conversions and settlement in the region began in the tenth century, primarily from Arab and Persian traders and preachers. The Europeans established trading posts in the area in the sixteenth century. Eventually, the area known as Bengal became part of British India. The partition in 1947 resulted in the formation of East Pakistan (Bangladesh after independence in 1971) in the Muslim-majority area of East Bengal (Schendel 2009).

Historically, Bangladesh was a prosperous part of the Indian subcontinent. Its mild and tropical climate, fertile soil, and ample water favoured the development of a rich agrarian economy. Since the Mughal and the British colonial period, East Bengal emerged as an important primary producer—mostly of rice and jute (see, Sinha 1962; Sen 1973; Islam 2012).

The partition of British India and the emergence of India and Pakistan in 1947 severely disrupted the economic system of East Bengal (known as East Pakistan at that time) with compulsions to create new industrial base and modernise agriculture. Between 1947 and 1971, the people of East Pakistan generally became poorer as Pakistan adopted a discriminatory

© The Author(s) 2020

M. K. Mujeri, N. Mujeri, *Bangladesh at Fifty*, Palgrave Studies in Economic History,
https://doi.org/10.1007/978-3-030-56791-0_1

development strategy based on industrialisation favouring West Pakistan, and resources were diverted from East Pakistan to West Pakistan (present day Pakistan).

With the dominance of West Pakistan and economic, social, cultural, political, and other exploitation of the eastern province, perpetual antagonism flourished between East and West Pakistan highlighting several factors, such as geographical absurdity, constitutional confusion and military takeover, economic disparity, language issues, political factionalism, and military dynamics (see Jahan 1972; Ahmed 1980; Ahmed 1981; Stern 2001). The ever-increasing escalation of the East–West divide led to Pakistan's disintegration and the emergence of Bangladesh as an independent state in 1971. The liberation war of Bangladesh began after the Pakistani military junta attacked the people of East Pakistan on the night of 25 March 1971; and the war continued until 16 December 1971 when the West Pakistani army surrendered to the Liberation Forces.

During the war, there was extensive destruction and damage to all types of establishments and infrastructures in both rural and urban areas across Bangladesh. An estimated 10 million Bengali refugees fled to neighbouring India, while 30 million were internally displaced. The atrocities committed by the Pakistani military constituted genocide and an estimated 3 million martyrs laid down their lives during the war.

The economy of Bangladesh suffered extensive losses, both direct and indirect, during the war. There is no reliable estimate of the economic costs of the war; some estimates put the direct costs at $9.53 billion and indirect costs at $14.08 billion even under the most modest assumptions (Choudhry and Basher, 2002). The war was not a minor event either by absolute or relative measures; and as Bangladesh emerged from the independence war in 1971, it had a devastated economy with little productive capacity; there were pervasive poverty and chronic malnutrition for the majority of the population; a high population growth rate between 2.5 and 3 per cent per year, and the dislocation of about 10 million people who had fled to India and returned to independent Bangladesh by 1972. Further, Bangladesh was still recovering from a severe cyclone that hit the coastal areas in 1970 and caused more than 250,000 deaths. In 1973, Cambridge Professor Austin Robinson wrote:

> *"The structure of the economy as it was in 1968–69, together with the trends of 1959 to 1969 and the growing inability to feed herself, would lead Bangladesh into widening balance of payments deficits, ever-increasing need for inflow of*

foreign capital if it was to be kept going, and ever-increasing debt obligations, which would sooner or later exceed the inflow. That structure cannot survive and needs to be changed..... Even before the massive upheavals of 1971 and 1972 flood, war, crop failure the eastern wing of Pakistan was one of the poorest countries in the world. Income per head was only about $70: with gross national product rising at about 4~5-% a year and population at almost 3%, even this low level was hardly improving. Imports of food were increasing, while earnings from the major export -jute were stagnant. In 1971 and 1972 flood and war caused tremendous damage to the transport system and seriously disrupted agriculture, on which 80% of the population depends for a livelihood. The establishment of political independence meant that the whole machinery of a separate state had to be created. The question now is whether Bangladesh can ever escape its grinding poverty....At present Bangladesh is the text-book example of Malthusian stagnation." (Robinson 1973: i and 46).

Overall, the economic viability of Bangladesh as a nation was in question. In 1972, the World Bank assessed the situation in Bangladesh as: *'Even under the best of circumstances, Bangladesh constitutes a critical and complex development problem. The population is poor (per capita income of $50 to $70—a figure which has not risen over the past 20 years), overcrowding (population density is nearly 1,400 per square mile) and becoming more so (population is growing at 3 per cent per annum) and largely illiterate (under 20 per cent literacy rate)'* (World Bank 1972). In 1976, Faaland and Parkinson termed Bangladesh as the 'test case for development' and stated: *'If development could be made successful in Bangladesh, there can be little doubt that it could be made to succeed anywhere else. It is in this sense that Bangladesh is the test case for development'* (Faaland and Parkinson 1976).

In sharp contrast to the initial pessimism, Bangladesh has achieved much in development over the last fifty years. Further, the acceleration in development over the last three decades has generated significant optimism about Bangladesh's growth potential. The country is much ahead today, relative to the rest of the world, than it was during its independence in 1971. In fact, the country stands at a new threshold, with greater triumphs and achievements in many aspects of economic life.

It is, in this background, that development economists and others are keenly observing the unfolding of Bangladesh's development drama over the past fifty years. The drama is full of development surprises and extraordinary resilience of the people in the face of frequent natural disasters and man-made calamities. In reality, the country has moved beyond the multiple development traps that it faced during its fifty-year journey to create one of the world's happiest development stories.

1.2 Pathway to Development: Exceptions and Innovations

Despite the dire predictions and pessimistic prophecies during the initial years, Bangladesh achieved an inflection point within a short time. Rising from the ashes, the country has now emerged as one of Asia's most remarkable phoenixes and has become one of Asia's most amazing and unexpected success stories of recent years.

Sustained rapid growth has enabled Bangladesh to reach the lower middle-income country status in 2015. No doubt, the upgradation of Bangladesh's development status to a 'lower middle-income country' is a remarkable milestone in the country's economic achievement.[1] In 2018, Bangladesh also fulfilled all three eligibility criteria for graduation from the UN's least developed countries (LDC) list for the first time and is on track for graduation in 2024. To achieve its growth aspiration of becoming an upper-middle income country by 2030 and a high income country by 2041, Bangladesh has adopted the 'Vision 2041' along with longer term development plans.

Thus, from a broader perspective, Bangladesh's development may be considered as a unique success story on many counts. Poverty incidence has fallen rapidly; gender parity has been achieved in primary and secondary school enrolment; the total fertility rate has fallen dramatically; infant and maternal mortality rates have declined sharply; and life expectancy has risen to nearly 73 years (more than four years higher than in India). Bangladesh is one of the few developing countries that achieved most of the millennium development goals (MDGs), and is now on track towards achieving the sustainable development goals (SDGs).

[1] The World Bank divides the world's economies into four income groups: high, upper-middle, lower-middle, and low. The income classification is based on a measure of national income per person, or GNI per capita. For the 2020 fiscal year, low-income economies are defined as those with a GNI per capita, calculated using the World Bank Atlas method, of \$1025 or less in 2018; lower middle-income economies are those with a GNI per capita between \$1026 and \$3995; upper middle-income economies are those with a GNI per capita between \$3996 and \$12,375; high-income economies are those with a GNI per capita of \$12,376 or more. See, World Bank 2019.

The developments achieved by Bangladesh are among the fastest improvements in basic living conditions in modern history; and many development observers are surprised because Bangladesh's achievements do not fit the traditional pathways of human and social development. In this context, Amartya Sen distinguishes between 'income-mediated' and 'support-led' pathways to human development (Sen 1999). The first refers to improvements in social indicators brought about by rapid and broad-based economic growth (as happened in South Korea), while the second is based on high public spending on social development programmes (e.g. the case of Sri Lanka).

However, Bangladesh does not clearly fit into either of the pathways. Economic growth in Bangladesh averaged below 4 per cent till the 1990s and rose significantly only after the 2010s. Similarly, public spending on social development especially education and health has been below the average of even the low-income countries. The average value of public spending on education as a share of GDP during the period of 1979 to 2016 was only 1.7 per cent per year. Similar spending on health averaged below one per cent of GDP during the period. Thus, although Bangladesh's GDP growth has witnessed impressive growth only in recent years, it does not fully explain the country's spectacular achievements in social development. Several countries in both South and Southeast Asia (e.g. India, Bhutan, Vietnam, Cambodia, and Lao PDR) have grown at similar or higher rates than Bangladesh in the last ten to fifteen years, yet Bangladesh's social development clearly stands out compared with these countries.

Alongside the progress in social sector including education, health and gender equity, Bangladesh successfully achieved a growth takeoff that reduced poverty and increased per capita income at rapid rates. The essential preconditions that allow private sector dynamism to fuel economic growth were also progressively ensured during the last two decades. Structural reforms in the 1980s and 1990s led to broad macroeconomic stability and low fiscal deficits. This allowed the banking system to cater to private investment needs and caused a significant rise in the investment—GDP ratio (currently at around 32 per cent of GDP). Successive governments also had considerable success in keeping inflation at a moderate level. Although foreign direct investment (FDI) inflow has been relatively modest, strong performance of remittance inflows succeeded in bolstering the foreign exchange reserves and smoothing out fluctuations in GDP due to varying domestic economic conditions.

Being a relatively more homogeneous country, there are fewer class- and ethnicity-based barriers to social mobility in Bangladesh and hence the benefits of economic growth have tended to reach most of the people in society, including the poor. The stimulus to economic growth has also come from labour-intensive garment exports; a vibrant and dynamic private sector; micro, small and medium enterprises (MSMEs) in manufacturing and services sectors; remittances from migrant workers; and the rise of the new middle class.

Bangladesh's reputation of low-cost, high-quality readymade garments (RMGs) exports has enabled the country to overcome various odds including image crisis and political instability to raise export earnings. With increases in wages in China and India, manufacturing in other industries may also shift to Bangladesh provided conducive policies are put into place. These may include pharmaceuticals, plastic and ceramic goods, leather goods, shipbuilding, and light machinery (such as bicycles and batteries). The rapidly emerging export-based IT sector may also contribute to higher growth.

Diversification of the country's export market can be achieved by increased access to major regional markets, including India and China. India has offered duty-free market access to nearly all Bangladeshi products, and China is likely to expand zero-tariff facilities to almost 95 per cent of Bangladeshi goods. The manufacturing and service industries will also be supported by robust growth in domestic demand, which will come about as Bangladesh reaps a demographic dividend of increased labour supply, lower dependency ratio, increased savings, and an emerging middle class.

1.3 A Unique Neo-liberal Development Model

Bangladesh's transformation from a 'basket case' in the 1970s into one of the most startling development successes of the twenty-first century within a span of fifty years provides a rare example of a neo-liberal development model under which social progress has far outstripped economic growth. The resulting pathway has also attracted the attention of many development analysts and practitioners across the world. In recent years, this so-called 'Bangladesh paradox' has been subjected to closer scrutiny, which evaluates the underlying public policies and their development outcomes applying diverse lenses.

While an early shift towards market-oriented reforms is identified by many as a major contributor to Bangladesh's success, others refer to a political settlement—in the nature of a social contract to protect against the crises of subsistence and survival—which united the elite, the masses, and the development partners in the wake of the devastating famine of 1974 (Hossain 2017). This laid a resilient foundation for human development and the emergence of a consensus across various political regimes during the post-independence period to pursue a pro-poor development pathway. The role of the state has also been recognised as critical in the pursuit of sound macroeconomic policies, disaster management, investments in public health and education, partnership with NGOs, reducing population growth rate and encouraging labour migration. The lessons of the 1974 famine led to a reasonably pro-poor growth and social policy agenda, along with women empowerment and grassroots activism.

In the post-1980s decades, Bangladesh's economic and social development is termed as a 'miracle' since the country's remarkable progress has been achieved under several unfavourable conditions for example weak governance and political instabilities, economic and social inequalities, risks emanating from rapid urbanisation, and frequent exposure to severe disaster risks. Some analysts attribute the country's successful development transformation to three country-specific characteristics: (i) penetration of MFIs and other NGOs into the rural communities that led to relaxed credit and other binding constraints of the rural poor households; (ii) development of the RMGs industry resulting in the rapid transformation of the economy from an agriculture-based to an industry-oriented one; and (iii) significant investments in infrastructure—particularly in roads and bridges—which helped to connect the formerly fragmented spatial economy (Sawada et al. 2018).

Several other studies identify major risks which could derail Bangladesh's upwards trajectory such as rapid development of robotics and artificial intelligence; uncertain global political and economic landscape; and the constant threat of climate change and natural disasters. In order to stay on track, the government needs to address various social, political, policy and institutional challenges facing the economy, including poor governance, inadequate physical infrastructure, skills and educational bottlenecks, demographic burden, dwindling social capital, and lack of transformational leadership (Quibria 2019). It is also suggested that, in the context of graduation of Bangladesh from the LDCs in 2024, there are some important synergies that can be drawn from the graduation journey in the era of the SDGs (Bhattacharya 2018). Obviously, several key analytical issues of the graduation paradigm including smooth transition and structural transformation, and post-graduation challenges and opportunities are important considerations for the future journey.

However, the important question for the present is: how can Bangladesh sustain its development trajectory as it advances into the new stages of development? Economically, a growth model that is dependent upon RMGs exports and migration renders the country especially vulnerable to global economic shocks. Socially, the challenge is how to effectively scale up and sustain the dual approach of state and NGOs service provision especially at the grassroots level. And politically, the individualistic empowerment approach that underpins the microfinance model faces the challenge of institutionalising collective empowerment and creating micro–macro transmissions to generate required impetus for social reforms. These challenges are further exacerbated by ecological challenges stemming from climate change.

One must also realise that the Bangladesh story is much wider than, for example, the RMGs boom, overseas migration bonanza, and the political consensus on social progress among the elites. Now a middle-income country, Bangladesh's successful outcome as one of the world's exciting laboratory for development has also generated lessons well beyond its borders, and Bangladesh continues to carve a pioneering pathway through the risks of rapid globalisation and deepening dangers of climate change. One of the key challenges for continued success for Bangladesh as a 'developmental state' would be to insulate and deepen the existing pro-poor development agenda from the technocratic macro solutions alone without integrating micro contexts of macro outcomes and from the grasping hands of the politicians, allowing chaotic politics to coexist with an effective developmental state.

1.4 Dynamics of 'Development Traps'

Countries at different stages of development usually face a number of 'development traps' that stand in the way of realising inclusive and sustainable development. The traps themselves result from longstanding weaknesses but, as the country progresses, new development challenges are also created. In this sense, as countries advance in their respective development pathways, the weaknesses are exacerbated. As development proceeds, earlier drivers of progress may no longer be sufficient. These include stagnant—or even declining—levels of productivity; persistent and increasing vulnerability of large segments of the population, with unequal access to public services across socioeconomic groups; growing dissatisfaction of citizens with public institutions; and an increasing pressure on natural resources that is deemed to be unsustainable.

Development traps refer to circular, self-reinforcing dynamics that limit the capacity of a country to move forward. The development literature has consistently used the concept of a 'trap' to illustrate certain dynamics that leave a country stuck with a particular development challenge. For example, the poverty trap is understood as 'a self-reinforcing mechanism which causes poverty to persist' and whereby 'poverty begets poverty, so that current poverty is itself a direct cause of poverty in the future' (Azariadus and Stachurski 2005). In a similar vein, the theory of development economics has been built around concepts such as the 'circular and cumulative causation' (Myrdal 1957), which stresses the self-fulfilling nature of poverty traps. There is also the concept of 'unbalanced growth' (Hirschman 1958), which introduced interest in policies that can support economies in moving from a 'bad equilibrium' to a 'good' one (Ray 2007). More recently, a relatively large body of literature has pointed to the 'middle-income trap' that affects a country's ability to sustain long-lasting growth when it reaches the middle-income range (Gill et al. 2007; Kharas and Kohli 2011; Melguizo et al. 2017).

The concept of 'development traps' used in this book refers to a combination of mutually reinforcing factors that could have limited the development of Bangladesh if left unaddressed. Over the last fifty years, Bangladesh has successfully overcome several of these traps while others are to be overcome in future. These development traps have been caused or may be caused by several sets of factors, including 'poverty trap', low-level equilibrium trap, low productivity trap, child labour trap, social vulnerability trap, institutional trap, environmental trap, and middle income trap (see, Collier 2007; Barrett et al. 2018)). As Bangladesh completes fifty years of its development journey, it has successfully overcome many of the above traps and is currently achieving remarkably rapid progress in meeting other challenges. In terms of per capita income, the country has transformed itself from being a laggard to a leader in many indicators of health, education and demographic outcomes (Mahmud 2008).

1.5 Explaining Bangladesh's Development

In sharp contrast to the initial pessimism after independence, Bangladesh has achieved much in development over the last fifty years. The economy of Bangladesh is the 2nd largest economy in South Asia and the 41st largest economy in the world in 2019; and is projected to become the world's 24th largest economy by 2033. Further, it is classified among the emerging market middle-income economies and a frontier market. Since independence, Bangladesh has become both a challenge and an inspiration of development policy. The growth story has been extraordinary so far. At the same time, the country is at an important juncture, when with right policies and timely action, it can quickly move up the middle income ladder.

This book explores the diverse experience of Bangladesh's development over the last fifty years and comes up with systematic explanations of its success in socioeconomic development, and assesses future trends on the basis of past experiences. It is widely acknowledged that Bangladesh provides one of the most striking examples in the study of present day development along with rapid growth and catching up. The analysis highlights the development traps that Bangladesh faced during its journey and the ones that may have to be faced in the coming decades for moving towards prosperity. The book asserts that explaining Bangladesh's development is not for the simpleminded; any single mono-causal explanation for Bangladesh's development is bound to fall down in the face of reality.

In this context, the question is: Why has Bangladesh succeeded in making this quiet transformation? As with all large-scale historical changes, there are many factors and no definite answers are likely to emerge. Still, one might argue that Bangladesh's economic transformation over the last fifty years has largely been driven by social changes, probably initiated by women empowerment. A large number of micro-level success stories of innovative, low-cost solutions, such as social development-intensive microfinance programmes targeted towards women empowerment and social mobilisation both by the government and the NGOs; women labour-intensive, export-based garments industry; and the boost to earnings and human capital provided by labour migration and inward remittances that has made significant strides towards educating girls and giving women a greater voice, both within the households and in the public sphere.

Bangladesh has also ripped large dividends through supporting grassroots initiatives in financial inclusion, the positive effects of which are visible in financial transactions. Among the Bangladeshi adults with bank accounts, 34.1 per cent have made digital transactions in 2017, compared with an average of 27.8 per cent for South Asia (World Bank 2018). Moreover, only 10.4 per cent of Bangladeshi bank accounts are 'dormant' (meaning that there were no deposits or withdrawals in the previous year), compared with 48 per cent of Indian bank accounts.

The relationship between the formal and informal labour markets in Bangladesh and the role of the informal sector in stimulating economic growth has also been significant. Although the informal sector accounts for the majority of employment (more than 85 per cent) in Bangladesh, the contribution of this sub-sector to the larger economy is not well recognised. The traditional view is that the labour markets are segmented; the informal sector provides subsistence income, and a pool of surplus labour for the formal sector. This is likely to disappear as the economy develops. However, informality in Bangladesh has also provided growth opportunities to the MSMEs and small entrepreneurs. Thus the developmental role of formal and informal sectors in Bangladesh has not been mutually exclusive; multiple relationships between formal and informal enterprises have developed, supportive of mutual growth. This labour market flexibility has also offered a better environment for the formal enterprises to achieve economies of scale and create a large number of jobs such as in the RMGs industry. Thus, Bangladesh's development over the last fifty years rests on a number of micro-foundations spread over both social and economic fundamentals.[2]

The book argues that the decades of the 1970s and 1980s—having slow economic growth and adverse macroeconomic fundamentals—may appear as 'lost decades' in Bangladesh's growth history in terms of traditional development yardsticks. On the contrary, these two decades had played important roles in Bangladesh's development through creating the

[2] While explaining development with micro-foundations, it is important to recognise that aggregate development is something more than mere sum of its components. Always, there exist some emergent properties at the aggregate level. In this context, King's metaphor of 'bridge' may be more appropriate to characterise the relationship between two sub-components. See, King 2012. Bidirectional causality between the two may be clearly visible. Micro-level decision making needs macro concepts as inputs. In addition, individual preferences are influenced by macroeconomic phenomena such as recessions and financial crises. Also, a large part of individual preferences are socially constructed. Therefore, not every element of development needs to have micro-foundations; and hence seeking across-the-board micro-foundation or every elements of development may be a futile exercise.

initial condition state at the micro-level by initiating socioeconomic transformation at the grassroots level by both the government (e.g. public works, safety nets, microcredit, and other social transformation programmes) and private (e.g. NGOs and their 'microcredit plus plus' and other social development programmes) efforts. These created the essential building blocks for developing critical linkages between micro- and macro-levels which were the unique features of Bangladesh's development model that ignited the rapid transformation of the later years. Further, the structural and policy reforms, both economy-wide and sector-specific, carried out during the mid-1980s, prepared the macroeconomy to effectively respond to the micro-signals for change and adopt appropriate transformations. These micro–macro transmissions and their role in overall development are seldom acknowledged in the traditional development literature.

In Bangladesh, microfinance to the poor (especially poor women) for undertaking income generating activities is widely treated as virtuous and is seen by many as valuable in the country's poverty reduction efforts. It is also argued that microfinance is a relatively efficient means for assisting the poor (Becker and Posner 2009). These views, however, have not gone unchallenged. Although the interest rates on micro-loans are relatively high, this is seen as a positive mechanism for rationing the limited volume of microfinance available to the borrowers who can earn sufficient returns to cover the costs. In practice, this self-selection process is far from perfect; because the poor may borrow in desperation and become locked into a vicious cycle of indebtedness. There may exist moral hazard problems as well (Banerjee and Jackson 2017). However, microfinance has expanded quite extensively in rural Bangladesh covering 35.2 million borrowers with a total loan disbursement of BDT 1494.4 billion and a savings of BDT 490 billion in 2018 (Table 1.1).

While the controversy about the effectiveness of microfinance in poverty reduction in Bangladesh is deep, an adequate assessment of the capacity of microfinance to reduce poverty needs to employ an economy-wide framework. Although microfinance can provide some short-term relief from poverty, it is probably not a long-term solution for poverty, especially in situations where the poor households own small amounts of land or other productive assets. In modern agriculture, there exist strong positive economies of scale which small farms are unlikely to tap to the required extent and benefit in the long term. The non-farm economic

Table 1.1 Financial performance of microfinance sector, June 2018

	No. of members, million	*No. of borrowers, million*	*Total loan outstanding, billion BDT*	*Total savings, billion BDT*	*Total loan disbursement, billion BDT*
MRA licensed NFIs	31.2	25.4	673.90	262.95	1201.91
Grameen Bank	8.3	8.3	152.19	205.39	243.21
Government departments/ agencies/ special programmes	1.4	1.0	26.87	12.93	27.68
Public and private banks	0.9	0.5	26.05	8.75	21.60
Total	41.8	35.2	879.01	490.02	1494.40

Source: Microcredit Regulatory Authority, Annual Report, 2018

opportunities may also remain limited in the absence of strong overall economic growth.

A more important aspect of microfinance is its role in increasing the status of women and their bargaining power in the family as most micro-loans are given to women (more than 90 per cent in Bangladesh). Although there exists counter evidence that increased access to microfinance does not improve the health and educational status of women, nor increase the availability of consumer goods to them, and fails to enhance their role in decision making within the household (e.g. Banerjee et al. 2015), these results may be context-specific, situational, and dependent on the nature of the patriarchy in society. If men have strong control over all finances in the household, micro-loans can do little to empower women. The overall picture in Bangladesh society is, however, more positive, where many women have been empowered and became successful microentrepreneurs through using microcredit as their stepping stone.

Over the years, civic organisations and NGOs worked with the local government institutions in Bangladesh to effect transformative change at the grassroots level and create linkages with the upwards—not just with the government initiatives, but also to transform underlying behaviours and ideas that underpin social development. In the aggregate, these micro efforts were powerful enough to create rapid social outcomes. As a result, Bangladesh's key development indicators leap-frogged past many wealthier countries in the region during the 2000s.

1.6 Uniqueness of Structural Transformation

The modern concept of structural transformation has three important dimensions (Herrendorf et al. 2013; Sumner 2017). These are: sectoral, factoral, and integrative. The sectoral dimension relates to the inter- and intra-reallocation of sectoral activity towards higher productivity. This includes the traditional measures of structural transformation, notably shares of GDP and employment. The factoral aspects are about the composition or drivers of economic growth in terms of factors of production and productivity. Underlying this are the issues of demography. On the other hand, the integrative aspect of structural transformation relates to the characteristics of global integration in terms of trade and investment pattern.

Bangladesh's structural transformation process since independence, as discussed in later chapters, has been very distinct on several counts. As traditionally happens, labour at the aggregate level did not move from agriculture into manufacturing and services sectors in the first phase followed by labour movement from agriculture and manufacturing into services. In Bangladesh, the share of services sector in output has been high at relatively low income per capita.

At the sectoral level, Bangladesh's agricultural modernisation trajectory since independence has been relatively rapid, leading it to shift from an ag-based to a transition country in only fifteen years (from the mid-1990s to 2010). This shift resembles the one that China experienced ten years earlier, from the mid-1980s to 2000. In fact, Bangladesh's agricultural modernisation model characterises the sequencing of chemicalisation and mechanisation. The successful case of land-saving technological change occurred after independence with the Green Revolution through an intensifying of input-based production characterised by the use of high-yielding and fertiliser-efficient new varieties of seed (rice and wheat). The policymakers in Bangladesh initiated this variety of agricultural transformation to increase food production and reduce poverty since the 1970s. Mechanisation has come with higher capital intensity later on, as chemicalisation has enabled the farmers to adopt practices that increased both the application and efficiency in the use of chemical fertilisers and other modern inputs required to produce higher levels of output per unit of land.

The pattern of industrialisation, on the other hand, has been closely linked with urbanisation resulting from a host of factors covering, for example, external market demand (e.g. export-oriented manufacturing products), internal supply of production inputs (cheaper skilled labour and infrastructure services), policy bias towards primate city favouritism, and migration of labour from rural areas and peripheries for better opportunities. Moreover, the spillover effects of industrialisation-induced growth encouraged local suppliers to be agglomerated in the cities and create informal activities that further accelerated the accumulation of labour in the cities. The concentration of low-income groups in the sub-urban areas to reduce the commuting costs attracted the small and informal businesses towards these locations. Bangladesh's urban growth dynamics was thus profoundly influenced by the key or strategic industry sectors (including the readymade garments). Moreover, the impacts on urban locations, livelihoods and the environment were strongly associated with the nature of industrialisation as well as broader growth forces. On the other hand, the lack of regulatory controls and other limitations intensified the negative externalities that emerged from the growth process, resulting in declining quality of life, degradation of the environment, and increased social instability. The developments have been more akin to the 'production cities' paradigm in contrast with the 'consumption cities' approach.

The services sector, on the other hand, has been highly heterogeneous with both tradable and non-tradable segments. The comparison of the sectoral total factor productivities (TFPs) shows that agriculture has been the least productive, followed by services and manufacturing. While sectoral TFP growth differentials can be the key driving forces of labour reallocation, such reallocations are also the result of interaction between distortions in the labour market and sectoral productivity.

The structure of country's employment shows that the industries with the highest labour productivity, namely tradable services and non-manufacturing industries, employ the smallest shares of the labour force. With time, tradable services are becoming more important due to their tradable nature and use of modern technologies such as information and communications technology (ICT); and these are skill-intensive. Specialising in these services therefore generates high-quality employment (with high salaries and learning opportunities), but Bangladesh also lacks the high-skilled labour needed for these services.

Moreover, since only a small fraction of the labour force can be employed in tradable services, structural transformation towards tradable services has not generated enough employment opportunities for the vast majority of the population. This explains why, even if successful, the ICT services industry in the country has not become a driver of growth for the large majority of the labour force. On their part, nonmanufacturing industries enjoy rapid productivity growth, but tend to remain isolated from the rest of the economy. Moreover, these can generate unsustainable growth patterns due to volatile global commodity prices and economic, social, and political inequalities that they tend to produce.

Thus, non-tradable services and agriculture still remain as the main sources of jobs in Bangladesh. However, their low labour productivity is reflected in low wages and limited opportunities for learning and accumulation of skills. The present challenge is to put the workers in these industries in a position to move out of these jobs in order to stimulate more virtuous processes of structural transformation. In addition, non-tradable services are characterised by high informality rates and high job vulnerability. Hence, structural transformation towards these services might fail to generate quality employment and shared prosperity.

At present, in terms of productivity and employment, manufacturing is located between tradable and non-tradable services, as it is less productive but employs more workers than tradable services, but is more productive but employs fewer workers than non-tradable services. Thus, future structural transformation towards manufacturing is the major route to industrialisation in Bangladesh.

As a matter of fact, the key would be to use industrial policy to push the limits of the country's static comparative advantage and diversify into new and more sophisticated activities (Rodrik 2016; Bosworth and Collins 1996). Historical evidence shows that the employment share of manufacturing increases until it reaches a threshold of about 30 per cent of total employment, and then it flattens out. There also exists a strong positive relationship between the share of employment in services and per capita income.

Further, productive structural transformation relies on both horizontal and vertical evolution, and both diversification and technological upgrading are essential to sustain high economic growth (Felipe et al. 2014; Ray 2015). For Bangladesh to sustain higher economic growth in future, the keys are to: (i) promote higher output and employment shares of secondary and tertiary sectors, especially with an expanding manufacturing industry; (ii) ensure both efficiency gains and changes in the economic structure; (iii) adopt manufacturing as the engine of productivity growth, while the services sector will act as the main source of employment; (iv) use productivity gains in agriculture to sustain economic growth, structural transformation, and poverty reduction; and (v) pursue economic growth with structural and productive transformation instead of economic growth alone, indicating that productivity enhancements within sectors should not come at the expense of employment. Such an approach will maximise the impact of structural transformation on decent employment generation, human development and poverty reduction in Bangladesh.

1.7 Bangladesh's Development: A South Asian Perspective

The South Asian development story over the last fifty years is highly perplexing in many respects. After the independence from the British colonial rule in 1947, South Asia showed a better prospect for development than many other parts of the developing world, such as East and Southeast Asia. But in reality, East and Southeast Asia moved ahead very fast; while South Asia was left behind. In fact, South Asia plunged into a deep crisis in the 1970s that made the future prospects look even worse than available predictions (e.g. highly pessimistic outlook on Asia's development prospects by Myrdal 1968).

Over the next fifty years, Asian countries have witnessed a profound transformation in terms of economic progress and living conditions of the people. By 2016, the Asian countries account for 30 per cent of world income, 40 per cent of world manufacturing, and over one-third of world trade, while its income per capita is rapidly converging towards the world average. However, the transformation during the period has been unequal across countries and regions.

East and Southeast Asia, with a population of nearly 2.4 billion relative to 1.9 billion in South Asia, has GDP per capita in US dollar terms which is more than six times that of South Asia. On human welfare indicators such as poverty rates, life expectancy, literacy, schooling and nutrition, most East and Southeast Asian countries are well ahead of South Asia. The 'Asian century' thus looks overwhelmingly East and Southeast Asian, not South Asian. The development gap between the two regions is huge and widening.

In general, East and Southeast Asia provides a much more integrated economic space. Intra-regional trade is more than half of total trade whereas, in South Asia, intra-regional trade is less than 5 per cent. To begin with, the East and Southeast Asian countries provided emphasis on getting the basics right. They followed prudent monetary and fiscal policies, competitive exchange rates, low domestic distortions (e.g. price controls and wasteful subsidies), flexible labour markets, openness to international trade, and investments in education and infrastructure. These economy-wide policies created environments for rapid catch-up growth. In contrast, industrial policies—subsidies, restrictions on imports and foreign investment, and other measures to promote targeted sectors—were much less successful in South Asia. As a consequence, East and Southeast Asia emerged as the global hub for manufacturing, particularly in information technology (IT) products. Further, production is fragmented across the region, but knitted together in vertically integrated supply chains to serve the global markets. This has been critical to the region's industrialisation, growth and global integration.

Bangladesh in South Asia and Vietnam in Southeast Asia are two countries which were liberated in 1971 and 1975 respectively and started their development journeys from similar conditions—war ravaged economies, wide incidence of poverty, and high susceptibility to natural disasters. Vietnam began its economic reforms, Đổi Mới (renovation), to transform its centrally planned economy to a regulated market economy in 1986. The reform programme was comprehensive, and covered all sectors of the economy. Along with domestic reforms, extensive reforms were undertaken to open the economy in 1989 (Thoburn 2009). The impact of these reforms was dramatic. Economic and political reforms under Đổi Mới have spurred rapid economic growth, transforming what was then one of the world's poorest nations into a lower middle-income country in 2010. Vietnam grew at 7.9 per cent annually between 1990 and 2000, and at 6.3 per cent between 2000 and 2017. Between 2002 and 2018, more than 45 million people were lifted out of poverty. Poverty rates declined sharply from over 70 per cent to below 6 per cent (US$3.2/day PPP), and GDP per capita increased by 2.5 times, standing over US$2500 in 2018.

Vietnam's recent success rests on several factors. Obviously, low wages and favourable demographics played a major role. Vietnam invested effectively in developing human resources, especially through promoting quality primary education and ensuring minimum quality standards thereby creating a better educated workforce. Along with political stability, the country also enjoyed the geographical advantage of locating close to major global value chains (GVCs), enabling it to emerge as an Asian manufacturing powerhouse specialising in assembly functions primarily for foreign firms. Vietnam's policy focus has been on attracting FDIs, especially in sectors that facilitate technology transfer, increase skill levels in the labour market, and enhance labour productivity to facilitate moving up the GVCs (Eckardt et al. 2018).

Thus, in the case of Vietnam, the success story lies in pursuing good policies. The core economic strategy has been rapid integration into the global economy, equipped with a diversified portfolio of exports and strong policies to attract FDI. This global economic integration is supported by successful growth in agriculture and a strong role of state-owned enterprises along with rapid growth of the private sector. In addition, Vietnam followed the 'East Asian' model of opening the domestic market slowly while encouraging export growth.

In contrast, South Asian growth has not benefited the poor nearly as much as in East and Southeast Asia. One reason is that South Asia has bigger reform gaps; the countries did not succeed in getting the basics right from the beginning. Public finances were ill-managed with persistent resource gaps and budget deficits. Internal and external trade barriers, price controls and hugely wasteful subsidies throttled most sectors. Most services sector activities were restricted by myriad regulations. The countries could not become FDI-driven export powerhouses in labour-intensive manufacturing sectors such as toys and IT products. Most South Asian countries faced persistent problems with politics, economic policies, governance and institutions. The region could not get integrated into the global supply chains as much as the other region, apart from Bangladesh and Sri Lanka in garments, and India in a few niche manufacturing and services sectors.

Despite the wide diversity between the two regions, there are common discernible patterns, such as rapidly rising GDP per capita driving economic growth, along with rising investment and savings rates and the spread of education providing the underlying impetus to development. Growth was driven by rapid industrialisation, often led by exports and linked with changes in the composition of output and employment. Rising per capita incomes also transformed social indicators of development, including a massive reduction in absolute poverty.

In Asia's economic transformation, the governments played a vital role, as both creating developmental states and catalysts. The success in development boiled down to managing the evolving relationship between the states and the markets, by creating the right balance in their respective roles that also changed over time. While several East and Southeast Asian countries (e.g. starting from South Korea, Taiwan and Singapore; followed by China and later on by Vietnam) could successfully coordinate policies across sectors over time and were able to become industrialised nations in just fifty years, the countries in South Asia could not successfully replicate these states.

Overall, the development experience of Asia, especially of the two most dynamic regions, brings out the core dynamics of the complex development processes of recent decades. The successes, as well as the failures, provide important insights into the economic prospects, especially of the latecomers in the development arena in Asia. These also reflect how the next twenty-five years are likely to unfold for Asia within the changing and evolving global context.

The Asian experience shows that the key is to get the 'policy basics' right for accelerated catch-up growth. The market liberalising process should be bottom-up rather than top-down. These reforms should be home-grown; and come from the national and sub-national levels rather than drawn by the external development partners. The East and Southeast Asian process followed the approach and opened up trade and foreign investment that enabled the emergence and expansion of manufacturing supply chains. For countries in South Asia, the need is to expand labour-intensive manufacturing, for which two issues are critical—attracting FDI and developing export capability. Potentially, this is the big engine of growth and employment for the poor, and the most effective way of linking up with regional and global supply chains. This, however, requires wider reforms in South Asia, especially in the case of labour market deregulation.

Another key area is to boost regional economic integration by reducing cross-border tariffs and non-tariff barriers and by improving cross-border infrastructure. Unilateral, bottom-up liberalisation is more important than bilateral and regional free trade agreements, although the others are complementary. The South Asian region, however, is in a much better shape than it was probably a generation ago. The region has enjoyed accelerated catch-up growth, narrowing the global and regional economic gap.

1.7.1 Growth Dynamics of South Asia

To begin with, around the middle of the twentieth century, the South Asian countries shared some similar initial conditions, arising from a common historical legacy. However, there were several important differences as well—stemming from cultural, geographical, political and historical differences—that had a significant bearing on their subsequent development. Nepal, with a landlocked and rugged, mountainous topography, is geographically very different from the rest of the countries. In contrast, Bangladesh is a plain riverine land which makes the pursuit of traditional rice-based agriculture profitable. The riverine topography also makes the development of physical infrastructure especially difficult. Pakistan, on the other hand, has a combination of rugged mountains and plain land. Sri Lanka, as an island economy, has a fair mix of rugged mountains and plain land. Sri Lanka is unique in the region in having a predominance of plantation agriculture (mainly tea, followed by rubber and coconut). India, the biggest country, has a varied economy with dominance of agriculture and some modern industries.

Despite many differences in the initial conditions, the countries shared one common initial condition that was fundamental to their subsequent developmental transformation. Inspired by the example of India, most of these countries adopted the strategy of state-led development through economic planning in which the state played the role of driver in the development process and heavy reliance on import substitution as the strategy of industrialisation.

During the later years, the development in South Asia was driven by economic growth characterised by high investment-savings rates and rapid industrialisation, often export-led, and associated with structural changes in the composition of output and employment. A number of South Asian countries now seem to have turned a corner and is looking forward to a much better future in the coming decades. This section describes and explains the story focusing on five major South Asian countries—Bangladesh, India, Nepal, Pakistan and Sri Lanka.

It should, however, be mentioned that, although South Asia could not keep pace with East and Southeast Asia, the region has made good progress over the last fifty years—in both economic and social terms (Table 1.2). Most importantly, the countries have succeeded in bringing down the rate of population growth. From an average of over 2.5 per cent per annum, population growth has come down to an average of about 1.5 per cent in

Table 1.2 Long-term trend of key development indicators in major South Asian countries

	Bangladesh		*India*		*Nepal*		*Pakistan*		*Sri Lanka*	
	Annual average during respective periods									
	1961–1965	*2010–2015*	*1961–1965*	*2010–2015*	*1961–1965*	*2010–2015*	*1961–1965*	*2010–2015*	*1961–1965*	*2010–2015*
GDP per capita, 2010 US$	392	882	322	1529	274	649	344	1088	594	3368
Population, million	52.6	157.6	477.8	1272.3	10.6	28.0	48.4	181.7	10.7	20.6
Population growth, % per year	2.9	1.2	2.0	1.3	1.6	1.2	2.5	2.1	2.4	0.8
Fertility rate, births per woman	6.9	2.2	5.9	2.4	6.0	2.3	6.6	3.7	5.1	2.1
Population density, person/sq. km.	404	1167	145	387	74	188	63	246	170	328
Life expectancy at birth, years	47	70	44	68	36	68	48	65	59	71
Gross enrolment at primary level, %	63.6	117.7	80.8	109.1	39.0	139.4	50.8	91.9	94.8	100.7
Share of manufacturing in GDP, %	5.4	18.6	17.1	15.8	3.3	5.9	14.1	13.5	16.5	17.9

Source: World Bank, World Development Indicators (WDI) database

the region, with the exception of Pakistan, where population growth still remains above 2 per cent. There has been an unusually early demographic transition that is still ongoing in most of the region. With the exception of Pakistan, where the fertility rate is still high at 3.7; all the countries of the region are fast approaching the replacement fertility level of 2.0.

Both the slowdown of population growth and reasonable economic growth have ensured that, despite more than a trebling of the region's population size, South Asia has experienced an improvement in living standards that was impossible to imagine fifty years ago. The per capita income has almost trebled in the region as a whole, life expectancy at birth has gone up from less than fifty years (except in Sri Lanka) to nearly seventy years, and enrolment at the primary level has become almost universal in several countries.

Although the South Asian countries shared several similar initial conditions—from their common historical legacy and nearly 200 years of British colonial rule—there were important differences in the initial conditions as well as those that arose from cultural, geographical and other differences. Among the countries, Bangladesh has its own specific characteristics. The country composes of plain riverine land, with its soil fertility regularly replenished by the rich alluvial deposits that come with the annual flooding of several mighty rivers (the Jamuna–Padma–Meghna) and their numerous tributaries criss-crossing the entire landscape. The geography of Bangladesh also favours the traditional rice-based agriculture; but this ease of subsistence agriculture comes with a price as well. Since the past, the subsistence agriculture-based livelihood induced high human fertility, which—once mortality began to reduce with the introduction of modern medical technology and family planning methods—resulted in high population growth and associated disadvantages in a low income economy. The riverine topography also made the development of physical infrastructure especially costly, in addition to making the country susceptible to excessive flooding and devastating tidal surges, which occurred almost regularly, causing immense loss of life, crops, physical assets and infrastructure.

With varying initial conditions, the countries witnessed significant structural changes over time along with economic growth. Table 1.3 shows how growth performance itself changed over the period from 1965 to 2015. Growth accelerated over the two periods in four countries—Bangladesh, India, Nepal and Sri Lanka—but the acceleration has been the sharpest in Bangladesh; the growth rate doubled from 2.7 per cent per year in the first half to 5.4 per cent in the second.

Table 1.3 Growth performance of major South Asian countries

	Per capita GDP growth, % per year		*GDP growth, % per year*		*Population growth, % per year*	
	1961–1990	*1991–2015*	*1961–1990*	*1991–2015*	*1961–1990*	*1991–2015*
Bangladesh	0.1	3.6	2.7	5.4	2.6	1.7
India	2.1	4.9	4.4	6.6	2.3	1.7
Nepal	1.1	2.7	3.3	4.4	2.2	1.8
Pakistan	2.7	1.8	5.8	4.1	3.1	2.3
Sri Lanka	2.8	4.5	4.6	5.4	1.8	0.9

Source: World Bank, World Development Indicators (WDI) database

Table 1.4 Structural Transformation in South Asia

	In per cent					
	Agriculture		*Industry*		*Of which: Manufacturing*	
	1966–1970	*2011–2015*	*1966–1970*	*2011–2015*	*1966–1970*	*2011–2015*
Bangladesh	54.7	16.5	9.1	27.3	5.9	17.2
India	44.6	18.2	23.6	31.0	15.6	16.8
Nepal	68.2	35.3	10.3	15.5	3.6	6.5
Pakistan	38.0	25.1	20.8	21.1	15.3	14.1
Sri Lanka	29.7	8.6	21.8	30.8	16.1	19.2

Source: World Bank, World Development Indicators (WDI) database

In comparison, the acceleration in India is modest, while in Nepal and Sri Lanka, it has been marginal. A deceleration is observed in the case of Pakistan, where the growth rate went down from 5.8 per cent in the first period to 4.1 per cent in the second.

The structural transformation that followed from economic growth can be seen from Table 1.4, where changes in sectoral contribution to GDP are compared between two periods, 1966–1970 and 2011–2015. The share of agriculture declined sharply in all the countries and the share of industry increased. Considering manufacturing alone, the extent of transformation is, however, relatively modest. This is true especially of Nepal, where the share of manufacturing remains at 6.5 per cent only. Even in the other four countries, the share is currently less than 20 per cent, but the rising share of Bangladesh is noteworthy.

Table 1.5 Investment rate, trade ratio and remittance inflows in South Asia

	% of GDP					
	Investment rate		*Trade ratio*		*Remittance inflows*	
	1966–1970	*2011–2015*	*1966–1970*	*2011–2015*	*1981–1985*	*2011–2015*
Bangladesh	11.5	28.3	21.1	45.7	2.7	9.1
India	16.5	35.9	1.2	3.5	1.2	3.5
Nepal	5.3	38.0	14.6	47.8	1.3	27.5
Pakistan	16.2	14.9	24.0	31.5	8.5	6.5
Sri Lanka	16.7	33.3	46.7	51.1	5.4	8.6

Note: Trade ratio refers to the ratio of the sum of exports and imports to GDP. For remittance inflows, Nepal's initial figures refer to the period 1993–1996

Source: World Bank, World Development Indicators (WDI) database

The past structural transformation is underpinned by increases in the rate of capital formation and trade orientation (Table 1.5). In Pakistan, the rate of investment actually declined over the two periods. This partly explains why Pakistan faced a growth deceleration during the period. In Bangladesh, investment rate significantly increased along with India, Nepal and Sri Lanka. As for trade orientation, Sri Lanka is the most trade-oriented country in the region raising its trade ratio, from 46.7 per cent in the beginning to 51.1 per cent at the end. Bangladesh and Nepal also performed very well. In all the countries, the inflow of remittances is high and has increased sharply over the years except for Pakistan. The magnitude of increase is most spectacular in Nepal, where remittances amounted to 27.5 per cent of GDP during 2011–2015. Bangladesh also increased its remittance inflows quite significantly.

The above analysis shows that, despite quite unfavourable initial conditions, Bangladesh started its transition to a higher growth path through a combination of policy interventions and favourable external conditions (see, Osmani et al., 2006). In agriculture, there was a major boost from the liberalisation of markets for agricultural inputs, resulting in expansion of irrigation and increase in the use of fertiliser. The growth in manufacturing was led by the export-oriented RMG sector, which benefitted from a combination of policy reform and other factors. During the late 1980s and early 1990s, Bangladesh embarked upon remarkable trade liberalisation which reduced protection; and this coupled with different incentives offered to export-oriented firms, resulted in a substantial reduction in anti-export bias in the incentive structure. The export growth was also facilitated by external factors such as the multi-fibre arrangement (MFA), which ensured easy access of Bangladeshi garments to the Western markets.

There also took place several growth-inducing changes such as greater mobilisation of domestic resources and increased flow of workers' remittances. Since the beginning of the 1990s, the practice of democratic governance and a relatively stable political environment also created a more favourable environment for development. Most importantly, Bangladesh did manage to evolve some institutional arrangements—though rather weak in effectiveness—that were conducive to industrialisation and development. In particular, the checks and balances of political democracies (in the context of two major political parties sharing the governance since the 1990s) have been crucial to making the government more orientated towards development and becoming more people-friendly.

The NGOs, which started operations after independence led by the Grameen Bank and BRAC, provided microcredit to the vast majority of the rural poor (by now more than 60 per cent of the rural population are covered under microfinance) along with various grassroots human development programmes (through innovative initiatives for providing informal education and healthcare to the poor, women's empowerment, nutrition, and other packages to improve the level of human capital of the poor and lagging population groups in society), softened the binding credit constraint of the poor and strengthened one of the major segments of the labour force especially the rural women. As a result, from an average of 3.8 per cent in the 1980s, the growth rate accelerated steadily, reaching an average of 6.3 per cent during 2010–2015 and further to more than 8 per cent in 2019.[3] Such a sustained acceleration in growth since the 1990s over more than quarter of a century has made Bangladesh an exceptional economic performer in South Asia.

1.7.2 Social Development Performance

The South Asian transformation encompassed not only income growth but also sharply falling poverty and human development. In terms of the

[3] One estimate suggests that, in the absence of microcredit, GDP of Bangladesh would have been around 9–12 per cent lower than it was in 2012–13 and rural GDP would have been around 12–16 per cent lower, depending on the assumptions made. See, Raihan et al. 2017.

international poverty line, the extent of poverty was in the range of 44–62 per cent in the early 1990s in the South Asian countries except in Sri Lanka, where it was less than 10 per cent. Since then, poverty has fallen drastically—to 15 per cent in Nepal, 13 per cent in Bangladesh, 6 per cent in Pakistan, and only about 2 per cent in Sri Lanka (see, World Bank, World Development Indicators (WDI) database).

In other dimensions of human development, impressive gains have also been made. Sri Lanka is well known for its welfare state structure, along with impressive health and educational outcomes. Since the early 1990s, other countries have also made impressive progress, as measured by indicators such as life expectancy, infant mortality, nutritional status, and primary schooling. South Asia (including India) has historically been notorious for having an exceptionally high prevalence of malnutrition, even compared with regions such as Sub-Saharan Africa, which have been economically more backward in most respects than South Asia.

Much has changed in the two decades since then. Although the level of malnutrition is still unacceptably high (referred to as 'Asian Enigma' by UNICEF) in all South Asian countries except Sri Lanka, the progress has been remarkable. The sharpest decline has occurred in Bangladesh, where the prevalence of stunting (which is usually taken as a general indicator of long-term nutritional stress among the population) has come down from around 69 per cent in 1995 to 36 per cent in 2014. Nepal has also achieved rapid improvement. Sri Lanka reduced it to 15 per cent by 2014. Pakistan is an exception to this pattern of sustained improvement; and poor progress in human development in Pakistan is underlined by low public spending on social sectors, which has actually declined as a share of GDP in recent years.

The overall progress in human development in Bangladesh is an exception in the developing world. Bangladesh's performance in health and education makes it a significant outlier—with a much better performance than might be predicted on the basis of per capita income. Further, Bangladesh has been able to achieve these outcomes with a low public expenditure on health and education (as a percentage of GDP) than countries with comparable performance (Asadullah et al. 2014).

This unique feature can partly be attributed to the grassroots activities of the government as well as the NGOs in promoting social development—with much higher intensity than any other country in South Asia. The focus was on women's empowerment; and women were kept at the centre of wide-ranging NGO-activities, involving microfinance, health, education, entrepreneurship development and other aspects of social development. Most NGOs are engaged in women-focused activities. The government provided special incentives for girls' education through stipends—first at the primary and later on at the secondary level. As a result, Bangladesh achieved gender parity in schooling much sooner than the rest of South Asia except Sri Lanka. The advancement in girls' education, along with the general empowerment of women, helped the country to achieve exceptional performance in health, nutrition, and other areas of human development.

Despite spectacular performance of Bangladesh and other South Asian countries in general, the critical issue is to face the challenges and the development traps that these countries are likely to face in their next stages of development. The critical challenges are the global competition that they will have to face in the increasingly globalised world and improving the skill base of the labour force to harness the potentials of technological revolution. Obviously, in all South Asian countries, the current level of human capital is very low by international standards as reflected in the low ratio of young people with access to tertiary education (Table 1.6).

Further, the region faces a number of common challenges, including rising inequality in all economic and social aspects, slow growth in the formal sector creating excessive dependence on low quality jobs, and rapid urbanisation which is becoming increasing unsustainable under present conditions. Further, the problem of climate change is likely to have far-reaching implications for all countries in the region, especially Bangladesh which is highly vulnerable to climate change impacts. Nevertheless, Bangladesh still seems to be the most favourably placed country in the region, and is highly likely to sustain the relatively rapid pace of socioeconomic development that the country has experienced in the past decades.

Table 1.6 Status of tertiary education in selected South Asian countries

	Gross enrolment in %	
	1981–1985	*2011–2015*
Bangladesh	4.3	13.4
India	5.5	24.7
Nepal	3.4	15.5
Pakistan	2.5	9.8
Sri Lanka	3.7	18.1

Source: World Bank, World Development Indicators (WDI) database

1.8 Structure of the Book

This book explores the diverse experience of Bangladesh's development over the last fifty years and come up with systematic explanations of its success in socioeconomic development, and assesses future trends on the basis of past experiences. It is widely acknowledged that Bangladesh provides one of the most striking examples in the study of present day development along with rapid growth and catch up. The analysis highlights the development traps that Bangladesh faced during its journey and the ones that may have to be faced in the coming decades for moving towards prosperity.

Capital accumulation is an ingredient of every conceivable development strategy. But high rate of investment is no guarantee for sustained growth of per capita output or total factor productivity. If the capacity to absorb investment is lacking, mobilising resources for investment results in waste and inefficiency. Human capital is also important in successful development experiences. But great success may be achieved in expanding the education system, while economic growth may stagnate or too much emphasis on institutions may result in 'institutional fundamentalism' such that failures of reform can be explained away, because reform has never gone far enough, or the difficulty of achieving institutional reform becomes an excuse for inaction.

The book is structured in ten chapters. Chapter 2 examines Bangladesh's growth dynamics since independence to offer perspectives on its growth prospects. The analysis of the long-term growth patterns is carried out in several ways. We decompose GDP growth across sectors—agriculture, industry and services; and across uses—consumption, investment, exports, and imports. We analyse the proximate factors that determine long-term GDP growth, such as capital, labour, productivity growth, trade openness, size of the external market, and institutions. Chapter 3 narrates the experience of Bangladesh's fight against poverty and deprivation including inequality. The analysis highlights that, for the medium term, Bangladesh needs to create effective economic institutions and proper policy incentives, while also pursuing sound macroeconomic policies and efficiency-enhancing reforms over time. The key for Bangladesh is to build a robust middle class and reduce extreme poverty and social marginalisation for creating a more equitable society.

Chapter 4 highlights on building human capabilities. Since independence, Bangladesh's development agenda incorporates a social development lens through adoption of an inter-sectoral approach and engaging with non-government and other actors in society. In recent years, the inclusion of the Sustainable Development Goals (SDGs) agenda within the policy framework has further contributed towards moving away from a technical approach for increasing human development towards an equity/inclusion approach that focuses on 'leaving no one behind'. These developments have put an increasing emphasis on social norms and understanding of social institutions, including political analysis.

Chapter 5 examines the issue of resetting priorities for adopting catching up strategies and refocusing strategic thrusts on structural transformation that complements export-led growth with strengthened role of domestic productive capacity, diversification of economic activities, improved technological capacity, and strengthened measures to stimulate a more inclusive and equitable development process. Chapter 6 is devoted to the analysis of the labour market and job creation. Bangladesh will have to create an increasing number of jobs in the coming decades to accommodate population growth, shifts in the age and sex composition of the population, changing age- and sex-specific labour force participation rates, rapid urbanisation and other socioeconomic changes.

Chapter 7 examines social vulnerability and exclusion in Bangladesh encompassing a broad set of concerns. People may be excluded from many domains of life—social, economic, political, civil or spatial—and the relative importance of each domain depends on the local contexts. The analysis maintains that Bangladesh has a reasonably good foundation on which social protection can be strategically scaled up to become a key component of poverty reduction and growth. Chapter 8, on the other hand, deals with the challenging issues of developing institutions for development in Bangladesh. The analysis maintains that the future development path of Bangladesh will significantly depend upon the quality of its economic institutions. Since the performance of economic institutions primarily reflects the nature of collective choices made by political institutions and the distribution of political power, the choice of Bangladesh's future development would require an understanding of why political institutions create bad economic institutions and what instruments are available to push the society to move from the bad to a good political, and consequently good economic, institutions.

The focus of Chap. 9 is on strengthening the financial-real sector nexus in Bangladesh. For transiting towards a high income Bangladesh, the analysis advocates for a developmental approach to financial sector growth, while at the same time attending to prudent regulations. Finally, Chap. 10 deals with Bangladesh's future perspectives. It is true that Bangladesh has shown remarkable catching-up records in recent years through raising economic growth and fostering overall development, but many development traps remain in its future journey. For the medium term, the analysis highlights four major concerns: First, design necessary domestic policies and institutions to ensure that the benefits of economic growth are more broadly and equitably shared within the society. Second, institutionalise deliberate efforts such that Bangladesh can derive greater benefits from the catching-up process. Third, put priority to move on technological—rather than factor-intensive mode of production—in order to close the development gaps. Fourth, provide more emphasis on policy coherence especially in agriculture.

References

Ahmed, E. 1980. *Bureaucratic Elites in Segmented Economic Growth: Pakistan and Bangladesh*. Dhaka: University Press Limited.

Ahmed, R. 1981. *The Bengal Muslims 1871–1906: A Quest for Identity*. Delhi: Oxford University Press.

Asadullah, M.N., A. Savoia, and W. Mahmud. 2014. Paths to Development: Is There a Bangladesh Surprise? *World Development* 62: 138–154.

Azariadus, C., and J. Stachurski. 2005. *'Poverty Traps', Chapter 5 in Handbook of Economic Growth, Volume 1, Part A: 295–384*. Amsterdam: Elsevier.

Banerjee, S.B., and L. Jackson. 2017. Microfinance and the Business of Poverty Reduction: Critical Perspectives from Rural Bangladesh. *Human Relations* 70 (1): 63–91.

Banerjee, A., D. Karlan, and J. Zinman. 2015. Six Randomized Evaluations of Microcredit: Introduction and Further Steps. *American Economic Journal: Applied Economics* 7 (1): 1–21.

Barrett, C.B., M.R. Carter, and J.P. Chavas, eds. 2018. *The Economics of Poverty Traps*. Chicago: University of Chicago Press.

Becker, G.S., and R.A. Posner. 2009. *Uncommon Sense: Economic Insights, from Marriage to Terrorism*. Chicago: University of Chicago Press.

Bhattacharya, D., ed. 2018. *Bangladesh's Graduation from the Least Developed Countries Group: Pitfalls and Promises, Routledge Research on Asian Development*. London: Routledge.

Bosworth, B.P., and S.M. Collins. 1996. The Economic Growth in East Asia: Accumulation Versus Assimilation. *Brookings Papers on Economic Activity* 27 (2): 135–204.

Choudhry, S. and S. Basher. 2002. *The Enduring Significance of Bangladesh's War of Independence: An Analysis of Economic Costs and Consequences, Journal of Developing Areas*, 36 (1): 41–55.

Collier, P. 2007. *The Bottom Billion: Why the Poorest Countries Are Failing and What Can Be Done About It.* Oxford: Oxford University Press.

Eckardt, S., D. Mishra, and V. Dinh. 2018. Vietnam's Manufacturing Miracle: Lessons for Developing Countries, *Brookings,* April 17. https://www.brookings.edu/blog/future-development/2018/04/17/vietnams-manufacturing-miracle-lessons-for-developing-countries/.

Faaland, J., and J.R. Parkinson. 1976. *Bangladesh: The Test Case for Development, C.* London: Hurst and Company.

Felipe, J., A. Mehta, and C. Rhee. 2014. Manufacturing Matters…But It's the Jobs that Count, Asian Development Bank Economics Working Paper No. 420, Asian Development Bank, Manila.

Gill, I., and H. Kharas, et al. 2007. *An East Asian Renaissance: Ideas for Economic Growth.* Washington, DC: World Bank.

Herrendorf, B, R. Rogerson, and A. Valentinyi. 2013. *Growth and Structural Transformation*, NBER Working Paper No. 18996, National Bureau of Economic Research, Cambridge, MA.

Hirschman, A.O. 1958. *The Strategy of Economic Development.* New Haven and London: Yale University Press.

Hossain, N. 2017. *The Aid Lab: Understanding Bangladesh's Unexpected Success.* Oxford: Oxford University Press.

Islam, M.M. 2012. *An Economic History of Bengal 1757–1947.* Dhaka: Adorn Publication.

Jahan, R. 1972. *Pakistan: Failure in National Integration.* New York: Columbia University Press.

Kharas, H., and H. Kohli. 2011. What Is the Middle Income Trap, Why Do Countries Fall into IT, and How Can It Be Avoided? *Global Journal of Emerging Market Economies* 3 (3): 281–289.

King, J.E. 2012. *Microfoundations Delusion: Metaphor and Dogma in the History of Macroeconomics.* Cheltenham: Edward Elgar.

Mahmud, W. 2008. Social Development in Bangladesh: Pathways, Surprises and Challenges. *Indian Journal of Human Development* 2 (1): 79–92.

Melguizo, A., S. Nieto-Parra, J.R. Perea, and J.A. Perez. 2017. *No Sympathy for the Devil! Policy Priorities to Overcome the Middle-Income Trap in Latin America,* Working Paper, No. 340. OECD Development Centre, Paris.

Myrdal, G. 1957. *Economic Theory and Under-developed Regions.* London: Gerald Duckworth & Co.

———. 1968. *Asian Drama: An Inquiry into the Poverty of Nations, (Volumes, I, II and III), A Twentieth Century Fund Study.* New York: Pantheon.

Osmani, S. R., W. Mahmud, B. Sen, H. Dagdeviren and A. Seth, 2006, The Macroeconomics of Poverty Reduction: The Case Study of Bangladesh, UNDP Regional Centre, Colombo.

Quibria, M.G. 2019. *Bangladesh's Road to Long-term Economic Prosperity: Risks and Challenges.* London: Palgrave Pivot.

Raihan, S., S.R. Osmani, and M.A.B. Khalily. 2017. The Macro Impact of Microfinance in Bangladesh: A CGE Analysis. *Economic Modelling* 62: 1–15.

Ray, D. 2007. Introduction to Development Theory. *Journal of Economic Theory* 137: 1–10.

Ray, A.S. 2015. *The Enigma of the "Indian Model" of Development. Discussion Papers from Centre for International Trade and Development*, New Delhi: Jawaharlal Nehru University.

Robinson, A. 1973. *Economic Prospects of Bangladesh.* London: Overseas Development Institute Ltd.

Rodrik, D. 2016. Premature Deindustrialization. *Journal of Economic Growth* 21: 1–33.

Sawada, Y., M. Mahmud, and N. Kitano, eds. 2018. *Economic and Social Development of Bangladesh: Miracle and Challenges.* London: Palgrave Macmillan.

Schendel, W.V. 2009. *A History of Bangladesh.* Cambridge: Cambridge University Press.

Sen, S.P., ed. 1973. *Modern Bengal: A Socio-economic History: Proceedings of a Seminar Held at the Institute in September, 1971.* Calcutta: Institute of Historical Studies.

Sen, A. 1999. *Development as Freedom.* Oxford: Oxford University Press.

Sinha, N.K. 1962. *Economic History of Bengal—From Plassey to the Permanent Settlement, Vol. II.* Calcutta: Firma K. L. Mukopadhyay.

Stern, R.W. 2001. *Democracy and Dictatorship in South Asia: Dominant Classes and Political Outcomes in India, Pakistan and Bangladesh.* New Delhi: India Research Press.

Sumner, A. 2017. *The Developer's Dilemma: Structural Transformation and Inclusive Growth, ESRC GPID Research Network Working Paper.* London: King's College.

Thoburn, J. 2009. Vietnam as a Role Model for Development, Research Paper No. 2009/30, World Institute for Development Economics Research, UNU-WIDER, United Nations University, Helsinki.

World Bank. 1972. *Report on the Mission of High Level United Nations Consultants to Bangladesh, March–April 1972,* Volume II, Sectoral Report IV p. 5, World Bank, Washington DC.

———. 2018. *Global Findex Database 2018.* Washington DC: World Bank.

———. 2019. *The Bangladesh Development Update 2019: Towards Regulatory Predictability.* Washington DC: World Bank.

CHAPTER 2

General Growth Performance

2.1 Introduction

Bangladesh's growth story since independence can be summarised as nothing short of remarkable. Over the last fifty years, Bangladesh has made impressive gains in both economic growth and human development. There has been significant increase in the GDP growth rate from an average of below 4 per cent in the 1970s and 1980s to more than 8 per cent in recent years. In 2019, Bangladesh has taken its place among the five fastest growing economies of the world (World Bank 2019). According to the 2019 UNDP Human Development Index, Bangladesh ranks 136th among 189 countries with an HDI score of 0.614 in 2018 that places it among the countries considered to have achieved medium human development (UNDP 2019).

This chapter gives a closer look at some of the key drivers which have contributed to Bangladesh's highly impressive growth story. More specifically, the chapter analyses Bangladesh's growth dynamics since independence and offers explanations on its growth variations during the period. It further examines the long-term growth patterns using alternative indicators. It decomposes GDP growth across sectors—agriculture, industry, and services—and across different uses—consumption, investment, exports and imports. Further, the analysis covers the proximate factors that determine long-term GDP growth, such as capital, labour, productivity growth, trade openness, size of the external market and institutions.

© The Author(s) 2020
M. K. Mujeri, N. Mujeri, *Bangladesh at Fifty*, Palgrave Studies in Economic History,
https://doi.org/10.1007/978-3-030-56791-0_2

Bangladesh's growth experience is also compared with that of the regional and comparable economies.

The analysis brings out several stylised facts. First, Bangladesh's long-term economic growth has been quite impressive. Despite variation around the long-term growth trend, average growth since the 1990s over a continuous ten-year period has steadily accelerated by about a percentage point, and has not reversed for a prolonged period (see, Figs. 2.1 and 2.2). Further, growth acceleration has been consistent with steadily improving proximate determinants of long-term growth. Economic growth has also become more stable (Fig. 2.3); firstly, due to growth rates stabilising in all major sectors, and secondly, due to the transition of the economy towards the services sector, which has a more stable growth rate.

Second, growth acceleration is characterised by productivity gains and not just by increased factor accumulation. Productivity gains have been reflected in both labour productivity and total factor productivity (TFP). Although the contribution of productivity gains to growth has been relatively insignificant in the initial years, it has been rising in recent decades. Overall productivity gains can be attributed both to within sector gains and reallocation of resources to more productive activities.

Third, the long-term growth potential of the economy is currently reflected in an ongoing upturn in the economy and appears to be firmly anchored in investment, exports, and the industrial sector. Investment rates have risen in recent years and Bangladesh has been gaining global export market shares. Further, credit growth has been sustained and protracted growth in major economic indicators may have implications for sustaining the current growth rate, for accelerating growth to Bangladesh's potential, and for enhancing the potential growth itself.

Fig. 2.1 GDP growth rate. GDP growth has accelerated over the long run

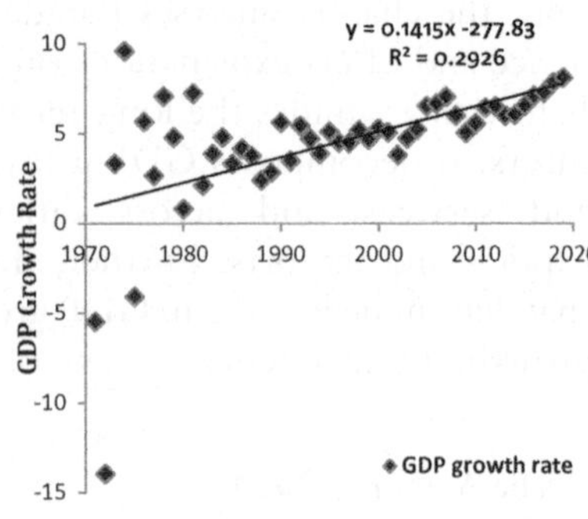

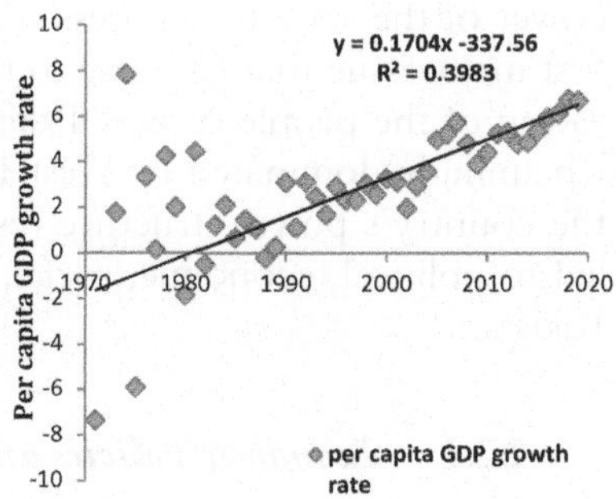

Fig. 2.2 GDP per capita growth rate. Per capita GDP growth has accelerated as well

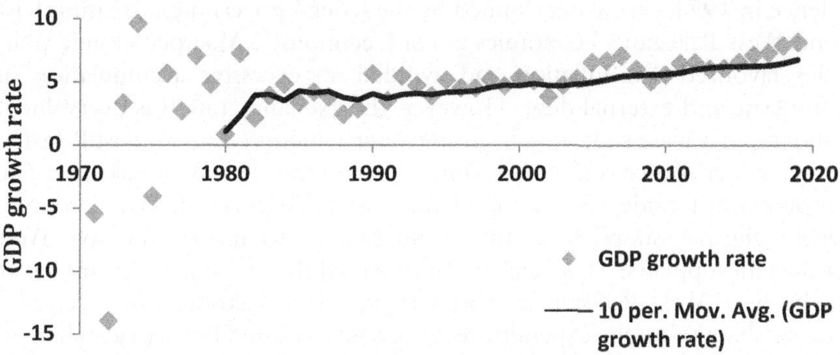

Fig. 2.3 10-year moving average of real GDP growth

2.2 The Economy before Independence

Pakistan, at the time of its creation in 1947, was a country bound with absurdity. It was divided into two parts, East and West Pakistan, separated by more than 1000 miles of Indian Territory. Besides, there were many socioeconomic and political differences. There existed a weak institutional structure along with a lack of political wisdom. The first signs of resentment among the people of East Pakistan appeared in March 1948 on the issue of state language when Urdu was declared as the only state language although the majority of the people of Pakistan spoke in Bangla language. Four years later on 21 February 1952, the police opened fire on a peaceful demonstration demanding Bangla as a state language in which many people (including students) were killed. The brutality of the coercive power of the state to suppress legitimate demands of the people was the first major issue that gave rise to the Bengali identity and a sense of deprivation of the people of East Pakistan. The central government was overwhelmingly dominated by West Pakistan and the lack of participation in the country's power structure resulted in denial of legitimate rights and led to political, economic, social, cultural and other deprivations of East Pakistan.

2.2.1 Economic Policies and Regional Disparities, 1947–1970

Bangladesh's fiscal, structural and trade policies—prior to its independence in 1971—were determined by the federal government treating East and West Pakistan's economies as 'one economy'. Macroeconomic policies favoured low inflation and avoided an excessive accumulation of domestic and external debt. However, the exchange rate was overvalued, and imports were subject to licensing and payments controls. East Pakistan was a larger source of export earnings (from jute) than West Pakistan. The protectionist trade regime raised the cost of imports, diverting sources from cheaper supplies on the world market to more expensive West Pakistani suppliers. This mechanism provided the much needed and costly subsidy to West Pakistan by East Pakistan. East Pakistan also received a lower share of public expenditure than was warranted by its larger share of population.

The central government of Pakistan adopted various means and methods to establish a firm grip over the economy of East Pakistan for which foreign exchange control and import licensing were the two most effective ways of appropriating agricultural surplus from East Pakistan and establishing import-substitution industries in West Pakistan. It also pursued the policy of single economy and fiscal and commercial policies were directed towards supporting private investment in East Pakistan through industrial houses based in West Pakistan. The thrust of the policies was not to develop East Pakistan, rather to use the eastern wing as a colony until its agricultural raw materials could be used to earn foreign exchange in order to develop West Pakistan.

The East Pakistan economy was mostly agriculture-based. Agriculture and services contributed 70 per cent and 10 per cent respectively to East Pakistan's GDP, while similar figures for West Pakistan were 54 per cent and 17 per cent respectively (see, Papanek 1967; Rahman 1968).

External trade was a major vehicle of creating economic disparities between East and West Pakistan. East Pakistan's exports were the main source of foreign exchange, which was used for the imports of industrial machinery and raw materials for West Pakistan. During the period of 1947–1958, East Pakistan's exports ranged from 50 per cent to 60 per cent of Pakistan's total exports. On the other hand, imports of East Pakistan were around 30 per cent of the country's total imports. Thus a large part of the trade deficit of West Pakistan was financed by East Pakistan. It is estimated that the resource transfer through international trade (in real terms) was nearly Rs. 1000 million per year during the 1950s.

The aid flow from abroad was also disproportionately allocated between East and West Pakistan; 77 per cent of the foreign resources were made available to West Pakistan as against only 23 per cent to East Pakistan (O'Donnell 1984). In 1968, 66 per cent of country's industrial assets, 79 per cent of insurance funds, 80 per cent of bank assets were controlled by twenty families from West Pakistan. As a result of the pursuit of discriminatory policies, disparity between the two regions of Pakistan rapidly increased.

Table 2.1 shows the Gross Regional Product (GRP) of East and West Pakistan during the period of 1950 to 1970. East Pakistan's GRP increased by an average annual growth rate of 2.0 per cent in the 1950s and 5.4 per cent in the 1960s; while the GRP of West Pakistan increased by an annual growth rate of 3. 6 per cent in the 1950s and 7.8 per cent in the 1960s.

In 1958, per capita income in West Pakistan was 30 per cent higher than in East Pakistan. But, the disparity increased to 45 per cent in 1965 and to 61 per cent in 1969. Further, there were consistently higher

Table 2.1 Gross regional product of East and West Pakistan, 1950–1970

	At 1959–60 constant factor cost in million Rupees			*Annual growth rate in per cent*	
	1949–50	*1959–60*	*1969–70*	*1950s*	*1960s*
East Pakistan	12,360	14,945	23,119	2.0	5.4
West Pakistan	12,106	16,494	31,157	3.6	7.8

Source: Planning Commission, Government of Pakistan, *The Third Five-Year Plan, 1965–70* and *Reports of the Advisory Panel of Economists for the Fourth Five Year Plan, 1970-7S*, Islamabad, July, 1970, Vol. 134

Table 2.2 Disparity in public expenditure between East and West Pakistan, 1951–1970

Period	*East Pakistan (Rupees in million)*			*West Pakistan (Rupees in million)*			*East Pakistan's share as % of total expenditure*
	Revenue	*Development*	*Total*	*Revenue*	*Development*	*Total*	
1951–1955	1710	1000	2710	7200	4000	11,200	19.5
1956–1960	2540	2700	5240	8980	7570	16,550	20.5
1961–1965	4340	9700	14,040	12,840	20,710	33,550	29.5
1966–1970	6480	16,550	23,030	22,230	29,700	51,930	30.7

Source: Report of East Pakistan Economists in the Report of the Panel of Economists on the Fourth Five Year Plan, 1970–75, Islamabad 1970

government expenditure (both revenue and development) in West Pakistan than in East Pakistan (Table 2.2).

The figures show that the regional disparity was far more endemic in revenue expenditure than in development expenditure, indicating a thriving permanent governance structure in West Pakistan at the cost of East Pakistan. Although East Pakistan's annual growth rate increased from an average of 1.7 per cent during 1955–1960 to 5.2 per cent during 1960–1965, it considerably lagged behind West Pakistan which recorded figures of 3.2 per cent and 7.2 per cent respectively over the same periods.

In addition to inequitable allocation of central government funds, inequality in provincial budgets was created by asymmetric fiscal rules of the Centre. To aid the process of industrialisation of West Pakistan, the central government systematically transferred visible as well as invisible resources from East to West Pakistan. Resource transfer occurred through inter-regional trade. West Pakistan exported to East Pakistan under a protective trade regime, at a higher than international price. Further, to support the process of industrialisation in West Pakistan, agricultural surplus (e.g. foreign exchange earned through agricultural exports by East Pakistan) was transferred to industry thereby masking the transfer of economic resources from the East to the West. In addition, by means of a complex system of taxes, the central government extracted from East Pakistan more than it injected income into there through expenditures

(Feldman 1971). According to one estimate, the resulting transfer was worth $2.6 billion (Rahman 1968).

The frustrations of East Pakistan found expression in the 'two-economy theory' in the 1960s realising that investment in one part of the country had been to their disadvantages and had not created any 'spread effect' on East Pakistan. Pakistan's peculiar geography and the disparities in different economic areas caused by the 'one economy' policy pursued by the Pakistani rulers deprived East Pakistan of its due shares in development. Consequently, the demand for regional autonomy and a two-economy policy gathered momentum over time. In 1959–60, the per capita income in West Pakistan was 32 per cent higher than the same in East Pakistan, but the difference in per capita income rose to 81 per cent by 1969–70 (Choudhary 1993). Finally, the autonomy movement led to the people's uprising in 1969 and the independence war of 1971; and the emergence of Bangladesh as an independent state after a nine-month long liberation war.

The war of liberation significantly destroyed the productive capacity of the Bangladesh economy. A survey of the United Nations Relief Operation (UNRO) in Bangladesh showed that the material damage caused by the war amounted to $1200 million; loss of agricultural output amounted to $300 million; damage of housing to $200 million; and transport facilities damage was $130 million. In addition, damage of agricultural potentials, loss of animals and fishing equipment, damage to the postal services and tele-communications, damage to sea ports and industries, and others had an extremely dampening effect on the Bangladesh economy and its production potential (UNRO 1972). In the first fiscal year of Bangladesh's independence (1972–1973), the country's GDP was well below that in 1969–1970 (Table 2.3). The total GDP declined by more than 14 per cent, while all major sectors experiencing huge declines in value added.

In addition, there were shortfalls in exports and imports, a sharp increase in money supply causing rises in the price level along with steep increases in the cost of living. The cost of living index was about 50 per cent higher in 1972–1973 than that of 1969–1970. The revenue collection of the government also lagged behind and failed to cover ever the current expenditures of the government. As Bangladesh's First Five Year Plan (1973–1978) observes:

> *"Bangladesh inherited a poor, undiversified economy, characterised by an underdeveloped infrastructure, stagnant agriculture, and a rapidly growing*

Table 2.3 GDP and its components of Bangladesh

	Tk. in million at 1972–73 prices		*% change over the two years*
	1969–1970	*1972–1973*	
Agriculture, livestock, forestry and fishery	28,830	24,970	-13.4
Manufacturing	5200	3580	-31.2
Construction	1840	1710	-7.1
Power and gas	150	1SO	0.0
Housing	2360	2360	0.0
Trade, transport and other services	11,650	11,070	-5.0
Total	50,030	42,940	-14.2

Source: The First Five-Year Plan, 1973–78, Planning Commission, Government of Bangladesh, Chapter 1, p. 15, Table 11–2

population. She had suffered from years of colonial exploitation and missed opportunities with debilitating effects on initiatives and enterprise. Superimposed on all these were the war of liberation, which caused serious damage to physical infrastructure, dislocation in managerial and. organisational apparatus and disruption in established external trading relationship." (Preface, The First Five-Year Plan, 1973–75, Planning Commission, November, 1973).

2.2.2 Disparities in Social Indicators, 1947–1970

Economic disparities and discriminatory allocation of resources between East and West Pakistan also led to big disparities in the development of infrastructure facilities and social sectors which, in turn, resulted in marked disparities in economic welfare of the people in two provinces (Auspitz et al. 1971; Islam 1972; Rao 1972; LaPorte Jr. 1975; Bhatia 1979). For instance, constrained supply of schools and health facilities, as a consequence of tightened public budget, directly affected educational opportunities and health status (Curle 1966). There also existed a systematic bias in the distribution of resources and facilities during 1947–1971 between East and West Pakistan.

For example, there was a decline in educational facilities, both in terms of relative and absolute availability of primary schools, in East Pakistan during the Pakistan period (Asadullah, 2006). Further, growing educational disparity fed into existing and growing regional economic inequalities. The two wings diverged significantly in socioeconomic outcomes over the years, owing to deliberate pro-West and anti-East policy adopted by the Pakistan's central government (Huq 1963; Falcon and Stern 1971; Mason et al. 1971). For instance, despite having more than 55 per cent of the country's total population, East Pakistan's share of central government development expenditure was as low as 20 per cent during 1951–1955 which rose to only 36 per cent during 1966–1970. In addition to unequal allocation of central government funds, inequality arose in provincial budgets following the asymmetric fiscal rules of the Centre. To aid the process of industrialisation in the Western wing, the central government systematically transferred visible as well as invisible resources away from the East to the West.

2.3 Growth of GDP and GDP per Capita

The growth of GDP is an important indicator of development. The process of growth of Bangladesh began in right earnest with the launch of the First Five Year Plan (1973–1978). It was a modest plan; and aimed largely to rehabilitate and restore stability to the economy after the devastation of the independence war in 1971. Well formulated strategy of growth was launched in the subsequent plans; giving primacy to accelerated and equitable growth, although modifications were made in response to the changing needs of the economy. The earlier plans aimed largely to build up the production capacity of the economy; and the strategy affected both the rate and the composition of growth. A new strategy of growth was adopted with the onset of the 1990s.

The rate of GDP growth slightly increased from 3.77 per cent during 1961–1970 (pre-independence period), to 3.99 per cent during 1976–1980; but decreased afterwards to 3.62 per cent during 1986–1990; and the next three decades saw average GDP growth rate rising by about one percentage point in each decade. The five-yearly average rose to 4.61 per cent during 1996–2000, to 5.52 per cent in 2006–2010, and accelerated further to 6.63 per cent during 2014–2018 (Table 2.4). In absolute terms, the country's GDP and GDP per capita have increased substantially: total GDP rose by nearly seven times in 2017 over its level in 1970, while GDP per capita increased by nearly three times over the same period (Table 2.5).

Table 2.4 Bangladesh's GDP growth rate at constant prices

	Average yearly growth rate, % (constant 2006 prices)	*Annual per capita GDP growth rate, constant 2006 prices, %*	*GDP per capita, constant 2006 BDT*	*GDP per capita Index, 2006 prices (2006=100)*
1961–1970 (pre-independence period)	3.77	1.01	22,700	68.41
1976–1980	3.99	1.40	18,293	55.13
1986–1990	3.62	1.07	20,490	61.75
1996–2000	4.61	2.62	25,346	76.39
2006–2010	5.52	4.60	36,637	110.42
2014–2018	6.63	5.54	54,485	164.21

Source: Tables B.1 and B.2 in the Statistical Annex, World Bank 2019

Table 2.5 Bangladesh GDP and GDP per capita, 1960–2017 (Selected years)

	GDP, BDT billion		*GDP per capita, BDT*	
	Current prices	*Constant 2006 prices*	*Current prices*	*Constant 2006 prices*
1960	20.52	940.70	425.72	19,516.70
1965	28.35	1180.67	507.79	21,146.06
1970	43.17	1390.91	663.59	21,382.90
1975	172.62	1228.33	2420.89	17,226.21
1980	280.78	1507.59	3446.35	18,504.61
1985	579.24	1857.70	6215.02	19,932.39
1990	1039.59	2234.01	9789.99	21,038.13
1995	1525.18	2787.66	12,848.27	23,483.55
2000	2685.03	3529.15	20,405.90	26,821.06
2005	4270.74	4521.69	29,775.56	31,525.15
2010	7975.39	6070.97	52,418.23	39,901.47
2015	15,158.02	8248.62	94,031.88	51,169.84
2017	19,758.15	9478.99	119,986.54	57,563.55

Source: Tables B.1 and B.2 in the Statistical Annex, World Bank 2019

Table 2.6 Distribution by uses of GDP at current prices, percentages

Use	*1960*	*1980*	*1985*	*1990*	*1995*	*2000*	*2005*	*2010*	*2015*
Household final consumption expenditure	86.22	NA	81.45	80.04	82.24	75.01	73.76	74.11	72.44
General government final consumption expenditure	6.19	6.14	4.03	4.05	4.63	4.97	5.18	5.08	5.40
Gross fixed capital formation	NA	NA	15.83	16.46	19.12	23.81	25.83	26.25	28.89
Exports	10.00	5.49	5.38	5.91	10.86	12.34	14.39	16.02	17.34
Imports	9.31	17.88	12.84	13.06	17.34	16.98	20.00	21.78	24.75
GDP, billion BDT	20.52	280.78	579.24	1039.59	1525.18	2685.03	4270.74	7.975.39	15.158.02

Note: NA = Not Available

Source: Table B.3 in the Statistical Annex, World Bank 2019

2.3.1 GDP: Distribution by Uses

Table 2.6 shows the distribution by uses of GDP at constant prices over the period 1960–2017. Household consumption, which was slightly higher than 86 per cent of GDP in 1960, declined to 81 per cent in 1985, declined further to around 80 per cent in 1990, rose to 82 per cent in 1995. For 2000 and 2005, household consumption was estimated at 75 per cent of GDP and it remained at around 74 per cent in 2005. Since 2010, there has been a fall in the proportion of private consumption and the figures for 2010 and 2017 were around 74 per cent and 69 per cent respectively. This suggests a downward shift in the share of household consumption in GDP during the beginning of the twenty-first century.

Government spending refers to public expenditure on goods and services and is a major component of GDP. Government spending policies like setting up budget targets, adjusting tax rates, increasing public expenditure and public works are effective tools for influencing economic growth. General government final consumption spending as a percentage of GDP was estimated at 6.2 per cent of GDP in 1960, increasing to 13.4 per cent in 1970. Bangladesh has one of the world's lowest government final consumption expenditures, at around 6 per cent of GDP in 2017. Among other factors, an inability to absorb resources by some ministries, in both the recurrent and development budgets, contributes to low expenditure. With significant development needs, including infrastructure requirements and a significant poverty challenge, public sector resources must be used efficiently to make progress. Between 2010 and 2015, public expenditure grew by an annual average of around 8 per cent. While both recurrent and development expenditure saw significant growth in real terms, the priority shifted towards public investment during the period.

Gross fixed capital formation (GFCF) accounted for only 5.6 per cent of GDP in 1970 and dipped to 2.3 per cent of GDP in 1972. It started to rise thereafter and was estimated at 15.8 per cent in 1985. The GFCF-GDP ratio was 16.5 per cent in 1990 which increased further to 23.8 per cent in 2000. Afterwards, a secularly rising trend can be observed reaching 26.3 per cent in 2010 and 30.5 per cent in 2017. This is a remarkable turnaround. It may be noted that some components of this higher levels of capital formation have been funded through private foreign investment, inflows of official development assistance (ODA), and international borrowing.

Exports of goods and services represent the value of all goods and other market services provided to the rest of the world. They include the value of merchandise, freight, insurance, transport, travel, royalties, license fees and other services, such as communication, construction, financial, information, business, personal and government services. However, they exclude compensation of employees and investment income (factor services) and transfer payments. The value of exports as a proportion of GDP was estimated at 10 per cent in 1960 which declined to 8.3 per cent in 1970 and further to 2.9 per cent in 1975. In 1980, the value was 5.5 per cent of GDP and rose to 5.9 per cent in 1990. Thereafter, exports increased rapidly to reach 12.3 per cent of GDP in 2000 and 17.3 per cent in 2015. The top exports of Bangladesh are non-knit men's suits, knit T-shirts, knit sweaters, non-knit women's suits, and non-knit men's shirts. In recent years, major export categories include: consumer goods (93 per cent), intermediate goods (3 per cent), raw materials (3 per cent), and capital goods (1 per cent).

The level of imports as a share of GDP was recorded at 9.3 per cent in 1960 which rose to 12.5 per cent in 1970. It then declined to a low of 8.1 per cent in 1975 and reached 17.9 per cent in 1980. The import share of GDP fluctuated around the 20 per cent level for more than a decade and reached a high of nearly 24.8 per cent in 2015. In 2017, the share was recorded at 20.3 per cent. Bangladesh's top imports are refined petroleum, heavy pure woven cotton, light pure woven cotton, raw cotton and non-retail pure cotton yarn. The product shares of different categories of imports in recent years are: intermediate goods (47 per cent), consumer goods (23 per cent), capital goods (17 per cent), and raw materials (13 per cent).

2.3.2 *GDP: Distribution by Industrial Origin*

For examining the distribution of GDP by industrial origin, we employ the International Standard Industrial Classification (ISIC) as adopted by the Bangladesh Bureau of Statistics (BBS). Agriculture corresponds to ISIC divisions 1–5 and includes forestry, hunting, and fishing, as well as cultivation of crops and livestock production. Industry corresponds to ISIC divisions 10–45 and includes manufacturing (ISIC divisions 15–37). It comprises value added in mining, manufacturing (also reported as a separate subgroup), construction, electricity, water and gas. Services

Table 2.7 Distribution of GDP by industrial origin at constant 2006 prices, percentages

Industrial origin sector	*1975*	*1985*	*1995*	*2005*	*2017*
Agriculture and forestry	56.00	28.93	20.33	15.74	10.98
i. Crops & horticulture	52.00	24.17	15.12	11.68	7.69
ii. Animal farming	2.00	3.42	3.31	2.38	1.93
iii. Forest and related services	2.00	1.34	1.90	1.69	1.37
Fishing	3.00	3.08	5.00	4.44	3.19
Mining and quarrying	0.00	0.55	1.01	1.09	1.83
i. Natural gas and crude petroleum	...	0.26	0.61	0.63	0.64
ii. Other mining & quarrying	...	0.30	0.41	0.47	1.18
Manufacturing	7.00	13.83	14.72	15.47	18.28
i. Large & medium scale	3.00	9.81	10.51	10.92	14.93
ii. Small scale	4.00	4.02	4.21	4.55	3.35
Electricity, water supply and gas	0.00	0.97	1.49	1.33	1.40
i. Electricity	...	0.86	1.25	1.11	1.09
ii. Gas	...	0.07	0.17	0.14	0.24
iii. Water	...	0.05	0.06	0.08	0.07
Construction	3.00	5.59	6.36	7.63	7.81
Wholesale and retail trade	9.00	12.87	12.37	13.25	13.05
Hotel and restaurants	0.00	0.59	0.58	0.66	1.03
Transport, storage and communication	7.00	9.94	8.87	10.34	10.00
i. Land transport	...	6.50	6.25	8.07	7.64
ii. Water transport	...	2.75	1.49	0.87	0.59
iii. Air transport	...	0.13	0.16	0.13	0.07
iv. Support transport services, storage	...	0.27	0.35	0.32	0.47
v. Post and telecommunication	...	0.29	0.62	0.96	1.24
Financial intermediations	1.00	1.25	1.47	1.56	3.91
i. Bank (monetary intermediation)	...	1.13	1.27	1.17	3.34
ii. Insurance	...	0.13	0.17	0.33	0.36
iii. Others (financial intermediation)	...	0.00	0.03	0.06	0.21
Real estate, renting and business activities	6.00	7.20	8.59	8.29	7.73
Public administration and Defense	2.00	1.51	2.42	2.59	4.19
Education	...	1.84	2.01	2.36	3.04
Health and social works	...	2.13	2.22	2.16	2.08
Community, social and personal services	5.00	7.39	8.57	9.02	11.46
GDP at producer prices	100	100	100	100	100

Source: Planning Commission, 2011. pp. 13–18 [6th five year plan (Part-3)] and Bangladesh Bureau of Statistics, 2016. p.399, Statistical Year Book Bangladesh 2015

correspond to ISIC divisions 50–99 and they include value added in wholesale and retail trade (including hotels and restaurants), transport, and government, financial, professional, and personal services such as education, healthcare and real estate services.

The share of GDP at constant prices by industrial origin for selected years from 1975 to 2017 is shown in Table 2.7. Over the entire period, agriculture's contribution to GDP (having the highest share at over 70 per cent in 1960) fell to a share of just about 14 per cent in 2017, while the share of the services sector rose to over 52 per cent and that of industry to around 34 per cent. Within agriculture, crops and horticulture has the leading share at 7.7 per cent in 2017 followed by the fishing sub-sector at 3.2 per cent. The share of animal farming is 1.9 per cent while that of forestry and related activities is only 1.4 per cent.

The share of the industry sector, which was around 15 per cent of GDP in the mid-1970s, witnessed a jump to 33.7 per cent in 2017 with some fluctuations over the period. Manufacturing is the leading sub-sector, with a share of nearly 18.3 per cent in 2017. Within manufacturing, large and medium scale enterprises are the dominant activities with a share of 14.9 per cent while the small scale ones contribute about 3.4 per cent. The mining and quarrying sub-sector has a share of 1.8 per cent while the share of electricity, gas and water supply is 1.4 per cent in 2017. Over the entire period, construction has emerged as one of the main subsectors; its share of GDP rose from around 4 per cent in the early years to nearly 8 per cent in 2017.

The services sector, with a share of over 52 per cent of GDP in 2017, has now emerged as the largest sector in the economy. The sub-sectors which show strong growth within the services sector are transport, storage and communications (share of 10 per cent in 2017); wholesale and retail trade including repair of motor vehicles, motorcycles and personal and household goods (share of 13.1 per cent in 2017); real estate, renting and business activities (share of 7.7 per cent in 2017); public administration and defence (share of 4.2 per cent in 2017); financial intermediations (share of 3.9 per cent in 2017); community, social and personal services (share of 11.5 per cent in 2017); education (share of 3.0 per cent in 2017); and health and social work (share of 2.1 per cent in 2017).

2.3.3 Savings and Capital Formation

In the development literature, much of the interest in savings is focused on the relation between savings and growth (see, e.g. Lewis 1954, 1955; Rostow 1960). It is usually argued that in low income countries there could be a vicious circle of low income leading to low savings, low investment and back to low income. Failure to break this vicious circle by raising the ratio of savings and investment to national income would result in perpetual stagnation and poverty. Across countries higher saving rates tend to go hand in hand with higher income growth—a fact that has been taken as proof of the existence of both virtuous cycles of savings and prosperity and poverty traps of inadequate savings and stagnation. But in a country like Bangladesh, saving is not only about accumulation and growth. It is about smoothing consumption in the face of volatile and unpredictable income, and helping to ensure the living standards of poor people whose lives are difficult and uncertain.

The part of GDP which is not used for private or government consumption is considered as gross domestic savings (GDS). Perhaps the worst problem that besets data on GDS is that saving is not measured directly but it is taken as a residual. In the national accounts, household saving is typically a residual among residuals. Fry (1988) notes that in many countries illegal capital outflows take place through 'overinvoicing' of imports and 'underinvoicing' of exports, so that if saving is calculated as the sum of domestic investment, government surplus, and trade surplus, saving will be underestimated by the extent of the illegal capital outflow. Because household saving is not measured directly, it is derived from national saving by deducting corporate and government saving, so that errors in measuring corporate saving or investment will be absorbed in the residual measure of saving. Given these deficiencies, even trends over time may be incorrectly observed, while real changes, especially those that involve foreign transactions (such as increased remittances) may affect the measurement as well as the reality of saving.

Table 2.8 shows GNI per capita and gross domestic savings rate for selected countries, including Bangladesh, during 1960–2017. The table provides evidence of some remarkable contrasts in development experience. Generally, a number of countries have sustained historically high savings rates despite having comparatively similar levels of per capita income. South Korea is a particular example which has moved from a very low level of savings in 1960 to an internationally high level of per capita

Table 2.8 GNI per capita and gross domestic savings in selected developing countries (per cent of GDP)

Country	*GNI per capita, 2017 PPP current international $*	*Gross domestic savings rate (% of GDP)*						
		1960	*1970*	*1980*	*1990*	*2000*	*2010*	*2017*
Bangladesh	4040	7.58	NA	14.84[a]	15.91	20.02	20.81	25.33
China	16,760	36.56	35.97	35.33	36.41	36.51	51.82	47.35
India	7060	6.15	11.37	12.47	21.52	24.16	33.70	29.77
Sri Lanka	12,470	9.39	13.48	17.87	17.71	18.01	23.09	29.32
Vietnam	6450	NA	NA	NA	2.91	27.12	27.45	25.49
South Korea	38.340	0.62	16.31	25.69	39.15	34.91	35.21	36.57

Note: [a] for 1981. NA: not available

Source: World Bank 2019

income and savings. The savings rate of China in recent years is remarkably high. Bangladesh, India and Vietnam have also achieved higher savings rates.

The savings and capital formation rates of the Bangladesh economy fluctuated, rather widely, since independence. For example, the rate of gross capital formation in 1970 was 5.6 per cent of GDP, it fell to 2.3 per cent in 1972, rose to 23.2 per cent in 1981; went down to 16.4 per cent in 1991, and then went up to 29.7 per cent in 2016. Table 2.9 shows the average and the marginal rates of gross savings at 2006 prices for selected periods between 1980 and 2017 for Bangladesh. As can be seen, there was significant variation in the savings rate across different periods and there has been a positive trend only since the 1990s.

2.4 Economic Growth and Structural Change

As is well-known, the process of economic development does not merely involve increases in the levels of economic growth and productivity, but also entails changes in the distribution of inputs and outputs across different economic sectors and population groups. Kuznets states that 'it is impossible to attain high rates of growth per capita or per worker without commensurate substantial shifts in the shares of various sectors' (Kuznets 1979). Structural change is considered as an important source of growth and productivity improvement in the growth-accounting literature which

Table 2.9 Average and marginal savings in Bangladesh (at 2006 constant prices)

	1981–1985	*1990–1995*	*2000–2005*	*2010–2015*	*2015–2017*
Average annual savings (BDT, million)	335,521.27	540,013.26	1,155,152.29	2,686,977.20	3,216,089.84
Change in annual savings over the period (BDT, million)	-16,296.70[a]	24,365.38	89,332.84	136,657.03	138,508.64
Average savings rate, % of GDP	19.85[a]	22.18	29.74	38.99	36.36
Marginal savings rate, %	-27.17	23.00	51.57	34.52	24.23
GDP, BDT billion	1657.65	2437.60	3873.04	6891.93	8854.33

Note: [a]Data for 1982–85

Sources: Table B.8 in the Statistical Annex, World Bank 2019.

is derived from the classical models of a dual economy (Lewis 1954). The analysis of the composition and development of economic sectors is a relatively new trend in economics and is known as 'structural economics'.

Structural change may be narrowly conceived as the reallocation of labour across economic sectors (Kuznets 1966). As labour and other resources move from traditional to modern economic activities, overall productivity rises and income increases. The nature and speed with which structural transformation takes place in an economy is one of the key factors that determines the economic success of a country; and the new structural economists argue that economic structures should be the starting point for economic analysis and the design of appropriate policies. Sustainable development of the Bangladesh economy is associated with increases in the living standards of the population through economic progress, largely encompassing the development of knowledge-based and innovation-prone sectors.

Economic growth and generation of income ultimately depends on the competitive performance of individual producers and enterprises in different sectors of an economy. The competitiveness of the producers, in turn, depends on the relative abundance (and hence cost) of resources, as well as the incentives and capabilities to use them in a productive and sustainable manner. There are many determinants, such as stability of macroeconomic fundamentals, operation of the factor and product markets, quality of the general business environment, relative intensity in factor use, incentives to pursue opportunities, and specific capabilities required for transforming into successful business, which vary across sectors and hence they differ greatly in their growth and performance.

2.4.1 Structural Changes in the Bangladesh Economy

Structural changes in the Bangladesh economy since independence can be studied with respect to various outcomes, such as output, employment, investment and consumption. These can further be studied using various dimensions of such changes including sectors and product groups; rural and urban locations; distribution across size of production units; income groups and consumption expenditure classes of households; technology and productivity variations across sectors and activities; and earning differences across activities, skills, gender, and social groups. In other words, the analysis of structural changes accompanying economic growth brings out different manifestations of the composition and distribution of growth.

This section highlights some important aspects of structural changes in the Bangladesh economy which have taken place after independence and have accelerated and undergone qualitative changes in recent decades. More specifically, several issues are highlighted in the analysis: (i) nature of structural changes in output experienced by the Bangladesh economy along with their secular trends, breaks, turning points and patterns over different periods; (ii) exploring the 'deviant' pattern of services sector growth prior to manufacturing growth and its implications for sustaining high GDP growth in the long term; (iii) long-term implications of growth pattern of different sub-sectors within the industry and services sectors; and (iv) changes in the structure of foreign trade and employment.

2.4.1.1 Post-Independence Economic Growth: Breaks and Turning Points

Since independence, economic growth in Bangladesh has seen several breaks and turns. Accordingly, different phases of economic growth with distinctive features in terms of rates of growth and structural changes can be identified. While analysing long-term growth, it is not very meaningful to highlight short-term fluctuations but, at the same time, it is also neither realistic nor analytically meaningful to discuss growth dynamics over the entire period disregarding major events or turning points, providing breaks or stimulus.

The introduction of economic reforms since the 199Os is often seen as a major turning point in Bangladesh's post-independence economic history, providing a break from the low growth trap in which the economy was caught in the 1970s and 1980s. The high GDP growth that was triggered by economic reforms in the 1990s and sustained thereafter is one of the most important achievements of Bangladesh's economic performance in recent years. However, policies which single-mindedly pursue economic growth alone suffer from serious analytical deficiencies in a country like Bangladesh, and can lead to rather simplistic and misleading framework that would disregard broader aspects of development which are important goals for Bangladesh.

Still, achieving higher growth is a major future challenge for Bangladesh, along with raising human capabilities for development. Bangladesh has already started the process of growth acceleration since the late 1990s and less short-term fluctuations through expanding TFP growth, ensuring macroeconomic stability, greater openness, human capital availability, higher growth of the services sector and other demand-driven activities.

During the last four decades, the sources of growth were mainly powered by factor accumulation, that is, higher investment and labour use. Since the end of the 1980s, investment has risen steadily relative to GDP. With greater availability of labour, capital per unit of labour is relatively scarce in Bangladesh. In such circumstances, most developing countries exhibit low marginal productivity; but there has been significant impact of labour availability on economic growth in Bangladesh.

Since the 1980s, the country's population growth started to slow down; but the growth of working age population experienced faster growth resulting from higher population growth of the earlier decades. Changes in the ratio of working age to total population also began to contribute to economic growth since the 1990s. This suggests that Bangladesh has been reaping the demographic dividend of the past population explosion in the recent decades. Moreover, labour market in Bangladesh has experienced a major qualitative and quantitative shift with the influx of more female labour in the labour force. Thus, Bangladesh's economic growth over the recent decades has been driven by growth in GDP per working age person, which can be viewed as a rise of labour productivity. Increased government expenditure on human resources for example health and education also positively influenced the outcomes.

Thus, human capital development efforts do have positive and significant impact on growth even at early stages, especially when these are productivity enhancing although the links in the dominant informal economy are complex and poorly understood.

Economic growth in the past in Bangladesh has largely been driven by the acceleration in capital accumulation and expansion of quantity and to some extent quality of labour, with a lesser role played by the human capital and insignificant role by technological growth. A major advantage for Bangladesh arose from the strong presence of local level organisations including the NGO-MFIs which provide an effective route for scaling up of innovative programmes and the spread of new ideas. The density of the settlements and their close proximity in the presence of an extensive network of rural roads and communication facilities were strong factors for promoting social interactions and mobility, especially for rural women. Besides, the economic impact of developing MSMEs and mobilisation of women groups had produced significant non-economic gains through enhanced agency, empowerment and mutual support, thus creating the social environment for development interventions to perform more effectively.

The approach had also been broad-based, since the NGO-MFIs primarily work with different groups of the poor and in remote and disadvantaged locations where the gains mostly come from low-cost solutions. The broad nature of these interventions had also helped in creating employment opportunities for the poor, such as in the rapidly-growing RMGs industry that employs mostly women from the rural areas. Overall, these proximate factors had also ushered in a broader process of social transformation affecting behavioural norms and attitudes. From a growth perspective, this included attitudes towards female employment, fertility behaviour and parental incentives for investments in children's health and education (Mahmud 2008).

The government's commitment and support for many innovative welfare-oriented programmes had also played important roles. The 'food for education' programme, for example, had helped to bring children from poor rural households to the formal school system since the early 1990s. Female school enrolment had been promoted by the introduction of a universal stipend programme for female students attending secondary schools creating a profound impact on parental attitudes and social norms regarding sending adolescent girls to schools. These programmes had also received sustained support from all types of ruling regimes to gain social legitimacy by delivering on welfare promises, albeit within the limits of adverse governance environments characterised by widespread corruption and vexing patronage politics (Mahmud and Mahmud 2014).

Obviously, many of these non-traditional innovations may not perform as effectively as before in the future or may not be sustained into the future. However, improvements in governance and macroeconomic policy and still not-fully exploited potential of economic globalisation to foster new industries through outsourcing and technology transfer are signs of hope for the future. Furthermore, there are drags that the rich countries exert on the world economy, the threats to globalisation, and the obstacles that Bangladesh faces as a late industrialiser. The relative weights of these diverse considerations and similar others would ultimately determine the new drivers of economic growth for the future. Extrapolation may not necessarily be a good guide to where Bangladesh should be heading.

The important issue is: how well are these models likely to perform under the changing dynamics of the Bangladesh economy? It is more likely that, as the gains from low-cost solutions are reaped, continued progress will have to increasingly depend on public social spending and improvements in service delivery systems. Further reductions in child mortality, for example, will require more expensive child survival interventions, such as hospital-based care to avert neonatal mortality resulting from birth-related complications. Similarly, lowering the currently high maternal mortality rate will also require the provision of relatively costly health services. It is more likely that the existing poor quality of schooling will not sustain the current gains in school enrolment, which is presently reflected in the high rates of school drop-outs.

In the above context, an important issue is to recognise that the present progress in social development has been achieved, to a large extent, through successfully bypassing the widespread problems of poor governance in public service delivery. For the purpose, several 'models' have been used. For example, immunisation and social marketing of contraceptives were pursued outside the established structure of service delivery and by involving the NGOs. However, further progress in many instances is likely to become difficult through using such routes. Still, the mainstream service delivery systems are highly centralised with very little mechanisms for transparency and accountability. The rural healthcare system, for example, is plagued by poor utilisation of services and widespread absenteeism of doctors.

In the case of alternative and past successful interventions (e.g. involving partnerships with NGOs and CBOs), the usual targets are the households or individuals, mostly poor women, instead of using 'the agency of the public', such as by involving local government institutions (Sen and Dreze, 1995: 190–91). As such, these interventions have mostly been effective in promoting self-interested behaviour for individual household welfare, even if the benefits accruing to the targeted households have elements of 'public good' (e.g. immunisation, family planning services, water supply and sanitation). In the absence of effective local government, NGO-MFIs in Bangladesh work almost in parallel with the 'ill-functioning' centralised public service delivery systems. This means that the NGO-MFIs can function as effective community-based organisations in support of the poor to claim quality public services and sanction service failures.

Clearly, the challenge for Bangladesh is to consolidate the gains achieved so far and make further progress with greater speed. This requires not only more resources for social spending, but also in improving the governance structure of service delivery. But, at the same time, Bangladesh should also continue to innovate, in the presence of multiple constraint and governance dysfunction, to streamline supportive service delivery channels by creating social awareness and using low-cost affordable solutions.

Beginning in the 1970s, the microfinance revolution, by providing smart loans and social development services, created a class of self-employed entrepreneurs, mostly women, who seldom existed in other countries in South Asia or elsewhere. The loan size gradually increased and the borrowers were provided with 'appropriate loans' to start their preferred income generating activities and/or microenterprises. This enabled, especially the 'empowered' rural women, to engage in gainful employment and play an important role in the Bangladesh growth story. Along with creating a successful growth story, Bangladesh has become a role model for other countries. It is widely considered as one of the rare examples of a poor country becoming a regional economic powerhouse within a few decades by following prudent economic policies.

2.4.1.2 Dominant Changes in Economic Structure

An exclusive focus on growth obviously leaves out important issues relating to structural changes which take place within a longer term perspective. No doubt, Bangladesh's structural transformation from an agricultural to a non-agricultural economy is a long-term secular phenomenon, but whether the shift takes place towards industry or services sector would very much depend on domestic policies and global economic environment during the transformation period. Economic growth, accompanied by specific structural changes, has its own implications for the rate and sustainability of growth itself. More importantly, composition of growth and associated structural changes has different implications for economic development in broader terms of equity, sustainability and improvement in the livelihoods and welfare of different groups of people in Bangladesh.

It is important to recognise that a simplistic description of Bangladesh's growth experience can lead to deceptive conclusions. After independence, indeed Bangladesh achieved a faster rate of growth in GDP than did East Pakistan during the pre-independence period. As seen earlier, the average GDP growth rate between 1961 and 1970 was 3.8 per cent per year while it rose to 4 per cent in the 1970s (see, Table 2.4). Within the post-independence period, changes in the rate of growth between sub periods were not significant except in the later periods: it was 3.6 per cent between 1986 and 1990, 4.6 per cent between 1996 and 2000, 5.5 per cent between 2006 and 2010, and 6.6 per cent between 2014 and 2018.

The above shows that a major break in the history of economic growth in Bangladesh occurred soon after Independence; an economy which was growing at about 3 per cent per annum, started growing at over 4 per cent from the early 1970s. A state controlled economic planning, although a much maligned issue at present could be identified behind this turning point.

The next break in terms of growth occurred during the second half of the 1990s, when GDP growth rate accelerated to between 4.5 and 5 per cent. In this respect, introduction of economic reforms in the early 1990s was not a 'break'; as the growth rate in the post–reform 1990s was not significantly higher than during 1980s. The growth rate, in fact, picked up significantly after 2000. The period since 2000, even after accounting for the slow down during financial crisis in 2008–09 represents a distinctive phase of high growth reaching more than 8 per cent in 2018.

Structural changes, as reflected in the changes in the shares of agriculture, industry and services in GDP, have broadly followed the same time pattern as changes in the rate of growth but the contents have varied over periods, As we have seen above, the share of agriculture (including fishing) consistently declined over the past five decades: from about 59 per cent in the mid-1970s to around 32 per cent in mid-1980s to 25 per cent in mid-1990s, and to about 14 per cent in 2017. Industry and services have both increased their share, but at different pace and in different periods.

Accordingly, their relative contribution to the growth of and importance in aggregate GDP has varied over different periods.

On the basis of the observed pattern of structural changes, economic growth in post-independence Bangladesh may be divided into the following three phases, each with its distinguishing features.

Phase 1: independence to mid-1990s: This period saw a moderate acceleration in the growth rate over pre-independence decades marked by a relatively high growth of industry, and a significant structural change with a large increase in the share of non-agricultural sector, especially of the services, in the national output.

Phase 2: mid-1990s to early 2000s: This period was marked by a relatively higher growth of GDP, accompanied by acceleration in the growth of industry and services, a higher pace of structural shift from agriculture to non-agriculture.

Phase 3: early 2000s onwards: This period saw a sharp acceleration in GDP growth rate, mainly contributed by services. Structural changes were also swift, with a large decline in the share of agriculture, higher growth in the share of industry; and services picking up the major share of the shift and emerging as the major sector.

Thus, since the 1980s, Bangladesh's GDP growth has been primarily services-led. The share of industry increased at a slower pace and picked up only after 2010. Within industry, the shares of manufacturing and construction increased their shares. The overall share of industry including construction was about 10 per cent in 1975, which rose to nearly 30 per cent in the recent years.

The acceleration in the services sector growth started in the 1990s and continued afterwards. As a result, the share of services sector is now more than 66 per cent in non-agricultural and 56 per cent in aggregate GDP. The share of services in total GDP used to be little more than 37 per cent in the mid-1970s. That the growth of the Bangladesh economy over the last decades has been primarily services–driven is thus well established. The key questions in this context are: (i) whether this represents a different growth path relative to the traditional growth pattern of industry-led growth acceleration followed by services sector growth; (ii) if the answer is affirmative, then why such a pattern emerged in the case of Bangladesh; and (iii) how sustainable is this services-led growth. In this context, it is useful to look at the composition of the services sector growth to see which services have contributed to the growth and dominance of the sector.

It appears that four broad services sub-sectors, namely, wholesale and retail trade; community, social and personal services; transport, storage and communication; and financial intermediation have contributed the most in services sector growth during the period. Their share in GDP was about 22 per cent in the 1970s and rose to nearly 39 per cent in the late 2010s.

2.4.2 *Implications of Services Sector-Led Growth*

The above analysis shows that the rate of growth of the secondary and tertiary sectors in Bangladesh has been significantly higher than that of the primary sector, with the secondary sector having an edge over the tertiary sector during the initial decades. In the subsequent period, the tertiary sector grew relatively fast than the earlier years. There may be a number of reasons for the higher growth of the services sector in recent years. As new technologies are adopted and competitive pressures built up, there are widespread outsourcings of non-core activities by the manufacturing firms, which show up as growth of services sector. Further, in Bangladesh's System of National Accounts (SNA), services are a residual category that ends up including several household and cottage/micro sector production activities. Nevertheless, the growth momentum of the services sector cannot be denied in Bangladesh.

As a result, the service sector has become the growth-driver of the Bangladesh economy. Presently, about two-thirds of the incremental growth in the Bangladesh economy can be attributed to the tertiary sector. One may note that this pattern of structural change in the Bangladesh economy deviates from the traditional pattern experienced by most of the currently developed Western and South East Asian economies. These economies experienced a shift from the primary to the secondary sector first; which was followed by a significant shift in favour of the tertiary sector at an advanced stage of their development.

The explanation for the shift runs in terms of relatively low Income elasticity of demand for agricultural products; as a result, with rising levels of income, the demand for agricultural products relatively declines and that for non-agricultural goods increases and, after reaching a certain level of income, demand for services of different sectors is also determined by the changes in the pattern of demand. On the supply side, agriculture, being mainly dependent on a fixed factor of production—namely land—faces a limit on its growth and is subjected to early operation of the law of diminishing returns.

Industry, specially manufacturing, on the other hand, offers large scope for use of capital and technology, which can be augmented almost without limit with human effort. The same applies to services sector where the application of technologies seems to offer much larger scope. It can be seen that over the period, the primary sector's share has fallen to about 15 per cent, while those of the secondary and tertiary sectors have increased. The above trend is likely to go further in the wake of the liberalisation of the economy. This may happen primarily due to encouragement to the private sector involvement in areas like software development and information services; and technological advances, and lower fixed capital requirements in the services sector.

Such a pattern of structural change enables to transfer the growing labour force from primary to secondary sector; in Bangladesh, such a labour transfer has not been possible because the secondary sector did not expand fast enough to absorb the growing labour force. As a result, the unskilled rural labour force continues to struggle in the labour-intensive primary sector and those who have been forced out by economic, social and other factors have joined the urban informal or the slum sector. Moreover, the sharp increase in the share of tertiary sector in GDP in Bangladesh seems to have taken place at a much lower level of per capita income than that in the developed countries when they experienced a similar transformation. This pattern of growth underlines the link between the growing poverty and unemployment and the inadequate growth of manufacturing and construction activities in the country.

In Bangladesh, the tertiary, i.e. the services (non-commodity) sector has grown at a much faster rate than the primary and secondary sectors. This means that income generated in the process of circulation grows faster than that in the directly productive process; resulting in an increase in the share of the services sector. This trend can be attributed to a number of factors.

A large part of the service sector consists of infrastructure and essential services such as banking, insurance, finance, transport and communication, and social and community services such as education and health. In Bangladesh, an urgent requirement for development is the rapid expansion of these services to cater to the needs of other sectors of the economy and meet the basic needs for the well-being of the people.

Further, public services are growing rapidly in Bangladesh since the government has to play a number of significant roles in the country's development process. In fact, the government policies over the last few decades have been increasingly directed towards the creation of necessary economic and social infrastructures. The operation of the demonstration effect as a consequence of rapid globalisation and increasing mobility is also an important factor.

Increasing urbanisation in the country may also be regarded as another factor in rapid expansion of the services sector in the economy. In fact, urbanisation is closely associated with a rise in demands for infrastructure services such as communication, public utilities and distribution services. A substantial change in the private consumption pattern is associated with increasing urbanisation. In particular, many new goods and services enter into the consumption basket.

Another emerging growth driver in the services sector is tourism which is being promoted through modern information technologies (IT) such as television and the Internet. Tourism including ecotourism, in turn, promotes all types of services. One very important recent factor has been the advent of IT and the knowledge economy which has enhanced the growth of the high productivity segment of the services sector.

With the rising complexities of modern industrial organisation, manufacturing industries have also become more service oriented. This has been reflected in the increasing adoption of accounting finance, legal services, advertisement, marketing, and public relations. Because of convenience, these services are being increasingly outsourced, resulting in growth in these service activities.

In addition, an increase in the share of the services sector in the country's GDP may be attributed to the failure of the commodity producing sectors to grow satisfactorily. While there are inherent difficulties in bringing about a fast growth in the primary sector, the country's secondary sector and its major components—manufacturing and construction—have not been able to grow at faster rates necessary to give the commodity sector a satisfactory share in the country's GDP.

During the coming decades, both domestic and international factors are likely to create favourable conditions for services sector growth in Bangladesh. As real per capita GDP grows, demand for services is likely to increase more than proportionately and this, in turn, will reinforce GDP growth itself. Within the services sector, demand for producer and government services, which constitute mainly intermediate consumption, have strong multipliers impacting on the real GDP. The growth of such dynamic service activities, which are intensive users of communication and information technology, will generate increasing employment opportunities especially for the educated youth.

The current process of economic growth will lead to the emergence and expansion of new services such as advertising, publicity, marketing, etc. These subsectors provide essential service inputs to other sectors in the economy, thereby developing strong linkages with the rest of the economy. Further, efficient delivery of required services will increase the productivity of both labour and capital in the economy as a whole. In the Bangladesh economy, the services sector appears to be highly growth inducing with positive externalities for other services, making services as an important catalytic agent of growth. Bangladesh can exploit several recent global developments to create wider opportunities for substantial growth of the country's services sector.

At present, the fastest growing segment of the global services economy is the knowledge-based services such as, professional and technical services. Bangladesh has advantages in the supply of such services because of a relatively developed structure of technological and educational institutions, sizable youth population, and lower labour costs. The progress in IT is unbundling the production and consumption of information-intensive service activities. These activities—research and development; computing; inventory management; quality control; accounting; personnel administration; secretarial, marketing, advertising and legal services—are performed in all economic sectors. Further, unlike most other prices, world prices of transport and communication services have fallen dramatically. The cost of communication is becoming independent of distance. Bangladesh's geographical distance from important industrial hubs is no longer an important element in the cost-structure of skill-based activities. Thus, it is possible now to provide value added services without waiting to 'catch up' in technology for production of sophisticated equipment or products.

The recent declining trend in the share of manufacturing in the output of rich countries implies a relative decline in their demand for industrial raw materials and fuels. It means that growth in exports of developing countries like Bangladesh in the future will depend less on natural resource endowments and more on efficiency in providing service-intensive goods. For instance, the aging of population in the developed world implies that the demand for different services will continue to grow. As a result, the sources of comparative advantage of Bangladesh may be vastly different now from what they were in the past. And, there are few developing countries which are as well placed as Bangladesh to take advantage of the phenomenal changes that have occurred in production technologies, international trade, capital movement and deployment of skilled human power.

Further, the expansion in the services sector has wider implications for population, employment, and trade prospects of the Bangladesh economy. The growing share of the services sector points to the need for policy initiatives towards introducing greater competition and efficiency in this sector so as to ensure its sustained contribution to exports (especially software) and to higher long-term growth. The gains in productivity in agriculture and industry sectors resulting from technological progress and innovation will have the effect of shifting employment towards the services sector. This may also result in a shift in real expenditures from commodities to value added services. For Bangladesh, the services sector is a vast but relatively unexploited potential tax-base, and its growth can therefore have important long-term implications for the fiscal policy.

For making services-led growth more widespread and sustainable, Bangladesh needs to adopt a coherent and integrated services policy (consistent with the agricultural and industrial policies). Further, reforms in services sector in Bangladesh so far have been implemented in an ad hoc manner rather than as part of an overall strategy. Consequently, the depth and pace of reforms lack uniformity across sectors. Given the strong interlinkages between different services, reforms in a particular services sector may not yield results if not backed by corresponding reforms in other complementary services. Such an integrated services policy should also define the sequence as well as the pace of reforms to be undertaken simultaneously in different services. Liberalisation should be followed in a phased manner accompanied by social policies in sectors that have surplus labour so as to avoid creating unemployment and social unrest. This will go a long way in sustaining the dynamism of services-led growth in Bangladesh.

2.4.3 GDP Growth and Occupational Structure

Occupational structure means the distribution of work force in different occupations. In a developing economy like Bangladesh, it is generally expected that the percentage of the labour force dependent on agriculture should decline over time; while the share of industry should increase. There may be an increase in the percentage of labour dependent on services. But, for a country in the early stages of industrialisation, this increase should be less than the increase in manufacturing. At a later stage of development, faster increase in the services sector may be expected.

The classical reasons for such a change are two-fold. With rise in incomes, the demand for agricultural goods does not rise proportionately. On the other hand, rise in incomes brings about a large increase in the demand for manufacturing goods and services, resulting in increasing demand for labour in the manufacturing and services sectors. With economic development, modern technologies and better techniques become available with agriculture, so that the productivity of land and labour rises. As a result, there is less need for labour in agriculture. On the contrary, in the industrial sector, although increase in capital and modern techniques makes it possible to bring about increases in productivity, demand increases at a faster rate than the rise in per head productivity resulting in increasing demand for labour in the industrial and the services sectors.

Table 2.10 gives the occupational structure of Bangladesh's labour force since the beginning of the 1970s. The data show that the occupational structure of the Bangladesh economy is lopsided. There is a heavy dependence on agriculture; about 41 per cent of the working population

Table 2.10 Changes in occupational structure and sectoral contribution to GDP, 1996–2010

	Agriculture		*Industry*		*Services*		*Total employed labour (million)*
	Employed labour, %	*Share in GDP, %*	*Employed labour, %*	*Share in GDP, %*	*Employed labour, %*	*Share in GDP, %*	
1995–96	48.85	21.44	13.22	21.79	37.92	56.76	**40.40**
1999–00	50.77	21.34	13.08	22.89	36.16	55.77	**42.80**
2002–03	51.69	19.77	13.56	24.08	34.75	56.15	**44.30**
2005–06	48.10	19.01	14.55	25.40	37.35	55.59	**47.40**
2010	47.33	18.38	17.49	26.78	35.18	54.83	**54.10**
2013	45.10	16.78	20.80	29.00	34.10	54.22	**58.10**
2016–17	40.60	14.74	20.40	32.42	39.00	52.85	**60.80**

Source: BBS, *Labour Force Survey* (LFS), 1995–96, 1999–00, 2002–03, 2005–06,2010, 2016–2017; BBS, *Labour Force Surveys* 1992 to 2010 and *Bangladesh Economic Review 2013* (As taken from: Ahmed and Khan (Internet source), Employment and Unemployment Situation in Bangladesh: A Dismal Picture of Development. pp.13 and 28–29)

derives its subsistence from agriculture, although its contribution of GDP is only 15 per cent. The changes in the occupational structure largely correspond to the celebrated Kuznets-Clark-Kaldorian path in the aggregate.

However, some significant developments in certain segments of the economy can be seen which are not revealed in the aggregate picture. For example, the number of workers in the formal sector is on the increase. The country is producing new products using new and modern techniques. Furthermore, there is an impressive expansion of job opportunities in services like education, health, science and technology, communications, etc. These changes are indicative that the process of modernisation of the economy is under way. But the pace of modernisation is slow so that it does not leave a significant mark on the occupational structure.

Overall, the proportion of working population engaged in agriculture has declined and that engaged in industries and services has gone up. The composition of GDP has shown a marked change over the years. There has been a marked fall in the share of agriculture in GDP, whereas the share of industry and services sectors has increased; although the share of services sector has increased at a faster rate than that of the secondary sector. These trends are indicative of the country-specific structural changes being experienced by the Bangladesh economy.

The above shows that structural changes in terms of key economic parameters have occurred in the Bangladesh economy as economic growth has proceeded since independence. More generally, in terms of percentage shares of GDP, saving rates have increased as income has grown; government revenues (and expenditure) have increased, growth in food consumption has decelerated, relative output of services—and, of industry as well—has increased, while that of agriculture has fallen.

In the case of employment, changes reflect the shift in output and changes in productivity. Labour in the primary sector (agriculture) of the economy has not fallen as rapidly as its share in output; the reverse is true for employment in industry where increase in labour productivity is more easily secured. Further, as development has proceeded and the economy has increasingly been integrated to the rest of the world, exports have accounted for a larger proportion of incomes and there have been a marked shift in the composition of exports, so that the value of export of manufactures has risen relative to that of primary products. Imports also have risen.

2.5 Economic Reforms and Growth Policies

2.5.1 Economic Policy and Planning

After independence, the main government institution responsible for coordinating national rehabilitation and development was the Planning Commission. The Planning Commission translates the multiyear development plan into public investment through the Annual Development Programme (ADP). The Commission also ensures that public programmes and policies are in conformity with its long-term strategy through its project approval process and through its advisory position on the country's highest economic decision-making bodies, the National Economic Council (NEC) and its Executive Committee (ECNEC). The ECNEC usually takes most of the decisions on major development projects and development issues in general. The Committee includes the ministers of key economic sectors (e.g. Finance, Planning, Industries, Commerce, and Public Works) and, according to the agenda, any other ministries concerned.

The First Five-Year Plan covered the period July 1973 to June 1978. It was succeeded by a two-year plan, covering the period July 1978 to June 1980, which was followed by a year-long hiatus. The Second Five-Year Plan (1981–1985) and the Third Five-Year Plan (1985–1990) put the planning process back on track. Currently, Bangladesh is implementing the Seventh Five Year Plan (2016–2020) while the process of preparing the Eighth Five Year Plan (2021–2025) is in progress. The 7th Plan centres around three themes: (i) GDP growth acceleration, employment generation and rapid poverty reduction; (ii) a broad-based strategy of inclusiveness with a view to empowering every citizen to participate fully and benefit from the development process; and (iii) a sustainable development pathway that is resilient to disaster and climate change; entails sustainable use of natural resources; and successfully manages the inevitable urbanisation transition.

2.5.2 Context and Determinants of Economic Reforms

During the Liberation War in 1971, there were extensive destruction and damages to all types of establishments and infrastructures in both rural and urban areas across Bangladesh. Since the Pakistani owners of most industrial enterprises fled during the war in 1971, the government had to undertake the responsibility of their enterprises as abandoned properties. As a result, the government started managing and operating more than 300 medium- and large-scale industrial enterprises, which represented nearly 90 per cent of the value of all such enterprises of the newly independent country.

The government established public corporations to oversee the major industries, such as jute, textiles, sugar, steel, paper and paperboard, fertiliser, chemicals, pharmaceuticals, engineering and shipbuilding, minerals, oil and gas, food and allied products, and forest products.[1] With government control over major industries and massive inputs of foreign aid, the economy gradually returned to the levels of the late 1960s by 1975.

After independence, socioeconomic developments were accompanied by significant changes in policy regimes as well as political ideals. The 'experiment' with the state controlled economy was reversed with the change in political regime in 1975. This was followed by policies of deregulation and liberalisation to create an open and private sector-led economy along with a liberal trade regime. The belief was that such a strategy would accelerate economic growth by relaxing several constraints of the small domestic market and providing access to foreign direct investment (FDI) thereby facilitating technology transfer, creating marketing network, and providing much-needed managerial and technical skills. Although the central thrust of the policies have not changed much since the period, the pace and content of the reforms varied considerably during different periods.

These reforms significantly influenced the country's socioeconomic performance through changing the underlying allocative and distributive policies and shifting the sectoral allocation of resources and ownership pattern of productive factors. The nature of impact of economic growth on poverty and social development was influenced by several other factors as well, such as initial conditions, development status in specific areas, socio-political conditions, nature of governance, and other socio-cultural contexts. Further, sustained political commitment resulting in policy consistence over a relatively longer period of time also brought impressive

[1]There were, for example, Bangladesh Jute Mills Corporation (BJMC); Bangladesh Textiles Mills Corporation (BTMC); Bangladesh Sugar Industries Corporation; Bangladesh Engineering and Shipbuilding Corporation; Bangladesh Paper Mills Corporation, Bangladesh Chemical Industries Corporation; Bangladesh Steel Mills Corporation; Bangladesh Oil and Natural Resources Corporation (Petrobangla); and others.

achievements in certain areas.[2] It is important, therefore, to explore Bangladesh's macroeconomic policy regimes in the light of its growth history.

Within the reform package, implementation pattern of reforms also varied over different sectors. The reforms were implemented rapidly in the trade sector resulting in significant reduction in tariff and non-tariff barriers.[3] The major aim was to liberalise the external trade and foreign exchange regimes and rationalise the trade regime by lowering tariff rates, phasing out quantitative restrictions, streamlining import procedures, and introducing tax reforms and export promotion measures.

Reforms in the industrial sector, on the other hand, were slow and generated mixed outcomes. Despite the emergence of a dynamic and export-oriented RMGs sector, the rest of the manufacturing industries (except a few like pharmaceuticals, leather goods, and others) suffered from deep-rooted governance, finance, infrastructure and other problems in the absence of wider and deeper reforms.

The reforms in agriculture covered several policy changes, such as liberalisation of the fertiliser and irrigation equipment markets, reforms in the public food grains distribution system (PFDS), and elimination of

[2]One of the factors that explain Bangladesh's significant social development at a relatively low level of income is the political commitment to human development creating policy consistency across all types of political regime since independence. Successive governments, irrespective of their ideological and political biases, emphasised on reducing population growth, investing on primary and girls 'education, improving primary health care, providing safe water and improved sanitation, women empowerment, and similar issues. One reason for this is that such concerns are universally appealing across a wide range of political beliefs and ingrained in all societies and cultures. This ignites actions and results in behavioural changes conducive to social development. See, Mujeri and Sen 2006.

[3]For details, see Mujeri 2002a, b, Mujeri 2004; Khondker and Mujeri 2006. Some major changes include: dismantling of tariff and non-tariff barriers; tariff bands were narrowed and import procedures simplifies; 24 slabs of import duty rates of the 1980s were replaced by only four slabs in 2000; highest customs duty rate was reduced from 350 per cent in 1992 to 37.5 per cent in 2000; mean tariff declined from 114 per cent in 1989 to 22 per cent in 1999 while weighted mean tariff declined to 19 per cent; number of commodities under the four digit code subject to quantitative restrictions declined from 550 in 1987 to 124 under the import policy 1997–2002; multiple exchange rate system was replaced by a unified exchange rate in 1992 and Taka was pegged to a currency-weighted basket; creeping devaluation was followed since 1992 to maintain exchange rate flexibility and export competitiveness within a more market-determined exchange rate regime and Taka was made convertible for all current account transactions. The exchange rate was made fully flexible in 2003. Further liberalisation has been followed afterwards.

subsidies. The overall impact of the policies was favourable and created significant positive impact on agricultural production and productivity (see, Ahmed 1995). However, reforms in other areas such as in the financial sector and infrastructure policies lagged behind creating serious deficiency in the quality and quantity of much-needed services.[4]

2.6 Policy-Based Periodisation of Growth

Over the last fifty years since independence, Bangladesh experienced several fundamental structural changes which altered the power structure within which social, economic and political processes unfolded. For the Bangladesh economy, this created distinct phases of growth, which could be traced by relating macroeconomic policy changes to major economic outcomes. For the present analysis, we have divided Bangladesh's growth-history into five phases using policy-based periodisation.[5] The five phases of growth are as follows:

Phase 1: 1972–1982—Reconstruction and recovery amidst political turbulence
Phase 2: 1983–1990—Slow growth and rising macro instability
Phase 3: 1991–1996—Crisis-driven reforms and favourable initial state
Phase 4: 1997–2008—Rising growth and social development
Phase 5: 2009–2019—Consolidating and enhancing growth

[4] These included, for example, power shortages including huge 'system loss', supply constraints, low reliability of service creating frequent supply disruptions; inadequate, inefficient and expensive telecommunications network; inefficiencies and problems in the ports resulting in high shipping costs; and poor governance and inefficiency in the banking sector creating in large incidence of non-performing loans.

[5] Periodisation is a process or study of categorising the past into discrete, quantified blocks of time. This is usually done in order to facilitate the study and analysis of history, understanding current and historical processes, and causality that might have linked those events. However, determining the precise beginning and ending of a period is often arbitrary, since it has changed over time in the course of history. To the extent history is continuous, periodisation is likely to be arbitrary. Yet, without periodisation a framework does not exist to analyse and understand scattered policies or developments in history. See, Besserman 1996. The present analysis has been adapted from Mujeri and Sen 2006. The above periodisation analysis for Bangladesh using policy criterion is also consistent with other plausible criteria, such as 'periodisation by crisis' or 'periodisation using structural breaks' in aggregate growth or sectoral growth.

Table 2.11 Macroeconomic indicators in different phases of growth

	Phase 1 1972–1982	*Phase 2* 1983–1990	*Phase 3* 1991–1996	*Phase 4* 1997–2008	*Phase 5* 2009–2019
GDP growth rate, % per year	2.30	3.86	4.53	5.40	6.60
Per capita GDP index, 2006=100	54.60	60.89	68.30	88.95	149.06
As % of GDP					
Gross investment	10.91	16.11	18.28	23.41	27.83
Gross national savings	3.61	21.74	22.19	30.63	38.11
Exports	5.27	2.65	3.87	9,68	17.81
Imports	12.97	5.80	6.28	13.43	21.14
Remittances	1.37	2.78	2.98	5.48	8.55
Total public revenue	6.27	6.33	8.83	9.66	11.05
Total public expenditure	13.04	12.79	13.77	14.03	15.90
Overall budget balance	-6.77	-6.45	-4.94	-4.37	-4.85
Current account balance	-3.26	-1.85	-0.31	0.16	1.10
CPI inflation, per cent per year	...	7.37	5.73	6.04	7.09

Source: BBS, *Statistical Yearbook*, various years

Major characteristics of the five phases using selected parameters are given in Table 2.11.

2.6.1 *Reconstruction and Recovery Amidst Political Turbulence, 1972–1982*

After independence, Bangladesh inherited an over-regulated economy characterised by import controls, foreign exchange rationing, overvalued exchange rate, subsidised pricing of food grains under public food distribution as well as for publicly provided agricultural inputs and institutional credit. It is estimated that about 34 per cent of the value of fixed assets in the modern manufacturing sector was contributed by public enterprises (Sobhan and Ahmad 1980).

The reconstruction phase faced big challenges. The GDP declined by more than 14 per cent in 1972–1973 over the last normal year before independence (see, Table 2.3). The newly independent country, however, boldly faced the challenges; and the country's per capital GDP and major macroeconomic indicators, such as gross savings and investment as shares of GDP, recovered to their normal levels within a short time. The period was also characterised by several socio-political and economic developments including economic nationalism emphasising inward orientation with strong state control, violent change of political power followed by partial liberalisation and privatisation, rapid spread of 'political loans' and the early signs of crisis of development financial institutions (DFIs), emergence of targeted employment programmes, emphasis on green revolution for increasing food production, and priority on population control programmes. The period, however, ended with a high and unsustainable reliance on external assistance and the emergence of 'crisis of external dependence' as a major policy concern (Sobhan 1982, 1991).

For setting economic priorities, the First Five-Year Plan (1973–1978) was prepared which was followed by a Two-Year Plan (1978–1980). The First Plan adopted socialist principles of distributive justice and spelled out an investment strategy dominated by the public sector and underscored the need for land reforms, extension of cooperatives, assistance to small farmers and landless labourers in the agriculture sector, and public sector control of industrial activities leaving only the small and cottage industries for the private sector. However, within a year of launching the First Plan, domestic events such as successive draughts (1972 and 1973) and devastating flood (1974) as well as global events including world commodity boom, international monetary disorder, and the recession during 1974–1975 in the developed world destroyed much of the relevance of the Plan. Further, political changes in 1975 brought about fundamental changes in the philosophy of development through a dominant public sector.[6]

During 1975–1982, more emphasis was put on promoting private sector development. After 1975, emphasis was placed towards developing new industrial capacity and rehabilitating the economy. The government gradually started to give greater scope to the private sector participation in the economy, a pattern that has continued since the period. Many state-owned enterprises were privatised, including banks, telecommunications, media, and jute industries. Economic policies aimed at encouraging private enterprises and investment, privatising public industries, reinstating budgetary discipline, and liberalising the import regime were accelerated.

[6] For an exposition of the developments and evolution of the ideas of the period, see Islam, 1978.

However, Bangladesh's reform programme remained in deep crisis because it had, over a decade, failed to accelerate growth, diversify the economy, stimulate investment and domestic savings and create the basis for sustained growth till the mid-1980s. One major characteristic of the policies and reforms of the period was that these were undertaken mostly in response to specific and/or exogenous shocks faced by the economy and were short-term in nature.

One may note that short-term shocks to the Bangladesh economy—due to the steep rise in oil prices and large deterioration in Bangladesh's terms of trade in the 1970s—forced the country to implement monetary stabilisation and exchange rate adjustment programmes during 1974–1975. A similar deterioration in the macroeconomic fundamentals again led Bangladesh to the International Monetary Fund (IMF) in 1980 for short-term financing under the Extended Fund Facility (EFF). The disbursements under the 1980 EFF, however, were suspended in early-1981 due to failure to keep within agreed borrowing targets.

2.6.2 *Slow Growth and Rising Macro Instability, 1983–1990*

The period witnessed slow growth (with yearly GDP growth averaging only 3.86 per cent over the entire period) along with wide yearly fluctuations.[7] The slow growth became increasingly unsustainable and the ensuing macroeconomic crisis led to the implementation of a range of stabilisation measures by the government. The reform measures were mostly driven by the balance of payments crisis and were a part of the conditionalities under the IMF and World Bank's structural adjustment programmes.

The macroeconomic instability during the early 1980s in most of the low income countries was regarded by the World Bank and the IMF not as the result of short-term exogenous shocks, rather the outcome of longer term structural maladjustment as a result of 'faulty' policies. As such, the 'prescription' was that the macroeconomic policies in developing countries were to be driven by considerations of price stability ('getting prices right'), based on the so-called Washington Consensus. As a remedy, these institutions promoted an agenda of macroeconomic stabilisation backed by reforms which broadly covered areas of import liberalisation,

[7] The coefficient of variation of yearly GDP growth rate was a high of 27 per cent during the 1980s which declined to less than 12 per cent during 1997–2007.

exchange rate adjustment, financial deregulation, fiscal reform, subsidisation of public goods, and development of private enterprises. These reforms were expected to make the low income countries realise a path of sustainable growth based on a more outward oriented development strategy (Sobhan 1992a, b).

In 1982, Bangladesh started implementing the above pattern of reforms. During 1986–1989, Bangladesh contracted with the IMF under its Structural Adjustment Facility (SAF) and again resorted to the IMF's Enhanced Structural Adjustment Facility (ESAF) during 1990–1993 (Rahman 1991). Both programmes involved agreements over a policy framework paper (PFP) which had set out the agenda of macroeconomic reforms during the period.

The PFPs were backed up by series of structural adjustment (SA) loans extended by the World Bank and Asian Development Bank (ADB), in terms of programme or sector loans. These loans provided foreign exchange to the government to carry out a series of policy and institutional reforms in particular sectors or areas of the economy. Some of the areas covered by these loans included the industrial, energy, financial and agricultural sector loans from the World Bank and the food crop sector loan and industrial sector loan of the ADB.

The IMF, on its part, related loans to the government to a policy regime of macroeconomic stabilisation on its budgetary and balance of payments account, financial stability and competitive exchange rates. The sectoral loans of the World Bank and ADB covered such areas as desubsidisation of agricultural inputs and public utility services, financial deregulation, import liberalisation, fiscal reforms, divestiture of public enterprises, improved revenue collection and management of public utilities.

Despite high enthusiasm about promoting macroeconomic reforms through structural adjustments, Bangladesh's economic stabilisation and adjustment programmes yielded little predicted outcomes (Rahman 1991; Sobhan 1993; Mujeri et al. 1993a, b). Nevertheless, structural reform of macroeconomic instruments transformed the once protective economic system into a market-driven one by deregulating the financial sector, encouraging foreign investment in industry and the money market, reducing import tariff rates, and most importantly, by withholding subsidies to the agricultural sector and privatising state-owned industries. Between 1991 and 1993, the government followed an enhanced structural adjustment facility (ESAF) with the IMF and carried out some economic reforms. However, in the absence of any comprehensive assessment of the country's economic, political and social priorities and the resulting uneven distribution of adjustment burdens on different socioeconomic groups, the adjustment programme did not provide realistic policy framework that could be backed by strong social and political commitment (Sobhan 1991; Mujeri et al. 1993a, b).

Thus, starting from the mid-1980s, Bangladesh gradually introduced various liberalisation measures. The process was initiated by liberalising international trade, which consisted of permitting the exporters of non-traditional items to convert some of their export earnings at higher exchange rate in the secondary market, reduction of the tariff level and tariff dispersion, simplification and rationalisation of the tariff structure, and deregulation of the import process as well as export incentives such as Export Performance Licensing, Export Performance Benefit Scheme, Special Bonded Warehouse Scheme, Back-to-Back L/C System, Export Credit Guarantee Scheme, Export Promotion Fund, bank loans, and tax holiday. The financial sector reforms which began during the first half of the 1990s included liberalisation of interest rates, improvement of monetary policy, abolishing priority sector lending, strengthening central bank supervision, deregulating banks, improving debt recovery and broadening the capital market development.

The reforms of the period signalled a qualitatively new phase of development in Bangladesh. The period, covering most of the 1980s, showed several characteristics having deep impact on the economy and the society. These included: slow and fluctuating economic growth; deteriorating macroeconomic stability with growing fiscal crisis; authoritarianism of governance, institutionalisation of corruption, and rise of 'crony capitalism'; decentralisation efforts for creating stronger local governance through introducing 'upazila' initiatives; emphasis on safety-net programmes; and the emergence of NGOs as important conduit of local development, especially in poverty reduction and social development initiatives.

2.6.3 Crisis-Driven Reforms and Favourable Initial State, 1991–1996

The period formed a period of transition in many respects, especially in terms of forming improved economic fundamentals and attaining a 'threshold' level of human and social capital. The period, although transitional in nature, saw more conscious efforts towards implementing wide-ranging social and economic reforms to facilitate the creation of a more liberalised and responsible policy regime.

The period witnessed significant outward orientation with the key developmental role assigned to the private sector along with a facilitating role for the public sector, a move towards macroeconomic stability, emphasis on development of human capital, emergence of NGOs as major service providers especially to the poor, recognition of government-NGOs partnership, and the transition towards parliamentary democracy. Thus, it was a period of rapid transition. During the period, there had been considerable economic reforms and greater nourishment of democratic values (Mujeri 2004). In particular, reforms in the external sector during the period led to the emergence of a more outward-oriented economy along with positive trends in major macroeconomic indicators.[8] The GDP growth rate also started to pick up especially since mid-1990s and followed a generally rising trend in the later years.

2.6.4 *Rising Growth and Social Development, 1997–2008*

With necessary conditions for graduating to higher growth in place, the period exhibited much improved performance both in terms of economic growth and social development. This was made possible through the unleashing of the second generation of reforms which differed significantly from the first generation gradual economic reform approach of the earlier phase. In particular, better performance of the period was the outcome of the interactions between the 'initial condition state' created over the last three phases and the policy and institutional changes of the period towards more market-responsive and democratic policy regimes.

Along with more prudent macroeconomic and other policies, several feature of the period were noteworthy, such as favourable macroeconomic fundamentals; continued emphasis on liberalisation, outward orientation, and the private sector; strong emphasis on agriculture and rural development; and greatly enhanced disaster management capacity. Building on positive conditions and through pursuit of more prudent policies, the period succeeded in achieving higher economic growth accompanied by

[8] The openness ratio, as measured by trade (merchandise exports and imports) to GDP ratio, increased from 20 per cent to 28 per cent between 1990 and 1996 compared with only one percentage point increase between 1985 and 1990. See Mujeri 2002a, b.

faster improvements in social indicators including reduction in income poverty and child malnutrition.

Since the mid-1990s, successive governments were committed to free-market policies, privatisation of state-owned enterprises, attracting overseas investment and financial and other sectoral reforms. In 2003, the government entered into a three-year Poverty Reduction and Growth Facility (PRGF) with IMF that aimed to support the government's economic reform programme up to 2006. Capital account liberalisation in Bangladesh started in 1997 which included easing restrictions in the capital and money markets, derivatives, credit operations, direct investments, real estate transactions, personal capital movements, provisions specific to commercial banks and institutional investors.

The period also witnessed the emergence of several areas of concern which threatened to undermine the socio-political stability and future economic progress, such as deterioration of governance including law and order situation, rising corruption, and political confrontation resulting in the declaration of emergency and formation of an interim government in January 2007; and the global financial crisis of 2007–2008 including terrorism and sharp increases in prices of oil and other commodities (especially essential food products which Bangladesh imports in large quantities) in the world market. However, Bangladesh successfully managed these crises and was able to ensure required domestic stability.

2.6.5 *Consolidating and Enhancing Growth, 2009–2019*

This period also saw a series of structural reforms (third generation reforms) which restored the Bangladesh economy to higher GDP growth rate and fiscal prudence. During the period, reforms were focused on restraining fiscal and current account deficits, and lowering the inflation rates. Various liberalisation measures and adjustment programmes (e.g. privatisation, rationalisation of sectoral loans and subsidies) were also pursued. While the pace and sequencing of these programmes was matters of concern, these measures, along with others, strengthened macro and sectoral policies, and created reasonably stable macroeconomic fundamentals. Fiscal deficits remained well below the widely accepted yardstick of 5 per cent of GDP. The current account also remained surplus during most of the years.

Bangladesh also relaxed its compulsions of following the strict conditionalities of the external lending agencies (e.g. World Bank and IMF). To a large extent, Bangladesh seems to have developed its own path of reform in the 2000s, especially with respect to sequencing and pacing of stabilisation and adjustment. With relatively low rates of inflation and a better debt sustainability, Bangladesh was able to significant reduce its dependence on conditional borrowing.

During the period, Bangladesh's macroeconomic policy framework has been more prudent, and the economy achieved a reasonable degree of stability during the entire period except some short-lived and small shocks. In particular, Bangladesh refrained from fiscal profligacy to drive growth and it managed to reduce the debt-GDP ratio to below 35 per cent, and external debt servicing to around 4.5 per cent of total export earnings. The global boom of 2002–2007, the falling fuel and commodity prices, and the growing significance of remittances were also vital to sustaining stability and growth. Rising remittances and exports also played significant roles in the growth of national savings and foreign exchange reserves; reduced the current account deficit and strengthened the country's import capacity.

The period also saw several positive developments that helped in building the country's resource balances, both internal and external. Export earnings rapidly increased with sustained high growth of RMGs exports, growth in food production helped to reduce the food import bills, and remittances from migrant workers grew significantly resulting in rapid growth in the country's foreign exchange reserves. The government debt reached 33.4 per cent in 2018 and remains steady at 34 per cent in 2020. Furthermore, the inflation rate was 6 per cent in 2018 and is projected at 6.1 per cent in both 2019 and 2020. The budget deficit also remains below the target of 5 per cent of GDP.

From the above, it is clear that macroeconomic performance significantly varied over the five phases. In particular, building on the favourable conditions of earlier periods, the period since 2009 has experienced a more facilitating macroeconomic environment and recorded higher and more stable economic growth (Table 2.12). It is seen that the country's growth rate has shown a consistent upward trend especially after the 2000s underpinned by strong macroeconomic fundamentals and favourable policy regime, indicating the beginning of a high and sustained growth phase of the economy along with the pursuit of the right policies.

The above analysis further shows that a significant feature of the country's political economy and associated economic policy regime has been the relatively rapid and significant changes within the short period of

Table 2.12 Select macroeconomic indicators during different policy regimes

	1972–1982		*1983–1990*		*1991–1996*		*1997–2008*		*2009–2019*	
	1975	*1982*	*1983*	*1990*	*1991*	*1996*	*1997*	*2008*	*2009*	*2019*
Annual growth rate, %										
GDP	3.4	2.4	4.0	5.9	3.4	4.6	5.4	6.0	5.1	8.1
Agriculture	-1.0	1.0	3.9	9.4	2.2	3.1	6.0	4.5	3.5	3.5
Industry	42.0	3.9	4.1	7.0	4.6	7.0	5.8	7.0	6.9	13.0
Services	1.1	3.4	4.2	3.3	3.3	4.0	4.5	5.8	5.1	6.5
Per capita GDP	0.4	0.5	1.9	2.8	1.2	2.9	3.9	4.6	3.7	6.9
As % of GDP										
Gross investment	7.5	17.8	17.0	17.1	16.9	20.0	20.7	26.2	26.2	31.6
Gross national savings	0.6	17.9	17.3	17.6	19.7	20.0	20.7	27.9	28.9	28.4
Total revenue	1.7	7.1	7.0	6.5	7.6	9.2	9.6	9.6	9.8	13.4
Total tax revenue	1.4	5.6	5.8	5.5	6.2	7.3	7.9	7.6	7.9	12.1
Total public expenditure	6.2	11.8	10.4	11.6	13.6	13.9	13.3	14.9	13.4	18.3
Overall budget balance (excluding grants)	-3.1	-16.9	-19.1	-7.4	-6.0	-4.7	-3.7	-5.3	-3.5	-4.9
Exports	2.5	5.2	5.7	6.1	5.5	9.5	10.4	15.4	15.2	9.0
Imports	8.7	15.9	15.1	13.5	11.2	17.1	16.9	21.3	19.8	12.5
Current account balance	4.9	-5.4	-1.9	2.7	-3.9	-2.3	-1.3	0.7	2.4	-1.4
Inflation, %	67.2	7.5	13.9	4.8	7.8	6.7	4.0	12.3	7.6	5.4

Note: Due to non-availability of data for 1972, data for 1975 are used. The high growth rate of industry in 1975 is due to recovery after the war of 1971. Similarly, relative high growth in 1990 (especially of agr culture) is due to recovery after two successive devastating floods in 1988 and 1989

Source: BBS, *Statistical Yearbook*, various years

50 years of Bangladesh's economic history. The analysis also shows that three important factors fuelled the process of policy development that was characterised by significant breaks and discontinuity. First, a rapid shift in the fundamental development philosophy from a democratic socialist system to a market-based economy through violent political changes in 1975. Second, a strong wave of globalisation that replaced the inward-looking import-substituting growth strategy with open, market-based and export-led growth as the framework for sustained growth. Third, emergence of repeated economic crises fuelled by economic and political mismanagement and recurrent natural disasters requiring urgent policy responses often 'dictated' by international financial institutions and the donor community.

Nevertheless, one important positive feature of the overall policy framework has been the presence of several continuing themes of policy consistency within the country's rather disjointed policy stream since independence, as discussed above. These included, for example, strong emphasis on social development and recognition of the importance of grassroots mobilisation, community interactions, and women empowerment in partnership with NGOs and civil society organisations (CSOs). No doubt, these aspects of development are underrated in conventional development discourse, but an early recognition of the importance of harnessing the potential of these factors ushered in, despite a slow pace of economic growth, a more conducive environment for social development at a relatively low level of per capita income in Bangladesh. In addition, socioeconomic compulsions and the urgent need for 'crisis management' at different points in time often played a major role in the evolution of specific policy regimes and shaping the dynamics of policy change in the country.

2.6.6 *Growth Impact of Reforms*

In the context of evolution of policy regimes in Bangladesh, an important question is: Did the reforms bring about any change in the country's growth prospects? Using the traditional growth theoretic framework, following growth impact of reforms may be provided.

The explanation is based on a simple interpretation using the equation for the speed of an economy's convergence to its steady state growth path. Mankiw et al. (1992) show that an economy closes approximately p per cent of the gap to its steady-state growth path each year and the value of p can be calculated as:

$$p = (1-\alpha)(n+g+\varphi) \tag{2.1}$$

where α is the share of capital in the aggregate production function, n is the rate of population growth, g is the trend growth rate of the efficiency of labour, and φ is the depreciation rate of capital.

Since we do not have firm estimates of several of these parameters for the Bangladesh economy, some plausible values derived in Sect. 2.7 of this Chapter have been used. We assume population growth rate (n) of 1.3 per cent, labour force efficiency (g) growth of 1.2 per cent, and a depreciation rate of capital (ϕ) of 4.2 per cent.[9] The share of capital (α) in the aggregate production function can have a wide range of values, depending on the definition of capital. For the present purpose, we have used a value of 0.45, which is the average value of α as estimated in Sect. 2.6. With these parameter values, the estimate of p is 0.0369.

In order to relate to the reforms, we use the simple growth theory prediction that the contribution of the reform measures to growth of the Bangladesh economy is through raising its long-term steady state growth path. With simplifying assumptions, it can be stated that the growth rate in the short run will accelerate by an amount equal to (p × Δy) where Δy is the proportional change in the economy's steady state growth path due to the reforms carried out in the economy.

We assume that the effects of the reforms can be captured as a one-time and once-and-for-all upward shift in the economy's steady state growth path. Then, for a value of p of 3.69 per cent and with an average annual acceleration of 1.5 per cent in economic growth since the 1990s, this implies that the policy reforms of the entire period boosted the long run steady state growth path of the Bangladesh economy by about 41 per cent. This shows that past reforms carried out in the Bangladesh economy brought about powerful changes in the economy's long run growth prospects, increasing the post-reform long run growth path by more than 40 per cent of the pre-reform one.

[9] The assumed values roughly correspond to their average values since the mid-1990s. The labour force efficiency growth rate also matches the real wage growth history in the formal sector.

2.7 Long-Term Growth Dynamics: Total Factor Productivity

The pace of economic growth in Bangladesh since independence shows that the growth rate has accelerated slowly, despite significant variation in the short term. Moreover, the growth rate has never reversed for a prolonged period. Further, different components of GDP have experienced varied rates of growth. To examine the underlying determinants of the growth experience, decomposition of output growth into input use and total factor productivity (TFP) growth is a useful framework. Decomposing the TFP, the trends in labour productivity may be analysed to see whether productivity growth was driven by within sector productivity gains or reallocation of labour to more productive sectors.

Generally, it is seen that the contribution of TFP to output growth depends on the share of physical capital in real output; and the higher this share, the lower would be the contribution of TFP to growth (Senhadji 2000). The accumulation of capital during the initial period is, therefore, of great significance in determining the rate of economic growth. According to the standard framework, the growth of output can be decomposed into accumulation of inputs, such as labour and capital, and technical progress (or improvement in production efficiency). Based on the assumptions of competitive factor markets, constant returns to scale and Hicks-neutral technical progress, Solow (1956) measures TFP growth (TFPG) by the output growth that is not explained by input growth:

$$\mathrm{TFPG} = \mathrm{A}'/\mathrm{A} = \mathrm{Y}'/\mathrm{Y} - \alpha\mathrm{K}'/\mathrm{K} - (1-\alpha)\mathrm{L}'/\mathrm{L} \tag{2.2}$$

where L and K refer to labour and capital inputs and A is the level of technology, while the dotted variable denote time derivatives and α is the elasticity of production with respect to capital (which is equal to the capital income share under the standard assumptions). In order to account for the contribution of human capital and reduce the omitted variable bias in the estimates of TFP growth, we have used 'quality-adjusted labour' as the labour input by taking the average years of schooling of employed labour as weights (Mujeri 2004). For our purpose, 'quality-adjusted labour' has been defined as

$$L_i^* = e^{0.1s}iL_i \tag{2.3}$$

where S stands for average years of schooling per worker, L is the total employed labour force, i stands for female and male labour force, and 0.1 is the return to education as estimated for Bangladesh (World Bank 2006). The use of exponential form for calculating L_i* reflects the implicit assumption that human capital grows faster at higher levels of schooling. The quality-adjusted labour input thus takes into account both the stock and the returns to education of the employed labour force. A widely used variant of the Perpetual Inventory Method (PIM) has been used for estimating capital stock as the accumulated stream of past investments:[10]

$$K_t = V_t I_t + V_{t-1} I_{t-1} + \cdots\cdots\cdots\cdots + V_{t-T} I_{t-T} \tag{2.4}$$

where $v_t = 1$; $0 < v_{t-1} < 1$: and t-T is the oldest surviving capital asset.

The capital stock series is constructed using the concept of initial capital stock, K(0):

$$K_t = (1-\varphi)^t K(0) + \Sigma I_{t-1} (1-\varphi)^I \, and V_t = (1-\varphi) V_{t+1} \tag{2.5}$$

where ϕ is the rate of geometric decay; and K(0) is the initial capital stock at period 0.

The present estimates of TFP growth are made using the familiar Cobb–Douglas production, using capital and labour as the two inputs. Consequently, the portion of output growth not explained by the growth of capital and quality-adjusted labour inputs has been taken as the TFP growth. The estimates of TFP growth during different phases of growth are given in Table 2.13.

The results indicate that the nature of economic growth in Bangladesh did not vary much over the five phases of growth distinguished in the present analysis. The annual growth rate of quality-adjusted labour consistently increased since the 1970s, reaching nearly 4 per cent over the last decade. The growth of capital stock also accelerated, and increased by nearly three percentage points in the last decade over the initial period.

[10] The PIM, though an indirect method, has many practical advantages over alternative techniques of estimating capital stock, e.g. through conducting direct surveys. However, a major limitation is that the application of PIM requires different assumptions on the length of asset lives, retirement and depreciation patterns which are often not very robust. See, Ward 1976; Nehru and Dhareshwar 1993; Rahman and Rahman 2002.

Table 2.13 Estimates of TFP growth in Bangladesh

Period	*GDP*	*Annual growth rate in per cent*		
		Quality-adjusted labour	*Capital*	*TFP*
1972–1982	2.30	2.45	4.05	0.25
1983–1990	3.86	3.35	4.12	0.27
1991–1996	4.53	3.54	4.96	0.06
1997–2008	5.40	3.74	6.79	0.36
2009–2019	6.60	3.96	7.01	0.89

Source: Mujeri 2004; Authors' calculation

As against the notable growth of labour and capital inputs, TFP had a secondary role in contributing towards the country's growth process. During the first two phases, the annual growth rate of TFP was 0.25 per cent and 0.27 per cent respectively, but this declined sharply to 0.06 per cent during the early-1990s, a period characterised by crisis-driven economic reforms and rapid trade liberalisation. Since 1997, the TFP growth has accelerated to an annual average of 0.36 per cent till 2008; and further to an average of 0.89 per cent during the period of 2009 to 2019.[11] The results indicate that the contribution of TFP to economic growth is rising consistently in Bangladesh, although TFP still remains a minor contributor.

Further, the analysis shows that the TFP growth has varied over the five policy regimes in the country's growth history differentiated in the present study. It shows that, from a value of 0.25 per cent per year in the first phase (1972–1982), it declined to only 0.06 per cent per year during the third phase (1991–1996) which was characterised by crisis-driven economic reforms. The trend, however, reversed afterwards, with an average annual growth rate reaching 0.89 per cent in the 2010s. This shows that the underlying factors which characterised different policy regimes also had a significant impact on TFP growth.

[11] It may be added that the contribution of TFP to output growth depends crucially upon the value of the share of capital in total output. The higher the value of capital's share, the lower is the contribution of TFP since decreasing the share lowers the contribution of capital and increases the contribution of labour. Generally, there is a negative correlation between the contribution of TFP and the level of capital's share due to the fact that capital generally grows faster than labour.

After independence, Bangladesh started its growth journey with a land-scarce and labour-abundant economy; having low stock of accumulated capital and physical infrastructure. The pattern of TFP growth over the years, therefore, is likely to be significantly influenced by these initial conditions and the nature of policy regimes that affected the overall growth conditions during different phases.

While the initial conditions do matter, Bangladesh's growth history suggests that, despite the country's unduly pessimistic assessments during the 1970s, Bangladesh did not perform poorly in terms of productivity growth despite the existence of adverse institutional and political set-ups, inherent dynamics of which could not create conditions to follow the right policies. In such an unstable situation, Bangladesh needed almost a decade to overcome adverse initial conditions and set up the pre-conditions for achieving higher productivity growth.

The second phase, covering most of the 1980s, shows that, in the absence of corrective mechanisms to keep deregulation and liberalisation on a competitive and efficient path, the economy may get derailed that is unlikely to promote productivity growth. The period also shows the importance of supportive socio-political environment that charts out the course of productivity growth, such as the type of political regime. In Bangladesh, the period was marked by a sequence of political instability leading to economic crisis and wide-ranging reforms in the following phase. As such, the rate of productivity growth could not increase during the period.

The analysis indicates that the most important turning point in the country's economic history was created by the crisis-driven economic reforms of the early-1990s through which a more liberalised, deregulated, and private sector-friendly policy regime was created. This phase itself was characterised by very low TFP growth no doubt, but it opened up the widows for higher productivity growth in the following phases.

The experience of the fourth (1997–2008) and fifth (2009–2019) phases indicates that, once accumulated distortions are removed and the economy can perform in a more efficient manner, TFP growth can be ignited and sustained. Obviously, fourth generation reforms are needed to ensure sustained and high TFP growth and a successful transition of the Bangladesh economy from factor-intensive growth to technology-driven growth.[12]

[12] It is now widely recognised that TFP growth needs to play the most significant role to accelerate the growth dynamics in a country. Among others, such conclusions emerge from studies that attempt to explain cross-country differences in GDP growth. See, Klenow and Rodríguez-Clare 1997; Easterly and Levine 2000.

The TFP analysis brings out the fact that the past GDP growth in the country is mostly driven by factor accumulation; with a lesser role played by technology growth. In view of Bangladesh's limited resource endowments, the major source of the country's future growth acceleration would have to come through TFP growth. This requires the exploitation of the multiple routes of raising TFP growth including infusion of new technology, more emphasis on R&D, and increased FDI inflows. This also requires more emphasis on human capital and technological skills development, and assimilation and adoption of appropriate technologies.

Furthermore, TFP growth is the outcome of productivity changes at the sector and enterprise level. To raise TFP growth, policies are needed to address issues that affect the productivity and competitiveness at the sector and enterprise level. The issues cover both economic and non-economic factors, such as critical bottlenecks in the supply of essential inputs and services (e.g. electricity, telecommunications, transport, port facilities, and others); human capital deficiencies, especially limited availability of quality education and demand-responsive training; lack of effective measures to improving trade facilitation and removing barriers to competitiveness; low absorptive capacity and weak base for adopting innovative activities and advanced technologies; weak economic institutions and low economic governance; and absence of investment-friendly climate.

Bangladesh needs to ensure that TFP growth emerges as the major driver of growth acceleration in future. Along with strengthening macroeconomic fundamentals, this requires harnessing sound economic and social policies, and further expansion of social entrepreneurship at the grassroots level. A well-articulated productivity and growth strategy that creates productive and decent employment opportunities for workers of every level of skill, education and training is necessary for Bangladesh for sustaining growth and development.

2.8 Bangladesh's Long-Term Economic Growth

The present analysis shows that Bangladesh's long-term economic growth has been steady and relatively stable; as well as diversified and resilient. A key issue is the following: Has Bangladesh succeeded in laying the foundation for a more sustained double-digit growth in the coming decades?

Bangladesh's long-term economic growth has steadily accelerated over the past fifty-year period, without any major reversals. The rate of growth has also become more stable. This has been true especially since the 1990s.

During the 1970s and 1980s, growth volatility was more pronounced, and annual growth rates were characterised by large and unsustainable annual variations.

Over the years, Bangladesh's economic growth has become more diversified too. The fastest acceleration has taken place in the services sector, followed by industry, and agriculture. Over the long run, growth has been driven by large consumption expenditures; and rising investments and exports. There have also been productivity gains, both labour productivity and total factor productivity (TFP), although the size of the gains is small.

Moreover, growth has broadly been resilient to shocks, both domestic and external. The resilience of Bangladesh's growth can be attributed to the country's spatially diversified economy, as well as to its diversified production structure. It can also be attributed to the country's progressively diversifying trade basket (mostly comprising essential commodities) and a broad range of trading partners, mostly in the developed world.

Yet, the present analysis shows that despite the growth rate recovering, attaining a double-digit growth on a sustained basis would depend on an effective structural reform agenda. Over the last five decades, there have been seven episodes of high growth exceeding 7 per cent, one each in the 1970s and 1980s, and the rest five in the 2000s of which four are consecutive during 2016–2019. The earlier episodes lasted for only one year, and corrected sharply in the year thereafter. In some of these cases, high growth was due to a low base impact of slow growth in previous year followed by unusually good agricultural output. The only durable episode of growth sustaining at levels above 7 per cent for four consecutive years is the one that lasted from 2016 to 2019. This episode benefited from the combined effect of important reforms undertaken in the 2000s, and from a favourable global economy, leading to high sustained growth across sectors and all components of GDP.

In future, sustaining a growth rate higher than the trend growth rate of 7.0 to 7.5 per cent, and reaching a growth rate of 9 per cent or higher, will require contributions from all domestic sectors as well as support from the global economy. Achieving this would require a concerted reform effort that maintains the reform momentum and widens its scope, and succeeds in raising investment, credit supply and exports (World Bank 2012a, b). Maintaining the hard-won macroeconomic stability, arriving at a definite and durable solution to banking sector issues, realising the expected growth and fiscal dividend from the tax reforms, and regaining the momentum on the unfinished structural reform agenda are other key components of attaining high growth.

It must also be acknowledged that the Bangladesh state has been more penetrated by social actors than many East and Southeast Asian countries since the beginning.[13] As is well-known, state-driven nationalisation or state-driven globalisation processes demand a state having adequate command over powerful social and interest groups in society. However, in the case of Bangladesh, successful reforms need to evolve in a gradual manner along with building a social consensus on the reforms. The country's development model is a partnership between the state and society, where the power of the state, even in its commanding moments, can be moderated by social actors.

Furthermore, economic policy reforms need to build upon the historical path of gradual changes in ideas and policies, punctuated by economic crises. Such dynamics explain the success of the politics of the green revolution and understanding of liberalisation after the 1990s. It is also important to realise that the trade, investment and infrastructure reforms of the 1990s, although they constituted a break from the past, were largely path-dependent. Without the experience of the 1970s and the 1980s, the conviction required to break the deadlock in favour of the status quo bias would not have arisen. It is a story of getting to higher rates of growth in a gradual manner after building a policy consensus among diverse stakeholders. No doubt, economic crises aid the arrival of new policy consensus.

2.8.1 Key Issues in Long-Term Growth

There are two key dynamics behind long-term growth (Rodrik 2007). First, the development of fundamental capabilities of human capital and institutions; long-term growth depends on the accumulation of education and health to improved regulatory frameworks and better governance (Acemoglu and Robinson 2012). Moreover, fundamental capabilities are multidimensional and possess complementarities. Second, the dynamics of structural transformation, which are the creation and expansion of higher productivity activities and the transfer of labour from lower productivity to higher productivity activities. The first requires investments in skills, education, administrative capacity, and governance, while the

[13] The complexity of Bangladesh's democracy and the inconsistent nature of its development policy are well known. The development state driven by the East Asian experience is largely preoccupied with the importance of autonomy—the East Asian state's ability to maintain independence from powerful social actors. See, Wade 1990.

second entails targeted remedies. As an economy develops, the dualism between modern and traditional sectors disappears; and if strong fundamentals cannot be ensured, growth driven by structural transformation becomes unsustainable. Historically, industrialisation and manufactured exports have been the most reliable levers for rapid and sustained growth. It is also seen that the most successful economies achieving high growth have not been the ones with the least state intervention.

The desired structural transformation is hampered by both government and market failures. The relevant government failures are well known in Bangladesh, such as excessive regulation, corruption, restrictive labour laws, financial repression, insecure property rights, poor contract enforcement, macroeconomic instability and similar other reasons. While there exists a wide number of such failures, it is unlikely that institutional reforms in all aspects are feasible and, in reality, many countries have grown fast without any across-the-board reforms. In many countries, successful economic transitions have been characterised by the sequential relaxation of important binding constraints, using policy tools tailored to local circumstances (Rodrik 2007). This shows that high growth is feasible in institutional environments which are quite distorted and policy remedies could be highly effective although they may be quite unorthodox in terms of conventional standards. In Bangladesh, one big challenge relates to stimulating new industries. A large number of constraints have already been identified which cover both government and market failures. Since Bangladesh is currently growing below its economic potential, a sufficiently well targeted measure can produce a large investment response.

2.8.2 *Moving beyond Middle Income Trap*

A major concern relates to Bangladesh's chance of developing beyond the so-called 'middle income trap'.[14] This relates to a situation, in which

[14] The term 'middle-income trap' contrasts the concept of 'poverty trap' (or 'low-income trap'), which is well-studied in the literature of development economics. For many years, development economics has paid much attention to 'poverty trap', i.e. '[a] bad equilibrium for a family, community, or nation, involving a vicious circle in which poverty and underdevelopment lead to more poverty and underdevelopment, often from one generation to the next'. See, Todaro and Smith 2012: 175. According to World Bank and DRC (2012), in past half a century, many countries have developed rapidly into middle-income status, but far fewer have gone on to high-income status. Of the 101 middle-income economies in 1960, only 13 made it to upgrade themselves to high-income status by 2008. Between 1995 and

middle-income countries fail to progress further to high-income economies, since they fail to shift their growth model towards more specialisation in production and employment, greater reliance on innovation, and more emphasis on ability to shape new products and processes (Gill et al. 2007). The Asian Development Bank uses the term to refer to 'countries stagnating and not growing to advanced country levels' and attributes the cause of the phenomenon to the failure to 'make a timely transition from resource-driven growth, with low cost labour and capital, to productivity-driven growth' (ADB 2011).

Development economics literature offers several plausible explanations for a middle-income trap or slowdown. The first is the rising labour costs after the economy reaches the Lewis turning point (Wang and Weaver 2013). The second is the exhaustion of the catch-up effect. After an economy reaches middle-income status, marginal returns to capital accumulation diminishes rapidly so that further labour productivity growth has to rely more on technological progress. However, with industrialisation progressing to the technological frontier, most of the 'low-hanging fruits' get picked up; and fewer technologies remain to be adopted.

Since low-cost labour and easy technology adoption are the main drivers that propel the growth of low-income economies such as Bangladesh, the disappearance of these drivers may cause significant slowdown if new engines of growth are not identified, especially in technological innovation and creative business models. The loss of these drivers is further aggravated through international links, which prevail in the globalised world. Even if there are no trade barriers or frictions, the Balassa–Samuelson effect may operate such that the fast-growing country's real exchange rate rises, either via faster domestic inflation or nominal exchange rate appreciation or both (Samuelson 1994). This reduces the middle income country's export competitiveness to slow down the export-led growth.

There are also social and environmental factors that may contribute to the middle income country slowdown. The inverted-U Kuznets curve suggests that in the early stage of industrialisation, the distribution of income tends to worsen before it eventually improves at a later stage (Kuznets 1955). Although empirical evidence on Kuznets curve exists in some historical cases but remains elusive in others, the hypothesis fits well

2005, the increase of per capita wealth in the upper-middle income group was only 11%, considerably slower than that of high-income OECD group (25%), lower-middle income group (48%), and low-income group (17%). See, World Bank 2011: 32.

with Lewis model's implication on changes of income distribution before and after the economy reaches the Lewis turning point. The plausible scenario of rising social inequality through the early stage of industrialisation may pave way to a period of social unrest, political instability and economic slowdown.

In the case of Bangladesh, many of the plausible causes of middle-income slowdown may be compounded by reality. For instance, the impact of Lewis turning point is likely to be intensified by the country's rapid demographic transition. The arrival of a fast-aging society bodes badly for the future of the country's social security burden and productivity growth. In addition, income inequality is rising; the Gini coefficient has increased from around 0.40 in the early 1990s to over 0.48 in 2016.

Several policy issues are important for Bangladesh in the context of moving beyond the middle income trap. First, the fiscal capacity of the government is a key condition for ushering a successful transition. Ultimately, fiscal capabilities are the ultimate determinants that define the quality and level of public goods that the government could provide to sustain the country's catching-up progress in the future.

Secondly, the trends and problems of the country's financial market show that the dominance of the state-owned financial enterprises distorts these markets and these distortions contribute significantly to the risks of stumbling on a middle-income trap. The markets need more freedom to act without these distortions so that a Schumpeterian process of 'creative destruction' can be set in motion and private entrepreneurship can play a greater role to promote productivity growth.

Thirdly, as Bangladesh moves from lower-middle income to upper-middle income status, the demand for urban housing is surging in the backdrop of massive urbanisation. How this housing market boom affects household savings may have important implications on national savings, the loanable fund market, and consequently the economy's growth trends.

The essence of economic growth shifts from deploying more capital, labour, and other inputs—that is, input accumulation—to using all those inputs more efficiently—that is, total factor productivity (TFP) growth. Such a growth pattern contributes significantly in the transition from middle income to high income; and catch-up, human capital, and research and development are significant sources of TFP growth.

Further, measures towards strengthening innovative capacity are important for successfully navigating the transition to high-income status. But growth based on productivity improvement poses new and different challenges—challenges sometimes seen as inherently more difficult—than growth based simply on additional inputs. Furthermore, as the share of manufacturing in employment and output peaks and gives way to employment and output of services, it may become more difficult to boost productivity, given that capital and technology have traditionally been difficult to apply to the production of services.

The process of industrial upgrading that Bangladesh needs to undergo as it enters the MIC stage, should shift the economy from labour-intensive to technology-intensive production, driving up wages and driving down competitiveness (World Bank, 2012a, b). In the process, Bangladesh faces two constraints in properly mobilising technical skills to increase productivity. The first is that the growth in industrial production is spurred, in most cases, by an influx of small and medium enterprises which decrease overall productivity. These firms are not sufficient to drive growth in technical skills. Unless this is properly resolved, Bangladesh may experience productivity-reducing structural change, where labour moves to activities with lower productivity.

The second reason is that a newly industrialising middle income Bangladesh could be outpaced by regional powerhouses such as China and India. Both China and India, for example, absorbs a large portion of cheap labour-intensive industry, creating a barrier to entry by its low wages and scale, even though, in some cases, regional powerhouses may pull up other neighbouring countries.

Bangladesh, as a newly graduating MIC, may initially benefit from factor accumulation in the secondary sector, which drives growth as did in South Korea, Nigeria and Egypt in the 1960s and 1970s. However, growth in industry is not sustainable without gains in total factor productivity (Satoru 1997). For example, South Korea's attention to productivity growth through its policies and institutions enabled it to sustain productivity growth. South Korea's productivity-specific institutions and policy focus provide useful policy lessons for Bangladesh which is starting to experience rapidly increasing industrial production and rising wages.

For Bangladesh, one important challenge to competitiveness is in establishing suitable institutions for industrial policy. In the past, at lower levels of industrialisation, gains in economic growth could be experienced by liberalising trade and safeguarding macroeconomic balances. Institutions did not require high importance. Growth in Bangladesh at early stages of industrialisation has therefore taken place in the absence of properly functioning institutions.

However, institutions for industrial policy are important for a middle income Bangladesh for three important reasons: (i) adjusting production across various sectors to learn what is profitable and feasible, which requires support from the government; (ii) managing investment and growth in the economy with expanding secondary sector production and lacking policy coordination among stakeholders; and (iii) ensuring an efficient and equitable distribution of public inputs in the form of infrastructure, legislation, and research and development.

Middle income countries that have seen great successes in industrial policy are also seen to have established effective institutions at the same time as they have carried out economic liberalisation (Cheng et al. 1998). This suggests the importance of institutional alignment in tandem with economic liberalisation for MICs.

The ability of the state to effectively participate in coordinating economic activity presents another important challenge to middle-income Bangladesh. Middle-income economies are especially susceptible to both falling into low equilibriums in sector productivity and inability to mobilise investment and entrepreneurial enterprises (Rodríguez-Clare 2005). This is because MICs with a rising skilled labour force but insufficient capital endowments are not able to properly invest in and profit from modern sector production.

The state may thus have to play a central role in encouraging economic growth, especially in negotiating market and coordination failures (World Bank 1993). However, the policies for the productive sector aimed primarily at correcting market failures should not be piece-meal, non-transparent and not well coordinated. More importantly, they should focus sufficiently on accumulation of technological capabilities, which allows for broad-based structural change towards higher value added activities and is therefore the driving force behind sustained productivity growth. It is seen that successful state attempts at coordinating economic activity have mobilised capital and investments efficiently.

Bangladesh's transition to the upper middle income status also faces the challenges in integrating economic activity since Bangladesh needs to establish economies of scale for its export industries and develop a wide variety of industries having scale and competitiveness. Firstly, there has to be vertical integration—to have control over supply chains and intermediary goods to reduce production costs and ensure supply of parts (Gill and Kharas 2007). Secondly, there is a need for spatial integration to benefit from economies of agglomeration (World Bank 2009). Finally, regional integration may be necessary to fully benefit from technical assistance and access to capital markets in the region (UN General Assembly 2011). Further, a key advantage of such integration for Bangladesh will be to facilitate the dynamic specialisation of trade and 'trade fragmentation' for developing niche local advantages to attract specific types of production in intermediary goods and allow the country's small and medium enterprises (SMEs) to get involved in regional production networks and upgrade their value added in production.

Bangladesh's success in moving up the global production chains also requires facilitating domestic policies, such as spatial integration. One way to achieve this is through industrial park planning and development. For the purpose, the government needs to take the responsibility of construction, location and functioning of the parks. This will help streamline foreign and domestic investments and technology transfers can be made easier and the needs of industries adjusting to rapid urbanisation could be taken into account. Thus proper integration of economic activity is a useful tool when implemented in tandem with new industrial growth policies of the middle-income transition.

Another important challenge for upper middle-income transition of Bangladesh is Increasing innovation. Although wage increases may not harm productivity if accompanied by increases in labour efficiency or overall efficiency of production, limited innovation, technical change and technological adoption may rapidly exhaust productivity gains from factor accumulation. In order to sustainably increase productivity and competitiveness, gains in innovation are required (Gill and Kharas 2007).

For a successful middle income country, three features are important: (i) ability of a significant share of local firms to adapt technological knowledge from more advanced countries to the enterprise and country-specific contexts; (ii) transition of transnational corporation (TNC) affiliates from the assembly of labour intensive, low-tech products towards production in medium and high-tech products; and (iii) emergence of skills training programmes and growing/high enrolments at the secondary school level for building key social capabilities.

There are two major obstacles to achieving more innovation in Bangladesh. The first is the very limited spending on research and development (R&D). Higher innovation is correlated to higher growth (World Bank 2011). Low public spending on R&D and a low share of R&D spending by the private sector adversely affect innovation (ADB 2011). The second is the lack of institutional capacity to absorb the existing technology and human capital that contributes to higher innovation. This includes the inability to guarantee a job market to accept a higher educated population, quality institutions for research and higher education, and collaboration between public and private sectors (Gill and Kharas 2007).

In the above context, the South Korean experience during its middle-income period provides several valuable insights. The first is in its use of economic and financial mechanisms to boost investment and direct production. The state initially offered credit subsidies and tax incentives to private sector, directing public investment into enterprises focusing on modern sector production and exports (Rodrik 1995). The state also subsidised specialised education, technology and innovation initiatives tailored to private sector needs (World Bank 2006).

Currently, Bangladesh is struggling to properly mobilise innovations. According to the Global Innovation Index 2018, published annually by Cornell University and the World Intellectual Property Organisation (WIPO), Bangladesh is ranked 116th, the lowest in South Asia. Bangladesh's R&D expenditure is the lowest in the region and the majority of the amount is spent by the government. Bangladesh's science and technology policies are not integrated with its education policies; and have very limited interaction between its institutions of higher learning and enterprises. The Bangladesh example highlights both the potential for economic gains via primary sector innovation and the constraints imposed by a lack of private sector involvement in R&D.

2.8.3 Bangladesh's Agricultural Modernisation Model: Sequencing of Chemicalisation and Mechanisation

Modernisation and structural transformation is a defining characteristic of the development process in all countries—both as a cause as well as an effect of economic growth. Such changes occur in agriculture and the rural economy as well, although the nature, magnitude and the pace of these changes vary among countries and in the same country over time. The general tendencies cover a number of dimensions, such as a consolidation of landholdings and agricultural production, reduced labour demand and increased mechanisation and use of purchased inputs, shifts in land-use patterns, a growing importance of nonfarm employment and other income sources in the rural areas, and changes in the commodity composition of agricultural GDP. These patterns are strongly influenced by demographics, agro-ecological resources, development of infrastructure, and changes in consumer demand and international markets. The Bangladesh agriculture has also undergone significant modernisation over the last fifty years.

The World Development Report 2008 (World Bank 2008) classifies different countries into five categories based on the share of agriculture in national GDP and employment—ag-based, pre-transition, transition, urbanising and mature. For ag-based countries, the focus of policy attention tends to be improving basic rural infrastructure; and raising output and productivity through opening up new agricultural areas and increasing the use of modern inputs. Primary goals relate to assuring food security, reducing rural poverty and contributing to the country's trade balance. For pre-transition countries, these goals are supplemented with efforts to support agricultural diversification and increase private investment. For transition and urbanising countries, greater attention is given to multi-sectoral concerns or opportunities, including nutritional outcomes, food safety, competitiveness, and reducing agriculture's environmental footprint. Safety nets tend to replace the physical supply of food to the poor.

Bangladesh's agricultural modernisation trajectory since independence has been relatively rapid, leading it to shift from an ag-based to a transition country in only fifteen years (from the mid-1990s to 2010). This shift resembles the one that China experienced ten years earlier, from the mid-1980s to 2000. For Bangladesh, the most significant change has been in the share of agriculture in employment, which fell from 49 per cent in 1995–1996 to 41 per cent in 2017. The rapidness of this trend, however, is mostly determined outside agriculture—notably by the growth of the services sector and growth and labour-intensiveness of manufacturing. The share of agriculture in Bangladesh's GDP has also declined rather sharply; from 62 per cent in 1975 to 27 per cent in 1995 and further to 17 per cent in 2010 (and further to 13 per cent in 2018).

Further, the largest gap between the contribution to value added and employment has been in agriculture; indicating that agriculture has the lowest productivity in the Bangladesh economy. Despite the advent of the 'Green Revolution' technologies in the late 1960s, most of the farmers used agricultural technologies largely based on traditional production methods and inputs (Alauddin and Tisdell 1991, 1995). Agriculture also faced high transaction costs due to the lack of infrastructure most of which was destroyed during the independence war. Low productivity in agriculture resulted in unstable and low paid jobs such that an overwhelming share of the agriculture-dependent households was poor. Almost four out of every five rural poor in the country worked in agriculture.

According to the Labour Force Survey 2017, agriculture provides employment for 24.7 million people out of a total of about 60.2 million employed labour although its share in GDP declined to 13.4 per cent in 2017. This shows that most of farming are small scale activities and aim to increase food security. Given its low productivity, increasing agricultural productivity is the only way to raise production in agriculture as Bangladesh has almost reached the agriculture frontier, as it uses almost all arable non-forest land for agriculture and the availability of these lands are declining rapidly due to high growth of non-agricultural activities.

Since independence, agricultural productivity improvement has therefore been the fundamental policy to initiate agricultural transformation and raise incomes of the poor in Bangladesh. The reasons were manifold: productivity improvement pushes labour out of agriculture and increases real agricultural wages, pulls jobs in sectors that use agriculture as inputs, and increases the supply of affordable food in the economy. The empirical literature also shows positive effects of rising agricultural productivity on poverty although the magnitude of poverty reduction has varied over time depending on the way the new technologies were developed and adopted (see, Glaeser 1987; de Janvry and Sadoulet 2010).

Available evidence shows that the innovation, selection and adoption of new technologies depend on the agriculture frontier, factor endowment, market imperfections and many other factors (see, e.g. Hayami and Ruttan 1985). For example, as a mechanisation strategy, labour-saving technological change consists of using tractors and machinery, whereas land-saving technological change focuses on biological and chemical innovations. In Bangladesh, the successful case of land-saving technological change occurred after independence with the Green Revolution through an intensifying of input-based production characterised by the use of high-yielding and fertiliser-efficient new varieties of seed (rice and wheat). The policymakers in Bangladesh initiated this variety of agricultural transformation to increase food production and reduce poverty since the 1970s. The Green Revolution increased agriculture and food production, and led to poverty reduction as it raised farmers' income and increased food affordability (see, Alauddin and Tisdell 1991).

Hayami and Ruttan's (1985) theoretical framework of biased technological change is based on the induced innovation hypothesis; according to which innovation is induced as a response to changes in relative prices, which push firms to innovate in order to use less of the resource that has become more expensive. However, the hypothesis may not have worked fully in Bangladesh over the last fifty years as labour may have been abundant, but land and capital have been scarce, and existing land inequality is very high where more than four-fifths are marginal and small farmers (cultivating less than 1.5 hectares of land). As a result, the theory of induced innovation could not work as the demands for innovation of small and large farmers were different, these groups had differing influences on public research and policy with the large farmers enjoying a clear advantage, and imported technologies remained outside the purview of the induced innovation theory.

Although the growth in agricultural productivity has contributed towards reducing poverty, the extent to which it has reduced inequality and benefited the small farmers still remains an issue of intense debate. For instance, the pro-poorness of the Green Revolution has been disputed, since its effectiveness in reducing inequality is not straightforward. The arguments emphasise that the Green Revolution worsens income distribution as it is biased in favour of large farmers and misses the poorer subsistence small farmers (Cleaver Jr 1972; Glaeser 1987). Further, it increases the number of landless farmers and the demand for unskilled labour, which in turn lowers real wages (Hazell 2009; Freebairn 1995).

Despite these controversies, the Bangladesh experience since the 1970s shows a positive role of strong public policies and investments in creating a 'pro-poor' Green Revolution. These policies included agricultural research and development, availability of high yielding varieties of seeds, irrigation, rural roads, access to credit and price support policies. In addition, these policies have been successful when they have been implemented within a package.

The process of agricultural modernisation in Bangladesh has involved both chemicalisation and mechanisation, but in a sequential way. Mechanisation has come with higher capital intensity whereas chemicalisation has enabled the farmers to adopt practices that increased both the application and efficiency in the use of chemical fertilisers and other modern inputs required to produce higher levels of output per unit of land. The scheme also included organic farming that maintained soil fertility to avoid the overuse of chemicals. Given the prices and subsidy levels, the technological path enabled the farmers to make effective and efficient use of the limited amount of fertilisers and other scarce inputs. The practices included crop rotation or integrated livestock crop rotation, intercropping, cover cropping or green manure, and composting waste materials, and other sustainable practices.

At present, high yielding varieties cover more than 80 per cent of the production of rice, wheat, maize and potatoes. The use of fertilisers and agrochemicals are also increasing every year. Water pumping for irrigation was first mechanised; and in 2017, total area equipped for irrigation was 5550 thousand hectares rising from 1047 thousand hectares in 1972 growing at an average annual rate of 3.45 per cent. At present, about 65 per cent of the cultivable area is under irrigation, mainly by pumped groundwater. The next operation that has been mechanised is the tillage operation mainly done by power tillers (single axle hand tractor) as the average farm size is very small. At present, about 80 per cent of the land preparation is by power tillers and tractors. The next operation undergoing rapid mechanisation was threshing. Farm power availability was only 0.24 kW/ha in 1960, which increased to 1.05 kW/ha in 2006. It is expected that the power will continue to increase at a faster rate as there are many important agricultural operations that are yet to be mechanised. Engines of shallow tube well pumps are also widely used to power country boats, small three wheelers, rice mills, and so on. Power tillers are used to some extent for haulage, but tractors are mainly used for this purpose (Justice and Biggs 2013; Biggs and Justice 2015).

Finally, it is worth noting that achieving agricultural mechanisation requires institutional changes that increase trust and encourage the private sector to adapt progressively proven technologies to local practices and production modes. For the future, more effective public interventions are required to improve the access to markets for inputs, outputs and finance, as transaction costs are still very high especially for small farmers.

The Bangladesh model for agricultural modernisation highlights that the apprehension that the adoption of capital-using technologies may lead to immiserating growth through the dominant redistribution effects which may outweigh the positive growth effects can be successfully avoided with appropriate sequencing of policies. The negative effects mainly result since capital-using technological change increases output in all sectors, but lowers rural unskilled and semi-skilled labour incomes inducing overall increases in inequality. As a result, rising inequality between the incomes of the rural labour with lower skills and the urban labour with higher and relatively scarce skills emerge, which is a key factor that explains the inequalising effects of capital-using technological change in a country like Bangladesh.

In contrast, the pursuit of labour-using technological change may be more effective in future in producing pro-poor effects in Bangladesh agriculture. This is also important in improving urban-rural income disparities. So far, the results of poverty decomposition analysis in Bangladesh show that growth impact has been the dominant factor over redistribution in changing poverty in the country (see, World Bank 2017). This suggests that labour-using technological change can emerge as a major route to reducing poverty via the income growth effects along with a high potential to enhance growth outside agriculture. From a policy perspective, this suggests that increasing the efficiency of agricultural value chains simultaneously with institutions and policies that increase farmers' market power and improve marketing efficiency is critical to accelerating labour-using technological change in Bangladesh agriculture. Further, reducing the distribution costs of modern inputs would increase access to market for small farmers leading to increases in income for all farmers including the small farmers.

The participation in decent off-farm activities is also a significant and strong determinant of pro-poor technological change in Bangladesh agriculture. There can be significant interactions between off-farm household income, access to credit and farm mechanisation in producing pro-poor welfare gains through transforming Bangladesh's future agriculture in an inclusive manner. Key issues are to promote the adoption of labour-using technologies to intensify and diversify the country's agriculture; increase the farmers' ability to evaluate, adapt, and disseminate proven technologies; increase investments in sustainable soil and water management methods, and in agriculture research and extension to improve farmer's ability to use modern inputs more efficiently; secure land tenure system among the small farmers and improve their access to land, especially for women farmers; help farmers organise themselves into farmer associations and cooperatives and increase marketing efficiency and farmers' power in the value chains; and carry out institutional reforms in the input supply and output marketing networks and increase investments in storage and infrastructures.

Bangladesh agriculture now sits at a crossroads. While there are several dynamic elements enabling the country to achieve cereal (rice) self-sufficiency from a persistent food deficit country after independence, there also exist a few trends and contextual realities that require different strategies and new approaches. These include, for example, declining rates of agricultural GDP and productivity growth; a growing gap between farm and non-farm incomes; and an erosion of natural capital base endangering sustainability. They also include growing competition for land, labour, water, and other resources; booming domestic demand not just for more food, but also for more diversified food, and more safety—all in the context of a changing climate.

Many of the challenges that Bangladesh agriculture faces at present stem from the need for its transition from an input-based system to an efficiency-based and higher value-added sector which cannot be met exclusively through changes in agricultural policies alone. For addressing the sector's transitional and longer-term competitiveness and sustainability challenges, the need is for implementing broader, economy-wide reforms, especially in relation to policies and institutions associated with science and technology, extension system and the role of the government. The government needs to invest more selectively, focusing on core public goods and services in agriculture. This may mean, for example, to invest more in rural infrastructure, early warning weather systems, land administration services, basic agricultural research, pest and disease surveillance and reporting, institutional capacity to enforce environmental and input regulations or to support certification systems, food safety inspection and related regulatory functions, and the provision of safety nets and agricultural insurance.

Adopting the right innovation policy that builds the sector's capacity for innovation—that is, for continuous improvement in how the business of agriculture can be carried out more effectively and efficiently—is vital for achieving the future aspirations of the sector. As in many other countries, the understandings of modern and sustainable agriculture are complex and vary across different contexts even in a small country like Bangladesh and hence agricultural development has to follow diverse pathways. For the future, the growing demands for an agricultural and food system that is more resilient, equitable and inclusive requires support for many divergent trajectories of agricultural modernisation that the farmers pursue under different agro-ecological conditions—trajectories that are often more attuned to the imperatives of ecology and to changing socioeconomic preferences in society.

2.8.4 *Bangladesh's Urbanisation: A 'Production Cities' Approach*

Globally, there exist established historical links between industrialisation and urbanisation; and the traditional form of industrialisation-led urbanisation is associated with development. In fact, urbanisation and industrialisation are considered as the two critical transformative processes for wealth generation and their complementarity is an important driver for development (see, e.g., Alvarez-Cuadrado and Poschke 2011). In recent times, the urbanisation of China—one of the most impressive political and human transformations—occurred along with unprecedented levels of industrialisation, job creation and poverty eradication.

The patterns of urbanisation in several developing countries over the last few decades have also diverged significantly from these historical trends: with the cities come the industries (Fay and Opal 2000). Although many countries are highly urbanised, they lack large industrial sectors. This divergence is more pronounced in the natural resource exporting countries (e.g. in Africa) which have urbanised without industrialising. The non-resource exporting countries maintain a close positive relationship consistent with the historical association between industrialisation and urbanisation, but no such relationships exist for countries that rely more heavily on natural resource exports.

Further, resource-exporting urban centres are more akin to 'consumption cities', where a larger fraction of the workers are employed in non-tradable activities, such as commerce and transportation or personal and government services. In contrast, industrialised urban centres may be characterised as 'production cities', where a larger fraction of the workers are engaged in manufacturing or in tradable services, such as finance (Gollin et al. 2016).

Industrialisation and urbanisation, however, are not necessarily synonymous. The urbanisation process is fuelled by income effects. Any income shock (both by the industrial and natural resources sectors) causes a shift away from economic activities in rural areas and encourage the movement of production and people into urban areas. However, with a shock emerging from the natural resources sector, there can be a Dutch disease outcome. The labour substitutes away from the tradable goods sector into the non-tradable. Hence, the cities grow into 'consumption cities', dominated by non-tradable employment.

In contrast, a productivity shock in the tradable sector pulls workers into the sector, and away from the rural areas, leading to urbanisation in 'production cities' dominated by tradable production (see, Gollin et al. 2016). This suggests that the source of urbanisation (resource exports or industrialisation), while may not have much implications for the level of urbanisation, may have significant repercussions for long-run development. Thus, understanding the dynamics of urbanisation is important for sustainable planning of the growth of the cities and the process of development in Bangladesh. In countries where there is a high reliance on resource exports, a significant degree of urbanisation may be driven by resources.

No doubt, Bangladesh is facing a very high pace of urbanisation, where major transformations are likely to happen along with a close interdependence with industrialisation and the knowledge economy. The past nature of the economic growth of Bangladesh—largely based on the primary sector (agriculture) of the economy—was rather short-lived; and the next steps of substantive development have moved towards more productive sectors, mainly manufacturing (secondary sector) and services (tertiary sector).

In 1973, the contribution of Bangladesh's urban sector to GDP was only 25 per cent which increased to 65 per cent in 2014 (Islam 2013). Meanwhile, the share of agriculture in terms of contribution to GDP also declined from 60 per cent (75 per cent for rural areas) in 1973 to 16.5 per cent (35 per cent for rural areas) in 2014. On the other hand, similar shares increased to about 30 per cent for industry and 54 per cent for services. This process of change has contributed to rapid urbanisation, as industrial and services activities are largely located in the urban areas that has led to rapid spatial restructuring of the economy since independence.

The economic density that is value added per sq. km is, however, low in relation to population. The country's economic geography is concentrated on economic production in Dhaka and Chittagong mega cities. About one-tenth of the country's population resides in Dhaka city but its contribution to GDP is about 40 per cent while the contribution of Chittagong is 11 per cent where 3 per cent of the population lives (World Bank, 2012). The economic density of Dhaka is $55 million per sq. km which is $88 million for Bangkok and $269 million for Singapore. Moreover, the primacy index for Dhaka in 2001 was 2.05 which means that the population of Dhaka was 2.05 times larger than other three large cities (Chittagong, Rajshahi and Khulna). The index has further increased to 2.12 in 2010 (World Bank 2012).

The pattern of urbanisation in Bangladesh has thus been closely linked with industrialisation in a broader term (including services activities) resulting from a host of factors covering, for example, external market demand (e.g. export-oriented manufacturing products), internal supply of production inputs (cheaper skilled labour and infrastructure services), policy bias towards primate city favouritism, and migration of labour from rural areas and peripheries for better opportunities. Moreover, the spill-over effects of industrialisation-induced growth encouraged local suppliers to be agglomerated in the cities and create informal activities that further accelerated the accumulation of labour in the cities. Further, the concentration of low-income groups in the suburban areas to reduce the commuting costs attracted the small and informal businesses towards these locations. Bangladesh's urban growth dynamics was thus profoundly influenced by the key or strategic industry sectors (including the ready-made garments). Moreover, the impacts on urban locations, livelihoods and the environment were strongly associated with the nature of industrialisation as well as broader growth forces. On the other hand, the lack of regulatory controls and other limitations intensified the negative externalities that emerged from the growth process, resulting in declining quality of life, degradation of the environment, and increased social instability.

With the strong relationship operating between urbanisation and industrialisation in the country, it is important to ensure that industrialisation facilitates the effective implementation of sustainable urban development in future. Sustainable urbanisation needs to address several issues relating to national urban policies, land use and its administration, urban and territorial planning, development of urban infrastructure and services, spatial planning of special economic zones (SEZs) and of border towns, human settlements and housing development, as well as policies for human settlements and city migrants.

In Bangladesh, the complementarities between urbanisation and industrialisation can be harnessed in several ways. For the formulation of national urban policies, urban and territorial planning, industrial development policies, industries layout and their distribution are important elements of policies and planning. Further, industrialisation will interact with urbanisation in a positive manner if both are harnessed in harmony in a balanced and sustainable manner. The right types of industries can provide sustainable urbanisation with immense driving force. This is particularly critical for spatial planning of the SEZs.

For developing improved urban basic services and housing, effective delivery requires advanced technologies provided by industries. Innovation and upgrading of industrial products and technologies need to drive the progress of applicable technologies in the field of basic urban services and housing in the process of urbanisation. Thus, integrating advanced industrial development ideas, technologies and products into urban development is an effective and efficient way to promote sustainable urbanisation in the country. Sustainable industrialisation can also provide strong support for financing of sustainable urbanisation.

The future policies should also explore as to how different partnership mechanisms (e.g. local government institutions, city/municipal organizations, private sector, etc.) can facilitate sustainable urban-industrial development in Bangladesh. These partnership platforms can play an important and positive role in formulating the new urban agenda and providing evidence-based and practical guidance to facilitate capacity building for the implementation of the agenda and the urban dimension of the SDGs. Within these partnership mechanisms, along with the private sector and enterprises, the entrepreneurs can also apply their creativity and innovation to solve sustainable development challenges in urban areas in Bangladesh. Their business activity, investment and innovation are the most important drivers of productivity, inclusive growth and job creation along with urban development.

By its very nature, urbanisation is one of the few social and political phenomena which generate a lot of value in the rapidly changing economy of Bangladesh. Urbanisation generates value through economies of location and economies of agglomeration. The location of an area, depending on its connectivity, can generate a lot of value, whereas the generation of value through agglomeration is due to factors of production which increase efficiency.

However, the present urbanisation in Bangladesh is not fully realising the potential of industrialisation. Urbanisation so far has been 'messy and hidden' in Bangladesh (Ellis and Roberts 2016). Messy urbanisation has been reflected in the widespread existence of slums and sprawl. Sprawl helps give rise to hidden urbanisation, particularly on the peripheries of major cities, which is not captured in official statistics. Messy and hidden urbanisation is symptomatic of the failure to adequately address congestion constraints that arise from the pressure of urban population. For Bangladesh cities, these congestion constraints undermine both liveability and the agglomeration economies that can produce greater prosperity.

2.9 Concluding Remarks

The economy of Bangladesh is the second largest economy in South Asia and the forty-first largest economy in the world in 2019; and is projected to become the world's twenty- fourth largest economy by 2033 (CEBR 2019). Further it is classified among the emerging market middle-income economies and a frontier market. Since its independence, Bangladesh has become both a challenge and an inspiration of development policy. The growth story has been extraordinary so far. At the same time, the country is at an important juncture, when with right policies and timely action, it can quickly move up the middle-income ladder.

To raise the income of at least 50 per cent of the country's population to the levels of the global middle class, the Bangladesh economy not only needs to attain a double-digit or close to such a level of growth but must also maintain such growth for the next three decades. Most evidence across the world highlights that this is no easy task; most countries that experienced high growth saw decelerations a few years later. Nonetheless, Bangladesh's remarkable growth experience lends credence to its long-term growth story. Further reform efforts and removing critical bottlenecks to specific drivers of growth will help accelerate growth to the desired high level.

Both theoretical reasoning and empirical evidence suggest that a well-developed financial system plays a positive growth-inducing role in development. For transiting towards an upper middle-income Bangladesh, a developmental approach to financial sector growth is necessary, while at the same time attending to prudent regulations. The country's progressive financial system must ensure a sound financial structure with varieties of financial products and services, including electronic trading system to trade derivatives in stock exchanges, a carefully outlined series of regulations that govern the market judiciously and allows market participants to contain systemic risks.

The development of the country's capital and equity markets will occur only as a part of a comprehensive endeavour that addresses all the factors that affect the profitability and attractiveness of private enterprises. The challenge is to ensure a delicate balance between a system that assures adequate protection of the investors and one that does not deter market growth.

However, for a successful journey, Bangladesh should not wait for the market to bring development. For example, since market outcomes of human capital are likely to be sub-optimal; a strong justification exists for state intervention. The need is to have 'smart' interventions. Instead of the top-down approach, the 'developmental state' approach is needed which uses 'market-following' policies, such as supporting the availability of skilled labour to attract enterprises towards greater productivity and value addition.

The developmental state paradigm holds that as an economy develops and its factor endowment becomes increasingly capital and skilled labour intensive, development demands a 'comparative advantage following' strategy of government support for structural transformation (Lin, 2012). An economy's specific factor endowment determines its optimal industrial structure, and each industrial structure demands a particular level of tangible and intangible infrastructure, from transport to human capital.

Bangladesh needs to bring rapid structural transformation by emphasising human capital-focused strategies, skill development and progressively higher value-added activities. The focus should be on upgrading the skills of the workforce and incentivising enterprises to invest in their own workers. A pre-condition for the above is to ensure strong public institutions so that the government can address 'government failure' before it can fix 'market failures'.

In the development process, one key issue for Bangladesh would be to introduce 'tripartism'—institutionalised cooperation of business, labour, and the government on economic issues—to help policymakers acquire the inputs for informed decision making and help build consensus. The strategy would be to advance in a planned way from labour-intensive industry to capital-intensive industry and finally to a knowledge-intensive economy that includes research, services, and high-end manufacturing.

In the Bangladesh context, investments in human capital can drive development for which the need is to ensure a combination of public investment, incentives for private investment, and close coordination with business and labour. This can rapidly upgrade skills and productivity; and ultimately the standard of living of the people.

However, rising inequality may pose a threat to Bangladesh's future development journey. The country's Gini coefficient of income and other measures of inequality are steadily creeping upwards. In this respect, the major challenge for Bangladesh is ensuring the inclusiveness of growth. Past growth has no doubt reduced poverty and improved the living conditions of the poorer groups in Bangladesh. But the gains of the middle and richer segments of the population have been greater than those of the poorer sections of society. This is evident from the fact that reforms in areas such as telecommunications, banks, stock markets, trade and industrial policy have not been matched by agricultural and human development. Bangladesh's industrialisation continues to be capital and knowledge intensive rather than led by MSMEs. This, along with slow progress in human development in areas such as education and health, will make it tougher for Bangladesh to grow in the long run. From a development perspective, the declining share of income going to wages might marginally benefit competitiveness, but this may face diminishing returns and threaten to undermine domestic demand.

For ensuring equity, the need would be to recognise vulnerabilities, challenges, and opportunities; and build strong institutions for equitable development. The past growth in Bangladesh has produced more benefits for the rich and the middle class than the poorer sections of society (Mujeri 2002a, b; Mujeri & Sen, 2003). Growth that increases economic inequality will be difficult to sustain within the Bangladesh's democratic polity.

In this respect, a key challenge is to successfully change the culture and ethos of the education system, finding a balance between rigour and standards and innovation and creativity. The efforts towards skill training can only succeed if employers are able to fairly reward workers and can take advantage of the new skills. A close linking of education institutions to economic growth trends and skill requirements in the labour market is essential to keep training relevant. Further, the path dependency nature of Bangladesh's economic policies would ensure that new policies build upon the lessons of the past and get embedded in politics to produce policy outcomes. This explains why economic change is more difficult but more stable in Bangladesh.

The country's high growth trajectory of the recent past, which is essential for development, has become reasonably stable. This is no doubt a substantial achievement. It has been achieved in the context of democratic politics where changes in policy orientation are inherently slow. Moreover, the coalition dominated by the new middle class favours growth and competition to overcome the status quo bias in favour of the slow growth of the past.

Bangladesh, having successfully completed the journey from low income to lower middle income country, now faces the more perilous journey to upper middle income status and then to a high income country. While the first leg of the journey provides grounds for optimism, Bangladesh must become more innovative and productive in order to successfully complete the second and the third stages, a journey in which all sectors need to play a more supportive role to bring higher levels of prosperity.

References

Acemoglu, D., and J. Robinson. 2012. *Why Nations Fail: The Origins of Power, Prosperity, and Poverty*. New York: Crown Business.

ADB. 2011. *Asia 2050: Realizing the Asian Century*. Singapore: Asian Development Bank.

Ahmed, R. 1995. Liberalization of Agricultural Input Markets in Bangladesh: Process, Impact, and Lessons. *Agricultural Economics* 12 (2): 115–128.

Alauddin, M., and C.A. Tisdell. 1991. *The "Green Revolution" and Economic Development: The Process and Its Impact in Bangladesh*. London: St. Martin's Press.

———. 1995. Labor Absorption and Agricultural Development: Bangladesh's Experience and Predicament. *World Development* 23 (2): 281–297.

Alvarez-Cuadrado, F., and M. Poschke. 2011. Structural Change Out of Agriculture: Labor Push Versus Labor Pull. *American Economic Journal: Macroeconomics* 3 (3): 127–158.

Asadullah, M. 2006. *Returns to Education in Bangladesh, Education Economics*. 14 (4): 453–468.

Auspitz, J., S. Marglin, and G. Papanek. 1971. *History of Economic and Political Dominance of East Pakistan*. Washington, DC: Ripon Society.

Besserman, L., ed. 1996. *The Challenge of Periodization: Old Paradigms and New Perspectives*. New York and London: Garland Publishing Inc.

Bhatia, B.M. 1979. *Pakistan's Economic Development 1948–78: The Failure of a Strategy*. New Delhi: Vikas Publishing House.

Biggs, S., and S. Justice. 2015. *Rural and Agricultural Mechanization: A History of the Spread of Small Engines in Selected Asian Countries*, Development Strategy and Governance Division, IFPRI Discussion Paper No. 01443, International Food Policy Research Institute (IFPRI), Washington DC.

CEBR. 2019. *World Economic League Table 2019*. London: Centre for Economics and Business Research.

Cheng, T., S. Haggard, and D. Kang. 1998. Institutions and Growth in Korea and Taiwan: The Bureaucracy. *Journal of Development Studies* 34 (6): 1.

Choudhary, G.W. 1993. *The Last Days of United Pakistan*. Dhaka: University Press Limited.

Cleaver, H.M., Jr. 1972. The Contradictions of the Green Revolution. *American Economic Review* 62 (1/2): 177–186.

Curle, A. 1966. *Planning for Education in Pakistan: A Personal Case Study*. London: Tavistock Publications.

de Janvry, A., and E. Sadoulet. 2010. Agricultural Growth and Poverty Reduction: Additional Evidence. *World Bank Research Observer* 25 (1): 1–20. https://doi.org/10.1093/wbro/lkp015.

Easterly, W., and R. Levine. 2000. *It's Not Factor Accumulation: Stylized Facts and Growth Models*. Washington DC: World Bank.

Ellis, P., and M. Roberts. 2016. *Leveraging Urbanization in South Asia: Managing Spatial Transformation for Prosperity and Livability*. Washington DC: World Bank.

Falcon, W., and J. Stern. 1971. Pakistan's Development: An Introductory Perspective. In *Development Policy II—The Pakistani Experience*, ed. W. Falcon and G. Papanek. Cambridge, MA: Harvard University Press.

Fay, M., and C. Opal. 2000. *Urbanization without Growth: A Not-so-Uncommon Phenomenon,* World Bank Policy Research Working Paper Series 2412, World Bank, Washington DC.

Feldman, D. 1971. *Unhappy East Pakistan: A Survey of Inter-regional Inequality in Pakistan*. Jersey, Isle de la Manche: St. Peter.

Freebairn, D. 1995. Did the Green Revolution Concentrate Incomes? A Quantitative Study of Research Reports. *World Development* 23: 265–279. https://doi.org/10.1016/0305-750X(94)00116-G.

Fry, M.J. 1988. *Money, Interest and Banking in Economic Development*. Baltimore: The John Hopkins University Press.

Gill, I., and H. Kharas. 2007. *An East Asian Renaissance: Ideas for Economic Growth*. Washington DC: The World Bank.

Gill, I., H. Kharas, et al. 2007. *An East Asian Renaissance: Ideas for Economic Growth*. Washington, DC: World Bank.

Glaeser, B. 1987. *The Green Revolution Revisited*. London: Allen & Unwin.

Gollin, D., R. Jedwan, and D. Vollrath. 2016. Urbanization With and Without Industrialization. *Journal of Economic Growth* 21: 35–70.

Hayami, Y., and V.W. Ruttan. 1985. *Agricultural Development: An International Perspective*. Baltimore: Johns Hopkins University Press.

Hazell, P. 2009. *The Asian Green Revolution*, IFPRI Discussion Paper 00911, International Food Policy Research Institute, Washington DC.

Huq, M. 1963. *The Strategy of Economic Planning: A Case Study of Pakistan*. Karachi: Oxford University Press.

Islam, N. 1972. Foreign Assistance and Economic Development: The Case of Pakistan. *Economic Journal* 82: 502–530.

———. 1978. *Development Strategy of Bangladesh*. LA: Elsevier Science & Technology Books.

———. 2013. *Overview of Urbanization in Bangladesh*. Dhaka: Urban Dialogue.

Justice, S., and S. Biggs. 2013. Rural and Agricultural Mechanization in Bangladesh and Nepal: Status, Processes and Outcomes. In *Mechanization for Rural Development: A Review of Patterns and Progress from Around the World*, ed. J. Kienzle, J.E. Ashburner, and B.G. Sims, 67–98. Rome: United Nations Food and Agriculture Organization, (FAO).

Khondker, B.H., and M.K. Mujeri. 2006. Globalisation–Poverty Interactions in Bangladesh. In *Globalisation and Poverty: Channels and Policy Responses*, ed. M. Bussolo and J.I. Round. London and New York: Routledge.

Klenow, P.J., and A. Rodríguez-Clare. 1997. The Neoclassical Revival in Growth Economics: Has It Gone Too Far?, *NBER Macroeconomics Annual*, 12, University of Chicago Press, Chicago.

Kuznets, S. 1955. Economic Growth and Income Inequality. *American Economic Review* 45: 1–28.

———. 1966. *Toward a Theory of Economic Growth, with Reflections on the Economic Growth of Modern Nations*. New York: W.W Norton & Co.

———. 1979. *Growth, Population and Income Distribution: Selected Essays*. New York: W.W Norton & Co.

LaPorte, R., Jr. 1975. *Power and Privilege: Influence and Decision-making in Pakistan*. Berkeley: University of California Press.

Lewis, W.A. 1954. Economic Development with Unlimited Supplies of Labour. *The Manchester School* 22 (2): 139–191.

———. 1955. *Theory of Economic Growth*. London: Allen and Unwin Ltd.

Lin, J.Y. 2012. Demystifying the Chinese Economy. Cambridge: Cambridge University Press.

Mahmud, W. 2008. Social Development in Bangladesh: Pathways, Surprises and Challenges. *Indian Journal of Human Development* 2 (1): 79–92.

Mahmud, W., and S. Mahmud. 2014. Development, Welfare and Governance: Explaining Bangladesh's 'Development Surprise'. In *Development and Welfare Policy in South Asia*, ed. G. Koehler and D. Chopra. London: Routledge.

Mankiw, N.G., D. Romer, and D.N. Weil. 1992. A Contribution to the Empirics of Economic Growth. *Quarterly Journal of Economics* 107: 407–437.

Mason, E., R. Dorfman, and S. Marglin. 1971. *Conflict in East Pakistan: Background and Prospects*. London: Bangladesh Students' Action Committee.

Mujeri, M.K. 2002a. Globalization–Poverty Links in Bangladesh: Some Broad Observations. In *Bangladesh Facing the Challenge of Globalization: A Review of Bangladesh's Development 2001*. Dhaka: Centre for Policy Dialogue and University Press Limited.

———. 2002b. *Bangladesh: Bringing Poverty Focus in Rural Infrastructure Development*, Issues in Employment and Poverty, Discussion Paper No.6,

Recovery and Reconstruction Department, International Labour Office, Geneva.

———. 2004. Changes in Policy Framework and Total Factor Productivity Growth in Bangladesh. *Bangladesh Development Studies* 30 (3 & 4): 1–29.

Mujeri, M.K., M. Alauddin, and C. Tisdell. 1993a. Consumption, Savings and Investment by Social Class in Bangladesh: Does the Rural Sector Support the Urban Sector? *Journal of Development Studies* 30 (1): 226–245.

Mujeri, M.K., Q. Shahabuddin, and S. Ahmed. 1993b. A Framework for Analysis of Macro-Micro Transmission Mechanisms in Bangladesh: Some Preliminary Considerations. *Asia-Pacific Journal of Rural Development* 3 (1): 20–43.

Mujeri, M.K., and B. Sen. 2003. *A Quiet Transition: Economic Growth in Bangladesh 1970-1990.* Washington DC: Global Research Project, World Bank.

———. 2006. Economic Growth in Bangladesh, 1970-2000. In *Explaining Growth in South Asia*, ed. K.S. Parikh. New Delhi: Oxford University Press.

Nehru, V., and A. Dhareshwar. 1993. A New Database on Physical Capital Stock: Sources, Methodology and Results. *Revista de Analisis Economico* 8: 37–59.

O'Donnell, A. 1984. *Bangladesh: Biography of A Muslim Nation.* London: West View.

Papanek, G. 1967. *Pakistan's Development: Social Goals and Private Incentives.* Cambridge, MA: Harvard University Press.

Rahman, A. 1968. *East and West Pakistan: A Problem in the Political Economy of Regional Planning*, Occasional Papers in International Affairs No. 20, Centre for International Affairs, Harvard University, MA.

Rahman, S.H. 1991. *Macro-Economic Stabilisation and Adjustment: The Experience of Bangladesh in the 1980s.* Dhaka: Bangladesh Institute of Development Studies.

Rahman, S., and A.K.M.A. Rahman. 2002. *The Estimation of Capital Stock for the Bangladesh Economy,* Focus Study No. 01, MIMAP Bangladesh, Bangladesh Institute of Development Studies, Dhaka.

Rao, V.K.R.V. 1972. *Bangladesh Economy: Problems and Prospects.* New Delhi: Vikas Publications.

Rodríguez-Clare, A. 2005. *Microeconomic Interventions after the Washington Consensus,* Working Paper 524, Inter-American Development Bank, Washington DC.

Rodrik, D. 1995. Political Economy of Trade Policy. Chapter 28 in Handbook in International Economics (3): 1457–1494, Elsevier.

——. 2007. *One Economics, Many Recipes: Globalization, Institutions and Economic Growth.* Princeton: Princeton University Press.

Rostow, W. 1960. *The Stages of Economic Growth: A Non-Communist Manifesto.* Cambridge: Cambridge University Press.

Samuelson, P.A. 1994. Facets of Balassa-Samuelson Thirty Years Later. *Review of International Economics* 2 (3): 201–226.

Satoru, O. 1997. Industrialization Policies of Korea and Taiwan and Their Effects on Manufacturing Productivity. *The Developing Economies* 35 (4): 358–381.

Senhadji, A. 2000. Sources of Economic Growth: An Extensive Growth Accounting Exercise. *IMF Staff Papers* 47 (1): 129–157.

Sobhan, R. 1982. *The Crisis of External Dependence: The Political Economy of Foreign Aid to Bangladesh*. London: Zed Press.

———. 1991. *Debt Default to the Development Finance Institutions: The Crisis of State Sponsored Entrepreneurship in Bangladesh*. Dhaka: University Press Limited.

———. 1992a. *Problems of Governance in Bangladesh*. Dhaka: University Press Limited.

———. 1992b. Rethinking the Market Reform Paradigm, Economic and Political Weekly, July 25.

———. 1993. Structural Maladjustment: Bangladesh's Experience with Market Reforms. *Economic and Political Weekly* 28 (19): 925–931.

Sobhan, R., and M. Ahmad. 1980. *Public Enterprise in an Intermediate Regime*. Dhaka: Bangladesh Institute of Development Studies.

Solow, R.M. 1956. A Contribution to the Theory of Economic Growth. *Quarterly Journal of Economics* 70 (1): 65–94.

Sen, A. and J. Dreze. 1995. *India: Economic Development and Social Opportunity*. Oxford: Clarendon Press.

Todaro, M.P., and S.C. Smith. 2012. *Economic Development*. 11th ed. New York: Addison-Wesley.

UN General Assembly. 2011. *Development Cooperation with Middle Income Countries*, United Nations General Assembly, 66th Session. Report of the Secretary General, New York.

UNDP. 2019. *Human Development Indices and Indicators 2018 Statistical Update*. New York: United Nations Development Programme.

UNRO. 1972. *A Survey of Damages and Repairs*. Dhaka: United Nations Relief Operation.

Wade, R. 1990. *Governing the Market*. Princeton: Princeton University Press.

Wang, X., and N. Weaver. 2013. Surplus Labor and Lewis Turning Points in China. *Journal of Chinese Economic and Business Studies* 11 (1): 1–12.

Ward, M. 1976. *The Measurement of Capital: The Methodology of Capital Stock Estimation in OECD Countries*. Paris: Organisation of Economic Cooperation and Development.

World Bank. 1993. *The East Asian Miracle: Economic Growth and Public Policy*. New York: Oxford University Press.

———. 2006. *World Development Report 2006: Equity and Development*. Washington DC: World Bank.

———. 2008. *World Development Report 2008: Agriculture for Development*. Washington, DC: World Bank.

———. 2009. *World Development Report 2009*. Washington DC: World Bank.

———. 2011. *The Changing Wealth of Nations: Measuring Sustainable Development in the New Millennium*. Washington D.C: World Bank.

———. 2012a. *Bangladesh: Towards Accelerated, Inclusive and Sustainable Growth—Opportunities and Challenges* (Vol. 2): Main Report No. 67991, World Bank, Washington, DC.

———. 2012b. Consolidating and Accelerating Exports in Bangladesh, Bangladesh Development Series No. 29, World Bank, Dhaka.

———. 2017. *Annual Report 2017 End Extreme Poverty • Boost Shared Prosperity*. Washington DC.: World Bank.

———. 2019. *The Bangladesh Development Update 2019: Towards Regulatory Predictability*. Washington DC: World Bank.

World Bank and DRC. 2012. *China 2030: Building a Modern, Harmonious, and Creative High-Income Society*. Washington, DC.: Development Research Center (DRC) of the State Council, People's Republic of China and World Bank.

CHAPTER 3

Poverty and Inequality

3.1 Introduction

After independence, Bangladesh's approaches to development were significantly influenced by the concept of 'population-poverty trap'. The argument runs as follows: with the persistence of a low level of per capita income, policies to reduce poverty and improve living conditions result in reduced mortality that lead to higher population growth which, in turn, reduces per capita income to its previous level (Nelson 1956). Thus, poor economies like Bangladesh would remain poor with high levels of poverty unless the rate of economic growth could receive a sudden boost to overcome the trap and break the cycle of 'circular causation'.

In reality, population and poverty dynamics is inherently complex; and changes in population size, structure and spatial distribution have a profound impact on economic, social and environmental aspects of sustainable development. Poverty is influenced by—and influences—population dynamics, including population growth, age structure, and rural–urban distribution. Investments in better health, including reproductive health, are essential for individual security and for reducing mortality and morbidity, which in turn reduce poverty and improve a country's productivity and development prospects. Bangladesh is currently passing through the phase of demographic dividend that emerged in 2007; with a fairly young population with 30 per cent aged 15 and younger and just 5 per cent aged 65 and older. At present, more than 65 per cent of the population is of

© The Author(s) 2020

M. K. Mujeri, N. Mujeri, *Bangladesh at Fifty*, Palgrave Studies in Economic History,
https://doi.org/10.1007/978-3-030-56791-0_3

Fig. 3.1 Population age structure in Bangladesh, 1911–2011. (Source: BBS, *Population and Housing Census 2011, National Report, Vol. 1, Analytical Report*, Bangladesh Bureau of Statistics, Statistics and Informatics Division, Ministry of Planning, Government of the People's Republic of Bangladesh, Dhaka)

working age, between 15 and 64; creating enormous economic growth and poverty reduction potential (Fig. 3.1).

For fighting poverty, the definition of poverty matters. The definition sets the standard by which we determine whether the incomes and living conditions of the low income people in society are acceptable or not. Definitions of poverty are also important, as they influence the way interventions and policies addressing poverty are shaped. Despite this, there is ambiguity as to how the term 'poverty' is used and, as a result, a range of definitions exists, influenced by different disciplinary approaches, views and ideologies (Handley et al. 2009).

In Bangladesh, the ultimate aim of development has always been the improvement in the living conditions and the quality of life of all population, especially of the poor and deprived sections in society. One of the fundamental principles of state policy, as laid out in the country's constitution, states that: '*It shall be a fundamental responsibility of the State to emancipate the toiling masses the peasants and workers and backward sections of the people from all forms of exploitation*' (14. Part II; Fundamental Principles of State Policy). Thus, development in Bangladesh should lead to sustained reductions in poverty in its multidimensional forms and inequality in all aspects of human lives.

The empirical analysis on economic growth nearly always is associated with a reduction in absolute poverty; while the relation between changes in inequality and rate of economic growth or between changes in inequality and level of national income is ambiguous (see, e.g. Ahluwalia 1976; Fields 1980; Sen 1973; Bourguignon 2003; Dollar and Kraay 2002; Ravallion 2001; UNDP 2014). Hence, the decisive factor in determining whether inequality increases or decreases is not the rate of economic growth, rather the quality of growth.

Further, no statistically significant relation exists between inequality in the initial distribution of income and subsequent economic growth (Barro 2000; Deininger and Squire 1998; Forbes 2000). This suggests that countries need not maintain unequal income distribution to grow rapidly. In general, high initial levels of inequality limit the effectiveness of growth in reducing poverty while growing inequality increases poverty directly for a given level of growth. As such, special attention is needed to reducing inequality in countries where income distribution is especially unfavourable.

3.2 Conceptualising Poverty and Inequality

Following the standard development theoretic approach, poverty in Bangladesh is defined in monetary terms, using income or consumption levels. As is well known, in order to be able to compare poverty levels across countries and over time, those that live below a given level of income—the poverty line—are classified as poor (Ravallion 2010). Over the last decades, this economic definition of poverty has been complemented by other approaches to conceptualise poverty, such as, basic needs approach, capabilities approach, human development approach and multidimensional poverty approach (Handley et al. 2009).

However, only by understanding the causes can the designing, implementing and evaluating interventions for attacking poverty begin. In designing poverty programmes, it is important to incorporate the perception of poverty as articulated by the poor people themselves. This may lead to begin by implementing income generation measures in some cases; but in the case of others, this may lead to begin by reducing the variability of income, or strengthening women's autonomy, or improving the quality of services the poor receive at the health centres. In practice, it is multidimensional poverty that matters for policy.

The Oxford Poverty and Human Development Initiative (OPHI) has developed an international measure of poverty—the multidimensional poverty index (MPI)—for the UNDP's Human Development Report

(HDR). The index goes beyond the traditional focus on income to reflect the multiple deprivations that a poor person faces with respect to education, health and living standard. Further, along with multidimensional definition of poverty, poverty dynamics are equally important determinants for designing appropriate interventions to eradicate poverty (Shepherd et al. 2014).

Vulnerability describes the likelihood of falling into poverty or into greater poverty. It is related to exposure to risks and the capacity to respond to prevent, mitigate or cope with risks (Ludi and Bird 2007). Poor people are particularly vulnerable to shocks and stresses and their resilience in resisting or recovering from the negative effects of a changing environment is particularly low, as they lack assets, entitlements and capabilities that would be required to deal with shocks and stresses. Policy interventions to address the vulnerabilities of the poor people include: social assistance, inclusive economic growth, human development of the hard-to-reach population groups (i.e. because of age, gender, geography, ethnicity, etc.), and transformative social change (i.e. change in norms, values and social relations that underpin development processes).

3.2.1 Aspects of Inequality

Although inequality is not poverty, but inequality—the absence of or limited access to human rights, freedoms and opportunities of specific population groups—is a central characteristic of poverty. Addressing inequalities is not only a moral imperative, but from a social perspective, increasing inequality is an impediment to economic growth and development, poverty reduction efforts and social stability.[1]

While inequality is mostly interpreted in economic and social terms, it has important civil and political dimensions as well. These relate to access to justice, political opportunity and redistribution of wealth and to enable the poor people to demand more inclusive and non-discriminatory policies (Tucker and Ludi 2012). In 2010, UNDP introduced the Inequality-adjusted Human Development Index/HDI (IHDI). It accounts for inequality of human development within a country and captures the losses

[1] According to available studies, of every \$100 worth of growth in world per capita income, the poor received only \$2.20 during 1981–1990, and this decreased to \$0.60 during 1990–2001, since inequality has been rising and the poor's share of income declining. See, Simms et al. (2010: 18); Woodward and Simms (2006: 16–17).

in human development due to inequality in health, education and income. The greater the difference between IHDI and HDI, the greater is the inequality in the country (UNDP 2010). In 2017, the inequality-adjusted HDI (IHDI) value of Bangladesh was 0.462 relative to an HDI value of 0.608; showing a loss of 24 per cent in HDI due to inequality (UNDP 2018).

3.3 Measuring Poverty and Inequality in Bangladesh

Two basic approaches to the concept of poverty are used in economic literature, namely, absolute poverty and relative poverty. The concept of absolute poverty is based on absolute norms for living (measured in terms of consumption expenditure) laid down according to specified minimum standard and all such individuals or households whose consumption expenditure is found to be below this standard are classified as poor. This concept is directly related to the minimum level of consumption. Under the relative concept of poverty, a household (or an individual) is deemed to be poor if its level of income or consumption expenditure falls below a predetermined level. Then the income distribution of the population in different fractile groups is estimated and a comparison is made between the level of living of people in the bottom layer and the top layers of the population to assess the relative standard of poverty. The concept of relative poverty is considered more suitable for developed countries while the absolute concept is relevant for the developing countries.

Bangladesh's official poverty measure uses money-metric poverty or poverty measured on the basis of a money value of expenditure, adopting the more commonly used headcount ratio (the number of the poor as a proportion of the population), which are derived from the familiar poverty line approach. Bangladesh's poverty line is anchored in a 'nutritional norm'; it is based on notions of what is a basic minimum of nutrition an individual must obtain every day in order not to be considered undernourished.

The national poverty line in Bangladesh is a monetary threshold below which a person's minimum basic needs cannot be met, taking into account the country's economic and social circumstances. The poverty line is also revised as the country develops. The government tracks how many people are living on less than the national poverty line so that it can monitor its development progress. The official statistics on poverty and inequality are provided by the Bangladesh Bureau of Statistics (BBS), the government statistical agency, using data from the Household Income and Expenditure Survey (HIES) series. These surveys are designed by BBS to make them comparable over time (e.g. in terms of methodology, questionnaire content, interviewing procedures, and others) and are carried out usually at five-year intervals. The BBS uses the cost-of-basic-needs (CBN) method to derive poverty lines and poverty measures which entails three main steps.

First, a food bundle yielding 2122 kcal per day per person is chosen comprising rice, wheat, pulses, milk, mustard oil, beef, fresh water fish, potato, other vegetables, sugar and bananas. The prices of various food items in this bundle are estimated for sixteen different geographic regions to ascertain the total cost of consuming the bundle in different parts of the country. The second step is to estimate the cost of basic non-food needs. For the purpose, two non-food allowance components are calculated: the first obtained by taking the amount spent on non-food items by those households whose total consumption is equal to their regional food poverty line (corresponding to the lower poverty line), while the second is obtained by taking the amount spent on non-food items by those households whose food consumption is equal to the regional food poverty line, corresponding to the upper poverty line (see, Ravallion 1994). The third step in calculating the lower and upper poverty lines for each region entails simply adding up the cost of purchasing the food bundle in each region to the respective non-food allowance components. The lower poverty lines thus incorporate a minimal allowance for non-food goods (the typical non-food spending of those who could just afford the food requirement) while the upper poverty lines made a more generous allowance (the typical non-food spending of those who just attain their food requirement).

The poverty measures used in Bangladesh are drawn from the Foster–Greer–Thorbecke class of functions written as

$$P_\alpha = \Sigma_{yi<z}\left[\left(z-y_i\right)/z\right]^\alpha / \quad (3.1)$$

where y_i is the consumption of the *i*th household or the *j*th class of household, *z* is the poverty line, *n* is the population size, and α is a non-negative parameter (Foster et al. 1984). The headcount ratio, H—given by the percentage of the population who are poor—is obtained when $\alpha = 0$. The poverty gap index (PG), given by the aggregate income shortfall of the poor as a proportion of the poverty line and normalised by the population size, is given by $\alpha = 1$, and the squared poverty gap index (SPG) is obtained when $\alpha = 2$.

Since prices and consumption patterns vary across different geographical areas, poverty lines are estimated for sixteen different geographical areas separately. For obtaining poverty estimates for previous years, the current poverty lines are deflated by price indices to represent identical purchasing power for all years. Estimates using alternative methodologies, which serve as important sensitivity checks for poverty trends, reveal similar trends for a wide range of methods for estimating and updating the poverty lines.

3.3.1 *Trends in Poverty*

Poverty in Bangladesh has declined remarkably since the early-2000s, as a result of decades of accelerated economic growth. It is widely recognised that, after independence in 1971, Bangladesh's poverty rate was extremely high, estimated at more than 80 per cent in 1972. According to the HIES data, national poverty headcount rate has declined to 24.3 per cent in 2016 (Table 3.1).

National poverty headcount rate declined by more than 57 per cent (32 percentage points) between 1992 and 2016. In 1991–1992, nearly 57 per cent of Bangladesh's population was poor (per capita consumption below the upper poverty line) as compared with 24 per cent in 2016. The percentage decline in poverty rate was almost similar in urban areas (nearly 56 per cent) and rural areas (55 per cent).

A notable feature of recent poverty reduction is a sizeable decline in the incidence of extreme poverty. The percentage of population under the

Table 3.1 Poverty headcount rates in Bangladesh

	% of population below upper poverty line					*% of population below lower poverty line*				
	1991–92	*2000*	*2005*	*2010*	*2016*	*1991–92*	*2000*	*2005*	*2010*	*2016*
National	56.7	48.9	40.0	31.5	24.3	41.1	34.3	25.1	17.6	12.9
Urban	42.8	35.2	28.4	21.3	18.9	24.0	19.9	14.6	7.7	7.6
Rural	58.8	52.3	43.8	35.2	26.4	43.8	37.9	28.6	21.1	14.9

Source: HIES reports, various years

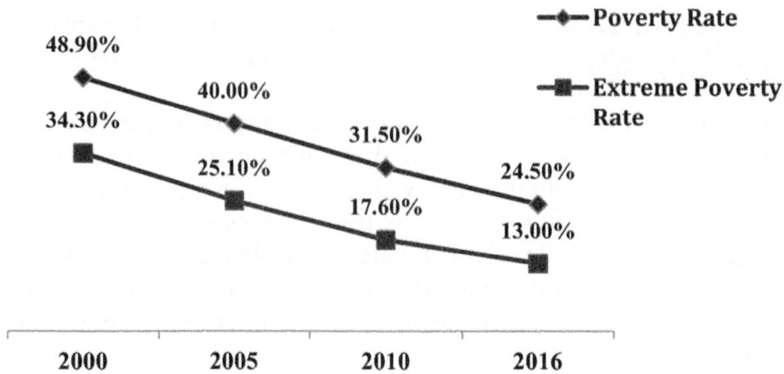

Fig. 3.2 Poverty and extreme poverty in the 2000s. (Source: HIES, various years)

lower poverty line—the threshold for extreme poverty—fell by nearly 69 per cent (or 28 percentage points) between 1992 and 2016. A fall of 68 per cent (or 16 percentage points) occurred in urban areas and 66 per cent (29 percentage points) in the rural areas (see, Table 3.1). The percentage decline in extreme poverty rate is thus more than that in the poverty rate, which shows higher growth in per capita consumption for the bottom two deciles (Fig. 3.2).

During the period, the fall in poverty headcount rates was large enough to significantly reduce the number of people in poverty or extreme poverty. The size of the population below the upper poverty and the lower poverty lines declined by 23.3 million and 22.9 million respectively between 2000 and 2016. However, it must also be remembered that an estimated 39.6 million Bangladeshis still live below the (upper) poverty line in 2016, and 24 million among whom are below the lower or extreme poverty line.

The depth (poverty gap) and the severity (squared poverty gap) of poverty have shown significant improvements as well; falling by 61 per cent and 67 per cent respectively (BBS 2017). The rates of decline are similar for urban and rural areas—the poverty gap declined by 57 per cent and 61 per cent and squared poverty gap by 64 per cent and 65 per cent for urban and rural areas respectively. These trends suggest significant improvement among those below the poverty line. A fall in poverty gap indicates that the average consumption of the poor has improved, while a decline in squared poverty gap implies more equitable distribution of consumption among the poor. These improvements have also taken place at similar rates for the urban and the rural poor.

It may, however, be noted that, while the rural–urban gap in poverty rate is narrowing down, the gap still remains considerable. The rural poverty rate in 2016 was 26.4 per cent compared with the urban poverty rate of 18.9 per cent. Thus, although the rural areas account for about 64 per cent of the total population of Bangladesh, they are home to more than 71 per cent of the poor people in the country.

The above shows that Bangladesh has experienced a substantial poverty reduction over the last 24 years (between 1991–1992 and 2016), with the pace accelerating during the 2000s. Since poverty is measured by consumption based indicators in Bangladesh, rapid growth in consumption is the primary contributing factor. However, since there exists a large disparity in the initial distribution of consumption between the poor and the non-poor, even similar growth rates for all consumption groups would necessarily imply an increase in the average size of the gap in consumption between the poor and the non-poor.

The HIES data show that absolute inequality or the size of the gap in consumption between different groups has expanded for the country as a whole (World Bank 2008). For rural areas, consumption growth has been the dominant force in reducing poverty; whereas in urban areas, a marginal reduction in inequality has also had a sizeable poverty reducing impact.

At the international level, poverty measured at the international poverty line of $1.90 a day is used to track progress towards meeting the target of reducing the share of people living in extreme poverty to zero by 2030 as measured by the international poverty line and set by the SDG1 (see, Ravallion et al. 2008). Using the international poverty line of $1.90, the poverty headcount ratio was estimated at 44.2 per cent in 1991 in Bangladesh which has come down to 14.8 per cent in 2016 (World Bank's Poverty and Equity DataBank).

On the other hand, MPI provides a comprehensive view of the various ways in which people worldwide experience poverty in their daily life. The MPI reflects both the incidence—headcount ratio (H) of poverty that is the proportion of the population that is multidimensionally poor—and the average intensity (A) of their poverty—the average proportion of indicators in which poor people are deprived. A person is identified as poor if he/she is deprived in at least one third of the weighted indicators.

Table 3.2 shows the multidimensional poverty rate (MPI) and its two components, H and A in Bangladesh. Those identified as MPI poor are deprived in at least 33 per cent of the weighted indicators. Those identified as vulnerable to poverty' are deprived in 20–33 per cent of weighted indicators and those identified as in 'severe poverty' are deprived in over 50 per cent (Fig. 3.3).

The 2019 global MPI shows that the population in multidimensional poverty in Bangladesh has dropped to 74.4 million in 2014 from 93.7 million in 2004. Thus Bangladesh got about 19.3 million people out of poverty between 2004 and 2014, which is the fastest reduction in MPI

Table 3.2 Changes in multidimensional poverty in Bangladesh

Survey	*Year*	*MPI = H × A*			*Incidence of poverty (H), %*			*Average intensity across poor (A), %*		
		Value	*95% CI*		*Value*	*95% CI*		*Value*	*95% CI*	
			Lower	*Upper*		*Lower*	*Upper*		*Lower*	*Upper*
DHS	2004	0.365	0.352	0.378	67.2	65.4	69.1	54.3	53.6	55.0
DHS	2007	0.292	0.279	0.304	57.8	55.7	60.0	50.4	49.9	51.0
DHS	2014	0. 198	…	…	41.7	…	…	47.5	…	…

Source: OPHI Country Briefing 2011 and 2019—Bangladesh

Note: DHS = Demographic and Health Survey; CI = Confidence interval; … data not available

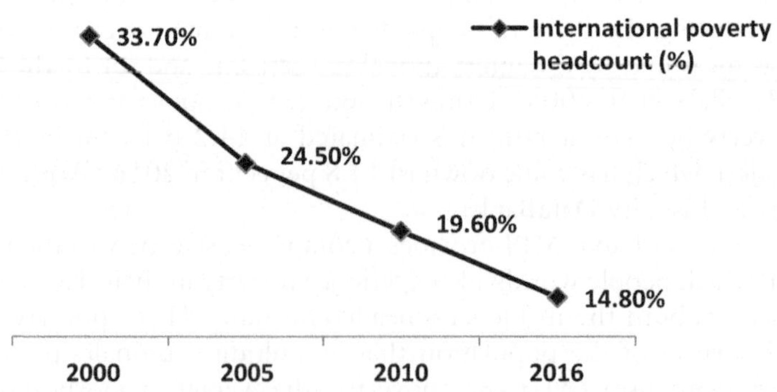

Fig. 3.3 International poverty headcount, Bangladesh (2011 1.90 PPP). (Source: World Bank (2019))

during the period across 101 countries of the world (see, OPHI/UNDP 2019). The data for Bangladesh from 2014 shows that 21.5 per cent of the population is vulnerable to multidimensional poverty and 16.2 per cent is vulnerable to severe multidimensional poverty. The data also reveal that a clear majority of the multidimensional poor live in the rural areas, where poverty rates are four times higher than that of urban areas. Further, nearly half of the people living in multidimensional poverty are eighteen years or younger. The data also show that a large majority of the people in Bangladesh are at risk of sliding into multidimensional poverty, which can be hastened by sickness, unemployment, climatic impacts and other adverse developments.

3.3.2 *Poverty in Bangladesh: A South Asian perspective*

Over the last two centuries, the global poverty rate dramatically dropped from 94 per cent in 1820 to 10.7 per cent in 2013 (Bourguignon and Morrisson 2002). However, South Asia's share of global poor has increased from 27.3 per cent to 33.4 per cent during the period of 1990–2013, while the largest share (50.7 per cent) live in Sub-Saharan Africa. Despite South Asia's share of global poor having increased, the number of poor people living in South Asia actually fell by 249 million during 1990–2013. Specifically, the headcount index of South Asia dropped from 44.6 per cent to 15.1 per cent during the period of 1990–2013.

The poverty headcount indices of the South Asian countries are highly heterogeneous (Fig. 3.4). Figure 3.5 shows the income poverty headcount indices of South Asian countries along with the world's and South Asia's average headcount indices. It shows that 21.2 per cent of the Indian population lives below the international poverty line of 1.90 US$. In fact, 270 million are considered poor, making India the poorest country in the region followed by Bangladesh where 18.5 per cent of population is below the poverty line. The headcount indices of Nepal, Pakistan and Maldives are 15.0 per cent, 6.1 per cent and 7.3 per cent respectively. In contrast, Sri Lanka has the lowest headcount index (1.9 per cent) while Bhutan reports the second lowest (2.2 per cent) in the South Asian region. Notably, the headcount indices of countries such as India, Bangladesh and Nepal are higher than that of the South Asia and global averages (Table 3.3).

Table 3.4 shows the percentage change in poverty and rate of poverty reduction in South Asian countries. Nepal has reduced poverty incidence

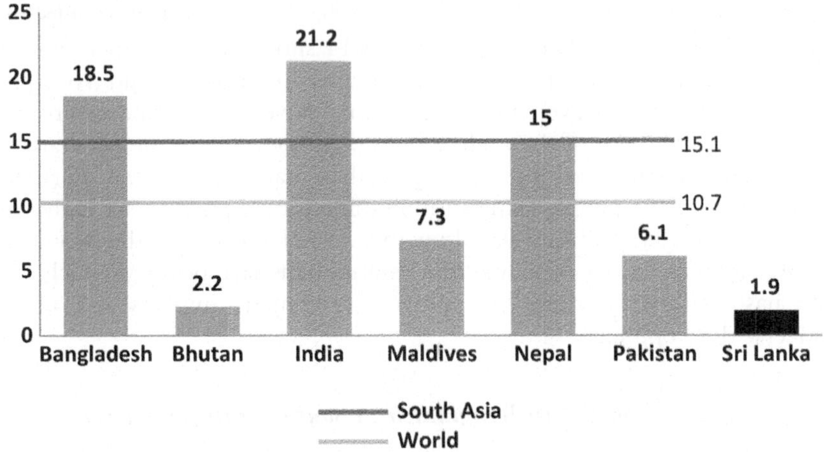

Fig. 3.4 Income poverty in South Asian countries, 2013. (Source: Based on World Bank, PavcalNet)

from 81.0 per cent to 7.3 per cent during the period of 1984–2010 and accounts for the highest poverty reduction and also the second highest rate of poverty reduction. Similarly, Pakistan and Bhutan have recorded the second and third largest poverty reduction respectively, while Bhutan has the highest rate of poverty reduction during the period 2003–2012. In fact, the headcount index of Bhutan has dropped from 35.2 per cent to 2.2 per cent within nine years: none other South Asian countries have achieved similar poverty reduction in such a short period. According to Bhutan Poverty Assessment 2014, three key drivers exist behind poverty reduction in Bhutan: increase in agriculture productivity and agriculture trade which is facilitated by trade agreements, expansion of road networks and other infrastructure facilities, and spreading spillovers from hydroelectric projects.

In contrast, both poverty reduction and rate of poverty reduction are lowest in Maldives where poverty reduction and its rate are equal to 2.6 per cent and 2.7 per cent respectively. The pace of poverty reduction of Sri Lanka has been modest, despite Sri Lanka's poverty incidence being the lowest in the region. Poverty reduction of Sri Lanka between 1985 and 2012 is only 11.4 per cent while the rate of poverty reduction is 85.5 per cent. In fact, Sri Lanka's headcount index has been the lowest among

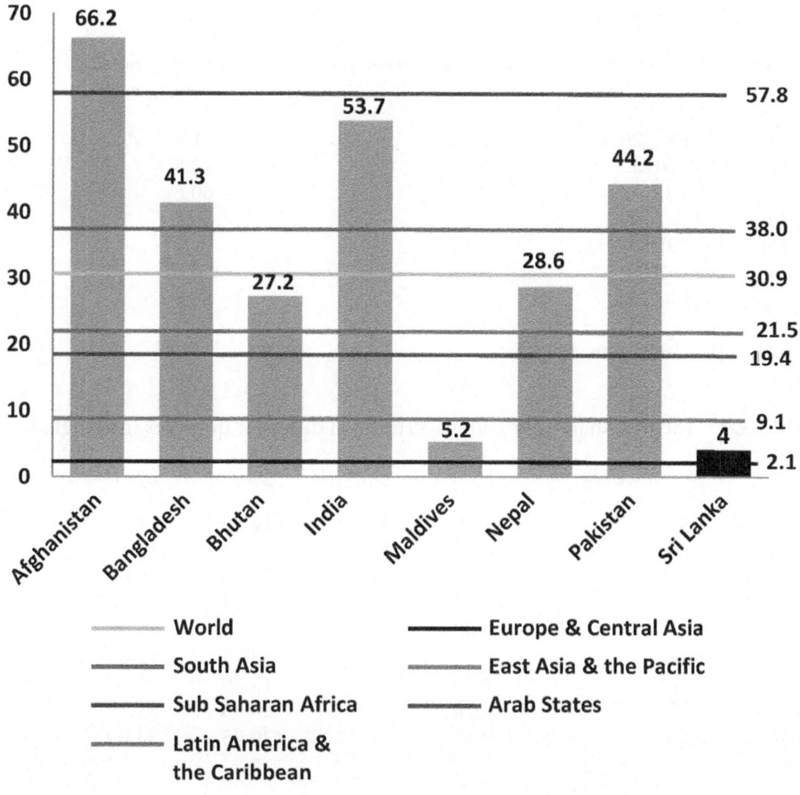

Fig. 3.5 Multidimensional poverty in South Asia. (Source: Based on data from OPHI)

South Asian countries throughout the history and Sri Lanka accounts for relatively low absolute poverty reduction compared with other South Asian countries. In general, Sri Lanka's growth performance fell well short of its potential in past decades and thus the process of growth-led poverty reduction has been inefficient.

Figure 3.5 shows multidimensional poverty in South Asian countries along with regional averages. Afghanistan has a remarkably higher multidimensional poverty headcount index (66.2 per cent), while 53.7 per cent and 44.2 per cent of the populations of India and Pakistan are respectively multidimensionally poor. Moreover, multidimensional poverty incidences

Table 3.3 Changes in poverty in South Asian countries

Country and period	*Change in poverty, %*	*Rate of poverty reduction, %*
Bangladesh, 1984–2010	20.2	51.9
Bhutan, 2003–2012	33.0	93.8
India, 1983–2012	32.6	60.6
Maldives, 2002–2009	2.6	26.7
Nepal, 1984–2010	73.7	91.0
Pakistan, 1984–2011	59.8	80.0
Sri Lanka, 1985–2012	11.4	85.5

Source: Based on World Bank, PavcalNet

Table 3.4 Income share (per cent) accruing to different quintiles in Bangladesh

Year	*Quintile 1 (Bottom)*	*Quintile 2*	*Quintile 3*	*Quintile 4*	*Quintile 5 (Top)*
1973–74	7.00	11.30	15.10	22.80	44.40
1981–82	6.64	10.72	15.20	22.12	45.32
1985–86	6.99	11.18	15.07	20.70	46.04
1991–92	6.52	10.89	15.53	22.19	44.96
1995–96	5.71	9.83	13.88	20.50	50.08
2000	6.15	9.68	13.17	18.79	52.01
2005	5.26	9.10	13.13	19.79	52.71
2010	5.22	9.10	13.33	20.56	51.79
2016	3.84	9.17	13.74	20.25	53.00

Source: HIES Reports, different years

of Afghanistan, India, Pakistan and Bangladesh are significantly higher than both world (30.9 per cent) and South Asian (38.0 per cent) averages.

In contrast, Sri Lanka, where only 4.0 per cent of the population is multidimensionally poor, has the lowest incidence of multidimensional poverty in the South Asian region. Furthermore, Sri Lanka's headcount index is considerably lower than all the regional averages and global average as well. South Asia accounts for the world's second largest income poverty incidence, despite the fact that a large number of people have moved out of poverty during the last two decades. Similarly, multidimensional poverty in South Asia is also considerably higher than that of world and other regional averages.

It is true that both income and multidimensional poverty in Bangladesh are rapidly declining, but these are still higher than regional and global averages. In fact, high growth in recent years and safety net programmes, state provided free education and health services along with other social protection programmes are the leading factors of this rapidly declining poverty incidence in Bangladesh—something that the many of the developing countries must consider in their efforts to reduce poverty.

Although there is a positive correlation between consumption and multidimensional measures of deprivation, but they are clearly not identical. Swaziland and South Sudan have similar monetary poverty rates (about 42 per cent of the population live below the International poverty line), but they have extremely different multidimensional poverty rates (around 20 per cent in Swaziland, compared with 91 per cent in South Sudan are living in 'multidimensional poverty'). This highlights the usefulness of tracking deprivation across multiple dimensions of well-being, including both standard and non-standard economic indicators (OPHI/UNDP 2019).

3.3.3 *Future of Poverty in Bangladesh*

Poverty change is not a consequence of economic growth alone. It also depends on the distribution of income and how income inequality changes during the growth process. If growth only lifts the incomes at the top, poverty levels are not likely to change. On the other hand, if growth is inclusive and lifts all boats, the country will be able to reduce absolute poverty over time. In Bangladesh inequality has been rising over time. Some studies on the link between growth, inequality and poverty reduction find that the share of income of the poorest quintile does not vary systematically with average income—or, in other words, the income of the poor on average rise proportionately with average incomes—and consequently, 'growth on average does benefit the poor as much as anyone else in society' (Dollar and Kraay 2002). Therefore, 'growth-enhancing policies should be at the center of any effective poverty reduction strategy'. However, the above 'do not imply that growth is all that is needed to improve the lives of the poor' or do not 'suggest a 'trickle-down' process or sequencing in which the rich get richer first and eventually benefits trickle down to the poor'.

Further, with a broadened concept of social welfare, the consequences of growth and changes in inequality, the analysis suggests that: 'Most of the cross-country and over-time variation in changes in social welfare is attributable to growth in average incomes. In contrast, the contribution of changes in relative incomes to social welfare growth is on average much smaller than growth in average incomes, and moreover is on average uncorrelated with average income growth' (Dollar et al. 2014). This suggests that persistent and high economic growth is a powerful force in poverty reduction. These consequences are valid for the long-run perspective of Bangladesh. Without the increase in productivity that brings economic growth, it would not be possible to lift millions of people out of poverty in the country.

The declared goal of the SDGs is to end extreme poverty by 2030. How realistic is this goal for Bangladesh? Answering this question obviously requires making assumptions. The historical decline in extreme poverty rates, from 1990 to 2016, along with the assumption that the average growth rate of consumption will be the same as the average growth rate over the past ten years and that the dispersion in the distribution of consumption will remain unchanged, suggests that the extreme poverty will continue going down significantly, but will not drop to zero by 2030 in Bangladesh. Thus, ending extreme poverty by 2030 will require growth with declining inequality in Bangladesh. This means that the shares of total consumption held by the poorest 40 per cent and the richest 10 per cent should steadily shift in favour of the poorest 40 per cent between 2020 and 2030.

3.4 Trends in Inequality

Since independence, Bangladesh has witnessed impressive average gains against multiple indicators of material prosperity. However, this is only part of the picture. Although Bangladesh is richer than ever before today, more than 30 million people still live in poverty. The richest 5 per cent of the households receives nearly 28 per cent of the total income, while the bottom 5 per cent gets only 0.23 per cent (BBS 2017).

Despite overall declines in maternal mortality, women in rural areas are still up to three times more likely to die while giving birth than women living in urban centres. Social protection has been extended, yet persons with disabilities are up to five times more likely than average to incur catastrophic health expenditures. Women are participating more in the work force, but continue to be disproportionately represented in vulnerable employment.

Over the last few decades, income inequality has been rising in Bangladesh. The Gini coefficient of income distribution stands at 0.483

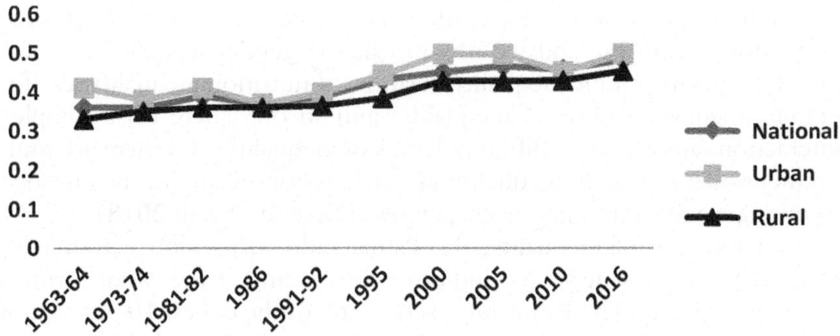

Fig. 3.6 Gini coefficient of income distribution in Bangladesh, 1963–2016. (Source: HIES, different years)

nationally in 2016; which is 0.498 in rural areas and 0.454 in urban areas (BBS 2017).[2] Figure 3.6 shows the trend of income inequality since 1963. Over the entire period of 1963–2016, national Gini has risen from 0.36 to 0.483—an increase by more than 34 per cent—while rural Gini increased by nearly 38 per cent and urban Gini by 21 per cent over the same period. These figures suggest that Bangladesh has experienced increases in the Gini coefficient over the period of last half century but the rate has accelerated especially since the 1990s. Table 3.4 shows that the share of income accruing to households belonging to the lower two quintiles has progressively declined with the richer quintiles gaining in income share.

The above widening income gap across the society is the consequence of a series of factors, including weak labour market institutions, inadequate social protection system, poor-quality education, inadequate access to credit and land, and high asset concentration.

It is seen that inequality increased rather sharply in the rural areas while urban areas experienced a somewhat moderate rise in income inequality. The income gap has deepened—and, with it, the difference in quality of life between the rich and the poor—despite the immense progress made through impressive growth performance. Economic progress in the country has not alleviated disparities. Overall, the Bangladesh society is more unequal today than at any point in time after independence!

[2] Gini coefficient is an inequality index that has value starting from 0 to 1. The higher the value, the greater the inequality. Thus, a value of 1 means highest unequal situation in a society and a value of 0 means there is perfect equality.

No doubt, inequality in Bangladesh society has many dimensions, such as economic (income and wealth) inequality; gender inequality; educational inequality; ethnic inequality; health and nutrition inequality; demographic inequality; political inequality; and so on. There exist complex interactions among these different forms of inequality; and there are multidimensional drivers of inequality. As such, a holistic approach is needed to mitigate and overcome the challenges (LSE and Oxfam 2018).

As a measure of inequality, the Palma ratio focuses on extremes of inequality. It is a widely used indicator for looking at the worst form of income inequality. The Palma ratio is the ratio of the richest 10 per cent of the population's share of gross national income (GNI), divided by the poorest 40 per cent of the population's share and is considered to be a more policy-relevant indicator than the Gini, especially when it comes to poverty reduction.

Palma suggests that 'middle classes'—more accurately the middle income groups between the 'rich' and the 'poor' (defined as the five 'middle' deciles, 5 to 9)—tend to capture around half of GNI almost universally. The other half of national income is shared between the richest 10 per cent and the poorest 40 per cent but the share of those two groups varies considerably across countries. He therefore holds that distributional politics is largely about the battle between the rich and poor for the other half of national income, and who the middle classes side with.

For a given, high Palma value, it is clear what needs to change: to narrow the gap, by raising the share of national income of the poorest 40 per cent and/or reducing the share of the top 10 per cent (see, Palma 2011; Cobham and Sumner 2013). In Bangladesh, it is changes in these extremes that are most noticeable; while the share of income in the middle is relatively stable (Appendix, Table 3.10). As can be seen from Figure 3.7, the Palma ratio at the national level has consistently increased from 1.68 in 1963–1964 to 2.93 in 2016; in urban areas, it rose from 2.00 to 2.96 while, in rural areas, it grew from 1.38 to 2.51 over the same period.

In Appendix, Fig. 3.9 shows the changes in the income shares of the poorest 40 per cent, middle 50 per cent and the richest 10 per cent in the income distribution at the national level; and Figs. 3.10 and 3.11 show separately for urban and rural areas respectively. These show that the share of the middle 50 per cent is relatively stable; while the poorest 40 per cent generally loses in terms of income share while the richest 10 per cent gains. The policy implication is that Bangladesh should focus on its 'extreme' inequalities, that is, inequalities that do most

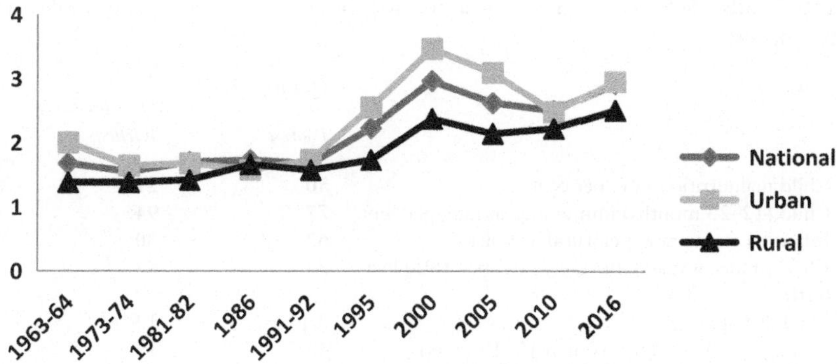

Fig. 3.7 Palma ratio in Bangladesh, 1963–2016. (Source: Authors' calculation using HIES data. Note: Due to data limitations, the Palma ratio has been constructed using total household income rather than gross national income (GNI))

harm to inclusive and sustainable economic growth and undermine social and political stability.

3.4.1 *Social Inequalities*

The HIES data show that income inequality is much higher than consumption inequality; and the ratio of income inequality to consumption inequality is rising over time (BBS 2017). This means that, given similar poverty thresholds for income and consumption, income poverty reduction would be slower than the reduction in consumption poverty. It is well-known that social indicators vary significantly across countries depending on their level of development; but these may vary widely across different income groups as well in the same country. Table 3.5 shows the glaring social inequalities that exist between the poorest and richest quintiles of Bangladesh population.

The table shows that inequalities in education, health and other basic services are significantly related to income and wealth. It shows that the percentage of malnourished children under 5 is about 50 per cent in poorest quintile whereas it is 21 per cent for richest quintile in 2011; whereas only about 12 per cent of women in the poorest quintile in 2014 are lucky enough to have the opportunity to be attended by skilled health staff during giving birth while it is around 64 per cent for the richest quintile.

Table 3.5 Selected social indicators for poorest and richest quintiles in Bangladesh

Indicator	*Quintile*	
	Poorest	*Richest*
Child malnutrition rate, per cent	50	21
Child (12–23 months) immunisation rate, per cent	77	94
Infant mortality rate, per 1000 live births	62	30
Child (under 5 years) mortality rate, per 1000 live births	78	38
Total fertility rate	3.1	1.9
Teenage mothers (% of women 15–19 years)	42	19
Per cent births attended by skilled health attendant	12	64
Per cent women receiving prenatal care	30	87
Primary school completion rate, per cent	65	97

Source: WDI (2014)

Bangladesh has already achieved gender parity in primary and secondary education at the national level. This positive development has occurred due to some specific public interventions focusing on girl students, such as stipends and exemption of tuition fees for girls in rural areas, and the stipend scheme for girls at the secondary level. This has contributed to promoting the objectives of ensuring gender equality and empowerment of women.

There has also been steady improvement in the social and political empowerment scenario of women in Bangladesh. The government has adopted the National Policy for Women's Development 2011 and a series of programmes for empowerment of women. Women participation in the decision making process has also marked significant improvement in the country. There has been a sharp increase in the number of women parliamentarians elected in 2014 (20 per cent) compared with 1991 (about 13 per cent). However, women employment is still low; around 30 per cent of women aged 15–24 are engaged in employment against 52 per cent of men (Gender Statistics, World Bank 2017).

The issue of inequality is thus multidimensional. An equal society can only be ensured if all individuals and social groups can use their productive abilities to the maximum extent for enjoying greater social welfare and inclusive development. In reality, while much progress has been made towards reducing gender inequality, inequality in income, wealth, and employment still remains high. To achieve universal realisation of equality and empowerment, it is critical to address key areas of inequality, in particular inequalities in opportunities; discrimination in law and in practice; women's and men's unequal opportunities in the labour market; unequal division of unpaid care and domestic work; poor's limited control over assets and property; and their unequal participation in private and public decision making and businesses.

3.5 Poverty Assessment

Poverty assessment provides information on the causes and consequences of poverty in the country and examines how public policies, expenditures and institutions affect the poor people. The assessment describes the poor, details their living conditions, describes their changing situation over time, and clarifies the main challenges facing the poor people when they try to move out of poverty. The assessment also considers how labour-intensive growth, human resource development and social protection programmes can alleviate poverty.

The official poverty measure in Bangladesh uses money-metric poverty or poverty measured on the basis of a money value of expenditure, adopting the more commonly used headcount ratio (the number of the poor as a proportion of the population), which are derived from a poverty line approach.

Bangladesh's poverty reduction, especially in the 2000s, provides a remarkable story of sustained progress. Between 2000 and 2016, the poverty rate fell by 1.2 percentage points per year relative to less than one percentage point decline in the 1990s (for per capita consumption growth see Fig. 3.8 and poverty trends, see Table 3.6). Moreover, poverty fluctuated widely till the end of 1980s since independence with no clear declining trend. Poverty incidence, using the international poverty line of $ 1.90 purchasing power parity (PPP) a day, also sustainably declined from 33.7 per cent in 2000 to 14.8 per cent in 2016. The period also saw significant improvements in other dimensions of well-being, including education and life expectancy. Between 2010 and 2016, about 8 million people were lifted out of poverty and 5.6 million out of extreme poverty (World Bank 2019).

The reduction in poverty was minimal in the decades till the 1990s and a more rapid pace is observed only recently. In 2016, nearly a quarter of the population, or nearly 40 million, continued to live below the national

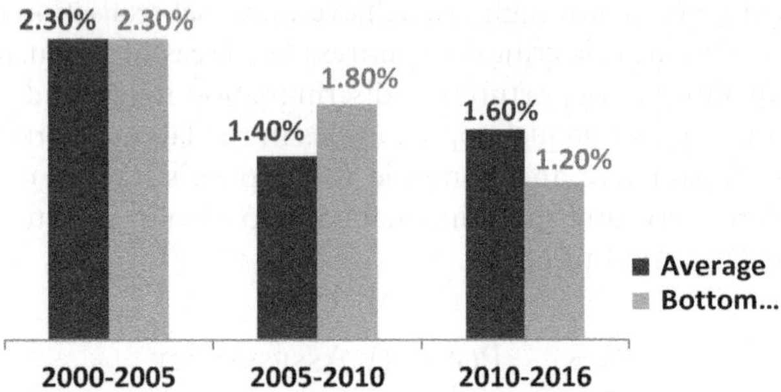

Fig. 3.8 Annualised per capita consumption growth. (Source: World Bank (2019))

Table 3.6 Poverty trends in Bangladesh, 2000–2016

	2000	*2005*	*2010*	*2016*
Poverty (Upper poverty line)				
Head count	48.9	40.0	31.5	24.5
Depth of poverty	12.8	9.0	6.5	5.0
Severity of poverty	4.6	2.9	2.0	1.6
Extreme poverty (Lower poverty line)				
Head count	34.3	25.1	17.6	13.0
Depth of poverty	7.5	4.7	3.1	2.3
Severity of poverty	2.4	1.3	0.8	0.6

Source: World Bank (2019)

poverty line. Using the international poverty line of US$1.90 a day and the poverty line for lower middle income countries (LMIC) of US$3.20 a day, both in 2011 purchasing power parity (PPP), the same trend of decline in the poverty rate is observed as with the national poverty line, although the magnitude and speed differ in the sub-periods. The number of poor has declined more rapidly in the recent years.

3.5.1 *Economic Growth and Poverty*

High and sustained economic growth has been the major driver of poverty reduction during the period. The Bangladesh economy has experienced good economic growth over the past decade. Along with impressive GDP growth, the growth of GDP per capita, which is more relevant for changes in poverty, has also been healthy. However, the elasticity of poverty reduction to growth (the extent of poverty reduction given by each percentage point growth in GDP per capita) has declined significantly: from 0.88 during 2000–2010 to 0.73 during 2010–2016. In the case of extreme poverty, the decline in elasticity has been from 1.24 to 0.86 over the same period. The above indicates that economic growth has not become inclusive enough as Bangladesh has raised its GDP growth.

Furthermore, since the poverty estimates are based on consumption, the above shows that average consumption growth has not kept pace with GDP growth. Data from HIESs show that although GDP growth has accelerated over the years, consumption growth has been slower. The HIES data show that the consumption growth rate of the poorest 40 per cent declined from 1.8 per cent during 2005–2010 to 1.2 per cent in 2010–2016 (World Bank 2019). Further, consumption growth has become more unequal over different income groups.

3.5.2 *Changes in Rural–Urban and Regional Poverty*

The progress in poverty reduction in urban and rural Bangladesh gives a divergent story in recent years (Table 3.7). As Table 3.9 shows, although the poverty has declined both in rural and urban areas, the rate of reduction has been much slower in urban areas. In particular, there has been virtually no reduction in extreme poverty in the urban areas after 2010. In this context, it is important to note that a rapid urbanisation is taking place in Bangladesh. The country's urban population is rising at an average annual growth rate of 3.9 per cent since 2000, relative to 2.7 per cent for South Asia (UNDESA 2018).

Furthermore, recent poverty reduction has been marked by significant regional divide across the seven geographical divisions of the country (Table 3.9). In general, the divisions located in the western parts of the country did not accrue similar gains as those by the eastern divisions giving rise to what is widely known as the 'east-west divide' in poverty reduction (Table 3.8). As Table 3.9 shows, poverty has actually risen in the western Rangpur division; while it has stagnated in Khulna and Rajshahi divisions after 2010. In terms of number, 45 per cent of the country's total poor and 48 per cent of the extreme poor are concentrated in Dhaka

Table 3.7 Rural and urban poverty in Bangladesh, 2000–2016

	2000	*2005*	*2010*	*2016*
Rural Bangladesh				
Poverty (Upper poverty line)				
Head count	52.3	43.8	35.2	26.4
Depth of poverty	13.7	9.8	7.4	5.4
Severity of poverty	4.9	3.1	2.2	1.7
Extreme poverty (Lower poverty line)				
Head count	37.9	28.6	21.1	14.9
Depth of poverty	8.3	5.3	3.7	2.6
Severity of poverty	2.6	1.5	1.0	0.7
Urban Bangladesh				
Poverty (Upper poverty line)				
Head count	35.2	28.4	21.3	18.9
Depth of poverty	9.1	6.5	4.3	3.9
Severity of poverty	3.3	2.1	1.3	1.2
Extreme poverty (Lower poverty line)				
Head count	20.0	14.6	7.7	7.6
Depth of poverty	4.1	2.6	1.3	1.3
Severity of poverty	1.2	0.7	0.4	0.4

Source: BBS, HIES Reports, various years

Table 3.8 Uneven poverty reduction across divisions in Bangladesh

Division	*Poverty rate, %*		*Extreme poverty rate, %*	
	2010	*2016*	*2010*	*2016*
Eastern divisions				
Barisal	39.4	26.4	26.7	14.4
Chittagong	26.2	18.3	13.1	9.0
Dhaka	30.5	20.5	15.6	9.9
Sylhet	28.1	16.2	20.7	11.5
Western divisions				
Khulna	32.1	27.7	15.4	12.1
Rajshahi	29.7	29.0	16.0	14.3
Rangpur	42.3	47.3	27.7	30.6

Source: World Bank (2019)

Table 3.9 Improvement in non-monetary dimensions of well-being

	2000	*2005*	*2010*	*2016*
Household demographics				
Average household size, number	5.2	4.8	4.5	4.1
Average number of children under eight	1.1	0.9	0.8	0.7
Access to services				
Households with tube well water, % of total	51.5	57.8	57.7	59.1
Households with piped water, % of total	6.8	7.6	10.6	12.0
Households with electricity, % of total	31.2	44.2	55.2	76.0
Households owning cultivable land, % of total	41.4	45.4	41.0	32.3
Education				
Literacy among population older than 18 years, %	43.0	49.6	53.9	60.1
Average years of schooling among older than 18, %	3.3	4.1	4.4	4.7
School attendance among 6–18 years old, %	63.9	66.6	73.9	80.4
Health				
Total fertility rate, births per woman	3.2	2.7	2.3	2.1
Female life expectancy at birth, years	65.7	68.7	71.5	74.6
Male life expectancy at birth, years	65.0	67.3	69.0	71.2
Life expectancy at birth, both sexes, years	65.3	67.9	70.2	72.8
Infant mortality rate, per 1000 live births	64.0	50.4	38.9	26.9
% of stunting, height for age, children under 5	50.8	45.9	41.4	36.1
% of underweight, weight for age, children under 5	42.3	37.3	36.8	32.6
Prevalence of undernourishment, % of population	20.8	16.6	16.9	15.2

Source: BBS, HIES and World Bank, WDI data

Note: Some data on health indicators for 2016 may vary over ±2–3 years depending upon data availability

and Rangpur divisions in 2016. Out of the country's 64 districts, most poor districts are located in the northwest and are concentrated in the periphery of the country.

3.5.3 *Proximate Determinants of Poverty Trends*

The strong economic growth contributed to steady decline in the unemployment rate from 4.2 per cent for males and 10.2 per cent for females in 2000 to 3.1 per cent and 6.7 per cent for males and females respectively in 2017. During this 17-year period, the labour force participation rate increased for both sexes: rising from 22.8 per cent to 36.3 per cent for females and from 73.5 per cent to 80.5 per cent for males. The total labour force participation rate rose from 49.2 per cent to 58.2 per cent over the period.

The female unemployment rate has consistently remained higher than the rate for males, with females constituting about half of the total number of the unemployed. Among age cohorts, young workers between ages 15 and 24 suffer the highest unemployment, making up almost half of the unemployed. As the age profile rises, the smaller becomes the share of the total unemployed. Despite the decline in unemployment, underemployment—those who work but are willing and available to work for more hours—remains persistently high, in the range of 18–20 per cent.

Nearly 41 per cent of the available jobs are in the agriculture sector, followed by services (39 per cent) and industry (20 per cent). In the recent decades, there has been a gradual shift in jobs away from agriculture and into industry sector, a structural change that started in the 1990s. The share of agriculture in total employment decreased from about 51 per cent in 2000 to 41 per cent in 2017, while the share of the services sector rose only marginally from about 38 per cent to 39 per cent. But the share of industry rose from about 13 per cent to nearly 21 per cent over the same period.

However, unlike the experience in many other countries, where a large share of the unskilled labour moved from agriculture to manufacturing jobs, with consequent higher productivity and higher wages, in Bangladesh the share of total employment in manufacturing did not increase much. Most of the employment in industry was generated in construction and allied activities. Similarly, bulk of unskilled employment moved to the informal services subsector, which is typically low-wage and low skill in nature. In the services sector, more than three-quarters is composed of low-pay or low-skill jobs, such as petty retail trade and similar informal activities. The low productivity in the services sector and non-manufacturing industry sector activities does not provide the basis for large wage increases, which limits the scope of poverty reduction and shared prosperity.

Changes in earned income, rather than transfers, are the key drivers of poverty reduction in Bangladesh, with earned income constituting more than 73 per cent of the total income on average and 82 per cent of the income of the poorest 40 per cent of the population (Jolliffe et al. 2013). In 2016, only about 5 per cent of all households received international remittances, while 13 per cent received internal remittances and 21 per cent received social protection transfers.

Favourable changes in several household demographics have also contributed to consumption gains over the years. As Bangladesh has succeeded in significantly improving human development outcomes since independence through joint efforts by the government and the NGOs, these non-monetary dimensions of well-being have also contributed to consumption and nutrition gains, particularly of the poor people (World Bank 2006). The trends in several selected indicators since 2000, given in Table 3.10, show sustained improvements in these indicators creating diverse channels of well-being. There has been sustained decrease in total fertility reducing the household size and dependency ratio; rise in life expectancy and decline in infant mortality; rise in school attendance and literacy; and access to safe drinking water and electricity and other well-being indicators, all contributing to poverty reduction. Without access to basic social services, the poor are vulnerable to illness, unemployment, and the country's increasing natural disasters due to climate change and other adverse impacts.

Further consolidation of the role of social development and its poverty reducing impact in Bangladesh needs comprehensive social policies for development. Social policy should be the foundation of national development strategies in the country. The key is to move to comprehensive social and employment policies as an essential part of balanced—socially, economically and environmentally—and sustainable development. Rather than neoliberal prescriptive policies of targeted benefits for the poor, equitable access and use of universal public services and human development agenda should become dominant in Bangladesh's development policy.

The driving forces of policy shift towards comprehensive social policies have to emerge from both the government's internal processes and external pressure from social advocacy groups such as NGO-MFIs, CBOs and other pressure groups. The key will be to create agency for triggering policy changes.

3.5.4 *Microfinance and Poverty Reduction*

Since independence, microfinance (or microcredit; in practice, the terms are used interchangeably) has emerged as a key policy and programme intervention for poverty reduction and 'bottom-up' socioeconomic development in Bangladesh. Bangladesh currently tops the ranking as the most microfinance-friendly country in the world with a microfinance penetration rate of 25 per cent (Gonzalez 2010; Rozas and Sinha 2010).

Microfinance to the poor (especially poor women) for undertaking income generating activities is widely treated as virtuous and is seen by many as valuable in poverty reduction. It is also argued that micro-financing is a relatively efficient means for assisting the poor (Becker and Posner 2009).

However, these views have not gone unchallenged. Although the interest rates on micro-loans are relatively high, this is seen as a positive mechanism for rationing the limited volume of microfinance available to the borrowers who can earn sufficient returns to cover the costs. In practice, however, this self-selection process is far from perfect; because the poor may borrow in desperation and become locked into a vicious cycle of indebtedness. There may exist moral hazard problems as well (Banerjee and Jackson 2017).

Further, an adequate assessment of the capacity of microfinance to reduce poverty needs to employ an economy-wide framework. Although microfinance can provide some short-term relief from poverty, it is probably not a long-term solution for poverty, especially in situations where the poor households own small amounts of land or other productive assets. In modern agriculture, there exist strong positive economies of scale which small farms are unlikely to tap to the required extent and benefit in the long term. The non-farm economic opportunities may also remain limited in the absence of strong overall economic growth.

A more important aspect of microfinance is its role in increasing the status of women and their bargaining power in the family as most micro-loans are given to women (more than 90 per cent in Bangladesh). Although there exists counter evidence that increased access to microfinance does not improve the health and educational status of women, nor increase the availability of consumer goods to them, and fails to enhance their role in decision making within the household (e.g. Banerjee et al. 2015), these results may be context-specific, situational, and dependent on the nature of the patriarchy in society. If men have strong control over all finances in the household, micro-loans can do little to empower women.

Regarding the impact on poverty, one study on three major MFIs in Bangladesh—BRAC, Grameen Bank, and RD-12—finds that up to 5 per cent of the participants are able to lift their families out of poverty every year by borrowing from one of these MFIs (Khandker 1998). Although later studies using more rigorous forms of impact evaluation, such as the randomised control trial (RCT) methodology, have generated mixed evidence, the believers of microfinance strongly hold that: '*A Grameen-type credit programme opens up the door for limitless self-employment, and it can effectively do it in a pocket of poverty amidst prosperity, or in a massive poverty situation'* (Yunus 1989: 156).

Notably, microfinance helps to build entrepreneurial activity, with many borrowers escaping poverty by growing their informal microenterprises into small and medium enterprises (SMEs). Microfinance, especially by providing microenterprise loans, reduces the credit constraints that the poor potential entrepreneurs (who are NGO-MFIs borrowers) often face and that preclude enterprise development in the poor communities.

Although average employment in micro- and cottage enterprises (MCEs) is low as these are mostly operated by family labour or the entrepreneur himself/herself, the total number of people engaged in MCEs is much higher than people involved in large, medium and small enterprises. In Bangladesh, around 89 per cent of all economic establishments are MCEs (BBS 2013). More than 7.8 million economic establishments operate in the country and the average employment per MCE is 1.98 persons. This means that the MCEs have created employment for 13.73 million persons; 56 per cent of total employment in all enterprises. The NGO-MFIs are significantly involved in financing MCEs; the total MCE loan outstanding by NGO-MFIs is Tk. 123.27 billion in 2015 (InM 2016). These enterprises have significant potential for future growth and are currently poised to become the emerging drivers of inclusive growth in Bangladesh. The MCEs are the pioneers of diversification of the rural economy and its transformation towards modernisation.

For unleashing the potential and making greater contribution to poverty reduction, NGO-MFIs need to focus on developing institutions that can promote productive entrepreneurship—institutions that can scale-up small businesses into those capable of productivity growth through innovation, technology transfer, subcontracting, skills-upgrading and serving additional non-local demand. By developing individual entrepreneurship, NGO-MFIs should also engage in developing the institutional vehicles and mechanisms of collective entrepreneurship that can facilitate organisational upgrading and learning.

Overall, Bangladesh seems to have shown little dynamism at both the low end (elimination of poverty) and the high end (decline in economic vulnerability and global middle class); and most of the newly 'well-off' households remain far from economically secure and are at risk of falling back into poverty if stricken by a negative shock. Bangladesh still has a small share of the economically secure middle class; and with such a very modest increase, there is still a long way to go for Bangladesh of becoming a middle-class society.

3.6 Poverty and Inequality Reduction Policy

Since both poverty and inequality are multidimensional, the poverty and inequality reduction policies have to be comprehensive covering not only inequalities in income but also social, political and economic exclusion and discrimination, and inequalities in opportunities and outcomes.

In Bangladesh, changes in the structure of output and income are one of the major sources of changes in inequality (World Bank 2008). Among different components of personal income, wage is the most equalising component; but its share is declining steadily in both rural and urban areas. For reversing the trend, policies for broad-based non-farm growth and expanding employment-intensive growth are needed. Over the medium term, this can be a powerful tool of reducing inequality in Bangladesh for which investments in both physical infrastructure and human capital are necessary.

According to the HIES data, there exist several sources of income inequality in Bangladesh: income from non-farm enterprises, land and non-land assets, and remittances from abroad (Khan and Sen 2001). Income from non-farm enterprises largely represents return to enterprise ownership and is the return to wealth. International remittances are also concentrated to relatively better-off households as overseas migration entails high costs beyond the reach of most poor households. Thus, the increase in the relative importance of incomes from non-farm enterprises and remittances are both highly inequalising as the incomes accrue mostly to higher income groups.

Obviously, curbing growth in these components is not a desirable policy as it could lead to reduced income growth. There are two options. First, to tax these income components in a way that does not reduce incentives. Second, introduce public transfer to the poor. However, the prospect for large transfers which can make a difference is somewhat limited due to inadequate availability of public resources and inevitable leakages in the distribution system. Appendix Table 3.12 provides a list of specific policies that may be considered for ensuring a more equitable development in Bangladesh.

The current status of inequality suggests that Bangladesh should focus on 'extreme' inequalities, that is, inequalities that do most harm to inclusive and sustainable economic growth and undermine social and political stability. For achieving inclusive and sustained development, Bangladesh cannot ignore extreme inequalities. The World Bank study on *Voices of the Poor* highlights that the poor suffer not just from a lack of income but from insecurity and a lack of voice.[3]

Since most of Bangladesh's poor live in rural areas and are engaged in farming, agricultural development is essential to directly increase the incomes of the poor who farm; but also for releasing labour and capital that can be used in non-agricultural enterprises and for stimulating the demand for non-agricultural goods. This emphasises the positive linkages between agricultural development and non-farm activity growth—local 'trickle-down' from improving farm productivity. Thus policies that encourage investment in the rural, non-farm sector may be the best means of reducing rural poverty and inequality.

But even in rural areas, rural non-farm activity ranges from household and village production on a very small scale producing simple, low-quality products on the one hand; to micro, small, and medium enterprises (MSMEs) on the other, sometimes using imported technology and producing modern high quality products. The high-quality products sector, that plays a central role in this framework, combines two separate elements: production of exportable goods that can be traded on a larger market and production of non-tradable goods and services.

Bangladesh's Seventh Five Year Plan (2016–2020) recognises that, since the existing distribution of assets and human capabilities are unequal, the benefit of growth favours the better endowed with these assets. The long-term income inequality reduction strategy must therefore focus on reducing this initial gap. Human development strategy with emphasis on alleviating the access gap for the poor is one powerful instrument for this purpose. Similarly, facilitating asset accumulation through better access to credit for the poor, social inclusion of the poor and disadvantaged by

[3] See also World Bank's World Development Report on Poverty in 2000. The International Commission on the Measurement of Economic Performance and Social Well-Being (2010) emphasises that metrics of performance (including output and inequality) should be expanded beyond just conventional measures of GDP and/or income. The OECD has carried on this work in their Better Living Initiative, including the construction of the Better Life Index. An important part of the agenda of OECD High Level Expert Group on Measurement of Economic Performance and Social Well-Being is the construction/evaluation of alternative measures of inequality.

eliminating physical and social barriers are important instruments for reducing income inequality in Bangladesh.

The Seventh Plan identifies two major areas for specific focus to ensure better income distribution—asset (land) redistribution and fiscal policy. In the case of land, the aim is to strengthen the land administration regime and related land market through a range of institutional, regulatory and fiscal policy reforms. A proper capital gains tax on land transactions can provide an important way to reduce windfall capital gains; it will also help to stabilise land prices by discouraging land speculation and providing additional revenues for spending on social services.

Clearly, a major way through which the government can help improve income distribution is by making faster progress in building up the human capital of the poor. Along with better health and education, a strong social protection system can be used as instruments for improving income distribution. One area where public spending should be increased is rural infrastructure—rural roads, rural electricity, irrigation and flood control. In addition, availability of rural credit is an important instrument for helping the poor to build up assets and also protect their consumption. Another area where public spending should be scaled up concerns social protection.

While the causes are complex, three factors may be identified that has been holding Bangladesh back compared with many high performing countries. These include: (1) lower pace and less inclusive pattern of growth; (2) rising inequality of income and wealth; and (3) adverse impacts of natural disasters and climate change. Per capita income and related data indicate that probably less than 10 per cent of the country's population has made it to the global middle class; and a large share of the population remains vulnerable to falling into poverty. Bangladesh's slow progress with poverty reduction is also linked to the limited progress achieved in providing economic mobility and growing the middle class. More rapid growth of the middle class can bring both intrinsic and instrumental benefits to Bangladesh society—not only it enjoys greater economic security and higher living standards, but it also provides instrumental benefits for other segments in society by being a key driver of growth; an influential constituency for good policies, better institutions and good governance; and a major provider of income tax revenues needed for investment in development.

The analysis presented above shows that Bangladesh has recently moved to a path that promotes booming manufacturing sector and provides large numbers of labour-intensive jobs, absorbing the surplus low-skilled labour from agriculture and give them significantly higher wage income. Creating such a manufacturing base helps poverty reduction; otherwise the workers who move out of agriculture generally end up in low-end service jobs, which limit the gains for labour from structural transformation. Wages are a major source of income for most households, hence rapid increase in real wages can make good progress in poverty reduction. In the long run, low wages for the highly educated and highly skilled are likely to damage Bangladesh's economic competitiveness by making it even more attractive for these groups to move abroad in search of more remunerative opportunities.

For Bangladesh, faster growth in agricultural productivity can also emerge as a key driver of poverty reduction. Agriculture, which employs most poor people in the country, has experienced minimal growth in the past decade. Further, the gains from structural transformation, or the shift from agriculture towards non-agricultural activities, are limited in Bangladesh compared with comparable countries, and growth in labour productivity relies disproportionately on within-sector productivity growth. As a result, the responsiveness of poverty reduction to growth is relatively slow.

Income inequality is rising in Bangladesh; there also exists high concentration of wealth. This may have contributed to strong vested interests in the status quo by hindering acceptance of the reforms needed to prompt more inclusive growth and faster poverty reduction. Differences in the quality of human resources, and in the incomes individuals and households can earn, drive a large degree of the inequality of outcomes in Bangladesh.

The effects of such inequality show themselves from the earliest days of life. Poorer children are at a disadvantage from their birth. They have limited access to good-quality healthcare and early childhood education, which undermines their ability to succeed later in life. Many poor people, including in the younger generations, have limited education. The low level of education and skills means that the poor cannot compete for productive jobs in the formal sectors, such as high-end services or business-process outsourcing positions, which require tertiary education. This constrains the total supply of skilled labour, which dampens the business environment for investors, perpetuating the cycle of inequality of opportunity and inequality of outcomes.

Frequent natural disasters, including cyclones that disproportionately strike the poor coastal regions of Bangladesh continually push vulnerable groups into poverty and jeopardise long-term human capital development. Natural disasters have caused significant losses and damages in Bangladesh since the 1970s, making it one of the most disaster-prone countries in the world. Further, lack of security and justice and economic stresses have intertwined to lock poor people in poverty. A review of the experiences of other

A closer examination of the profile of the poor clarifies the importance of each of the above three factors, and how the drivers of poverty work together to hold the poor from achieving a better life. The poor live in relatively large households, with low educational attainment, headed by individuals who are self-employed or work in agriculture as labourers or small/marginal farmers. Households that rely on agriculture as the main source of income are the poorest. Female headed households, which receive a large share of income from remittances, are less likely to be poor. Like most countries, Bangladesh shows a strong negative correlation between poverty risk and the level of education of the household head. Secondary education stands out as the key threshold—graduation reduces the risk of poverty.

There are large regional disparities in poverty across Bangladesh; usually growth is higher in the central and eastern regions while regional growth is low in the lagging northwestern regions of the country. Most of the poor live in the rural areas, and the rural poverty rate is higher than that of urban areas. In addition, people living in informal settlements in urban areas suffer high levels of multidimensional poverty; almost 40 per cent of these informal settlers are located in Dhaka.

Poor households rely disproportionately on income from agriculture (including subsistence farming, agricultural wages, and agriculture-related self employment), domestic remittances, and government transfers. While the share of income provided by agriculture has declined over time, dependence on wages and salaries from agricultural activities remains high—about two-thirds of the microenterprises are agriculture-related. Domestic remittances and government transfers form low shares of total household income in poor households.

The poor start their life at a disadvantage. They are constrained by undernourishment, limited resources, poor access to quality healthcare, and low education and skills, along with many other deficits. They earn low incomes, save little for the future, and are vulnerable to shocks. Lacking the requisite skills to take advantage of job opportunities, the poor are generally limited to agricultural work or other low-paid jobs in rural areas; in urban settings, many end up in slums.

The high concentration of income and wealth limits equality of opportunity and impedes equitable public service delivery, which is necessary for inclusive growth. With a low rate of investment, the economy is largely driven by consumption, which limits the potential for more rapid structural transformation and improvement in productivity. The slow increase in real wages, while it might be attractive in the short run, is likely to negatively affect the competitiveness of the economy in the long run with the better skilled people leaving the country for more attractive job opportunities.

Bangladesh has solid macroeconomic fundamentals and its growth prospects are strongly positive. With a healthy current account, strong international reserves, significant fiscal space, and low and stable inflation, the economy is in a strong position to adopt multiple policies to seize opportunities, mitigate domestic and global shocks, and provide the basis for productive job creation and poverty reduction.

The population of Bangladesh is relatively young. In 2011, about 65 per cent of the population was in the working age group of 15–64 years. Three in 10 of the household population is of school age and, for every 100 people in the working-age population, there are about 54 dependents (46 young dependents and 8 old dependents). The demographic structure presents a clear opportunity for the country to reap the economic benefits of demographic dividends in the coming years if it can manage to improve the skills of the labour force and create productive jobs. At the same time, it raises significant challenges for more inclusive growth for providing the growth benefits to the poorer households.

Making the pattern of growth more inclusive, particularly creating more well-paying jobs, will help the people to achieve higher and more stable incomes. The government can help end the vicious cycle of unequal opportunity and outcomes that trap people in poverty, and establish mutually reinforcing positive cycles that will create a growing middle class that is well-integrated with other groups. It can help improve service delivery for all and increase non-farm employment opportunities through increased demand for manufacturing goods and services. Finally, more progressive and better-administered revenue system can help finance needed investments in both physical and human capital.

For the future, strong economic growth will be the basis for productive job creation and poverty reduction. In the long run, productivity is the fundamental. Addressing the key factors—creating more well-paying jobs; improving productivity in all sectors, including agriculture; reducing income and wealth inequality through more investment in people and skill development; and better managing the risks and protecting the vulnerable—will help accelerate poverty reduction.

3.6.1 Constraints to Poverty Reduction

In the Bangladesh economy, three key constraints trap the people in a vicious cycle of 'low skills and low wages' and 'low investment and low-quality jobs'. Most of the poor work in very low productive jobs or suffer from underemployment. Although employment has grown at roughly the same rate as the working-age population in the past decades, but only a small share of the jobs created are well-paying jobs. Real wages of the labour force has increased at a slow rate which indicates low effective demand in the labour market, particularly for the skilled labour force. Demand side solutions are therefore necessary to move up the value chain and create more gainful employment opportunities and, on the supply side, measures are needed to equip the labour force with better education and skills.

The first key constraint is the rising inequality of incomes and wealth. This negatively affects the business environment, limiting long-term investment, inclusive growth, and productive job creation. The rich has a strong interest in maintaining the status quo. This hinders the reforms needed to facilitate more inclusive growth and poverty reduction. The elite capture and corruption in the governance structure have been highly corrosive, not only to public service delivery but also to political and economic performance. These risks limit the attractiveness of long-term investment hampering rapid structural transformation and increased productivity.

The second key constraint relates to low and inequitable distribution of human capital. The learning outcomes in Bangladesh are very weak. In particular, the poor suffer disproportionately from the low endowment of human capital. Children from poor households have limited education. The low level of education and skills renders the poor uncompetitive for productive jobs in the formal sectors which require tertiary and technical education. This constrains the total supply of skilled labour, which dampens the business environment for investors, perpetuating the cycle of inequality of opportunity and inequality of outcomes.

The third constraint is natural disasters and regionally depressed locations with inadequate economic opportunities. Frequent natural disasters, including recurrent floods, river erosion and deadly cyclones that disproportionately hit the poor and coastal regions, continually push vulnerable groups into poverty and jeopardise long-term human capital development. While the macro economy has become more resilient with swift capacity to recover from different shocks—due to sound macroeconomic fundamentals and strong flows of remittances (which cushion household consumption)—the poor and vulnerable suffer more from these shocks than the rich. As weather patterns shift with climate change, the poorest regions where agriculture is the predominant economic activity and the capacity to manage risk is particularly weak, face increased vulnerability to shocks. The high level of natural disaster risks reduces the risk taking capacity of households and firms, through lower investment or the selection of safer and less promising technologies, which in turn lead to a reduction in local growth and job creation.

3.6.2 Policy Priorities

Although a comprehensive approach to poverty reduction is necessary, the key areas for achieving faster poverty reduction are to ensure more rapid and inclusive growth, tackle inequality of opportunity and outcomes, reduce vulnerability, and protect the poor.

3.6.2.1 Create Decent and Well-Paid Jobs

Since a significant share of the poor have employment with very low wages or suffer from underemployment in the informal sector, support for the creation of more better paid jobs, particularly semi skilled jobs, for the majority of the current labour force who have less than high school education, can help reduce poverty and address inequality through higher wage incomes.

Underinvestment in human and physical capital is a major constraint to improving labour productivity and results in low quality and highly informal jobs. Investment in productive capacity, in particular, lags in the manufacturing sector. To attract more private investment, the business environment needs to be improved, particularly through addressing institutional constraints, strengthening competition in key sectors, securing better governance, providing risk management solutions, and simplifying business regulations. To attract foreign and domestic investment, the government will have to play a more active role by improving infrastructure and basic services delivery, as well as by providing targeted support to the self-employed or those working in MSMEs, where large numbers of the poor are employed.

For creating better jobs, improving labour productivity and moving up the value chains are necessary. Bangladesh is rapidly transforming from an agricultural economy to a (low-end) service economy, without a booming manufacturing sector which traditionally creates large numbers of labour-intensive jobs absorbing the surplus labour from agriculture. But, manufacturing can still deliver productivity gains and well-paid employment opportunities for the unskilled workers in in potential activities. Bangladesh needs to find its specific niches in both manufacturing and services sector and in regional and global value chains to capitalise on its growing non-agriculture economy and enhance the productivity gains from structural transformation.

Linkages between the services sector and manufacturing and agriculture are critical to upgrading the domestic value addition in Bangladesh. This would include proficiency in communication and information technology skills, as well as taking advantages of Bangladesh's locational and other advantages. In doing so, Bangladesh could leverage business process outsourcing and expand other service-based sectors. This, in turn, would contribute to successful transformation by creating more productive employment opportunities, including opportunities with skill requirements compatible with those of individuals from poor households.

3.6.2.2 Increase Productivity, Especially in Agriculture

Further, as a lower middle-income country, Bangladesh economy is becoming less dependent on agriculture for output and employment. But agriculture still remains important for poverty reduction and employment as well as sustainable and equitable growth. Agriculture sector performs below its potential for contributing towards growth, employment, and poverty reduction. Improvements in productivity, diversification, and value-addition are crucial, as well as progress in making agriculture more resilient to natural disasters and climate change.

Agricultural productivity is low in Bangladesh with wide scope to raise productivity to the levels of the best performers in Asia. Reasons for the persistent low productivity of agriculture include high input costs; small land sizes; insufficient ability to manage rainfall variability and other natural hazards; limited access to finance, applied research, and extension services; and inadequate connectivity and links to market outlets resulting in low and fluctuating prices. As evidenced in other middle-income countries in the region, structural transformation will attract workers out of agriculture as the manufacturing and service sectors expand. But agriculture will continue to remain a large employer as absorption of surplus labour by manufacturing and service sectors is unlikely to be undertaken at a fast pace in the short run. Improving income from agriculture will help address persistent poverty issues and contribute to employment opportunities in rural areas.

Thus, within the structural transformation agenda, the role of agriculture will evolve; with the share of agribusiness in GDP rising higher than that of agriculture. As agriculture's share in GDP continues to fall and incomes and urbanisation continue to rise in Bangladesh, the composition of agricultural output will change as part of agricultural diversification. To reduce poverty in the rural areas, policies will be needed for agricultural development and diversification through support for the development of agribusiness, bringing in various input providers and agro-processors, distributors, and retailers for value chain development in agriculture.

3.6.2.3 Ensure Skills for the 21st Century Economy

For meeting the human development needs, one key issue for Bangladesh is to ensure that the people can acquire the skills they need for the 21st century economy. In recent years, Bangladesh has made admirable strides in education with critical advances in primary and secondary education. Key challenges now include making sure that the students in schools are learning, reducing high dropout rates for the poor, and developing practical learning skills. Two critical areas to address are quality challenges and 'learning crisis' (World Bank 2017) and increase secondary enrolment among the poor beyond the primary level.

The importance of socio-emotional skills is growing for competitiveness in the global economy (World Bank 2017). A higher level of socio-emotional skills is associated with greater probability of being employed and with higher earnings. Therefore, worker competitiveness increasingly requires not only traditional technical and cognitive skills but also improved socio-emotional skills. Moreover, such skills are associated with the greatest wage differential among workers with low educational levels. As a substitute for traditional technical and cognitive skills, socio-emotional skills offer a route to higher earnings for workers with limited formal education. To take this advantage, it will be necessary for Bangladesh to develop preparedness and training among teachers to actively foster these skills in all education and training, including early childhood education, K–12 (publicly supported school grades prior to college; these grades are kindergarten (K) and the 1st through the 12th grade, 1–12) education, and tertiary education, as well as regular and vocational training.

3.6.2.4 Invest in Health and Nutrition

Although Bangladesh has a long way to go to ensure universal health coverage, it has significant weaknesses in existing health access and quality. The rates of child malnutrition remain high and the country has faced challenges in implementing its health policies. A series of efforts in these areas are needed to boost human capital and make possible the demographic dividend. Bangladesh has made great progress in expanding access to healthcare but the scope and quality of care available in public facilities remains limited and uneven. To break the cycle of poor health and poor income, public investment in healthcare needs to be increased to ensure easy access to basic good-quality care and alleviate the burdens of out-of-pocket payment. The top policy priority is to expand the essential health benefits package available to the poor. The next priority is to develop a national strategy for quality of healthcare improvement. Limited and uneven access and quality of healthcare contribute to the general health challenges of the poor as well as to weaknesses in reproductive health and nutrition.

Around one in three children in Bangladesh under age 5 is stunted—the principal indicator of malnutrition—and stunting rate is mostly stagnant although other socioeconomic indicators have seen progress. Malnutrition in the womb and during the first two years of life inhibits brain development and a permanent damage, resulting in lower levels of schooling, reduced cognitive function, and lower earnings later in life. As such, the returns from investments to reduce malnutrition are extraordinarily high in Bangladesh. The critical needs are to focus on health interventions during the 'first 1000 days' of a child's life from conception through the first two years of life, combined with multi-sector efforts involving education, social protection, agriculture, and water and sanitation.

3.6.2.5 Help Manage Risks and Vulnerability

The poor are more vulnerable to negative shocks. They are more exposed to different types of risks due to lack of resources; more sensitive to the impacts due to an inability to cope with them; and lack the capacity needed to adapt to potential risks and hence suffer repeated setbacks. Children from the poor families are particularly vulnerable to not getting the needed education and healthcare. Providing targeted support to the poor and vulnerable to mitigate shocks, build up human capital, and provide effective safety nets when needed, is crucial. Managing risks and protecting the vulnerable maintain public investments in individuals and private assets; it also supports growth and capital accumulation through reducing repeated losses of physical and human capital, and through increasing thresholds of natural risks for investors.

Poor people are more likely to live in coastal and disaster- and flood-prone areas in fragile housing, with a large share of their low income spent on staples—and are more vulnerable given their lack of capacity for prevention and limited ability to cope with and recover from shocks. Effective disaster prevention measures can yield high returns, especially when they are correctly designed and implemented as part of a larger programme of poverty reduction.

Early warning systems, financial inclusion, insurance policies, and social assistance (such as, cash transfers and public works programmes) can improve the capacity of individuals to cope with and recover from shocks and avoid well-being losses.

Bangladesh has adopted the integrated National Social Security Strategy (NSSS) in 2015, seeking to streamline and strengthen the existing social protection programmes. The NSSS aims to reduce poverty, improve human development and reduce inequalities. The core is programme coordination and consolidation along lifecycle risks—with programmes for children, working age people, the elderly, and persons with disabilities—which goes beyond the safety net and ladder models. It is important to implement the NSSS to keep up with the evolving needs of the poor.

3.7 Concluding Remarks

No doubt, despite rapid reduction in poverty, rising inequality is a big policy issue in Bangladesh. This has serious implications for ensuring secure, sustainable lives and livelihoods for all. Obviously, *'when inequality creates discriminatory outcomes, it becomes a human rights issue'*. In Bangladesh, rising vertical inequality that concentrates greater amounts of wealth among a small group of elites along with horizontal inequalities that marginalise specific groups and communities undoubtedly create discriminatory outcomes.

At present, the combined effect of the ongoing demographic transition and the growing labour force participation of women are increasing the size of the working population in Bangladesh. Providing quality jobs to the new entrants and increasing productivity of the employed population, especially in agriculture and services, are no doubt major challenges. Accelerated economic growth is a pre-condition for meeting these challenges. This requires macroeconomic stability, efficient investments in human and physical capital including infrastructure, better and efficient regulation, and well-functioning financial institutions. At the same time, focused attention is needed on four key elements of economic policy: (1) inclusive and sustainable economic growth within and across generations; (2) greater investment in building human capital of the poor; (3) prudent use of safety nets; and (4) environment-friendly policies to make growth greener.

Despite resource constraints, many tools are available with the government for reducing poverty and inequality. Universal social protection policy, including healthcare and microinsurance, can ensure that all people have access to basic services and social protections. Similarly, an effective and progressive tax system can help produce a more equal distribution of wealth. The critical challenge is to address social and cultural inequalities that are deeply rooted and woven into the fabric of the society.

For the medium term, Bangladesh needs to create effective economic institutions and proper policy incentives, while also pursuing sound macroeconomic policies and efficiency-enhancing reforms over time. The key for Bangladesh is to build a robust middle class and reduce extreme poverty and social marginalisation for creating a more equitable society.

Clearly, a major way through which the government can help improve inequalities is by making faster progress in building up the human capital of the poor. Along with better health and education, a strong social protection system can be used as instruments for improving income distribution. One area where public spending should be increased is rural infrastructure—rural roads, rural electricity, irrigation and flood control. In addition, availability of rural credit is an important instrument for helping the poor to build up assets and also protect their consumption. Another area where public spending should be scaled up concerns social protection.

While the causes are complex, three factors may be identified that has been holding Bangladesh back compared with many high performing countries. These include (1) lower pace and less inclusive pattern of growth; (2) rising inequality of income and wealth; and (3) adverse impacts of natural disasters and climate change. Per capita income and related data indicate that probably less than 10 per cent of the country's population has made it to the global middle class; and a large share of the population remains vulnerable to falling into poverty.

Bangladesh's slow progress with poverty reduction in recent years is also linked with the limited progress achieved in providing economic mobility for growing the middle class. More rapid growth of the middle class can bring both intrinsic and instrumental benefits to Bangladesh society—not only it enjoys greater economic security and higher living standards, but it also provides instrumental benefits for other segments in society by being a key driver of growth; an influential constituency for good policies, better institutions and good governance; and a major provider of income tax revenues needed for investment in development.

Bangladesh has recently moved to a path that promotes booming manufacturing sector and provides large numbers of labour-intensive jobs, absorbing the surplus low-skilled labour from agriculture and give them significantly higher wage income. Creating such a manufacturing base helps poverty reduction; otherwise the workers who move out of agriculture generally end up in low-end service jobs, which limit the gains for labour from structural transformation. Wages are a major source of income for most households, hence rapid increase in real wages can make good progress in poverty reduction. In the long run, low wages for the highly educated and highly skilled are likely to damage Bangladesh's economic competitiveness by making it even more attractive for these groups to move abroad in search of more remunerative opportunities.

For Bangladesh, faster growth in agricultural productivity can also emerge as a key driver of poverty reduction. Agriculture, which employs most poor people in the country, has experienced minimal growth in the past decade. Further, the gains from structural transformation, or the shift from agriculture towards non-agricultural activities, are limited in Bangladesh compared with comparable countries, and growth in labour productivity relies disproportionately on within-sector productivity growth. As a result, the responsiveness of poverty reduction to growth is relatively slow.

Income inequality is rising in Bangladesh; there also exists high concentration of wealth. This may have contributed to strong vested interests in the status quo by hindering acceptance of the reforms needed to prompt more inclusive growth and faster poverty reduction. Differences in the quality of human resources, and in the incomes individuals and households can earn, drive a large degree of the inequality of outcomes in Bangladesh.

The effects of such inequality show themselves from the earliest days of life. Poorer children are at a disadvantage from their birth. They have limited access to good-quality healthcare and early childhood education, which undermines their ability to succeed later in life. Many poor people, including in the younger generations, have limited education. The low level of education and skills means that the poor cannot compete for productive jobs in the formal sectors, such as high-end services or business-process outsourcing positions, which require tertiary education. This constrains the total supply of skilled labour, which dampens the business environment for investors, perpetuating the cycle of inequality of opportunity and inequality of outcomes.

Frequent natural disasters, including cyclones that disproportionately strike the poor regions of Bangladesh continually push vulnerable groups into poverty and jeopardise long-term human capital development. Natural disasters have caused significant losses and damages in Bangladesh since the 1970s, making it one of the most disaster-prone countries in the world. Further, lack of security and justice and economic stresses have intertwined to lock the poor people in poverty.

The high concentration of income and wealth limits equality of opportunity and impedes equitable public service delivery, which is necessary for inclusive growth. With a low rate of investment, the economy is largely driven by consumption, which limits the potential for more rapid structural transformation and improvement in productivity. The slow increase in real wages, while it might be attractive in the short run, is likely to negatively affect the competitiveness of the economy in the long run with the better skilled people leaving the country for more attractive job opportunities.

Bangladesh has solid macroeconomic fundamentals and its growth prospects are strongly positive. With a healthy current account, strong international reserves, significant fiscal space, and low and stable inflation, the economy is in a strong position to adopt multiple policies to seize opportunities, mitigate domestic and global shocks, and provide the basis for productive job creation and poverty reduction.

The government can help end the vicious cycle of unequal opportunity and outcomes that trap people in poverty, and establish mutually reinforcing positive cycles that will create a growing middle class that is well-integrated with other groups. It can help improve service delivery for all and increase non-farm employment opportunities through increased demand for manufacturing goods and services. Finally, more progressive and better-administered revenue system can help finance needed investments in both physical and human capital.

For the future, strong economic growth will be the basis for productive job creation and poverty reduction. In the long run, productivity is the fundamental. Addressing the key factors—creating more well-paying jobs; improving productivity in all sectors, including agriculture; reducing income and wealth inequality through more investment in people and skill development; and better managing the risks and protecting the vulnerable—will help accelerate poverty reduction in Bangladesh.

Appendix

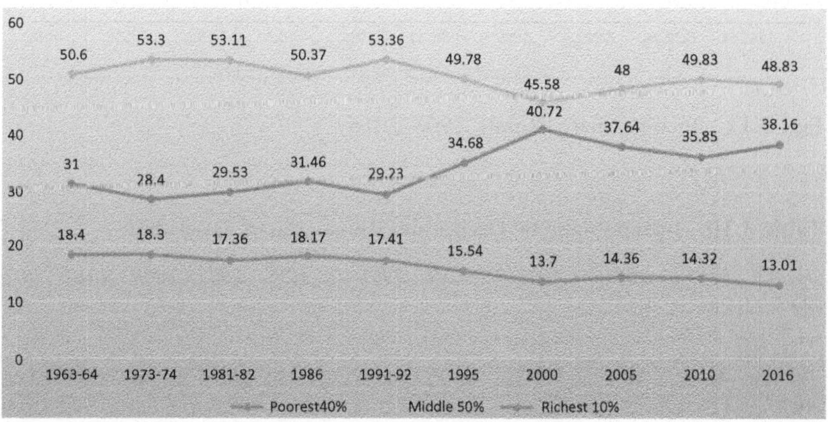

Fig. 3.9 Share of Deciles in Total Household Income at National Level, 1963–2016

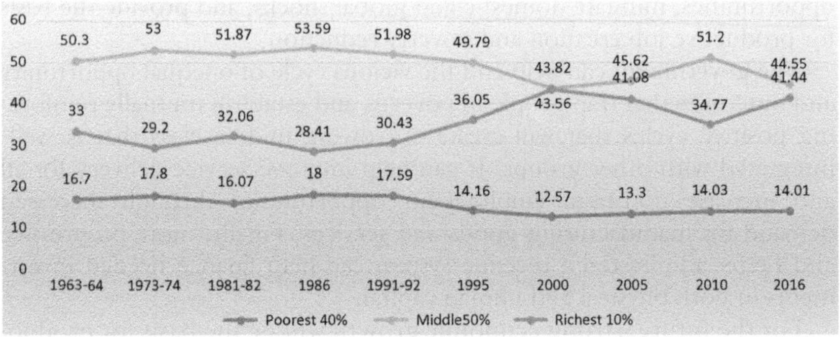

Fig. 3.10 Income Share (Urban), 1963–2016

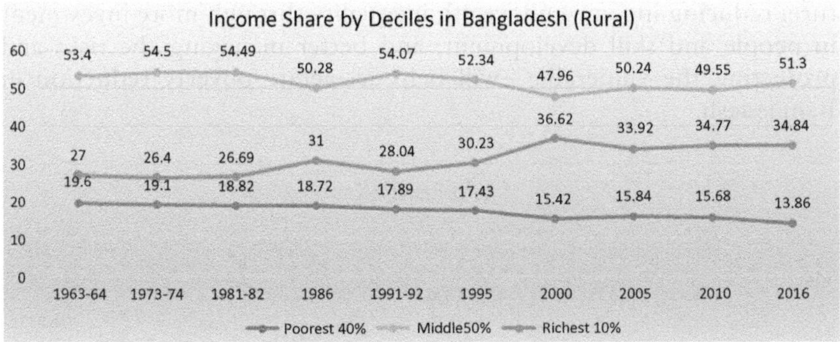

Fig. 3.11 Income Share (Rural), 1963–2016

Table 3.10 Income share by Deciles and Palma ratio in Bangladesh

Income share	*1963–64*	*1973–74*	*1981–82*	*1986*	*1991–92*	*1995*	*2000*	*2005*	*2010*	*2016*
National										
Poorest 40%	18.4	18.3	17.36	18.17	17.41	15.54	13.70	14.36	14.32	13.01
Middle 50%	50.6	53.3	53.11	50.37	53.36	49.78	45.58	48.00	49.83	48.83
Richest 10%	31.0	28.4	29.53	31.46	29.23	34.68	40.72	37.64	35.85	38.16

(*continued*)

Table 3.12 (continued)

Income share	*1963–64*	*1973–74*	*1981–82*	*1986*	*1991–92*	*1995*	*2000*	*2005*	*2010*	*2016*
Palma ratio	1.68	1.55	1.70	1.73	1.68	2.23	2.97	2.62	2.50	2.93
Urban										
Poorest 40%	16.7	17.8	16.07	18.00	17.59	14.16	12.57	13.30	14.03	14.01
Middle 50%	50.3	53.0	51.87	53.59	51.98	49.79	43.82	45.62	51.20	44.55
Richest 10%	33.0	29.2	32.06	28.41	30.43	36.05	43.56	41.08	34.77	41.44
Palma ratio	2.00	1.64	1.68	1.58	1.73	2.55	3.47	3.09	2.48	2.96
Rural										
Poorest 40%	19.6	19.1	18.82	18.72	17.89	17.43	15.42	15.84	15.68	13.86
Middle 50%	53.4	54.5	54.49	50.28	54.07	52.34	47.96	50.24	49.55	51.30
Richest 10%	27.0	26.4	26.69	31.00	28.04	30.23	36.62	33.92	34.77	34.84
Palma ratio	1.38	1.38	1.42	1.66	1.57	1.73	2.37	2.14	2.22	2.51

Source: Authors' calculation from HIES data

Table 3.11 Growth in real per capita household income (average and bottom 40 per cent)

	National		*Urban*		*Rural*	
	Average	*Bottom 40%*	*Average*	*Bottom 40%*	*Average*	*Bottom 40%*
1986–1995	0.94	-0.40	4.34	0.91	-0.49	-1.61
1995–2005	1.93	-0.72	2.61	-0.89	0.52	-1.14
2005–2016	3.99	1.09	4.45	2.48	2.28	0.37
1986–2016	1.43	0.28	2.28	0.68	4.41	-0.24

Source: Authors' calculation using HIES data

Table 3.12 Specific policies for more equitable development in Bangladesh

Broad agenda	*Policy measures*
Policy 1: Moderate income inequality	
Induce changes in the pattern of growth such that incomes of low-income population grow faster than average	**Decent employment creation and labour market reforms**: Create sufficient employment (quantity); that gives adequate income, security and stability (quality); and accessible to all groups (equal access); target MSMEs by providing access to finance (both start-up and for expanding operations) and markets, assist in adopting new technologies and identifying strategically important sectors; provide information on improved production methods, technical support services, vocational training, establishing/strengthening business links and subcontracting; adopt strategies to ensure that MSMEs are integrated with the industrial sector as providers of inputs and raw materials to bigger firms.
	Employment guarantee schemes: Implement government-sponsored employment guarantee schemes to absorb low-skilled poor workers and allow them to earn a basic income which act as a safety net to guarantee a certain level of income for those otherwise unemployed, while putting in place much needed economic and social infrastructure. Scaling up of employment guarantee schemes can be effective in reducing inequality, including horizontal inequalities. Moreover, the infrastructure built will increase labour productivity; cost per net job created could be much lower than for alternative policies, and the programme wage may emerge as the de facto minimum wage, reducing minimum wage enforcement costs.
	Labour market policies: Create stronger labour market institutions along with effective minimum wage legislation, collective bargaining to reduce wage inequality; manage drivers of inequality associated with financial and trade globalisation.
	Macroeconomic strategy to promote inclusive growth: This will prioritise three elements—economic growth, employment creation and macroeconomic stability.

(*continued*)

Table 3.12 (continued)

Broad agenda	*Policy measures*
Adopt effective redistributive measures to improve income inequalities	**Social protection providing minimum income security**: Social insurance (e.g. microinsurance) and social assistance programmes to cope with contingencies and adverse events. **Consumer subsidies:** For reducing the costs of household goods for which low-income households spend a disproportionate share of their incomes which can have an immediate impact on nutrition and consumption as well as general well-being of low-income households. **Progressivity of tax system:** Strengthen direct taxation including income and property taxes and adopting well-designed tax brackets and rationalising personal exemptions and deductions; make VAT progressive by taxing goods and services consumed by the rich and poor at different rates, such as basic food items.
Promote income opportunities for the low income population groups	**Administrative reforms to improve access to employment and income:** Address all discriminatory provisions and discriminatory practices including statutory or customary barriers to access or ownership of assets; use affirmative action policies for improving income-generating opportunities of specific groups, allocate jobs, public contracts, credit, access to higher education and legislative seats on the basis of belonging to a disadvantaged group; barriers to participating in productive employment. **Access to labour markets:** Remove barriers to skill sets, information gaps or mobility constraints of individuals and groups; design policies to promote higher employability of the poor and disadvantaged groups involving a package of instruments that address different barriers to access employment and income generation opportunities; improve access of women to labour market by addressing gender-based discrimination and specific barriers that women face when entering productive employment; ensure on-site child care centres and other worksite facilities (e.g. medical aid, drinking water, toilet facilities and shade) in informal employment locations. **Access to finance:** Ensure financial inclusion for all by removing both price and non-price barriers in both demand and supply sides.

(*continued*)

Table 3.12 (continued)

Broad agenda	*Policy measures*
Policy 2: Reduce gaps in health, nutrition and education	
Ensure better targeting and pro-poor composition of public expenditures	**Increase level of public expenditures in education, health and nutrition sectors:** Ensure that these basic social services are available in sufficient quantity; physically and economically accessible; affordable without being a disproportionate burden for the poorest; and of good quality in terms of relevance and cultural acceptability; ensure greater flow of public expenditures to social services with the biggest gaps (e.g. expenditures on health sector in rural areas need to grow faster than expenditures in urban areas; as secondary school enrolment rates lag behind primary completion rates, more resources should be directed towards secondary education, large gaps in nutrition outcomes across wealth quintiles imply that expenditures should target those at the tail end of the distribution etc.); increase investments in early childhood development having strong redistributive power while being highly cost-effective; direct public investments in infrastructure, especially in rural and geographically isolated areas, with strong positive growth and inequality-reducing benefits. **Create better access for poor, excluded and disadvantaged groups:** Focus on sectors, geographic locations and groups that are more isolated and disadvantaged by increasing availability and quality of social services and programmes for the poorest and most excluded groups; investments in infrastructure like basic water and energy reduce the time women spend in household unpaid labour, allowing them to spend more time in paid labour to reduce income inequality across genders and improve mothers' health, which benefits children's well-being.

(*continued*)

Table 3.12 (continued)

Broad agenda	*Policy measures*
Improve delivery channels of quality services	**Focus on (1) multi-sector early childhood development programmes, (2) integrated local service delivery systems, and (3) community-based programmes:** **Early childhood development:** Early childhood development programmes work across sectors to achieve a series of mutually reinforcing objectives to improve the well-being of children, directly providing health and nutrition services to participating low-income and disadvantaged children while also providing the stimulation, support and attention to improve their school readiness and chances to earn higher future incomes. **Integrated service delivery systems:** Integrated delivery systems that group relevant services under one scheme and overcome issues of fragmentation can improve access to services and avoid dropout of beneficiaries. Integrated delivery systems are networks of providers and organisations that aim to deliver a coordinated continuum of services to a defined population and are accountable for the outcomes of the population served. **Community-based programmes:** Interventions that support participatory, community-based programmes focused on improving outcomes in education, health and nutrition can have an important impact in closing gaps in well-being. By involving beneficiaries in programme design, implementation and evaluation, participatory programmes help empower communities, create a sense of ownership and foster accountability to poor clients. Community outreach and community-based services are also useful strategies for reaching isolated groups or those who would not otherwise seek services.
Strengthen institutions and improve capacity for provision of quality services	Focus on three important tools to build institutional capacity: (1) improving the quantity and quality of human resources to deliver services, (2) strengthening local governments so that services reach the most marginalised communities, and (3) enabling inter-sectoral coordination so that services are comprehensive.
Implement governance reforms for installing greater responsiveness to disadvantaged groups	Ensure that institutions operate not only efficiently, but also responsively to the needs and aspirations of those who are lagging behind. Effective accountability mechanisms are needed to ensure full implementation of inequality-reducing measures, particularly those based on public expenditures. A variety of instruments within the broad realm of social accountability, such as social audits, citizen report cards and public expenditure tracking surveys, can be used for the purpose.

(*continued*)

Table 3.12 (continued)

Broad agenda	*Policy measures*
Expand access to un/underserved population and regions	Disadvantaged groups need to be reached through specific reforms that address the particular access barriers that they face, including social norms that allow for exclusion and discrimination. Social norms are significant in explaining inequality in education, health and nutrition outcomes across gender and place of residence.
Policy 3: Remove social and gender exclusion and discrimination	
Expand civic/political/economic engagement for socially excluded/marginalised population groups including women	**Broaden participation in political and public life:** Create civic and political space for inequality reduction such as involvement of civil society in policy debates on national development plans and budget priority setting; resolve specific economic, social and cultural barriers that prevent the poor and marginalised from participating in public life; CSOs must themselves be inclusive, accountable and transparent if they are to effectively promote greater social justice; work towards a truly inclusive democracy—in which nobody is left out of the public dialogue based on income or other grounds—which is critical to distributional outcomes; new technologies hold great potential to create inclusive citizen networks e.g. platforms based on simple SMS capacity for collecting and mapping inputs from citizens can enable initiatives of mapping community needs.
Adopt affirmative action and anti-discriminatory laws/policies	**Promote conditions that are conducive to inequality reduction:** Prejudice and discrimination are based not only on gender, racial, ethnic or cultural grounds, but also on economic grounds; use the space for specific interventions to revise the norms underpinning inter-generational transmission of inequalities using effective enactment of anti-discriminatory legislation; improving access to justice for the poor, marginalised and disadvantaged; introduction of affirmative action policies; and engagement with the media and other public opinion makers. Affirmative action interventions that aim at directly promoting the socioeconomic status of specific groups in the areas of education, employment and business creation can improve the opportunities for disadvantaged groups; these policies can use quota system for racial and ethnic groups, women and persons with disabilities.

References

Ahluwalia, M.S. 1976. Inequality, Poverty and Development. *Journal of Development Economics* 3: 307–342.

Banerjee, S.B., and L. Jackson. 2017. Microfinance and the Business of Poverty Reduction: Critical Perspectives from Rural Bangladesh. *Human Relations* 70 (1): 63–91.

Banerjee, A., D. Karlan, and J. Zinman. 2015. Six Randomized Evaluations of Microcredit: Introduction and Further Steps. *American Economic Journal: Applied Economics* 7 (1): 1–21.

Barro, A. 2000. Inequality and Growth in a Panel of Countries. *Journal of Economic Growth* 5: 5–32.

BBS. 2013. *Economic Census 2013*. Dhaka: Bangladesh Bureau of Statistics, Ministry of Planning, Government of the People's Republic of Bangladesh.

———. 2017. *Report of the Household Income and Expenditure Survey 2016*. Dhaka: Bangladesh Bureau of Statistics, Ministry of Planning, Government of the People's Republic of Bangladesh.

Becker, G.S., and R.A. Posner. 2009. *Uncommon Sense: Economic Insights, from Marriage to Terrorism*. Chicago: University of Chicago Press.

Bourguignon, F. 2003. The Growth Elasticity of Poverty Reduction: Explaining Heterogeneity Across Countries and Time Periods. In *Inequality and Growth: Theory and Policy Implications*, ed. T.S. Eicher and S.J. Turnovsky. Cambridge, MA: MIT Press.

Bourguignon, F., and C. Morrisson. 2002. Inequality Among World Citizens: 1820–1992. *American Economic Review* 92 (4): 727–744.

Cobham, A., and A. Sumner. 2013. *Putting the Gini Back in the Bottle? 'The Palma' as a Policy-Relevant Measure of Inequality*. London: King's College.

Deininger, K., and L. Squire. 1998. New Ways of Looking at Old Issues: Inequality and Growth. *Journal of Development Economics* 57: 259–287.

Dollar, D., and A. Kraay. 2002. Growth Is Good for the Poor. *Journal of Economic Growth* 7 (3): 195–225.

Dollar, D., T. Kleineberg, and A. Kraay. 2014. *Growth, Inequality, and Social Welfare: Cross-Country Evidence*. Policy Research Working Paper 6842. Washington, DC: World Bank.

Fields, G.S. 1980. *Poverty, Inequality, and Development*. New York: Cambridge University Press.

Forbes, K. 2000. A Reassessment of the Relationship Between Inequality and Growth. *American Economic Review* 90: 869–897.

Foster, J., J. Greer, and E. Thorbecke. 1984. A Class of Decomposable Poverty Measures. *Econometrica* 52: 761–766.

Gender Statistics, World Bank. 2017. *The Gender Statistics Database*, data@worldbank.org. … *Gender Data Portal*. New York: World Bank.

Gonzalez, A. 2010. *Is Microfinance Growing Too Fast?* Washington, DC: Microfinance Information Exchange (MIX).

Handley, G., K. Higgins, and B. Sharma. 2009. *Poverty and Poverty Reduction in Sub-Saharan Africa: An Overview of Key Issues.* Working Paper 299. London: Overseas Development Institute.

InM. 2016. *Diagnostics of Micro-enterprise (ME) Lending by MFIs in Bangladesh: Opportunities and Challenges.* Dhaka: Institute for Inclusive Finance and Development.

Jolliffe, D., P. Lanjouw, S. Chen, A. Kraay, C. Meyer, M. Negre, E. Prydz, R. Vakis, and K. Wethli. 2013. *A Measured Approach to Ending Poverty and Boosting Shared Prosperity: Concepts, Data, and the Twin Goals.* Policy Research Report. Washington, DC: World Bank, 2014. https://doi.org/10.1596/978-1-4648-0361-1. http://www.worldbank.org/AMeasuredApproach.

Khan, A.R. and B. Sen. 2001. Inequality and Its Sources in Bangladesh, 1991/92 to 1995/96. *An Analysis Based on Household Expenditure Surveys, Bangladesh Development Studies* 27 (1): 1–49.

Khandker, S.R. 1998. *Fighting Poverty with Microcredit: Experience in Bangladesh.* New York: Oxford University Press.

LSE and Oxfam. 2018. *World Inequality Report 2018.* London: London School of Economics and Oxfam.

Ludi, E., and K. Bird. 2007. *Understanding Poverty.* London: Brief No 1, The Poverty-Wellbeing Platform, Swiss Agency for Development and Cooperation and Overseas Development Institute.

Nelson, R.R. 1956. A Theory of the Low-Level Equilibrium Trap in Underdeveloped Economies. *American Economic Review* 46 (5): 894–908.

OPHI/UNDP. 2019. *Global Multidimensional Poverty Index 2019: Illuminating Inequalities.* New York and Oxford: United Nations Development Programme and Oxford Poverty and Human Development Initiative.

Palma, J.G. 2011. *Homogenous Middles vs. Heterogeneous Tails, and the End of the 'Inverted-U': The Share of the Rich is What It's All About.* Cambridge Working Papers in Economics (CWPE) 1111, January 2011. www.econ.cam.ac.uk/dae/repec/cam/pdf/cwpe1111.pdf.

Ravallion, M. 1994. *Poverty Comparisons.* Chur, Switzerland: Harwood Academic Publishers, GmbH.

———. 2001. Growth, Inequality and Poverty: Looking Beyond Averages. *World Development* 29 (11): 1803–1815.

———. 2010. *Poverty Lines Across the World.* Policy Research Working Paper 5284. Washington DC: World Bank.

Ravallion, M., S. Chen, and P. Sangraula. 2008. *Dollar a Day Revisited.* Policy Research Working Paper 4620. Washington, DC: World Bank.

Rozas, D., and S. Sinha. 2010. Avoiding a Microfinance Bubble in India: Is Self-Regulation the Answer?. *Microfinance Focus,* January 10.

Sen, S.P., ed. 1973. *Modern Bengal: A Socio-economic History: Proceedings of a Seminar Held at the Institute in September, 1971.* Calcutta: Institute of Historical Studies.

Shepherd, A., L. Scott, C. Mariotti, F. Kessy, R. Gaiha, L. da Corta, K. Hanifnia, N. Kaicker, A. Lenhardt, C. Lwanga-Ntale, B. Sen, B. Sijapati, T. Strawson, G. Thapa, H. Underhill, and L. Wild. 2014. *The Chronic Poverty Report 2014–2015: The Road to Zero Extreme Poverty.* London: Overseas Development Institute.

Simms, A., V. Johnson, and P. Chowla. 2010. *Growth Isn't Possible.* London: nef.

Tucker, J., and E. Ludi. 2012. *Empowerment and Equity.* Paris: Organisation for Economic Cooperation and Development.

UNDESA. 2018. *World Urbanization Prospects; The 2018 Revision.* New York: Population Division, Department of Economic and Social Affairs, United Nations.

UNDP. 2010. *Human Development Report 2010 the Real Wealth of Nations: Pathways to Human Development.* New York: United Nations Development Programme.

———. 2014. *Humanity Divided: Confronting Inequality in Developing Countries.* New York: United Nations Development Programme.

———. 2018. *What Does It Mean To Leave No One Behind?* A UNDP Discussion Paper and Framework for Implementation. https://www.undp.org/content/dam/undp/library/Sustainable%20Development/2030%20Agenda/Discussion_Paper_LNOB_EN_lres.pdf.

Woodward, D., and A. Simms. 2006. *Growth Isn't Working: The Unbalanced Distribution of Benefits and Costs from Economic Growth.* London: nef.

World Bank. 2006. *World Development Report 2006: Equity and Development.* Washington, DC: World Bank.

———. 2008. *Global Economic Prospects 2008: Technology Diffusion in the Developing World.* Washington, DC: World Bank.

———. 2017. *Annual Report 2017 End Extreme Poverty • Boost Shared Prosperity.* Washington, DC: World Bank.

———. 2019. *The Bangladesh Development Update 2019: Towards Regulatory Predictability.* Washington, DC: World Bank.

WDI. 2014. *World Development Indicators 2014.* Washington, DC: World Bank. https://openknowledge.worldbank.org/handle/10986/18237 License: CC BY 3.0 IGO.

Yunus, M. 1989. Grameen Bank: Organization and Operation. In *Microenterprises in Developing Countries*, ed. J. Levitsky. London: Intermediate Technology Publications.

CHAPTER 4

Human and Social Development

4.1 Introduction

Since independence, Bangladesh's development agenda incorporated a social development lens through adoption of an inter-sectoral approach and engaging with non-government and other actors (e.g. NGO-MFIs, CBOs, private sector participants) in society. The discourse was also influenced by the millennium development goals (MDGs) focus on human development outcomes in the 1990s. The inclusion of the sustainable development goals (SDGs) agenda within the policy framework in the 2000s has further contributed towards moving away from a technical approach to increasing human development towards an equity/inclusion approach that focuses on 'leaving no one behind'. These developments have put an increasing emphasis on social norms and understanding social institutions, including political dimensions.

Social development, within a narrow framework, suggests improvement in the conditions and quality of life of the population. Additionally, social development may be interpreted in terms of the processes of social differentiation and social complexity associated with economic and social transformations giving rise to more advanced societies. On the other hand, the capability approach provides the theoretical underpinning of human development which expands individuals' capabilities or freedoms (Sen 1999; Nussbaum 2000). The approach maintains that freedom of individual choice is central to satisfactory development.

© The Author(s) 2020

M. K. Mujeri, N. Mujeri, *Bangladesh at Fifty*, Palgrave Studies in Economic History,
https://doi.org/10.1007/978-3-030-56791-0_4

Nevertheless, social institutions are important in determining individual capabilities as (i) most individual capabilities would not exist without social competencies; (ii) societal institutions, together with social norms, determine people's choices within a capability set; (iii) social institutions and competencies affect the functioning of all societal institutions, including both state and market institutions; and (iv) they affect the power and influence of particular groups at the macro-, meso- and micro-levels (Stewart 2013). As such, social development comprises many non-economic processes and outcomes of development, including reduced vulnerability; inclusion; well-being; accountability; people-centred approaches; and freedom from violence.[1] This shows that social development is also concerned with human rights, power relations, inequality and possibilities for building greater equality among individuals and groups within society.

4.2 Bangladesh's Social Development Agenda

Since the beginning, human and social factors have been considered as important components of Bangladesh's development process with the realisation that economic growth on its own does not guarantee a reduction in poverty and improvements in well-being of the poor. Development occurs more readily when the opportunities of the individuals are maximised. These opportunities emerge when the capabilities of the persons are realised, allowing them to use their own skills, knowledge, experiences, and strengths to raise themselves to a way of life and/or standard of living which they value. The empowerment of the individuals also speaks to his/her increased ability to interact with others in meaningful, positive and mutually beneficial ways.

The root of the country's social development focus lies in the microcredit movement after independence when the NGOs undertook the relief and rehabilitation efforts in the war ravaged Bangladesh economy. The approach started with an array of financial services—including loans and savings—available to women in the poor households, who had no collateral and, otherwise, would not qualify for an institutional loan. The NGOs generally believed that such access would help the poor people out of poverty. Over time, the approach to microcredit was broadened

[1] World Bank, Social development overview: http://www.worldbank.org/en/topic/socialdevelopment/overview#1

covering microcredit along with broader social development packages. The success of the microcredit model rests with a number of factors, such as minimum entry requirements, manageable risk with joint-liability principles, and insignificant non-performing loans coupled with social development inputs.

In practice, for many, microcredit was a way to promote development, employment and growth through the support of micro-entrepreneurship and small businesses; for others, it was a way for the poor to manage their finances more effectively and take advantage of economic opportunities while managing the risks. The area which, however, has received less attention within microcredit at least in the initial years is the contribution of NGOs in social performance, which broadly is an indication of how well an NGO meets the social goals outlined in its mission and vision. Social performance may be reflected in a wide range of indicators, including an NGO's policies towards its own employees; success in targeting the poorest of the poor; policies on environmental conservation; how low an NGO keeps its interest rates; and, finally, how the NGO's services translate into social well-being and improved lives for the poor.

In fact, the scope of the work of the NGOs went well beyond providing microcredit to the poor women of Bangladesh society, especially in the rural areas. The NGOs worked to build a unique micro-level development approach combining financial inclusion, livelihood sustainability and social development to empower the marginalised sections of the communities with women taking a frontal role. Broadly speaking, the NGOs were involved, through group based and other techniques, in capacity building, financial literacy, livelihood promotion, preventive healthcare, education and training, water and sanitation, and other social development areas besides their core financial functions such as microcredit to the poor. Over time, the NGOs have not only expanded their geographical outreach in Bangladesh but also consolidated their footprints in social development arena in a big way. These efforts have made significant contributions in adding value to the lives of the poor by the time-tested interventions to enhance overall quality of their life and empower them meaningfully.

In other words, microcredit model works with the presumption that just offering small loans or savings is not enough; financial service needs to be bound up within a social programme if it is to achieve positive changes. Embedding financial services into social benefits can deliver positive results faster and on a larger scale than isolated credit is likely to do. The focus is that microfinance on its own may not have any explicit social benefit: a loan can be just a loan but, to be effective, microfinance needs to focus on the double bottom line of financial sustainability and social benefits. These perspectives led the sector to diversify beyond microcredit, notably with more savings-led approaches to help the poorest people build up assets. New cross-sectoral partnerships have also emerged, offering the potential to deliver more innovation and greater scale.

These developments provided the impetus to a bottom-up approach to social development enabling Bangladesh to achieve rapid and spectacular improvements in many social development indicators. For example, the decline in infant and child mortality; elimination of gender disparity in primary and secondary school enrolment; achieving universal basic education; fast reduction of population growth rate; and many others are unique among countries at similar per capita income levels (Mahmud 2008). The increased awareness created by the NGOs through effective social mobilisation, such as for immunisation, contraceptive use, safe water and hygienic sanitation, girls' schooling, use of oral rehydration saline (ORS) for diarrhoea treatment resulting in decline in child mortality, and many others as well as scaling up these and other programmes by thousands of NGOs throughout Bangladesh have made a difference in social development in the country, which was effectively supported by government initiatives and government-NGO partnerships. The NGOs, by targeting the poor rural women, expanded social interactions and mobility of rural women along with enhanced agency, empowerment and mutual support, thus creating an environment within which rapid and broad-based social development can flourish. This explains why Bangladesh's performance is a welcome outlier providing a unique social development model which fits neither into typical 'income-mediated' or 'support-led' pathways to social and human development (Sen 1999).

4.2.1 *Social Context in Bangladesh*

According to the Human Development Report (HDR) 2018, Bangladesh is one of the countries that made the greatest progress in recent decades, as measured by the Human Development Index (HDI). Bangladesh's HDI has increased by nearly 60 per cent in the past 28 years, from 0.388 in 1990 to 0.614 in 2018.

Along with the home to one of the highest concentrations of NGO activity in the world, Bangladesh has a rich history of what may be described as civil society activity and organisation. Civil society owes its origin in the country's struggle for independence. Many NGOs were formed in the aftermath of the independence and, over the last five decades, NGOs have increasingly shifted in favour of service delivery programmes, along with earlier efforts at social mobilisation and community activism. The relationship between the government and civil society has been strongly influenced by the country's political history. The government's attitude towards the civil society has played a major role in shaping the choices available to Bangladeshi NGOs and the character needed to engage with state institutions and the political elite.

Bangladesh has experienced impressive human and social development in recent decades—people live longer, more children are in school, and more people have access to employment opportunities and basic social services. The Human Capital Index (HCI) quantifies this progress by showing the contribution of health and education to the productivity of the next generation of workers.[2] The worldwide average HCI is 0.57, while Bangladesh's score is 0.48 (with an HCI rank of 106 out of 157 countries in 2018). This shows that a child born in Bangladesh today will be 48 per cent as productive when he/she grows up as he/she could be if he/she enjoyed complete education and full health. While youthful populations offer potential demographic dividend in Bangladesh, this relies on quality jobs and maximising productivity of the working population.

The guiding factors of social development in Bangladesh are basic social values, such as equality of opportunity, solidarity, and participation; and social investments to promote sustainable development and economic growth. Education, health and social protection systems provide people with an opportunity to develop from their own resources and live decent lives. Education is a powerful driver of social development; and it promotes economic and social integration and empowerment of youth.

[2] The HCI consists of knowledge, skills, experience and health that people accumulate throughout their lives and represents productivity relative to a benchmark of complete education and full health on a scale of 0 to 1. The HCI measures the amount of human capital that a child born today can expect to attain by age 18. It conveys the productivity of the next generation of workers compared with a benchmark of complete education and full health. It is made up of five indicators: the probability of survival to age five, a child's expected years of schooling, harmonised test scores as a measure of quality of learning, adult survival rate (fraction of 15-year olds that will survive to age 60), and the proportion of children who are not stunted See, World Bank, Human Capital Project.

4.2.2 Leave No One Behind

While accepting the 2030 agenda for sustainable development, 193 UN Member States promised to 'leave no one behind' (LNOB) and make 'endeavour to reach the furthest behind first'. In practice, this means taking direct and practical action to reduce and end all forms of discrimination. People are discriminated when they lack the choices and capabilities that enable others to participate in or benefit from development. As UNDP (2018) highlights, discrimination and lagging behind may stem both from (i) absolute deprivation, that is when people live in multidimensional poverty or below other minimally accepted standards of security, income, public services, infrastructure or well-being; and (ii) relative deprivation, when they face exclusion, discrimination and/or entrenched inequalities; are less able to gain influence, get educated, survive setbacks, acquire wealth, and access job markets or technologies.

In reality, deprivation dynamics is inherently complex in Bangladesh; and changes in population size, structure and spatial distribution have a profound impact on economic, social and environmental aspects of sustainable development. Poverty is influenced by—and influences—demographic dynamics, including population growth, age structure, and rural-urban distribution.

With its central pledge to leave no one behind, SDGs recognise that development will only be sustainable if it is inclusive. Promoting inclusion is fundamental to achieving a socially, economically and environmentally sustainable future. No single set of policies or strategies is applicable in all contexts to tackle exclusion and promote inclusion. Instead, the government will have to apply a strong equity lens to policy making to address the structural causes of exclusion and social injustice.

The issues of LNOB are closely linked to marginality in which disadvantaged people fail to gain access to resources and full participation in society. Whether or not people are left behind can be explained by one or more of five factors: (i) discrimination, (ii) geography, (iii) socioeconomic status, (iv) governance, and (v) shocks and fragility (UNDP, 2018). The key factors for lagging behind are not one-dimensional rather these are multidimensional and are not mutually exclusive.

In Bangladesh, the deprivation and lagging behind process is multidimensional, although their sources and multiplicity vary over different lagging communities/population groups and geographic regions. For understanding the leaving behind drivers in Bangladesh, it is important to consider several issues such as, types of deprivation; extent of disadvantageous situation; violation of basic rights; apparent and underlying causes; the state of psychological construction of deprived population groups; and involvement of second or third parties as contributing factors.

4.3 Progress in Education

The concept of human capital, which was introduced in the early 1960s, is deeply connected to education and is one of the major ways of investing, maintaining and shaping human capital as a 'perpetual machine' for sustainable development. In the earlier neoclassical models, education was not considered a major input for production and hence was not included in growth models (Harberger 1998). In the 1960s, mounting empirical evidence stimulated the 'human investment revolution in economic thought' (Bowman 1960) and led to a series of growth accounting studies pointing to education's contribution to the unexplained residuals in the economic growth of western economies. Other studies looked at the impact of education on earnings or estimated private rate of returns (Becker 1964; Mincer 1974).

Education is a human right and is central to achieving many other sustainable development outcomes. A quality basic education gives children and youth the knowledge and skills they need to face daily life challenges, and take advantage of economic and lifelong learning opportunities. It is also a key driver for reducing poverty, fostering economic growth, achieving gender equality, and social development.

The constitution of Bangladesh recognises education as a basic right of all citizens and obligates the state to adopt effective measures to ensure access to education as a goal in its own right and as a means to improving the quality of life and human welfare. Article 17 of the Constitution mentions that it is the responsibility of the state 'to provide uniform, mass-oriented and universal education and to extend free compulsory primary education to all children to such stage as may be determined by the law'.

Bangladesh has re-affirmed its commitment to basic education through the two world conferences on 'Education for All' (EFA) in 1990 and 2000; and is a signatory to the World Declaration on 'Education for All', adopted in the Dakar Conference 2000. Following the Framework of Action adopted in the Conference, a post-Dakar National Plan of Action (2003–2015) was formulated. Prior to the Dakar Conference, the government signed Jomtien Declaration (1990) and adopted 'Education for All by 2000' under which the priority agendas included eradication of illiteracy and ensuring universal primary education.

4.3.1 *Education in Bangladesh: A Progress Report*

Since independence in 1971, the primary focus of education policies and programmes has been to deal with the problems of access, equity and quality. Despite the priority accorded to education in the country's development strategy, the progress towards realising these goals has been slow. As a result, Bangladesh still remains a poorly educated country, especially in terms of quality.

This section uses selected indicators to assess the overall record of progress in the country's education sector. Despite significant quantitative expansion, the record of progress suggests that the past success in rapid expansion in enrolment has been achieved at the cost of quality, indicating the increasing importance of quality-enhancing measures in promoting human rights to education in Bangladesh.

4.3.1.1 Structure of the Education System

The structure of the education system in Bangladesh is diverse and complex. The government institutions are dominant at the primary, technical, and tertiary levels while private institutions are pre-dominant at the secondary level. A significant recent development, moreover, is the rapid expansion of the NGO-run non-formal primary schooling and private tertiary institutions. The 2010 National Education Policy proposes a new tier of pre-primary education for one year. The traditional religion-based system (madrasah), both at primary and secondary levels, is also prevalent. A simplified summary of the structure of the country's education system is given in Table 4.1.

The structure of the diverse system has several characteristics: (i) the system normally starts with one or two years of pre-primary education offered by various institutions (e.g. private schools, kindergartens, and religious schools like maktabs); (ii) the primary education system covers a five-year period for children of 6–10 years age group; (iii) the secondary education offers five years of schooling (grades 6 to 10) at the end of which the students are screened through a public examination (Secondary School Certificate, SSC). For the religious schools, a separate public examination is conducted; (iv) students, with demonstrated competence at SSC examination, can enter into two-year (or vocational/technical)

Table 4.1 Education system in Bangladesh

Education	*School/Level*	*Grades*	*Age*	*Years*	*Remarks*
Primary	Primary education	1–5	6–10	5	....
Secondary	Junior secondary education	6–8	11–13	3	....
	Secondary education	9–10	14–15	2	Includes trade certificate/SSC vocational
	Higher secondary education	11–12	16–17	2	Includes 2 years of 4 year Diploma in Engineering & Nursing, HSC Vocational
Vocational	Diploma in engineering	...	...	4	Not a Bachelors, similar to Associates
Tertiary	Fazil	13–14	...	2	Similar to Associates degree
	Bachelor's	...	...	3–5	....
	Kamil	15–16	...	2	Similar to Bachelor's degree
	Bachelor (Engineering & Technology)	15–16	...	3	Engineering & Technology
	Master's	...	...	1–2	...
	Master of Philosophy	...	...	2	...
	Doctorate	...	...	3–5	...

Source: Mujeri 2010

institutions. At the end of the period, the students appear at the Higher Secondary Certificate (HSC) examination for screening and successful students become eligible to pursue higher education; (v) a mix of degree, certificate and diploma education of various durations is available at colleges, universities, and other specialised institutions for higher education. It may be mentioned here that successful completion of a degree (or equivalent) education is a requirement for entry into white collar jobs; (vi) the post-graduate education (1–2 years) is usually provided in the universities and affiliated institutions.

The Bangladeshi education system is thus unusually complex in that primary, middle, senior and tertiary education are oriented towards general, madrasah (religious) or technical/vocational preferences. Even private schools and universities are heavily subsidised—in fact the constitution decrees that children between ages 6 and 10 shall pay nothing. To complicate things further, local education is controlled by a hierarchy of school boards.

Those who choose to complete the last two of their 10 school grades at general secondary schools may specialise in humanities, science, or commerce to mention but a few. At the end of this, they may write a secondary school certificate (SSC) examination supervised by no less than eight school boards. Alternatively, they may elect to follow the religious (madrasah) education route that culminates in a different series of similar level tests. Other students may switch across to vocational training institutes or technical training centres administered by the Ministry of Education and the Ministry of Labour and Employment respectively. Choices here are between longer-term professional certification and shorter term job-specific orientation. Students who stay either course have choices once again. These include writing their higher secondary certificate (HSC) examination after two more years at a technical/polytechnic institute where they hone their practical skills further. Alternatively, they may enter one of many private or state-funded universities for five years of undergraduate study.

4.3.1.2 Literacy

Great strides have been made in improving literacy rates since Independence of the country in 1971. Yet, with a huge backlog of illiterate population, the literacy rate in Bangladesh is still low by international standards (Table 4.2). Despite the fact that adult literacy rate has more than tripled since 1970, as many as 27 per cent of the adult population were still illiterate in 2017. Moreover, 7 per cent of the youth population (15–24 years) was illiterate in 2017, implying that a large number of the young entrants into the labour force have no education and skills to pursue productive and remunerative income earning opportunities, especially in the nonfarm sector. A significant gender disparity in literacy among the adult

Table 4.2 Adult and youth literacy rates in Bangladesh

	1970	*1981*	*1991*	*2001*	*2011*	*2015*	*2017*
Adult literacy rate (15 years and above), %	24	29	35	48	47	65	73
Female	11	18	26	41	47	62	70
Male	35	40	44	54	48	68	76
Youth literacy rate (15–24 years), %	31	36	45	64	66	88	93
Female	18	27	38	60	73	90	94
Male	43	44	52	67	56	86	92

Source: UNESCO data base

population also remains, although it must be acknowledged that the gender gap has narrowed considerably over the years, especially in respect of youth literacy where the gender gap has disappeared; and more young women are now literate than young men.

4.3.1.3 Primary Education

The government 'nationalised' the primary education sector in 1973. Between 1975 and 2017, the number of primary schools more than tripled and the number of teachers more than doubled, both of which exceeded the rate at which the number of students increased during the same period (Table 4.3). As a result, both the average number of students per school and the student–teacher ratio show declining trends. It is important to note, however, that the declining trend in these ratios is a relatively recent phenomenon. The number of students per school started to decline in the 2000s and the recently declining student–teacher ratio shows that the last couple of years have witnessed a sharp acceleration in the availability of schools and teachers at the primary level.

There also exists a pluralist and heterogeneous structure of the primary schooling system in Bangladesh. In addition to primary school operated directly by the government, there are registered and non-registered non-government primary schools, community schools, satellite schools, kindergartens, madrasahs and other types of schools. Most of the non-government schools receive subsidy from the government including teacher salaries and text books for the students. The curriculum also adheres to the national competency-based curriculum developed by the National Curriculum and Textbook Board (NCTB). In addition, about 2 million children (10 per cent of total primary enrolment) receive primary schooling through the NGO run schools. Since the late 1990s, the

Table 4.3 Expansion of primary education in Bangladesh

	1975	*1985*	*1995*	*2005*	*2015*	*2018*
Number of schools	39,914	43,588	62,617	80,397	122,176	134,147
Number of teachers, thousand	164.62	183.86	248.78	262.08	322.77	349.22
Number of students, million	8.35	10.08	16.43	16.23	19.07	17.34
Ratios						
Number of students per school	209	231	262	202	156	129
Number of students per teacher	51	55	66	62	59	50

Source: UNESCO data base

government initiated a programme to provide grants to NGOs, CBOs (community-based organisations) and PVOs (private voluntary organisations) to set up primary schools including satellite schools in villages having no schools.

The government also supports non-formal education (NFE) which aims at providing literacy and basic functional education to those who remain out-of-school or to the drop-outs before completing primary education. During 1996–2001, 34.4 million learners (covering age groups 8 to 45 and hard-to-reach groups) were covered under these programmes. In adult literacy, about 330 NGOs are directly involved in the non-formal education programmes of the government aiming to cover nearly 30 million adult learners.

At the output level, there has been a rapid progress in quantitative expansion of primary education. The gross and net enrolment rates increased to 114 per cent and 98 per cent respectively by 2018 (Table 4.4). Another significant achievement is the gender parity in primary education. An important factor that contributed to rapid progress in primary schooling is the policy emphasis on appointing female teachers in primary schools. Currently, more than half the teachers at the primary level are females.

4.3.1.4 *Secondary Education*

In Bangladesh, the secondary education system consists of two levels—secondary education (grades 6–10) and higher secondary education

Table 4.4 Selected indicators of primary schooling in Bangladesh

	1970	*1980*	*1990*	*2005*	*2010*	*2018*
Gross enrolment rate, %	54	61	72	99	108	114
Female	35	46	66	97	112	118
Male	73	75	77	97	103	110
Net enrolment rate, %	51	60	64	94	95	98
Female	33	45	60	93	92	98
Male	66	74	68	91	98	98
Student-teacher ratio	46	54	63	47	40	30
Repetition rate, %	NA	18	7	10.8	12.6	5.4
Share of pupils reaching grade five, %	NA	21	48	52.9	60.2	81.4

Source: UNICEF data base and Annual Primary School Census, Ministry of Primary and Mass Education, various years

Table 4.5 Selected indicators of secondary schooling in Bangladesh

	1980	*1985*	*1990*	*1997*	*2005*	*2016*
Gross enrolment rate, %	18	19	19	19	43	61
Female	9	11	13	NA	47	67
Male	26	27	25	NA	39	54
Net enrolment rate, %	18	21	22	22	44	55
Female	10	13	15	16	NA	61
Male	25	29	28	27	NA	50
Student-teacher ratio	24	28	28	29	31	42
Private sector share in total enrolment, %	NA	93	90	82	97	97

Source: World Bank and BANBEIS websites

(grades 11–12). Despite its growing trend, enrolment rate at the secondary level is still low. Between 1980 and 2016, gross enrolment rate rose from 18 per cent to 61 per cent along with a significant increase in female enrolment rate (Table 4.5). The major function of secondary schooling is the screening of students to pursue higher education and, in this respect, the system appears to be inefficient. In 1999, for every 100 students who entered the system at grade six, only six survived through passing the final examination at the higher secondary level which is a pre-condition to continue higher education.

Moreover, the rapid expansion of the system has aggravated the quality problems. Poor achievement of students and low quality in secondary education can be attributed to well-known causes, such as deficiencies in teachers' skills and capability, inadequate facilities and learning materials, poor enforcement of rules and criteria for approval of government subvention, inadequate resources reflected in low per student expenditure, and poor governance and management of schools.

4.3.1.5 Higher Education

The access to higher education is limited with very low enrolment ratios (Table 4.6). Two separate systems exist: the universities and the degree colleges. Enrolment in the universities is selective which accounts for about 15 per cent of the total enrolment and mostly serves the urban elites. Due to lack of employment opportunities at the lower levels, nearly three out of four students who pass the higher secondary level

Table 4.6 Gross enrolment ratio in tertiary education in Bangladesh

	1970	*1980*	*1990*	*2000*	*2005*	*2010*	*2014*
Gross enrolment ratio, total,%	2.1	3.2	4.1	5.4	6.2	13.3	13.4
Share of female students, %	9.7	13.9	15.9	32.3	33.5	40.5	41.7

Source: World Data Atlas Bangladesh, Tertiary Education

examination continue with some form of higher education.[3] Although Bangladesh's gross graduation ratio for tertiary education has fluctuated substantially in recent years, it tended to increase in the 2000s rising from 4.7 per cent in 2002 to 7.3 per cent in 2012.

4.3.2 Status of Vulnerable Groups

The progress in Bangladesh's education sector, as shown above, highlights several features for example commitment to primary education and expansion of girls' enrolment rates. Despite the progress achieved so far, significant disparity in basic education remains.

4.3.2.1 Spatial Disparity

Significant disparity exists in literacy rate between urban and rural areas, between females and males, and among different administrative divisions of the country. Similarly, geographical disparity exists in access to and participation in primary education.

4.3.2.2 Disparity by Household's Poverty Status

The children from poor families are less likely to attend schools. Moreover, such disparity has gender and location (rural and urban) dimensions (Table 4.7). Although the disparity is less at the primary level (aged 6–10), the gap is much wider at higher levels. Gross enrolment at the junior secondary level (aged 11–15) is only 68 per cent for the poor compared with

[3] At present, along with 41 public universities, there are 103 private universities which were permitted first time in the 1990s. The private universities are not subsidised by the government, tuition fees arc high, and hence these provide education mostly to children from the richer segment of the population. In order to make university education more accessible, the Bangladesh Open University was established in 1992 which enrolled 0.53 million students in 2018.

Table 4.7 Gross enrolment disparity by poverty status, 2016

	Urban			*Rural*			*National*		
	Boys	*Girls*	*Total*	*Boys*	*Girls*	*Total*	*Boys*	*Girls*	*Total*
Children aged 6–10									
Poor	86.6	85.0	85.8	89.5	93.2	91.3	89.0	91.5	90.2
Non-poor	93.6	95.2	94.4	94.9	95.4	95.1	94.6	95.4	95.0
Children aged 11–15									
Poor	61.8	74.3	68.1	72.7	85.7	79.0	70.5	83.4	68.1
Non-poor	83.0	85.7	84.3	84.4	91.7	87.8	84.1	90.0	86.9

Source: BBS, *Preliminary Report on Household Income and Expenditure Survey 2016*, Bangladesh Bureau of Statistics, 2017

87 per cent for the non-poor. Similarly, the non-poor to poor ratio is nearly four at the secondary level and close to six at the higher secondary level.

4.3.2.3 Poverty and School Enrolment

Crucial to improving educational outcomes is the calculation that households make when assessing the returns to education against the costs involved. For the poor families, the cost of educating their children is a significant deterrent. Although the direct costs are low in the early years of education, they increase rapidly with each grade. The composition of direct education costs changes with age and varies between income groups. Tutoring costs—that is, costs for supplementary private teaching outside school hours—become progressively more important at higher grades, and is a cost that poorer families can less frequently afford (either in monetary terms or in terms of children's time free of household tasks).

More important than direct costs for poor households, however, are the indirect costs. In Bangladesh, child labour is common and begins at an early age. In both rural and urban settings, poor families often rely heavily on their children to help with a variety of tasks (generally household-based) essential to the well-being of the family. These forms of child labour include both income-earning or subsistence oriented productive or trading activities, and household reproductive tasks (caring for younger siblings, cooking, cleaning, carrying water, etc.) much of which is necessitated in order to free up both parents for economic activity.

For many poor children, work and school attendance are largely substitutes for one another, and this trade-off becomes more pronounced as children get older. The burden of housework and productive work is a particular problem for rural children of poor families, and girls. In particular, from age 12 onwards, household work is significantly more likely to interfere with girls' education than boys'. Such children, especially girls, start to fall behind in grade attainment compared with their peers who only attend school. The high proportion of children who both attend school and work suggests that the household need for child labour contributes to outright dropout from school.

Access to education also has important inter-generational, inter-sectoral, and inter-societal dimensions. Statistically significant positive relationship between parental education and net enrolment is observed: mothers with secondary and higher education are more likely to send their children to school than those with primary and no education. Similar relationship also holds for father's education. Moreover, it is observed that, out of 20 per cent of the eligible children (age 6–10 years) who are not enrolled in schools, nearly 18 per cent did never go to school while the rest had enrolled but dropped out before reaching the age of 10 years.

The socioeconomic background of the non-enrolled children shows that most of them (more than 50 per cent) come from food deficit households, nearly 88 per cent live in rural areas, and over three-quarters of the fathers and 85 per cent of the mothers of the non-enrolled children have no schooling. Even in the case of enrolled students, only about 22 per cent of the eligible students are 'in the right grade in the right age' and more than 47 per cent are in a class behind their age. The analysis by age shows that less than 45 per cent of the children of age six are enrolled in grade one and, of the children aged 10, only 15 per cent are in grade six.

While the overwhelming majority of the non-enrolled, drop-outs and poor performers of the basic schooling system belong to the poor families, the 'rural-urban divide' in the education sector is reflected in significant variations in the type of primary schools that the students attend. Most of the rural students (around 92 per cent) are enrolled in government and government-subsidised schools and madrasahs while similar share in urban areas is 76 per cent and relatively more urban students have access to Bangla and English medium private schools (e.g. kindergartens).

Since the quality of education in private schools is usually higher than that in government schools, which also have better qualified teachers and improved facilities in urban areas, urban students tend to get higher quality education than their counterparts in the rural areas. Obviously this quality differential has far reaching implications on future educational prospects of the children living in rural areas compared with those in urban areas.

The above indicates significant progress in the education sector particularly in increasing literacy and enrolment rates in primary education and in closing the gender gaps at primary and secondary levels in Bangladesh. The progress is the outcome of a series of affirmative actions taken by the state, the private sector and the NGOs. Several such actions are noted, such as the enactment of the Primary Education Act in 1990 to provide free and compulsory primary education to all children; free education for girls up to grade twelve in rural areas; stipends for girls at the secondary level; food for education (recently substituted by cash for education) programme for children from poorer families; creation of a space along with financial support by the government for the private sector and NGOs to function; and proliferation of NGO-run non-formal schools for the children deprived of formal schooling due to poverty, gender or other reasons. It may be argued, however, that most of these actions contributed to improving the performance in quantitative terms with inadequate efforts towards addressing the quality aspects of education.

4.3.2.4 Public Expenditure and Education

Bangladesh's development strategy considers education more as a precondition for sustained economic growth which leaves little space for its human dimension. The existing inadequacy in educational attainments is seen as a manifestation of poverty, resulting in low labour productivity and inadequate living conditions, but it is not explicitly recognised as violation of people's right to education. Nonetheless, the role that the government plays in the education sector has an impact on the fulfillment of this right, even though the government does not adopt an explicitly rights-based approach.

The government policies recognise that inadequacies in educational investments are caused in part by poverty, which in turn contributes to its perpetuation. The poor households, with limited resources, face a difficult trade-off in meeting educational expense of their children which has a future pay-off at the cost of current consumption that is urgently needed for survival. As a result, education, particularly for the poor in Bangladesh, acquires the characteristics of public goods with positive externalities and the government is, therefore, required to spend more on education. This is necessary to ensure that the poor do not become the victims of both market and government failures. In view of such strong arguments, the case for rapid growth in public expenditure has been generally accepted. The government has also followed active policies for expanding the delivery of educational services along with creating the institutional capacity to reach the poor.

A noteworthy feature of government policy is the pursuit of different approaches to the expansion of primary and secondary education. The strategic thrust for expanding primary education is through public provisioning and expanding the net of non-government schools. Since the 1990s, the approach also covered efforts at expanding the role of community schools organised by NGOs and communities with government support. The advantage of community schools lies in their lower cost of teacher salaries, higher number of students per class and higher student-teacher ratios, resulting in lower per-pupil costs compared with the government schools. The strategy for expanding secondary education, on the other hand, emphasises more on partnership with private providers. The policy of wider partnership with the private sector contributes to lower per-pupil cost through lower teacher-student ratios and lower teacher salaries (since the government pays 90 per cent of the base teacher salary in approved non-government secondary schools).[4]

4.3.2.5 Public Expenditure Policy

Three sources of educational financing are available in the country: the government, the households, and community financing including NGOs. Survey evidence shows that the household sector is the most important source of educational financing in the country. Although the publicly provided primary education is tuition-free, the non-government schools collect fees and contributions. Moreover, the households pay for supplementary educational materials, private tutoring, and other education-related expenditures.

The average annual education expenditure by the households is almost similar to government expenditures at the primary and tertiary levels (Table 4.8). The level of private expenditure is, however, more than two-and-a-half times that of public expenditure at the secondary level. Although primary education is 'free' in the country, in the sense that tuition fee does not have to be paid, households do need to incur a variety of other

[4]The unit cost per student is estimated at USS 16 in non-government schools compared with US$ 68 in government secondary schools (including all recurrent costs incurred by the schools irrespective of their financing). Sec World Bank 2002.

Table 4.8 Public and private expenditures in education

Level of education	*US $ per student per year, 2001*	
	Public	*Households*
Primary	13	13
Secondary	27	73
Tertiary	155	151

Source: World Bank 2002

Table 4.9 Public expenditure by level of education

	Total public expenditure in billion Tk. at 2005–06 prices	*% share in total expenditure*					
		Primary	*Secondary*	*Technical*	*University*	*Others*	*Total*
1992	33.5	51.3	32.0	2.6	8.8	5.3	100
1996	60.1	50.3	39.5	1.5	6.0	2.7	100
2000	71.9	44.6	43.5	2.6	7.4	1.9	100
2009	94.4	40.1	42.0	2.6	6.2	9.1	100
2019	296.1	31.0	39.0	9.4	12.0	8.6	100

Source: GOB 2008; BBS 2009

expenses. Thus, the so-called 'free' primary education is far from free, with the households having to pay at least the similar amount per student than does the government.

Over the years, Bangladesh's public policy has increasingly emphasised the importance of education. Correspondingly, public resources devoted to education have increased in both absolute and relative terms (Table 4.9). Still, despite devoting around 15 per cent of total government spending to education, the level of government spending is low and constitutes only 2.2 per cent of GDP. As a share of GDP, aggregate public spending on education in South Asia is reported by the World Bank at 2.5 per cent in 2016. The ratio varies widely across other South Asia countries: 4.7 per cent in Bhutan, 3.2 per cent in India, 6.8 per cent in the Maldives, 4.7 per cent in Nepal, 2.2 per cent in Pakistan, and 2.0 per cent in Sri Lanka.

The distribution of government education expenditure shows that the share of primary education has declined from more than 51 per cent in 1992 to 31 per cent in 2019, whereas the share of secondary education increased representing a shift of resources from the primary to the secondary level (Table 4.9). Along with the need to accommodate the increasing demand for continuing education for the cohort that completed the primary education, the trend also reflects a policy shift towards expanding the provision of secondary education, especially for girls.

A feature of public education expenditure which reflects its unbalanced nature, however, is the very high share of resources that is devoted to teachers' salaries in government schools and salary-related subsidies to non-government institutions. At the primary level, the revenue expenditure is almost entirely devoted to meeting expenses on pay and allowances. It is estimated that nearly 97 per cent of expenditure is accounted for by salary and salary-related expenditures.

At the secondary level, the share of pay and allowances is estimated at around 80 per cent when grants to non-government institutions are added since these are spent on salaries of teachers (Mujeri 2000). As a result, very little resources can be made available to meet other educational needs, such as teaching materials, essential supplies, in-service training and maintenance, and text book related expenditures which contribute towards improving the quality of basic education. In effect, the present expenditure pattern indicates low priority to complementary expenses needed for the delivery of quality education services, indicating an imbalance between labour and non-labour teaching inputs.

Despite increased allocations of public resources over the years, education expenditure is still low in Bangladesh compared with many South Asian and other developing countries. It appears that the government spends too little on education in relation to requirements and does not use the resources efficiently. Moreover, there exist imbalances in public education spending over different levels as well as its nature and composition (Mujeri 2000). With the overriding concern for human resource development as an end in itself and a major avenue of poverty reduction, the government needs to substantially increase its expenditure on education (from the current level of 2.2 per cent to around 5–6 per cent of GDP within the next decade) along with measures for increasing its efficiency and equity.

4.3.3 Education Policies and Strategies

The government's education policies and strategies have largely attempted to bring about reforms in the education sector for expanding enrolment and improving its quality and governance. The government has approved the National Education Policy 2010 with the objective to foster humanity among the future citizens of the country. The policy assists to grow the students as creative, rational, tolerant to others' opinion and liberal who will be able to lead the country towards inclusive development and progress.

4.3.3.1 Education and Child Labour

The government has taken several measures to combat the problem of child labour through providing access to education. The Compulsory Primary Education Act 1990 and interventions like the food for education (FFE) and stipend programmes, flexibility and child-centred nature of non-formal education is now accepted as a complementary approach to formal education, especially for the underprivileged, drop-outs, and out-of school children of poor families. A special programme was launched in 2000 for the working children in urban areas to provide them with two years of basic literacy courses. The experience from other countries shows that, even when compulsory schooling laws cannot be fully enforced, the mere availability of 'good schools' and quality education can succeed in diverting children to schools from the long hours at the work place (Basu 1999).

Bangladesh, by ratifying the ILO-Convention No. 182 on the Worst Forms of Child Labour, has committed itself to the goal of a child labour-free country. Despite significant efforts to combat child labour, the country still faces the daunting challenge of addressing the problem of a large number of working children and younger siblings at risk. The International Programme on the Elimination of Child Labour (IPEC), sponsored by the ILO, is an innovative programme in Bangladesh that integrates the right to education with other dimensions of human rights.

4.3.3.2 Assessment of Educational Policies

Despite the recognition of the right to education, the educational policies and processes constrain Bangladesh in performing its responsibilities in the education sector. The factors are complex and interrelated; but these have four components, namely, availability, accessibility, acceptability, and adaptability—the so-called four A's of the right to education.

Since the quality of education depends on several factors, such as the status, morale and professionalism of the teachers; physical facilities and supervision mechanism; and management, governance and accountability procedures, any effort to improve the quality must deal with all these issues. For an effective system, the management of basic education needs decentralisation and community participation.

Over the years, the share of domestic financing has increased in the education sector; and Bangladesh has succeeded in raising the education budget in absolute amount every year, but lags behind in terms of share for education in the national budget. Bangladesh is yet to achieve the international benchmark of 15–20 per cent of the national budget for education and 4–6 per cent of GDP for education. Bangladesh seems to have fallen into the '2 per cent of GDP trap' for education over a long period. Unless the government invests more in education, many of the nation's aspirations will remain unfulfilled. Similarly, ensuring quality education requires a comprehensive review of all curricula, deployment of trained teachers, and increased use of ICT for education.

Several critical concerns for education in Bangladesh relate to the capacity gaps in education; centralised decision-making process and inadequate decentralisation; corruption and governance issues; increased trend of the commercialisation of basic education; and the lack of a legislative framework for the right to education.

Furthermore, quality remains the biggest challenge across all levels of education. Attracting qualified, motivated, and trained teachers remains challenging; and providing them with a congenial working environment, decent remunerations, and adequate time for preparation by adopting guidelines for teachers are bigger challenges. There is a lack of a comprehensive policy on teachers' issues that is aligned with the UNESCO-ILO recommendations.

What is required is a systematic effort under the sector-wide programme. The relevant government departments should work together to improve the quality of education by (i) revisiting the curricula at the primary and secondary levels; (ii) increasing the use of ICT to foster the progress of educational attainment (planning, teacher's preparedness, learning enhancement, monitoring and reporting); (iii) improving physical infrastructure; and (iv) increasing the supply of teaching-learning materials along with ensuring the supply of competent, professionally developed, and motivated teachers and academic supervisors.

In the present era of globalisation, promoting human rights and global citizenship among the youth is critical for improving living standards and ensuring sustained development For the purpose, special programmes are required, the curriculum needs to be re-visited regularly for integration with global developments, and efforts need to be strengthened to promote peace, tolerance, and pluralism to support social coherence and societal harmony along with global citizenship.

4.3.4 Conclusions

Despite substantial achievements in the education sector as a whole, major challenges remain in Bangladesh. These relate to a number of issues, such as to increase access to education, improve equity and quality, and to speed educational reforms. In Bangladesh, more children now wish to go to quality secondary schools than are able to enroll, and the demand for higher education is in general increasing faster than the supply.

The issue of equity mainly affects several overlapping disadvantaged groups, including the rural poor, ethnic minorities, street and working children. The different access that boys and girls have to the education system is also important because it contributes to gender differences later in life. The gender gap in expected years of schooling is still large in the country and it is not closing fast enough. The quality of education is poor at all levels. Students in Bangladesh have a mean level of achievement below that in developed countries, and their performance shows a much greater variation around the mean.

The traditional definition of educational quality in Bangladesh is mostly based on content mastery. But using the traditional schooling approaches during the precious years that the children spend in schools lead to wasted resources and forgone opportunities for individuals and communities. The government's approach to promote quality education for all children must move beyond traditional models to help children develop the knowledge, skills, and attitudes that are relevant to their lives and that can lift them out of poverty and deprivations. So far, investment in education in the country has been guided mostly under the unquestioned assumption that improved test scores are clear evidence that the investments have paid off. But if a mastery of the basic primary school curriculum is not the best way of improving life chances and alleviating poverty, then Investing in such interventions may not reflect the priorities for allocating scarce resources and the time available for developing the young minds. It is time to seek out the interventions that lead to the greatest social and economic impact for the poor in the country.

Any delays in reforming the education system to keep pace with economic structures may adversely affect the quality of the country's growth process and the speed with which the country can move forward and achieve the development goals. Thus lags in reform can hinder growth; conversely, timely reform can pay off in terms of economic growth and poverty reduction, as evidenced by the East Asian countries that have generally invested heavily in basic human capital, both male and female.

Bangladesh needs to focus on the most critical issues in education equity, inclusion, quality, and financing. For the purpose, it is necessary to (i) revisit the boundary, particularly legal, technological, physical, and moral boundaries that set the norms of educational operations; (ii) enact a comprehensive right to education act using the rights-based approach; (iii) ensure free and compulsory basic education up to grade 12; and (iv) reduce commercialisation of education.

Improving the internal capacity, strengthening governance, and ensuring effective citizen's participation, particularly the civil society engagement in educational planning, implementation, monitoring, and evaluation are essential to achieving the education goals in Bangladesh and ensure that no one is left behind.

The strategic framework for future educational development of Bangladesh needs to focus on some basic principles, such as: (i) universality; (ii) the rights-based approach recognising that education is a public good; (iii) comprehensive policies, plans and systems; (iv) effective governance, accountability and partnerships; (v) effective coordination; (vi) sufficient financing; (vii) efficient monitoring, follow-up, and review for evidence-based policies and sector plans; (viii) emphasis on equity, inclusion, and gender equality; (ix) focus on quality, learning outcomes, and relevance; and (x) preparedness for and provision of education during emergency situations and natural calamities.

It is true that systematic obstacles, such as poverty, socio-cultural constraints arising out of existing social divides, and serious flaws in the educational vision stand in the way of translating educational goals into reality, However, if poverty has to be reduced and the poor have to be empowered, the capability of the poor must be enhanced through ensuring their access to education.

4.4 Progress in Health and Nutrition

The role of the state in the provision of health rights stems from the state's obligation to provide minimum healthcare to every individual. The right to health imposes three obligations on the state: (i) to respect; (ii) to protect; and (iii) to fulfil and to promote the enjoyment of the right to health.

The state needs to respect the health rights of every individual through protecting them from illness and diseases, facilitating and providing minimum basic services, and through health promotion.

The healthcare industry in Bangladesh may be seen as one of the most important sectors of the economy, since medication counts as a basic need for living and has a strong stable demand. Growth in living standards and aging of population are likely to ensure that this industry grows much faster than the country's economy. This reveals a strong correlation between income and healthcare spending—mainly due to the fact that the healthcare demand rises in response to rise in income.

4.4.1 Healthcare System in Bangladesh

The developments of the healthcare system in Bangladesh may be analysed under three broad frameworks: (i) health sector policies and programmes; (ii) healthcare industry and expansion of health facilities and medical personnel; and (iii) volume and pattern of health expenditure and its trend and composition.

4.4.1.1 Policies and Programmes in Health Sector

Policy making for the design, implementation, and management of effective, efficient, and equitable health system is critical to addressing Bangladesh's health challenges. Health policy is needed not only to address the pressing needs of infectious diseases and malnutrition, but also for mitigating the emerging problems of non-communicable diseases and obesity. The evidence is strong that sound health policy making can contribute to rapid and inclusive development and social well-being and security. For the purpose, not only must policy making be knowledge-based —it must also be result-oriented.

Bangladesh did not have any coherent health policy until the 1990s; and all health-related policies and programmes were guided by the health sector strategies of the successive five year plans during the period. The first National Health Policy was approved in 2000, and a new policy was adopted in 2011. While the policy documents provide broad directions for action, the practical operations in the health sector are guided by strategies under the sector-wide approach (SWAp) since 1998 with a view to coordinating government and external funding in the health sector.

Under the SWAp, the government and the development partners (DPs) pursued a series of multi-year strategies, programmes and budgets for management and development of the health nutrition and population (HNP) sector. The Ministry of Health and Family Welfare (MOHFW) is currently implementing its fourth sector programme named '4th health, population and nutrition sector programme (4th HPNSP)' covering a 5.5-year period between January 2017 and June 2022. The 4th HPNSP encompasses three components: (i) governance and stewardship; (ii) HNP systems strengthening; and (iii) provision of quality HNP services. The Programme's objective is 'to ensure that all citizens of Bangladesh enjoy health and well-being by expanding access to quality and equitable healthcare in a healthy and safe living environment'.

The first major nutrition project was the Bangladesh integrated nutrition programme (BINP) in 1995. This was followed by the national nutrition programme (NNP) in 2004 in conjunction with the HPNSP. The project had three inter-related objectives: (i) improve the capacity of national level nutrition institutions in Bangladesh in the areas of advocacy, analysis of causation and consequences of malnutrition, policy advice, operational research, and operational support of national programmes; (ii) improve the capacity of communities, households and individuals to better understand their nutritional problems in practical terms and take appropriate actions to address them at their own level; and (iii) improve the nutritional status of the population, with particular emphasis on children and pregnant and lactating women.

4.4.1.2 The Drug Policy

Bangladesh is one of the pioneers in formulating and implementing a coherent drug policy in the early 1980s. The government adopted the National Drug Policy in 1982, and updated and revised it in 2004. The policy played a critical role in improving the supply of quality essential drugs in Bangladesh at an affordable price (Islam 1999). Under the policy, an essential drug list (EDL) was prepared, which initially included 150 items (45 for rural PHC facilities) with controlled prices, which was later reduced to 117 in 1993. The EDL has recently been revised to reflect advances in medical science and now contains 209 drugs.

The drug policy has been instrumental in stimulating the development of the pharmaceutical industry in Bangladesh and in raising the market share of local manufacturers (Reich 1994). Since the adoption of the Policy, pharmaceuticals emerged as one of the fastest growing industries in the country, and have now emerged as the second largest exporter after RMGs (Begum 2007). The drug policy also stimulated the production of essential drugs by requiring all manufactures that 60 per cent of production capacity should be devoted to producing medicines under the EDL. As a result, the local pharmaceutical industry is now capable of producing all the 209 items under the EDL and can meet the demands of the country. The prices of these have also been kept affordable by subjecting 117 out of 209 drugs listed under EDL to price control. The combination of these policies with the requirement that raw materials must be procured from internationally competitive markets has resulted in a substantial decline in the prices of essential drugs in real terms (Ahmed 2004).

4.4.1.3 Immunisation

The first large-scale programme of immunisation for children began in 1979, under which vaccines for tuberculosis, DPT, measles and polio were administered. But the provision was inadequate and vaccines were frequently not available; as a consequence, very limited progress was made in raising coverage, which remained well below 5 per cent until the mid-1980s.

The real breakthrough came in 1985, with the launching of the expanded programme of immunisation (EPI) with financial support from several donors. The programme was revised to include community-level delivery through outreach centres, bringing about very rapid increases in immunisation rates towards the end of the decade and the percentage of those having no vaccination at all continued to decline, reaching less than 10 per cent by the end of the 1990s (World Bank 2005).

In the early 2000s, immunisation continued to be provided in the rural areas through outreach centres, complemented by services at district and upazila-level hospitals, union-level clinics, annual campaigns, and catch-up days to reach children who had missed doses. National immunisation days were instituted during the 1990s to deliver two doses of polio vaccine a year. Immunisation was included under the essential services package (ESP) developed for HPSP, and subsequently as part of essential service delivery (ESD) under HNPSP, according to which immunisation was to be made available from community clinics. As a result of these efforts, more than 82 per cent of children came to be fully immunised by 2016, a truly spectacular rise from the base of less than 5 per cent in the early 1980s.

4.4.1.4 Healthcare Industry Ecosystem

The Ministry of Health and Family Welfare (MOHFW) has an extensive health infrastructure. The service delivery structure follows the country's administrative pattern, starting from the national to the district, upazila, union and finally to the ward levels. It provides promotive, preventive, and curative services such as outdoor (outpatient), indoor (inpatient), and emergency care at different levels—primary, secondary and tertiary.

In Bangladesh, depending upon the type of services patients required, the level of healthcare can be divided into three broader categories:

Primary care: Basic or general healthcare traditionally provided by doctors trained in: family practice, paediatrics, internal medicine, and occasionally gynaecology.

Secondary care: Medical care provided by a physician who acts as a consultant at the request of the primary physician.

Tertiary care: Specialised consultative care, usually on referral from primary or secondary medical care personnel, by specialists working in a centre that has personnel and facilities for special investigation and treatment.

For ensuring equitable healthcare to every citizen, an extensive network of health services has been established in the country. It takes a circuitous form of healthcare network spread over the country, ranging from the policy-making bodies to healthcare facilities down to the community level. The infrastructure of healthcare facilities may be divided into three levels: medical university, medical college and specialised hospitals exist at the tertiary level; district hospitals as well as mother and child welfare centres are located at the secondary level; and upazila health complex, union health and family welfare centres, and community clinics are located at the primary level.

Further, the healthcare system in Bangladesh covers a wide range of public and private providers within the above intricate network (see, World Bank 2003, 2005; Mahmud 2008; Osman 2008). In fact, several sources of health services exist in the country. Apart from the government services, there are private providers, traditional (e.g. ayurvedi, kabiraji) and homeopathic providers, NGOs, other non-profit facilities, and qualified and unqualified drug sellers. Additionally, modern private care is provided by qualified practitioners and government doctors engaged in private practice.

The level of urbanisation is a major determinant of the location and service mix offered by both public and private providers. The tertiary and advanced level services are offered by public and private providers in major metropolitan areas (e.g. Dhaka). The secondary level services are offered at the district headquarters, and the primary level services are offered at the upazila level. There are generally no in-patient and specialised services below the upazila level.

Community Clinics (CCs), as the first tier public health facility, provide primary healthcare (PHC) services to the rural community of the whole country especially in remote and hard-to-reach areas. The initiative, taken in 1998, has extended coordinated health and family planning services to the door steps of the rural population. A total of 10,723 CCs have been constructed during 1999–2001. At present, 13,539 CCs are on operational mode and 27 items of medicine and two items of contraceptives are supplied from the CCs. With other services, normal delivery service is also available in many CCs.

4.4.1.5 Primary HealthCare

Bangladesh has achieved significant success in providing free healthcare services at the grassroots level from various types of field level healthcare facilities. Diarrhoea, malaria, filaria, kala-zar, tuberculosis, leprosy control, removal of Vitamin A related blindness, deworming medicine distribution and vaccination programmes have been strengthened by rural level field workers and volunteers. As a result of proper implementation of these programmes, maternal and neonatal mortality rate have been reduced as well as average life expectancy has increased. Now dengue, swine flu and SARS disease have been controlled successfully in Bangladesh. Detection of smear positive pulmonary tuberculosis rate has increased up to 100 per cent under directly observed treatment short-course (DOTS) programme.

4.4.1.6 Medical Education

There has been a notable expansion in the number and availability of health service institutions as well medical personnel over the last few decades. The government has continued its efforts for expansion of modern and updated education in medical sciences. In 2019, five new government medical colleges launched their academic journeys raising the total seats in MBBS course in 36 government medical colleges to 4068. In addition, 6231 students get chance to study MBBS course in 69 non-government medical colleges. There are 250 seats in six army medical colleges and 125 seats in one armed forces medical college.

In total, 532 students can get higher studies at one government dental college and eight dental units of medical colleges. In addition, total seats in BDS course are 940 in 12 private dental colleges and 465 seats in 14 non-government dental units. In addition, 716 students can study in nine government assistant training institutions. Likewise, 12,824 students can study in 192 non-government medical assistant training institutions. In total, there are 2585 seats in 11 government institutes of health technology. In the private sector, there are 8940 seats in 97 institutes of health technology. Moreover, in 22 government medical colleges, 1541 students can study at the post-graduate level. In addition, there are 580 seats in the Bangabandhu Sheikh Mujib Medical University for post graduate courses.

4.4.1.7 Nursing Services

Altogether, 29,407 registered nurses are working in various hospitals at present. Former seven nursing institutes have been converted into nursing colleges. Four new nursing colleges have also been established. Two nursing colleges have been set up to provide master's degree. In order to increase the midwifery activities in the prevention of maternal and child deaths, a total of 3000 posts of certified midwives have been created in the public sector and 1143 midwives are deployed in upazila health complexes. A three-year diploma in midwifery course has been started in 38 (10 nursing colleges and 28 nursing institutes) nursing educational institutes of the country.

4.4.1.8 Growth in Health Infrastructure

Between 1975 and 2016, the number of government hospitals has increased from 131 to 1220 and the number of government hospital beds has increased from 15,452 to 50,527. That is, the number of government hospitals has increased more than nine-fold during the period, while the bed strength has more than tripled. This divergence between the rates at which hospitals and hospital beds have expanded shows that the government has paid greater attention in recent decades on expanding small-scale hospital facilities for semi-urban and rural areas.

In addition, private clinics and hospitals have expanded at a rapid pace. Their number has grown from about 150 in the early 1980s to over 4596 in 2016, thus outnumbering public hospitals by a huge margin. Further, the number of private registered diagnostic centres has risen to 9741. The number of beds in private registered hospitals is 78,426 in 2016. Thus, more than 60 per cent of the total hospital beds in the country are accounted for by the private sector—up from only one-sixth in the early 1980s.

Table 4.10 Distribution of beds in public health facilities

Type of hospital	*Number of hospital*	*Number of beds*
Secondary and tertiary public health facilities		
District hospital	53	7850
General hospital	11	1350
Infectious disease hospital	5	180
Medical/dental college hospital	22	11,960
Specialised hospitals affiliated with post-graduate institutes	7	2300
BSMMU (medical university)	1	1212
Others	28	2201
Total	126	27,053
Public health facilities at upazila level and below		
Upazila health complex	436	18,290
Union hospital	31	490
Trauma Centre	5	100
Total	472	18,880

Source: MOHFW, Bangladesh Health Bulletin 2013

The distribution of beds in the public health facilities is skewed in favour of secondary and tertiary public health facilities. It is seen that nearly 60 per cent of the beds are located in secondary and tertiary facilities while 0nly 40 per cent are located in public health facilities at the upazila level and below (Table 4.10).

4.4.1.9 Private Sector Health Services

In the private sector, providers can be grouped into two main categories. First, the organised private sector (both for-profit and nonprofit) which includes qualified practitioners of different systems of medicine. Second, the private informal sector, which consists of providers practicing in rural areas not having any formal qualifications, such as untrained allopaths, homeopaths, and kobiraj.

4.4.1.10 Diagnostic Centres

Along with private clinics and hospitals, the number of diagnostic centres in the private sector is growing. In 2016, a total of 9741 laboratories and other diagnostic centres were registered with the Ministry of Health and Family Welfare (MOHFW 2016). In the private for-profit sector, there are some large diagnostic centres in the cities (e.g. Lab Aid, Ibn Sina, Popular and Medinova) providing laboratory and specialised radiological tests. Some of these facilities maintain a high standard. In the nonprofit private sector, there are centres like the International Centre for Diarrhoeal Diseases and Research, Bangladesh (ICDDR,B), which has a modern laboratory providing research facilities and extends laboratory services to the general community.

4.4.1.11 NGOs and Professional Groups

Bangladesh is known worldwide for having one of the most dynamic NGO sectors, with 2472 NGOs registered with NGO Affairs Bureau working in the population, health and nutrition sector in 2018. The NGOs are active in health promotion and prevention activities, particularly at the community level, and in family planning, maternal and child health areas.

Multiple donors, both multilateral and bilateral, are also active in healthcare financing and planning. The main bilateral donors to the health and population sector in Bangladesh are the governments of Australia, Belgium, Canada, Germany, Japan, Netherlands, Norway, Sweden, the United Kingdom and the United States. The multilateral donors include the World Bank, European Union, UNICEF, ADB, and the Global Fund to Fight AIDS, Tuberculosis and Malaria (GFATM).

Moreover, there are a number of professional organisations in Bangladesh who address the rights of medical professionals at different levels, such as the Bangladesh Medical Association (BMA), Bangladesh Private Medical Practitioners Association (BPMPA), Public Health Association of Bangladesh, Bangladesh Paediatric Society and the Nephrology Society of Bangladesh.

However, there is no organised body, either in the public or private sector, for overseeing the interests of the patients. The Consumers Association of Bangladesh (CAB) is an NGO addressing the rights of consumers in general, and does not have a separate agenda on health focusing on the rights of consumers as patients.

4.4.1.12 Availability of Health Personnel

The availability of health personnel is critical for health service delivery and, despite considerable expansion in recent years, this still remains a major problem. The number of registered physicians (including dental surgeons) has increased by more than eight-fold over the last four decades— rising from just about 10,000 in 1980 to 85,587 in 2016.

During the same period, the number of registered nurses has increased about 14-fold—from 3000 to nearly 42,000; and the numbers of registered midwives, skilled birth attendants and other medical technicians have also increased even faster.

The expansion in each of these dimensions has been rapid enough in relation to population growth to mark a significant expansion of facilities per person. As can be seen from Table 4.11, the number of persons per hospital bed has come down from 3600 in 1986 to 1110 in 2016. During the same period, the number of persons served by a doctor has declined more than three times—falling from 6600 to 2039, and the number of persons served by a nurse has come down even faster—from 15,000 to 3432. It should be noted, however, that most of the improvement in the availability of hospital beds has come from exceedingly rapid expansion of private hospitals rather than of government hospitals.

However, although the size of the professional health workforce is consistently increasing over time, it has not been according to the requirements. Bangladesh has been identified by WHO as one of the 57 countries having critical shortage of health workforce (WHO 2006). A recent report of WHO suggests that there are 0.3 doctors and 0.3 nurses per 1000 population and cumulatively less than 23 doctors, nurses and midwives per 10,000 populations [see, MOHFW, Bangladesh Health System Review, 2015].

Table 4.11 Growth of medical facilities and personnel

	Number of persons per				
	Hospital bed			*Medical personnel*	
	Public	*Private*	*Total*	*Doctor*	*Nurse*
1986	4300	21,000	3600	6600	15,000
1991	4100	16,000	3200	5400	12,000
1996	4100	15,000	3100	4500	8700
2001	3900	11,000	2800	4000	7200
2006	4000	8600	2700	3300	6900
2009	3500	4000	1900	2800	6000
2016	2832	1825	1110	2039	3432

Source: BBS, *Statistical Pocket Book*, various Years; Ministry of Finance, *Bangladesh Economic Review*, various years; and Ministry of Health and Family Welfare, *Health Bulletin*, various years

Although medical facilities and personnel have expanded rapidly in recent years—both in absolute numbers and relative to the size of the population—a number of inadequacies still exist. One must realise that the number of qualified doctors and nurses per person is still quite low by international standards. In 2015, Bangladesh has low ratios of medical professionals—only 0.5 doctors per 1000 (increasing from 0.1 in 1980) and 0.2 nurses per 1000 people, far less than the minimum standard of 2.28 per 1000 recommended by WHO. Bangladesh also has a shortage of skilled health workers, with twice as many doctors as nurses clustered disproportionately in urban areas. According to WHO (2006), the density of medical workers (doctors, nurses, and midwives together) is only 0.58 per 1000 people in Bangladesh, whereas international evidence suggests that the optimal density is about 2.5.

Further, the distribution of different categories of medical workers is lopsided. For example, according to international best practice, the nurse-doctor ratio should be 2:1, but the current ratio in Bangladesh is reverse—with twice as many registered doctors as nurses. The availability of existing facilities is also skewed towards the urban sector—with only about 16 per cent of qualified doctors practicing in rural areas where the majority of the population still live (BHW, 2008). The problem is further aggravated by widespread absenteeism in public facilities, which is especially severe in the rural areas.

4.4.2 *Healthcare Expenditure*

The total healthcare expenditure includes spending by both public and private sources like medical goods and services, prevention programmes, and health administration. The public healthcare expenditures are usually financed through social security contributions, government revenue earnings, and from external sources (Poullier et al. 2001). On the other hand, the private healthcare expenditures encompass private insurance premiums and prepaid schemes, mandated enterprise health expenditure, expenditure on health through non-profit health services and direct out of pocket expenditure on health goods, which includes co-payments as well as direct payments by uninsured individuals (Novignon et al. 2012). Adequate and efficient healthcare spending is essential for improving the health status of individuals (see, Mahmud et al. 2013).

In 2016, health expenditure per capita (that is, expenditure on healthcare goods and services in current US dollars) for Bangladesh was $34, which grew substantially from $9 in 2002. Out of the amount, about 28 per cent is contributed by the public sector, while the remaining 72 per cent consists of out-of-pocket payments (OPP), which are spending on health directly out-of-pocket by households on a diverse range of providers of modern and alternative services. The OPP share increased from 62.3 per cent in 2002. The direct household expenditure on purchasing drugs from pharmacies is estimated at around $ 4 per head, far outstripping the public expenditure of less than $1 per head on drugs.

The above share of OPP in Bangladesh is exceptionally high by international standards. The 72 per cent share of out-of-pocket sources in Bangladesh compares unfavourable with 15 per cent in Bhutan, 24 per cent in Thailand, 51 per cent in Sri Lanka, and 54 per cent in Indonesia. In general, richer countries rely more on government resources and social insurance funding for healthcare, but even in comparison with other low-income developing countries, a disproportionate share of the financing burden is placed on households in Bangladesh.

A few more unusual features of the pattern of health expenditure in Bangladesh may be noted. Bangladesh is an outlier in terms of the share of total national spending allocated to in-patient care. Bangladesh spends around 15 per cent of recurrent expenditure on in-patient services compared with 25–40 per cent in other countries. This suggests that Bangladesh may be under-spending on in-patient care. Further, an unusually large share (about 45 per cent) of total spending is devoted to expenditures on medical goods purchased from retail outlets (for the most part medicines).

4.4.2.1 Structural Shift in Health Spending

A significant structural change has occurred in the health sector in recent years as the private sector has come to acquire increasing dominance. The Bangladesh National Health Accounts (NHA) 1997–2015 shows that total health expenditure (THE) for Bangladesh in 2015 is Tk. 452 billion, which comes to Tk. 2882 per person (US$37 per capita). The share of THE in GDP accounted for less than 1 per cent of GDP in 1997; in 2015, it is 3 per cent of GDP. In Bangladesh, THE is dominated by private sector financing. In 2015, private sector financing accounted for 77 per cent of THE, and public sector's share was 23 per cent. Donor funds utilised directly by the private providers is 7 per cent, while such funds channeled through the government are included under public financing. Despite the government's continued increase in public sector financing, their relative share has declined from 36 per cent of THE in 1997 to 23 per cent in 2015.

Traditionally, a large part of the government's health budget was spent to service facilities at the upazila level and below. During the 1980s and 1990s about half of total expenditure on health was spent on primary healthcare, which is provided mostly at lower level facilities (MOHFW, 1995). The share went up to 60–70 per cent in the late 1990s with the introduction of the ESP, which was successful in diverting resources into primary level care and vital services such as maternal care and in shifting resources from secondary and tertiary hospitals to lower-level facilities (MOHFW 2001).

Since these facilities are mostly used by the rural people, this pattern suggests a degree of vertical equity in the distribution of public health spending. Moreover, the equity effect is reinforced by the fact that most of the services provided at these levels are in the nature of free primary healthcare and nutritional and family planning services, which are more pro-poor than the services provided at higher levels (Glinskaya, 2005). This pattern has, however, been reversed in recent years. The share of resources going to the upazila level and below has declined from 60 per cent in 2002 to 51 per cent in 2004 and further to 42 per cent in 2006 (MOHFW 2008).

Over the years, private sector financing of health expenditure has been dominated by household OPP spending. It has ranged from 83 per cent to 89 per cent during the 1997 to 2015 period. The pattern of public expenditure on health and related information can be seen in Tables 4.12 and 4.13. Table 4.12 shows that total health expenditure as a share of GDP in Bangladesh is one of the lowest in the SAARC countries. Further, public health expenditure as percentage of total health expenditure in Bangladesh is also low and declining.

4.4.2.2 Out-of-pocket Payments

Out-of-pocket payments (OPPs) are direct payments by individuals to healthcare providers at the time of service use. This excludes any prepayment for health services, for example, in the form of specific insurance premiums or contributions and, where possible, net of any reimbursements to the individual who made the payments. OPPs are part of the health financing landscape in all countries including Bangladesh. Table 4.13 shows that household OPP is around 60 per cent in Bangladesh and shows a rising trend.

Table 4.12 Health expenditure in Bangladesh

	1997	*2000*	*2005*	*2010*	*2015*
Total health expenditure, % of GDP	2.27	2.35	2.70	3.08	2.98
Public health expenditure, % of GDP	0.83	0.77	0.72	0.79	0.68
Private health expenditure, % of GDP	1.44	1.58	1.98	2.30	2.31
Per capita total health expenditure, at constant Tk.	1038	1189	1617	2343	2882
Per capita total health expenditure, at current US$	9	10	14	24	37
	2004	**2007**	**2010**	**2012**	**2014**
Total health expenditure as % of GDP in SAARC countries					
Afghanistan	8.8	6.7	9.2	8.5	8.2
Bangladesh	2.6	2.8	3.1	3.1	2.8
Bhutan	4.4	5.9	5.2	3.7	3.6
India	4.2	4.2	4.3	4.4	4.7
Maldives	5.9	6.6	7.9	9.2	13.7
Nepal	5.8	5.8	6.4	5.9	5.8
Pakistan	2.6	3.4	3.0	2.8	2.6
Sri Lanka	4.3	3.8	3.4	3.2	3.5
Public health expenditure as % of total health expenditure in SAARC countries					
Afghanistan	11	8	31	34	36
Bangladesh	40	35	34	32	28
Bhutan	72	87	88	73	73
India	24	26	27	27	30
Maldives	66	69	67	71	78
Nepal	27	39	45	42	40
Pakistan	26	24	32	37	35
Sri Lanka	47	49	45	38	56

Source: MOHFW 2018, Bangladesh National Health Accounts 1997–2015; Global Health Expenditure Database, WHO website

Household OPP on healthcare is normally seen as a burden on households in a developing country like Bangladesh, especially when the share of household OPP is on the rise. Thus a close review of OPP by economic quantile may be warranted to explore whether the burden of OPP lies on the poor or the share of OPP is rising due to increasing healthcare expenditures by the rich. A quintile analysis of healthcare expenditure using Household Income and Expenditure Survey 2010 (HIES 2010) data shows that the spending of the richest 20 per cent of the population accounts for the major share of OPP in both urban and rural areas (Table 4.14).

Table 4.13 Household OPP as percentage of total health expenditure in SAARC countries

	2004	*2007*	*2010*	*2012*	*2014*
Afghanistan	89	92	69	65	64
Bangladesh	58	61	61	63	67
Bhutan	28	13	11	26	25
India	68	65	63	65	62
Maldives	23	23	27	24	18
Nepal	55	50	45	46	48
Pakistan	61	68	61	55	56
Sri Lanka	44	42	45	49	42

Source: Global Health Expenditure Database, WHO website

Evidence suggests that increased allocation of public funds to the health sector leads to a decrease in OPP health expenditure as well as catastrophic OPP health spending (WHO 2016). Thus, insufficient public health financing over the years may be a major driver for high levels of OPP health spending in Bangladesh. This shows the urgency with which policy makers should increase public healthcare funding and provide social health protection plan against informal OPP health payments in order to provide financial risk protection which is currently absent among the poor households in the country. A pro-poor policy reform with improved quality of care, availability of essential medicines and equitable distribution of health workers will improve the coverage and utilisation of healthcare services for the poor and most vulnerable households.

4.4.3 *Progress in Health Status*

4.4.3.1 Trends in Health and Nutritional Status

Bangladesh has made significant progress in improving the health status of its people since independence. During the 1980s, the crude death rate (CDR) remained somewhat static but it started to come down afterwards. The CDR has nearly been less than halved in about two and a half decade since 1990—from 11.3 in 1990 to 5.1 in 2017 (Table 4.15). However, as in most aspects of standard of living, rural people lag behind their urban counterparts in health as well, and rural CDR remains consistently higher than in the urban areas.

Table 4.14 Household consumption and out-of-pocket healthcare expenditure by quintiles

Quintile	*Urban*			*Rural*		
	Annual household consumption expenditure, million Tk.	***Annual household OPP health expenditure, million Tk.***	***OPP as % of annual household consumption***	***Annual household consumption expenditure, million Tk.***	***Annual household OPP health expenditure, million Tk.***	***OPP as % of annual household consumption***
Quintile 1 — Poorest 20%	131,792	2962	2.25	272,506	7304	2.68
Quintile 2	197,813	4353	2.20	376,727	10,405	2.76
Quintile 3	261,416	5730	2.19	472,459	16,316	3.45
Quintile 4	368,690	9800	2.66	608,270	22,990	3.78
Quintile 4—Richest 20%	739,235	29,177	3.95	1,081,430	48,017	4.44
Total	1,698,950	52,022	3.06	2,811,390	133,213	4.74

Source: MOHFW, Bangladesh National Health Accounts 1997–2015

Table 4.15 Trends in mortality and life expectancy in Bangladesh

	Crude death rate, per 1000 people			*Life expectancy at birth, years*		
	National	*Rural*	*Urban*	*Total*	*Male*	*Female*
1960	20.3	...	...	45.8	46.1	44.6
1970	18.9	...	...	47.5	47.7	46.2
1980	14.2	...	...	53.5	53.4	52.4
1990	10.3	11.3	7.5	58.4	58.2	58.2
2000	6.9	7.1	4.2	65.5	65.0	66.0
2010	5.6	5.9	4.9	70.2	68.7	71.3
2015	5.2	5.8	4.6	72.2	70.0	73.3
2017	5.1	5.7	4.2	72.8	70.4	74.0

Source: Estimates Developed by the UN Inter-agency Group for Child Mortality Estimation (UNICEF, WHO, World Bank, UN DESA Population Division)

The changes in life expectations at birth depict a similar story. Since independence, life expectancy at birth in Bangladesh has increased by more than 25 years— going up from 47.5 years in 1970 to nearly 73 years in 2017. The urban population has had a distinct advantage over their rural counterparts in terms of living longer, but the advantage has declined over time.

The overall decline in mortality and the resulting increase in life expectancy is perhaps more influenced by the impressive decline in infant and child mortality in Bangladesh. The infant mortality rate (IMR) in Bangladesh was reported at 170 per 1000 live births in 1960; it was estimated at 162.6 in 1971. The IMR started to decline in the 1980s—coming down from 130.6 per thousand live births in 1980 to 97.7 in 1990, and the rate of decline further accelerated afterwards. Over the last two decades, IMR has less than halved—from 62.4 per thousand in 2000 to around 26 in 2018.

The decline in under-5 mortality (child mortality) rate during the same period is probably more impressive—falling from 243.2 per 1000 live births in 1971 to 31.5 in 2018 (Table 4.16). The rural areas always have higher IMR than in urban areas, but the rural-urban gap has narrowed over time. Improvements in child health, widespread child immunisation along with use of oral rehydration therapy against diarrhoeal diseases have contributed towards bringing about this remarkable improvement in child mortality throughout the country.

Table 4.16 Infant and under-5 mortality rates in Bangladesh

	Infant mortality rate, per 1000 live births			*Under-5 mortality rate, per 1000 live births, national*
	Total	*Male*	*Female*	
1960	173.6	NA	NA	260.2
1970	148.9	NA	NA	223.1
1980	133.6	NA	NA	198.7
1990	99.6	106.6	92.2	143.7
2000	63.9	68.1	59.5	87.3
2010	38.9	41.4	36.2	49.1
2015	29.6	31.5	27.6	36.1
2018	25.1	26.9	23.3	30.2

Source: Estimates Developed by the UN Inter-agency Group for Child Mortality Estimation (UNICEF, WHO, World Bank, UN DESA Population Division)

Table 4.17 Neo-natal mortality and probability of dying at age 5–14 in Bangladesh

	Neo-natal mortality, per 1000 live births	*Probability of dying at age 5–14 years (per 1000 children age 5)*
1960	102.5	NA
1970	94.1	NA
1980	86.9	NA
1990	64.1	25.6
2000	42.4	11.1
2010	27.4	9.5
2015	20.8	5.5
2018	17.1	4.1

Source: Estimates Developed by the UN Inter-agency Group for Child Mortality Estimation (UNICEF, WHO, World Bank, UN DESA Population Division)

Further, the reduction in the rural-urban gap in infant and under-5 mortality has been achieved mostly in recent years. These are phenomena of the 2000s, when a rapid convergence is observed. The convergence seems to be the outcome of a sharp decline in rural IMR since 2001 when the urban IMR has remained mostly unchanged. One can also observe a similar trend in neo-natal mortality, which has experienced a sharp fall in the rural areas but hardly declined in the urban areas (Table 4.17).

4.4.3.2 Nutrition

While improvements in mortality are quite impressive in Bangladesh, the success in overcoming the problem of malnutrition is somewhat blurred. Two major sources of child nutrition data in Bangladesh are: the Child Nutrition Surveys (CNS) of Bangladesh Bureau of Statistics (BBS) and the Bangladesh Demographic and Health Surveys (BDHS) carried out by Macro International with the help of local collaborators. The two sets of surveys differ in coverage and methodology, but they reveal similar broad trends.

The CNS shows that between 1985 and 2005, the proportion of malnourished children—as measured by the percentage of children who are underweight i.e., low weight for age—has declined from 71 per cent to 48 per cent (Table 4.18). Despite the improvement, it shows that nearly half of the country's children were malnourished in 2005. The improvements

Table 4.18 Child malnutrition in Bangladesh

	% of children aged 6–59 months		
	National	*Rural*	*Urban*
Underweight (low weight for age)			
1985	70.9	72.0	62.3
1990	65.8	66.7	62.7
1992	68.3	69.8	57.2
1995	57.4	59.3	46.3
2000	51.0	52.6	41.8
2005	47.8	50.1	38.5
Stunting (low height for age)			
1985	67.5	68.9	57.1
1990	64.6	66.7	58.3
1992	64.2	65.8	52.8
1995	51.4	52.8	42.9
2000	48.3	50.2	37.5
2005	42.4	44.9	32.5
Wasting (low weight for height)			
1985	15.3	15.4	14.0
1990	14.4	14.7	14.0
1992	16.7	16.9	15.1
1995	16.6	17.2	13.3
2000	12.0	12.2	10.9
2005	12.7	13.1	10.8

Source: BBS (2007), Table 27, p.50

during the period are mostly due to the reduction in chronic malnutrition (as measured by stunting i.e., low height for age), which has declined from 68 per cent to 42 per cent during the same period, while the prevalence of acute malnutrition (as measured by wasting i.e., low weight for height) has remained mostly unchanged—falling only marginally from 15 per cent to 13 per cent.

The BDHS data cover the period from 1997 to 2014 (Table 4.19). During the period, the proportion of underweight children went down from 56 per cent to 33 per cent—and a major reduction took place in the period after the 2000s. Further, there has been hardly any improvement in stunting (low height for age) during the period.

One worrying feature in the nutrition sector is the relatively unchanged rural-urban differential in child malnutrition over the years. Both CNS and BDHS data (Tables 4.18 and 4.19) show that while the malnutrition gap between rural and urban areas has declined a little, a substantial

Table 4.19 Recent estimates of child malnutrition in Bangladesh

	% of children aged 6–59 months		
	National	*Rural*	*Urban*
Underweight (low weight for age)			
1996–97	56.3	57.8	41.9
1999–00	47.7	49.2	39.8
2004	47.5	48.8	42.2
2007	46.3	48.1	39.7
2014	32.6	34.8	26.1
Stunting (low height for age)			
1996–97	54.6	56.2	39.4
1999–00	44.7	46.6	35.0
2004	43.0	44.3	37.6
2007	36.2	37.6	30.5
2014	36.1	37.9	30.8
Wasting (low weight for height)			
1996–97	17.7	18.2	12.8
1999–00	10.3	10.6	9.3
2004	12.8	13.2	11.5
2007	16.2	16.9	13.5
2014	14.3	15.1	12.2

Source: National Institute of Population Research and Training (NIPORT), Mitra and Associates, and ICF International. 2016. Bangladesh Demographic and Health Survey 2014. Dhaka, Bangladesh, and Rockville, Maryland, USA: NIPORT, Mitra and Associates, and ICF International

differential still persists. Children in rural Bangladesh have traditionally been at a disadvantage relative to the urban children in terms of both mortality and malnutrition. With respect to mortality decline, catching up of rural children has been quite fast—achieving near parity in recent years, but in respect of malnutrition the catching up process still remains slow.

4.4.4 *Gender Dimension in Health Status*

Behaviour has an important role in health disparities—for example, young men take greater risks, causing injury and violent death. In developed countries, women are born with an advantage—their healthy life expectancy is two years longer and their life expectancy six years longer than those of men (WHO, World Health Report 2003). This advantage is prominent in childhood—girls are more likely to survive the first five years of life than boys. For Bangladesh, the relevant question is: does this female advantage persist in Bangladesh where gender discrimination exists?

From many perspectives, women are disadvantaged with regard to health, healthcare and nutrition. Most of the evidence shows that gender inequalities have led to a systematic devaluing and neglect of women's health and nutrition in Bangladesh. The extent of progress achieved in narrowing the gender divide can be seen from Tables 4.15 and 4.16, which show the trends in sex-specific infant mortality and life expectancy. While interpreting the figures, it is important to recognise that as females have a natural biological advantage over males in terms of survival, the life outcomes should be better for females compared with males provided they are treated equally with respect to health and nutritional care. This is reflected to some extent in infant mortality, which shows that mortality in the first year of life was lower for female children than male children in the early 1990s. As overall mortality has declined over the years, male infants have gradually been able to overcome their natural disadvantage so that the gap between male and female infant mortality has narrowed down consistently.

In contrast to infant mortality, life expectancy reveals lower achievement for females in the 1990s, indicating a distinctly inferior survival outcome for females despite having a natural biological advantage over males. This disjuncture between potential and actual differential in female and male life expectancy is suggestive of gender discrimination against women in post-infancy period. But this unnatural trend has been reversed and, by the 2000s, female shortfall in life expectancy has almost disappeared, and by 2010 females have emerged with a lead of more than 2 years. However, since the actual lead is much lower than the potential (six years), this suggests that gender discrimination in terms of health and nutritional care still persists in Bangladesh.

It can be seen that discrimination against females start quite early in life. Table 4.20 divides childhood mortality into several time-spans — neonatal mortality (within first month of life); post-neonatal mortality (after first month but within first year of life); infant mortality (within first year of life); child mortality (between end of first year and end of fifth year of life); and under-five mortality (mortality within first five years of life).

As expected, neonatal mortality is higher among boys than girls as by nature from the time of conception, boy babies are more vulnerable than girl babies. All other mortality rates, except neonatal mortality, are higher for girls than for boys. In general, the results indicate both higher post-neonatal and child mortality for girls than for boys—a pattern that is observed in other countries of South Asia as well where strong son preference is thought to result in relative nutritional and medical neglect of girl children (Das Gupta 1987; Basu 1989). The 2014 BDHS indicates that under-5 mortality is 9 per cent higher in girls than boys (48 deaths and 44

Table 4.20 Gender disparity in child mortality

	Mortality rate per 1000 live births				
	Neonatal	*Post-neonatal*	*Infant*	*Child*	*Under-5*
1993–94					
Male	71	37	107	47	149
Female	56	38	93	62	150
2001					
Male	52	23	75	23	96
Female	42	26	67	29	94
2007					
Male	42	19	61	16	76
Female	36	17	54	20	72
2014					
Male	31	6	37	8	44
Female	26	14	39	9	48

Note: Neonatal, post-neonatal, infant, child, and under-5 mortality rates for the 5-year period preceding the survey

Source: NIPORT, Mitra & associates and Macro International (1994, 2003, 2009, 2014)

deaths per 1000 live births respectively). The above shows that, soon after the first month of life the girl's advantage begins to erode, with the result that the male-female gap is much lower in terms of post-neonatal mortality (and infant mortality) compared with neonatal mortality. However, what is more revealing is child mortality i.e. death after the first year of life up to the end of the fifth year. The evidence is thus clear that the female child is discriminated against soon after she is born; but the intensity of gender discrimination is declining over time.

4.4.4.1 Gender Disparity in Nutritional Status

Nutritional status is the result of complex interactions between food consumption, overall health status, and care practices. Adequate nutrition is a prerequisite for attaining good health, quality of life, and high productivity. Although poor nutrition affects the entire population, women and children are especially vulnerable because of their unique physiology and socioeconomic characteristics. The period from birth to age two is crucial for optimal growth, health, and development. In Bangladesh, this period is often characterised by protein-energy and micronutrient deficiencies that interfere with optimal physical growth and cognitive development. Malnourished children have lower resistance to infection and are more likely to die from common childhood ailments, such as diarrheal diseases and respiratory infections (Black et al. 2008).

Malnutrition in adults results in reduced productivity, increased susceptibility to infections, slow recovery from illness, and for women, increased risk of adverse pregnancy outcomes (Victor et al. 2008). A woman of poor nutritional status—indicated by a low body mass index (BMI), short stature, anemia, or other micronutrient deficiencies—has a heightened risk of obstructed labour, having a baby with low birth weight, producing low quality breast milk, and dying from postpartum hemorrhage. Morbidity, in general, is also high for both the woman and her baby. Effects of undernutrition are passed from one generation to the next, as undernourished girls tend to become short adults and thus are more likely to have small children (Victor et al. 2008).

Poor nutritional status is one of the most important health problems in Bangladesh. Young children and women of reproductive age are especially vulnerable to nutritional deficits and micronutrient deficiencies. At the individual level, inadequate or inappropriate feeding patterns lead to malnutrition. Numerous socioeconomic and cultural factors influence patterns of feeding and nutritional status. Overweight and obesity is also a

Table 4.21 Gender disparity in nutritional status of children

	% of children aged 6–59 months					
	Underweight (low weight for age)		***Stunting (low height for age)***		***Wasting (low weight for height)***	
	Girls	*Boys*	*Girls*	*Boys*	*Girls*	*Boys*
1996–97	58.0	54.6	55.0	54.3	16.8	18.6
1999–00	49.6	45.8	45.8	43.6	10.1	10.6
2004	48.7	46.4	43.5	42.5	12.5	13.2
2007	48.6	44.1	36.7	35.6	16.0	16.5
2014	33.1	32.2	35.4	36.7	13.6	15.0

Source: NIPORT, Mitra & associates and Macro International (1994, 2003, 2009, 2014)

growing concern in Bangladesh. Overweight individuals are predisposed to a wide range of health problems such as diabetes and heart disease as well as poor birth outcomes for women. Maternal overweight and obesity at the time of pregnancy increases the risk for childhood obesity that continues into adolescence and early adulthood, with the potential to transmit obesity to the next generation (Black et al. 2013).

The gender differential in nutritional status of children is shown in Table 4.21. These data show some degree of female disadvantage in terms of underweight (low weight for age) measure. However, the picture is not very clear in terms of stunting (low height for age), which is a better indicator of chronic deprivation.

Thus, both mortality and nutritional status indicators suggest that gender discrimination against female child is still present in Bangladesh, although the degree of discrimination is declining over time.

4.4.4.2 Maternal Mortality

Another important aspect of gender dimension in health is maternal mortality, which is affected both by the nutritional input and healthcare experiences over a woman's life span and by the quality of maternal care taken during pregnancy. Maternal mortality refers to deaths due to complications from pregnancy or childbirth. According to UN estimates, from 1990 to 2015, the global maternal mortality ratio (MMR) has declined by 44 per cent—from 385 deaths to 216 deaths per 100,000 live births.

Almost all maternal deaths can be prevented, as revealed by the lifetime risk of maternal death in high income countries of 1 in 3300, compared with 1 in 41 in low income countries.

Due to life-long gender discrimination and lack of modern maternal care, the women in Bangladesh suffer from a high maternal mortality (Table 4.22). Although the MMR is declining, the rate is rather slow. The current MMR of 181 (in 2015) is still high and the target under the 4th Health, Population and Nutrition Sector Programme, 2017–2022 is to attain an MMR of 105 per 100,000 live births in 2022. Because of constraints in data availability on MMR over time, it is not possible to assess how progress has been distributed across income groups or between rural and urban areas. However, it is reported that inequalities exist between income quintiles and place of residences. 'National as well as community-level data also show substantial use-inequities in maternal health services by asset quintiles, education, distance to facility and place of residences' (UNESCAP 2008).

Overall, it is seen that gender inequalities of health in Bangladesh are declining. The fact is that the health hazards are present at every stage of a woman's life cycle. Health problems which pose the greatest hardship to women in Bangladesh include: reproductive health problems, excess female mortality in childhood, violence against girls and women, occupational and environmental hazards, and cervical and breast cancer. Many of these lead to maternal mortality which is one of the most important indicators of women's health.

Gender inequalities of health originate in the Bangladesh society from the definitions of health status and medical practices, which reflect the

Table 4.22 Maternal mortality ratio in Bangladesh

	Deaths per 100,000 live births		
	National	*Rural*	*Urban*
1986	650	NA	NA
1991	472	484	402
2000	316	329	261
2010	216	230	178
2015	181	191	162
2017	173	NA	NA

Source: UNESCAP using BBS data from the Vital Registration System, in World Bank, 2007

subordinate social status of women. Gender inequalities in health are manifested in medical practices which attribute women's illnesses to behavioural lapses by women and differential access to and utilisation of modern healthcare services by women and girls, including maternal care, general healthcare, family planning and safe abortion services.

Reasons for gender inequalities in health include—emphasis on women's childbearing roles resulting in early childbearing; sex preference manifested in discrimination against female children in health and general care; women's workloads which not only expose them to health hazards but also make it difficult for them to take time off for healthcare; lack of autonomy by women leading to lack of decision-making power and access to independent income; early marriage which exposes women to the complications of early childbearing. Gender inequality in health is one of the social dimensions in which gender inequality is manifested in Bangladesh, and hence efforts to eradicate gender inequalities in health must include ways to improve the status of women in the households and society.

4.4.4.3 *Assessment of Progress*

The above analysis shows that Bangladesh has made great progress in improving the health status of the people during the last five decades after independence. Indeed, Bangladesh's achievements in the social sector, including the health sector, are widely acclaimed as exceptional across countries at comparable levels of development (see Mujeri and Sen 2006). The success no doubt is a move in the right direction.

However, along with speedy improvement in the overall health of the people, there are several other considerations that are also important for creating an inclusive and equitable society. These include equity and non-discrimination, participation of the people in all relevant health related decisions, and effective accountability mechanisms for delivering health services to the people, especially the poor and disadvantaged sections in society.

4.4.4.4 *Equity in Healthcare Services*

The concept of equity has many dimensions. For example, the gender dimension of health equity shows that, despite considerable progress, gender discrimination still persists in the health sector. The relative neglect of the girl child and adult women is still a matter of concern in the health scene of Bangladesh.

However, a more significant inequity that persists in the health sector is the inequality between the rich and the poor (see Gwatkin et al., 2000, Gwatkin et al. 2007; Ensor et al. 2002; Chowdhury and Osmani 2010). There is evidence that inequity exists both in the provision of and access to healthcare as well as in health outcomes. Table 4.23 shows that the degree of undernutrition for children from the lowest wealth quintile is more than two-and-a-half times as high as that for children from the highest wealth quintile. One would, of course, expect the poorer children to suffer more from lack of nutrition than the richer ones, but what is especially important to note is that the differential has increased since the mid-1990s. The relative position of the poorest children has also become worse in terms of stunting. While the extent of both underweight and stunted children has declined for both groups of children as a part of overall progress of the health sector, it has declined faster for the highest wealth quintile, so that the differential has increased over time. This shows that progress in the health sector is associated with persistent inequity.

A similar picture emerges for child mortality and morbidity. As in the case of undernutrition, the mortality levels of children from the poorest quintile is almost double that of the richest quintile (Table 4.24). Again, although both infant and under-five mortality have declined for all groups

Table 4.23 Rich-poor differential in children's nutritional status

	% of children aged 6–59 months	
	1996–97	*2014*
Underweight		
Lowest wealth quintile	65.2	45.1
Highest wealth quintile	37.6	17.4
Ratio (lowest to highest quintile)	1.7	2.6
Stunting		
Lowest wealth quintile	61.4	49.2
Highest wealth quintile	34.8	19.4
Ratio (lowest to highest quintile)	1.8	2.5
Wasting		
Lowest wealth quintile	NA	17.1
Highest wealth quintile	NA	11.7
Ratio (lowest to highest quintile)	NA	1.5

Source: Gwatkin et al. 2007 for 1996–97; NIPORT, Mitra & Associates and Macro International 2014 for 2014

Table 4.24 Inequity in child mortality and morbidity

	among children under age 5	
	1996–97	*2014*
Infant mortality		
Lowest wealth quintile	97	43
Highest wealth quintile	57	24
Ratio (lowest to highest quintile)	1.7	1.8
Under-5 mortality		
Lowest wealth quintile	141	53
Highest wealth quintile	76	30
Ratio (lowest to highest quintile)	1.9	1.8
Prevalence of fever		
Lowest wealth quintile	31.6	36.6
Highest wealth quintile	30.0	32.1
Ratio (lowest to highest quintile)	1.1	1.1
Prevalence of diarrhoea		
Lowest wealth quintile	8.8	37.0
Highest wealth quintile	6.4	25.5
Ratio (lowest to highest quintile)	1.4	1.5
Prevalence of acute respiratory infection (ARI)		
Lowest wealth quintile	12.7	6.8
Highest wealth quintile	10.6	3.5
Ratio (lowest to highest quintile)	1.2	1.9

Source: NIPORT, Mitra & Associates and Macro International 1997, 2014

of people, but the differential between the poorest and richest quintiles has remained mostly unchanged. As for morbidity, for three most common childhood diseases in Bangladesh—common fever, diarrhoea, and acute respiratory infection (ARI)— the incidence is consistently higher for children from the lowest wealth quintile. Further, no systematic decline is observed in the prevalence of these diseases since the mid-1990s (except in the case of ARI).

Further, a growing inequity in women's health is observed between the rich and the poor (Table 4.25). It shows that the women from the lowest wealth quintile suffer from more malnutrition (with BMI less than 18.5) than their highest wealth counterparts; and the differential is rising over time. In 1996–97, the extent of malnutrition among women in the lowest wealth quintile was twice as high as that of women in the highest wealth quintile; but the gap has increased by 4.6 times in 2014.

Table 4.25 Rich-poor differential in women's nutritional status

	% of ever-married women age 15–49 with undernutrition (BMI< 18.5)			
	1996–97	*2004*	*2007*	*2014*
Lowest wealth quintile	64.5	46.1	43.4	32.2
Highest wealth quintile	32.6	16.7	13.4	7.0
Ratio (lowest to highest quintile)	2.0	2.8	3.2	4.6

Note: The body mass index (BMI) is expressed as the ratio of weight in kilograms to the square of height in meters (kg/m2)

Source: NIPORT, Mitra & Associates and Macro International 1997, 2014

It is observed that inequity is widening not just in terms of health outcomes but also in terms of accessing healthcare services (Chowdhury and Osmani 2010). It is natural that the provision of healthcare by the private sector will be inequitable in the unequal society of Bangladesh, but the concern for Bangladesh is to develop the public health facilities in a manner in which the poor can have equitable access and from which they can benefit. In Bangladesh, public health facilities are either free or heavily subsidised; and are designed to serve as the main vehicle through which the poorer segment in the society can access healthcare services.

There exist a number of problems in the public healthcare facilities. Although these facilities are supposed to provide most services free of charge, in reality they are not free for the poor patients; they have to make various kinds of unofficial and informal payments. Further, absenteeism is high in public facilities and the opportunity of government doctors to do private practice makes the matter worse. There is also non-availability of essential drugs and equipment. A review of HPSP finds that only one in five persons using government health services receives all prescribed medicines (CIET 2001). As a consequence, there exists a poor rate of utilisation of public health facilities. The poorly functioning public health facilities hurt the poor, as they tend to avail these services more than the rest of the population.

4.4.5 *Issues in Healthcare Services*

Bangladesh suffers from both a shortage of and geographic mal-distribution of human resources for health (HRH). Health workers are concentrated in urban secondary and tertiary hospitals, although 70 per cent of the population lives in rural areas (GHWA 2008). Major challenges include: an overly- centralised health system, weak governance structure and regulatory framework, weak management and institutional capacity in the Ministry of Health and Family Welfare (MOHFW), fragmented public service delivery, inefficient allocation of public resources, lack of regulation of the private sector—which employs 58 per cent of all physicians, shortage of HRH, high turnover and absenteeism of health workers, and poor maintenance of health facilities and medical equipment.

Despite these challenges and the fact that HRH is not considered a priority in the sector programmes, there have been recent successes including: increase in the number of graduates and health worker training facilities, and an increased number of rural health facilities. The MOHFW has prepared its new sector programme—the Health, Population and Nutrition Sector Development Programme (HPNSDP) and has adopted the National Health Policy, based on lessons learned from previous programmes. Goals include: developing an HRH plan, creating a functional HRH Information System (HRIS), scaling up the production of critical health workers, introducing incentive packages to deploy and retain critical health workers in remote and rural areas, addressing the challenge of skilled birth attendance by training community-based SBAs and/or nurse-midwives and family welfare visitors, and streamlining the recruitment and promotion of nurses (World Bank 2011).

To be effective, health services should be available, accessible and affordable. Mere availability of health facilities does not result in their utilisation. Accessibility has a number of key dimensions (Osmani, 2003). These include: (i) physical accessibility (e.g. distance, travel time and travel costs); (ii) economic accessibility (e.g. cost of medicine, cost of consultation, cost of hospitalisation, cost incurred with respect to tests/investigations); (iii) social and cultural context (gender) affecting accessibility; and (iv) perceived quality of services including availability of doctors, availability of medicine and attitudes of doctors/nurses.

Now is the time to realise that achieving universal healthcare (UHC) in Bangladesh is not an impossible dream. The need is to ensure:

- **Insightful leadership:** Health sector reform is a crucial step in providing wide-scale services. This requires diverting resources to the health sector, building a strong base of human resources, seeking international accreditation, and creating a sustainable and equitable funding pool for healthcare.

- **An operational agenda:** This should adequately prioritise the agenda based on Bangladesh's disease profile, demographic considerations and epidemics.
- **Private sector involvement:** Based on the out-of-pocket spending rates, it is realistic that the private sector should play a positive role by increasing the funding pool for the health agenda. This can be achieved in two ways: first, with the 'competition and choice' idea, where national and private hospitals offer the same, efficient service, giving patients the ability to choose which to go to; second, with 'complementary actions', where private sector hospitals take on advanced health interventions that state hospitals cannot perform. Banks, private companies and pharmaceutical industries can participate in lifting the overall health quality.
- **Advocacy and civil society involvement:** It is socially unacceptable to see the poor people suffer due to insufficient healthcare. There is a need for advocating for equality in health rights.
- **Monitoring and evaluation:** The metric of progress would be based on health outcomes and out-of-pocket expenditure such that the government and the health system can be held to account. Effective evaluation tools of successes and failures will guarantee resources are not wasted, and will contribute to the progression of a successful, inclusive healthcare system in Bangladesh.

4.4.6 Conclusions

No doubt, Bangladesh has made impressive strides in improving the health status of its people over the last 50 years since independence. This is especially true for child mortality and morbidity and women's reproductive health—leading to a sharp fall in fertility. The achievements of Bangladesh with respect to mortality and fertility are widely hailed by the international community as exceptional for its level of economic and social development. Mortality decline is still continuing without much interruption after the 2000s, but progress in nutritional improvements especially of children and mothers has been slow in the recent period. Similarly, fertility decline stalled for a long time till the end of the 1990s.

An important factor behind the slowdowns is the exhaustion of the avenues for easy and quick gains over the last few decades—such as by launching massive campaigns for immunisation, safe water, and contraception. The health status in Bangladesh has now reached a stage where further gains can only be made by reorienting the strategy such that matching resources are available to reach specific goals in the most efficient manner. This would require targeted focus on those segments of the population who have gained relatively less from the health progress of the last five decades, which in turn would call for participatory planning at both local and national levels involving the disadvantaged groups, and strengthening the voice and accountability mechanisms.

As the analysis in this chapter suggests, despite impressive gains in the health sector, the health system of Bangladesh is characterised by many features that militate against the rights-based approach to health. For example, discrimination against the girl child in particular and women in general is still a problem even though the gender gap in health and nutrition has narrowed down significantly over the years; but the health system remains stubbornly biased against the poorer segments of the population, and in some cases, the bias has even become more pronounced, partly because the relative roles of public and private provision have been reversed reducing the relative importance of public facilities to which the poorer people tend to turn more for their healthcare needs, and partly because numerous inadequacies and distortions have compromised the potential equity of the public health system.

In addition, since health status does not depend on health interventions alone, promotion of other health related interventions must also be involved in the process of promoting the right to health. A person's health is a joint outcome of a multiplicity of causal influences; and interventions on different fronts are needed if the right to health is to be fulfilled. For example, education, especially health and nutrition education particularly for women, is especially important as the status of children's health is systematically related to mother's education. Mothers' own health and nutritional status is also instrumental for child health, in addition to being important for women themselves. Since mothers' health is itself a function of women's empowerment, these relationships suggest that the fulfillment of all kinds of rights that enhance women's empowerment is also causally important for the health of a nation, not just for women's health.

The vision of the government includes ensuring optimum nutrition and healthcare services as well as aligning the sector as a fundamental component of human and economic development. Bangladesh has made tremendous strides in different health indicators like survival of child, immunisation, and tuberculosis control. Despite its resource constraints, Bangladesh has successfully evolved a pluralistic healthcare system that combines the technology in healthcare with a focus on women's participation in its health indicators such as family planning, immunisation, oral rehydration therapy, and vitamin supplements. Bangladesh's healthcare system has also successfully addressed the first generation of poverty-linked infections, and nutrition and maternity related diseases.

As a mean to minimise the financial burden of the people, the government is examining ways to adopt a universal medical health insurance. The government aims to achieve universal health coverage by 2023 that will pay 70 per cent of the medical expenses.

There are two sides to the access problem in healthcare. On the supply side, good quality, effective healthcare is not offered. On the demand side, individuals do not utilise services from which they could benefit. The two are obviously related. Poor quality care will arouse little interest from the public. A high level of demand, made effective by purchasing power, will induce the provision of quality care. Solving the access problem requires tackling both demand and supply side issues. There is an urgent need to establish mechanisms that can increase the availability and improve the quality of healthcare in Bangladesh.

It is often seen that public healthcare interventions are underutilised in Bangladesh, and income-related disparities in use are large. The causes of the problem are diverse including insufficient system resources; inappropriate allocation of resources across different levels of care, programmes, and regions; inadequate quality; insufficient household incomes; lack of access to credit; prohibitive charges (formal and informal); travel costs; cultural barriers to the acceptability of services; and misperceptions of illness and the effectiveness of care. Solutions, at a general level, must address one or more of these causes. The difficulty lies in the design of detailed policy initiatives that tackle root problems within usually severe economic, institutional, and political constraints.

Solutions to the access problem need to be developed at a general strategic level, but more crucially at the level of detailed policy measures. There is consensus support for universal access to essential services, priority to services close to the community but with measures to improve the quality of care, strengthening of the stewardship role of the state, targeting of diseases of poverty, and more effective protection of the poor from user charges.

Under the rapidly changing socioeconomic conditions in Bangladesh, many of the existing business models for accessing health services might not suffice in the future. In order to maintain sustainability, health supply must adapt to market forces, technological transformation and digital innovation. Apart from these, the government needs to account that a large proportion of the population is unable to receive proper medication and requires the access to healthcare services.

While there is some consensus on the general lines of a strategy for improving access to healthcare, details of the precise policy measures required to implement such a strategy are more difficult to identify. A general strategy can be defined at the national level, while policy measures should be heterogeneous, varying with the local conditions in which they are implemented.

Community financing, microcredit schemes, entitlement cards, vouchers, and conditional cash transfers have all been demonstrated to raise healthcare utilisation in many developing countries. But their application is still very limited in Bangladesh, both geographically and with respect to the services covered. The common characteristic of these initiatives is that they work through demand side economic incentives. Community financing and fee waivers implemented through health cards remove, or at least reduce, the constraints of income and price. Microcredit schemes relax the income constraint from current to lifetime income. Vouchers reduce the price constraint on demand. Conditional cash transfers provide a positive financial incentive to consume healthcare interventions. Community financing, microcredit, and fee waivers provide different degrees of insurance against unforeseen expenditures, although the nature of the risk pooling is different in each case. Community financing and microcredit, with relatively small risk/saving pools may find it difficult to cover against high cost interventions.

Health cards and targeted health insurance are financed at the national level and can cover such risks. Vouchers and conditional cash transfers are essentially price incentives to induce demand for preventive care for which there is a predictable, easily verifiable need. There may be scope for extending the use of vouchers to low cost, high frequency curative care, such as primary care for small children. Further consideration should be given to the combination of these instruments to cover different needs for preventive and curative, predictable and unpredictable, and high and low cost care.

One must also recognise that the evidence base on the effectiveness of these initiatives still remains thin. Therefore, implementation should be accompanied by evaluation for at least two reasons. First, post-evaluation, since the design of a scheme can be modified by the effort to improve effectiveness. Second, such evaluation provides lessons for implementation in different contexts.

In Bangladesh, the dream of equitable and affordable healthcare is a dream of justice. Falling ill is a weakening situation that all of us go through, but illness in the context of poverty is disastrous. A functional universal healthcare system in Bangladesh can prevent the death of thousands, alleviate the pain of millions, and provide justice to countless families.

4.5 Women Empowerment

The integration of women into the development process and their participation in economic activities facilitate women's access to physical resources such as food, land, income and other forms of wealth; and social resources such as knowledge, power, participation and prestige within the family and the community. Education, for example, enables women to assume more autonomy or power both in traditional gender-stratified family setting and in more egalitarian ones, giving them greater control over their own lives and stronger voice in matters affecting themselves and their families.

It is a well- established fact that in a patriarchal society like Bangladesh, women are ascribed a lower status than men who have the sovereign power to control households and society, while women are often isolated in their homes. In Bangladesh, women have a limited role in household decision-making, limited access and control over household resources (physical and financial), low level of individual assets, heavy domestic workloads, restricted mobility and inadequate knowledge and skills that lead to their extreme vulnerability. The status of women in Bangladesh is ranked among the lowest in the world on the basis of multiple indicators related to health, marriage, children, education, employment and social equality.

Women's economic participation and empowerment are fundamental to strengthening women's rights and enabling women to have control over their lives and exert influence in society. It is about creating just and equitable societies. In Bangladesh, women often face discrimination and persistent gender inequalities, with some women experiencing multiple discrimination and exclusion.

Thus in Bangladesh society, women empowerment is seen not only as an extrinsic control over resources (human, financial, intellectual, and others), but also as a growing intrinsic capability, seen through greater self-confidence and an inner transformation of women's consciousness that enables them to overcome external barriers.

4.5.1 Conceptual Issues in Empowerment

The basis of empowerment is an unequal distribution of power which results in a situation in which some people have power while others experience powerlessness. Power may emerge from different sources, such as personality, organisation, property, wealth, social class and other socioeconomic or other constructs (Lord and Hutchison 1993). Some argue that empowerment is a relational construct that creates dependency or interdependency relationship among people. Empowerment is when the diversity of power is redistributed and decreased. In this sense, to empower is to delegate sources of power to people (Conger and Kanungo 1988).

Sen (1993) notes that empowerment is reflected in a person's capability set and capability depends on many factors including personal characteristics of a person, proper food, good health, good shelter, and social arrangements. Empowerment is a process that follows a series of steps sequentially in which ownership of one type of power increases the ability to exercise other forms of power. This creates a positive 'power spiral' (Allsopp and Tallontire 2015).

Thus, when unequal power distribution exists in a society (such as, between women and men in Bangladesh) women empowerment programmes should start with outlining the power relations among men and women and their possibilities to participate and benefit from the interventions. For success, one needs to understand the women's life worlds so that the changes in power distribution and the motivation to influence are accepted by and convenient to women. Important issues to analyse, for example, are what aspects of women's life worlds influence their possibilities to participate and benefit from these programmes and what the needs are of the programme's target groups. Also, one must follow up the programmes as the conditions, under which it is implemented and developed, change.

Women empowerment is a necessity for the development of any society, since it enhances both the quality and the quantity of human resources available for development. Empowerment is one of the main procedural concerns when addressing human rights and development. Women empowerment and gender equality is critical for Bangladesh to ensure sustainable development of the country. It is widely recognised across the world that sustainable development can be ensured through gender equality and women empowerment. Sustainable development requires environmental protection as well as social and economic development; and without women empowerment, they are unlikely to achieve their full participation in the process of development. Without gender equality and empowerment, women would not be able to benefit from or contribute to the development of the country.

Economic empowerment increases women's agency, access to formal government programmes, mobility outside home, economic independence, and purchasing power. Strengthening women's access to property inheritance and land rights is another way of economically empowering women. This allows them better means of asset accumulation, capital, and bargaining power needed to address gender inequalities. Often, women are legally restricted from their land on the sole basis of gender. Having a right to their land gives women bargaining power that they wouldn't normally have; in turn, they gain more opportunities for economic independence and accessing formal financial institutions.

Women empowerment and improvement of their political, social, economic status is an important end in itself; essential for sustainable development of Bangladesh. The full participation and partnership of both women and men is required in productive and reproductive life, including shared responsibilities for the care and nurturing of children and maintenance of the household. In Bangladesh, women traditionally face threats to their lives, health and well-being as a result of being overburdened with work and of their lack of power and influence.

Clearly observable dimensions of women empowerment are women's absolute well-being and women's relative well-being. For absolute well-being, women's empowerment is considered as the process of improving the success of women which is indicated by outcomes that measure current status regarding literacy, good health and nutrition, labour force participation, mobility and ownership of assets. For relative well-being, women's empowerment is observed as the process of improving the position of women relative to men within the household which is indicated by women's involvement in the household process such as decision-making, control over household income, assets and loans taken. Women empowerment begins when they become aware of the socio-psycho-cultural inequity imposed on them and how imbalance and socio-cultural, economic and political forces adversely affect them. It starts with the understanding of women's positive self-image, self-esteem, self-confidence, rights and duties, capabilities and potentialities.

The empowerment of rural women is about expanding women's assets and capabilities to participate in, negotiate with, influence, control and hold accountable the institutions that affect their lives (FAO, 2015). As women participate in microcredit organisations, they usually become more empowered and less vulnerable. Women's economic empowerment is fast becoming a key instrument in promoting their abilities to achieve their rights and well-being which successively reduces household poverty and increases economic growth, productivity and efficiency (Golla et al., 2011).

Over the years, Bangladesh has emerged as a role model in women empowerment, and the country has been experiencing appreciable changes in gender relations in the society. The country has achieved a steady progress in gender equality, which has helped Bangladesh to secure the top position in gender equality among the South Asian countries for the second consecutive year as reflected in the 2017 Gender Gap Index. The index—prepared by the World Economic Forum (WEF)—measures education, economic participation, health, and political empowerment to assess gender equality in a country. Bangladesh secured the 47th position among 144 countries in 2017 as per the Global Gender Gap Report, ahead of other South Asian countries. In this context, Bangladesh's achievement in the past decade has been remarkable in many areas, such as in reducing infant and child mortality, poverty reduction, increase in women entrepreneurship, education, health and other socioeconomic indicators.

Presumably the origin of these changes can be located in the aftermath of Bangladesh's struggle for independence in 1971, when visible ruptures to the patriarchal society emerged in the background of the crisis in social reproduction. This led both the government and the NGOs to provide attention to the plights of the poor and landless rural women, creating a space for their inclusion in both NGO programmes (e.g. group-based microcredit model) and the government's targeted social protection programmes. While non-state action and human development policies emerged out of these crisis responses, a major impact has been on women empowerment and the gains women have made during the critical juncture in gender relations in Bangladesh.

4.5.2 *Women in Bangladesh*

Women in Bangladesh are in many ways dependent on men from their early childhood. Traditionally, girls were married at an early age (the legal age at marriage has now been fixed at 18 years) and thereafter had to pursue the rules of purdah (Hartman and Boyce, 1998). Violence against women was also common. Even though the Constitution has guaranteed equal rights to women, women still suffer from discrimination and violence that occurs in home, at workplace, and communities as well. Within the household, women have less access to and control over resources and limited influence over household decisions. Beyond the household, women have limited access to communal resources, are under-represented in public decision-making bodies; have limited bargaining power in markets (such as the labour market), and often lack opportunities to improve their socioeconomic position. Therefore, efforts to reduce gender inequality are required on multiple fronts.

Bangladesh has enacted consistent policies and programmes since the 1970s to improve women's conditions and reduce gender inequality. Women's participation in the workplace, leadership role in the political and social arenas, and access to credit can be regarded as empowerment of women. Relevant policies consider women's engagement in political and economic activities as a cross-cutting issue with women empowerment as one of the main drivers of transformation.

The government policy has been to ensure women's overall development by affording them equal and active participation in the mainstream socioeconomic activities and removing various impediments to their empowerment. To expedite women's economic empowerment, comprehensive initiatives have been undertaken by providing extensive training, creating job opportunities, ensuring participation in labour market and providing support to small and medium women entrepreneurs. Extensive social safety net programmes have been undertaken to provide various kinds of allowances, such as destitute women allowance, maternity and lactating mother allowance, disabled women allowance, divorced women allowance etc. Vulnerable Group Feeding (VGF) is carried out for ensuring food security to vulnerable extreme poor women.

For the economic empowerment of rural women, collateral free micro-credit is given at subsidised rates. Women entrepreneurs receive 10 per cent of the Small Enterprise Fund (SEF) and 10 per cent of the industrial plots in industrial estates are kept reserved for women. Currently, more than 3 million women are working in the RMG sector alone. Bangladesh's women labour force has expanded rapidly: from 24 per cent in 2010 to 32 per cent in 2017. The government has been preparing gender sensitive budgets for 40 ministries since 2015.

For building an inclusive and equitable society, the government has taken an innovative initiative, called JOYEETA. This is an initiative of the Ministry of Women and Children Affairs (MoWCA) targeted to empowering rural women of Bangladesh. It is a business platform to support and facilitate the grassroots women entrepreneurs to showcase and market their own arts, crafts, products, and services. To promote the products of women entrepreneurs, an independent sales centre has been opened under the programme of Development Efforts of Women Entrepreneurship of the Department of Women Affairs. Disabled and oppressed women entrepreneurs are also provided with these facilities.

4.5.2.1 Education

Bangladesh is the first country in South Asia to achieve gender-parity in primary education. Achieving this milestone is a result of effective public policy, adequate resource allocation, and strong commitment from public and non-government sectors.

Primary education is free and compulsory for all children aged between 6 and 10. All children attending primary and secondary schools receive textbooks free of cost. The education of girls up to grade twelve in public institutions is also free. To encourage girl students to continue their studies and also to reduce the drop-out rates, stipends are awarded. This proactive strategy for girls' education has resulted in gender parity. For example, in primary schools, female enrolment is 51 per cent and in secondary schools it is 53 per cent, a sharp departure from a few years ago when male students overwhelmingly dominated the school enrollments.

4.5.2.2 Violence Against Women

In 2010, the Domestic Violence (Prevention and Protection) Act 2010 was enacted by the Parliament recognising the problem of domestic violence in Bangladesh. This Act signifies Bangladesh's fulfillment of state obligations under the Convention on the Elimination of All Forms of

Discrimination against Women (CEDAW) as well as Article 28 of the Constitution, guaranteeing special measures for the advancement of women and children. In order to effectively implement the law, the government has formulated the Domestic Violence (Prevention and Protection) Rules 2013.

Other laws enacted by the government for combating violence against women include Prevention and Restraint of Human Trafficking Act 2012 and the Pornography Control Act 2011. In addition to enactment of laws, One Stop Crisis Centres in seven divisions provide medical treatment, legal support, policy assistance and rehabilitation to the victims. DNA profiling lab and DNA screening labs have been established in several national hospitals for effective investigation of gender based offences such as rape. Further, 80 One Stop Crisis Cells are established, among them 40 in district hospitals and 20 in upazila health complexes.

4.5.2.3 Women in Different Occupations

In order to enhance women empowerment, the number of seats for women in the Parliament has been increased to 50. There has also been a continuous increase in the number of women parliamentarians elected in the national elections. To create opportunities for women's increased participation in politics, reserved seats for women in union councils, upazila parishads and municipalities have been increased to one-third of the total and women are to be directly elected to these seats. More than 12,000 women are elected as public representatives in the local government elections. Women's participation in local level elections is treated as an important milestone in Bangladesh.

The increasing number of women in the judiciary, administration, armed forces, and even in UN peacekeeping forces indicates improvement in women's empowerment. This has been possible due to a reserve quota created by the government for women employment at every level of administration to enhance women participation.

Gender perspective has also been integrated into Bangladeshi peacekeeping missions. Bangladesh is the top contributor of female police officers to the United Nations Peacekeeping Operations as Formed Police Unit. Bangladesh female peacekeepers have placed themselves as key driving force to reduce gender-based violence, conflict and confrontation, providing sense of security especially for women and children, mentoring female police officers in the local area and thus empowering women in the host country and promoting social cohesion.

The policy framework in Bangladesh highlights that the country should adopt targeted efforts at improving the conditions for women instead of relying on economic development, with its attendant rising incomes and resources, eventually leading to gender equality on its own. Rather, gender equality is considered as a prerequisite to achieving the country's development goals. To implement such policies, the government has widely used several policies for empowering women—through microfinance and cash transfer programmes given only to women, scholarships, parliamentary/government quotas aimed at increasing female participation, or laws designed to protect women's rights—which do change the way families make decisions. Compared to income or assets in the hands of men, income or assets in the hands of women is associated with larger improvements in child health, and larger expenditure shares of household nutrients, health, and housing.

4.6 Concluding Remarks

In Bangladesh, development discourse since its independence identified human and social factors as integral components of the country's development process. The grassroots experience by both the government and the NGOs after independence made it clear that development occurs more readily when the opportunities of the individuals are maximised. These opportunities evolve when individual capabilities are allowed to flourish through using their own skills, knowledge, experiences, and strengths to raise themselves to pursue a way of life and standard of living which they value. The empowerment of the individuals also enhances their abilities to interact with others in meaningful, positive and mutually beneficial ways.

In recognition and adoption of this people centred definition of development, one of the government's priority agenda since the beginning has been to remove the barriers which would otherwise prevent the citizens from pursuing their dreams with confidence and developing programmes on social protection, social safety nets, child abuse, juvenile justice, domestic violence and care for the more vulnerable including the elderly, disabled and the poor.

Women empowerment and gender equality enhance economic development, improve prospects for future generations and strengthen political and social systems. Although women now comprise about 32 per cent of Bangladesh's total labour force, they still lag behind men in terms of earnings and productivity. Women also face greater obstacles when it comes to participation in social and political institutions. The gender gap hinders economic and social development and destabilises the social environment.

Bangladesh's policy framework identifies four priority areas for improving gender equality: reducing gender gaps in human capital, specifically in female mortality and education; improving female access to education and economic opportunities; addressing women's under-representation in communities and political systems; and understanding how gender inequality applies across generations.

At present, several factors are contributing towards women empowerment and promoting gender equality in Bangladesh. Globalisation and increased access to information provide women with stronger connections to markets and economic opportunities. These factors also contribute to increasing knowledge about women's roles in other cultures throughout the world. Perhaps most importantly, there seems to be a broad understanding and growing consensus about the importance of women's economic, political, and social empowerment in the country.

One area where gender equality seems particularly important for Bangladesh is that of agricultural production and food security. Bangladesh has significant scope of improving resource access for women which would increase agricultural productivity. Improving gender equality will enhance economic production and create stronger social and political systems. Bangladesh has certainly made progress when it comes to women empowerment and gender equality. However, with more and more evidence confirming the importance of empowering women, policymakers in Bangladesh would be well served to improve women's access to healthcare, education, and economic opportunities as well as increasing female participation in social and political systems.

It is also important to recognise that, with Bangladesh's commitment to women empowerment, the state is duty-bound to ensure the normative benchmarks for gender equality in the country. These benchmarks should spell out what the government aims to achieve in the sphere of women empowerment which should be formulated and implemented in a transparent and accountable manner. At present, Bangladesh is far from achieving these benchmarks as reflected in the high level of gender inequity and wide gaps that persist in ensuring women empowerment. Moreover, the current approach to women empowerment provides singular emphasis on achieving the outcomes with little concern about the process, for example how the outcomes will be realised.

The strategy of implementing the above approach has well-defined principles such as participation, accountability, transparency, equality, non-discrimination, universality and indivisibility which will significantly facilitate achieving of the women empowerment goals in Bangladesh. Obviously, systematic obstacles such as poverty, inequality and other socioeconomic constraints arising out of existing social and gender divides stand in the way of translating women empowerment into reality in the country. However, if poverty has to be reduced and the poor women have to be empowered, the capability of the women must be enhanced. Since human rights are about development and gender disparity is a major impediment to Bangladesh's development, women empowerment has positive human rights components.

For bringing out multiple linkages between gender and empowerment, the country's policy agenda needs to go beyond the household-headship approach to address, for example, gender discrimination experienced by women even in non-poor households resulting from gender bias in the distribution of resources within households. Further, at the microeconomic level, it is important to understand the gender and age-based power relations within households, the mechanisms of cooperation and conflict including the dynamics of bargaining that shape the distribution of work, income, and assets.

Such processes of bargaining are affected by social norms and the differential access to opportunities and resources men and women have outside the household. The relevant policies therefore should be extended to the meso-level, where the interaction of households and household members with other economic and social institutions, such as the state or markets, takes place. Often it is found that institutions, which are not inherently gender-biased, operate with a gender bias. Similarly, policies at the macroeconomic level are important since the economic, social, political and other environments in which households survive are shaped by the macroeconomic realities. Finally, it is important to recognise that the critical catalysts are political will, right policies, and an understanding that it takes time to change the mind set and beliefs regarding gender inequity and women empowerment that have persisted for long. The unfair and unjust social systems need to be challenged constantly through production of new and better knowledge for the empowerment of women and the disadvantaged and ensure gender mainstreaming at all aspects of social life.

Gender gaps in several domains are still large in Bangladesh. We should not expect these gender gaps to shrink and disappear over time; although several mechanisms exist through which women's lot should improve as Bangladesh grows. First, a sectoral shift away from agriculture towards services which opens up new employment opportunities for women. Second, technological advances reduce the time needed for household chores. Third, the frequency and risk of childbearing also decline. Each of these factors increases women's participation in the labour force, which in turn increases human capital investment in girls and women's personal autonomy.

However, there are certain cultural and other practices and norms that could make gender inequality persist even in the face of economic growth in Bangladesh. These cultural norms help explain the extremely male-skewed social and cultural behaviour in Bangladesh. Similarly, the low female labour force participation rate in Bangladesh is likely to be rooted in the high value the culture places on women's subjugation. The cultural institutions favouring males might themselves fade naturally with economic modernisation, enabling gender gaps to close, but there is also scope for policy makers to expedite the process.

In view of the realities in Bangladesh, it is true that neither economic development nor women's empowerment is the magic bullet; gender equity is only likely to be achieved by continuing policy actions that favour women at the expense of men, possibly for a long time.

References

Ahmed, M. 2004. *Effects of Regulations on Pharmaceutical Market in Bangladesh*, Available at: www.pharmadu.net/articlesdetail.php?art=2&pg=1.

Allsopp, M.S., and A. Tallontire. 2015. Pathways to Empowerment? Dynamics of Women's Participation in Global Value Chains. *Journal of Cleaner Production* 107: 114–121.

Basu, A.M. 1989. Is Discrimination in Food Really Necessary for Explaining Sex Differentials in Childhood Mortality? *Population Studies* 43: 193–210.

Basu, K. 1999. Child Labor: Cause, Consequence and Cure with Remarks on International Labor Standards, *Journal of Economic Literature*, September.

BBS. 2009. *Compendium of Environment Statistics of Bangladesh 2009, Bangladesh Bureau of Statistics, Ministry of Planning*. Dhaka: Government of the People's Republic of Bangladesh.

Becker, G.S. 1964. *Human Capital*. New York: Colombia University Press.

Begum, R. 2007. Pharmaceutical Industries: Potentials and Possibilities. *NDC Journal* 6 (1): 2.

Black, R.E., et al. 2008. Maternal and Child Undernutrition: Global and Regional Exposures and Health Consequences. *The Lancet Maternal and Child Health Series* 371 (9608): 243–260.

———. 2013. *Maternal and Child Undernutrition and Overweight in Low-Income and Middle-Income Countries,* The Lancet, June 2013. https://doi.org/10.1016/S0140-6736(13)60937-X

Bowman, W.D. 1960. Area Resource Development, *Transactions of the New York Academy of Sciences,* https://doi.org/10.1111/j.2164-0947.1960.tb00707.x.

BHW. 2008. *Bangladesh Health Watch (BHW) Report, James P. Grant School of Public Health.* Dhaka: BRAC University.

Chowdhury, O.H., and M.R. Osmani. 2010. Towards Achieving the Right to Health: The Case of Bangladesh. *Bangladesh Development Studies* 33 (1 & 2): 2.

CIET. 2001. *Health and Population Sector Programme (1998-2003), Service Delivery Survey, Second Cycle, 2000, Final Report, CIET Canada and Ministry of Health and Family Welfare.* Dhaka: Government of the People's Republic of Bangladesh.

Conger, J., and N. Kanungo. 1988. The Empowerment Process: Integrating Theory and Practice. *Academy of Management Review* 13 (2): 471–482.

Das Gupta, M. 1987. Selective Discrimination against Female Children in Rural Punjab, India, *Population and Development Review,* 13(1), March.

Ensor, T., P. Dave-Sen, L. Ali, et al. 2002. Do Essential Service Packages Benefit the Poor? Preliminary Evidence from Bangladesh. *Health Policy and Planning* 17: 246–256.

FAO. 2015. *The State of Food and Agriculture 2015—Social Protection and Agriculture.* Rome: Breaking the Cycle of Rural Poverty, Food and Agriculture Organization of the United Nations.

GHWA. 2008. *Scaling Up, Saving Lives, Task Force for Scaling Up Education and Training for Health Workers.* Geneva: Global Health Workforce Alliance and World Health Organization.

GOB. 2008. *Bangladesh Climate Change Strategy and Action Plan 2008.* Dhaka: Ministry of Environment and Forests, Government of the People's Republic of Bangladesh.

Golla, A.M, A. Malhotra, P. Nanda, and P. Mehra. 2011. *Understanding and Measuring Women's Economic Empowerment—Definition, Framework and Indicators, International Center for Research on Women (ICRW).* Retrieved from: http://dmeforpeace.org/sites/default/files/Understanding-measuring-womenseconomic-empowerment.pdf

Glinskaya, E. 2005. Education and Health Expenditures in Bangladesh: Benefit Incidence Analysis. *Journal of Developing Societies* 21 (1–2): 91–120.

Gwatkin, D.R., S. Rustein, K. Johnson, et al. 2000. Socio-economic Differences in Brazil, HNP/Poverty Thematic Group of the World Bank. DC: Washington. http://www.worldbank.org/poverty/health/data/index.htm#lcr

Gwatkin, D.R., S. Rutstein, K. Johnson, E. Suliman, A. Wagstaff, and A. Amouzou. 2007. *Socio-Economic Differences in Health, Nutrition, and Population (HNP) within Developing Countries*. Washington DC: Produced by the World Bank in collaboration with the Government of the Netherlands and the Swedish International Development Cooperation Agency.

Harberger, A.C. 1998. A Vision of the Growth Process. *American Economic Review* 88 (1): 1–32.

Hartman, B., and J.K. Boyce. 1998. *A Quiet Violence*. Zed Book: View From a Bangladesh Village.

HIES. 2010. *Report of the Household Income and Expenditure Survey 2010, Bangladesh Bureau of Statistics, Ministry of Planning*. Dhaka: Government of the People's Republic of Bangladesh.

Islam, N. 1999. Bangladesh National Drug Policy: An Example for the Third World ? *Tropical Doctor* 29 (2).

Lord, J., and P. Hutchison. 1993. The Process of Empowerment: Implications for Theory and Practice. *Canadian Journal of Community Mental Health* 12 (1): 5–22.

Mahmud, W. 2008. Social Development in Bangladesh: Pathways, Surprises and Challenges. *Indian Journal of Human Development* 2 (1): 79–92.

Mahmud, M., N. Asadullah, and A. Savoia. 2013. *Bangladesh's Achievements in Social Development Indicators: Explaining the Puzzle, Policy Brief 31012*. London: International Growth Centre.

Mincer, J.A. 1974. *Schooling, Experience, and Earnings, (Human Behavior and Social Institutions No. 2)*. Cambridge, MA: National Bureau of Economic Research.

MOHFW. 1995. *Health, Population and Nutrition Sector Development Program*. Dhaka: Ministry of Health and Family Welfare, Government of the People's Republic of Bangladesh.

———. 2001. *Public Expenditure Review of the Health and Population Sector Programme, 1999/2000*. Research Paper 19, Health Economics Unit (HEU) and Management Accounting Unit (MAU), Ministry of Health and Family Welfare, Government of the Bangladesh, Dhaka. Bangladesh.

———. 2008. *Bangladesh Health Nutrition and Population Sector Programme: Mid-Term Review, Ministry of Health and Family Welfare*. Dhaka: Government of the People's Republic of Bangladesh.

———. 2016. *Health, Nutrition and Population Strategic Investment Plan (HNPSIP), 2016-21, Ministry of Health and Family Welfare*. Dhaka: Government of the People's Republic of Bangladesh.

Mujeri, M.K. 2000. *Social Sector Investments and Policy Priorities to Address Poverty Reduction in Bangladesh*. (Processed). Report prepared for the Asian Development Bank, Manila.

———. 2010. The Rights Based Approach to Education in Bangladesh. *Bangladesh Development Studies* 33 (1-2): 139–203.

Mujeri, M.K., and B. Sen. 2006. Economic Growth in Bangladesh, 1970-2000. In *Explaining Growth in South Asia*, ed. K.S. Parikh. New Delhi: Oxford University Press.

Novignon, J., S. Olakojo, and J. Nonvignon. 2012. The Effects of Public and Private Health Care Expenditure on Health Status in Sub-Saharan Africa: New Evidence from Panel Data Analysis. *Health Economics Review* 2 (1): 1–8.

Nussbaum, M.C. 2000. *Women and Human Development: The Capabilities Approach*. Cambridge: Cambridge University Press.

Osman, F.R. 2008. Health Policy, Programmes and System in Bangladesh: Achievements and Challenges. *South Asian Survey* 15 (2): 20.

Osmani, S.R. 2003. *Exploring the Employment Nexus: Topics in Employment and Poverty* (mimeograph). Geneva: International Labour Office.

Poullier, J.P., et al. 2001. *National Health Accounts: Concepts, Data Sources, and Methodology*. Geneva: World Health Organization.

Reich, M.A. 1994. Bangladesh Pharmaceutical Policy and Politics. *Health Policy and Planning* 9 (2): 2.

Sen, A. 1993. Capability and Well-being. In *The Quality of Life*, ed. M. Nussbaum and A.K. Sen, 30–53. Helsinki: World Institute of Development Economics Research.

———. 1999. *Development as Freedom*. Oxford: Oxford University Press.

Stewart, F. 2013. *Capabilities and Human Development: Beyond the Individual—The Critical Role of Social Institutions and Social Competencies, Occasional Paper 2013/03*. New York: Human Development Report Office, United Nations Development Programme.

UNESCAP. 2008. *Multi-Sectoral Determinants of Maternal Mortality in Bangladesh*, Workshop on Addressing Multi-Sectoral Determinants of Maternal Mortality in the ESCAP Region, Hefei, 20-22 October.

UNDP. 2018. *Statistical Update: Human Development Indices and Indicators*. New York: United Nations Development Programme.

Victor, C., S. Scambler, and J. Bond. 2008. *The Social World of Older People: Understanding Loneliness and Social Isolation in Later Life*. Maidenhead: Open University Press.

WHO. 2006. *The World Health Report 2006: Working Together for Health*. Geneva: World Health Organisation.

———. 2016. *Public Financing for Health in Africa: From Abuja to the SDGs*. Geneva: World Health Organization.

World Bank. 2002. *Bangladesh: Public Expenditure Review, Poverty Reduction and Economic Management Sector Unit*. Washington DC: World Bank.

———. 2003. *Private Sector Assessment for Health Nutrition and Population (HNP) in Bangladesh*. Washington, DC: World Bank.
———. 2005. *Maintaining Momentum? An Impact Evaluation of Interventions to Improve Maternal and Child Health and Nutrition in Bangladesh*. Washington, DC: Operations Evaluation Department, World Bank.
———. 2011. *World Development Report 2011: Conflict, Security, and Development*. Washington DC: World Bank.

CHAPTER 5

Creating Opportunities

5.1 Introduction

Bangladesh has achieved impressive growth and development over the last fifty years, but economic growth needs further acceleration along with measures to enhance its quality and make it more broad-based and inclusive. In line with the SDGs and national imperatives, the focus of Bangladesh is on sustainable development which introduces both new dimensions and challenges relating to harnessing the complementarities between investments in social, economic and climate change areas. The basic precepts of sustainable development requires that financing must be aligned with development outcomes which integrate and synergise the three dimensions of sustainable development for example economic, social and environmental dimensions—as outlined in the Rio+20 outcome document—to ensure intra- and intergenerational equity as well as recognise planetary boundaries.

For Bangladesh, the implementation of the sustainable development agenda requires significant investments in public goods, such as social services, clean air, water and the continued flow of ecosystem services, upon which economies and people depend (Mujeri 2015). While economic goals are relatively straightforward, the complementarities between the three broad groups (economic, social and climate change) of investments are somewhat complex to comprehend in Bangladesh; but these are essential to opening up new frontiers of investments and exploiting market

© The Author(s) 2020

M. K. Mujeri, N. Mujeri, *Bangladesh at Fifty*, Palgrave Studies in Economic History,
https://doi.org/10.1007/978-3-030-56791-0_5

forces for positive social change and for adapting to climate change impacts.

At its current development phase, social investments in Bangladesh are varied as social impact and complex social relationships play a large role in determining their outcomes. In terms of composition, social investments are also dependent on several sources, such as traditional instruments like public and private investments, short and long-term debts, equity including public-private partnerships (PPP) and other hybrids. Grants are also a factor in social finance as are quasi-equity and other structured products.

Since the nature of adaptation to climate change and disaster prevention are mostly horizontal, careful consideration of economic, social and other policy areas is necessary for pursuing synergies along with taking into account each specific activity. Synergies should be pursued with activities under all major activities including technological development and innovation for adaptation to climate change, support for MSMEs, taking up adaptation measures and technology, knowledge transfer and information actions, and actions to preserve and protect the environment and promote resource efficiency. In particular, the inter-sectoral links are important since many of the priorities and measures dealing with adaptation, risk prevention, water management, and eco-system preservation could be designed to maximise the synergies and complementarities among different aspects of development and human welfare.

For adopting an integrated view and harnessing the potentials, it would be important for Bangladesh to ensure coordination, complementarities and synergies; and avoid overlapping with segmented approaches. For instance, adaptation to climate change is related to water issues and hence, where relevant, the links with water management in the country and region/sub-region need to be carefully taken into account as well as the synergies with possible investments in other water-related sectors, adopting the framework of the Bangladesh Delta Plan (BDP) 2100. Moreover, given the horizontal nature of adaptation to climate change and disaster prevention, careful consideration of and synergies with other policy areas and regional policies have to be taken into account. Synergies and complementarities between overall structural and investment opportunities, particularly in agriculture and rural development sectors, should also be looked at.

5.2 The Delta Plan 2100 and Vision 2041

The Bangladesh Delta Plan 2100 (BDP 2100) seeks to integrate the medium term aspirations of Bangladesh to achieve SDGs and UMIC status and eliminate extreme poverty by 2030 and emerge as a HIC in 2041 through realising Vision 2041 with the longer term challenge of sustainable agri-food sector transformation and management of water, ecology, environment, and land resources in the context of their interaction with natural disasters and climate change.

The BDP 2100 comes up with an adaptive, holistic and long-term integrated master plan to steer the opportunities and vulnerabilities created by the interface of water, climate change, natural disasters, environment, ecological balance, agriculture, land use and inland water management for national development (GED 2018). The Plan looks primarily at the delta agenda up to 2050; keeping in view the integrated nature of the decisions as today's decision will have implications up to 2050 and beyond.

In this regard, it sets up a long-term vision for the evolution of the Bangladesh Delta by the end of the twenty first century, but defines short and medium term goals as steps to reach that vision of 'achieving safe, climate resilient and prosperous delta'. These goals, associated strategies, policies, institutions and investments are shifting targets and adaptive in nature. They are adaptive to changing natural events in order to respond appropriately and stay in course of the long-term Delta vision. The sustainable use of water resources and prevention of water-related natural disasters are the backbones of the Delta Plan.

Considering the climate change threat, the important long-term issue is: can Bangladesh ensure food and nutrition security with increased agricultural productivity? In this context, the main challenges to achieving and sustaining food security over the longer term include: (i) expanding urbanisation; (ii) impacts of climate change and sea level rise; (iii) loss of agricultural land; and (iv) uncertainty in surface water availability from upstream.

With an integrated, comprehensive and long-term delta vision of 'achieving safe, climate resilient and prosperous delta', the BDP 2100 mission is to 'ensure long term water and food security, economic growth and environmental sustainability while effectively reducing vulnerability to natural disasters and building resilience to climate change and other delta challenges through robust, adaptive and integrated strategies, and equitable water governance'.

The BDP 2100 proposes three higher level national goals which have been aligned with the Second Perspective Plan 2021–2041 (SPP, 2021–2041) and six water, ecology and land use specific goals that contribute to these higher level goals. The higher level goals are:

Goal 1: Eliminate extreme poverty by 2030;
Goal 2: Achieve upper middle income status by 2030; and
Goal 3: Become a high income country by 2041.

Six water, ecology and land use specific goals that contribute to the above higher level goals are: Goal 1: ensure safety from floods and climate change related disasters; Goal 2: enhance water security and efficiency of water usages; Goal 3: ensure sustainable and integrated river systems and estuaries management; Goal 4: conserve and preserve wetlands and ecosystems and promote their wise use; Goal 5: develop effective institutions and equitable governance for in-country and transboundary water resources management; and Goal 6: achieve optimal and integrated use of land and water resources.

While setting goals and targets for the agri-food sector, these goals will have to be in alignment with: (i) risk management of floods in the wet season and other climate change related disasters; (ii) water resources management; (iii) sustainable management of river systems; (iv) safeguard and maintaining the wetlands; and (v) ensuring efficient integration and proper interaction between land and water use aspects.

5.2.1 *The Vision 2041*

For realising the Vision 2041, Bangladesh is finalising the Second Perspective Plan 2021–2041 (SPP 2021–2041) which is underpinned by two major visions:

(i) Bangladesh will be transformed into a developed country by 2041, with a per capita income of over $12,500 in 2019 prices, and will be fully tuned with the digital world.
(ii) There will be no poverty in 2041.

The strategic goals and milestones in the journey towards a high-income country include the following:

- Eradication of extreme poverty by 2030; and reducing moderate poverty to less than 5 per cent by 2041.
- Emerge as an upper middle income country (UMIC) by 2030 and a high income country (HIC) by 2041.
- Industrialisation with export-oriented manufacturing will be the driver of future structural transformation.
- Paradigm shifts in agriculture will enhance productivity and ensure future nutrition and food security.
- The future services sector will provide the bridge for the transformation of the rural agrarian economy into a primarily industrial and digital economy.
- The urban transition will be an essential component of the strategy to move to a HIC.
- Efficient energy and infrastructure will be essential components of the enabling environment that would facilitate rapid, efficient and sustainable growth.
- Bangladesh will be built such that it is resilient to climate change and other environmental challenges.
- Bangladesh will establish itself as a knowledge hub country for promoting a skill-based society.

The institutional foundations of Bangladesh as a HIC will rest on the people who are the principal drivers of growth along with labour, embodied skill, capital accumulation, and management capacity. Four institutional pillars—good governance, democratisation, decentralisation, and capacity building—will ensure the inclusive growth path throughout the Vision 2041 journey covering the period, 2021–2041.

The underlying poverty reduction strategy covers multidimensional efforts to address the poverty dynamics in the country. Along with securing sustained rapid rate of GDP growth, the quality of growth will be improved through making GDP growth more inclusive and pro-poor by ensuring the required structural transformation of the production base of the economy. Further, the human capital base of the poor will be strengthened along with improving the access to finance for the poor. The urbanisation process will be made more balanced along with ensuring more equitable regional development. The access of the poor to migrant labour market will be enhanced. The vulnerabilities of locations/districts to climate change and natural disasters will be lowered along with sharply improving the poverty focus of the social protection programmes.

The strategic approaches to ensuring a sustainable agriculture for food security and rural development in the high income Bangladesh in 2041 under the SPP 2021–2041 cover four major areas:

- **Sustainably intensify agricultural production systems** with a key defining principle for agricultural technologies and innovations to support food and nutrition security as well as poverty reduction and meet the needs for sustainable agricultural intensification.
- **Increase the resilience of crop and livestock production systems** in the face of climate change.
- **Diversify agricultural output and livelihoods** involving more plant species/varieties, animal breeds, off-farm activities and employment.
- **Cope with uncertainty and develop responses to uncertainty** about the scale and eventual nature of adaptation needed to address climate change.

In addition, higher investment in adaptation and risk prevention means preserving socioeconomic development and enhancing the capacity for further development in the country. It is useful to recognise that the cost of inaction may significantly be higher than the required investments for harnessing the complementarities and synergies between social, economic and climate change areas and decreasing the overall vulnerability to climate impacts.

In Bangladesh, there exists a situation of apparent market failure in these respects as institutions and individuals cannot afford the high risk premiums needed to ensure integration and cover potential losses due to climate change impacts. Also, returns on investment may not be in line with the timeframe of the infrastructure investments, increasing potential economic losses at a later stage. Moreover, exploring complementarities between social, economic, and climate change areas has spillover effects on downstream activities (e.g. infrastructure users) not necessarily integrated into infrastructure and other investment decisions. Hence, it makes economic sense for Bangladesh to explicitly consider complementarities across all relevant dimensions to ensure sustainable and efficient investment decisions.

In practice, harnessing the complementarities between social, economic and climate change issues would involve a process which is mostly horizontal in nature. This means that solid and effective governance should be in place to ensure the required quality of investments. This would require that the responsibilities among ministries and agencies, in particular for the cohesion of policy related aspects, should be clearly established, including the involvement of relevant local authorities. In addition, weak capacities, including at the administrative level, can often act as a major hurdle that would require necessary investments in trainings and capacity building.

5.3 Narrowing Development Gaps: The Role of Technology

Technology has always played a central role in socioeconomic development of a country, and change in technology has been seen as an essential ingredient of development strategies throughout the world (Bell and Pavitt 1993; Evenson and Westphal 1995). As such, there is an intense interest in processes of technological change; such as technology innovation, diffusion, adaptation, implementation, and their uses that make the connection between technology and development. It is these processes—more than the context within which they occur, or the impact of technological change—which is important for a country such as Bangladesh.

Bangladesh—and developing countries in general—faces the unique challenges in promoting sustainability and rapid growth, although technology and globalisation has created many opportunities and ushered in advancements into areas which were never conceived in the past. Technology has been playing a key role in helping move Bangladesh towards sustainable development, with innovative solutions that promote the welfare of the people. In many areas, such as using solar energy to power villages and generate free Wi-Fi, setting up mobile phone systems to track births and provide healthcare information, or expanding education to un- and underserved children through digital means, technology has emerged as a critical resource for sustainability.

One key issue related to technology in Bangladesh is the wider application of artificial intelligence (AI) and robots; how they take the jobs away, and skills development as the policy response. In this context, the important consideration for Bangladesh is to recognise the implications of rapid technological change for poverty and inequality and its impact on the world of work in Bangladesh. For the purpose, it is useful to distinguish between three different ways through which digital technology affects the world of work: automation, connectivity, and innovation. These forces change the relative cost of labour and capital, the cost of transaction, the potential for economies of scale and market competition, and the speed of innovation. These interactions determine the nature of production of goods and services and hence the characteristics of the world of work.

Automation replaces human effort with machine effort; and it is undoubtedly the most direct, and also the most visible way through which technology affects employment in a country. In Bangladesh, the direct effects of automation on the demand for labour are still limited, as enterprises are slower to adopt digital technologies. Yet, some workers and firms are already using such technologies (e.g. in the RMGs industry), which help them become more productive. Also there are indications that automation leads to polarisation in the country's labour market, putting upward pressure on inequality in Bangladesh. There can also be several important indirect consequences. If the labour-scarce developed countries adopt labour-saving technologies, developed country enterprises may find it more profitable to produce goods at home using machines rather than workers in low-wage countries such as Bangladesh. This will threaten to disrupt labour markets in countries such as Bangladesh. It would also prematurely close the door to formal wage job creation in export-led manufacturing sectors in Bangladesh, a country with a huge youth bulge.

Technology is also rapidly changing the cost of transactions. Access to markets and resources, due to improved connectivity, helps enterprises to grow and create jobs, or attract work to new markets that are more competitive. The power of lowering transaction costs for job creation and better earnings is especially relevant to Bangladesh. The cost of transaction is obstructively high in Bangladesh, preventing enterprises, both agricultural and nonagricultural, from expanding supply in domestic and external markets. Mobile phones are already easing farmers' access to market information and improving their income. The internet-based tractor renting platform enables smallholders to capture the productivity increases from mechanisation without needing to have the scale. In urban contexts, car-sharing services like Uber link riders with underutilised drivers. However, one should also be aware that technologies may weaken the market power of existing enterprises; and create new oligopolies when there are significant economies of scale from increased use of technology services. The World Development Report 2016 shows for example that many internet-based markets—such as web searches, mobile payments, or online bookstores—are dominated by a few firms sometimes of foreign origin (World Bank 2016).

5.3.1 *Technological Change Processes*

One can identify three different processes within which technology and development interact in a developing country like Bangladesh. The first is the context (e.g. policy, infrastructure, markets and other institutions), the second is the process, while the third is impact (i.e. the development outcomes). While it is difficult to disentangle these elements, the process dimensions are important in developing countries (Bell and Albu 1999; Juma and Yee-Cheong 2005; Niosi 2008; Kaplinsky 2011). In the 1960s, the main process of interest was adoption; with the simplistic assumption that technology as embodied in fixed capital needs merely to be moved from its point of invention in the developed North to its point of use in the global South for development (Evenson and Westphal 1995).

In the 1970s and 1980s, attention shifted more towards transfer: opening to greater scrutiny the choices, channels and mechanisms by which the move from North to South should take place, and changing the view of technology from a physical artefact to a system of artifact plus 'people, procedures and organisational arrangements' (Bell and Albu 1999: 1717). In the 1990s, the process of adaptation was incorporated: that is to understand the changes in various system components that should be made in order to get technology to work effectively in developing country contexts (Barnett 1990). In the 2000s, and particularly since the 2010s, there has been a growing interest in innovation: seeing technology as embodied knowledge developed by learning supported by networks of organisations and institutions (Wignaraja 2003; Johnson and Andersen 2012).

In terms of the conceptual framework, the major development has been the shift from exogenous to endogenous growth theory (Mayer 2002). While exogenous growth theory focuses on developing countries as passive adopters of the global stock of externally invented artifacts, the latter views technological processes and endowments of knowledge in a developing country as central to long-term economic growth. In the process, this also opens up the entire chain of technological change processes—transfer, adaptation, innovation, etc.—in the developing countries. The early models of technological change in development characterise the process as a set of discrete stages along the lines of invention—production—transfer—implementation—use (e.g. UNIDO 1984). The critics, however, argue that the processes of technological change contain activities that run synchronously, iteratively, and even cyclically (Lundvall et al. 2009). Typical approaches to processes of technological change in development cover the national policies; networks of organisations and institutions which both shape and enact the processes; and organisational subcomponents which also shape and enact these processes (e.g. World Bank 2008; Montobbio and Sterzi 2013; Hwang and Choung 2014).

5.3.2 *R&D Intensity and Technology Adoption*

For Bangladesh, the key issue in development centres around expanding people's choices and creating opportunities for all. Education is the key to creating, adapting and spreading knowledge for technological transformation in the country. Basic and secondary education create ability to learn and interpret information and technology while tertiary education is necessary for producing new knowledge and technology; and adapting technology produced in other countries.

For rapid development, emphasis is needed on productivity growth—rather than accumulating more labour or capital—as the main driver of economic growth. In addition, innovation is the main engine of productivity growth. Countries that invest more resources into research and development (R&D) expand the technological frontier and grow (Romer 1990).

Generally, innovative activity remains concentrated in very few rich countries; these 'leaders' expand the technology frontier; and countries behind the technology frontier—the 'followers'—can also grow by importing technology from the leaders. The transfer of technology and knowledge from leader to follower countries is an important source of economic growth for the latter (Rosenberg 1982). Transfer of knowledge can occur through imported technology (Coe et al. 1997; Keller 2004; Santacreu 2015) and/or multinational activity (Burstein and Monge-Naranjo 2009; Guadalupe et al. 2012), among other channels. Multinational corporations in innovating countries, for example, transfer knowledge to their affiliates or suppliers in other countries. Therefore, innovation and technology transfer are two sources of productivity growth.

With need for faster technological development, the policies have emphasised science and technological research to develop technologies through adoption of imported technology as well as development of indigenous technologies in Bangladesh. For imported technologies, proper planning is required for its effective transfer through acquisition, assimilation and adoption. Bangladesh's National Science and Technology Policy 2011 provides the directions for science and technology (S&T)

activities and research, institutional and manpower development, and dissemination and documentation facilities (MOST 2011). The Policy aims to ensure applications of science, technology and innovation (ST&I) for achieving sustainable economic growth with due attention to employment generation, poverty alleviation, gender equity and environmental sustainability. The National Council for Science and Technology (NCST) determines S&T policies, reviews the activities of different institutions and provides direction towards S&T research and activities.[1]

Research and innovation are considered the warranted drivers of business and economic growth as well as social transformation. Innovation does not come automatically; demand-driven research and testing the ideas for demonstration are essential. Since Bangladesh has started moving towards an upper-middle-income country, Bangladesh needs to intensify its efforts to improve R&D by spending at least 1.5 per cent of GDP on R&D. Further, a separate allocation for the R&D in the national budget is desirable at the present stage of Bangladesh's development.

5.3.3 *Knowledge Development and ICT*

The Information and communication technology (ICT) is a fast-growing technological domain in Bangladesh. The ICT is entering both in education and in the job market in Bangladesh at a rapid rate. The UNDP Human Development Report 2001 introduces the technology achievement index (TAI) which aims to capture how a country is creating and diffusing technology and a human skill base, reflecting the capacity to participate in the technological innovations of the network age. The TAI is a new measure of the countries' ability to participate in the present network age. It focuses on four dimensions and selected indicators. The dimensions and indicators are shown in Table 5.1. Out of the four dimensions of TAI measures, Bangladesh's achievement value for creation of technology and diffusion of recent innovations is negligible in comparison with seventy-two countries covered in the analysis. For the other two dimensions, diffusion of old innovations and human skills, the values are

[1]The Global Innovation Index 2018, published by Cornell University and the World Intellectual Property Organisation (WIPO), ranks Bangladesh 116th, the lowest in South Asia, for its capacity for innovation and the quality of its scientific research institutions. Bangladesh invested only 0.38 per cent of its AgGDP in agricultural research in 2016—well below the level needed to address multiple challenges, including rapid population growth and severe climate change impacts.

Table 5.1 Dimensions and indicators of TAI

Dimension	*Indicator*
Creation of technology	1.1 Patent granted per million people (1998) 1.2 receipt of royalties and license fee per thousand people (US$ 1999)
Diffusion of recent innovation	2.1 internet hosts per 1000 people (2000) 2.2 high and medium technology exports as percentage of total exports (1999)
Diffusion of old innovation	3.1 telephone including cellular per 1000 people (1999) 3.2 electricity consumption kwh per capita (1998)
Human skills	4.1 mean year of schooling age 15 and above 4.2 gross tertiary science enrolment ratio (1995–97 percentage)

Source: UNDP 2001

also very low. The values of two indicators of diffusion of old innovations; telephone including cellular per 1000 people (1999) and electricity consumption k kwh per capita (1998) for Bangladesh are 5 and 81 compared with India's 28 and 384, South Korea's 938 and 4497, and Japan's 1007 and 7322 respectively. The values of two indicators of human skills: mean year of schooling age 15 and above and gross science tertiary enrolment ratio (1995–96 percentage) are 2.6 and compared with India's 5.1 and 1.7, South Korea's 10.8 and 23.2, and Japan's 9.5 and 10.

Compared with Bangladesh, the achievement level of TAI of most countries is higher with higher level of human skills in terms of the two indicators; mean year of schooling and gross tertiary science enrolment ratio. These two indicators depend on the level, type and quality of education in the country. In particular, Bangladesh requires more professional researchers and mid-level technicians to acquire, absorb and use ICT in order to enter and grow in the technology-based global chain of the economy.

The values of four dimensions and eight indicators of TAI at the country level indicate three trends: (i) significant disparities among the countries; (ii) diversity and dynamism in technological progress among the developing countries; and (iii) existence of technology hubs in countries at different levels of development. While consulting with the government, industry and media, four criteria were used to rate and identify the technological hubs: ability of the local universities and research facilities to train highly skilled workforce or develop new technologies; presence of established companies and multinational corporations to provide expertise and economic stability; population's entrepreneurial drive to start new ventures; and the availability of venture capital to ensure that the ideas make it market.

One must, however, remember that TAI measures only technological achievements; it does not indicate how well these achievements have been translated into development outcomes. The TAI shows high correlation with the human development index (HDI); it correlates better with HDI than with income. The World Development Report 2002 states that the poor countries and the poor people differ from the rich ones not only because they have less capital but because they have less knowledge as well (World Bank 2002). The balance between knowledge and resources has shifted towards the former: knowledge has become perhaps the most important factor determining the standard of living; more than land, the tools and the workforce.

The employment pattern of the country's employed workforce reflects an uneven distribution of skills with most skilled jobs occupied by workers without having the required education and training. They occupy the mid-level technician jobs as well; as the country's secondary general education is, to a large extent, non-responsive to the needs of the job market. The secondary and post-secondary vocational and technical education faces different problems and fails to produce graduates with employable skills. Most of the boys and girls in the secondary schools end up with a poor quality of education. The education system also breeds inequality and inequity in society.

For Bangladesh, the shining prospects of demographic transition of least dependency with the highest proportion of active working population are lying ahead. At present, there is acute shortage of researchers and mid-level technical persons to absorb and use ICT in education and in production and services. There is a need to adopt an integrated approach to resolve these issues, problems and barriers of the education system of the country. The key is to ensure strong political commitment, willingness, understanding, and tolerance for building sound institutional and professional capability in the education sector and establish S&T linkages.

5.3.4 *Innovations in Agriculture*

Although the availability of productive resources is limited, the potential for enhancing the productivity of these resources is wide in Bangladesh.

The country has a long way to go to fully exhaust its potentials for enhancing social productivity; and hence the potential for employment generation is also wide. Since this is true for material resources, it is much more applicable for technology, organisation, knowledge, skill and other less tangible social resources. The enhancement in computer performance over the past thirty-five years according to Moore's Law is only one dramatic instance of a general truth about technological productivity in all fields.[2] While the power of computers keeps increasing, the cost of producing them keeps falling because of technological developments that reduce their size, material consumption and labour inputs.

In the coming years, the present fourth industrial revolution (4IR) will bring an unprecedented pace of technological change, building on the digital revolution to combine technologies and transform systems, production structure in agriculture and other sectors—including the Bangladesh society itself. For Bangladesh, advances in computing power, connectivity, artificial intelligence (AI), biotechnology and GIS, and more capable technologies hold tremendous promise of generating decent employment, especially in the rural areas. This will accelerate inclusive agriculture, rural growth and structural transformation to high-productivity agriculture and rural nonfarm activities. One key policy for realising the positive outcomes of 4IR is to bridge the widening gap between the skilled and unskilled labour.

For reaping the benefits of technology, the key will be to transform the country's rural economy and create skilled jobs in rural areas. The need is to ensure more investments in transportation, power, and internet access to create more employment for women and youth in the rural areas.

The access to new technologies enables the small farmers to shift from input-intensive to knowledge-intensive agriculture. Further, precision agriculture can improve the timeliness of planting, secure the best market prices through market information and e-market reforms, provide fertiliser subsidies via direct bank transfers that eliminate or reduce the cost of

[2] Moore's Law refers to the perception that the number of transistors on a microchip doubles every two years, although the cost of computers is halved. Moore's Law states that we can expect the speed and capability of our computers to increase every couple of years, and we will pay less for them. Another tenet of Moore's Law asserts that this growth is exponential. Moore made the statement based on noticing emerging trends in chip manufacturing at Intel. Eventually, Moore's insight became a prediction, which in turn became the golden rule known as Moore's Law. The Law implies that computers, machines that run on computers, and computing power all become smaller, faster, and cheaper with time, as transistors on integrated circuits become more efficient.

financial intermediaries, and improve agricultural extension. Combined with improved seed supply and land and water management, this can increase double and triple cropping; farmers' income can grow and employment can increase. The expansion of crop insurance will reduce the risks of small farmers.

Additionally, investments in mapping the country's aquifers and using technology to manage water demand will help quantify the relationship between rainfall and groundwater levels under alternative modes of irrigation and farming should enable prioritisation of prospective water and irrigation investments.

Greater investment in research is needed to develop multi-resistant crops. Bangladesh needs to invest more in genomics, to increase the supply of genetically modified crops developed by Bangladeshi scientists. These crops will not involve multinational monopolies, can be grown by poor farmers, and offer increased resistance to extreme climatic conditions.

Digitised land registration, mobile phones and 'Uberised' tractor services can contribute to improved farm management. Such efforts will provide title guarantees and increased security of land tenure to the farmers; while stimulating land rentals by nonviable smallholders and land consolidation.

The thrust would be to directly utilise agriculture as an engine to raise on-farm incomes and purchasing power, generate additional on-farm employment opportunities, and stimulate rural industrialisation and develop rural services. These would in turn increase demand for agricultural products, and nonfarm goods and services throughout the economy, creating a multiplier effect that generates new jobs in other sectors. The specific focus of the strategy would be on raising on-farm productivity and fostering closer linkages with other sectors and markets through innovative approaches to the organisation of the rural economy. These will lead to agricultural diversification and dramatic increase in production of fruits and vegetables, dairy products, and growth of inland aquaculture.

The scope for improving farm productivity, the potential for improving linkages with processing industries, and the scope for dietary enhancement is wide in Bangladesh. However, the organisational mechanisms required to fully tap these potentials need to be re-examined in the light of the current role of the government and private sector in the development process. In addition, we need to take into account changing external conditions that open up new opportunities and present new challenges. Several critical areas for rural technological advancement may be identified as follows:

- Establish/strengthen village-based farm schools to demonstrate and impart advanced technology to farmers on their own lands. A network of soil test laboratories could be established capable of high volume precision analysis of 13 essential plant nutrients coupled with development of expert computer systems to interpret soil test results and recommend individualised packages of cultivation practices for each crop, location and soil profile.
- Strengthen upazila information and service centres (UISCs) to act as a medium for transmission of soil test data and recommended practices, access to current input and market prices, and other essential information for upgrading agriculture.
- Undertake policy and legal measures to encourage contract farming arrangements between agri-business firms and small/marginal farmers in order to increase small farmers' access to advanced technology, quality inputs, bank credit, processing, marketing and crop insurance.
- Since the rural labour force suffers from a severe shortage of employable skills at all levels, and that intensive development of vocational skills can act as a powerful stimulus for employment and self-employment generation, establishing a network of government-certified, rural vocational institutes can provide training and certification in vocational skills not covered by the technical institutes. In order to offset the shortage of qualified trainers and the costs of replicating institutions throughout the country, a national network of 'Job Shops' can be created linked with the UISCs. Similarly, televised multimedia training programmes and computerised vocational training programmes can be introduced.
- While the number of employment opportunities is rising, the type and quality of these opportunities does not match the expectations especially of educated job seekers, which reflects inadequacies both in the type of employment generated and type of education being imparted to youth. There are also mismatches between the educated workforce and workforce with required work capabilities to meet the growth in demand in specific areas such as business process outsourcing, automotive component production and many other fields.
- There are also gaps in specific occupational skills for example carpentry, masonry, electrical, mechanics and many other trades. Although there is a vocational training system, it is grossly inadequate to impart skills to the new job entrants as well as the huge number of current unskilled workers. Absence of reliable information on the actual

growth in employment by specific occupational categories makes it difficult to determine either the number of jobs being created in each field or the unsatisfied demand for various types of skills.

- There is an increase in casual and migratory employment which reflects deterioration in the quality of jobs in the rural areas as well as rising expectations of the workforce that impels increasing numbers to abandon traditional occupations in search of better employment opportunities.
- While the share of the workforce employed in agriculture is declining, total employment in this sector continues to rise, though at significantly slower rates than in the past. A reduction in the proportion of the population employed in the primary sector is a natural and inevitable trend that is spurred by rising expectations and changing attitudes as much as by rising levels of farm productivity and mechanisation. However, this does not mean that the potential for employment in this sector is being fully exploited. In the short term, strategic initiatives to modernise and diversify agriculture can generate employment opportunities for a very large numbers of rural people, thereby providing time for the more gradual expansion of employment potentials in other sectors.
- The traditional path to development is the progression from agriculture to manufacturing and then to services. However, Bangladesh's service sector has grown rapidly showing that this formula need not necessarily apply in the context of today's global economy where the demand for services can rapidly expand employment opportunities domestically. In addition, changing social expectations are stimulating rapid growth in demand for services in the country, as indicated by the proliferation of courier companies, Internet cafes, fast food restaurants and retail boutiques. There is also a surging demand for health care services, telecommunications, media, entertainment, and financial services. A more adequate understanding of the growth of the services sector, particularly its informal portion, is needed to assess the potential demand and most effective strategies for accelerating growth of employment, especially in the rural areas. These trends suggest that rural Bangladesh has the opportunity to leapfrog over the traditional path to development, moving directly from agriculture into services.

Agriculture and food processing represent an untapped reservoir of opportunities for the rural youth. While local and regional demand for food is rising, the scope for developing and integrating rural youth into the local value chains remains largely underexploited. Most rural youth engaged in agriculture are currently involved in production and very few are involved in downstream activities in the value chain. There are many reasons why investing in local value chain development in the agri-food sector could become an engine for decent job creation and food security. From a rural perspective, local food processing is compatible with the relatively low level of skills possessed by the rural youth, and is more likely to remain located in small towns and rural areas to ensure proximity to the production source. Additionally, it can create strong forward and backward linkages with other food and non-food system activities, paving the way for a virtuous cycle of territorial development.

The labour market's major problem is not a shortage of jobs; it is the shortage of employable skills. The speed of a nation's development is directly related to the quantity and quality of vocational skills possessed by its workforce. The wider the range and the higher the quality of vocational skills, the faster is the growth and more prosperous the society. The availability of employable skills is one of the major determinants of how readily new job seekers find employment. The very low level of employable skills makes the search for work much more difficult. It reduces the market value of the job seeker and adds to the costs of employers who must train new recruits from scratch.

The rate of growth of the economy cannot be accelerated, in particular in the labour intensive sectors, if there is a general lack of skills among the work force. This requires strengthening of the existing training system. The role of public sector has to be restructured and conditions created for inflow of funds at a much larger scale than at present. Role of private sector has to be expanded sharply if the requisite resources are to be brought in to bridge the large capacity gaps that exist. The vocational training policy has to respond to this challenge.

5.4 Vision for Microenterprises

Historically, the production sector in Bangladesh is characterised by an overwhelming dominance of both small scale production units (cottage, micro, and small enterprises, CMSEs) and an extensive informal economy. Because of the scale, smaller enterprises are especially vulnerable to the problems of bad governance, poor policies and weak institutions; and are also more adversely affected by high bureaucratic costs than larger enterprises. Moreover, being in the informal sector places significant constraints on an enterprise's growth by reducing access to financial and other inputs, limiting access to public services and narrowing the kind of contracts or investments that they can make.

In practice, although the definition of CMSEs in Bangladesh focuses on quantitative criteria, such as employment and/or capital and sales turnover, from a conceptual standpoint these quantitative size-related characteristics also influence organisational behaviour. Apart from independent ownership, which can result in a more limited internal resource base (particularly finance and management resources) than is the case of larger firms, these characteristics include: a lesser ability to shape or control relationships with different dimensions of external environment (such as customers, suppliers, labour markets and sources of finance) compared with larger firms; and a coalescence of ownership and management, which is often associated with distinctive types of organisational behaviour. Whilst these are commonly recognised characteristics of CMSEs, it is important to emphasise the heterogeneity of the CMSE sector, especially in the context of the Bangladesh economy.

According to the Labour Force Survey (LFS) 2015–2016, total employment is 59.5 million in Bangladesh, of which 52.3 million (88 per cent) are employed in the informal sector; for females, the share of informal employment is 97 per cent while 84 per cent of male labourers are employed informally. This share is high in all sectors: 98 per cent in agriculture, 90 per cent in industry and 71 per cent in services sector. Further, nearly one-third of the informal labourers belong to youth labour in the age group 15–29. In urban areas, informal employment is 78 per cent, and it is 89 per cent in rural areas. Thus, in both rural and urban areas, females and youths are more likely to be in informal employment.

The BBS Economic Census 2013 shows that the total number of economic units has increased nearly four-fold in Bangladesh within a span of twenty seven years—rising from 2.17 million in 1986 to 7.82 million in 2013. In 1986, 72 per cent of these were permanent establishments; but the share has declined to 58 per cent in 2013. The above shows two emerging trends: first, since temporary establishments and household economic units mostly involve informal activities, their rising share suggests that the informal sector has been expanding quite rapidly providing supplementary sources of household incomes and employment especially for the rural and urban poor; and second, the consistent increase in the number of permanent establishments is expanding the nonfarm (and varied) economic base starting a process of formalisation of economic activities. Also there is a clear positive relationship between educational attainment and formal employment—educated persons are more likely to be in formal sector employment.

For Bangladesh, increased income, by itself, is not a synonym for development. The critical concern is to use income skilfully, such that income can emerge as the entry point for other aspects of development. The key is to use income as a catalyst to the development of other aspects for example education, health, nutrition, community participation, women's empowerment, social justice and harmony, and discarding of social prejudices—in short, igniting a process of revitalisation, both economic and social, of marginalised rural and urban communities.

Promoting CMSEs therefore lays the foundation for a domestic economic structure in which the smaller enterprises can gradually emerge as suppliers to larger-scale enterprises. Small enterprises also mobilise entrepreneurial initiative and autonomy. This strengthens not only economic but also pluralistic and social transformation processes, which benefit women in particular, who are heavily represented in the small enterprise sector. Thus the development of CMSEs favouring the disadvantaged social groups, especially women and young entrants into the labour force, could contribute to poverty reduction within a wide variety of cultural contexts.

To support these initiatives, there is a need to create enabling conditions to facilitate expansion and technological upgradation of these enterprises and mobilise social capital for comprehensive training and non-formal education in literacy and numeracy. Through targeting the marginalised youth, these trainings can also address product diversification issues, book keeping and financing, use of innovative technology and ICT, and marketing. The design methodology and employment-oriented training may also be integrated into the school curricula such that interested students may have access to a viable alternative for future employment.

For the CMSEs targeted to the extreme poor, employment generation policies should possess three essential features: (i) workers must have access to training. There must also be a demand for the skills as well as a supply of people who can be trained; (ii) semi- and low-skilled workers must have access to markets where they can sell their goods. Moreover, market access is linked with access to information, transportation facilities and telecommunications; and (iii) financial services (including microfinance) must be expanded and existing intermediary national financial institutions must be equipped with adequate financing and appropriate risk-sharing programmes for the CMSEs. The support of Bangladesh Bank and international financing institutions is also extremely important.

The creation of an entrepreneurial class is a part of the above process. However, in promoting the role of CMSEs in entrepreneurial transformation, it is important to make a distinction between 'entrepreneurship' (a person's commitment to capital accumulation and business growth) and 'proprietorship' (ownership of property and other assets that may be used to realise profits but are not utilised for the longer term processes of capital accumulation). In reality, 'proprietors' in Bangladesh are more likely to consume the surplus that is generated rather than re-invest it in their businesses. One may argue that it is the 'proprietors' rather than 'entrepreneurs' who dominate in the majority of small businesses that have been established in Bangladesh, as they mostly strive to protect themselves by generating cash flows that can be consumed for raising general living standards, rather than for business expansion.

Thus, probably a minority of the CMSE owners can be considered as 'entrepreneurs' in the classical sense. Therefore one must recognise that not all CMSE owners aim to grow their businesses and CMSE development in the Bangladesh context is more than an economic process. Under the current rapid transition of the country's economy, the emergence of a divergent class of small traders is a part of the social transformation process contributing to wider consumer choice and the emergence of the middle class. Therefore, the role of CMSEs will have to keep pace with different stages of this transformation process.

With rising income and greater role of the middle class, the consumer markets will be more fragmented and differentiated reflecting changing patterns of consumer demand. This will open up new business opportunities (and thus employment creation) in CMSEs. This will also expand opportunities for self-employment as well. An important challenge in this respect is to identify the specific CMSEs which have employment generating potential and how the potential can be achieved. The conventional wisdom suggests that young firms tend to create more jobs than older firms since most CMSEs grow in the first few years after start-up and then stabilise. Similarly, the smallest young firms tend to grow faster than the rest.

Thus, it appears that the best way of generating employment in the longer term is to focus on firms with the greatest growth potential. Whilst for entrepreneurs, growth objectives are more typically defined in terms of sales or profits than in terms of employment, policy makers need also to recognise that employment growth is a consequence of significant output growth.

With respect to CMSEs, another issue of concern is the quality of jobs created by these enterprises. It is generally held that the job quality provided by these smaller firms is lower than that in larger firms, wages are lower, and job trainings are absent to develop better skills. This suggests that CMSEs require the right kind of support for improving their skill and working conditions and wage levels.

There are other characteristics of CMSEs which are positive from an economic perspective. One characteristic of CMSE owners is their education levels: nearly 86 per cent of the head of establishments are educated in Bangladesh. Although education is not a guarantee of business success, it does tend to influence management behaviour, including a greater willingness to make use of technology in managing and developing the business. They have greater ability to identify areas of management weakness (particularly in sales and management) and upgrading the firm's management skills. Clearly, access to an effective system of business support and management training can help to increase the competitiveness of CMSEs in the country.

There seems to have emerged a consensus among the policy makers and practitioners around the world on what has been described as a 'bootstraps' approach, in which local institutions and initiatives emerge as the 'common sense' of the present development agenda. On the other hand, strategies based on the principles of flexible specialisation emphasise the emergence of small firms in local networks that resemble Marshallian 'industrial districts'. In this type of approach, the emergence of local democratic structures is not simply seen as enhancing local democracy but also to act as a countervailing force in the face of the power of large firms, particularly TNCs. Despite these theoretical differences, there is a common acceptance of a role for CMSEs in local development which clearly presents particular challenges in the context of Bangladesh.

In this context, the relative importance of policies designed to increase the rate of new business start-up and the survival of young firms on the one hand, and those which aim to encourage and support growth in existing firms on the other are likely to vary: first, according to overall policy objectives (such as reducing unemployment or improving competitiveness), and second, between different regions of the country, because of differences in the strengths and weaknesses of local economies. Nevertheless, at the national level, resource scarcity, together with the differences that exist between CMSEs in their relative contribution to development, would justify a targeted approach. In view of the close connection between sales growth and employment growth, there is a strong case for linking policy support to a firm's growth orientation and performance. Moreover, there is a strong case for giving high priority to growth oriented firms that are seeking either to break into foreign markets, or increase their foreign sales.

5.5 Harnessing Globalisation Opportunities

Globalisation improves the prospects for developing countries to catch up economically with the industrialised countries; but the benefit from globalisation will not flow automatically. Domestic economic policies ultimately determine whether a country can benefit from the process. The challenges for the developing countries in the era of globalisation emerge from different sources, such as missing institutionalised links to regional integration and a low level of inter-firm technology cooperation with developed countries, and a high concentration of foreign direct investment (FDI) flows to only a few developing countries. Technology transfers between industrialised countries and developing countries mainly occur through FDI and trade in capital goods, rather than through inter-firm technology cooperation. Recent trends in FDI and international trade show that Bangladesh is becoming increasingly more closely integrated into globalisation strategies.

The quality of developing country economic policies determines whether the country will succeed in joining the globalisation process. The experience suggests some basic policy conclusions: openness towards world markets is a precondition for becoming involved in globalisation strategies of transnational corporations. Liberalising all forms of international investment cooperation and removing barriers to international trade should rank high on the policy agenda of a successful developing country. Under conditions of globalised production, developing country governments are increasingly constrained in pursuing policies of their own liking.

Over the past decades, many emerging economies (including Bangladesh) have enjoyed faster growth in GDP per capita than the rich ones, leading to convergence in incomes. Bangladesh has also done well by implementing the reforms that are required for higher catch-up growth: it has opened the economy to global markets; it has reformed the laws to make them more business-friendly; it has invested in infrastructure and educated its workers. And convergence will work the way it has worked in other countries. In China, for example, low-wage manufacturing of cheap goods for export eventually evolved into the production of more sophisticated goods and services, as workers and enterprises accumulated knowledge and experience.

Yet the forces that drive convergence may also act as a drag on growth of these countries. The expansion of supply-chain oriented trade allows the developing countries quickly to become export powerhouses by importing complex components (like computer chips) for assembly into finished goods that could be re-exported. Although this enables faster growth, supply-chain trade may not contribute much to the technological sophistication of these economies. If trade and commodity prices grow slowly, developing countries may find it harder to build on these successes. The sustainable solution is to reform the domestic economy and boost education in order to continue catching up with the developed world.

One major constraint in opening up the domestic economy is that the local interest groups have little incentive to open up the domestic market to foreign firms with more advanced technologies. Moreover, even with opening the borders, the country may still remain trapped in lower middle-income levels. There are instances of many countries (e.g. in Latin America) who have tried to attract FDI but have not been very successful; even if they do attract FDI, they are still unsuccessful in climbing out of the income trap.

For benefiting from globalisation, Bangladesh needs to prepare itself to take the unprecedented opportunity for industrialisation and growth from the dynamic economic growth of China and other large emerging markets. The graduation of these countries will open up a large number of labour intensive jobs in low skilled manufacturing. The successful strategy for Bangladesh will be to exploit its late-comer advantage by building up industries that are growing dynamically in more advanced countries with similar resources, in terms of land, labour and capital (Lin 2011).

Lin (2011) suggests a six-step process that a country should pursue for the purpose: (i) identify goods and services that have been produced for about 20 years in rapidly growing countries, with similar resources and a per capita income that is about 100 per cent higher than its own; (ii) prioritise those industries identified in Step 1 in which some domestic private firms have already entered spontaneously and identify and remove obstacles to their development; (iii) adopt specific measures to attract firms from higher income countries, identified in Step 1, to invest in industries that are completely new to domestic firms; (iv) provide support to scale-up industries that have been spontaneously discovered by private enterprises but not identified in Step 1; (v) invest in industrial parks or export processing zones to attract domestic private firms and/or foreign firms to invest in the targeted industries; and (vi) provide limited incentives for domestic pioneer firms or foreign investors that work with the list of industries identified in step 1, to compensate for public knowledge created by their investments. The key is to carefully follow the comparative advantage, tap the potential of the latecomer advantage and engage in activities that will dynamically transform its economic structure.

5.5.1 *Participation in Global Value Chains*

Over the last two decades, global trade and production have become increasingly organised around what is commonly known as global value chains (GVCs) or global supply chains. The advances in information and transportation technologies and falling trade barriers across different countries have allowed the enterprises to unbundle production into tasks performed at different locations to take advantage of different factor costs (Feenstra and Hanson 1997; Grossman and Rossi-Hansberg 2008). Such production fragmentation means that intermediate goods and services cross borders several times along the chain, often passing through many countries more than once. These complex global production arrangements have changed the nature of trade.

In developed countries, GVCs provide access to more competitively priced inputs, higher variety, and the economies of scale (Baldwin and Lopez-Gonzalez 2013). Meanwhile, for developing countries, GVCs are viewed as a fast track to industrialisation. Baldwin (2011) argues that internationally fragmented production allows these economies to join existing supply chains instead of building them. With increased sophistication of goods, joining a supply chain removes the need to gain comparative advantage in a broad range of production stages domestically.[3]

[3] Theoretical literature offers support for these views. Studies have shown that productivity gains associated with offshoring and GVCs can arise through multiple channels: finer division

The participation in GVCs—the international fragmentation of production—can lead to increased job creation and economic growth. In order to reap the gains from value chain participation, the important prerequisite is to put in place the right kind of trade and investment policies. The traditional practice has been to produce goods and services primarily in one country. But this production system is changing fast under globalisation: a single finished product now results from manufacturing and assembly in multiple countries, with each step in the process adding value to the end product. Through GVCs, these countries trade more than products; they trade know-how, and make things together. Imports of goods and services matter as much as exports to successful GVCs. The GVCs integrate the know-how of lead firms and suppliers of key components along stages of production and in multiple offshore locations. The international, inter-firm flow of know-how is the key distinguishing feature of GVCs. How a country engages with GVCs determines how much it benefit from the chains.

At present, GVCs have emerged as powerful drivers of productivity growth, job creation, and increased living standards. The countries that participate in GVCs grow faster, can import skills and technology, and boost employment. With GVC-driven development, the countries generate growth by moving to higher-value-added activities and by embedding more technology and know-how in their agriculture, manufacturing and services production. Further, the GVCs provide the countries with the opportunity to leap-frog their development process.

Several developing countries have fully embarked on the GVC revolution, but there are still challenges in aligning GVCs with their national development strategies. The critics view GVCs as a process of recreating the core versus periphery relationships, with the 'good' jobs concentrated in the developed countries while the 'bad' ones in the developing countries. Yet, the GVC-driven success of countries like China and India illustrates the significant boost in a country's competitiveness that can be delivered by combining competitive costs of production with high

of labour across countries (Grossman and Rossi-Hansberg 2008), availability of greater input varieties (Halpern, Koren, and Szeidl, 2015), increased competition, learning externalities, and technology spillovers. While some of these gains are associated with conventional trade as well, welfare gains can theoretically be larger if one uses a multiple-sector framework and considers the input-output linkages (e.g., Caliendo and Parro 2015; Ossa 2015).

technology. With the right strategies, developing countries can maximise their participation in GVCs.

For successful participation in GVCs, the government needs to have a clear vision and strategy to improve coordination among the government institutions and ensure the involvement of the private sector. Opening of borders and attracting investments help jump-start the entry in GVCs. The greatest benefit can be derived by maximising the absorption potential of the domestic economy and by strengthening its linkages with GVCs. Many diverse policy areas affect the success of GVCs. They include, among others, trade policy, logistics and trade facilitation, regulation of business services, investment, business taxation, innovation, industrial development, conformity to international standards and the wider business environment fostering entrepreneurship.

Moreover, the country should identify measures that will complement its GVC strategies. These include a large number of dimensions, from investment in education and vocational training to environment and urbanisation, from ICT and infrastructure building to labour market mobility.

Recent theoretical research shows that countries can benefit from participation in GVCs through multiple channels. Research further shows that GVC-related trade, rather than conventional trade, has a positive impact on income per capita and productivity (Ignatenko et al. 2019). However, there is large heterogeneity and the gains appear more significant for upper-middle and high-income countries. Further, 'moving up' to more high-tech sectors while participating in major supply chains does take place; but this is not universal, suggesting other factors do matter. This includes the findings of the standard gravity literature for GVC trade that highlights the key role of institutional features such as contract enforcement and the quality of infrastructure as determinants of GVC participation.

Bangladesh's present participation in GVCs is relatively small. Both upstream and downstream links exist in exports although the use of foreign intermediaries in Bangladesh's exports (i.e. backward participation) is higher than the use of Bangladesh intermediaries in other countries' exports (i.e. forward participation). Bangladesh participates in manufacturing GVCs for RMGs, electronic and electrical equipment, chemicals, pharmaceuticals, and other manufactures. The participation is mainly due to sourcing of intermediates from abroad. Bangladesh also shows participation in GVCs in services sector, especially in business services.

While the ability to participate in GVCs in instrumental for global economic integration of Bangladesh, but benefiting from GVCs depends on how much value Bangladesh creates in the GVCs. Similar to the stylised approach applied for the individual products, the contribution of different industries along the value chain can be calculated at the aggregate level (Timmer et al. 2012). Obviously, the majority of the final demand for manufactured goods and market services in Bangladesh represents value added that has been created domestically. The foreign value added share is small.

Like other countries, Bangladesh creates and captures value added in domestic markets as well as in foreign markets (through exports). In an era of GVCs, gross export shares are less meaningful in measuring external sector performance of individual countries. Individual economies increasingly specialise in specific activities (e.g. assembly, logistics and R&D) instead of entire industries within GVCs. Since there exist international dispersion of productive activities across countries and uneven distribution of value along the value chain, export shares in value added terms become more accurate indicators of country competitiveness in the global economy. In the present situation, the share of Bangladesh in value added exports will be similar to the share in gross exports, reflecting very small use of imported intermediates in its exports.

For Bangladesh, it is also important to recognise that manufacturing at present involves much more than just production of goods; the process increasingly includes service-related activities, both in the upstream and downstream value chain. Manufacturing exports include significant value added from services sector: firms increasingly use logistics, communication, and business, financial and many other services to facilitate the efficient functioning of the GVCs. In addition, services such as design, development, marketing, warranties, and after sales care services help to differentiate, customise, and upgrade products; enabling firms to capture higher values.

With GVCs emerging as a dominant feature of world trade, the entire process of producing goods, from raw materials to finished products, is increasingly carried out wherever the necessary skills and materials are available at competitive cost and quality. Similarly, trade in services is essential for the efficient functioning of GVCs, not only because services link activities across countries but also because they help enterprises to increase the value of their products. This fragmentation highlights the importance of designing a complementary policy agenda to leverage engagement in GVCs into more inclusive growth and employment in Bangladesh.

The poverty responses to globalisation are not a one-way phenomenon. It is hard to predict that there will be an unequivocal positive (or indeed a negative) outcome for all types of households in all kinds of circumstances. As suggested by McCulloch et al. (2001), there are many channels of effect in translating the macro-level initial shock to the micro-level impact on households and individuals. The more easily identifiable (and quantifiable) channels include price responses and labour market responses—both on the demand and supply sides, including changes in wage rates in different market segments. Other channels, such as changes in infrastructure, may also affect social well-being although these are often much harder to quantify. Nevertheless, the variety of price and factor market responses demonstrate that the direction and level of effects crucially depend on household endowments; differential price responses in markets (e.g. prices of goods and factors); rigidities (e.g. supply constraints); and, of course, heterogeneity in individual responses. There are other factors as well, such as the importance of good institutions, for example financial institutions, governing the availability of credit; agricultural and industrial extension services; etc. (McCulloch 2006; Khondker and Mujeri 2006).

Trade reforms have neither readily nor necessarily benefited the poor in Bangladesh. The standard argument that trade liberalisation improves resource allocation, enhances growth, and hence benefits the poor (through the 'trickle-down' channel) does not seem to have worked in the context of Bangladesh. Moreover, it has been observed that tradable goods production does not use unskilled (or less skilled) workers as the most intensively used factor and, indeed, many non-tradable sectors (such as products and services of the informal sector) are more labour intensive than the tradable sector. As a result, with a segmented labour market, the opening up of the economy benefits a few groups who have specific skills while the poor workers at the lower end of the skill profiles remain the losers.

It also needs to be recognised that there is no automatic association between trade liberalisation and growth, and that Bangladesh needs to adopt appropriate phasing and sequencing of trade reforms to liberalise the economy in more strategic ways and to participate in the global economy on its own terms. An open trade regime, on its own, will not necessarily set the economy on a sustained growth path. The reforms are likely to be beneficial when complemented by measures aimed at strengthening the domestic economy, addressing structural bottlenecks and improving the policy regimes and institutional capabilities.

What is important for Bangladesh is the quality, timing and scope of liberalisation and its success in promoting or facilitating factors such as strengthening of local enterprises, human resource and technological development, and building up export capacity and market access. Specific and sound policies are required in areas such as infrastructure, market facilitation and access, and competitiveness to meet the challenges.

Furthermore, the risks of job and income losses for poor groups in a situation of continuing high unemployment and in a liberalised environment are too high for Bangladesh. This may have a negative effect on growth prospects via deficient demand. Such risks highlight the importance of consistency of the macroeconomic policy regime with trade liberalisation efforts. The liberalisation process thus needs to be far more sensitive to social costs consistent with appropriately targeted social safety nets for the affected poor, and guided by institutional capacity to better manage the transition period of trade liberalisation.

Finally, effective measures are also needed to increase the supply response of poor households and their ability to cope with risk and uncertainty through complementary policies for developing small and medium enterprises and agro-based industries, improving access to the credit market, ensuring better asset distribution, increasing labour market flexibility, disseminating market and technical information, and investing in skill development. At the same time, the international environment needs to be supportive of, and reduce the transition costs of, economic restructuring of the country. On the global front, along with preferential access to Bangladesh's exports in general, this means importing countries reducing tariffs on garments and other labour-intensive exports from Bangladesh where the country may have an increasing comparative advantage.

5.6 Expanding Fiscal and Policy Space

The responses to economic crisis in developed countries prominently feature automatic stabilisers compared with those of the developing countries. Some developed countries incorporate specific measures in their stimulus packages in order to address the social dimensions of the impact of a crisis. The measures may include instruments to strengthen the automatic stabilisers that exist in a country for example unemployment benefits, introduction of subsidy for employers who adopt the practice of 'short-time work' as opposed to retrenchment, investment in infrastructure that would have a direct impact on employment and others. Depending on the availability of fiscal space, it may be possible to strengthen such instruments (for example, an extension of the coverage and/or duration of the unemployment benefits, where they exist). Likewise, the existence of programmes like employment guarantee or conditional cash transfers also makes it easier for policy makers to address the social concerns.

If Bangladesh wants to incorporate social dimensions more explicitly in response to an economic downturn, a useful beginning could be made with the position articulated in Article 22 of the Universal Declaration of Human Rights (1948): 'Everyone, as a member of society, has the right to social security'. Article 25 of the Declaration formulates this right in a more precise manner as '… the right to security in the event of unemployment, sickness, disability, widowhood, old age or other lack of livelihood in circumstances beyond his control'. The Social Protection Floor (SPF) Initiative of the UN defines the term as 'global and coherent social policy concept that promotes nationally defined strategies that protect a minimum level of access to essential services and income security for all in the present economic and financial crisis and beyond' (ILO and WHO 2009: 1). According to this initiative, the main elements of SPF are: (i) essential services: that is geographical and financial access to essential services (such as water, sanitation, adequate nutrition, health and education, housing, and other services including life and asset saving information); and (ii) essential social transfers: that is social transfers, in cash and in kind, paid to the poor and vulnerable to provide a minimum income and health security." (ILO and WHO 2009: 2).

The ILO defines what it calls 'the basic social security floor' (BSSF) as 'a basic and modest set of social security guarantees—implemented through social transfers in cash and in kind— for all citizens …'. (ILO 2008: 2). This set of guarantees includes (i) access to basic/essential health care benefits, (ii) income security for children at least at the poverty level through various family/child benefits, (iii) targeted income support to the poor and the unemployed in the active age group, and (iv) income security for the old and the disabled—at least at the poverty level—through pensions for old age, disability and survivors. The BSSF thus consists essentially of a guaranteed set of basic social transfers in cash or in kind to all.

Table 5.2 Addressing employment and labour market impact of economic downturns

Goal	*Instruments*
Minimise the adverse effect on employment	(i) Automatic stabiliser in the form of unemployment benefits (if appropriate, through schemes for guaranteeing employment) (ii) incentives for job preservation (iii) investment and adoption of labour based approaches in infrastructure
Mitigate the adverse effects of economic Downturn on retrenched workers	Introduction of severance pay
Enhance employability and redeployment of Retrenched workers	Introduction of active labour market policies
Protect investment in human capital	Conditional and unconditional cash transfers With particular focus on education and skill Training

Source: Islam et al. 2011

It may be reasonable for Bangladesh to assume that it would create a basic social floor below which the poor would not be allowed to fall. As income and living conditions depend crucially on employment and the labour market, it may be useful to consider these elements. Table 5.2 gives a list of instruments that may be applied to various goals.

5.6.1 *Employment and Labour Market Policies: An Illustration*

A number of programmes exist in Bangladesh that provides social protection and social safety nets, especially to the poor. Apart from 1.2 million government employees who are eligible for pensions after they retire at the age of fifty-nine years, the rest are basically programmes targeted to the poor and do not carry any defined benefits. The latter can be grouped into several categories: (i) employment generation programmes; (ii) anti-poverty programmes aimed at providing food security; (iii) programmes in the areas of education and health; and (iv) special allowances for various groups like the old, disabled, etc. These programmes provide a good foundation for creating a basic social floor for the poor in Bangladesh. They can be used to create a strong floor for the poor so that they can be protected from possible adverse effects of external shocks (like the global economic crisis of 2008–2009) to which they are vulnerable.

However, a number of gaps in the social safety net programmes of Bangladesh need to be filled in. For example, although there are employment generation programmes, there is no legal basis for providing employment and unemployment benefits on a guaranteed basis. Another important gap is the absence of severance pay and of programmes of retraining and redeployment for retrenched workers. A more comprehensive package of programmes can be formulated by filling these gaps so that Bangladesh can have an effective social floor for the poor.

The critical element in such a package would be to upgrade the employment programme into a truly nationwide programme providing guaranteed employment and unemployment benefits so that it can serve the purpose of an automatic stabiliser during periods of sharp economic downturns. The employment programme should be integrated more effectively with the country's infrastructure development programme so that employment generation can be combined with strengthening of infrastructure that can act as a catalyst for future development. The other elements that should be considered include possible means of preventing job losses due to economic downturns and active labour market policies including retraining and redeployment for retrenched workers.

For Bangladesh, for a basic minimum policy package consistent with reality and relevant to addressing potential adverse impact of an economic downturn, a key consideration would be to combine priority social transfers in an articulated manner to protect the poor and vulnerable from becoming trapped in debilitating poverty by providing security to a minimum level of income and enhancing the capacity to respond to labour market opportunities. Keeping the above considerations in view, a package may consist of the following four employment and labour market components:

(i) guaranteed employment programme with a component of unemployment benefit;
(ii) scheme for subsidising job preservation through work sharing;
(iii) scheme for introducing active labour market policies including retraining and redeployment; and
(iv) provision for an increase in public investment in infrastructure especially focusing on labour based approaches and linked with the proposed guaranteed employment programme.

One study (Islam et al. 2011), while estimating the total budgetary and fiscal implications of the four components of the proposed package, shows that the total cost of the package comes to about BDT 187 billion per year at 2009–2010 prices which is only 2.6 per cent of GDP (Table 5.3). In the context of the existing budgetary and other constraints, it is important to look at options for enhancing the fiscal and policy space needed for implementing such a package. There can be several alternatives such as: (i) increasing the efficiency of utilisation of existing resources; (ii) raising additional domestic resources; (iii) ensuring more efficient utilisation of remittances received from migrant workers; and (iv) promoting public private partnership especially in infrastructure and in undertaking active labour market policies.

Efficiency in resource utilisation can be increased by raising the efficiency of administration and by rationalising the composition of budgetary allocation among different activities. Other routes for increasing efficiency would include infusion of technology (especially ICT), emphasis on R&D, and development of human capital (especially the ability to cope with new technology). While the current revenue-GDP ratio is around 10 per cent, the potential for Bangladesh is regarded as 14 to 15 per cent of GDP. This implies that simply by removing the weaknesses in the collection system, an additional revenue of BDT 170-BDT 230 billion could be collected. Thus the entire cost of the programme for the basic social floor in terms of employment and labour market programmes could be financed through an improved revenue effort. Measures needed to improve revenue collection include expansion of the tax base, curbing tax evasion, checking leakages in the tax collection system, simplifying tax rules and improving transparency, and strengthening of revenue administration. It is important to note that the basic social floor outlined in the present section

Table 5.3 Total cost of employment and labour market policies within a social floor

Component	*Cost, billion BDT at 2009/10 prices*
Guaranteed employment programme	132.00
Subsidising job preservation through work sharing	9.85
Introducing active labour market policies	5.00
Increasing public investment in infrastructure	40.00
Total	186.85

Source: Islam et al. 2011

can be attained by raising public investment to 6–7 per cent of GDP from its present level of less than 5 per cent of GDP.

In Bangladesh, it is thus possible to create the necessary fiscal space for implementing a package of employment and labour market programmes within the framework of a basic social floor through the country's own resources if the country is prepared to make a serious effort to attain its revenue potential. Of course, it would be essential to strengthen the institutional capacity to formulate and implement such a programme.

5.7 Fighting 'Crony Capitalism'

The concept of 'crony capitalism' or 'cronyism' is closely connected with the idea of rent-seeking and corruption. It incorporates both an ethical judgment and a positive description of a feature of an economic process. Crony capitalism rests on the notion of plunder and bad governance whose purpose is to divert national wealth for personal and political use by influential groups. Further, it refers to a type of rent-seeking society where the rent-seeking structure is somehow legitimised. A rent-seeking elite, weak public institutions, a bureaucracy uninsulated from the meddling of politicians and vested interests, a political culture founded on coercion and patron-client relations, corruption, and absence of concern for redistribution serve as fertile grounds for persistence and growth of crony capitalism. The essence of crony capitalism is a relationship between business and politics.

Thus crony capitalism arises when business cronyism and related self serving behaviour by businesses or business people spills over into politics and government, or when self-serving friendships and family ties between businessmen and the government influence the economy and society to the extent that it corrupts public-serving economic and political ideals. The manifestation of crony capitalism may take distinct forms depending on its level of development and the presence or absence of the rule of law. For example, the use of 'crony relations' is a mechanism through which property rights are secured in the absence of rule of law creating a crony and personal overlap. Often, in developed countries, corruption is a complement to the official economy rather than a substitute; whereas in countries like Bangladesh the situation is reversed.

In practice, crony capitalism manifests as a system in which those close to the political authorities who make and enforce policies receive favours that have large economic value. In the system, leading businessmen enjoy close personal relationships with key politicians. It enriches the privileged through use of political power. With crony capitalism, the person with political power joins hands with influential businesses to block competition for mutual benefit. Further, these people may award government contracts to their favoured businesses at inflated prices/reduced quality in order to collect a percentage.

Often the ruling elites find cronyism too handy in establishing legitimacy; and the businesses promoting the system can use it to ensure their hold over the economy's commanding heights. The collusion among business enterprises, government officials, and ruling parties results in business-friendly policies and investments that serve private interests at the expense of public interest.

In a crony capitalism economy, businesses thrive through a return on money amassed through a nexus between the business and the political elites. This is done using state power to remove competition in handing out favours over resources where the state exercises monopolist control over public goods; for example, contracts for public works. Money is then made not merely by making a profit in the market, but through profiteering by 'rent seeking' using the monopoly or oligopoly. Entrepreneurship and innovative practices, which seek to reward risks, are stifled, since the value-added is little by crony businesses as hardly anything of significant value is created by them, with transactions taking the form of 'trading'. Crony capitalism spills over into the government and the politics and the nexus distorts the economy and affects society. In its worst form, crony capitalism can devolve into simple corruption, and bribes to politicians and government officials are considered lawful and tax evasion is common.

Development literature shows that sustained growth in developing countries is often hampered by the middle income trap, where crony capitalism kills transparency and competition and creates oligarchies that slow down growth. The rich and the influential receive land and resources in return for payoffs to corrupt politicians. It substitutes vested interests for public interest. In countries like Bangladesh, the provision of public goods becomes mostly biased against access by the poor. The system also tolerates corruption. There is also a link between poor public service, patronage, and corruption that grows more worrisome over time.

The massive losses due to alleged scams are prime examples of deeper rots that exist in Bangladesh's banking sector. In most cases, it is alleged that the banks are being milked dry by 'influential people' including politicians and their cronies. Many of the current problems in the financial sector and the huge non-performing loans (NPLs) of the banks stem from the collusion and influence-peddling that happens during sanctioning loans. This leads to extensions, moratoriums and restructuring packages. With banks having directors and even independent directors appointed by the government, crony capitalism has its feet firmly stuck in the mess.

In Bangladesh society, businesses compete for the goodwill of those in power, rather than the consumers. This is truer of those involved in big business; small business owners usually find a completely different, less-regulated environment. This allows those connected with power to tap into rich sources of corruption, including in public procurement, project implementation, and tax administration. These governance failures have created an economy which is largely built around redistribution of rents that is excess returns above the normal levels that are generated in competitive markets.

Since independence, Bangladesh has been struggling with widespread discontent over deep-seated corruption and state capture. Oligarchs dominate large sectors of the economy, extracting rents and exerting their influence on the state often through representation in the Parliament. Further, politically connected businesses use various channels to access economic rents: public procurement, subsidised loans, transfers from the budget, trade regulations that restrict imports, privileged access to state assets through privatisations, and beneficial tax regimes.

Cronyism may rule widely in a country if it scores poorly (as Bangladesh does) on widely accepted corruption indices (such as Transparency International's Corruption Perceptions Index in which Bangladesh has a score of 26 out of 100 in 2018). In such cases, ruling parties and business elites work together in ways that increase their hold on power and wealth, and close off opportunities to the competitors. They may also be assisted by investments from foreign corporations, often in the energy or mining sectors, seeking to gain favour with local authorities in order to secure exploration rights.

Similarly, a country that lags on political pluralism, independence of its judiciary, gender equality, or human rights (like Bangladesh does), cronyism can be an active factor. The Rule of Law Index produced by the World Justice Project puts a value of 0.41 for Bangladesh in 2017–2018 indicating very low ratings on measures of government powers, absence of corruption, open government, fundamental rights, order and security, regulatory enforcement, civil justice, and criminal justice. It is also held that if a country's economy is highly reliant on exports of raw materials or low value-added goods (like Bangladesh's dependence on readymade garments) rather than productivity or innovations, cronyism can become a dominant factor.

Moreover, high-income inequality that exists in Bangladesh can mean that cronyism plays a key role in reducing competition in the country's economy. The wealth that the ruling elites accumulate through cronyism also flows into the developed economies. The Tax Justice Network estimates that $12 trillion from developing countries alone was parked in offshore havens in 2016.

Despite the clear economic cost of crony capitalism, the ultimate success of economic reforms in Bangladesh will depend in large part on overcoming resistance from vested interests to any efforts to establish a rule-based system and regulations. A strong Independent Anticorruption Commission (ACC) is a first step of an effective anti-corruption framework. The government must also deliver on its promise of real change and transparent governance. These expectations are the strongest counterweight to corruption and state capture in Bangladesh. Further, an engaged and vocal civil society is the country's best bet at breaking the vicious cycle of crony capitalism. After all, as we have learnt from Adam Smith, what is in the best interests of business is not always the same as what is in the best interests of the individuals—and 'business friendly' is not the same as 'market friendly'.

It is proven that rapid growth generates strong virtuous circles of prosperity and opportunity. Strong growth and employment opportunities improve incentives for parents to invest in their children's education by sending them to school. This may lead to the emergence of a strong and growing group of entrepreneurs, which should generate pressure for improved governance. Strong economic growth therefore advances human development, which, in turn, promotes economic growth and equity.

But the extent to which growth reduces poverty/inequality depends on the degree to which the poor participate in the growth process and share in its proceeds. Thus, both the pace and pattern of growth matter. A successful strategy of poverty/inequality reduction must have at its core measures to promote rapid and sustained economic growth. The challenge for policy is to combine growth-promoting policies with policies that allow the poor to participate fully in the opportunities unleashed and so contribute to that growth. This includes policies to make labour markets work better, remove gender inequalities and increase financial inclusion. Bangladesh must increasingly tackle this agenda of 'inclusive growth'.

No doubt, future inclusive growth will have to be based on an increasingly globalised world that offers new opportunities; but also new challenges. New technologies offer not only 'catch-up' potential but also 'leap frogging' possibilities. New science offers better prospects across both productive and service sectors. Future growth will also need to be environmentally sustainable. Improved management of water and other natural resources is required, together with movement towards low carbon technologies. With proper institutions, growth and environmental sustainability may be seen as complements, not substitutes. Bangladesh needs to identify more and better drivers of growth to improve policies; but the biggest determinants of growth will be the quality of leadership, policies and institutions. Overarching lessons from the development experiences from different countries for reducing inequalities may be summarised as follows:

- There is no unique way to poverty and inequality reduction and development

It is futile to translate general policy principles into a unique set of policy actions. There are no best-practice policies that will always yield the same positive result. To sustain growth requires key criteria to be met, but there is no unique combination of policies and institutions for fulfilling them. For example, creating stronger incentives for private investment may require improving the security of property rights in one country, but enhancing the financial sector in another. Technological catch-up may call for stronger or weaker patent protection, depending on the level of development. This helps to explain why growing countries should have diverse policy configurations, and why attempts to copy successful policy reforms in another country often end up in failure.

- Institutions matter

The institutional context is perhaps the single most important factor in determining whether a given policy will be appropriate or not. Institutions may be crudely seen as the framework in which markets operate: the basis of the rule of law and enforcement of property rights. Institutions are often deeply rooted and are difficult to change, though unlike some other contextual factors (such as climate and location), change is possible. A wide variety of events and policies are influenced by different institutional settings. For example, natural resource endowments can be beneficial to countries with well-defined and enforceable property rights, but are often detrimental in countries without these rights. This is because without well-defined property rights, there is a temptation for individuals to attempt to obtain the resources of others either illicitly (theft) or using the legal process (disputed ownership). Incentives for investment in physical and human capital, the scope for technology transfer and a whole host of other key conditions for growth depend on the institutional setting.

- Timing is the key

Too often, research has focused simply on what is needed. The question of when it is needed has seldom been investigated, which has led to disastrous outcomes. Two separate factors are crucial: the sequencing of policies; and the speed at which they are introduced. In Eastern Europe, market-based reforms were introduced as 'shock therapy': quickly and simultaneously. Institutional reforms were left incomplete even as large parts of the state-run economy were privatised and deregulated. This contributed to the collapse in output in many of these countries in the early 1990s. In Brazil in the early 1990s, trade reforms were introduced rapidly, without much concern for the competitiveness of the exchange rate regime and the response of the manufacturing sector. In contrast, during the same period in India, trade reforms were introduced at a gradual pace, and so were designed to enable domestic firms to restructure and spread the costs of adjustment over time. The exchange rate was kept competitive to ensure export growth, and the Indian industrial sector flourished.

- Right focus is crucial

Reform efforts need to be selective and focus on the 'binding constraints' on economic growth and inequality. The government must avoid the temptation to implement only the uncontroversial policies and instead focus attention where it is needed. This makes it vital to avoid the formulaic approach of the Washington consensus, to recognise the individual characteristics of a country and to undertake more rigorous economic analysis. While there is no fool proof method of identifying the binding constraints, common sense and economic analysis can help. For example, when investment is constrained by poor property rights, improving financial intermediation will not help fuel growth. When investment is constrained by a high cost of capital, improving institutional quality will not catalyse growth. Experimentation and learning about the nature of the binding constraints are an integral part of the reform process. It is not easy for the government to identify the binding constraints at a given point in time and stage of development, but 'growth diagnostics' could provide important starting points for Bangladesh.

5.8 Harnessing the Middle Class Dynamism

The world is reaching a tipping point, where the global middle class will expand dramatically over the next several years. The global middle class, numbering 3.8 billion people in 2018, is likely to grow at 170 million per year in the coming years; and nearly 88 per cent of the next billion people in the middle class will be from Asia. The middle class market is also growing at about 4 per cent per year in real terms, faster than global GDP growth. Although China and India are at the forefront of the expansion of the global middle class, more than a fifth or about 33 million of the country's total population belong to the middle class category (defined as having income ranging between $2 and $3 per day) in Bangladesh. The share is likely to reach 25 per cent by 2025 and 33 per cent by 2030.

The expansion of a country's middle class is often regarded as a sign of development, resulting in economic prosperity, as well as a potential for more social security. Rapid growth in middle class clearly has economic consequences; it also has social ones. The middle class is important for growth as Income elasticities of demand by these people are usually greater than one especially for durables; their preference for product differentiation leads to value added in branding; they culture 'middle class values' such as hard work, meritocracy, savings, and education; their impetus to growth is more sustainable than export-led growth; and there is less risk of falling into the middle income trap. Cross-country empirical evidence shows that a larger middle class influences consumption growth primarily through higher levels of human capital accumulation.

The middle class also has growing expectations regarding quality health care, good education, social protection, affordable living, and other social services. They no longer remain satisfied with simply having access to public services; they are increasingly concerned with their quality. This, in turn, may have implications on poverty, assuming that the government is able to meet public demands. It is well known that the causes of poverty include insufficient access to public resources such as education and healthcare, especially for rural inhabitants.

Thus, the middle class may not be satisfied with simply having access to public services; they may be increasingly concerned with their quality. The middle class would demand greater access to high-quality, inexpensive education and healthcare. Providing quality services that the middle class demands is far more complicated than providing access and this can be a source of friction and conflicts. With rapid growth of the middle class, the demand for public services soars, the capacity of the government to respond to these demands also expands, but at a slower rate.

Bangladesh's emerging middle class can be a critical factor because of its potential as an engine of growth. History tells us that those belonging to the middle class vigorously accumulate capital, both physical and human, so that a stable middle class can provide a solid foundation for economic progress by driving consumption and domestic demand.

The experience of Brazil and South Korea illustrates major differences in the role of the middle class. In the 1960s, both these countries had similar levels of income and economic growth rate; but by the 1980s, the middle class made up only 29 per cent of the population in Brazil due to high income inequality; in contrast, South Korea's share of middle class was 53 per cent. The high share of the middle class enabled South Korea to shift away from export driven growth towards domestic consumption, a transition that did not happen in Brazil.

Moreover, the middle class is not only a driver of consumption and domestic demand, its social role is equally important. The middle class is usually progressive, supports democracy and moderate political platforms. A strong middle class can therefore influence inclusive development through more active participation in the political process, expressing support for inclusive political programmes and electoral platforms.

Although a larger middle class may imply a happier population—especially for the new entrants—this may also create pressures for better delivery of public services or for more democratic governance as middle class citizens recognise their potential to bring about positive changes. Strength often comes in numbers as well.

However, despite having incomes above the poverty line, some middle class segments are quite vulnerable. Many of them work in the informal sector, their education and skill levels do not permit them to move up to better occupations, and social protection systems fail to reach these vulnerable groups. Their susceptibility to economic shocks is striking. This vulnerability is especially worrying, since if they have vulnerable incomes and unstable employment, their consumption levels may not support sustainable development and stable social progress.

Usually, the middle class possesses rising expectations, which follow Hirschman's 'tunnel effect'. The tunnel effect highlights initial tolerance of increased inequality resulting from uneven economic growth processes on the part of relatively disadvantaged members of society, who, expecting to catch up and benefit in the near future, draw satisfaction from the improved income situation of others. If the moment of catching up does not arrive, initial tolerance may switch, giving way to feelings of falling behind, resulting in social upheaval.

The government's role is to put policies in place to fight the vulnerabilities of the middle class and benefit from middle-class support. These policies should promote upward social mobility such as quality education, and provide safety nets that protect the vulnerable segments when facing life risks. If high quality of publicly provided services can be ensured, a constituency for comprehensive contribution-based social protection system can be built with support from the middle class. However, if publicly-provided services are of low quality, the middle class will perceive themselves as losers in the fiscal bargain and may not be willing to finance the public system.

No doubt, the concept of middle class is somewhat vague and corresponds to different lifestyles; and it may be hard to see how this heterogeneous group would position itself in society. Moreover, it is widely noted that these classes are driven mostly by self-interest; they strongly feel that their interests should be protected and are likely to oppose even good reforms that affect them in any negative way. They are extremely unwilling to compromise their group's interests and privileges.

People also cite evidence for representatives of the middle class who are more likely to guard their relative privileges against the incursions of poorer classes than champion alternatives that would help to reduce poverty. The middle class is often branded to be more concerned with retaining its privileges and remaining loyal to the government that made its social advancement possible than in greater social justice and equality. The middle class helps a regime to maintain the status quo. Thus, they may not become progressive drivers of social reforms that would benefit the majority.

Despite these structural limitations of the middle class, the rising expectations of the expanding middle class in Bangladesh signal its awakening with its own specificities; and the key question is: will this middle class be the country's agent of change?

5.9 Mobilising Resources for Development

Domestic revenue mobilisation (DRM) has gained increasing prominence in recent policy discourse in Bangladesh due to several factors, including potential benefits of taxation for development and equity, gaining freedom from long-term dependence on foreign assistance and shifting aid paradigm, fiscal effects of trade liberalisation, and continuing acute financial needs for meeting development aspirations. Currently, Bangladesh collects only about 10 per cent of its GDP in tax revenue which is much higher in many other developing countries at similar levels of development. Bangladesh's tax effort index—revenue collection relative to estimated revenue potential—is also low. Bangladesh generates and collects revenues through taxes and other sources; but still it is most in need of revenues, and often faces the steepest challenges in collecting taxes.

DRM creates additional space for sustainable budget expenditures, fosters ownership and reduces dependency on external assistance. When assessing DRM, not only the volume of revenue must be considered (e.g. tax to GDP ratio); the content and fairness of tax policies also matters (e.g. to avoid distortions and inequity).

Globally, it is suggested that countries collecting less than 15 per cent of GDP in taxes must increase their revenue collection in order to meet basic needs of citizens and businesses. This level of taxation is an important tipping point to make a state viable and put it on a path to development. The Addis Ababa Action Agenda of 2015 for financing the SDGs calls on countries to step-up their efforts to mobilise domestic resources, recognising that much of the increased public financing to achieve the SDGs needs to be generated domestically.

In the case of taxation, a key policy issue is to recognise that making it easier to pay taxes improves competitiveness. Modern tax systems seek to optimise tax collections while minimising the burden of taxpayers to comply with tax laws. A low cost of tax compliance and efficient tax-related procedures are advantageous for the businesses as well. Overly complicated tax systems are associated with high levels of tax evasion, large informal sector, more corruption, and less investment. Undue burden on taxpayers can occur in connection with the filing or correction of mistakes in tax returns, claiming refunds on taxes, undergoing tax audits, and appealing tax assessments.

The need is also to ensure that the tax system is fair and equitable. The government needs to balance goals, such as increased revenue mobilisation, growth, and reduced compliance costs along with ensuring that the tax system is fair and equitable. Fairness considerations include the relative taxation of the poor and the rich, corporate and individual taxpayers, cities and rural areas, labour and investment incomes, and the older and the younger generations.

The tax effort index captures how much the government would be able to collect in tax revenue given the specific characteristics of the economy, such as the level of development and trade openness by calculating the ratio of the actual tax revenue to the estimated tax revenue that a national economy with some specific characteristics should be able to raise. The estimate of tax is typically obtained using econometric models that predict the tax share using 'tax determinants' such as, the agricultural share of the economy, the share of manufacturing or industrial activities, GDP per capita, sum of exports and imports as a share of GDP, inflation, indices of corruption, and governance. The tax effort index then tells what percentage of the potential (estimated) tax revenue is actually collected. In terms of both tax efforts and tax collection, Bangladesh is placed in the 'low' category among the developing countries.

In the fiscal literature, 'tax gap' refers to the difference between revenue collected and what could be collected. However, it is hard to estimate the tax gap for a developing country like Bangladesh. Tax evasion and avoidance, tax exemptions, and inequitable rent-sharing are all significant sources of tax gap. As a result of globalisation, competition between countries to attract capital creates large grey areas in tax legal systems, and transnational corporations (TNCs) make widespread use of aggressive tax planning and transfer mispricing in order to minimise their tax payments. These practices lead to revenue loss for countries like Bangladesh. Further, although these have been proven largely ineffective in attracting foreign investment, tax incentives still result in large revenue losses in Bangladesh. In many sectors, rent-sharing agreements are often negotiated directly between companies and politicians, in a way that is often not transparent and which leads to highly favourable terms for investors at the expense of lower public revenues.

Bangladesh faces extensive political, economic and administrative challenges in closing tax gaps. Tax reform is often difficult due to interest groups who benefit from the existing system. Meanwhile, tax authorities also suffer from weak capacity due to a shortage of skilled staff and the lack of modern infrastructure such as IT systems and property registers. The structure of the Bangladesh economy has also some challenges for taxation given the large size of the agriculture sector, small tax bases, and high degree of informality.

Tax reforms and technical assistance and training to tax and customs administrations can go a long way in raising revenue in Bangladesh. Bangladesh also needs to be more active on the issues of tax evasion and avoidance. Initiatives may also be directed towards signing new tax information exchange agreements along with providing assistance in implementing guidelines on transfer pricing. The South Asian countries may, for example, promote good governance in tax matters and strengthen the fight against tax fraud and tax evasion.

The debate on tax issues at the global level currently focuses on two main agendas: one on increasing transparency and information exchange, and the other on base erosion and profit-shifting (BEPS). The former involves establishing automatic information exchange as the new global standard for cooperation in tax matters and ending legal secrecy of ownership of companies and trusts, especially those based in tax havens. The latter involves a range of potential actions relating to transfer mispricing, country-by-country reporting by transnational companies, international tax laws, standards for international tax treaties, limits on tax planning activities, and the tax treatment of the digital economy. Further, these agendas have been endorsed by the G8 and the G20, thus giving them high level support and momentum.

Bangladesh can adopt a framework for developing action plans for raising domestic revenues. The framework can help develop coordination with other actors involved in the area of taxation to ensure coordination and prevent duplication. This will also provide pathways for Bangladesh for greater involvement in global initiatives in developing the domestic revenue system.

The global agenda should promote reforms in the global tax system, ensuring that international tax evasion efforts is accompanied by actions to support tax mobilisation efforts of countries like Bangladesh. There should also be more emphasis on increased financial and technical assistance to support local capacity in tax administrations, that still face great administrative and capacity constraints, and support building/strengthening regional organisations in developing, for example, shared principles on tax exemptions, standard tax regimes for natural resource contracts, and proposals for minimum withholding taxes on dividends paid by subsidiaries of TNCs.

Although there are some successful reforms in the tax system, still there remain many challenges pressing domestic revenue mobilisation in Bangladesh. Dealing with 'hard to tax' sectors, poor administrative capacity, legislative and enforcement obstacles, and other customs-related problems are aggressive challenges that still remain. For moving forward, there need to be comprehensive efforts to reduce the base of informal activities, build administrative capacity, create a secure environment, develop a robust fiscal framework, reform customs operations with effective policy for trade facilitation, and update the tax legislations.

5.9.1 *Extending and Enlarging the Fiscal Space*

For Bangladesh, a prudent financing strategy during the post-2021 period would increasingly depend on enhancing the fiscal space to scale up expenditure in relevant areas in order to close the development gaps. For the purpose, four major mechanisms may be conceived: (i) enhancing domestic revenues from tax and non-tax sources; (ii) increasing ODA including grants, concessional loans and debt relief; (iii) reprioritising expenditures, including enhancing their allocative and technical efficiency, and (iv) financing public expenditures by borrowing from domestic and international sources. In practice, the extent to which Bangladesh can expand the fiscal space would depend critically on two elements: (i) scope of generating fiscal savings from improved allocative and technical efficiency of existing spending; and (ii) capacity to raise additional fiscal resources from new revenue measures, additional aid or new borrowing.

For a country which already raises significant revenue, has a high initial stock of debt, or receives relatively high aid inflows, the scope to raise additional revenue from any of the above sources would be limited. On the other hand, the lower the allocative and technical efficiency of the existing budget and the larger the volume of such spending, the greater would be the scope for efficiency gains as a source of expanding the fiscal space. In reality, the scope of raising additional revenues from all the above sources appears to be wide for Bangladesh.

It is also important in Bangladesh not to assign the role of fiscal policy as a tool for reducing government deficits or restoring macroeconomic balances alone. Its role as a powerful instrument for promoting employment and economic growth should also be recognised. Similarly, monetary policy is not only a means of controlling inflation rather it should be treated as a versatile instrument through which both the price and volume of credit can be effectively used in the pursuit of development objectives. The policy framework needs to adopt a developmental approach based on an integration of short-term counter-cyclical fiscal and monetary policies with long-term development objectives. In addition, the term 'resource' should be interpreted having a wider connotation covering not only financial but also human, institutional, social, technical and other forms of capital that play important roles in the process of development in Bangladesh.

For closing the development gaps, Bangladesh needs to strengthen the existing institutional mechanisms and modalities for financing its sustainable development agenda along with leveraging new, emerging and innovative avenues of financing from different sources, both domestic and external. However, such sources of finance should be stable and predictable and they should supplement—and not substitute—traditional sources of finance. Table 5.4 provides both domestic and external sources of potential funding and also looks at both public and private dimensions of these sources. Although these sources are treated as distinct, it is important to recognise that resource mobilisation from public sources and supportive policies can leverage private financing to meet the growing and emerging requirements of finance in the country.

The future development agenda requires adequate resources to meet significant investment needs in public goods, such as closing huge infrastructure gaps; providing required education, health and other basic services; ensuring continued flow of ecosystem services in view of the threats of climate change and other challenges; and creating the environment for enhanced private investments both from domestic and external sources. In Bangladesh, such investments need to be leveraged from public resources as these investments are characterised by high social rates of return but having low private returns. In addition, both supportive public finances and domestic capital markets are needed including innovative sources of finance such as carbon taxes, diaspora bonds, financial transaction taxes and similar other revenue sources.

Table 5.4 Potential Sources of Development Financing for Bangladesh

Traditional		*Innovative*	
Domestic	*External*	*Domestic*	*External*
Public Tax revenue Other (non-tax) revenue **Private** Household saving Corporate saving	**Public** Bilateral and multilateral donors (e.g. ODA) Multilateral development finance institutions **Private** Global financial market FDI Multinational corporations Remittances from overseas migrant workers	**Public** Leveraging financial inclusion Islamic banking finance Introducing new and innovative taxes (e.g. carbon tax) Ensuring trade finance for MSMEs Encouraging PPPs **Private** Developing capital markets Involving institutional investors	**Public** Accessing climate finance Using aid for trade Deepening south-south cooperation and triangular development cooperation **Private** Blended finance Loans, equity investments, guarantees

Source: Mujeri 2015

5.10 Concluding Remarks

This chapter provides an overview of several areas where Bangladesh needs to reset priorities to overcome the challenges of the post-2021 era. Over the coming decades, Bangladesh has large financing requirements, but there also exists wide scope of raising significant resources from the traditional sources and tapping new and innovative sources of finance at national and regional levels. While the numbers may appear large and beyond the country's available resource mobilisation capacity, with rapidly rising prosperity, Bangladesh can generate enough savings to finance its resource requirements for bridging the development gaps. The challenge, however, is how to mobilise these savings for financing the development gaps.

An essential prerequisite for collecting increased revenues for development is to promote and nurture strong, diversified and stable financial system which is the key to ensuring financial inclusion along with financial stability and sustainability. For developing a more inclusive financial system and generate increased development resources, Bangladesh needs to: (i) raise tax-GDP ratio through different measures such as broadening tax bases, addressing loopholes, removing irrational exemptions, improving collection and administrative efficiency and adopting other revenue generating measures; (ii) rationalise and reorient public expenditures towards more productive activities, increase expenditure efficiency, reduce unproductive expenditures including high defense expenses and subsidies; (iii) undertake effective measures to create well-diversified and competitive financial systems that would facilitate the broadening and deepening of equity and debt markets, create the conditions for expanding the institutional investment sector to generate required liquidity; (iv) strengthen the legal and regulatory frameworks and supervisory systems to heighten investor confidence and promote financial inclusion especially for providing financial services to the low-income groups, women and micro-entrepreneurs; (v) create conducive environments and well-designed incentive frameworks for leveraging innovative models of blended finance and PPPs in infrastructure and other key areas of development; and (vi) undertake measures for developing the capital market having high potential for raising resources for financing development. In this context, a critical issue is to increase the capacity to install effective regulatory frameworks for efficient functioning of capital market institutions.

Bangladesh also needs to take effective measures to rapidly develop the domestic institutional investors especially in the areas of asset management and pension fund. The country should prepare itself to exploit the large potential of the rapidly growing presence of high-net worth and mass affluent sections of individuals in the Asia-Pacific region. Bangladesh should increasingly exploit all potential domestic sources of financing and work together to ensure a fair share of ODA commitments and distributions. The private sector must also be given proper incentives to participate in development activities for which the country needs to create supportive policy framework for blended finance and PPPs, adapt innovative climate financing mechanisms, provide financial services to all, and promote South-South and triangular development cooperation especially for expanding its knowledge base and building development capacities.

References

Baldwin, R. 2011. *Trade and Industrialisation After Globalisation's 2nd Unbundling: How Building and Joining a Supply Chain Are Different and Why It Matters, No. w17716*. Cambridge, MA: National Bureau of Economic Research.

Baldwin, R., and J. Lopez-Gonzalez. 2013. *Supply-Chain Trade: A Portrait of Global Patterns and Several Testable Hypotheses, No. w18957*. Cambridge, MA: National Bureau of Economic Research.

Barnett, A. 1990. The Diffusion of Energy Technology in the Rural Areas of Developing Countries: A Synthesis of Recent Experience. *World Development* 18 (4): 539–553.

Bell, M., and M. Albu. 1999. Knowledge Systems and Technological Dynamism in Industrial Clusters in Developing Countries. *World Development* 27 (9): 1715–1734.

Bell, M., and K. Pavitt. 1993. Technological Accumulation and Industrial Growth: Contrasts Between Developed and Developing Countries. *Industrial and Corporate Change* 2 (2): 157–210.

Burstein, A.T., and A. Monge-Naranjo. 2009. Foreign Know-How, Firm Control, and the Income of Developing Countries. *Quarterly Journal of Economics* 124 (1): 149–195.

Caliendo, L., and F. Parro. 2015. Estimates of the Trade and Welfare Effects of NAFTA. *Review of Economic Studies* 82 (1): 1–44.

Coe, D., E. Helpman, and A. Hoffmaister. 1997. North-South R&D Spillovers. *Economic Journal* 107 (440): 134–149.

Evenson, R.E., and L.E. Westphal. 1995. Technological Change and Technology Strategy. In *Handbook of Development Economics*, ed. J. Behrman and T.N. Srinivasan, vol. 3A, 2209–2299. Amsterdam: North-Holland.

Feenstra, R.C., and G.H. Hanson. 1997. *Productivity Measurement and the Impact of Trade and Technology on Wages: Estimates for the US, 1972–1990, No. w6052*. Cambridge, MA: National Bureau of Economic Research.

GED. 2018. *Bangladesh Delta Plan 2100 (Bangladesh in the 21st Century), Volume 1: Strategy, General Economics Division, Bangladesh Planning Commission, Ministry of Planning*. Dhaka: Government of the People's Republic of Bangladesh Dhaka.

Grossman, G.M., and E. Rossi-Hansberg. 2008. Trading Tasks: A Simple Theory of Offshoring. *American Economic Review* 98 (5): 1978–1997.

Guadalupe, M., O. Kuzmina, and C. Thomas. 2012. Innovation and Foreign Ownership. *American Economic Review* 102 (7): 3594–3627.

Halpern, L, M. Koren and A. Szeidl. 2015. *Imported Inputs and Productivity, American Economic Review* 105 (12): 3660–3703.

Hwang, H.-R., and J.-Y. Choung. 2014. The Co-evolution of Technology and Institutions in the Catch-up Process. *Journal of Development Studies* 50 (9): 1240–1260.

Ignatenko, A., F. Raei, and B. Mircheva. 2019. *Global Value Chains: What are the Benefits and Why Do Countries Participate?, IMF Working Paper WP/19/18*. Washington DC: International Monetary Fund.

ILO. 2008. *Can Low-Income Countries Afford Basic Social Security?*, Social Security Policy Briefings, Paper 3, Social Security Department, International Labour Office, Geneva.

ILO and WHO. 2009. *Social Protection Floor Initiative, Manual and Strategic Framework for Joint UN Country Operations*. Geneva: International Labour Office and World Health Organization.

Islam, R., M.K. Mujeri, and Z. Ali. 2011. *Fiscal and Policy Space for Crisis Response with a Focus on Employment and Labour Market: A Study of Bangladesh*. Geneva: Employment Policy Department, International Labour Office.

Johnson, B., and A.D. Andersen. 2012. *Learning, Innovation and Development*. Aalborg, Denmark: Aalborg University Press.

Juma, C., and L. Yee-Cheong. 2005. *Innovation: Applying Knowledge in Development*. London: Earthscan.

Kaplinsky, R. 2011. Schumacher Meets Schumpeter: Appropriate Technology Below the Radar. *Research Policy* 40 (2): 193–203.

Keller, W. 2004. International Technology Diffusion. *Journal of Economic Literature* 42 (3): 752–782.

Khondker, B.H., and M.K. Mujeri. 2006. Globalisation–Poverty Interactions in Bangladesh. In *Globalisation and Poverty: Channels and Policy Responses*, ed. M. Bussolo and J.I. Round. London and New York: Routledge.

Lin, J.Y. 2011. *From Flying Geese to Leading Dragons: New Opportunities and Strategies for Structural Transformation in Developing Countries*. Maputo, Mozambique: WIDER Lecture.

Lundvall, B.-A., K.J. Joseph, C. Chaminade, and J. Vang, eds. 2009. *Handbook of Innovation Systems and Developing Countries*. Cheltenham, UK: Edward Elgar.

Mayer, J. 2002. Globalization, Technology Transfer and Skill Accumulation in Low-income Countries. In *Globalization, Marginalization and Development*, ed. S.M. Murshed, 62–79. London: Routledge.

McCulloch, N. 2006. The Impact of Structural Reforms on Poverty: A Simple Methodology with Extensions. In *Globalisation and Poverty: Channels and Policy Responses*, ed. M. Bussolo and J.I. Round. London and New York: Routledge.

McCulloch, N., L.A. Winters, and X. Cirera. 2001. *Trade Liberalization and Poverty: A Handbook*. London: Centre for Economic Policy Research and Department for International Development.

Montobbio, F., and V. Sterzi. 2013. The Globalization of Technology in Emerging Markets: A Gravity Model on the Determinants of International Patent Collaborations. *World Development* 44: 281–299.

MOST. 2011. *National Science and Technology Policy 2011, Ministry of Science and Technology*. Dhaka: Government of the People's Republic of Bangladesh.

Mujeri, M.K. 2015. *Financing Development Gaps in the Countries with Special Needs in the Asia-Pacific Region, WP/15/12, Discussion Paper, Third International Conference on Financing for Development, Addis Ababa, Ethiopia, Macroeconomic Policy and Development Division*. Bangkok: United Nations Economic and Social Commission for Asia and the Pacific.

Niosi, J. 2008. Technology, Development and Innovation Systems: An Introduction. *Journal of Development Studies* 44 (5): 613–621.

Ossa, R. 2015. Trade Wars and Trade Talks with Data. *American Economic Review* 104 (12): 4104–4146.

Romer, P.M. 1990. Endogenous Technological Change. *Journal of Political Economy*, 98 (5, Part 2): The Problem of Development: A Conference of the Institute for the Study of Free Enterprise Systems: S71-S102.

Rosenberg, N. 1982. *Inside the Black Box: Technology and Economics*. Cambridge: Cambridge University Press.

Santacreu, A.M. 2015. Innovation, Diffusion, and Trade: Theory and Measurement. *Journal of Monetary Economics* 75: 1–20.

Timmer, M.P, A.A. Erumbana, B. Los, R. Stehrer, and G. de Vries.2012. *New Measures of European Competitiveness: A Global Value Chain Perspective*, Background paper for the WIOD project presentation at the high-level conference on "Competitiveness, Trade, Environment and Jobs in Europe: Insights from the New World Input Output Database (WIOD), European Commission, Brussels.

UNDP. 2001. *Human Development Report 2001, Making New Technologies Work for Human Development*. New York: United Nations Development Programme.

UNIDO. 1984. Technological Self-reliance of the Developing Countries. In *Technology Policy and Development*, ed. P.K. Ghosh, 97–174. Westport, CT: Greenwood Press.

Wignaraja, G. 2003. Competitiveness Analysis and Strategy. In *Competitiveness Strategy in Developing Countries*, ed. G. Wignaraja, 15–60. London: Routledge.

World Bank. 2002. *World Development Report 2002: Building Institutions for Markets*. Washington, DC: World Bank.

———. 2008. *Global Economic Prospects 2008: Technology Diffusion in the Developing World*. Washington, DC: World Bank.

———. 2016. *Annual Report 2016 Digital Dividends*. Washington DC: World Bank.

CHAPTER 6

Creating Jobs

6.1 Introduction

Bangladesh is the eighth most populous country in the world with a total population of about 165 million in 2019 which, according to the UN, is projected to grow to more than 202 million in 2050 (WDI 2015). Although the large size of population has traditionally been considered as a bottleneck for rapid growth in a low income country, the recent development literature highlights two-way positive interactions between population and economic growth, especially in terms of its changing age structure (see, e.g., Bloom et al. 1999, 2011, Prskawetz et al. 2004). Changes in age structure lead to decline in dependency ratio which favours higher economic growth if supportive policies enhance employability prospects of the labour force. Understanding how demographic changes unfold in future is essential for the design and implementation of the sustainable development agenda for a country like Bangladesh.

While the relationship between population size, consumption, technology and the environment is complex, the demographic trends in countries like Bangladesh highlight the importance of integrating population dynamics into development planning while also promoting sustainable patterns of consumption and production. As Bangladesh embarks on an ambitious development agenda for the future, there is an urgent need to strengthen the evidence base on the country's population-labour

© The Author(s) 2020

M. K. Mujeri, N. Mujeri, *Bangladesh at Fifty*, Palgrave Studies in Economic History,
https://doi.org/10.1007/978-3-030-56791-0_6

force-development dynamics in order to design development pathways, monitor progress, and promote sustainable development.

6.1.1 Population Dynamics in Bangladesh

Population dynamics—more particularly demographic changes in Bangladesh—are intertwined with almost all critical questions that human beings face today. In the past, changes in the size and structure of population needed centuries to evolve and remained mostly unnoticed. But now the world, and especially countries like Bangladesh, is undergoing profound demographic changes within short periods of time.

As Table 6.1 shows, the total number of population in 2018, estimated by the US Census Bureau, is 159,453 thousand, whereas the United Nations estimate counts 169,775 thousand in 2020 with a population growth rate of 1.0 per cent per year. According to US Census Bureau, the annual number of births in Bangladesh currently stands at 2963 thousand with a crude birth rate of 19 and total fertility rate (TFR) of 2.2. Accordingly, the annual number of deaths is 863 thousand with 5 deaths per 1000 populations. Infant mortality rate and under-five mortality rate stand at 31 and 37, respectively with a slight higher infant mortality among male children than that of their female counterpart. Moreover, the life expectancy at birth currently stands at seventy-fouryears and again higher for females than that of males. The net migration of Bangladesh shows a negative value. Indeed, population density is 1304 people per square kilometre in 2020 (United Nations 2019).

The above figures indicate that changes in fertility in Bangladesh have been extraordinary; total fertility levels dropped from high levels at a very fast pace. This is due primarily to voluntary decisions to reduce family sizes. The TFR declined by nearly 200 per cent within a period of three decades. However, fertility levels still vary considerably among different income groups and between rural and urban areas. Capital city and other urban areas have lower fertility. These differences can also be observed if other indicators of social differentiation, such as education levels, are used. They are the expression of inequalities in choices and opportunities among different social sectors and geographic areas.

Major improvements in longevity have come about due to advances in public health, infrastructure, education and medicine. Further, Bangladesh has made dramatic improvements in child mortality since the 1980s. Life expectancy in Bangladesh rose by almost twenty years since 1950 and has reached nearly seventy-four years in 2018.

Table 6.1 Selected demographic trends, Bangladesh

Indicator	*Source*					
	US Census Bureau			*United Nations*		
	1995	*2018*	*2025*	*1990*	*2020*	*2030*
Mid-year population in thousands	117,374	159,453	170,281	106,189	169,775	185,585
Growth rate, %	1.9	1.0	0.9	2.6	1.0	0.8
Number of births, in thousands	3757	2963	2917	3144	2548	2297
Crude birth rate, per 1000 population	32	19	17	38	19	15
Total fertility rate, births per woman	3.8	2.2	2.1	4.98	2.07	1.84
Sex ratio at birth (males per 100 females)	...	...	...	105	105	105
Number of deaths, in thousands	980	863	976	943	727	826
Crude death rate, per 1000 population	8	5	6	11.4	5.3	5.5
Infant mortality rate, per 1000 births	86	31	24	109	27	18
Under five mortality rate, per 1000 births	116	37	28	159	33	22
Life expectancy at birth	62	74	75	57.0	73.0	75.7
Male	...	...	...	56.7	71.3	73.9
Female	...	...	...	57.3	74.7	77.6
Net number of migrants, in thousands	-553	-482	-480	219	-2350	-1500
Net migration rate, per 1000 population	-5	-3	-3	-0.4	-2.8	-1.7
Population density, no. per sq. km.	...	...	...	816	1304	1426

Source: US Census Bureau, 2010; United Nations 2017

6.1.2 *Key Demographic Issues*

Bangladesh has achieved considerable success in reducing fertility but population momentum will carry its population close to 250 million, unless some unforeseen developments occur to bring fertility below replacement level within a decade. Future trends in fertility will depend on further improvements in child survival, which has been stagnant for the past decade, following impressive gains in the 1980s. It will also depend on the changing status of women and girls, and that will require continued inputs in primary and secondary female education linked with developing formal sector employment opportunities in the rural areas, not only in the cities.

A key demographic shift that demands a response is the rapid ageing of the population due largely to the fertility decline. The numbers of the elderly people will increase by nearly six-fold by the mid-century, while numbers in the working ages will less than double. This decrease in the relative size of the working age tax base to the growing demands for healthcare by the elderly group, who are more prone to non-communicable diseases, should be a matter of concern, as Bangladesh evolves health insurance schemes, and more expensive health services, in response to the changing needs.

A second demographic phenomenon that demands an urgent response is that of rural-urban migration. The future of Bangladesh agriculture suggests that the country is close to the limits of availability of agricultural land and productivity, at least in the short-term. This is, partly, due to challenging problems of satisfactorily controlling the flow and timing of water for irrigation and, partly, due to the very high population densities in the rural areas. The inevitable consequence of this situation will be urbanisation on a scale which risks overwhelming the capacity of the urban authorities to provide housing, water and sanitation, healthcare, education and other essential services to the incoming migrants.

In the case of fertility, the recent cessation of outreach family planning services seems to have selectively disadvantaged the poor, among whom fertility has risen. This shows that the importance of services for different population subgroups need to be better understood. The same pattern may also apply to women, for example, in Sylhet division, who may be economically better-off, but have limited mobility. Their fertility has been consistently higher than in other parts of the country. Learning how to develop health systems to identify high-fertility families and target these families for additional services is a challenge to the health system.

Bangladesh still has a pattern in the use of short-term family-planning methods which are rather inefficient where most women marry while young and complete their childbearing in their mid-twenties, leaving another twenty years of fertile life to ensure protection from unwanted pregnancies. It is possible that concerns about poor quality of care and fear of surgical procedures underlie much of the hesitation to adopt long-term or permanent contraceptive methods. The issue needs to be addressed effectively.

In the case of rural–urban migration, it is not clear whether and how the provision of rural microfinance affects the migration process. Many rural people migrate to urban areas with the hope of finding employment. In many cases, the hope remains unfulfilled as well. It is important to assess the nature of employment in the urban informal sector and how employment opportunities can be increased in the urban areas.

6.2 Labour Force in Bangladesh

The rising size of the Bangladesh labour force presents an opportunity to drive economic expansion and increase GDP, but it also presents many challenges. Nearly two-thirds of Bangladesh's population, or more than 111 million people in total, are of working age in 2017, the highest share in the last few decades. The United Nations projects that the potential labour force will continue to grow throughout the second half of the present century (United Nations 2017). Bangladesh, like many other developing countries, will face the challenge of expanding its labour market to provide jobs for the growing workforce. A vital labour force is an asset, but when its proportion is too high relative to the rest of the population, low wages and unemployment become a risk.

A good government has the ability to adopt right policies that can mitigate that risk by fostering sustainable jobs that offer good wages and working conditions. This is easier to accomplish where rights-based population policies encourage balanced age distributions, and where sound health and education policies improve employment potential. The age structure of a country's labour force depends primarily on the fertility rate followed by the rate of migration. Bangladesh has a falling fertility rate and about 111 million people in the working age group, a number that is likely to increase in future and may push economic growth. Bangladesh's labour force participation rate is low at about 57 per cent due to the fact that just one-third of women work outside the home.

6.2.1 Labour Force Growth in Bangladesh

Although the labour force in Bangladesh is defined in the Labour Force Surveys (LFS) using two alternative concepts termed as 'usual' (which uses 15 years as the lower age limit for inclusion in the labour force) and 'extended' (which uses 10 years as the lower age limit for inclusion) definitions, the usual definition is most widely used in labour market analysis. We also follow the same tradition in the present analysis.

The total labour force includes all persons both in employment and unemployment. These two groups together represent the current supply of labour force in the country. The 'youth labour force' covers persons of the labour force who belong to the age group of 15–29 years. On the other hand, the proportion of country's working age population in total population that is involved actively in the labour market (either currently working or looking for jobs) provides the labour force participation rate (LFPR). Bangladesh uses the standard ILO definition of employment and unemployment. Employed labour force comprises all persons of 15 years and above who during a specified period was actively involved at least for one hour, in any form of work for wage or salary, profit or family gain, including production of goods for own consumption. Unemployment, on the other hand, indicates the proportion of the labour force that is willingly looking for work but don't have a job. Underemployment is another terminology that shows the mismatches between labour supply and demand, measured in Bangladesh mostly in terms of hours of work per week (BBS 2018).

The labour force in Bangladesh has expanded considerably since the 1970s. The total labour force was 63.6 million in 2017 compared with 35.9 million in 1991 and 20.5 million in 1974 (Table 6.2). This shows that around 1 million people have entered the labour force annually during the 1990s and, given the present demographic trend, the growth of the labour force is unlikely to taper off during the coming decade. Over the years, the increase in the labour force has come mostly from the growth in the working age population. During the 1990s, population aged 15 years and above grew by nearly 25 per cent although the refined activity rate, that is, the ratio of economically active population of ages 15 years and above to the population of same ages remained almost unchanged at around 49 per cent during the period. The rural–urban variation in the labour force growth has also been significant. Between 1974 and 2017, the rural labour force grew by nearly two-and-a-half times while the increase in urban labour force was by nearly nine times. This reflects the impact of significant urbanisation that has taken place in the country: the urban population increased by more than five times between 1974 and 2011 from 6.3 million to 33.6 million compared with an increase of rural

Table 6.2 Labour force in Bangladesh, 1974–2017 (in million)

Year	*Both sex*			*Male*			*Female*		
	Total	*Rural*	*Urban*	*Total*	*Rural*	*Urban*	*Total*	*Rural*	*Urban*
1974	20.50	18.50	2.00	19.60	17.70	1.90	0.90	0.80	0.10
1985	29.51	25.37	4.14	26.81	23.14	3.67	2.70	2.23	0.47
1991	35.90	28.40	7.50	31.00	24.40	6.60	4.90	4.00	0.90
2000	45.04	34.77	10.27	35.02	27.31	7.71	10.02	7.46	2.56
2010	56.70	43.40	13.30	39.50	30.20	9.30	17.20	13.20	4.00
2017	63.60	45.70	17.90	43.60	30.70	12.90	20.00	15.00	5.00

Source: BBS, Labour Force Surveys, various years

population by nearly 70 per cent (from 65.2 million to 110.5 million) during the same period.

In urban areas, females accounted for 5 million (28 per cent) of the labour force in 2017 compared with only 0.1 million in 1974. Although the size of the female labour force has expanded in the rural areas, but the urban female labour force has steadily expanded. This has also been associated with increase in the female labour force participation rate. These changes suggest that the urban labour market has been emerging as more attractive to women, presumably due to the rapid expansion of women's employment opportunities in the readymade garments and similar other sectors. The composition of female participation in the labour market seems to have undergone some changes as well through a lowering of the rate of marginalisation of the female labour in exclusive non-paid household activities. Nevertheless, the extremely disadvantaged situation of women is evident: the female labour force participation rates are much lower than similar rates for the males (Table 6.3).

The numbers of employed and unemployed populations along with sex composition and rural–urban residence are given in Table 6.4. The number of employed population more than doubled from 27.9 million to 60.8 million between 1984 and 2017; although total unemployed population also registered a significant increase during the same period. A total of 2.7 million people are unemployed in 2017 compared with 0.51 million in 1984. A noteworthy feature is that the period witnessed a more rapid expansion of female employment which increased from 2.4 million to 18.6 million whereas the growth of male employment was from 25.5 million to 42.2 million. Also, the expansion of urban employment was faster than

Table 6.3 Labour force participation rate in Bangladesh

Year	*Labour force participation rate, %*			*Distribution of labour force, %*			
	Total	*Female*	*Male*	*Female*	*Male*	*Rural*	*Urban*
1985	43.9	8.2	78.2	...	...	...	...
1991	48.8	14.1	79.6	14	86	78	22
2000	49.2	22.8	73.5	22	78	77	23
2010	59.3	36.0	82.5	30	70	77	23
2017	58.2	36.3	80.5	31	69	72	28

Source: BBS, Labour Force Surveys, various years

employment in the rural areas as a result of which the share of urban employment in total employment increased from less than 14 per cent to nearly 28 per cent over the period.

6.2.2 *Employed Population by Employment Status and Sector*

The status of employment in terms of various categories, such as self-employed, unpaid family helper and day-labourer is provided in Table 6.5. The data reveal significant changes in the distribution of the working population in terms of their status of employment over the last few decades. Between 1991 and 2017, the share of the self-employed persons increased from 22 per cent of the employed population to 44 per cent; while the share of unpaid family helpers declined from 24 per cent to 12 per cent. As we shall see later on, this is largely explained by the significant increase in employment in the services sector (e.g. transport and trade) during the period which employs the largest share of the self-employed labour. The rapid decline in the share of unpaid family helpers may broadly be associated with relative decline in agricultural employment and declining participation rates of labour in agricultural activities. The share of the wage-employed population (employee) rose significantly (from 17 per cent to 39 per cent) showing structural shift towards formal employment in the labour market.

In terms of sector of employment, agriculture provides employment to the vast majority of the labour force in Bangladesh. As can be seen from

Table 6.4 Employed and unemployed labour force in Bangladesh, 1984–2017

	Employed labour force, million									*Unemployed labour force, million*			
Year	Total			Rural			Urban			Rural		Urban	
	Both sex	Male	Female	Both sex	Male	Female	Both sex	Male	Female	Male	Female	Male	Female
1984	27.9	25.5	2.4	24.2	22.2	2.0	3.8	3.4	0.4	0.3	0.1	0.09	0.02
2000	42.8	33.6	9.2	33.2	26.4	6.8	9.7	3.3	2.4	0.9	0.6	0.4	0.2
2006	47.4	36.1	11.3	36.1	27.5	8.6	11.3	8.6	2.7	0.9	0.7	0.3	0.2
2010	54.1	37.9	16.2	41.7	29.1	12.6	12.4	8.8	3.6	1.1	0.6	0.5	0.4
2013	58.1	41.2	16.8	41.9	29.6	12.3	16.2	11.6	4.5	0.8	0.8	0.4	0.6
2017	60.8	42.2	18.6	43.9	29.8	14.1	16.9	12.4	4.6	0.9	0.9	0.4	0.5

Source: BBS, Labour Force Surveys, various years

Table 6.5 Employment status of employed population

Employment status	*Employed labour force, million*				
	1991	*1996*	*2000*	*2010*	*2017*
Self-employed/own account worker	7.7	16.0	18.8	22.0	26.8
Employer	5.7	0.2	0.1	0.1	2.7
Employee	5.9	6.8	7.7	20.0	23.8
Unpaid family helper	8.4	7.6	6.0	11.8	7.2
Day labourer	7.0	9.8	10.2	...	...
Others	0.2	...	...	1.4	0.4
Total	34.9	40.4	42.8	54.1	60.8

Source: BBS, Labour Force Surveys, various years

Table 6.6, employed population in agriculture was 24.7 million (41 per cent of employed labour) in 2017 compared with 17 million (49 per cent of total employment) in 1996. The share of agricultural labour in total employed labour has declined over the years largely due to the continuing rural-urban migration and expansion of non-agricultural employment opportunities. Nevertheless, it is still true that, despite the expansion of the urban sector, there has not taken place any significant change in the sectoral distribution of employment over the last few decades.

A more significant change, however, may be noted in the distribution of employment within the non-agricultural sector. The sectoral pattern of non-agricultural employment shows that the shift in the labour force in the non-agricultural activities was directed more towards the services sector. During 2017, nearly 39 per cent (23.7 million) of the employed labour was engaged in the services sector compared with 35.6 per cent (13.9 million) in 2000. Within the services sector, the dynamic components in terms of labour absorption included trade, hotels and restaurants, community and personal services, construction and transport. The strong growth of many of these activities can also be related to the high rate of urbanisation of the period.

The most striking development in the non-agricultural sector, however, is the trend in the manufacturing employment. Employment in the manufacturing sector increased from 2.5 million in 1984 to a high of nearly 7.0 million in 1989. Afterwards, the number declined dramatically to 5.9 million in 1991 and further to around 4.0 million in 1996 and increased marginally to 4.3 million in 2000. The above trends are perplexing,

Table 6.6 Employed population by broad sectors

Year	*Agriculture*				*Industry*				*Services*			
	Both sex		*Male, million*	*Female, million*	*Both sex*		*Male, million*	*Female, million*	*Both sex*		*Male, million*	*Female, million*
	Million	*% of total*			*Million*	*% of total*			*Million*	*% of total*		
1996	16.99	48.84	15.61	1.38	4.68	13.45	3.33	1.35	13.12	37.71	10.88	2.24
2000	19.99	51.31	16.23	3.76	5.10	13.09	3.52	1.58	13.87	35.60	11.33	2.54
2010	25.73	47.56	15.22	10.51	9.59	17.72	7.43	2.16	19.12	35.35	15.57	3.55
2013	26.19	45.10	17.18	9.01	12.07	20.79	8.08	3.99	19.81	34.11	15.96	3.85
2017	24.69	40.60	13.57	11.13	12.42	20.42	9.28	3.15	23.71	38.98	19.34	4.37

Source: BBS, Labour Force Surveys, various years

particularly in view of the fact that the manufacturing value added increased at a relatively robust rate of about 7 per cent per year during the period.

Even if we exclude the 1989 data, the trend in manufacturing employment shows a mixed pattern: first, an increase from 2.7 million in 1985 to 5.9 million in 1991 and then a decline to 4.0 million in 1996 followed by a marginal increase to 4.3 million in 2000. The total manufacturing employment during the first half of the 1990s declined for both females (from 1.6 million to 0.9 million) and males (from 4.2 million to 2.6 million). A more detailed examination of the 2000 data shows that most of the manufacturing workers (particularly the females) in the rural areas are involved in the manufacture of food products and beverages and belong to the unpaid family workers category. Under the situation, it seems probable that a significant part of such workers were classified as manufacturing unpaid family workers prior to the 1990s and as agricultural unpaid workers afterwards.

6.2.3 *Labour Force and Education*

The level of productivity and earnings, and hence the access to remunerative employment, of an individual is positively related to his/her level of education. With significant increase in enrolment rates in Bangladesh, the educational profile of the labour force has improved over the years creating better potential for skill development.

The data on the level of education of the labour force, presented in Table 6.7, show that the share of the labour force with no education has significantly declined since the 1980s (32 per cent in 2017 compared with 62 per cent in 1984) and the proportion of the labour force with basic schooling (grades 1–5) and secondary education (grades 6–10) has greatly increased: from 18 per cent to 26 per cent having primary education and from 12 per cent to 31 per cent with secondary education. The proportion of the labour force with no education, however, remains relatively high amongst the female workers.

6.2.4 *Unemployment and Underemployment*

The standard definition of unemployment is based on three criteria which should hold simultaneously: without work, currently available for work, and seeking work. In Bangladesh, the job search criterion is applied to people not employed in the seven days prior to the interview for

Table 6.7 Employed labour and level of education

	No education	*Primary (grade 1–5)*	*Secondary (grade 6–10)*	*Higher secondary*	*Graduation and above*
1984 (% of total employed labour)					
Both sex	62.19	17.67	12.22	6.01	1.92
Male	69.20	18.71	12.94	6.16	1.99
Female	83.07	6.72	4.57	4.45	1.19
2017 (% of total employed labour)					
Both sex	31.90	25.80	30.80	6.00	5.60
Male	29.80	26.50	30.40	6.70	6.50
Female	36.40	24.20	31.70	4.30	3.50

Source: BBS, Labour Force Surveys, various years

measuring unemployment. It is often maintained that unemployment in developing countries such as Bangladesh arises because 'capacity and effective demand never have been great enough'. The standard explanation for the existence of labour surplus or unemployment and underemployment in developing countries like Bangladesh is that as compared with the magnitude of population and labour force there is limited availability of capital or complementary resources which include land, factories, machines, tools and implements-the means with which labour produces.

If the population grows faster than the stock of capital of a country, the entire addition to the labour force cannot be absorbed in productive employment because not enough instruments of production would be there to employ them. Since in less developed countries, the stock of capital has not been growing at a rate fast enough to keep pace with the growth of population, the ability to offer productive employment is limited. This results in surplus labour which is manifested in the existence of huge magnitude of underemployment or disguised unemployment and open unemployment in both the rural and urban areas.

Capital as the major bottleneck to growth of employment was made popular by the Harrod-Domar model of economic growth in which capital accumulation plays a pivotal role and according to which the rate of growth of output depends on the proportion of national income saved, divided by the capital-output ratio ($g = s/v$, where g stands for growth rate, s for the proportion of income saved and v for the capital–output ratio).This model assumes capital coefficients (i.e. capital-output ratio and capital–labour ratio) to remain constant. With constant capital–output and capital–labour ratios, the more the capital, the more will be both output and employment. Therefore, when adapted to the less developed countries, this model suggests that the rate of growth of output and therefore of employment is determined by the growth of capital stock.

An alternative view regarding the cause of unemployment and underemployment in developing countries is the deficiency of the availability of essential consumer goods, often called wage goods. It suggests that when the unemployed people or disguisedly unemployed people who are withdrawn from agriculture are engaged in some public works, they will have to be supplied with wage-goods so that employed labourers can subsist. If the wage-goods are not sufficiently available, their employment in capital-creation works cannot be sustained.

Given the real wage rate, a particular number of people can be employed in the economy, depending upon the supply of wage-goods in the economy. Now, the total quantity of wage-goods required to employ all the disguised unemployed workers in agriculture would exceed the actual available supply of wage-goods even when the release of wage-goods by the withdrawal of disguised unemployed is taken into account. Thus, there exists a wage-goods gap which is the fundamental cause of unemployment in labour-surplus developing countries. The quantum of wage employment in the economy depends on the total supply of wage-goods on the one hand and the real wage-rate on the other. If the supply of wage-goods is less than the required supply to provide all labour force, then all workers cannot be fully employed, which will result in the emergence of unemployment. Thus, to generate enough employment and solve the problem of unemployment and underemployment, the wage-goods industries, especially agriculture, must be accorded a high priority in the strategy of economic development.

Considering the total size of the population, the number of unemployed population is rather low in Bangladesh (Table 6.8). As per the ILO definition of unemployment, the total number of unemployed population increased from 2.2 million in 2000 to 2.7 million in 2017, representing nearly a quarter-fold increase in the absolute number of the unemployed population. This represents an unemployment rate of 4.2 per cent in 2017. In view of the existing realities, such low rates of open unemployment are expected in a country such as Bangladesh since the participants

Table 6.8 Unemployed population in Bangladesh

	2000				*2010*				*2017*			
	Total unemployed labour, thousand		***Unemployment rate, %***		***Total unemployed labour, thousand***		***Unemployment rate, %***		***Total unemployed labour, thousand***		***Unemployment rate, %***	
	Male	Female	Male	Female	Male	Female	Male	Female	Male	Female	Male	Female
Total	1353	872	4.21	10.19	1595	972	4,04	5.66	1347	1330	3.09	6.65
Rural	947	657	3.77	10.25	1071	639	3.55	4.85	929	882	3.03	5.88
Urban	406	215	5.73	10.00	524	334	5.65	8.35	417	448	3.23	8.96

Source: BBS, Labour Force Surveys, various years

in the labour force are compelled to engage in some work—even for few hours and at low wages in the informal sector—in order to subsist with his/her family. As a result, the 'standard' unemployment rate does not provide a real picture of the supply–demand balance of the labour market and adequately reflect the degree of inefficiency that prevails in the labour market. In a situation like this, alternative indicators such as underemployment rates and work intensity are necessary to supplement the standard indicator of unemployment rate and reveal the labour market reality in Bangladesh.

6.2.5 *Level of Underemployment*

Conceptually, the notion of underemployment is related to a situation when a person's employment is inadequate in terms of hours of work, income earnings, productivity and use of skills, and the person is looking for better or additional work in conformity with his/her education and skills. In practice, the measurement of underemployment faces a number of difficulties and the adopted methodology in Bangladesh is to estimate underemployment on the basis of hours worked alone. The adopted norm is to treat those who work less than 40 hours during the reference week of the survey as underemployed.

As such, BBS defines time-related underemployment rate as the percentage of employed persons who work less than 40 hours during the reference period and are willing and available to work more hours than what they actually work. It includes all employed persons whose working time in all jobs is 'insufficient in relation to an alternative employment situation in which the person is willing and available to engage'. The criteria for defining time-related underemployment are: willingness to work additional hours; availability to work additional hours; and having worked less than a threshold of working hours (40 hours per week), which is the normal number of working hours per week—eight hours per day, for five days.

Of all employed persons who worked less than 40 hours in a week in Bangladesh in 2017, a total of 1.5 million employed persons (2.4 per cent) are looking for new/additional jobs. Of them, 1.0 million are employed male (2.2 per cent) and 0.5 are employed female (2.9 per cent). And the majority of them live in rural areas; 1.1 million persons (2.6 per cent), compared with 0.3 million persons (1.9 per cent) in urban areas. Further, of all employed persons, 0.66 million (45.2 per cent) are underemployed in the age group 15–29 years and 0.79 million (53.8 per cent) are in the age group 30–64. The proportion of underemployed in the total employed persons is higher in youth (3.7 per cent), followed by adults (1.9 per cent) and old age (0.6 per cent).Almost two-thirds of the time-related underemployed persons are engaged in agriculture (61.6 per cent), while more than one-fourth works in services sector (28.2 per cent) and the rest 10.3 per cent are engaged in the industry sector.

Thus, the perception of the labour market substantially changes when underemployment is taken into account in assessing the status of the labour force in Bangladesh. The information on hours worked shows that a total of 8.3 million (which is more than 19 per cent of the employed labour of 42.8 million) were underemployed in 2000 compared with 1.4 million (4 per cent of the employed labour) in 1984. This shows an extremely high increase in the number of the people who work less than 40 hours per week.

Also the information reveals relatively high incidence of underemployment in rural areas and among the female labour force (Table 6.9). During 2000, the share of the employed labour force who worked less than 40 hours per week was nearly 29 per cent in the rural areas compared with 19 per cent in the urban areas and was as high as 68 per cent among the females against 16 per cent for the males. Of the total number of underemployed labour, nearly 60 per cent were females.

The distribution of the employed labour by hours of work per week reveals some striking features (Table 6.9). The average duration of work is estimated at 46 hours. The distribution of working hours is, however,

Table 6.9 Distribution of working hours of labour force in Bangladesh, 2000

	Total employed labour, million	*Hours worked per week (per cent of respective total employed labour)*			*Average hours of work*
		Less than 40	*Less than 20*	*50 and more*	
Total	39.0	26.3	3.9	40.6	46
Rural	30.3	28.5	4.2	40.0	45
Urban	8.7	18.7	3.0	42.7	48
Male	31.1	15.6	1.3	47.9	49
Female	7.9	68.3	13.1	11.8	33

Source: BBS, Labour Force Survey 1999–2000

relatively wide. While 26 per cent of the labour forces work less than 40 hours a week, nearly 4 per cent work for less than 20 hours per week only. On the other hand, a large proportion of the labour force (41 per cent) works for 50 hours or more per week.

Although the differences are not much between rural and urban areas, the differences are significant between male and female labour. In particular, the underemployment rate is significantly high for the female labour which is 68 per cent (compared with 16 per cent for the male labour). The data, however, do not reveal the nature of the constraints that result in low working hours of women and whether these underemployed female workers would be able to work for longer hours if such opportunities are available in view of their exclusive burden of working in reproductive and household activities. At the same time, it is also true that a large part of the working population is pushed to working for long hours presumably to meet survival needs due to low productivity of their work.

The status of employment of the underemployed labour shows that two categories—self-employed labourers and unpaid family helpers—are mostly affected: self-employed and unpaid family helpers constitute 2.8 million (43 per cent) and 2.6 million (40 per cent) of the total underemployed labour respectively. The rural areas are the home of the majority of the underemployed persons. In particular, the female unpaid family helpers form the largest category (34 per cent) of the underemployed labour force in Bangladesh.

6.3 Informal Sector Employment

In Bangladesh, the informal economy plays an important role both in employment generation and in production and distribution of goods and services. The informal sector activities are mostly small in size and transient in nature. The production units of the informal sector have the characteristic features of household enterprises. The fixed and other assets do not belong to the production units and hence the units, in most cases, cannot engage in transactions or enter into contracts with other units, nor incur liabilities, on their own behalf. The owners have to raise the necessary finance at their own risk and are personally liable, without limit, for any debts or obligations incurred in the production process. The expenditure for production is often indistinguishable from household expenditure of the owners. Similarly, capital goods such as buildings or vehicles may be used indistinguishably for business and household purposes.

Bangladesh's official statistical agency (BBS) adopts the definition of informal employment as a combination of both the informal character of the individual job and employment in the informal sector covering all employed persons in the non-agriculture sector, both wage and salaried workers (employees) with no pension or no contribution to a retirement fund; all contributing family workers; all employers and own-account workers in the informal sector enterprises (operationally defined as all private unincorporated enterprises engaged in non-agriculture work that do not have any registration); and all own-account workers employed in a private household.

According to the Labour Force Survey 2017, informal employment overwhelmingly dominates the country's labour market: 85.1 per cent of all employed population is engaged in informal employment. For the females, the share is 91.8 per cent while it is 82.1 per cent for the males. In the rural areas, the informal employment's share is 88.1 per cent (93.3 per cent for females and 85.6 per cent for males) and, in urban areas, the share is 77.3 per cent (87.3 per cent for females and 73.6 per cent for males). The informal sector usually accounts for around 40 per cent of the total gross value added, with the highest contributions in agriculture, fisheries, trade, and industries (micro, small, and medium enterprises, MSMEs) where capitalisation is relatively low. Over the years, there has not been much change in the level of informality. In 2000, 75.2 per cent of employment has been informal, and the share rose to 86.2 per cent in 2017. The rising share of informal employment, however, is not due to declining levels of formal employment, but due to more rapid growth in informal employment than formal jobs.

In 2017, a total of 51.7 million persons are engaged in informal employment; of them 31.0 per cent are 15–29 years old while 64.9 per cent are 30–64 years old, and only 4.1 per cent are 65 or older. The share of informally employed persons in total employment is very high in all sectors; in particular, it is 95.4 per cent in agriculture, followed by industry (89.9 per cent) and services (71.8 per cent). There exists a clear negative correlation between higher educational attainment and informal employment that is, highly educated persons are more likely to be in formal rather than in informal employment. It is seen that nearly half of those who are engaged in informal employment have no schooling while only a small fraction (less than 0.5 per cent) has received any vocational/technical/skills development training. Further, protective labour regulations and unions do not cover informal sector employment.

6.3.1 Skill Development in the Informal Sector

Given the overwhelming dominance, skills development in the informal sector is an issue of great importance for Bangladesh. It concerns almost all the sectors in the economy. For ensuring greater efficiency and higher productivity, it is necessary to develop technical and vocational skills for these young people and other stakeholders in the sector. The informal apprenticeship programmes that currently exist in the informal sector have better external efficiency although it costs about three times less than formal training courses. Skills development in the informal sector means focusing on the needs and capacity building of the MSMEs. The skill development initiatives for enhancing skills improvement in the informal sector, are no doubt challenging tasks. There is over six million children out-of-school in Bangladesh who have either dropped out or never enrolled in schools. Most of these children are engaged in informal employment, as unskilled labour, involved in hazardous or non-hazardous, paid or unpaid work. These children, especially from the large urban slums have to be given an opportunity to not only complete courses in non-formal basic education but also stream into training on livelihood skills. Still, informal skills development remains outside the scope of government programmes. A large number of NGOs—both large and small—have adopted various programmes of skilling young people, especially from the marginalised and disadvantaged sections in the society.

Close linkage with the labour market is a vital requirement for a training system. Labour market demands are dynamic in nature and they change frequently. These likely changes have to be identified in advance and factored into the skills training. Enterprise-based skill trainings, for instance, create a built-in mechanism to provide training in accordance with the labour market trends. In Bangladesh, the Directorate of Technical Education (DTE) and the Bangladesh Technical Education Board (BTEB) have been adopting different models towards skill training delivery options for the disadvantaged, particularly for the working children. It is expected that these models will be institutionalised through government run vocational training centres. Supervised informal apprenticeship model has been designed to deliver livelihood skills training to out of school children with low level of educational qualification (depending on trade). This innovative intervention ensures that 14+ years aged urban working children have the opportunity to acquire competency based skills under a trade based master crafts person (MCP) who is based in a local market.

In addition to cater to the demand for skill shifts in response to changes in economic regime and management, the process of skill formation for informal sector is further challenged by inadequate capacity of the formal sector institutions and non-affordability of formal training by those who want to acquire skills. The traditional system is further constrained by its inability to reach the disadvantaged who mostly compose the informal sector and reduce discrimination in access to training and education. Formal work environment in Bangladesh is also undergoing rapid transformation in the context of globalisation and technological change, leaving the majority of the workforce in the informal sector, composed of non-farm or off-farm rural activities and work in family-run micro-enterprises. The informalisation of the labour market with changes in the concept of employability risks exclusion from employment for those without appropriate skills. Further, the rapid expansion of the country's informal sector is an outcome of the inability of the formal sector to generate adequate employment opportunities.

In Bangladesh, the labour force has been growing much faster than the employment opportunities in the formal sector, and therefore, the problems of un- and underemployment remain high in the country's policy agenda. Although the informal and modern economic sectors are closely interdependent and have many forward and backward linkages, the organised sector in Bangladesh has never provided a very large employment base. According to the Labour Force Surveys, the growth of formal sector employment is very low over the years. Most of the additional labour force has been absorbed in the informal sector. Therefore, the changing concept of employability requires an innovative approach to education, training and skill development for the informal sector. One of the principal development challenges for Bangladesh is the creation of employment for new entrants into the labour force, most of whom are underemployed.

6.3.2 Issues and Challenges

One of the key challenges for Bangladesh is the creation of employment for the large number of new entrants into the labour force which is growing, at almost twice the rate of population growth. The provision of education, training and skills development of the labour force can increase labour productivity; economic growth and wage increase of the labourers are inter-linked. The current state of the informal sector in Bangladesh demands education, training and skills for decent work in the informal sector. The urban informal sector also shows low productivity. Obviously, a labour force with low levels of education and skills is one of the principle determinants of low productivity in most sectors including the urban informal sector.

Comprehensive and detailed information are needed to develop a clear picture of the state and the workings of the informal enterprises since the informal economy is the largest segment of the country's economy. For such an analysis, data on several issues are needed for identifying the policies for ensuring the best utilisation of the opportunities of the informal sector to create decent employment: (i) number employed in the informal sector, (ii) prevalence of workers in the informal sector compared with the formal sector, (iii) socioeconomic profile of the workers engaged in the informal sector; and (iv) present skill and skill needs to develop them into formal enterprises.

In recent years, there has been a rapid informalisation of the labour market due to depressed level of employment, increased job insecurity and displacement, growing risk of exclusion from employment for those without appropriate skills, highlighting the urgency of continuous acquisition of skills through training and education. The changes in the concept of employability in an increasingly complex and uncertain labour market warrants modifications in job content, skill requirements and knowledge. The government policy, therefore, needs to provide adequate attention to the informal sector as the informal sector has become a living reality covering the vast segment of the labour force in Bangladesh. It is of utmost importance that the country's employment policies plan for the proper development of the informal sector which is emerging as a growing and productive source of employment covering diverse activities such as fisheries, trade, tourism, small-scale manufacturing, real estate and other business activities.

6.4 Gender Wage Gap in Labour Market

In Bangladesh, wages provide a crucial link to poverty—particularly for the poor who rely on earnings derived from their labour—and it is important to ascertain why wages vary among different groups, such as women and men. Moreover, as expectations regarding returns to labour are likely to influence individual and household decisions especially on investments in education and other productive factors, understanding gender wage differentials can lead to more efficient and equitable allocation of resources within households. If, for instance, it is seen that women earn less than men, this could discourage parents from investing in girls and lower girls' future employability. On the other hand, if women earn less than men because of differences in educational and skill endowments, policies should be adopted and awareness created to address specific underlying causes. Better labour market information can thus lead to more appropriate and effective labour market interventions in the context of more inclusive development in Bangladesh.

From a gender perspective, women have made important advances in the labour market since the 1970s. Although still far behind that of men, women's labour force participation rate has increased from 8.2 per cent in 1985 to 36.3 per cent in 2017. This has been associated with an increased share of women in the urban labour force, particularly in manufacturing employment (often in the ready-made garments industries). But this increase has not been enough and gender inequalities continue to persist in the labour market in Bangladesh. Women workers are still heavily concentrated in rural areas (employed in low productivity daily work for poor wages and often concentrated in public food for work programmes) and in unpaid family businesses. On the contrary, despite a strong convergence in the distribution of characteristics (for example, in terms of educational attainment) since the 1990s, wages of men and women have not converged to the same extent and a sizeable gender gap persists. This is possibly a reflection of discrimination that women face at work.

Some researchers suggest that the wage inequality is caused by labour market discrimination against women (Ahmed and Maitra 2010), while others connect the gender wage gap with the significantly lower level of female human capital relative to men (Hossain and Tisdell 2005). The Global Wage Report 2018 of ILO shows that Bangladesh is the only country in the world where the factor-weighted hourly wage gender pay gap is positive. The gender pay gap shows the difference on overall pay between women and men employees. According to the report, the global average monthly gender pay gap is 21.2 per cent in 2017, while Bangladesh gender pay gap is only 2.2 per cent, the lowest in the world.

The BBS conducted a national occupational wage survey in 2007 covering 202 non-farm occupations in 37 industry groups. According to the survey, the average hourly wage among males is BDT 17.20, compared with BDT 14.20 per hour for women, representing 21.1 per cent higher hourly wages for men (Table 6.10). With regard to literacy and education, 17 per cent of women have no education versus 12 per cent of men.

Table 6.10 Gender wage gap in Bangladesh, 2007

	Hourly wage, BDT			*Weekly hours worked*		*Education level, %*									
	Male	*Female*	*% female*	*Male*	*Female*	*No education*		*Below primary*		*Primary*		*Secondary*		*Tertiary*	
						M	*F*	*M*	*F*	*M*	*F*	*M*	*F*	*M*	*F*
Manufacturing	15.2	11.5	75.7	55.3	51.6	17	30	40	35	32	26	9	7	2	2
Electricity, gas, & water supply	27.0	…	…	56.1	…	1	…	4	…	33	…	58	…	4	..
Construction	18.8	11.2	59.6	54.8	54.4	22	72	44	28	31	1	3	0	0	0
Wholesale and retail trade	13.2	…	…	60.6	…	7	…	32	…	44	…	15	…	2	…
Hotels and restaurants	12.3	8.5	69.1	67.3	57.4	17	71	32	24	25	4	20	0	5	1
Transport, storage & communications	17.8	…	…	59.5	…	5	…	17	…	37	…	34	…	6	…
Financial intermediation	40.0	28.3	70.8	47.7	43.8	0	0	0	0	4	15	39	51	57	33
Education	15.6	13.2	84.6	40.6	36.8	1	4	6	14	18	18	44	37	31	28
Health & social work	17.4	14.0	80.5	53.6	51.7	1	4	7	16	26	24	41	34	24	22
Other services	20.1	16.9	84.1	50.4	49.2	4	5	10	6	17	23	42	48	27	17
Total	17.2	14.2	82.6	56.0	47.5	12	17	28	19	30	20	22	27	9	17

Source: BBS, Occupational Wage Survey, 2007

However, a larger share of women completed secondary education (27 per cent versus 22 per cent for men) as well as tertiary education (17 per cent versus 9 per cent for men). Overall, 57 per cent of men are literate, but have less than a secondary education. The average education level of women is therefore somewhat higher than that of men, which shows that the gender-based gap in education has narrowed substantially in the country.

The survey further shows that manufacturing is the most preferred industry for employment for both women and men, after which the picture diverges. The second and third most prevalent industries for women are, respectively, education and health and social work, while for men they are transport, storage and communications and construction (followed closely by hotels and restaurants). This indicates significant gender-based segregation with respect to employment. Indeed, women make up only 10 per cent of manufacturing workers; 7 per cent of workers in construction; and less than 1 per cent in transport, storage and communications, wholesale and retail trade, and electricity, gas and water. Women comprise 14 per cent of workers in 'other services' industry, 28 per cent in financial intermediation and health and social services industries and over 47 per cent in education-related activities. Women's employment is therefore heavily skewed towards service-sector activities.

In terms of hourly wages, the largest gender gap is in construction, where the average hourly wage for women is about 60 per cent that of men; followed by hotels and restaurants (69 per cent); financial intermediation (71 per cent) and manufacturing (76 per cent). The smallest gaps are observed in the service industries in education, health and social work and other services industries in which women have a fairly high share of employment.

Women work fewer hours on average than men across all industries, although the differences are very small in the construction and other services industries. The gap in hours worked is largest in the hotels and restaurants industry, where women work an average of 57.4 hours per week versus 67.3 hours for men. There are also sizeable gaps in financial intermediation, education and manufacturing.

In every industry outside financial intermediation, there is a larger share of women with no education than men. In manufacturing and construction the bulk of both women and men have less than a secondary education. In the hotels and restaurants industry, women are largely uneducated, whereas 25 per cent of men have secondary education or higher. In service industries including financial intermediation, education and health and social work, the majority of workers of both sexes have at least completed secondary education. In financial intermediation, a greater share of men has tertiary education, while in education and health and social work almost the same proportion of women and men have completed tertiary education.

The above shows that wages remain very low in Bangladesh and it is equally true that there is a persistent and large gap in earnings between women and men. Controlling for differences in age, educational background, industry, occupation and geographic location, the estimated gender wage gap is between 15.9 per cent (which excludes the effects of industrial and occupational segregation) and 23.1 per cent (which includes the effects of segregation). Further, across various industries, around 60 per cent of the gap can be explained by differences in endowments, and in most industries less than half the difference is explained, which could be indicative of labour market discrimination (Kapsos, 2008). Thus, there is evidence that there exist gender-based wage differentials in the country, particularly in the construction, hotels and restaurants and manufacturing industries. This also points to the need to reduce industrial and occupational segregation and promote education for all as a means to reduced gender wage differentials and improved gender equity.

6.5 Incidence of Child Labour

Child labour is an issue of concern in Bangladesh. The precise estimate of the incidence of child labour is, however, difficult to arrive at, particularly in view of the diversity of work in which the child labour is involved in both rural and urban areas.[1] In Bangladesh, child labour is usually defined as those children in the age group 5–14 years who were found to be working during the survey reference period (12 months preceding the day of the survey).[2] This means that a child will be taken as a child labour if he/she is found either working one or more hours for pay or profit or working

[1] Two extreme points in defining child labour may be conceived. At the one extreme, one can count all non-educational, non-leisure time of children below a certain age as part of child labour. On the other, child labour may be defined as those involved in full-time employment in an economic activity. A realistic definition, however, may lie between the above two extremes.

[2] See, 1995–96 Child Labour Survey in Bangladesh, BBS. The 2002–2003 National Child Labour Survey, however, adopts a different criteria and estimates child labour as (i) all chil-

in a family farm or enterprise during the reference period, or is found not working but has a job or business from which he/she is temporarily absent during the reference period.

The information on child labour from two Child Labour Surveys (conducted in 1995–1996 and 2002–2003) shows that total child population (5–14 years) in the country was 34.5 million (28 per cent of the total population) in 1995–1996 which marginally increased to 35.1 million, but as a share of total population declined to 26 per cent, in 2002–2003. It may be noted that the child population is estimated at 32.6 million (26.3 per cent of the total population) in the 2001 Population Census, comprising of 15.4 million girls and 17.2 million boys.

The total number of working children declined from 6.3 million to 5 million between 1995–1996 and 2002–2003, indicating an overall reduction in the participation rate from 18 per cent to 14 per cent.[3] Although the participation rates for both girls and boys showed declining trends, the decline was sharp for the girls. The share of total children attending school increased by nearly 8 percentage points during the period reaching 83 per cent in 2002–2003. While important achievements in the fight against child labour have been made by Bangladesh, some 1.2 million children are still trapped in its worst forms, according to the National Child Labour Survey, published in 2015. The UNICEF Multiple Indicator Survey for Bangladesh finds that of the children between 6 and 17 years, 21 per cent of boys and 4 per cent of girls are working. The proportion of children working increases with age, but the very low proportion of girls is attributed to the fact that most work on domestic chores, which is usually a hidden form of child labour.

In Bangladesh, domestic work is the most common form of child labour. Estimates for Dhaka city alone range from 200,000 to one million, almost all girls (Stalker 1996). Other forms of child labour include street children selling various goods and services, waste collectors combing through the rubbish dumps and wandering the streets with sacks over

dren aged 5–17 years who are working/ economically active excluding those children between 12 and 14 years old who spend less than 14 hours a week on

their jobs unless their activities or occupations are hazardous by nature or circumstances; and (ii) 15–17 years old children in the worst forms of child labour or who work 43 hours or more in a week.

[3] One should, however, note that the scope of the survey covered the child population living in the households and excluded street children and children living in institutions such as prisons, orphanages or welfare centres.

their shoulders, and other petty professions. As far as small informal factories are concerned, children aged 5–15 years account for about 40 per cent of the total workforce. Such industries seem to engage children of different age groups. The younger boys, aged 5–12 years, are to be found in industries such as jewellery, shoes, lock making, and book binding. Older boys aged 12–15 years are more likely to be engaged in engineering and automobile workshops as well as in furniture, glass, and electric wire industries. Factories with the highest proportion of child workers include candle making, kite-making and electronics.

Children in Bangladesh engage in the worst forms of child labour, including forced child labour in the production of dried fish and bricks. Children also perform dangerous tasks in the production of garments and leather goods. In addition, the labour law does not prohibit children from working in informal economic sectors, and does not specify the activities and number of hours per week of light work that are permitted for children ages 12 and 13. Moreover, the number of labour inspectors is insufficient for the size of Bangladesh's workforce, and penalties are inadequate to deter child labour law violations.

The government has adopted the 2010 National Child Labour Policy and the National Plan of Action to implement the policy over the period 2012–2016. The Domestic Worker's Protection and Welfare Policy 2015 has set a minimum age for child domestic workers paving the way to address the issues of thousands of child domestic workers in the country. Since 1995, nation-wide sample surveys, baseline surveys and research studies have been conducted which form the basis of various policy and field-level interventions to combat child labour. A National Child Labour Survey report has been published in 2015. A 'Women and Children Labour Unit' in the Ministry of Labour and Employment has been formed in 2015 to facilitate proper coordination of child and women issues in the labour market. The government has undertaken the 'Country Level Engagement and Assistance to Reduce Child Labour' (CLEAR) project to improve the capacity of the government to reduce child labour, including its worst forms. The project is designed to make direct contribution to various strategic areas of intervention of the National Plan of Action thus assisting the government to realise its commitment to eliminate the worst forms of child labour within a time bound manner in the light of the SDGs.

6.5.1 Eradication of Child Labour

Legislation alone has proved inadequate for eradication of child labour in Bangladesh as in other developing countries. Pursuant to the 1973 United Nations convention, Bangladesh has made provisions of law that set a minimum required age for working, but apparently this has not been effective. The Constitution of Bangladesh (Articles 23 and 34) also contains provisions conveying similar spirit. It prohibits the employment of children in factories, mines or in any hazardous work. Bangladesh has also passed a compulsory Primary Education Act, 1990 providing penal prescription on parents for not sending a child to school. But to create enforcement mechanism is a costly proposition. Therefore, the making of laws has to be accompanied by the provision of alternatives acceptable to children and their families.

Citing unemployment, poverty and illiteracy are a superficial way of looking at the issue. Adult unemployment may be the immediate reason why parents send their children to work. Thus abolition of child labour may well open up employment opportunities for adults in the same places where their children work. Often adults, incapacitated by years of labour in their own childhood send their children to work to continue the same vicious cycle of poverty, ill-health and death. Poverty and illiteracy create a mindset that employers exploit for their profit. Employers prefer children for their easy manipulation and low cost, not for their expertise or capacity for hard work. If one is to witness the elimination and proper rehabilitation of child labourers, the issue of releasing the children from their work places and subsequent rehabilitation should occupy an important agenda for policy. The socioeconomic reality of Bangladesh may not permit the total and sudden elimination of child labour, as children released without proper rehabilitation are bound to drift towards some other sources of employment. This is the paradox of child labour reform (Berlau 1997).

Bangladesh ratified the ILO Convention on the Worst Forms of Child Labour, 1999 (No. 182) in March 2001. National legislation on hazardous child labour was subsequently revised in 2006 and a list of hazardous forms of child labour was adopted in 2013. Bangladesh, with support from ILO, has been working since 1994 through its International Programme on the Elimination of Child Labour (IPEC). In addition to the government, IPEC also works with employers and workers organisations, civil society actors as well as a wide range of NGOs to implement various projects and activities. About 75,000 child labourers have directly benefited from these interventions.

Technical cooperation is a significant step in this direction. Technical cooperation programmes like the ILO's International Programme on the Elimination of Child Labour (IPEC) can play and has played a significant role in the release and rehabilitation of child labourers in Bangladesh. In particular, Bangladesh's garment industry is one example of the implementation of a unique action programme under IPEC. Started in 1995 after observing the plight of the released child labourers, the programme began with the signing of a Memorandum of Understanding (MOU) between the Bangladesh Garments Manufacturers and Exporters Association (BGMEA), ILO and UNICEF, detailing areas of cooperation. The MOU provides that all child labourers below 14 years of age in the garment sector be removed from factories and enrolled in schools and paid a monthly stipend. By September 1996, 130 MOU schools for former child workers have opened, serving nearly 2300 children, a figure that quadrupled by the next year (Berlau 1997). The project is unique in that the employers play an active role for educating their former underage workers. The government, trade unions or NGOs implement other projects under IPEC in Bangladesh. The model shows that for an effective elimination of the child labour, legislation and economic incentives have to work together, whereas technical cooperation has an important role. Technical assistance in the form of aid and know-how are important which can help defray the expenses relating to: (i) free and compulsory primary education for all children; (ii) implementation of part-time income generating schemes; (iii) developing the technical and managerial capacity of those involved in the rehabilitation of child labour; (iv) strengthening institutional capacity in the form of organisation development; (v) research for combating child labour; and (vi) awareness raising and social mobilisation.

The Ministry of Labour and Employment adopted the National Child Labour Elimination Policy (NCEP) in 2010. The policy suggests adopting six working strategies of action: (a) determining the goals and objectives, (b) identifying the scope of strategic action; (c) setting up programmes; (d) determining the time frame; (e) selection of key implementation agencies for policy implementation; and (f) selecting the associate and collaborative organisations. The NCEP 2010 also suggests ten programmatic strategies for intervention. These are: policy implementation and institutional development, education, health and nutrition, social awareness raising and motivation, legislation and enforcement, employment and labour market, prevention of child labour and safety of children engaged in labour, social and family integration, research and training, and monitoring and evaluation. The policy suggests establishing a Child Labour Unit under the Ministry of Labour and Employment to coordinate various activities undertaken by different actors. It calls for establishing a National Child Labour Welfare Council, participation of NGOs and collaboration with different international and national organisations for ensuring Bangladesh as a hazardous child labour free country.

In 2017, Bangladesh made some advancement in efforts to eliminate the worst forms of child labour. The government extended its Child Labour National Plan of Action through 2021. The Department of Inspection for Factories and Establishments also provides comprehensive training to the majority of labour inspectors, and institutionalises the use of a factory inspection checklist that includes child labour components.

Along with increasing the access to and quality of primary education, Bangladesh should also reconsider its system of imparting formal education at fixed hours. The system has to be informal and flexible, as only non-formal education can serve as a bridge for working children to enter the world as productive and healthy adults. Several programmes have been devised in Bangladesh to address the paradox of child labour reform (Berlau 1997). The Underprivileged Children's Education Programme (UCEP) is a step in this direction. The main objective of UCEP is to impart general and vocational education to the underprivileged children and provide them with jobs through UCEP job placement centres. Many students of the UCEP schools also do odd jobs like shining shoes in the footpath, some work as vendors, some in rickshaw garages or as garbage pickers, and so on.

Education systems have to be reoriented to suit the needs of child labourers and designed for different age groups in such a way that in due course the children, irrespective of the age at which they enter the system, become healthy and productive adult members of society. The education to be given should attain the objectives of non-formal education that is community development, self-help, leadership, awareness raising, decision-making and participation. It is also important to consider fruitful activities in which released and rehabilitated children may engage after school hours in order to prevent their drifting towards unlawful and criminal activities. Combining beneficial work and education in the form of non-formal education as mentioned above is necessary, as such forms of child work help to fill leisure time, especially in places where organised outside activities are absent to keep children away from streets, crimes and criminals.

Much depends on addressing the special needs of the different groups of child labourers. The needs of the domestic child labourer and the needs of the bonded child labourer have to be addressed differently. Child labourers working within closed doors of a household as domestics face different risks than child labourers working in a factory or in the streets. As far as domestics are concerned, there is a need to address the multiple developmental risks faced by child domestic workers. There is the special group of child labourers, the street children, whose needs are different from that of the domestics. Many of these children do not have contacts with their families and many of them do not want to go back to their families.

Many children also work in the undocumented informal sector, where conditions are harsh and sometimes inhumane. What is required is to assist NGOs in eliminating child labour in a phased manner. A safety net is a good way to relocate the released children to other beneficial activities. Progress may be slow, but similar ventures like the one adopted in the garments industry of Bangladesh is a necessity. Codes of conduct that have already appeared in the garments industry through policies that address child labour and other working conditions is required for other industries too. Parties involved in technical cooperation have to be aware of issues to be monitored. In Bangladesh, the garments industry is now required to terminate the services of its child labourers and provide stipend and schooling to them, until they come of age to work legally. In some cases, industries may deny the existence of child labour by hiding the children or disclaim responsibility by sub-contracting. Codes of conduct should be applicable to all involved in the supply chain. These should not be used by firms merely as an advertising gimmick for selling their products.

Imposition of restrictions may simply prompt the industries to close down, putting many adults out of work and closing the avenues of future adult employment. A way out could be to involve organisation of industries in that sector to make this economically viable. It is also important to ensure that corporate social responsibility (CSR) is voluntary and extends to all domestic industries and not confined to a select few. Mobilisation of civil society has to be a necessary component of the strategy. The problem of child labour has reached the consciousness of the society in Bangladesh. A movement for attitude change and raising awareness is gaining ground.

This involvement will facilitate the formation of interest groups which are essential for enforcing legislation.

The state, the society, all relevant institutions and individuals as well as the international agencies need to play complementary roles in eliminating child labour. The interests may differ; but the process needs to be economically viable and in the interests of the children who may not have the maturity to decide for themselves. In Bangladesh, child labour cannot be considered in isolation from the socioeconomic realities. This means that total and sudden elimination of child labour at a point in time may threaten the delicate socioeconomic balances of the transitional society. But the price of child labour is continued illiteracy, backwardness, ill-health and adult unemployment. Hence, sector-wise elimination in a phased manner may be the reality.

6.6 Issues in Youth Employment

Full and productive employment and decent work for all is indispensable to eradicate extreme poverty and hunger: employment is the poor people's main route out of poverty. As decent work for all is considered a key driver of inclusive growth, employment with a focus on youth is a key development agenda for Bangladesh. Youth employment outcomes need to be analysed in the perspective of a life-long career. A lack of decent work, if experienced at an early age, threatens a person's future employment prospects and frequently leads to undesirable labour market outcomes over longer periods (ILO 2012a, b). In addition, the impact of a job on individual well-being reaches far beyond current and future earnings and employment prospects, through giving a young person self-esteem and social identity, including a sense of belonging in society (World Bank 2012).

At the same time, if new families are formed despite poor access to stable and productive employment, this can have intergenerational spillover effects through investment in their children's schooling and health. Youth from poor households are likely to become working poor, while unemployed youth are found in households without any employed members (ILO 2012a, b). Young women's work has an additional intergenerational impact, as mothers' labour force participation is a strong predictor of the labour force participation of their daughters.

The youth-focus in the employment debate in Bangladesh is warranted by the sheer size of youth cohorts in the country. Today's youth population is the largest in the country's history. These large youth cohorts enter in the labour market every year with higher expectations than former generations. Bangladesh is still in earlier phases of the demographic transition, with relatively high fertility rates. The need for Bangladesh is, therefore, to turn the demographic challenges into a youth dividend as productive employment of youth is key to sustaining development and inter-generational equity. A direct consequence of large number of youth is that youth unemployment and non-productive employment bears high economic cost. Instead of contributing to society, unemployed or unproductively employed youth create direct costs, for example, through public support programmes. Examples of indirect economic costs are the loss of investment in education, forgone earnings, lower savings and lower aggregate demand (ILO 2010).

Further, Bangladesh warrants a specific focus on the vulnerable groups of youth, for whom the labour market situations are likely to deteriorate if no targeted actions are taken. Rural-urban migrants, for example, are likely to be the first ones losing out in the urban labour market. Moreover, young women are likely to be discouraged since female labour force participation has been relatively low. Other vulnerable groups are low-educated youth, ethnic minorities, and young people with disabilities.

Labour market in Bangladesh, like in many other developing countries, presents a complex combination of realities, including paid employment and self-employment, often characterised by persistent informality, low productivity and limited access to social security. Since regular wage employment is often the exception rather than the rule, understanding the position of youth in the labour market requires an integrated analysis of labour market outcomes.

6.6.1 Youth Employment in Bangladesh

There are different typologies of young people, defined as the population age 15 to 29, in the labour market. Table 6.11 shows how the youth population can be classified into different groups according to their employment or activity status. The main quantitative indicators are the youth employment rate, unemployment rate and the share of youth not in employment education or training (NEET).

The employment-to-population rate measures the share of employed youth in the total youth population. The unemployment rate measures the share of unemployed youth, which are those not working but searching

Table 6.11 Labour market status of youth population

Labour force status	*Employment status*	*Employed/ unemployed*	*Employment type*
In the labour force	Wage employment	Employed	Wage employment
	Self-employment		Vulnerable employment
	Contributing family labour/ unpaid labour		
	Unemployed	Not employed	NEET
Out of the labour force	Discouraged		
	Inactive/household work		
	In education		Student

Source: Adapted from African Development Bank, 2012

for a job, as a percentage of the youth labour force (those employed or unemployed). The NEET rate captures a broader group of inactive youth, also including those that are discouraged from searching for work and those inactive for other reasons (many women, for example, do housework that is not considered to be work in employment statistics). It considers youth with employment but also youth still in education as being active. It is calculated as the share of NEET youth in the total youth population. Regarding the quality of work, an indicator that is often used is the so-called vulnerable employment share. This is calculated as the share of self-employment and unpaid family work in total employment. Another indicator that captures the quality of work is working poverty. This measures the share of workers living below the poverty line.

Youth population in Bangladesh is growing in absolute numbers. The growth rate of the number of youth has been particularly high across most countries in South Asia including Bangladesh, and it is now tapering off. The Labour Force Survey (LFS) 2016–2017 of BBS shows that, while the national unemployment rate is 4.2 per cent, youth unemployment rate is high at 10.6 per cent. This shows that around 2.68 million youths are unemployed; among them, 1.36 million youths are between 15 and 24 years of age. In 2011, youth unemployment rate was 7.27 per cent. The share of unemployed youth in total unemployment is 79.6 per cent. Moreover, unemployment rate among youth having a tertiary level education is 13.4 per cent (BBS 2018). The LFS 2016–2017 also indicates that unemployment is highest among youths having secondary level education (28 per cent). Further, 29.8 per cent youth are not in education, employment or training (NEET). This suggests that, in Bangladesh, education is not empowering the youth with the right set of skills to be employable in the economy. Such high unemployment among the young population implies that Bangladesh has not been able to benefit from the 'demographic dividend'—which implies that as the share of working-age population increases, there will be a fall in the dependency ratio.

The LFS 2016–2017 shows that more than 20.1 million youth aged 15–29 participate in the labour force; the number of males being 13.1 million and females being 7.0 million. Youth labour's share in the total labour force is 33.5 per cent. The youth labour force share is higher in rural areas, at 32.0 per cent, than in the urban areas, at 30.8 per cent. An estimated 17.9 million youth (89.4 per cent) are employed of the total 20.1 million youth labour force aged 15–29 years, with large difference in numbers between male youth (12.0 million) and female youth (5.9 million). Of the total youth labour force population aged 15–29 (20.1 million), 2.1 million (10.6 per cent) are unemployed. The unemployed male youths (1.08 million) are larger than the female youths (1.05 million). The proportion of unemployed youth in total unemployment is smaller in rural areas (78.3 per cent) than in the urban areas (82.4 per cent). Overall, 79.6 per cent of total unemployed are youth. The youth unemployment rate is 10.6 per cent (8.2 per cent for males and 15.0 per cent for females). In urban areas, the youth unemployment rate is 11.6 per cent, with a higher rate for females at 16.7 per cent compared with 8.7 per cent for males, while the results reveal a youth unemployment rate of 10.2 per cent, with a higher rate for females at 14.3 per cent compared with 8.1 per cent for males in rural areas.

The self-employed and unpaid family workers can be treated as a proxy for vulnerable employment. Self-employed and unpaid family workers are considered vulnerable because they are less likely to have formal work arrangements, and therefore often lack employment protection, access to adequate social security, and voice through effective representation. Low productivity and earnings, and lack of decent working conditions further characterise vulnerable employment. The vulnerable employment share of total employment is high in Bangladesh, at more than 75 per cent. Further, the majority of youth vulnerable workers are active as unpaid family workers, while adults are more likely to be own account workers.

The NEET youth can either be unemployed or inactive and not involved in education or training. Young people who are neither in employment nor in education or training are at risk of becoming socially excluded—individuals with income below the poverty line and lacking the skills to improve their economic situation. This indicator is also a better measure of the current universe of potential youth labour market entrants compared with the youth inactivity rate, as the latter includes those youth who are not in the labour force and are in education, and thus cannot be considered currently available for work. More generally, a high NEET rate and a low youth unemployment rate may indicate significant discouragement of young people.

The LFS 2016–17 shows that, among the NEET youths, 13.0 per cent are males and the rest 87.0 per cent are females. A high NEET rate for young women suggests their engagement in household chores, and/or the presence of institutional barriers limiting female participation in the labour market. The largest share of the NEET youth is from the age group 25–29 (4.9 million or 40.1 per cent), followed by those who belong to 20–24 age group (4.6 million or 37.3 per cent) and 15–19 age group (2.8 million or 22.6 per cent). Of the total NEET youths, 69.5 per cent are from the rural areas and the rest 30.5 per cent are from the urban areas. Overall, 29.8 per cent of the working age population aged 15–29 is not in education, employment or training.

6.6.2 *Youth Employment Challenges*

Youth employment challenges in the country can be grouped under three broad heads: labour demand, labour supply, and the functioning of the labour market. Demand for labour is driven by growth and structural change: job creation depends on the growth and labour-intensity of production in different sectors. Further, youth employment challenges are closely related to the informal non-agricultural economy, including manufacturing and services.

The majority of youth labour in Bangladesh work in agriculture in rural areas. Typically, the most vulnerable people in agriculture are the landless, who work for a wage on the land of others. Agricultural labour demand depends on factors such as the labour-intensity of production technology and land distribution, and varies seasonally. The rural poor increasingly diversify into non-agricultural activities as part of their livelihood strategies, mainly in the form of informal, unpaid or self-employment. The urban poor are also concentrated in the informal non-agricultural economy, and are not any better off than the rural population.

In a dynamic economy such as Bangladesh, youth employment challenges are interconnected especially through the proliferation of production fragmentation. Jobs in manufacturing—and more recently in services as well—have become increasingly mobile with possibility to jump-start industrialisation. It is also apprehended that mismatches between labour demand and labour supply at the sectoral and regional level may keep arising due to the increasing global interconnection of jobs, as well as labour-saving technological change, urbanisation, and the transition to more energy efficient production and consumption. When labour demand slows down, self-employment may be the only alternative opportunity. The self-employed thus consist of necessity-driven on the one hand, and voluntary entrepreneurs on the other.

The main supply side determinants of youth employment outcomes are education and skills, in terms of quantity, quality, and relevance. Migration is another important supply side factor. Skills are built through formal general education, formal vocational education and training (VET) and apprenticeships, and through non-formal education and training. Better cognitive skills are associated with reduced idleness and increased school enrolment, with lower incidence of vulnerable employment, and with reduced agricultural employment (Lee and Newhouse, 2012). At the same time, lack of non-cognitive skills is often mentioned by employers in the private formal sector as an obstacle to hiring young workers.

The importance of the relevance of education in Bangladesh is illustrated by the fact that higher education is no guarantee for a successful school-to-work transition. Although highly educated youth is less likely to be in vulnerable employment, unemployment tends to increase with education. This may be due to large numbers of youth completing higher education degrees fit for public sector jobs, while public sector employment is not expanding rapid enough in Bangladesh. Unemployment can then be accompanied by unmet demand for highly skilled workers in the formal private sector. Such mismatches between young people's skills and the structure of employment growth may hamper future economic growth, because new generations of the working age population may not possess the skills demanded by the employers. Lack of adequate skills is all the more worrying as the number of years of education attained by youth has been increasing rapidly.

Preparing youth for successful entrepreneurship is extremely important in Bangladesh, as self-employment is often the only opportunity when the private formal sector does not create enough jobs. There is little youth-specific research on self-employment; but it is true that a substantial share of working youth is self-employed in Bangladesh. Most of the young self-employed come from the poorest households and have at most incomplete secondary education. They tend not to hire any employees, thus only creating employment for themselves as owners of micro-enterprises. Important determinants of self-employment entry and success are a person's basic and entrepreneurial skills, and access to credit. The perceived status of self-employment is also particularly relevant among the highly educated youth: where a majority of self-employed youth has little education and unemployment rises with education, this can be a signal that highly educated youth do not aspire to running their own businesses.

In Bangladesh, labour supply in different places is also affected by rural-urban and international migration. Due to rural–urban migration patterns, urban labour supply tends to grow faster than the working age population, further increasing the pressure on the urban labour market. Most of Bangladesh's international migrants are labour migrants, related to the lack of opportunities for full employment and decent work in the country. Labour migration is determined by many factors such as existing job opportunities, wage levels, and working conditions. The facilitation of foreign employment is also a strategy for alleviating labour market pressures and increasing remittance receipts and thus household income for families left behind. Evidence suggests that this strategy can be effective if a number of conditions are met in terms of working conditions, access to social protection, portability of benefits, social costs of family disruption or gender-related risks.

On the other hand, there may be negative effects of migration ('brain drain'), as normally those having the capacity to leave are the more productive in the labour market. Most rural–urban migrants are young people, while young people make up a significant share of international migrants as well. Youth migration can serve to build human capital if young migrants attend school or gain work experience in the host region/country. In contrast, for some young people migration exposes them to several risks, including lack of access to basic rights and exploitation. This can also be due to weak social networks and limited access of young migrants to information on their rights and entitlements.

Further, little is known about the livelihood opportunities and the risks associated with migration of young people especially young women, the policies and measures that help them reap the benefits and contribute to development of both countries of origin and of destination, and the mechanisms that exist for migrant workers to avoid falling into risky situations. Young international migrant workers tend to be concentrated in a few occupations. For young men, these are mainly in construction and agriculture, while young women often work in domestic services, sales, or restaurants. Female domestic workers are vulnerable and isolated, often working in their employer's home. Furthermore, according to the United Nations Report on Trafficking in Persons, human trafficking for forced labour has significantly increased from the developing countries in recent years. Women and girls account for the majority of all trafficking victims.

It is seen that youth employment outcomes are shaped by the institutions governing the matching of job seekers to vacancies, notably information, intermediation, and labour market regulation. The availability and quality of information play a key role in the labour market, for job seekers to identify relevant opportunities and for employers to find adequate workers. Evidence from School-to-Work Transition Surveys in many developing countries shows that the most important channel of job search for youth is the social network: via family and friends. Reliance on informal networks and connections may be efficient when employers find it costly to assess competencies of potential employees, or when there are no formal institutions mediating short notice hiring. However, it does mean that young job seekers are unlikely to find work outside their own network, which limits social and intergenerational mobility.

Lack of information about job opportunities can contribute to skill shortages and mismatches, because parents and children are not well equipped to assess the returns to education. Formal sources of information are public employment services and private recruitment agencies. Their services, however, are typically confined to jobs in the public sector and large formal private firms. And their relevance may be limited if hiring happens through family and political connections, which is a major problem according to young job seekers in Bangladesh. The role of information thus also includes providing transparency in hiring practices. Labour market functioning further depends on regulation, such as minimum wages. However, with the majority of workers in informal employment, labour market regulation may have little direct effect on youth employment outcomes. Indirectly, however, regulation could affect aggregate outcomes if there are large spillovers to the informal economy.

As noted earlier, Bangladesh has high vulnerable employment share, informality, and working poverty. Despite high growth rates compared with other countries, a large share of workers remains in agriculture, in the urban informal sector or in informal jobs in formal enterprises. Employment growth in the formal sector is too low to absorb large numbers of young labour market entrants. Manufacturing still accounts for a low share of total output and employment. This mostly affects low- and medium-skilled workers, who are still predominantly confined to working in agriculture and informal services. Besides structural change towards more low-skilled intensive manufacturing production, increasing productivity in agricultural and informal activities are the keys to improving youth employment outcomes.

On the supply side, although primary school enrolment has increased, the transition rate from primary to secondary schooling is still low. Due to the poor quality of basic formal education and persistent gender gaps in secondary attainments, the most vulnerable groups of youth fail to get a good chance at decent work. Another striking feature of youth employment in Bangladesh is the persistently low female labour force participation. The main challenge for Bangladesh is the poor quality of employment for the majority of workers, as still the vast majority of the country's employed are in vulnerable employment. Further, vulnerable employment rates for women remain significantly higher than for men. In Bangladesh, the services sector and export-oriented (e.g. readymade garments) employers will remain a significant driver of demand for skills, and with import growth it is likely that imported technology will become more important in overall production. A large share of firms reports difficulties in finding skilled workers for professional (white collar) jobs. There is some evidence that inadequate skill certification is an important constraint in job matching (World Bank 2010).

6.6.3 *Youth Employment Policy Agenda*

6.6.3.1 *Comprehensive Youth Employment Strategies*

To develop youth employment strategies, Bangladesh needs an integrated youth employment approach involving different levels of government and other stakeholders, ranging from relevant ministries to education and training providers and social partners. Although youth needs to be targeted with specific policies, it is important to link youth employment strategies with overall development and employment policy. Because of the complex nature of the country's labour market, and the diversity of income generating activities that people undertake, youth employment challenges require policy action beyond education and the labour market, in areas such as credit markets, infrastructure, business regulation, and rural development. Responsibilities therefore need to lie with a government agency that has appropriate capacity and political and administrative support to ensure coherence and coordination.

Social dialogues need to include youth and the private sector, and effective programmes require the target groups of youth to be involved in the design, implementation, and evaluation processes. Evidence-based policies addressing youth employment challenges require strong labour market information and analysis systems. Information is crucial for setting realistic targets and measuring outcomes. The ILO School-to-Work Transition Survey and the ETF school-leaver survey are examples of targeted data collection, and it may be possible to integrate certain components into regular labour force surveys. To understand youth's pathways to decent work and inform policy making, employment measures need to be available for different subgroups of youth (male and female, rural and urban, youth at different income levels, and youth at different education levels).

Growth promoting job-rich inclusive growth is a key to youth employment promotion in the long-term. Although achieving job-rich growth is a major general challenge, strategies to expand labour demand are needed to complement interventions targeting more short-term and youth-specific goals, such as wage subsidies and skills training (IEG 2013). Thus, macro and growth policies need to stimulate private investment especially in labour-intensive sectors or sectors with large employment multipliers (ILO 2012a, b).

In Bangladesh, there is a need to focus on labour- and resource-intensive production activities, rather than prioritising capital-intensive industries. There could be a priority to so-called 'soft' industrial policy (Harrison and Rodríguez-Clare 2010), aiming to facilitate collaboration between the government, industry and cluster-level private organisations, to reduce coordination failures in order to increase productivity.

6.6.3.2 Entrepreneurship Promotion

Youth entrepreneurship and self-employment promotion require increased access to credit by strengthening financial infrastructure, bank competition and nonbank financing. The financial sector typically has insufficient banking skills for dealing with micro-enterprises and the cost of small-scale lending is high. Youth micro-entrepreneurship promotion also requires reform and more consistent enforcement of business regulation, in order to reduce red tape and increase transparency (ILO 2012a, b). The most effective entrepreneurship training combines 'core' business administration skills, such as accounting, with 'softer' entrepreneurial skills, such as problem solving. It is important to systematically screen youth for latent or active entrepreneurial characteristics, such as innovative thinking, leadership attributes, passion and results-orientation.

Training also needs to include support services, such as coaching, mentoring, and financing. Programmes should clearly separate training and financing functions by forming partnerships with financial institutions to provide and manage credit for youth. To improve entrepreneurs' ability to benefit from trade liberalisation and foreign investment, they also need skills for developing their networks and linking with higher levels of the value chain.

In Bangladesh, livelihood self-employed may be targeted as a different group than entrepreneurs. Measures to improve the situation of the most vulnerable groups of self-employed, such as the poor and disadvantaged women, may take many forms from capacity building and training, to social protection measures, through improved access to social services and finance. Well-designed interventions should be specifically targeted to their needs, integrating several components. Programmes also need to address people's empowerment as a way to provide informal workers with tools for defending their interests and rights in the long term. Empowerment can have an individual and/or collective dimension (e.g. small workers or employers' associations and cooperatives). Such a holistic approach is India's 'Self Employment Women's Association (SEWA)', which offers various support services, coordinates many local organisations, and manages to give poor, self-employed women a voice.

6.6.3.3 Public Work Programmes

The most direct way to increase labour demand in the short term is through Public Works Programmes (PWPs). The PWPs create temporary jobs for the poorest and most vulnerable, with the primary goals of income smoothing, poverty reduction, and asset building. Many PWPs are organised around infrastructure development, but there is significant scope for PWPs to provide social services. This is a highly labour-intensive sector and could be better targeted at young women's participation.

Beyond providing a safety net, PWPs can also be used to improve participants' employability in paid jobs or self-employment in order to graduate from the programme especially through investing in skills and human capital building. Bangladesh has several such programmes which are implemented by the Local Government Engineering Department (LGED) and other local government institutions. To increase employability, youth or participants with high re-employment opportunities receive skills training and education that may result in some type of accredited certification. Training may be related to the area of activity of the PWP or they can link beneficiaries to growing sectors where the scope for hiring new entrants is high. In some cases, they can get access to employment services, finance, or business development support services for starts-up. These components partially address the concerns raised the by beneficiaries about the short-term nature of PWPs and their inability to link beneficiaries to future, long-term employment opportunities (Subbarao et al. 2013; Mujeri 2002). Moreover, it is possible to design broader PWPs—such as 'public works plus' programmes—to target beneficiaries' employability and adopt graduation strategies to enhance youth's labour market outcomes.

6.6.3.4 Skill Development

Addressing skill shortages and mismatches requires action on several fronts, including formal and non-formal general education, VET, and apprenticeship training. Improving literacy skills through quality primary education is also urgent. Education policies should also aim at improving access to secondary education for disadvantaged youth. They are often constrained by the cost of schooling and, in the case of young women, by social and cultural barriers. Mentoring and remedial teaching in primary education can be a means to improving not just literacy and numeracy skills, but also social skills, self-esteem, and information about further education. For the current youth cohort, who has already passed basic secondary schooling age, second-chance education is the only option to address basic literacy and numeracy deficiencies.

Existing programmes in the country reach very few of these young people. The use of ICT, especially radio and mobile phones, in education is a promising way of reaching disadvantaged youth (UNESCO 2012). New technologies in education and access to open educational resources (OER) could enhance flexible course delivery and customised training for specific groups of youth. Policies that increase the permeability of education systems are also needed, to allow youth to move more easily between different levels and types of education. In Bangladesh, more mobility in education and training systems is necessary to facilitate social mobility, such that youth can re-enter education in later stages of life. Permeability is not only about institutional and bureaucratic barriers. Family background and choices and early tracking systems are major factors influencing education and training choices and careers. Mobility would also include allowing students to move between VET and other higher education tracks, which could increase the attractiveness of VET.

Since the benefits of formal VET depend largely on the relevance of skills to actual demand in the private sector, a widely adopted policy is to build public–private partnerships in the design and provision of VET. Almost by definition, however, formal VET policies cannot address challenges for the majority of youth in the country working in the informal sector. It is crucial that skills development policies include youth in agricultural and non-agricultural informal employment, where poverty reduction is most urgent. This could be achieved by improving and expanding traditional apprenticeship schemes, for example, through local training committees and training schemes for agricultural (or agriculture-related) occupations.

To begin with, education and training organised by informal actors may first be identified and strengthened before developing new learning schemes. The government may also organise the recognition and certification of skills acquired in non-formal learning, and integrate non-formal schemes in the national skills development strategies. Regulations may be introduced for traditional apprenticeships in order to set limits to the number of years of training and daily and weekly working hours. These programmes should combine complementary interventions. Training programmes are effective only if they target and include work experience, rather than focusing on skills first and job later. The most effective programmes are those that combine private sector involvement in training, classroom instruction combined with internships or apprenticeship, and employment services like job search assistance. Personal monitoring and follow up of individual participants also increase the probability of success.

In Bangladesh, with a large informal economy, the applicability of employment services is somewhat limited. Alternative channels, such as local media and advertising, may be beneficial for spreading information on the labour market and job opportunities. Further, the pace, components, content and teaching approaches should be adjusted to the capacities and interests of different types of youth. Some key groups are male versus female youth, younger versus older youth, and married versus unmarried women. Graduation rates can be maximised by addressing common reasons for dropping out, such as transportation costs and lack of family support. In addition, soft skills (such as communication, team work, responsibility, motivation) matter a great deal for improving youth employability.

6.6.3.5 Labour Market Information

When jobs exist, youth can be helped by providing information and employment exchange services through educational institutions, or by offering these in youth centres. For poorer youth and those living further from urban centres, support may be provided to benefit from employment exchange services. Besides improving labour market information, policies also need to aim at increasing transparency and fairness in hiring practices. Bangladesh should enact laws requiring firms to publicly announce their job openings as well as improve the enforcement of these laws.

However, in the informal labour market, information laws have little relevance. Although little is known about the functioning of the informal labour market, usually informal networks are the key in the job search process. The use of new technologies, particularly mobile phones, could help in expanding job search networks for youth, linking formal and informal networks, and increasing the effectiveness of these networks. In Bangladesh, overseas employment can also be an important solution for youth employment deficit. It can stimulate local labour market through remittances and through the youth's incentives to invest in education. Overseas employment services exist in Bangladesh, through the Bangladesh Overseas Employment and Services Limited (BOESL)—the only the State owned manpower exporting agency in Bangladesh established in 1984 to export both skilled and unskilled manpower— and private manpower recruiting agencies and these should therefore be part of the national youth employment strategies.

6.6.3.6 Regulatory Framework

Bangladesh, with a relatively high unemployment among educated youth, needs a restructuring of public administration hiring and promotion processes, to reduce public-private dualism in the labour market. This requires labour regulations and social insurance reforms and more social dialogue, including with youth organisations and representatives. Minimum wages could be important for young workers to sustain a decent earnings level, while a lower youth minimum wage can be used to stimulate youth labour demand. In terms of employment protection, special first job contracts or reducing restrictions on temporary contracts may be used to stimulate youth labour demand.

In designing labour market policies for youth employment, it is important to realise the trade-off between short-term increases in temporary or part-time jobs on the one hand, and the risk of decreasing the quality of employment in the long term. While youth wage subsidies or extended periods of fixed term and other flexible contracts may induce firms to hire more young workers, they also lengthen the time it takes for youth to reach job security. Similarly, since Bangladesh has large informal economy, strong regulations may create dualism between the formal and informal labour markets. Reforms of labour regulation can be used to facilitate entrance of workers into the formal sector and encourage hiring of youth. However, since the existing formal sector may not be able to absorb most of the current youth cohort in the short term, policies need to consider social protection and social security to the self-employed, to workers in informal enterprises and to those working informally in formal enterprises.

6.6.3.7 Knowledge Gaps

In Bangladesh, labour market characteristics are such that youth are mostly absorbed in agriculture, non-farm informal jobs, or self-employment. But very little is known about the functioning of informal and agricultural labour markets, and even less about youth-specifics of these labour markets. Therefore, investing in youth labour market data is an important first step in developing proper policy and programme design in the country. Improving data infrastructure will also increase attention to the labour market situation of the vulnerable youth. Further, more efforts are needed to analyse the role of urbanisation and the location of jobs, new technologies in production and in job search, micro-franchising for stimulating entrepreneurship, green growth strategies, and similar other areas in youth employment.

Further, an important challenge for the majority of youth in Bangladesh is to improve the quality of employment, since they remain mostly trapped in some form of low quality employment. Nonetheless, unemployed youth are arguably the group with most visibility and voice, and the ones who spur the current interest in youth employment. When addressing youth employment challenges from the development perspective with poverty reduction as the principal objective, policies need to have a specific focus on the most vulnerable groups of youth, i.e. youth in rural areas and those with lower levels of education. However, keeping in view the broader role of decent work in promoting social cohesion, development policies need also to target the large group of openly unemployed youth in general. In order to promote and safeguard progress towards gender equality, which can erode rapidly with growing competition for scarce jobs, young women are another key subgroup in employment-related strategies and interventions in Bangladesh.

In the short term and for the current youth cohorts, more targeted policies and programmes are needed in Bangladesh. One clear message in the context of the country's informal economy where most of the labour force is engaged is that reaching the vulnerable groups of youth can only be achieved by targeting productivity, skills, social safety nets and proper labour market functioning in the informal economy. Supporting the organisation of informal workers can be an effective means towards reinforcing their position in the value chain and identifying available opportunities for training, finance and insurance structures, as well as information networks. Public works programmes also appear as a promising tool for addressing employment challenges for the vulnerable youth, through the inclusion of additional components such as training and labour market counselling.

Reaching young women remains a particular challenge, especially in Bangladesh with a historically low female labour force participation rate. Programmes targeting adolescent girls are among the most effective and can have wider long-term impacts on health and well-being. Because many important early life transitions may coincide during adolescence, it is important to generally analyse youth employment within the broader framework of the multidimensional nature of social inclusion of young people and with differentiation among different age groups and family situations when designing programmes for young women.

Finally, effective design, implementation, and evaluation of youth-targeted policies and programmes require two ingredients regardless of the specific context. First of all, the inclusion of youth, particularly vulnerable youth, and the formal and informal private sector in the process is the key. And second, there is a need of better data, particularly on the pathways to work and the quality of jobs, as well as on the impact of youth labour market policies and programmes. Investing in information systems in cooperation with statistical offices, as well as strengthening evaluation of labour market policies and interventions targeting young people will be an important step towards strengthening the employment perspective, enhancing the functioning of the labour market, and improving effectiveness of employment interventions.

6.7 Rural Employment Strategy

For Bangladesh, a critical question is how to create the required jobs for the poor with limited purchasing power and limited capital for investment. The idea that most of these jobs could be created in the corporate sector or by government-sponsored activities is not realistic. Currently, 56 per cent of the country's labour force is self-employed/own account workers or unpaid family helpers. The self-employed represent 46 per cent of the workforce. For any employment strategy to be successful in Bangladesh, it must give central importance to self-employment and entrepreneurship, with emphasis on agriculture, agro-industry and small firms in the informal sector.

A policy vision is needed to harness the potential of the rural labour force, especially rural youth, through vibrant, sustainable and inclusive domestic food systems anchored in local value chains. Bangladesh can make this happen, but decisions and actions should be initiated now. Several policy priorities are important to create the enabling environment:

- Promote local value chains as an engine for decent job creation and food security.
- Link rural and urban development using a territorial approach.
- Adopt a comprehensive approach to rural development to develop regional advantages.
- Exploit the opportunities in regional and international markets.
- Invest in agriculture and rural infrastructure.
- Green and diversify the rural economy.
- Apply social and environmental safeguards.
- Raise the voices of rural youth in policy dialogue.
- Provide skills development and second-chance programmes for the rural youth.

Agriculture as an engine: Nearly 41 per cent of the workforce is still engaged in agriculture. Agriculture will continue to remain the largest single occupation in the medium term. Historically, agriculture has also played a major role as an engine for economic growth and employment. For the coming years, Bangladesh's rapid growth can only be sustained by rising productivity and incomes in agriculture that increases the demand for manufactured goods and various services. Rising agricultural productivity and a shift to value-added crops will be the dynamic engines for economic growth, job creation, higher incomes and rural purchasing power, wider markets for produce, and the growth of downstream industries. Bangladesh needs to adopt a conscious strategy to utilise agriculture to stimulate job creation and domestic demand. The vast technological gap between the levels of agricultural productivity achieved by Bangladesh and the potential yields that can be achieved represents an enormous untapped potential for stimulating economic growth and job creation. Thus, an agriculture-led job creation strategy can generate sufficient jobs to eradicate poverty in the rural areas of Bangladesh.

Utilise agriculture as a source of economic growth and job creation by a selective shift to high value-added crops including processing; supported by policy measures to upgrade technology, improve skills, raise productivity, ensure the supply of essential inputs, establish marketing and distribution channels, create linkages between agriculture and industry, and cater to export markets.

A new deal for the self-employed: Self-employed persons and the microenterprises which they establish have enormous potential for rapidly generating large numbers of new jobs and raising productivity to increase incomes, provided the right policy measures are in place to support them. Japan's economic growth has relied heavily on the proliferation of small rural enterprises. China created 101 million jobs between 1985 and 1991, 70 per cent in 'township and village enterprises' (TVEs), of which nearly half are privately owned. In many countries, a large proportion of small enterprises is established by women and employs predominately female labour.

According to the Economic Census 2013, out of 7.82 million economic units in Bangladesh, 72 per cent are located in the rural areas and nearly 89 per cent of these are cottage and microenterprises. These can emerge as the new drivers of rural job creation with an appropriate mix of policies focusing on access to technology, training, finance, marketing and distribution channels which can substantially accelerate self-employment, particularly in the informal sector and rural areas, and among women.

Promote micro and small enterprises by policies to make technology, training, credit, and marketing and distribution channels more easily accessible to these enterprises, and by forging linkages between universities, research institutes and microenterprises for technological innovations. The creation of microenterprise banks and credit unions specifically designed to cater to the needs of the self-employed and microenterprises can be especially effective. There are a growing number of these institutions targeting clients that lack access to commercial lending institutions, particularly women, providing unsubsidised loans, and achieving very low levels of default.

Expand services: The services sector represents around 39 per cent of the labour force in Bangladesh. Contrary to the common conception, services can be a major contributor to rural job growth even in countries at earlier stages of development such as Bangladesh. This sector is as amenable to stimulation by government policies as agriculture or manufacturing, and it also provides impetus for the growth of other sectors.

Actively encourage and support growth of the service sector through programmes similar to those utilised to support the expansion of small and medium enterprises. Adopt supportive policies to enable trade, transport and other services to generate more jobs in many activities, including private day-care centres, nursery schools and computer training institutes, which are multiplying rapidly but can be expanded much further in Bangladesh. Bangladesh can adopt, for example, innovative, low-cost, self-employment strategy to expand availability of long-distance telecommunications services by setting up small private telephone and fax centres throughout the country. Informal private service enterprises in construction, commerce, food catering, repair and transport have vast growth potential. Rapid expansion of education, training and public health, especially rural health and education, can also serve as a conscious strategy for employment generation.

Innovate organisationally: Significant improvements in the competitiveness and growth of businesses in Bangladesh can be achieved through raising organisational efficiency and dynamism through better internal management practices and better commercial systems in the marketplace.

Conduct a comprehensive study of successful management practices, systems and institutions from both developing and developed countries that can be transferred and adapted to local conditions in order to accelerate development in each field of activity. Evolve new organisational patterns for existing industries based on adaptation of new technologies in small, geographically decentralised, labour-intensive production units in order to make these industries more responsive, flexible, efficient and competitive.

Extend basic education: A distinguishing feature of the East Asian countries has been their emphasis during the early stage of industrialisation on primary and secondary education, especially in rural areas. This strategy increases the productivity of the mass of the workforce; helps promote income equality, consumer spending power and broad support for high growth and pro-business policies.

Raise the educational qualifications of the workforce to the level existing in more economically advanced nations. Place particular emphasis on primary and secondary education, rural education and education of young girls.

Revamp higher education: In Bangladesh, the existing educational systems which 'manufacture graduates' compound the problem rather than alleviating it. The problem of the educated unemployed is not so much the amount of education they receive, but the type of knowledge and attitudes imparted.

Reorient the educational curriculum at all levels, especially higher education, to impart the knowledge and attitudes needed to promote self-employment and entrepreneurship rather than salaried employment.

Upgrade skills: Absorbing new technology, raising productivity, improving the quality and competitiveness of exports—all depend on the skills of the workforce. For raising labour productivity in Bangladesh, there is a need to invest more in education and technical skills. Training institutions and programmes in Bangladesh provide only a narrow range and low level of skill acquisition to a small portion of the population.

Raise skills to increase productivity by vastly expanding the lower tiers of the agricultural, craft, technical and vocational training systems at the local level to provide practical training in job-related skills to the saturation point. Imbalances between supply and demand for skills exist at all levels in Bangladesh. Make a careful assessment of present supply and demand for key skills. Compare the density of different types and levels of skill in countries at the next higher stage of development and evolve programmes to raise the quantity and quality of skills to that level.

Technology of organisation: We place much emphasis on the widening gap in technology between Bangladesh and the fast growing countries, but the gap in the technology of organisation is even greater. Creation of new types of systems and organisations can create markets and jobs in many ways. The Dutch system of flower auction cooperatives is so successful that 68 per cent of the entire world's exports of cut flowers pass through markets in the Netherlands. The franchise system has led to a rapid proliferation of new businesses and new jobs in many countries in such widely diverse fields as food services, home remodelling, dry cleaning and real estate. Industrial estates, export processing zones, export promotion councils, export insurance, warehouse receipts, quality standards, and thousands of other organisational innovations have been either created or borrowed by many countries to accelerate social progress.

Undertake a comprehensive study of successful systems and institutions that can be transferred and adapted to local conditions in Bangladesh; this will indicate the enormous untapped potential for stimulating faster economic and job growth by inventing, imitating and further improving social systems.

Improve marketing: The organisation of marketing is typically one of the weakest links and, therefore, one of the greatest barriers to economic growth and job growth in Bangladesh. As labour costs have risen in East Asia, greater opportunities are emerging for lower-wage countries such as Bangladesh to take a larger share in growing international markets. In order to take advantage of the increasing opportunities opened up by liberalisation of world trade, Bangladesh should accelerate steps to expand export-oriented markets by forging foreign collaborations and overseas subsidiaries, acquiring technology, creating an attractive commercial environment for foreign investment, and continuously building the skills of the labour force.

Improve distribution and marketing systems, especially for agricultural produce, by identifying missing links and establishing successful model programmes that bridge the gap between rural producers and urban or overseas markets.

Employment planning: Conscious employment planning is an essential requirement for generating 'decent employment for all'.

Place the employment objective high on the national agenda and evolve a comprehensive plan to achieve employment for all by identifying untapped growth potentials in agriculture, industry, exports and services. Launch a nationwide programme to implement all employment-related strategies on a high priority basis.

Comprehensive strategies and action plan: While most of the policies and programmes listed above are not new, the major problem lies in the absence of their systematic and efficient application. Bangladesh can benefit enormously by applying strategies that have worked in many Southeast Asian countries. Employment generation is a product of multiple factors that combine together. Stimulating job creation requires a comprehensive approach, rather than partial policies or piecemeal strategies. Rapid increases in employment generation can be achieved based on comprehensive strategies. While broad prescriptions should not be indiscriminately applied to the widely disparate situations, the availability of a number of tested methods underlines the fact that effective and proven policy measures can be formulated to meet the employment needs of Bangladesh.

Encourage the establishment of new institutions, programmes and systems to speed and extend the dissemination of practically useful information as a powerful catalyst for more rapid employment creation and social progress. Encourage a national climate of open-mindedness to new ideas, influences and success stories. Adopt a comprehensive approach, the right mix of policies, good governance and a conducive environment for trade, technology transfer and investment, to create the capacity to develop and meet the employment needs of all people, including the rural labour force, in Bangladesh within the next decade.

Policy implications.

Given that improving the efficiency of agricultural production is a key to rural employment growth both in farm and nonfarm activities, improvements in agricultural technology are the principal means of doing this. Agricultural technology can affect small farmer income, labour opportunities for the poor, food prices, environmental sustainability, and linkages with the rest of the rural economy.

Agricultural technology has been a primary factor contributing to increases in farm productivity and rural employment in Bangladesh over the past half-century. New technology can provide additional rural employment, but there are always countervailing pressures to reduce labour input and lower its costs. The adoption of technology requires adequate incentives for producers. Investments in labour or cash will not be made unless there are adequate returns. One of the most important supporting factors is the adequacy of markets for outputs and inputs. Because agricultural technology addresses multiple, and at times conflicting, objectives, there is a need for careful planning. But there is a trade-off between investment in micro-level technology screening, on the one hand, and support to basic institutional capacities and political responsiveness, on the other.

The rhetoric of technological revolutions should be avoided in favour of consistent attention to building technological capacity in response to changes in the rural economy of Bangladesh. An important challenge is to ensure adequate and coherent support for public research and extension in the face of resource constraints. Private sector technology generation (and technology delivery) is of growing relevance to employment generation, but it is probably unreasonable to place high expectations on vastly expanded formal public–private partnerships, especially in the short run.

Support to NGO-MFIs in agricultural technology generation should focus on their role in building local institutions and capacities; a strong rural civil society is essential for articulating technology demand. There are no easy rules for guiding investments in particular types of technology, and pragmatic, case-by-case analysis and follow-up is required. Much current rhetoric (e.g. related to biotechnology or low external input agriculture) does little to promote responsible policies. Among the most important policy challenges related to support for agricultural technology innovation in Bangladesh are

- Identification of an effective investment portfolio of technologies;
- Structuring linkages among producers, consumers, public institutes, civil society and the private sector to elicit effective technology demand and innovation options;
- Locating technology innovation policies in the wider national policy arena; and
- Setting and articulating clear policy goals that relate technology generation to employment generation and regional and local development.

There are a number of implications of technological advancement for rural employment generation. There is a need to develop in-house capacity to monitor the processes and outcomes of technology generation. This implies a commitment to developing institutional memory and to coordinating central syntheses and guidance with country-level experience. Policies in support of technology generation should place strong emphasis on local institution building and should see that rural employment issues are addressed in a coherent fashion in national and local planning. An understanding of the multiple impacts and second-order effects of technology should inform the policy process.

6.8 Future Labour Force: Issues and Challenges

Bangladesh is the eighth most populous country in the world with a total population of 161 million in 2015 which is projected to grow to more than 202 million in 2050 (Fig. 6.1). Changes in age structure lead to

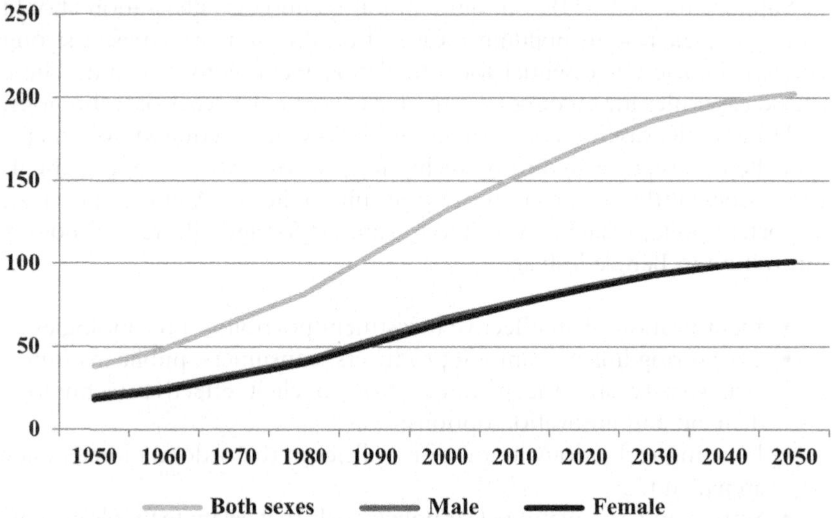

Fig. 6.1 Population in Bangladesh (medium variant, in million), 1950–2050. Source: *World Development Indicators 2015,* World Bank

decline in dependency ratio which favours higher economic growth if supportive policies enhance employability prospects of the labour force.[4]

The initial decline in dependency ratio starts with a demographic transition from high to low birth and death rates which results in demographic dividend for the economy that continues until the share of working-age population reaches the peak. Afterwards, the dependency ratio starts rising due to aging that is, increasing proportion of people in 65+ age which raises the old-age dependency ratio. During this phase of population dynamics, a country can reap a second demographic dividend over an infinite time horizon if high income levels can be maintained and people accumulate adequate savings and assets for their retirement (Mason and Lee 2006). However, the benefits of these demographic dynamics can only be realised if human capital can play its due role in economic growth and development (see Dobson 2013; Page 1994; World Bank 1993).

[4] Total dependency ratio is defined as the ratio of population 0–14 and 65+ age to population 15–64 age. In Bangladesh, the standard dependency ratio as calculated above may not reflect the true picture due to widespread prevalence of child labour which is very common with 4.7 million or 12.6 percent of children aged below 14 in the labour force.

Demographic transitions across the world suggest that the low income countries have high child dependency ratio and low old-age dependency ratio while the situation is reverse for high income countries. As income rises, child dependency ratio declines while old-age dependency ratio rises in low income countries. In 2015, total dependency ratio in low income countries is estimated to be 84.8 per cent in contrast to 50.5 per cent in high income countries. In the low income countries, child dependency ratio is 78.5 per cent and old-age dependency ratio is 6.3 per cent while these ratios are 26.0 per cent and 24.5 per cent respectively in high income countries (UN 2016). It may, however, be argued that, despite a high total dependency ratio in the low income countries relative to the high income countries, the composition of the dependency ratio (with a high share of child dependency ratio) in the low income countries has a potential growth advantage since the large share of child populations can be transformed into future contributors to economic growth and development with proper investment in their human capital and supportive policies.

How has the dependency ratio changed over time in Bangladesh? Figure 6.2 shows the past trends and future projections of changes in dependency ratios of Bangladesh. Between 1950 and 2010, the country's total dependency ratio fell by 24 percentage points from 82.3 per cent to 58.3 per cent which is entirely due to fall in child dependency ratio (which fell by 24.4 percentage points). On the other hand, the period experienced a minor increase in old-age dependency ratio (by 0.3 percentage point). This shows that Bangladesh is currently passing through a period of demographic dividend.

The projections show that Bangladesh will continue to experience a continuously falling, albeit gradual, child dependency ratio to reach 25.6 per cent in 2050 from 50.8 per cent in 2010 while old-age dependency ratio will face a gradual rising trend to move to 23.1 per cent in 2050 from 7.4 per cent in 2010. As a result, total dependency ratio will decline to 48.7 per cent in 2050 from 58.3 per cent in 2010.

In the case of working age population, the number rose from 17.9 million (54.8 per cent of total population) in 1950 to 83.5 million (63.2 per cent of total population) in 2010 and is projected to reach its peak of 137 million (69.5 per cent of total population) in 2040 and thereafter start declining both in absolute number and share to 136 million (67.3 per cent of total population) in 2050 (Fig. 6.3). This shows that the size of the country's labour force will increase by nearly 53 million between 2010

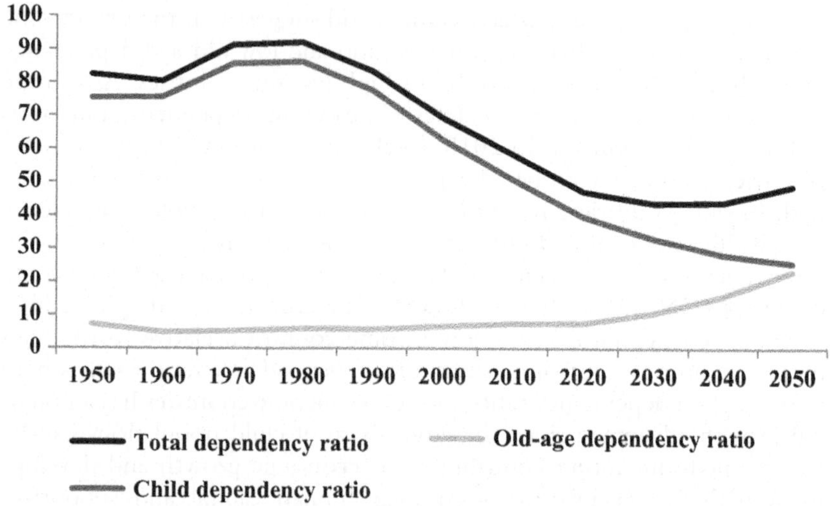

Fig. 6.2 Dependency ratio in Bangladesh, 1950–2050. Note: Total dependency ratio is the ratio of population 0–14 and 65+ per 100 population 15–64; child dependency ratio is the ratio of population 0–14 per 100 population 15–64; old-age dependency ratio is the ratio of population 65+ per 100 population 15–64. Source: World Development Indicators 2015, World Bank

and 2050 which gives a wide window of opportunities for Bangladesh to raise economic growth by developing the human capital of the young children of today who would join the labour force over the next two decades. The policy choice is clear: Bangladesh must adopt required measures to create a workforce with highly skilled labour prior to aging sets in during the middle of the 21st century when a different set of problems would emerge for the Bangladesh economy.

The government has adopted a comprehensive National Skills Development Policy in 2011 to guide skill development strategies and coordinate skill training in the country (MoE 2011). The policy covers both formal and non-formal vocational, technical and skill based education and training for wage employment and/or self-employment including (i) pre-employment and livelihood skill training, including technical and vocational education and training (TVET), apprenticeships and school based TVET, (ii) education and training for employed workers, including workplace training, and (iii) employment oriented and job-related short

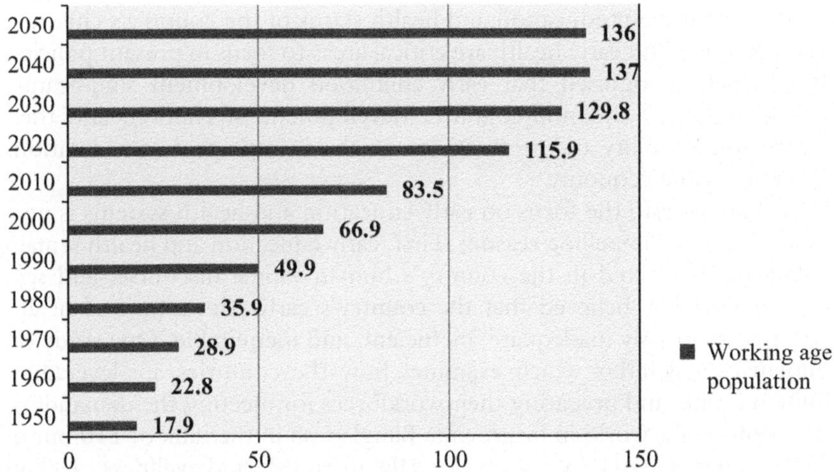

Fig. 6.3 Working Age Population in Bangladesh, 1950–2050. Note: Population age 15–64 in million. Source: World Development Indicators 2015, World Bank

courses for both domestic and international markets. The policy also recognises the need of providing skills to enhance employability and secure safe and decent work for the huge labour force currently working in the informal economy.

While the implementation of the present policies for skill development is expected to make significant contributions towards reaping the benefits of demographic dividends, Bangladesh also needs to transform its labour force in the medium term for meeting the challenges of a knowledge economy for which the work force should be dynamic, highly-skilled and broad-based in competence. Along with meeting the current requirements of education and skills, it is also time for Bangladesh to prepare its labour force for addressing the challenges of the country's future vision. In this context, demographic changes that the country will undergo in the coming decades provide wide opportunities for the age-groups who are in their infancy today to realise their potentials in the envisaged knowledge economy of the future if right policies are integrated with the current policy initiatives.

The above concerns highlight the importance of early childhood development of the present generation of children as a key element of education and skill development of the future labour force. In this context, in view of the present education and health status of the country's children, pre-schooling and early health are critical areas to focus in present policies. It is widely recognised that early childhood development significantly affects cognitive and non-cognitive development of children and their future employability and productivity which are important considerations in a knowledge economy.

In Bangladesh, the focus on early education and health systems is necessary for two compelling reasons. First, early education and health remain somewhat neglected in the country's human capital discourse; and second, it is widely believed that the country's early education and health systems are grossly inadequate, inefficient, and inequitable. One study on human capital index which examines how the countries are leveraging human capital and preparing their workforces for meeting the demands of the competitive world in future puts Bangladesh in the rank of 110 out of 122 countries—104 in education, 104 in health and wellness, 103 in workforce and employment, and 110 in enabling environment.[5] This shows the extremely disadvantaged situation of Bangladesh in terms of human capital which, if remains unchanged, will make the country's transition to the middle income category difficult to realise within the stipulated time.

6.8.1 Labour Demand in the Knowledge Economy

The current focus of skill development policies and skills training in Bangladesh covers both formal and non-formal vocational, technical and skills based education and training for wage employment and/or self-employment of the country's labour force.[6] Overall, the implicit target

[5] The human capital index measures the state of human capital development using four pillars: (i) education covering quantitative and qualitative aspects across primary, secondary and tertiary levels and information on both present and future workforce; (ii) health and wellness containing indicators on physical and mental well-being from childhood to adulthood; (iii) workforce and employment covering experience, talent, knowledge and training of the working-age population; and (iv) enabling environment which captures legal framework, infrastructure and other factors that enable return on human capital. The index contains a total of 51 indicators with 12 in education, 14 in health and wellness, 16 in workforce and employment, and 9 in enabling environment. For details, see WEF 2013.

[6] Conventionally, skills are classified into two categories: cognitive skills and non-cognitive/soft/character skills. Cognitive skills refer to the rate at which people learn (fluid intelligence) and their acquired/crystallized intelligence. It is widely recognized that cognitive skills significantly depend on personality/character traits. Non-cognitive skills are now widely

group is the existing labour force with the prime objective of equipping them to gain productive and gainful employment. In this context, the issue of employability is critical for which, in addition to technical and vocational skills, cognitive and non-cognitive skills also play important roles.[7] Thus, for ensuring occupational and inter-sectoral mobility, the concept of employability needs to be interpreted in a broad sense covering all aspects of skills including good health and quality education.

6.8.2 Early Childhood Development

In the literature, the role of early childhood development (ECD) is widely recognized as a key element of productive labour force in any country. The ultimate goal of ECD is to improve young children's capacity to develop and learn for which he/she must be socially and emotionally healthy, confident, and friendly; has good peer relationships; tackles challenging tasks and persists with them; has good language skills and communicates well; and listens to instructions and is attentive. The ECD interventions include educating and supporting parents, delivering services to children, developing capacities of caregivers and teachers, and using mass communications to enhance parents and caregiver's knowledge and practices.[8] In addition to negative impact on children's educational performance, the lack of ECD has profound implications for later-life employability, productivity, and professional mobility (see, Knudsen et.al, 2006; World Bank 2013). Bangladesh's future economy is likely to be more human capital intensive and hence investments in human capital have to be made early on today's children to begin with.

In this respect, the Skills towards Employment and Productivity (STEP) provides a comprehensive framework to visualize skills development covering the determinants of ECD and reforms in the present vocational and

considered as the dominant employability characteristics with far greater returns than those targeted to building cognitive skills. See, Holmlund and Silva 2009, Heckman et al. 2006

[7] The term 'employability' is interpreted as (i) values and attitudes compatible with the work along with a desire to learn and apply the learning to improve and take advantage of changes; (ii) basic skills e.g. literacy and numeracy; (iii) key skills e.g. communication, application of numbers, information technology, improving own learning and performance, problem solving, working with others etc. (iv) other generic skills such as modern language and customer service skills; and (v) job specific skills with ability to manage own career. See, Heckman and Kautz 2013.

[8] See, World Bank, http://go.worldbank.org/BJA2BPVW91

technical education systems and labour markets (see, Banerji et al. 2010). The STEP framework provides the elements of a successful skills development strategy covering five interlinked steps: (i) getting children off to the right start; (ii) ensuring that all students learn; (iii) building job-relevant skills that employers demand; (iv) encouraging entrepreneurship and innovation; and (v) matching the supply of skills with the demand (Table 6.12).

The framework shows that the efficacy of training, behavioural skills, and ability to acquire higher cognitive skills later in life is significantly influenced by the quantity and quality of stimulation and education

Table 6.12 The STEP framework: Integrated programmes across workers' life cycles

	Pre-school age	*School age*	*Youth*	*Working age*
Step 1: Getting children off to the right start	Nutrition, psychological and cognitive stimulation, basic cognitive and social skills	School health and remedial education		
Step 2: Ensuring that all students learn		Cognitive skills, socialization, behavioural skills	Second chance education, behavioural education	
Step 3: Building job-relevant skills that employers demand		Basic vocational training, behavioural skills	Vocational training, higher education, apprenticeships, targeted programmes	Firm provided training, re-certification, re-skilling
Step 4: Encouraging entrepreneurship and innovation		Fostering inquiry	Universities, innovation clusters, basic entrepreneurship training, risk management systems	
Step 5: Matching the supply of skills with the demand			Apprenticeships, skills certification, counseling	Intermediation services, labour regulation, social security portability

Source: Banerji et al. 2010

received in childhood. The workers who have poor early childhood environments and inadequate basic education are less likely to acquire higher level skills and be employable or productive. The relative priorities of different steps will depend on a country's specific situations, its future ambitions, and existing constraints. While steps 3 and 5 are important in the short run in the context of Bangladesh, improvement of the entire system of producing skills is necessary for the medium and long runs including ECD. This will enable Bangladesh to ensure the supply of required skills and adjust the skills to continual changes in demand and contribute to productivity increase, innovation, and economic growth.

For Bangladesh, it is important to recognise that ECD enhances the ability to learn, work with others and develop a wide range of foundational skills for formal learning and interactions during school years and beyond. Moreover, one should not forget the fact that any failure to develop these skills during the childhood will create long-term and irreversible adverse effects on education, health, productivity, and earnings in the labour market. Studies from different countries show that inadequate nutrition between conception and age 2 leads to serious cognitive delays among school-age children. Associations between poverty and cognitive, physical and socio-emotional aspects of child development are observed within 18 months of age in Bangladesh (see, Grantham-McGregor et al. 2007). The failure to make required investments in ECD is costly since the resulting deficiencies cannot be compensated later in life thereby reducing skills, abilities and productivity of the future labour force.

Moreover, strong evidence exists on the positive impact of ECD over the life time of an individual. Children participating in ECD programmes have higher cognitive development, lower repetition and dropout rates in early primary school grades, better learning, and higher school completion rates. One study in Bangladesh shows that children who received centre-based pre-school education outperformed their peers without such education by 58 per cent in terms of a standardised test of school readiness (Aboud, 2006). The positive outcomes of ECD reach far beyond childhood and affect labour productivity when they are grown up. The evidence shows that ECD is among the most cost-effective investments that a country can make in its people. It is proposed that a country, especially low labour productivity countries like Bangladesh, should invest at least 1 per cent of its GDP on ECD (Taylor and Bennett 2006).

The government has recognised that pre-primary education (PPE) is the most common and promising intervention of early childhood care and development in Bangladesh. The National Education Policy, approved in 2010, includes PPE as an integral part of primary education and the government's commitment is to introduce one year pre-primary education through the government primary education system. For the purpose of ensuring effective implementation of the PPE services throughout the country, the Ministry of Primary and Mass Education (MoPME) has taken initiatives to bring all PPE activities under one framework. In 2008, an operational framework has been adopted to introduce one year pre-primary education for all children of 5–6 years age along with a long-term goal of bringing all children, 3–5 years of age, under pre-school programmes along with access to programmes of health, nutrition, social, physical and intellectual development, and preparing their entry into the formal education system.

Although significant progress has been made in recent years in participation of 3–5 year olds in some forms of pre-primary education, still about 2.9 million out of a total of 3.7 million PPE age children (as per the 2011 Population Census data) remain out of pre-school coverage. Moreover, in terms of quality, there are wide variations in available PPE services. Many of the pre-schools do not have required physical environment and facilities and fail to meet minimum standards for pedagogical issues, such as trained teacher, minimum contact hour, teacher-student ratio, and curriculum planning. There also exists widespread disparity in PPE participation both by expenditure quintiles (about half of the non-poor but only one-fifth of the poorest children participating in some form of pre-primary education) and between urban and rural areas (with about half in urban areas and a fifth in the rural areas attending pre-schools). Also, in view of diverse linguistic background, there is a need for provision of multi lingual education (MLE) for children belonging to different ethnic/indigenous populations living in the three Chittagong Hill Tract (CHT) districts and other parts of the country.

Although the enrolment rate at the primary level has risen relatively fast in recent years, still more than 0.62 million children remained out of primary school in 2010 (WDI 2015). The primary completion rate as a proportion of the relevant age group is 75 per cent while the gross enrolment rates at the secondary and tertiary levels are estimated at only 54 per cent and 13 per cent respectively in 2012. Moreover, basic literacy has progressed modestly as reflected in the adult literacy rate (persons aged 15 years and above) of 60 per cent in 2013. In addition, the youth literacy rate (as a share of people aged 15–24 years) is 81 per cent in 2013 showing that nearly one-fifth of the country's population belonging to the most productive age group of the population are illiterates having no ability to read and write.

Given the above status of the country's education system and the levels of enrolment at various stages, it is not surprising that the educational status of the country's current labour force is poor (Table 6.13). Nearly two-thirds of the labour force has either no or primary education while only about 4 per cent of the labour force is at least graduates. With the poor levels of functional literacy and professional skills, this shows that the level of employability and productivity of the labour force is low with consequent implications on growth and development dynamics of the country.

For the future, what is more worrisome is the quality and other differentials among different streams of education, especially at the primary level. In view of the foundational significance of the primary education, such differences raise both educational inequality and inequality of opportunity at the basic levels. Thus, the current developments in the education sector are more likely to contribute to deep-rooted inequalities in human capital for the coming generations with a limited number of fortunate people getting the opportunities of acquiring higher levels of skills to get remunerative jobs at home and abroad while the vast majority with low education and skills struggling to get a decent job at home or resort to 'distress' migration with unskilled and/or semi-skilled jobs at low wages.

Table 6.13 Educational status of Bangladesh's labour force, 2010 (in per cent of respective total)

Education level	*Total*	*Female*	*Male*
No education	40.2	40.7	39.9
Primary (grades 1–5)	22.8	22.7	22.9
Secondary and below (grades 6–10)	29.5	31.4	28.6
Higher secondary (grades 11–12)	3.7	3.0	4.0
Graduates and above	3.8	2.2	4.6
Total	100	100	100
Total labour force (million)	56.65	17.17	39.48

Source, BBS, Report on Labour Force Survey 2010.

6.8.3 *Child Health and Nutrition*

In the policy discourse on skill development and labour productivity, early childhood health and nutrition is a somewhat neglected issue although child health and nutrition is an important determinant of labour force productivity. Recent studies highlight a number of pathways through which the impact of health and nutrition is transmitted to the labour market (see, Becker 2007; Bartley 1994; Butterworth et al. 2012; Schuring et al. 2013; Wagenaar et al. 2012). Despite these recognitions, the impact of early health on employability and productivity of the labour force still remains less understood.

One important indicator of good health is the prevalence of stunting among the children. Stunting (low height-for-age) is the outcome of chronic malnourishment and exhibits that the body has failed to receive adequate nutrition over a long period of time. The children, who are stunted, are unlikely to realise their cognitive potential due to poverty and poor health and nutrition which affects their educational outcomes. The poor health and nutritional status of these children results in low cognitive performance, educational achievements and mental retardation which adversely affect their performance in the labour market, employability prospects, and reach their full potential in later life.

Overall, the provision of healthcare services is grossly inadequate in Bangladesh which is also considered inefficient and inequitable (see, e.g. BHW 2008). It is reported that the share of out-of-pocket (OOP) expenditure is 63 per cent in total health expenditure while the share of public expenditure is 34 per cent.[9] Obviously, if the burden of OOP health expenditure could be reduced through greater access to public health systems especially for the poor households who can hardly afford it, this would have enabled them to invest more in human capital development of their children leading to less inequity in ECD, higher skill achievement and productivity in later years, and better social outcomes in terms of creating a level-playing field for pursuing future educational and job-related opportunities.

[9] The rest is accounted for by other components of total expenditure on health. For details, see World Development Indicators 2012.

6.8.4 Policy Implications

The major challenges of the Bangladesh's labour market relate to two aspects—employability and inequity—that significantly undermine the development potential of the economy and its transition to a higher growth trajectory. While the short-term responses to these challenges require adoption of both formal and non-formal vocational, technical and skill based education and training for wage employment and/or self-employment of the labour force, the medium/long-term strategy involves appropriate adjustments in the country's education and health systems with emphasis on early childhood education and healthcare. For graduating to a knowledge-based economy in the medium to long term, what is important for Bangladesh is to effect major changes in its education and health care systems to effectively reap its demographic dividends.

The present policies of the government emphasise on developing the skills of the existing labour force and the new entrants for which a comprehensive national skill development policy has been adopted in 2011. While these are steps in the right direction, the present approach has limitations in meeting the requirements of the knowledge economy as envisaged for the future. It is well recognized that Bangladesh's future knowledge economy will require a labour force whose skills are broad enough to cover both cognitive and non-cognitive skills rather than having a narrow focus on technical and vocational skills alone. It needs to be recognized that a dynamic economy is unlikely to be sustained with sector- and industry-specific skills for long in the context of rapidly changing demands for skills as the structure of the economy undergoes changes. For the future, the emphasis needs to be on developing flexible skills to meet the changing requirements of the economy.

While strategies for providing flexible skills and enhancing employability of the existing labour force are difficult to implement within a comprehensive approach, the scope is wide for the children who are the potential entrants of the future labour force. For the approach, the challenge is to put the required emphasis on early education and health of the children with emphasis on both cognitive and non-cognitive skills as illustrated in the paper. The aim should be to develop and enlarge the human capital profile of the future labour force.

While the government has put emphasis on expanding the pre-primary education along with primary education for all, the approach should also enhance the quality and equity aspects of education and incorporate the comprehensive elements of a successful skills development strategy covering the entire life cycles of the future labour force. As we have noted, the central role in the approach is the development of soft skills, which needs to start at the pre-primary level. This requires a close coordination between pre-primary schooling and child health initiatives, the two central pillars of early childhood development. Bangladesh can also learn from success stories of early childhood development and their employability/productivity implications in later life working age from other countries, such as South Korea.

6.9 Overseas Employment

The growing importance of overseas employment for the Bangladesh economy is clearly evident in recent years. Remittances rose to over $15 billion in 2018 or about 8 per cent of GDP—rising from only $10 million in 1975. Remittances have become a major source of foreign exchange earnings, second only to ready-made garments. Overseas employment itself represents over one-fifth of the annual addition to the country's total labour force and over half of additional manufacturing jobs created in recent years. Close to half a million people found jobs abroad every year from 2012 to 2015; and this exceeded 0.9 million in 2017.

After independence, short-term migration for employment started in the 1970s, which picked up pace by the end-1980s. In recent years, the number of workers going abroad fluctuated around half a million every year. In the past, female migrant workers from Bangladesh accounted for a small and negligible proportion of the total, but the annual trend rose consistently since 2000. In 2017, nearly 122,000 were women workers, accounting for 12 per cent of the total migrant workforce from Bangladesh. By skill composition, the unskilled constitute the largest number of Bangladesh workers, at 45 per cent in 2014. The share of skilled is 23 per cent, while 3 per cent is semiskilled and 0.01 per cent is professional. For women, data from 2005 to 2014 reveal more unskilled migrant workers, at 67 per cent, compared with 55 per cent for men.

Several economic, demographic, and social factors are the keys in influencing the flow of overseas migration of workers. Migration flow is positively correlated with GDP growth in Bangladesh (World Bank 2012) and the long-term trend remains positive for more than two decades as economic growth has accelerated. This steady flow of overseas employment, despite economic progress, suggests other factors at play, including limited employment opportunities at home and expected higher earnings in countries with demand for migrant workers.

Whether migration is induced by poverty is a contentious issue in Bangladesh, although this does not imply that the poor benefit more from migration than upper-income groups. The associated high costs of migration brought on by the imposition of expensive recruitment fees make access to migration opportunities highly skewed in favour of upper-income groups. Other costs and potential risks, such as payment to intermediaries at various stages of the recruitment process, increase the burden of prospective migrant workers. Those from lower-income groups, therefore, potentially find themselves using illegal channels to migrate abroad, leaving them more prone to abuse and violence, particularly for women.

The impact of overseas employment at the macro level has been significant. Migrant workers' remittances to Bangladesh are the second largest source of foreign exchange, after ready-made garments. This has enabled Bangladesh to steadily increase foreign exchange reserves, which allow increases in imports without necessarily putting pressure on exchange rates. Remittances also have a positive impact on the balance of payments and help offset deficits in the balance of trade in goods and services.

Overseas employment has also been an important factor in easing the pressure on the domestic labour market. With about 1.8 million people entering the labour force annually during the 2000s, present rates of economic growth has not been able to create employment opportunities quickly enough to fully absorb the unemployed and the newly entrant workers. On overage, the annual flow of migrant workers represents about 22 per cent of the additional labour force annually. If the multiplier effect generated by the inflow of remittances and investment in economic activities by the receiving households of remittances are taken into account, the contribution of overseas employment becomes quite significant.

At the micro level, the contribution of migration to poverty reduction has been notable, with remittances boosting household consumption and savings significantly. The World Bank (2012), using the Household Income and Expenditure Survey (HIES) 2010, shows that the monthly income, consumption, and savings are on average 82 per cent, 38 per cent and 107 per cent higher, respectively, for remittance receiving households than households not receiving remittances. In the same year, only 13 per cent of remittance receiving households is below the poverty line, compared with 34 per cent in non-remittance—receiving households.

On the use of remittances, available surveys (see, BBS, 2014) show three primary expenditures of remittances: food (39 per cent), land purchases (17 per cent), and loan repayments (9 per cent). Education and health account for 4 per cent and 5 per cent, respectively. Data on savings and investment by remittance-receiving households show that 57 per cent are savers and 25 per cent are investors, largely in purchases of land and construction of houses, while only about 7 per cent invest in businesses.

However, the results of small-scale surveys on the impact of remittances on education and health are mostly unclear and mixed. Some surveys report that allocation to education and health is lower in the priority of remittance expenditure (e.g. Mamun and Nath 2010), while others find allocations to education and health precede the purchase of land and construction of houses (World Bank 2012; Kumari and Shamim 2010). These studies also underscore the contribution of migration to empowerment of women—both as migrants and family members left behind, through the decision-making roles they play in household affairs, particularly on the education and health of children and in running economic activities.

6.9.1 Future Prospects

The continuation of the present trend of the number of Bangladeshi migrant workers suggests that about 650,000 overseas employment would be created in 2020 (ADB 2016). Many factors will shape the future landscape of overseas employment for Bangladeshi workers. These factors include the needs of prospective migrant workers, nature of bilateral relations of the sending and receiving countries, potential skills of migrant workers, and the governance of the recruitment process and deployment of overseas workers. The significant restriction of countries, such as Kuwait, Malaysia, and Saudi Arabia on migrant workers from Bangladesh illustrates this point. On the other hand, with strong incentives to emigrate, such as kinship and other networks in receiving countries, the presence of reliable and reputable recruitment agencies, and a proactive and facilitating attitude of the government can help strengthen the country's potential to increase overseas employment.

6.9.2 Matching Skill Composition of Migrant Workers

The skill composition of workers from a sending country to a destination country depends on many factors, and countries employing foreign labour usually associate particular occupations and skills with specific countries for which the sending country needs to adopt right overseas employment policies and strategies. Table 6.14 compiles the labour market needs and potential opportunities for Bangladeshi migrant workers in selected key destination countries.

Table 6.14 shows that the demand for a broad range of skill categories—with high-level technicians for manufacturing and professionals in the service sectors at one end, and workers in construction and maintenance that require very little skill at the other. The main determinants for low-skilled labour from South Asian countries are: price (wages), availability, general health and physique, connections, recruiter catchment area and other criteria such as perceptions about attitudes and behaviour as well experiences of certain nationalities (ILO 2015).

As such, it may not be easy for Bangladesh to attain a desired skill or occupational composition of its migrant workers. However, supply-side interventions, such as skills training, changing stereotypes about country perceptions, and entering into bilateral negotiations and agreements are essential first steps to move in the right direction. It would be useful to promote Bangladesh as a potential supplier of skilled workers. This, however, involves effective investments by the government for developing required skill training facilities by the public sector. The key is to change the perception of Bangladesh as a supplier of unskilled and low-skilled workers alone. This involves the ability to generate qualifications that are internationally recognised. Training facilities need to be upgraded and international recognition of certificates obtained. Bilateral contracts, marketing of available skills, and showcasing of cutting-edge skills-training facilities are required to address the perception issue.

For Bangladesh, one major challenge is to sustain and raise the flow of overseas employment at desired levels. This requires in-depth reviews, on a regular basis, of the economic prospects of the present destination countries and to identify potential destinations; and their requirement for expatriate labour for responding to the evolving demand for workers—both in terms of destination countries and skill composition.

Other relevant issues are the high cost of migration in overseas employment of Bangladeshi workers; abuse and exploitation of migrant workers at different stages of migration cycle; and developing common frameworks for employing expatriate workers in destination countries. Further, monitoring and analysis of labour markets (including the broad direction and skill composition) in prospective labour-receiving countries; monitoring

Table 6.14 Labour market needs and opportunities for Bangladeshi workers in selected countries

Country	*Skill type of Bangladeshi workers, 2005–2012*	*Demand prospects and labour market needs*	*Potential opportunities/ constraints*
Saudi Arabia	Labour (unspecified), Agricultural workers and Farmers (unspecified), Construction workers, drivers.	Manufacturing, trade, and services sectors have Higher growth potential, while growth of construction Sector is likely to taper off. Employers have a high degree of confidence In training programmes in Philippines and, hence, Likely to recruit workers with high-level skills for trade And service sector but without such perception about the construction sector.	Skills and occupations on greater demand are technicians and higher level skills for manufacturing, qualified professionals in education, health, retail trade, construction workers.
United Arab Emirates	Labour (unspecified), worker (unspecified), private service, construction workers, cook, driver, cleaner, machine operator, tailor, salesperson, agricultural workers.	Construction, real estate, tourism and hospitality, Manufacturing and logistics, education and health Care are among the sectors likely to grow rapidly, With significant rise in expected demand for qualified personnel.	No new visas have been issued for workers from Bangladesh since August 2012.
Kuwait	Labour (unspecified), cook, Driver, houseboy, salesperson, Welder, technician (unspecified), cleaner	Growth sectors include oil capacity, utilities, Infrastructure (including residential), and services Especially health care and education	No recruitment of Bangladeshi Workers has been made by Kuwait in the past five years

(*continued*)

Table 6.14 (continued)

Country	*Skill type of Bangladeshi workers, 2005–2012*	*Demand prospects and labour market needs*	*Potential opportunities/ constraints*
Qatar	Labour (unspecified), Construction workers, cook, Driver, fitter, foreman, private Service, engineer	Due to hosting of 2022 soccer world cup, sectors likely to grow at high rates include construction, hotel and restaurants, and services	More workers to deliver these services and run the newly constructed facilities effectively are expected
Jordan	Garment workers	Construction sector and garments industry are Considered growth sectors	More construction and garment workers
Republic of Korea	…	Construction (including skills in civil engineering, Masonry and carpentry), domestic and care work, Housekeeping in hospitals are among the sectors where Foreign labour is employed	More domestic and care work, Construction workers and Housekeeping in hospitals

Source: Compiled from ADB 2016

of domestic labour supply in various skill categories; ways of linking skill providers with the recruitment process for overseas employment; flow of remittances and their use; monitoring and analysis of return migration including reintegration of returning workers in the domestic labour market; and utilisation of their savings and skills, etc. are important areas on which effective measures are required (ADB 2016).

6.10 Concluding Remarks

The demographic transition provides a window of opportunity for raising economic growth and prosperity in Bangladesh. The country is also blessed with unprecedented youth human resources. Although demographics do not directly determine the pace of economic growth, but these are certainly key determinants for an economy's growth potential.

An aging population coupled with a declining birth rate in the coming decades may lead to decline in future economic growth. Increases in productivity can lessen the impact of such population shifts, and technological advances are the ideal source of productivity boosts. This, however, is a double-edged sword: technological progress can increase productivity, but at the same time it can eliminate jobs, increasing unemployment. As the age composition of the workforce will change in the future, so will the kinds of jobs that the Bangladesh economy will require.

Currently, Bangladesh's labour market is experiencing deep structural changes, but there is a dearth of reliable data to capture these shifts. The debate tends to focus narrowly on the pace of job creation, but there is need for a new emphasis on the notion of gainful or decent employment that focuses on improved quality of work and the income derived from it. Decent employment covers a range of issues, including the quantity and type of work done by people already in employment, growth in labour productivity, higher earnings, and aspects of work quality such as safety, cleanliness, flexibility, income security, and intellectual challenge.

There are three forces that are particularly relevant in shaping the workforce landscape: (i) urbanisation and the need to bridge infrastructure gaps; (ii) automation and knowledge-intensive work: and (iii) new digital ecosystems and independent work. However, these are not unique to Bangladesh and the government policies and actions need to adopt the right policies. A wide range of initiatives, both government-led and undertaken by the private sector, can help increase decent employment in the country. There are possibly three areas with considerable potential: more appropriate statistical measurement of employment; establishing targeted government programmes to stimulate decent employment; and removing hurdles standing in the way of investment and innovation.

In the coming decades, population ageing and growth will place additional pressure on government service delivery in Bangladesh. These pressures will be ameliorated to some degree as urban density increases. However, population ageing will drive up demand for services related to seniors, carers and the disabled, which tend to be more complex and require more face-to-face interactions. These emerging trends will present challenges to the current service delivery system, which remains reliant on manual processes and face-to-face transactions. These will require transformational reform, necessitating a movement away from discrete programmes built around government agencies to citizen-focused service delivery. A modern service delivery model will need to use resources more efficiently.

Bangladesh will have to create an increasing number of jobs in the coming decade to accommodate population growth, shifts in the age and sex composition of the population, changing age-and sex-specific labour force participation rates, rapid urbanisation, and other socioeconomic changes. Since the 1990s, population growth stands out as the primary driver of employment growth, with its effect dampened somewhat by decreasing labour force participation rates and little to no impact from changes in unemployment rates. But, during the coming decade, although population growth will remain the primary driver of employment growth, but this will be magnified by general increases in labour force participation rates, a general shift in the age structure whereby population becomes more concentrated in higher participation age groups. Thus demographic change will ensure a continuing job creation challenge in Bangladesh.

Job creation requirements in the coming decade will primarily reflect population growth in the prior two decades, which reflected high levels of population growth in the country. Because of these lags in the effect of fertility, currently decreasing fertility and population growth rates imply that this is a transitive phase. During the period, youth population will start growing at lower rate than the adult population growth rate due primarily to decreasing fertility and population growth leading to low rates of replacement in the youth working-age population.

A much-discussed hypothesis proposes that there is a U-shaped relationship between economic development and women's participation in the labour force. The stylised argument is that when a country is poor, women work out of necessity, mainly in subsistence agriculture or home-based production. As the country develops, economic activity shifts from agriculture to industry and services, which benefits men more than women. At higher stages of economic development, education levels rise, fertility rates fall, and social stigmas weaken, enabling women to take advantage of new jobs emerging in the service sector that are more family-friendly and accessible. At the household level, these structural shifts can be described in the context of the neoclassical labour supply model: as a spouse's wage rises, there is a negative income effect on the supply of women's labour. Once wages for women start to increase, however, the substitution effect will induce them to increase their labour supply.

Clearly, not all countries follow such a U-shaped path as their economies grow. For example, the female labour force participation rate rose from 23.9 per cent in 1990 to 36.0 per cent in 2010 in Bangladesh, a low-income country, while it stagnated or declined during the period in India especially in rural areas. Participation rates for women in Bangladesh started at much lower levels before increasing over the 2000s due to the boom in the garments industry and microcredit, which support agricultural livelihoods. Thus, there is a complex evolution of female labour force participation which portrays the reality of multiple forces at play.

Further, education levels of girls and young women have improved considerably in Bangladesh in recent decades and this should help increase opportunities for women to enter the labour market. In Bangladesh, there seems to exist a linear relationship between education and female labour force participation, as opposed to a nonlinear or U-shaped correlation in India. In poorer countries, the uneducated women are likely to participate in subsistence activities and informal employment, while women with a high school education can afford to stay out of the labour force. Once women have more than a secondary school education, higher wages pull them to join the labour force, particularly if appropriate jobs are available.

Overall, the quality of employment and opportunities for better jobs continue to be unequally distributed between men and women in most countries including Bangladesh. When women work, they tend to earn less (well-known gender wage gap), work in less productive jobs, and overrepresented in unpaid family work and other forms of vulnerable jobs. In terms of employment status, more women than men work as contributing family workers, which adds to their labour market vulnerability. In Bangladesh, still a high proportion of working women are active in the agriculture sector, although the share have fallen in recent years as more women have taken up work in the manufacturing (readymade garments) and services sectors.

Beyond standard labour force participation rates, policymakers in Bangladesh should address the barriers that constrain women to access better jobs and take advantage of new labour market opportunities that arise as the country grows. For the purpose, policies should consider both supply- and demand-side dimensions, including better quality education and training programmes and access to childcare, as well as other supportive institutions and legal measures to ease the burden of domestic duties, enhance women's safety, and encourage private sector development in industries that can increase job opportunities for women. Particular emphasis is needed on keeping young girls in school and ensuring that they receive a good quality education, beyond secondary level, and are able to take advantage of training opportunities. That, in turn, will increase their chances of overcoming other barriers to finding decent employment.

It is true that a small segment of Bangladesh's 67 million strong workforce is already reaping benefits from strong GDP growth, increasing shift into non-farm employment, and the country's high-tech skills—but millions more could also do better. The workforce aspires to higher pay, better and more productive working conditions, and safer, cleaner, and more stimulating work. A new emphasis on decent employment would help the workforce meet these aspirations. It will require a conscious effort on the part of the government, including in terms of measuring employment more holistically, targeting spending on initiatives, and changing regulation of private-sector investment and innovation to remove barriers to gainful employment. While these and other possible policy steps are challenging, the effort and energy required to put them in place will be highly rewarded if they achieve their end goal of a more fulfilled, better rewarded, and more productive workforce.

References

Aboud, F.E. 2006. Evaluation of an Early Childhood Preschool Program in Rural Bangladesh. *Early Childhood Research Quarterly* 21: 46–60.

ADB. 2016. *Bangladesh: Looking Beyond Garments.* Manila: Employment Diagnostic Study, Asian Development Bank.

Ahmed, S., and P. Maitra. 2010. Gender Wage Discrimination in Rural and Urban Labour Markets of Bangladesh. *Oxford Development Studies* 38 (1): 83–112.

Banerji, A., W Cunningham, A. Fiszbein, E. King, H. Patrinos, D. Rubalino, and J.P. Tan. 2010. *Stepping Up Skills: For More Jobs and Higher Productivity.* Washington DC: World Bank.

Bartley, M. 1994. Unemployment and Ill Health: Understanding the Relationship. *Journal of Epidemiology and Community Health* 48 (4): 333–337.

BBS. 2014. Education Household Survey 2014. Dhaka: Bangladesh Bureau of Statistics, Statistics and Informatics Division (SID), Ministry of Planning, Government of the People's Republic of Bangladesh.

———. 2018. *Bangladesh Labour Force Survey 2016-17, Bangladesh Bureau of Statistics, Ministry of Planning.* Dhaka: Government of the People's Republic of Bangladesh.

Becker, G.S. 2007. Health as Human Capital: Synthesis and Extensions. *Oxford Economic Papers* 59 (3): 379–410.

Berlau, J. 1997. The Paradox of Child-Labor Reform. *Insight on the News* 13 (43): 20–21.

BHW. 2008. *The State of Health in Bangladesh 2007, Health Workforce in Bangladesh, Who Constitutes the Healthcare System?, Bangladesh Health Watch (BHW)*. Dhaka: BRAC University.

Bloom, D, D. Canning, and P. Malaney. 1999. *Demographic Change and Economic Growth in Asia*, CID Economic Paper No. 15, Center for International Development, Harvard University, Cambridge. MA.

Bloom, D, D. Canning, and L. Rosenberg. 2011. *Demographic Change and Economic Growth in South Asia,* PGDA Working Paper No. 67, Program on the Global Demography of Aging, Harvard Initiative for Global Health, Cambridge. MA.

Butterworth, P., L. Leach, J. Pirkis, and M. Kelaher. 2012. Poor Mental Health Influences Risk and Duration of Unemployment: A Prospective Study. *Social Psychiatry and Psychiatric Epidemiology* 47 (6): 1013–1021.

Dobson, W., ed. 2013. *Human Capital Formation and Economic Growth in Asia and the Pacific.* Oxford and New York: Routledge.

Grantham-McGregor, S., Y.B. Cheung, S. Cueta, P. Glewwe, L. Richter, and B. Strupp. 2007. Development Potential in the First 5 Years for Children in Developing Countries. *Lancet* 369: 60–70.

Harrison, A., and A. Rodríguez-Clare. 2010. *Trade, Foreign Investment, and Industrial Policy for Developing Countries.* NBER Working Paper No. 15261, Chicago.

Heckman, J., and T. Kautz. 2013. *Fostering and Measuring Skills: Interventions that Improve Character and Cognition*, IZA Discussion Paper No. 7750, Institute for the Study of Labor, Bonn.

Heckman, J., J. Stixrud, and S. Urzua. 2006. The Effects of Cognitive and Non-Cognitive Abilities on Labour Market Outcomes and Social Behaviour. *Journal of Labor Economics* 24 (3): 411–482.

Holmlund, H., and O. Silva. 2009. *Targeting Non-Cognitive Skills to Improve Cognitive Outcomes: Evidence from a Remedial Education Intervention,* No 4476, IZA Discussion Papers, Institute of Labor Economics (IZA), Bonn.

Hossain, M.A., and C.A. Tisdell. 2005. Closing the Gender Gap in Bangladesh: Inequality in Education, Employment and Earnings. *International Journal of Social Economics* 32: 439–453.

IEG. 2013. *Annual Report 2013.* Washington DC: Independent Evaluation Group, World Bank.

ILO. 2010. *Global Employment Trends for Youth.* Geneva: International Labour Office.

———. 2012a. *Global Employment Trends for Youth.* Geneva: International Labour Office.

———. 2012b. *The Youth Employment Crisis: Time for Action,* International Labour Conference, 101st Session, Report V. Geneva.

———. 2015. *Global Wage Report 2014/2015*, International Labour Office, Geneva, http://www.ilo.org/wcmsp5/groups/public/@dgreports/@dcomm/@publ/documents/publication/wcms_324678.pdf.

Kapsos, S. 2008. *The Gender Wage Gap in Bangladesh, ILO Working Papers 994134173402676*. Geneva: International Labour Organization.

Kumari, R., and I. Shamim. 2010. Gender Dimensions of International Migration from Bangladesh and India: Socio Economic Impact on Families Left Behind. http://www.saneinetwork.net/Files/10_07___Ranjana_Kumari.pdf.

Knudsen, E. I, J. J. Heckman, J. L. Cameron, and J. P. Shonkoff. 2006. *'Economic, Neurobiological, and Behavioral Perspectives on Building America's Future Workforce', Proceedings of the National Academy of Sciences* 103 (27): 10155–10162.

Lee, J. N and D. Newhouse. 2012. *The Role of Sectoral Growth Patterns in Labor Market Development*. Background Paper for the World Development Report 2013, Washington DC: World Bank. https://openknowledge.worldbank.org/handle/10986/12145 License: CC BY 3.0 IGO.

Mamun, K., and H. Nath. 2010. Workers' Migration and Remittances in Bangladesh, Welch College of Business Faculty Publications Paper 84. http://digitalcommons.sacredheart.edu/cgi/viewcontent.cgi?article=1084 context=wcob_fac.

Mason, A., and R. Lee. 2006. Reform and Support Systems for the Elderly in Developing Countries: Capturing the Second Demographic Dividend. *Genus* 62 (2): 11–35.

MoE. 2011. *National Skills Development Policy 2011*. Dhaka: Ministry of Education, Government of the People's Republic of Bangladesh.

Mujeri, M.K. 2002. *Bangladesh: Bringing Poverty Focus in Rural Infrastructure Development,* Issues in Employment and Poverty, Discussion Paper No.6, Recovery and Reconstruction Department, International Labour Office, Geneva.

Page, J. 1994. The East Asian Miracle: Four Lessons for Development Policy. *NBER Macroeconomic Annual* 9: 219–282.

Prskawetz, A, T. Kogel, W. Sanderson, and S. Scherbov. 2004. *The Effects of Age Structure on Economic Growth: An Application of Probabilistic Forecasting in India,* Vienna Institute of Demography Working Paper No. 03/2004, Austrian Academy of Sciences, Vienna.

Schuring, M., S. Robroek, F. Otten, C. Arts, and A. Burdorf. 2013. The Effect of Ill Health and Socioeconomic Status on Labor Force Exit and Re-employment: A Prospective Study with Ten Years Follow-Up in the Netherlands. *Scandinavian Journal of Work, Environment & Health* 39 (2): 134–143.

Stalker, P. 1996. *Child Labour in Bangladesh: A Summary of Recent Investigations.* Dhaka: United Nations Children Fund.

Subbarao, K., C. del Ninno, C. Andrews, and C. Rodríguez-Alas. 2013. *Public Works as a Safety Net: Design, Evidence, and Implementation*. Washington DC: World Bank.

Taylor, C., and J. Bennett. 2006. *Starting Strong II: Early Childhood Education and Care*. Paris: OECD.

UN. 2016. *World Economic and Social Survey 2014/2015: Learning from National Policies Supporting MDG Implementation*. New York: United Nations. https://doi.org/10.18356/e109dc22-en.

UNESCO. 2012. *Shaping the Education of Tomorrow: 2012 Report on the UN Decade of Education for Sustainable Development*. Paris: United Nations Educational, Scientific and Cultural Organization.

United Nations. 2017. *World Population Prospects 2017*. New York: Population Division of the Department of Economic and Social Affairs of the United Nations Secretariat.

———. 2019. *Asia and the Pacific SDG Progress Report 2019*. Bangkok: Economic and Social Commission for Asia and the Pacific.

Wagenaar, A., M. Kompier, I. Houtman, S. van den Bossche, and T. Taris. 2012. Employment Contracts and Health Selection: Unhealthy Employees Out and Healthy Employees In? *Journal of Occupational and Environmental Medicine* 54 (10): 1192–1200.

WDI. 2015. *World Development Indicators 2015*. Washington DC: World Bank.

WEF. 2013. *The Human Capital Report 2013*. Geneva: World Economic Forum.

World Bank. 1993. *The East Asian Miracle: Economic Growth and Public Policy*. New York: Oxford University Press.

———. 2010. *World Development Report 2010: Development and Climate Change*. Washington DC: World Bank.

———. 2012. *Bangladesh: Towards Accelerated, Inclusive and Sustainable Growth—Opportunities and Challenges* (Vol. 2): Main Report No. 67991, World Bank, Washington, DC.

———. 2013. *World Development Report 2013: Jobs*. Washington DC: World Bank. https://openknowledge.worldbank.org/handle/10986/11843 License: CC BY 3.0 IGO.

CHAPTER 7

Social and Climate Change Vulnerability

7.1 Introduction

Vulnerability refers to exposure to contingencies and stress, and difficulty in coping with them. It relates to the diminished capacity of an individual or group to anticipate, cope with, resist and recover from the impact of a natural or man-made hazard or disaster. The concept is relative and dynamic. Vulnerability is most often associated with poverty, but it can also arise when people are isolated, insecure and defenceless in the face of risk, shock or stress.

Many factors contribute to vulnerability, that act to undermine capacity for self-protection, blocks or diminish access to social protection, delays or complicate recovery, or expose some groups to greater or more frequent hazards than other groups. They include factors, such as rapid population growth, poverty and hunger, poor health, low levels of education, gender inequality, fragile and hazardous location, and lack of access to resources and services, including knowledge and technology, disintegration of social relations. Other causes include, for example, lack of access to information and knowledge, lack of public awareness, limited access to political power and representation (Aysan 1993). When people are socially disadvantaged or lack political voice, their vulnerability is exacerbated. The economic vulnerability is related to a number of interacting elements, including its importance in the overall national economy, trade and foreign exchange earnings, aid and investments, international prices of commodities and

© The Author(s) 2020

M. K. Mujeri, N. Mujeri, *Bangladesh at Fifty*, Palgrave Studies in Economic History,
https://doi.org/10.1007/978-3-030-56791-0_7

inputs, and production and consumption patterns. Environmental vulnerability concerns land degradation, earthquake, flood, cyclone and hurricane, drought, storms (monsoon rain, El Niño), water scarcity, deforestation, and the other threats to biodiversity.

In the context of poverty, there are two differing perspectives on vulnerability. One may be called the 'risks-centric view' whereby vulnerability is typically defined as variability in the living standard caused by consumption or income shocks. The second perspective, on the other hand, may be called the 'rights-centric view' whereby vulnerability is caused by the lack of social and political rights. However, both views are important in understanding how poverty and vulnerability are interlocked. These views attach importance to differing dimensions of poverty. The risks-centric view tends to highlight transient poverty while the rights-centric view focuses on chronic poverty although there are considerable overlaps between the two.

Counteracting vulnerability requires several actions, such as (1) reducing the impact of the hazard where possible (through mitigation, prediction and warning, preparedness); (2) building capacities to withstand and cope with hazards; and (3) tackling the root causes of vulnerability, such as poverty, poor governance, discrimination, inequality and inadequate access to resources and livelihoods.

Bangladesh, located in the low-lying areas of the Ganga–Brahmaputra–Meghna (GBM) Delta with high population density, experiences intense climate change impacts like sea level rise, coastal erosion, salinisation, frequent cyclones and floods, and other calamities which severely stress especially the highly natural resource dependent communities. The situation is further complicated by the multi-dimensional deprivations of poverty and lack of social well-being such as poor access to education, health services, child mortality, food and nutrition security, lack of safe drinking water and sanitation facilities. The communities, with varying adaptive capacity to respond to climate impacts, are experience different levels of vulnerability.

7.2 Social Vulnerability in Bangladesh: Challenges and Practices

Social vulnerability refers to potential harm to the people and involves a combination of factors that determine the degree to which someone's life and livelihood are put at risk by a discrete and identifiable event in nature or in society. Social vulnerability is related to the susceptibility of social groups to potential losses from hazard events of society's resistance and resilience to hazard (Blaikie et al. 1994; Hewitt 1977).

In the Bangladesh context, the concept of 'marginality' is often used to indicate social vulnerability in poverty discourse as a crosscutting issue within a trans-disciplinary framework.[1] Marginality generally applies to socio-cultural, political and economic spheres in which disadvantaged people fail to gain access to resources and full participation in society. In other words, marginalised people are socially, economically, politically, and legally ignored, excluded or neglected and are therefore vulnerable to livelihood insecurity (Müller-Böker et al. 2004).[2] Thus marginalisation is a process that emerges and evolves uniquely under distinct socioeconomic and geo-political environments. Marginalised people are usually discriminated against, stigmatised, ignored, and often socio-politically suppressed on the basis of ethnicity, gender, age, culture, religion, occupation, education, and economic status by the mainstream.[3] Although spatial marginality is usually linked to geographical remoteness, it may also exist in urban slums of metropolitan cities where geographical proximity is essentially irrelevant.

There exists significant overlap between poverty and marginality in Bangladesh, and the marginalised communities have always been and continue to be the outcome of severe socioeconomic discrimination. Some

[1] Marginality remains a subject of much debate, especially relating to its measurement and how to differentiate it from broader issues of inequality, poverty, and social exclusion (see Klasen 2001; Kabeer 2005; World Bank 2005; Ferreira and Gignoux 2008). The controversy, however, should not obscure the imperative to combat social vulnerability and marginalisation. As Sen (2009: vii) argues, "What moves us is not the realization that the world falls short of being completely just [...] but that there are clearly remediable injustices around us which we want to eliminate."

[2] Marginality is primarily defined by two conceptual frameworks—societal and spatial. The societal framework refers to human dimensions such as demography, religion, culture, social structure, economics, and politics in relation to access to resources by individuals and groups. The emphasis is placed on understanding the underlying causes of exclusion, inequality, and social injustice. The spatial dimension of marginality is primarily based on physical location and proximity to centres of development, or existing at the edge of, or poorly integrated into society (see Leimgruber 2004).

[3] In practice, determining who is marginalised is problematic because there is seldom an agreed definition of the term within a country, let alone across countries. Nevertheless, understanding marginalisation is one of the conditions for helping people to overcome it. It is important to identify the marginalised in a country in terms of identifiable indicators to make them more visible, to identify areas of concentrated disadvantages, to understand the extent of absolute and relative deprivations, and to suggest remedial measures.

marginalised groups, including indigenous people occupying both plains and hilly areas, have a long history of being subject to social humiliation and oppression (Ali and Mujeri 2016). In Bangladesh, the extreme poor experience poverty in its multiple deprivations, that manifest in having little or no income, employment or education, poor housing, ill health, malnutrition, social marginalisation and the lack of voice and political power. These poor groups subsist at the bottom of the social hierarchy. It is important to keep a number of issues in view for understanding marginalisation in the context of Bangladesh, such as (1) types of deprivation; (2) extent of disadvantageous situation; (3) violation of various rights; (4) apparent and underlying causes; (5) state of psychological construction; and (6) involvement of second or third parties as contributing factors (Ali and Mujeri 2016).

Traditionally, development programmes do not differentiate between the severity levels of the poor and the socially vulnerable, treating them as a group with similar characteristics and needs that require homogenous forms of assistance. It is now widely recognised that effective poverty alleviation efforts require more than a unidirectional approach, and must be adapted to the specific needs and capacities of people at different levels of poverty. Most importantly, the extreme poor and vulnerable must be targeted specifically in order to be properly reached. Social exclusion processes are extremely complex since they involve a range of economic, social, political and cultural phenomena that are often related to each other in many different ways.

Deep-seated and extreme inequalities tend to generate structures and institutions that are inaccessible to large population segments, usually because excluded groups lack skills or live in neglected geographical areas in the country. As a consequence, vast components of the population are unable to meet such basic needs as food and healthcare. It should be added that the vast gaps separating different social groups are in themselves factors of exclusion, for they aggravate the state of disregard for the neediest.

In addition to economic growth, the strategies of poverty reduction in Bangladesh rely on both broad-based social expenditures and targeted poverty programmes. Broad-based social expenditures are devoted to areas including education, healthcare, social security, skill training and housing. Targeted poverty alleviation programmes focus on investing in the human capital of the poor, such as improving food security, promoting income and employment opportunities, improving physical infrastructure in poor (rural and vulnerable) locations, and similar programmes. In an environment of inequality that promotes exclusion, egalitarianism as a value lacks social roots. An important factor affecting the severity of the phenomenon of exclusion is in the obstacles to integration of those who have been excluded. This is a problem which is commonly experienced in vulnerable social sectors and that is growing worse because the country's heterogeneous structure is an obstacle to the success of general measures to all social groups and regions.

7.3 Environmental Vulnerability

Over the last fifty years, one particular issue that is gaining increasing importance in sustaining development efforts in Bangladesh is the challenge of overall environmental management problems in the face of adverse impacts of climate change. Environmental health risks are rising rapidly as a result of industrial growth and urbanisation which is occurring at one of the fastest rates in South Asia. Moreover, almost all future population growth is likely to occur in urban areas, pointing to the growing importance of addressing urban and industrial contamination. With high population density, two-thirds of the land area is under crops and the cropping intensity has also increased by more than 40 per cent over the last fifty years. Most of the natural forests are now significantly degraded; and pressure on wetlands and aquatic life is a particular concern (World Bank, 2005a, b). Also, Bangladesh is highly vulnerable to the impacts of climate change, which will increase the already high risk of disasters, exacerbating existing vulnerabilities both to flooding and drought, and threatening agricultural productivity.

The Country Environmental Analysis (CEA) of the World Bank (2006) identifies five critical environmental constraints to sustainable, poverty-reducing growth in Bangladesh. These are: (1) environmental risks to human health; (2) protection of water quality in Dhaka; (3) management of capture fisheries; (4) sustaining soil quality; and (5) strengthening institutions for environmental management. Further, the estimated economic losses associated with the above sources of environmental degradation amount to more than 4 per cent of Bangladesh's GDP; and in all cases, the poor suffer disproportionately.

7.3.1 Environmental Risk Analysis

While economic growth is essential to reduce poverty, a careful balancing act is necessary for Bangladesh such that economic growth is maximised without compromising the environment. The development efforts need to explicitly recognise both the dependency of the poor on natural resources as well as the vulnerability of the poor to environmental health and other risks.

7.3.1.1 Environmental Health Risks

While the burden of disease in Bangladesh is comparable to other South Asian countries, the share attributable to respiratory infection and diarrhoeal disease is significantly higher in Bangladesh. Both are associated with poor environmental conditions, highlighting the importance of focusing attention on environmental quality in Bangladesh. The CEA, mentioned earlier, estimates that environmental factors account for as much as 22 per cent of the national burden of disease, principally in the form of respiratory infection and diarrhoeal disease. Achievable goals for reduced exposure to environmental health risks could result in economic savings equivalent to as much as 3.5 per cent of GDP. This can be achieved by improving access to adequate sanitation and safe water supplies, better hygienic practices, reducing exposure to indoor and urban air pollution, and to a lesser extent, by better management of agro-industrial toxics.

7.3.1.2 Environmental Quality of Dhaka City

The environment of the capital Dhaka city faces the triple threat of air pollution, inadequate solid waste management, and contamination of surface water. The total economic cost of poor management of water resources in Dhaka city is estimated at US$670 million annually, including impacts on human health, as well as industrial and natural resources productivity. Unless prompt actions are taken, these costs will continue to rise in line with Dhaka's continued rapid growth. Given that economic activity in Dhaka contributes about one-fifth of the country's GDP, environmental constraints to growth in the capital constitute a national priority.

7.3.1.3 Depletion of Natural Resources

The pressure on natural resources in Bangladesh is very high. Natural forests remain significantly degraded; and the ability of the soil to sustain agricultural production is an issue of concern. Fertiliser usage is imbalanced and nutrient mining occurs suggesting the need to regular monitoring of soil quality. Bangladesh's fisheries provide two-thirds of the country's animal protein needs. Capture fisheries and associated wetlands play a particularly important role in the nutrition of the poor. There is general consensus, however, that inland and coastal capture fisheries are declining. Threats include losses of floodplain habitat due to agriculture and urbanisation, lost connections along critical fish migration routes, significant reductions in dry season river flows, overfishing, and rapidly increasing industrial, human and agricultural pollution. Almost 30 per cent of all inland fish species are in some danger of extinction, and there is a fear that the inland major carps, Indian Salmon and other coastal inshore fisheries, may be in danger of collapse, with adverse consequences for the people, especially the poor.

7.3.2 *Environmental Governance*

An over-arching theme for improving environmental governance in Bangladesh is to strengthen incentives for behaviour and investments that lead to better environmental quality. The most important governance element to support such incentives is the access to environmental information, transparency and consultation for accountable decision making, adequate institutional capacity for credible enforcement and economic policies that promote improved environmental performance.

At the household level, for example, greater awareness of the risks of indoor air pollution could significantly reduce exposure through simple changes in behaviour. Similarly, sustainable management of capture fisheries requires information on necessary dry season flows, and monitoring of soil productivity depends on the development of appropriate indicators of soil quality. Greater access to environmental information and understanding of the impacts of degradation also create higher demand for environmental investments, both in the public and private sectors. For instance, public investments in necessary infrastructure to protect water quality around Dhaka city will require strong civil society support, based on an understanding of the costs of inaction. Private investment to control pollution will require public pressure for compliance, based on information regarding sources of pollution and their performance.

Transparency and public consultation are essential elements of environmental decision making, which strengthen the accountability of environmental institutions and thereby build their credibility. There is considerable scope to introduce greater transparency and broaden environmental consultation in Bangladesh.[4] As regulatory enforcement is central to environmental governance, establishment of institutional capacity to deliver such enforcement is crucial. Strong environmental enforcement capacity is necessary in the Department of Environment (DoE) and outside it, particularly for sustainable management of natural resources.[5] An important element in the battle to control urban air pollution is to ensure that the sulphur content of imported diesel is reduced to 500 ppm, reflecting the economic cost of the health damage caused by lower quality fuel. Economic incentives can also be used to complement regulatory approaches to improve environmental management.[6]

7.3.3 Environmental Policies

The environmental conservation issues in the national policy regime have been explicitly recognised and major policy initiatives, strategies and plans emphasise environment and natural resources management to achieve sustainable development. Although there was no specific environmental policy in Bangladesh after independence, the concerns for environmental protection were reflected in national planning documents and policies.

The Ministry of Environment and Forests was established in 1989 to address the emerging environment related issues. The government started to take measures, drafted the National Conservation Strategy, adopted the National Environmental Policy (1992) and revised the old law by enacting the Bangladesh Environment Conservation Act (1995) which has also restructured the Department of Environment (DoE). Moreover, National Environment Management Action Plan (NEMAP) has been adopted. Bangladesh is a signatory to forty-four international conventions, treaties

[4] At the local level, for example, the issuance of No Objection Certificates (NOCs) could be subject to consideration by an open meeting of the Union Parishad; and at the national level all EA information should be publicly available, with high-risk projects presented for public review.

[5] The success of the Department of Fisheries in protecting the *hilsa* fish, for example, serves to demonstrate the potential effectiveness of regulatory enforcement in ensuring the long-term productivity of the nation's capture fisheries.

[6] In the industry sector, promotion of waste-minimisation and eco-labeling initiatives may be encouraged. While this would primarily attract export-oriented businesses, consideration may also be given to the promotion of an eco-level for the domestic market.

and protocols in connection with the conservation and protection of environment and ecology.

Since the 1990s, environmental management has emerged as a priority issue in Bangladesh and successive governments have developed detailed policy framework. These include National Environment Policy (1992), National Forestry Policy (1994), Energy Policy (1995), National Fisheries Policy (1998), National Policy for Safe Water and Sanitation (1998), National Agricultural Policy (1999), National Water Policy (1999), National Water Management Plan (2004), National Land Use Policy (2001), Bangladesh Climate Change Strategy and Action Plan (2009), and National Bio-Safety Framework (2010). A National Conservation Strategy (NCS) and a National Environmental Management Action Plan (NEMAP) have been formulated. Both NCS and NEMAP contain national strategies and programmes for conservation of sites, important from biodiversity consideration. The Sustainable Environment Management Programme (SEMP) has a total of twenty-six components of which three components are directly concerned with the conservation of biodiversity in the wetlands and in the floodplains of the country through community participation.

The decade of the 1990s marked the beginning of innovation in environmental policy in Bangladesh which gave a new direction to the policy concerns in the field of environmental protection. Beginning with explicit concern on environment and sustainable development, the emphasis gradually shifted towards the interface between environment and sustainable livelihood with focus on environment, climate change and disaster management for sustainable development.

7.4 Climate Change and Social Vulnerability

With Bangladesh's high dependence on natural resource management, environmental issues assume special significance in the country. However, one particular issue under the overall environmental problems is the issue of climate change (CC) which is now a stark reality and a complex development challenge for Bangladesh. People are already feeling the 'heat' of climate change. While one may at one level consider climate change like any other problem of environmental degradation, the problem runs far deep and its reach in destabilising many of the natural systems is potentially immense (Asaduzzaman et al. 2011).

Bangladesh is a lower riparian country to a total of fifty-seven trans-boundary rivers coming down to the country: fifty-four from India and three from Myanmar. Bangladesh is located at the bottom of the mighty Ganges, Brahmaputra and Meghna (GBM) river basin. Also, nearly a quarter of Bangladesh is less than seven feet above sea level. The earth's temperature is likely to increase by 2.0 to 4.5 degrees Celsius by the end of the century. According to the Intergovernmental Panel on Climate Change (IPCC), the sea levels are expected to rise by 0.18 to 0.59 metres during the time. The US Environmental Protection Agency states that if polar ice continues to melt in step with increase in global average temperature, sea levels could increase by 0.49 to 0.79 metres by 2100. IPCC findings also state that a 45 cm sea level rise will inundate almost 11 per cent of the territory of Bangladesh and is likely to displace 5.5 million people in the coastal regions.

Although only about 15 per cent of the country's GDP comes from agriculture, nearly 41 per cent of the total labour force is engaged in the sector which makes the country's economy sensitive to climate variability and change. Bangladesh is widely recognised as one of the most climate vulnerable countries in the world. It experiences frequent natural disasters, which cause loss of life, damage to infrastructure and economic assets, and adversely impacts on lives and livelihoods, especially of the poor people.

Most of the climate change impacts in Bangladesh come from the south—that is, the Bay of Bengal and the adjoining North Indian Ocean. These waters are the sources of tropical cyclones and storm surges, coastal erosion, monsoon wind, evaporation for monsoon rainfall, floods and droughts. The geographical location and geo-morphological conditions of Bangladesh have made the country one of the most vulnerable ones to climate change. The country has a very low and flat topography, except in the northeast and southeast regions. About 10 per cent of the country is hardly 1 metre above the mean sea level (MSL), and one-third is under tidal excursions.

The natural hazards such as tropical cyclones, river erosion, flood, landslides and drought will increase both in frequency and intensity as a result of climate change. Rising sea levels will gradually inundate Bangladesh's coast and river erosion will destroy land and homes. These and many other adverse impacts of climate change will have profound and far-reaching consequences for the economy. This is largely due to its unique geographic location, dominance of floodplains, low elevation from the sea, high population density and overwhelming dependence on nature.

Moreover, one of the most intense impacts will be the forced movement of the people throughout Bangladesh as a result of losing their homes, lands, property and livelihoods due to climate change. Rising sea levels alone may displace 18 million Bangladeshis within the next 40 years. The vast majority of these people will be displaced domestically—not across international borders—presenting the government with enormous challenges especially when it comes to finding places to live and work for those who have been displaced. The number of 'climate change refugees' in Bangladesh may rise dramatically in the coming decades. If sea levels rise by just 3.2 feet, one-fifth of the country located on the delta formed by some of Asia's largest rivers, is expected to be covered in water. Needless to add, poor people are the most vulnerable to the changing conditions. Bangladeshis have already started to move away from the lowest-lying villages in the river deltas of the Bay of Bengal: 1.5 million of the five million slum dwellers in Dhaka city moved from villages near the Bay of Bengal.

Biodiversity would be adversely affected in some of the most fragile environments, such as the Sundarbans and other tropical forests. Bangladesh possesses a wide diversity of ecosystems including mangrove forests at the extreme south of the country. The Sundarbans, a World Heritage is the largest mangrove forest in the world, comprising 10,000 square km (mostly in Bangladesh) of land area along the Bay of Bengal. Around 425 species live there including the famous Royal Bengal tigers. Climate change impacts will have negative effects on the ecosystem of the forest resources in Bangladesh, with the Sundarbans likely to suffer most.

7.4.1 Climate Change and Sea Level Rise

All available projected climate change scenarios predict a steady increase in temperatures for Bangladesh. With regard to precipitation, whether there is an increase or decrease under climate change is a critical factor in estimating how climate change will affect Bangladesh given the country's extreme vulnerability to water related disasters. The key is what happens during the monsoon. More than 80 per cent of the 2300 mm of annual precipitation that falls on Bangladesh comes during the monsoon period (April–August) and the prediction is that precipitation will increase during the summer monsoon. Moreover, with higher temperatures increasing evapo-transpiration combined with a small decrease in precipitation, dry winter conditions, even drought, are likely to be made worse.

Bangladesh currently has extreme vulnerability to cyclones, both on account of its somewhat unique location and topography (that creates an inverted funnel effect), and because of the low (though growing) capacity of its society and institutions to cope with such extreme events. A partial listing of major cyclones and accompanying surge heights is given in Table 7.1. Given that over two-thirds of the country is less than 5 metres above the sea-level and densely populated, storm surges contribute to

Table 7.1 Major cyclones along coastal Bangladesh

Cyclone event	*Season*	*Storm surge height (metres)*	*Max. wind speed (km/hour)*
November 1876	Post-monsoon	3.0–10.0	…
May 1941	Pre-monsoon	4.0	…
May 1960	Pre-monsoon	3.2	…
October 1960 (First Event)	Post-monsoon	5.1	…
October 1960 (Second Event)	Post-monsoon	6.6	…
May 1961 (First Event)	Pre-monsoon	3.0	…
May 1961 (Second Event)	Pre-monsoon	6.0–8.0	…
May 1965	Pre-monsoon	7.6	161
December 1965	Post-monsoon/ winter	8.8	217
October 1967	Post-monsoon	7.6	139
May 1970	Pre-monsoon	5.0	…
October 1970	Post-monsoon	4.7	…
November 1970	Post-monsoon	9.0	224
September 1971	Monsoon	5.0	…
December 1973	Post-monsoon/ winter	4.5	…
August 1974	Monsoon	6.7	…
November 1975	Post-monsoon	3.1	…
May 1985	Pre-monsoon	4.3	154
November 1988	Post-monsoon	4.4	…
April 1991	Pre-monsoon	4.0–8.0	225
May 1997	Pre-monsoon	3.1–4.6	232
November 2007 (SIDR)	Post-monsoon	…	223
May 2009 (AILA)	Pre-monsoon	…	92

Source: DMB (2010)

Note: Surge height varies based on location

flooding and loss of life and livelihoods far beyond the coast. Although in recent years greater success in disaster management has significantly reduced the human lives lost, the potential for economic and infrastructural damage remains very significant. Given the current vulnerability, a critical question is whether (and how) climate change might affect cyclone patterns and their intensity in the Bay of Bengal.

While some tentative assessments are available, there is no reason to assume that cyclone tracks will shift under climate change—meaning that Bangladesh is likely to expect to continue to be hit with cyclones and storm surges. The possibility that peak intensities may increase has potentially serious implications for the country which is already very vulnerable to storm surges driven by strong winds. A potential implication would be that future storm surges might be even higher than those observed currently. And a projected increase in 20–30 per cent in the associated precipitation could only make the concerns more serious given that Bangladesh is also prone to inland flooding because of its topography and lying as it does at the mouth of three major river systems (the Ganges, Brahmaputra, and Meghna).

Another critical variable that determines the vulnerability of Bangladesh to climate change impacts is the magnitude of sea level rise. There is no specific regional scenario for net sea level rise, in part because the Ganges–Brahmaputra delta is still active and the morphology is highly dynamic. Evidence suggests that the coastal lands are receiving additional sediments due to tidal influence, while there are parts where land is subsiding due to tectonic activities (Huq et al. 1996). Since the landform is constituted by sediment decomposition, compaction of sediment may also play a role in defining net change in sea level along the coastal zone.

7.4.2 Climate Change and Agricultural Vulnerability

Agricultural crops in Bangladesh are influenced by seasonal characteristics and different climatic conditions, such as temperature, rainfall, humidity, day-length, and such other factors. It is also constrained by different disasters such as floods, droughts, soil and water salinity, cyclone and storm surges. Since climate is changing and becoming more unpredictable every year, its variability in extreme weather events is being experienced more frequently than ever before. Hazards like floods, droughts, cyclones and salinity intrusion are being aggravated by climate change and sea level rise. Flood and water logging in the central region, flash-flood in the northeast region, drought in the northwest and southwest region, and salinity intrusion and coastal inundation in the coastal region are likely to become more acute in future. All of these will have an extra bearing on the agriculture sector.[7]

Extreme temperature due to climate change would affect livestock as well. High temperature affects livestock in a number of ways: causes great discomfort as in the case of human, decreases feed intake and alters nutrient metabolism leading to high loss of energy, and the combined effects of discomfort and nutrient metabolism reduces their productivity, resulting in financial loss of the farmers. Apart from extreme temperature, natural disasters such as cyclone and tidal surge, cause immense loss and sufferings to livestock through destruction of forage crops as well as housing.

7.4.2.1 Northwest Region

The northwest region is characterised by high temperature and low rainfall compared with the average conditions in Bangladesh. The region is primarily prone to drought which is likely to become more frequent and intense along with horizontal expansion due to climate change. It is also important to note that changes in timing of drought will be the other phenomenon, resulting from erratic behaviour and distribution of rainfall, and temperature rise. The major impacts would be on agriculture and availability of water resources for agriculture and domestic use particularly in the dry season.

There is a strong possibility that moisture content of the topsoil would decrease substantially resulting from decrease in winter precipitation and higher evapo-transpiration. Late Kharif II drought in December would adversely affect aman crop at the ripening stage, while an early *rabi* drought would more severely affect wheat and *boro* crops at both germination and vegetative growth stages (Karim et al. 1998). Furthermore, increasing moisture stress in early Kharif I would significantly affect aus production. In the case of boro rice, it is seen that up to 30 per cent

[7]Available models predict different level of impacts for yield reduction under different climate change scenarios. The GFDL model predicts about 17 per cent decline in overall rice production in Bangladesh and as high as 61 per cent decline in wheat production under 4 degree changes in temperature. The highest impact would be on wheat followed by rice (*aus* variety). Of the three varieties of rice grown in Bangladesh, *aus* rice (grown during the summer, monsoon period under rain-fed conditions) seems to be the most vulnerable. The Canadian Climate Change Model (CCCM) also predicts a significant fall in food grain production.

moisture stress results in 1 to 4 per cent yield reduction while reduction is 10 to 33 per cent at 60 per cent moisture stress condition.

7.4.2.2 Coastal Region

Degradation of productive land including quality and physical loss are key concerns for the coastal agriculture due to salinity intrusion and sea level rise. Recent assessments suggest that about 13 per cent more area (469,000 ha) will be inundated in monsoon due to 62 cm sea level rise in addition to the existing inundated area. The most vulnerable areas are the areas without polders as in the districts of Patuakhali, Pirojpur, Barisal, Jhalakati, Bagerhat and Narail. Due to increased rainfall, in addition to 62 cm sea level rise, the inundated area will be increased by about 16 per cent (551,500 ha). On the other hand, due to 62 cm sea level rise in the dry season, about 364,200 ha (10 per cent) more area will be inundated by the year 2080 (IWM and CEGIS 2007).

Drainage congestion and water logging are very likely in the coastal region as a result of combined effect of higher sea water levels, subsidence, sedimentation of estuary branches, higher riverbed levels and reduced sedimentation in flood-protected areas. It is estimated that about 25 polders in the southwest region may experience severe drainage congestion due to 62 cm sea level rise and 13 polders embankment will be overtopped due to increased water level in the peripheral rivers. Due to the overtopping of the embankment, about 120,200 ha of these polders will be deeply inundated whereas the present inundated area is only 42,200 ha. About 32 per cent more area will be deeply inundated due to overtopping of embankment (IWM and CEGIS 2007).

Salinity will intrude more inward especially during the dry season due to sea level rise. Consequently, brackish water area would increase and a sea level rise of 27 cm causes 6 per cent increase of brackish water area compared with base condition. About an additional area of 327,700 ha would become high saline water zone (>5 ppt) during the dry season due to 60 cm sea level rise. In the monsoon about 6 per cent of the sweet water area (276,700 ha) will be lost (IWM and CEGIS 2007). The effect of saline water intrusion in the estuaries and into the groundwater would be enhanced by low river flow, sea level rise and subsidence.

7.4.2.3 Central Region

The central region of the country is already facing frequent flooding; and situation is likely to be aggravated due to increased rainfall, melting of

Himalayan glaciers in the short to medium term. In an 'average' year, approximately one quarter of the country is inundated. An analysis of the country's flood history over the last 25 years shows that now once in every 4 to 5 years, there could be a severe flood that may cover over 60 per cent of the country's area and cause loss of life and substantial damage to infrastructure, housing, agriculture and livelihoods.

Higher discharge and low drainage capacity, in combination with increased backwater effects, would increase the frequency of such devastating floods under climate change scenarios. Prolonged floods would tend to delay *aman* (paddy) plantation, resulting in significant loss of potential *aman* production, as observed during the floods of 1998 and 2007. It is estimated that the 1988 flood caused reduction of agricultural production by 45 per cent (Karim et al. 1996) and approximately 1.2 million acres of crops were destroyed or partially damaged in 2007 floods with an estimated damage of over $1 billion.

7.4.2.4 Northeast Region

The northeast region of the country is characterised by highest rainfall and relatively low temperature compared with the annual average of the country. The average annual rainfall in the region is 4130 mm which is almost double of the country average. The average maximum temperature of Sylhet shows an increasing trend at the rate of 0.039 °C per year. The lowest maximum temperature was recorded in 1977 which was 28.5 °C and the highest maximum temperature was recorded in 1998 which was 31.25 °C.

The Sylhet region is highly vulnerable to river flood, flash flood, intensive rainfall, and landslides. The *haor* area of this region is single cropped and is cultivated only transplanted (T) *aman* in the *kharif* season. This crop is damaged almost every alternative year by flash flood. In the recent years, the frequency of flash flood has increased. Tornado and hailstorm are also two important climate induced disasters for this region which damage crops, houses, trees and even cause human death. Intensive rainfall causes landslides and erosion in the hillocks area. Soil degradation, due to the sandification of arable land, is also seen as a hazard in this area as well as siltation of river and water bodies that enhance the strength of floods and provoke water logging.

7.4.3 *Climate Change Adaptation*

Although Bangladesh is an insignificant and a virtually zero contributor to the greenhouse gas (GHG) emissions that affect global climate change, it has to suffer so disastrously from the effects of climate change that is likely to occur in the coming decades. It must, therefore, adapt itself to the changing circumstances. Adaptation requires assessment of vulnerability from the viewpoint of different disciplines, which requires an integrated approach.

Bangladesh has established the Bangladesh Climate Change Trust Fund (BCCTF) and the Bangladesh Climate Change Resilient Fund (BCCRF) to address the challenges due to climate change. There also exist plans such as the National Action Plan on Adaptation (NAPA) of 2005 and the Bangladesh Climate Change Strategy and Action Plan (BCCSAP) of 2009. Various countries have pledged to provide funding for adaptation and mitigation in developing countries including Bangladesh. This funding is available to build the capacity of these countries to reduce emissions and to respond to impacts of climate change. The funding is used for mitigation and infrastructure adaptation in various sectors including forestry. The Copenhagen Accord (COP 15) pledges $100 million of public and private financing by 2020.

Bangladesh places emphasis on capacity building and disaster management, institutional and infrastructure strengthening, development of research and low-carbon technologies in order to create an inclusive and comprehensive mitigation scheme. The government's priority is to develop national action plan on climate change adaptation and allocate necessary funds in the national budget to monitor the impacts of climate change in different sectors and spheres of the national economy. Engagement in constructive debate on the issues of technology and production transfer is also encouraged.

With higher population and rapid industrialisation, Bangladesh would embark on developing a low-carbon path with financial and technical support from the international community. Bangladesh also plans to prepare the long-term adaptation strategy and identify all vulnerabilities and future opportunities, to adjust sectoral priorities and policies especially in agriculture while promoting training and education to create awareness among the masses in all possible spheres.

The findings of a farm-level study on identifying the factors affecting farmers' adaptation strategies to environmental degradation and climate change effects in coastal Bangladesh which are likely to be caused or exacerbated under global climate change offer several interesting insights (Nasir Uddin et al. 2014). The study examines four central components: (1) rate of self-reported adoption of adaptive mechanisms/coping strategies as a result of change in climate; (2) ranking the potential coping strategies based on their perceived importance to agricultural enterprises; (3) identification of socioeconomic factors associated with adoption of coping strategies; and (4) ranking potential constraints to adoption of coping strategies based on farmers' reporting on the degree to which they face these constraints.

The empirical analysis shows that a majority of the farmers self-identified themselves as having engaged in adaptive behaviour. Out of 14 adaptive strategies, irrigation ranked the first while crop insurance was ranked as the least utilised. The logit model explains that out of eight factors surveyed, age, education, family size, farm size, family income and involvement in cooperatives are significantly related to self-reported adaptation. Despite different support and technological innovations available, lack of water, shortage of cultivable land, and unpredictable weather ranked highest as the respondent groups' constraints to coping with environmental degradation and climate change effects. These results provide policy makers and development service providers with important insights, which can be used to better target interventions which would promote or facilitate the adoption of coping mechanisms with potential to build resiliency to changing climate and resulting environmental impacts.

In principle, one may conceive of three adaptive options in Bangladesh: retreat, accommodation, and protection. Considering the high population density, future population projections, and shortage of land, retreat is not a feasible option for Bangladesh. For Bangladesh, the relevant options are accommodation and protection. Moreover, the country should also strive to get land from the sea.

Bangladesh has adopted the climate change strategy and action plan (BCCSAP) as the basis of all efforts to combat climate change (GOB 2008). The strategy prioritises adaptation and disaster risk reduction, and addresses low carbon development, mitigation, technology transfer and the provision of adequate finance. In short, the BCCSAP is built on six pillars:

- **Food security, social protection and health:** Ensure that the poorest and most vulnerable in society, including women and children, are protected from climate change and that all programs focus on the needs of this group for food security, safe housing, employment and access to basic services, including health.

- **Comprehensive disaster management:** Further strengthen the country's already proven disaster management systems to deal with increasingly frequent and severe natural calamities.
- **Infrastructure:** Ensure that existing assets (e.g. coastal and river embankments) are well-maintained and fit-for-purpose and that urgently needed infrastructure (e.g. cyclone shelters and urban drainage) is put in place to deal with the likely impacts of climate change.
- **Research and knowledge management:** Predict the likely scale and timing of climate change impacts on different sectors of the economy and socioeconomic groups to underpin future investment strategies and to ensure that Bangladesh is networked into the latest global thinking on climate change.
- **Mitigation and low carbon development:** Evolve low carbon development options and implement these as the country's economy grows over the coming decades.
- **Capacity building and institutional strengthening:** Enhance the capacity of government ministries and agencies, civil society and the private sector to meet the challenge of climate change.

The Action Plan has worked out the details of the programmes and sub-programmes to be implemented along with identifying the potential sources of finance. The programmes have been identified applying a participatory framework and adopting indigenous knowledge and technology wherever appropriate. These also build on the past efforts of adaptive responses.

The experience of Bangladesh strongly suggests that one of the best ways to adapt to climate change is to involve the people at the grassroots level. The people of Bangladesh are very enterprising and innovative. They have been living with disasters for a long time. Adapting to changing situations is a familiar traditional practice in Bangladesh. What is important is to carry out detailed scientific studies, make the people aware of the impending dangers and develop, adopting their traditional knowledge and experience, effective methods of adaptation.

As climate change adaptation action is mostly local, the need for Bangladesh is to link organized and local adaptation strategies and approaches. This will provide a better understanding of ways of improving coping and adaptation strategies by communities impacted by climate change along with providing support to creating an environment that would make such practices sustainable and more effective by fostering participation, empowering the participants, and incorporating indigenous knowledge.

Since there are strong links between adaptation and development, the two should be addressed in Bangladesh in an integrated manner through mainstreaming. There are a number of options for operationalising mainstreaming at the national level. Ayers et al. (2014) suggest that sustainable mainstreaming should involve national and sub-national institutions and processes. Obviously, there exists no single approach to successful mainstreaming—it emerges as a patchwork of climate-proofing and more integrated strategies that build climate resilience in interconnected ways. In Bangladesh, different processes contribute to such mainstreaming, involving blends of information, capacity building, resource mobilisation and governance changes, underpinned by political and social compulsions.

7.5 Urbanisation and Social Vulnerability

Urbanisation is the process through which a society changes from a rural to an urban way of life. It refers also to the gradual increase in the proportion of population living in urban areas. At present, the urban lifestyle is not confined to the city as the urban-rural continuum has replaced the historical urban–rural divide (Heineberg 2000). The United Nations (UN) applies three different concepts for the delineation of urban areas: (1) urban agglomeration being the 'built-up or densely populated area containing the city proper; (2) suburbs; and (3) the continuously settled commuter areas. It may be smaller or larger than a metropolitan area; it may also comprise the city proper and its suburban fringe or thickly settled adjoining territory'; metropolitan area as the 'set of formal local government areas that normally comprise the urban area as a whole and its primary commuter areas'; and the city proper comprising the 'political jurisdiction that contains the historical city centre' (UN-Habitat 2006: 5).

The patterns of urbanisation in developing countries over the past few decades have diverged significantly from the historical trends. For most of the developed world, urbanisation was associated with industrialisation. But today, many developing countries, though highly urbanised, do not have large industrial sectors. The historically strong relationship between urbanisation and industrialisation has broken down for much of the developing world that have urbanised without industrialising.

A high degree of concentration—the share of large metropolitan areas in total urban population—characterises the rapid urbanisation process in many developing countries including Bangladesh. The concentration is also reflected in urban primacy—the share of the largest city in national urban population. And it involves megacities of unparalleled size, presenting major problems in health and quality of life, management and institution building, social cohesion, and stability. Today's developing countries face greater urbanisation challenges than developed countries faced in the past as their urbanisation process had a comparatively leisurely pace.

In a market economy, city size reflects a trade-off between the scale productivity benefits of local employment growth and the cost of living increments of local population growth. Improvements in commuting technology which reduce local costs of living, and local knowledge accumulation which accentuates scale economies, suggest that efficient city sizes increase over time. As commuting technology continues to improve and human capital investments rise in developing countries, the size of cities is likely to increase in the future. At the same time, national population growth means that the number of cities may need to grow to accommodate population increases. Generally, both the size and number of cities have grown with national population growth in most countries over the past century.

South Asia remains at an emerging stage of urbanisation. Further, the official statistics tend to understate the region's level of urbanisation—indicating the existence of significant 'hidden' urbanisation. A key characteristic of urbanisation is that agglomeration economies, which are the unintended benefits that firms and workers gather from one another as they cluster together, enhance productivity and job creation, especially in manufacturing and services. In South Asia, the process is visible in the structural transformation of the region's economy, with manufacturing and services now accounting for more than 80 per cent of GDP.

According to the agglomeration index (AI), the share of South Asia's population living in urban areas in 2010 was 52.5 per cent (Ellis and Roberts 2016). India's urban population share, as estimated using the AI, is 55.3 per cent, which is also very similar to the AI-estimated urban shares of Maldives and Pakistan. The other South Asian countries (Afghanistan, Bangladesh, Bhutan, Nepal and Sri Lanka) have urban shares (according to the AI) of less than 50 per cent.

South Asia has a growing number of multicity agglomerations, where the multicity agglomeration is defined as a continuously lit belt of urbanisation containing two or more cities, each of which had a population of at least 100,000 living within its administrative boundaries in 2010. In 1999, there were 37 such agglomerations; and the number rose to 45 in 2010 (Table 7.2). Bangladesh saw the emergence of its first two agglomerations—the Dhaka agglomeration (Dhaka and Rupganj) and the Brahmanbaria agglomeration (Brahmanbaria and Bhairab).

7.5.1 *Urbanisation in Bangladesh*

Historically, towns and cities in Bangladesh were few in number, and until recently, the country was largely rural. In 1951, slightly more than 4 per cent of the population lived in the urban areas which exceeded 28 per cent in 2011 and has been estimated at more than 36 per cent in 2018 (Table 7.3). It is projected to reach 40 per cent in 2020. During the last few decades, Bangladesh has experienced extremely high rates of urbanisation far exceeding the national growth in population. This rapid urbanisation in Bangladesh is perhaps inevitable in a situation of a globalised market economy. Across the world, high- and middle-income countries are more urbanised, and their urban areas have higher economic densities (that is, value-added per unit of space) than low-income countries (World Bank 2012).The correlation between urbanisation and GDP is indicative of the productivity advantages of the urban areas.

In Bangladesh, the urban–rural value-added and productivity differentials are larger than the population density differential as well. The population density in the urban areas (1800 people per km^2) is more than double that in the rural areas (800 people per km^2), but urban economic density (USD 2.7 million per km^2) is eight times as high as rural economic density (USD 320,000 per km^2). The average GDP per capita in the urban areas (USD 1500) is almost four times as high as in the rural areas (USD 400).

Urban concentration, metropolitanisation and primacy are yet other features of contemporary urbanisation in Bangladesh. There is a heavy concentration of urban population in the capital city of Dhaka, where more than a third of the country's total urban population lives. Along with population, there is also a heavy concentration of economic activities in Dhaka. The next largest city is Chittagong, where about 9 per cent of the total urban population resides. It is a port city and has attracted considerv-vvthan 42 per cent of the country's total urban population and serve as the

Table 7.2 Growth of multicity agglomerations, South Asia

Country	*No. of agglomerations*		*No. of cities in agglomerations*				*Area, square kilometres*		
	1999	*2010*	*1999*		*2010*		*1999*	*2010*	*Annual growth, %*
			Mean	*Maximum*	*Mean*	*Maximum*			
India	23	30	4.09	17	4.73	38	22,240	75,499	11.75
Pakistan	12	10	4.00	10	6.50	29	1536	2558	4.75
Bangladesh	…	2	…	…	2.00	2	…	1340	…
Sri Lanka	1	2	5.00	5	3.50	5	182	205	1.08
Nepal	1	1	2.00	2	2.00	2	12,979	12,495	-0.30
South Asia	37	45	3.92	17	4.89	38	36,927	92.097	8.66

Source: Ellis and Roberts (2016: 63)

Table 7.3 Urbanisation in Bangladesh, 1951–2018

Year	*National population (million)*	*Yearly growth rate of national population (%)*	*Urban population (million)*	*Level of urbanisation (%)*	*Yearly growth rate of urban population (%)*
1951	44.17	0.50	1.82	4.33	1.69
1961	55.22	2.26	2.64	5.19	3.72
1974	76.37	2.48	6.27	8.87	6.66
1981	89.91	2.32	13.23	15.18	10.66
1991	111.45	2.17	20.87	19.63	4.56
2001	123.10	1.47	28.61	23.10	3.15
2011	150.40	1.37	42.11	28.40	4.12
2018 (est.)	166.37	1.23	60.73	36.50	3.27

Source: BBS, Report on Bangladesh Population Census, various census years, and Report on Urban Areas 1997

primary growth centres over the past four decades. The other two regional city centres, Khulna and Rajshahi have less than 3 per cent and 2 per cent of total urban population respectively and have mostly failed to take-off as growth centres.

The above shows that nearly half of the country's total urban population is concentrated in four biggest metropolitan cities (Dhaka, Chittagong, Khulna, and Rajshahi). However, Dhaka alone enjoys a clear primate status in the country's urban structure. In 1961, Dhaka's share of the urban population of Bangladesh was 20 per cent. The share rose to 24 per cent in 1974, 26 per cent in 1981, and 30 per cent in 1991, and exceeds 33 per cent at present.

The primacy of Dhaka is stronger in socioeconomic arenas than in terms of population. Administrative headquarters and civil employments, financial and banking services, international commerce and business except port functions are all largely concentrated in Dhaka. Educational, cultural and other activities are also concentrated in the capital city. A disproportionately large concentration of industrial and various public sector investments have been made in the city. In spite of the declared governmental policy of decentralised administrative and economic development, the actual development in the huge export-oriented readymade garments (RMGs) sector, for example, shows an overwhelming concentration in Dhaka city. The dominance of Dhaka is also visible in several other manufacturing activities such as furniture (97 per cent), publishing (96 per cent), footwear (84 per cent), leather goods (82 per cent), and electrical machinery (72 per cent).

7.5.2 *Migration and Urbanisation*

The role of migration in urbanisation is obvious in all societies and at all times. Urbanisation and urban growth are the outcomes of the combination of three components: (1) natural increase of the urban population; (2) area redefinition or reclassification or annexation; and (3) rural–urban (or other forms of internal) migration. It is estimated that migration contributed about 40 per cent to the urban growth in Bangladesh during 1974–1981 (BBS 1984). The share is probably similar in the later periods. For some large cities, this share could even be higher, up to 70 per cent, as in the case of Dhaka. Rural to urban migration in Bangladesh takes several forms, such as permanent migration, temporary migration, seasonal migration, circular migration, and commuting. By and large, the process ranges from short distance mobility (commuting) to long-distance and long-term movement or permanent migration.

The causes of rural-urban migration may vary widely depending upon specific contexts. Migration can be a domestic phenomenon; but it can be the outcome of an international politico-economic framework. The most popular explanation of domestic migration is the push–pull model. It indicates that migration is the combined effect of both push and pull factors; and it is often difficult to separate out the role and impact of these two. Within the push–pull model, push factors (at the rural end) working in Bangladesh cover population pressure; inadequate availability of productive assets such as land and other inputs; landlessness and poverty; natural disasters (including floods and river bank erosion); feeling of insecurity; inadequate employment and livelihood opportunities; limited access to basic services such as health, education, water and sanitation; inadequate availability of social and cultural opportunities. The pull factors operate at the urban destination end. Real or perceived job opportunities and higher wages in the city are the main pulls. Rural-urban disparities in other opportunities and services are also responsible.

Generally, migration to the urban areas tends to be a highly selective process; and characteristics such as age, sex, education, marital status, occupation, skill and socioeconomic status, have impact on the urbanisation process. Although majority of migrants are the rural poor, some also belong to the rural middle class or even rich. Migrants are generally young adults but increasingly more and more old people and children are coming to the city as accompanying family members. While young adults tend to assume the role of main bread earner, older members of the family is vested with the responsibility of 'keeper' of children in city life. In the past, the migrants used to be mostly males, but in recent years, females, including unmarried girls, are also coming to the city in large numbers for example to work in the RMGs sector. Women in the past would only migrate to city as spouses or female members of the family. Now they also come as unmarried singles.

The impact of rural to urban migration is both diverse as well as deep, both at the urban destination and the rural origin. These can be both positive and negative. Several positive benefits may accrue, such as economic benefits (e.g. higher productivity, and better income), demographic benefits (higher age at marriage for girls, reduction in fertility rate etc.), socio-cultural benefits (modernisation, attitudinal change etc.), political benefits (empowerment, democracy etc.) and improved access to information and communication technologies (ICTs). On the other hand, there can be negative environmental consequences such as water and air pollution. Rapid urbanisation without proper planning results in massive degradation in the urban environment. There can also be high level of noise pollution, and degradation of land. Uncollected garbage adds to increase in noxious odour. Massive traffic congestion also becomes regular features. Congestion causes significant economic losses as well. That rapid growth of population of a massive scale causes negative impact on environment is obvious in Bangladesh both in its rural and urban settings. Deforestation, cutting down of hills, encroachment and filling of water bodies, or such other situations are caused mainly by excessive population and poor governance.

7.5.3 *The Economics of Agglomeration*

Economic activities agglomerate in cities because of local external economies of scale in production—a plant's productivity is enhanced if other plants are located nearby. Urban models of the micro-foundations of urban externalities follow Marshall's (1890) description of spillover benefits for a plant from others in the neighbourhood—information spillovers about technology, suppliers, purchasers, and market conditions (Fujita and Ogawa 1982); scope for local intra-industry specialisation of plants in specific activities (Becker and Henderson 2000); increased diversity of local suppliers to local export producers (Dixit and Stiglitz 1977; Abdel-Rahman and Fujita 1990); and search for and matching improvements between workers and firms in local labour markets (Helsley and Strange 1990). In addition, the proximity of buyers and sellers reduces transport costs of trade (Krugman 1991) and search costs in retailing (Caplin and Leahy 1998).

There may also be dynamic components to externalities. One is local knowledge accumulation (Rauch 1993), as in endogenous growth models (Romer 1986). Black and Henderson (1999) develop an urban growth model that suggests city sizes will grow over time, as local human capital development enhances economies of agglomeration. They document the strong empirical relation between human capital accumulation in individual cities and growth of city size.

7.5.3.1 Urbanisation and Economic Growth

For developing countries, studies suggest that urban concentration increases in the early stages of economic development as part of increasing regional disparities, and then decreases in later stages of development as part of decreasing regional disparities, or regional convergence (Williamson 1965; see also Parr 1985; El-Shakhs 1992; Wheaton and Shishido 1981). Hansen (1990) suggests that in the early stages of development, when resources are scarce (especially infrastructure capital) it is impossible to invest enough in public infrastructure to support widespread urban agglomeration and a system of interconnected cities joined by paved highways, rail transit, and communication.

An efficient allocation of economic infrastructure requires concentration in just one or two cities (perhaps megacities) initially, conserving on spending that would go instead to linking cities or developing other cities. Such concentrated investment induces immigration and industrialisation of focal megacities and increases urban concentration. With accompanying economic growth, the country will develop some appropriate institutions and a pool of skilled technocrats. Eventually, the country will be able to invest in hinterland regions, allowing other major urban centres to develop as well as smaller and medium-size cities. This leads to urban deconcentration. Although the concentration phase is observed in many developing countries, but subsequent deconcentration appears to be modest. Bangladesh, in particular, reflects the Asian megacity phenomenon where high concentration seems to stem from political and institutional forces that lead to a high centralisation of resources, so that a high concentration of industry accompanies population concentration in the megacities.

Normally, industrial deconcentration may start with deconcentration from the core primate city into its suburbs or satellite cities and then to the rest of the country. Deconcentration into the rest of the country enhances specialisation across cities, as industrialising cities focus on a specific activity. South Korea experienced the first stage of deconcentration into satellite cities prior to 1980 and the second into the hinterlands over the past few decades. Currently, Thailand and Indonesia seem to be experiencing some of the first stage of deconcentration of industry into satellite cities. However, such a process is yet to take roots in Bangladesh.

On the other hand, excessive concentration may reduce economic growth as wage, land, and infrastructure costs escalate with megacity size relative to scale benefits for standardised products, making it more difficult to attract foreign investment and to remain competitive in world markets. Also, excessive concentration leads to degradation of the quality of life as population concentration rises. Problems with congestion, contamination of ground water, gastrointestinal and infectious diseases, and poor air quality are severe in Dhaka. The quality of life and public service issues are exacerbated by a lack of technical expertise in planning and managing megacities. As environmental quality in the megacity declines, infrastructure investment becomes increasingly focused on trying to alleviate the effects of these unpriced negative externalities.

7.5.3.2 Influencing Deconcentration

Better pricing of goods, negative externalities in large metropolitan areas, and liberalisation and decentralisation of financial markets, licensing and permits can help avoid excessive concentration. The role of intercity infrastructure investments, economic openness, and appropriate government structure and institutions are also important.

A key condition for urban deconcentration is investment in modern inter-city transport and communications. Manufacturers cannot move from the main city (e.g. a port city) to hinterland locations unless they are linked to the port and national and international markets by good transport and communication. Containerisation and ready movement of freight are essential for purchasing inputs and getting products to market at reasonable delivered prices in a timely manner. In a globalised world where just-in-time production and minimised inventories are needed to reduce costs, reasonably fast, cheap and reliable transport is essential. Good communications are also critical for interaction with buyers, suppliers, parent firms and government regulators.

The government structure and institutions play a key role in determining the deconcentration of urban activity. Decentralised governments and institutions may lead to greater deconcentration. A key element in decentralisation is revenue sources for the operating and capital accounts for autonomous local governments. Efficient levels of long-term (intergenerational) investment cannot readily be financed from current taxes; they need to be financed over the long term, generally by floating bonds and establishing sinking funds to pay them off. This requires a sophisticated capital market to monitor local government creditworthiness, good communications and information gathering, and an adequate level of financial development.

The rapid urbanisation in Bangladesh over the past half century seems to have been accompanied by excessively high levels of concentration of the urban population in very large cities. This is most prominent in the recent growth of Dhaka as a megacity. Often some degree of urban concentration is considered desirable at initial stages to reduce inter- and intraregional infrastructure expenditures. But in a mature system of cities, standardised manufacturing production tends to be deconcentrated into smaller and medium-size metropolitan areas, whereas production in large metropolitan areas focuses on services, R&D, and nonstandardised manufacturing. The problem of Bangladesh is that there appear to exist strong biases towards excessive concentration.

Such concentration reflects several forces. Externalities of congestion and pollution are relatively underpriced in megacities relative to smaller cities, encouraging overpopulation of larger cities. Rent seeking and urban bias of the policy makers and government bureaucrats result in centralisation, often in capital cities, of capital markets and licensing for exports, imports, production, and material allocations, forcing a centralised location of production. Further, infrastructure investments and public services provision outside of main cities and interregional linkages remain at too low levels for too long. The costs of excessive concentration stem from the large sizes of megacities and underdeveloped institutions and human resources for urban planning and management. These costs include traffic congestions, health costs from exposure to high levels of air and water pollution, and time lost to inordinately long commutes.

In many developing countries, a large proportion of the national population live in the largest city, which in many cases is also the capital, such as Dhaka in Bangladesh. This is not the case in more developed countries, which tend to have more advanced urban networks. The concentration of population in the largest city (Dhaka) is particularly striking in Bangladesh where more than a third of the country's total urban population resides.

The speed and scale of increase of the largest city (Dhaka) can create enormous stresses on the immediate and surrounding environment and pose major challenges for sustainable urban development. A long-standing urban bias in social infrastructure investments has contributed to the creation of living conditions which is far better in Dhaka than in smaller cities or towns. At the same time, high population pressure, together with significant rural–urban migration, has contributed to the rapid and unplanned expansion of low-income settlements on the outskirts of Dhaka city, which has occurred without a concomitant expansion of public services and facilities. Further, congestion costs in Dhaka city can indeed be very real.

In Bangladesh, there are good reasons for putting smaller cities more centrally on the development agenda. First, when combined, the total population of smaller cities and towns is demographically very significant in Bangladesh. Second, because by definition they are starting from a smaller base, small cities typically grow faster than large cities. Third, residents of small cities in Bangladesh are extensively underserved with respect to basic services such as urban infrastructures. As such, residents of small cities suffer a marked disadvantage in the provision of piped water, waste disposal, electricity, and schools than residents of medium or large cities. Furthermore, there is some evidence to suggest that rates of poverty are higher in smaller cities; and often the levels of infant and child mortality are negatively proportional to city size. Finally, local government (e.g. municipalities) capacity is weaker in smaller cities. In view of the role that will be played by small cities in accommodating future population growth, it is clear that their need for improved basic services should be urgently addressed.

Currently, many small cities lack the necessary institutional capacity to be able to manage their rapidly growing populations in the country. As cities grow and evolve, the task of managing them becomes ever more complex. In addition, the nature and tasks of urban management and governance are also undergoing fundamental changes. The policy and programme environment is likely to be altered as the government pursues the decentralised service delivery and revenue-raising to lower tiers of government agendas more vigorously. In the areas of health, education, and poverty alleviation, already the government has begun to allow hitherto untested local governments to operate the levers of many policy and programmes. However, few small city local governments are fully equipped with the technical and managerial expertise they need to take on these new responsibilities.

At the same time, there are advantages to being small. Small cities have time to address the residents' basic infrastructure and service needs before the magnitude of the service gap becomes too overwhelming. Further, small cities that are growing rapidly also offer critical opportunities for bypassing old technologies and for implementing efficient, ecologically sound practices that can contribute to shaping a more sustainable future for these cities.

At present, urbanisation in Bangladesh appears to have become largely decoupled from the country's development in many respects. The vast majority of the cities are economically marginalised and most cities are growing despite poor investments in city development. In such a situation, the cities in Bangladesh are serving as weak engines of growth and structural transformation; rather, they have become a part of the cause and a major symptom of the socioeconomic constraints that retard sustained and healthy growth of the country.

7.5.4 *Issues in Social Vulnerability*

A majority of the urban population in Bangladesh works in the informal sector and is irregularly employed. For example, the informal sector in Bangladesh accounts for 89 per cent of all employment and contributes more than 40 per cent to GDP. This is partly due to the fact that the formal sector is unable to provide the increasing urban population with sufficient jobs and employment opportunities. Another reason is that the formal sector frequently sources out services to the informal sector. The share of women, who work in the informal sector, is disproportionally high. In Bangladesh, 95 per cent of women, as compared with 82 per cent of men, are engaged in informal employment. Within cities, the extent of socioeconomic inequalities, often called intra-city inequalities are especially manifest. Income inequality, which is one aspect of intra-city inequality, is especially pronounced.

Furthermore, only parts of the population are fully involved in mainstream economic activities; and thus the divide between the rich and the poor is relatively sharp in Bangladesh. Huge sections of the urban population live in conditions of deprivations. In the country, compared to 35 per cent of the rural population, 21 per cent of the urban populations live below the poverty line. Whereas poverty lines are not visible, slums are an obvious sign of urban poverty and extreme deprivation. Since the mid-1990s, the term 'urbanisation of poverty' has been used to describe the interrelationships of urban growth, lack of employment opportunities, and extreme deprivation (Piel 1997; Ravallion 2001; Ravallion et al. 2007).

7.5.4.1 Slum Dynamics

According to the 2014 BBS census on slum dwellers and floating population, a total of 2.23 million people live in slums across the country compared with 1.39 million in 1997. It is observed that 51 per cent of the shanty people relocate to cities in search of jobs, 29 per cent due to poverty, and 7 per cent after losing their lands and houses to river erosion.

However, slum households are not a homogeneous group, but differ in the extent to which they lack the five above mentioned requisites. While some households lack just one requisite, such as secure tenure, others may suffer from multiple deprivations. Further, as shelter deprivations add up, not only the labour but also the disease burden increases, especially for women and children. One of the major reasons for slum households with multiple deprivations lies within local authorities who do not extend their services (water, sanitation, education, and healthcare) to informal settlements, or do not have the capacity to keep step with the rapid urban growth, not to mention the capacity to spatially direct urban growth, (Malik and Breckenkamp 2007; UN-Habitat 2006).

Although the definition of slums focuses on the physical dimensions of poverty, urban poverty also encompasses social, economic, and political dimensions which form a structure of disadvantage (Stephens 1995; UN-Habitat 2006). For a multidimensional view on urban poverty, UN-Habitat stresses on the following: inadequate and often unstable income; poor quality, hazardous, overcrowded and often insecure housing; inadequate provision of basic services; inadequate, unstable or risky asset base; inadequate public infrastructure; inadequate protection of rights through the operation of law; and voicelessness and powerlessness within non-responsive political systems and bureaucratic structures.

While the definition of slums is a first step towards operationalisation and measurement of urban poverty, this is still inadequately done for different dimensions of urban poverty. The prevalence of slums indicates that traditional income based indicators inadequately capture and underestimate urban poverty. Although not all inhabitants of slums are poor or live in a slum household, this discrepancy suggests that the income-based poverty lines applied in cities are inappropriate for measuring poverty in urban areas.

7.5.4.2 Urbanisation and Health

There are two, although apparently contradictory, views on the interrelationship between urbanisation and health. The first one posits that urbanisation is basically good for health and that there is something called an 'urban health factor'; while the second qualifies this factor as a myth. This myth is rooted in the fact that rural–urban migration is selective, which means that it is predominantly the young and the qualified that move to the city (Bähr 2004). In fact, it is the intra-city inequalities in living conditions (slum households vs. non-slum households, slum households with one shelter deprivation vs. slum households with multiple shelter deprivations) that correspond to intra-city health inequalities. Moreover, it is shown that health related figures for slums (e.g. diarrhoea, acute respiratory illness, and under five mortality), resemble and, in some cases, even exceed those of rural areas (UN-Habitat 2006). Nevertheless, cities offer advantages of spatial proximity and thus better availability of services (UNFPA 2007).

The majority of the urban population in countries like Bangladesh lives in the midst of the epidemiological transition which developed countries has already gone through. This means, apart from chronic, non-infectious diseases, which have in the past been associated with industrialised countries; there is still a high prevalence of infectious diseases (Stephens and Stair 2007).

Inadequate access to water and sanitation constitutes the main reason for digestive tract diseases, one of the leading causes of death, especially for children in Bangladesh. For example, diarrhoea affects the health status of children by preventing the absorption of nutrients and thus the proper growth of children (UN-Habitat 2006). Overcrowding, another shelter deprivation indicated by shift-sleeping or several children sharing one bed, facilitates the spread of infectious diseases (e.g. diarrhoea, measles and tuberculosis). The generally high concentration of people within cities, and slum settlements in particular, further add to this menace (UN-Habitat 2006).

A lot of the slum settlements are located in hazardous locations as well. These locations, often flood plains, unstable cliff sides or places near industrial plants, are the result of exclusion due to a lack of available land and settlement sites. Consequently, people in these places have a higher vulnerability to disasters. The negative consequences of locational disasters are directly attributable to 'poor infrastructure, substandard housing, haphazard city planning and often non-existent response measures (IRIN & UN-Habitat 2007).

Based on the urbanisation trends as well as the living and health conditions, current and future health challenges may be identified for Bangladesh. They can conceptually be divided into general challenges for a more humane urbanisation, and more specific challenges for the improvement of the health situation of the urban populations. Acknowledging the link between general challenges on a global, national and subnational levels as well as on a neighbourhood and individual level, is at the heart of the conceptual urban health model by Galea et al. (2006). Their model focuses on the exposure of urban populations to specific local living conditions defined by the physical, social and service environment, which is being shaped by more distal determinants on the municipal, national and global level. The model includes health determinants at several levels and as such it provides a comprehensive framework to answer the question of how and why cities influence the health of urban populations, and to place the subsequently defined challenges

The most relevant report to explicitly deal with the challenges posed by urbanisation worldwide is the WCED report, titled 'Our Common Future', its wider concern being the sustainability of human ways of production and living (WCED 1987). In the chapter titled 'Crisis in Third World Cities' (WCED 1987: 237), the report argues that there is a need to develop national urban strategies, strengthen local authorities, promote self-reliance and citizen involvement, provide housing and services for the poor and tap more resources. National urban strategies ought to formulate explicit goals and priorities for developing a national urban system including small cities. Furthermore, such strategies need to be intersectoral and should go beyond the traditional areas of building and city planning, thus providing a basis to reorient and assess key policy areas. The development of national urban strategies relates to the strengthening of local authorities, which need to have the capacities to manage local problems as well as opportunities with regard to their particular context.

Therefore, local authorities need political power, decision making capacity and access to revenues based on the wealth generated in the cities. Promoting self-reliance and citizen involvement refers to the support of the informal sector, which in its own way contributes to city development and represents an important employment source. This includes facilitation of loans to small entrepreneurs and MSMEs, building cooperatives and neighbourhood associations, provision of tenure to illegal dwellers and easing of building and housing regulations. As a result, the urban poor would be empowered to exercise local governance as well as fill service gaps. Citizen involvement is also at the core of providing houses and services for the poor as it is believed to reduce costs and improve needs orientation. The task of the local government and local authorities is primarily to provide 'cheaper, better serviced, better-located, legal alternatives to illegal plots' (WCED 1987: 250) as well as advice and technical assistance on how to improve building, health and hygiene.

Many of the challenges raised by WCED, i.e. national urban strategies, strengthening local authorities and citizen involvement, are still being articulated in recent documents such as the 'State of the World's Cities' (UN-Habitat 2006). It raises the point that a permanent and consistent political will by national and local governments is the necessary basis for all efforts to improve the urban poor's access to shelter, income and services. Political will, according to UN-Habitat, is characterised by the implementation of political reforms (land and housing policies), the expansion of slum upgrading programmes as well as the introduction of city planning measures and equitable economic policies. The role of the national government is stressed in particular as they shape the local environment by their political support, legislation and macroeconomic policy. To be successful, political will have to go along with long-term strategies including realistic targets, an adequate allocation of budgetary funds and a political, legal and regulatory reform programme, which is linked to the national development agenda. The latter comprises provision of tenure rights and well located, affordable and serviced land, changes in the land market (e.g. simpler land registration process, more flexible approval of building materials and standards, reduced minimum plot sizes) and land use planning, investment in water and sanitation and the establishment of pro-poor policies.

Strengthening local authorities and citizen involvement is treated as democratisation and decentralisation to the lowest appropriate level, in order to achieve a balance of power enabling the poor to put across their interests, also against higher social strata (UN-Habitat 2006). This has to be based on the acknowledgement that every person has a right to live in the city. The overarching concept of democratisation and decentralisation is local governance characterised by inclusive, participative decision making processes and the devolution of political, administrative and financial power away from the central government to subnational and local authorities. The aim is to reorient governance to the needs of the urban population and make it transparent, accountable and responsive. The role of the central government is to facilitate a conducive environment, that is through fiscal transfers, municipal elections and spatial planning.

UN-Habitat stresses, like the WCED, the importance of national urban strategies including explicit targets, specified budgets and expenditure frameworks (UN-Habitat 2006). Furthermore, local authorities should adapt these national strategies to the local level and integrate them into all sectors of urban development. For assessing the achievement of targets, spatially disaggregated information is needed, i.e. on population size, age structure, shelter location, access to water, sanitation and electricity, income and income generating strategies as well as crime (UNFPA 2007).

7.5.4.3 Malnutrition

A considerable share of the urban population in developing countries like Bangladesh finds it difficult to cover their dietary needs, which is due to high food prices in cities and the inability to grow their own food (Stephens and Stair 2007). The situation is further aggravated by global food price hikes caused by weather related production shortfalls, a gradual reduction in levels of stocks, increasing fuel costs on the supply side as well as an emerging need for biofuels on the demand side (FAO 2008). Difficulties in covering dietary needs negatively impacts on children in particular, for whom underweight is often the underlying cause of death as demonstrated by Black et al. (2003). The study shows that, for the leading causes of child mortality worldwide (neonatal disorders, diarrhoea, pneumonia and malaria), about half of the deaths can be attributed to underweight. However, it is not only undernutrition, which is problematic, but also the consumption of street food. Its biological contamination can lead to digestive tract diseases. Although being rather inexpensive, street food is often dense fatty, sugar rich or salty, and as such it is also a cause of overweight, which in turn is associated with an increased risk for diabetes as well as cardiovascular diseases (Stephens and Stair 2007).

7.5.4.4 Environmental Pollution

Another health risk is posed by indoor air pollution. This is because the poor households often use solid fuels (biomass and coal) for cooking while not having proper cooking facilities and ventilation. Women and children of poor families are among the most severely affected as they spend more time within the house than men. Furthermore, indoor air pollution adds to outdoor air pollution which affects the entire urban community. Besides, the density of industrial facilities, lorries, cars and motorbikes also influences the level of outdoor air pollution. Industrial facilities, and the by-products of their production processes, often contaminate urban water and soil. This creates a paradoxical urban development: immediate economic benefits, but at high expenses for the health of current and future urban generations, disproportionately borne by the poor who live and work in these facilities (Stephens and Stair 2007: 138).

7.5.4.5 *Traffic Congestion*

Motorised traffic is not only associated with air pollution but also with traffic congestion and accidents. The association is amplified in Bangladeshi cities by poorly planned, overburdened urban transport systems. In 2012, a total of 21,316 road traffic deaths are estimated by the WHO (WHO 2015). According to the Road Safety Global Report (2015), Bangladesh lacks best practice legislations for all five road safety risk factors, including speeding, helmet use, drink driving, seatbelt use and child restraint use, which make the situation even worse. These figures are likely to increase if motorised traffic in Bangladesh increases further without an adequate improvement of urban transport systems. The road traffic injury (RTI) is emerging as a leading cause of death, illness and disability in Bangladesh, especially among the younger age groups.

7.5.4.6 *Urban Violence*

Urban violence is emerging as a serious development constraint in Bangladesh; and it increasingly dominates the daily lives of citizens in the country. The accompanying increase in fear and insecurity leads to a wide-scale preoccupation with the phenomenon, but there is little agreement on the underlying causes of such endemic violence or of its costs and consequences. Equally, the capacity of various sector-specific violence reduction interventions to address this pervasive problem is often questioned.

The effects of urban violence on mortality rates are especially visible in younger age groups. Usually, mortality rates are higher in poorest neighbourhoods than in wealthiest neighbourhoods. Along with its direct and harmful consequences, a high prevalence of violence in a neighbourhood also affects the mental well-being of its residents because fear, critical life events, a lack of control over resources and social support, increase the risk of suffering from a depression (Stephens and Stair 2007).

The above provides the necessary contexts for framing an integrated policy, one that reconciles the bottom-up views of the local people with the top-down solutions offered by professionals. A useful matrix for urban violence prevention or reduction policies needs to cover a wide range of interventions such as criminal justice and public health, through conflict transformation and human rights—more commonly associated with conflict reduction—to newer more innovative urban solutions such as citizen security, crime prevention through environmental design (CPTED), and the community-driven social capital approach. As the government, the private sector, and civil society increasingly prioritise violence reduction, they need to take up the challenge to provide more innovative cross-sector solutions that better address the complexity of the endemic violence, fear, and insecurity that permeates the everyday lives of urban populations.

7.5.4.7 *Climate Change*

Climate change probably poses the biggest (urban) health challenge in future. Its manifold consequences range from more frequent and severe droughts, floods and heat waves (amplified by the urban heat island effect) to an increasing sea level as well as a geographic spread of (previously) tropical diseases. However, cities do not just fall victim to the consequences of climate change, but as already mentioned, they also cause them, by the combustion of fossil fuels, through traffic and industry (Stephens and Stair 2007).

The urban poor, especially in slums located on steep hill sides, in poorly drained areas or in low elevation coastal zones (LECZ), are disproportionally affected by the effects of climate change (UNFPA 2007). A prominent example for the vulnerability of LECZ is Bangladesh, where the cyclone 'Sidr' killed 3000 people and left millions homeless (cf. http://news.bbc.co.uk/1/hi/world/south_asia/7100957.stm). Furthermore, the flooding of latrines led to contaminated water sources and promoted the spread of water borne diseases. For instance, the area of Dhaka, the capital, lies between two and thirteen metres above the sea level, which continues to rise.

7.5.5 *Constraints to Orderly Urbanisation*

Several factors may be identified that constraint orderly urbanisation in Bangladesh. These cover institutional as well as financial and other drawbacks, such as unclear legal mandates, overlapping functional responsibilities and accountabilities, weak capacities, poor governance and weak finances.

In Bangladesh, the evolution of the legal framework underlying the local government institutions (LGIs) has not followed an orderly growth. The shape of LGIs that emerged in recent years has five tiers: two in urban areas and three in rural areas. The two urban LGIs are: municipalities (small towns) and city corporations (large cities). The three rural LGIs are: Zilla Parishads (District Councils), Union Parishads (Union Councils) and Thana Parishads (Thana Councils). However, proper allocation of responsibilities and financing has not emerged.

It is seen that only a limited number of functions have been assigned to the urban LGIs. Moreover, the demarcation of responsibilities is unclear and overlapping. For example, in Dhaka city, there are as many as nine specialised institutions and several line ministries that provide urban services with little or no coordination, overlapping mandates, weak capacities and financial limitations. Although the governance structure appears democratic and is elections based, but in practice LGIs enjoy little autonomy and are controlled by the national government. Further, resources available to LGIs are extremely limited. There is little financial autonomy that creates a huge dependency syndrome on the national government.

However, the most fundamental constraint is the inadequacy of resources available to urban LGIs and associated weak financial autonomy. Under the legal framework, urban LGIs can obtain resources from a number of sources. These include: (1) property tax; (2) rents from markets owned by urban LGIs; (3) fees from licenses issued to traders and non motor vehicles; (4) fees from advertisements, cinema and entertainment; (5) sale of property/assets and (6) grants and loans from the government.

In practice, the returns are very low and resources are grossly inadequate in comparison with their needs. Other than property tax, all other taxes are assigned to the national government. Transfers from national government to LGIs are ad-hoc and are not based on well-defined principles in the context of a legal framework. The evolution of urban finances in Bangladesh shows that government transfers account for about 54 per cent of total urban LGI resources, charges and fees account for 30 per cent, while taxes account for only 16 per cent (Table 7.4). The government budget is the source of all transfer funding including grants and loans. Since the urban LGIs do not have capacity for loan servicing, these government loans stay in the books as outstanding dues.

Table 7.4 Urban finance in Bangladesh (in million BDT)

Items	*1974*	*1978*	*1992*	*2001*	*2011*
Taxes	27	88	995	3027	8154
Charges and fees	57	112	681	2360	15,103
Total own resources	84	200	1676	5387	23,257
Government transfers	33	58	1319	8909	27,802
Total resources	117	258	2995	14,296	51,059
Total spending	110	261	2984	14,296	51,059

Source: BBS, Statistical Yearbooks, various years

The traditional way of measuring financial autonomy of LGIs is the amount of public spending assigned to them. Financing arrangements usually vary over countries. While tax collections normally tend to be centralised, many countries assign a significant number of tax instruments to city governments to raise their own resources. Moreover, countries with effective decentralisation usually have a system of transfers that is based on clearly defined principles. These are important elements of a decentralised fiscal system. They provide predictability of resources and support the proper planning and implementation of assigned services by urban LGIs.

In Bangladesh, urban LGIs account for only about 4 per cent of total government spending (which in terms of share of GDP is less than 1 per cent); while the Ministry of Local Government Rural Development and Cooperatives controls and manages most urban and rural development public spending and government transfers constitute the biggest instrument of resource transfer.

Although the urban LGIs are heavily dependent upon transfers from the national government, there is no formal resource transfer mechanism and there is often little or no correlation between assigned responsibilities and resource transfers. The resource transfers are determined centrally based on political considerations and competing national priorities. While urban LGIs account for less than 3 per cent of total government revenues, almost all potent sources of revenues are controlled by the national government while the only tax source assigned to urban LGIs is the property tax. Yet, yields are insignificant mostly owing to lack of political will. LGIs cannot decide on their own to change rates or property valuation.

Reforms in both urban governance and urban finances are critical to improving the pattern of urbanisation and urban services in Bangladesh. This needs to go together to get the desired results. Strong political will of the national government is important for materializing the reform agenda. In particular, fiscal decentralisation is essential to establishing accounting LGIs at both the urban and rural levels.

The strategy for urban financing needs to combine taxes, service charges, predictable transfers and responsible borrowing. Since tax administrative capacity is generally weak even at the national level, the scope for decentralisation of tax responsibilities to LGIs is very limited. This is not even necessary at this stage of Bangladesh's development. However, in the property tax, LGIs have a potentially powerful source of revenue that must be better used. A properly designed property tax could yield 1.0–1.5 per cent of GDP equivalent of tax revenues that will significantly improve urban LGI financing. With better efforts, urban LGIs should be able to increase resources from service fees and charges equivalent to about 0.5 per cent of GDP.

Government transfers should be reformed to assign greater transparency and predictability of the transfers. The transfers will also need to match assigned responsibilities. There should be a better balance between spending by the central ministries and LGIs based on a clearly articulated devolution of responsibilities and matching transfers that is enshrined in the legal framework This requires the designing of a proper transfer system that would work in the context of Bangladesh. Basic principles that could be included may relate to factors like population, poverty, endowment and performance. Similarly, a two-tier transfer system combining equity and incentives (performance) may also be possible.

Similarly, responsible borrowing by urban LGIs from the local market can be a major source of funding urban infrastructure. However, borrowing is not risk free and requires careful management with special attention to the debt repayment capacity of the borrowing entity. In general, loan financing should be responsibly focused on well-designed projects and in line with debt servicing capacity of the concerned LGI. Borrowing strategy of urban LGIs also needs to be made consistent with national debt management.

7.5.6 *Urban Vulnerabilities: Building 'slum resilience'*

The urbanisation process changes inequality by many ways. As urbanisation continues, the urban share rises; and changes are observed both in between and within urban and rural inequalities. The path that inequality follows is determined by the internal dynamics and specific socioeconomic structure of the country. As part of this process, 'leading' areas emerge, characterised by higher average standards of living than in 'lagging' areas. The spatial inequalities that emerge are often viewed as an inevitable part of the development process, rewarding higher productivity, economies of scale, and agglomeration effects in the more advanced sectors of the economy. While 'leading' and 'lagging' areas often correspond to urban-rural divides, spatial disparities may also be replicated on larger geographical scales, for instance in the form of East–West divides or intra-urban inequalities in Bangladesh.

Even if urban inequalities are linked to the process of development, these inequalities can be far from benign. Such inequalities may increase total inequality, which can diminish the impact of growth on poverty reduction. While unequal outcomes are expected to some degree as the country develops, if left unchecked these inequalities may emerge as structural inequalities that translate into inequalities of opportunity. Appropriate policies and institutions can play a crucial role in rural-urban transformations and addressing urban inequalities. For example, as urban-rural welfare inequalities are strongly associated with differences in education attainment, policies must focus on equal provision of education (both in terms of quantity and quality) so as to narrow productivity and income gaps between leading and lagging areas.

It is observed that, among all migrants in Bangladesh, more than 55 per cent migrate from rural to urban areas for better livelihoods and higher earnings. But the reality can be very different. Several studies show that migrants, as the first shelter, choose urban slums; and living conditions in urban slums are often appalling and, in fact, much worse than those in most rural areas. The Slum Census 2014 counts 2.2 million slum dwellers—more than 6 per cent of the country's total urban population. The Census shows that slum/floating population has increased by 214 per cent over a similar Census done in 1997. The 2014 Slum Census identifies eight reasons for migration to Dhaka city and taking refuge in slum areas: river erosion, uprooted, driven out, abandoned, meagre income, insecurity, for jobs and others.

Social inequalities among the slum dwellers are extremely high relative to any other population groups and, because of the conditional status, they are the most vulnerable segment among the all populations. Slum settlements are characterised by tenure insecurity and evictions, and controlled by *mastaans*-gang lords who charge exorbitant rents and charges for basic services. Such a situation deters investments for improving living conditions by slum residents and agencies.

Poor quality and densely built housing is typical in Dhaka's slum settlements and basic public infrastructure for water, energy, sanitation and hygiene are non-existent or very limited. A combination of human and natural factors results in various urban hazards with serious impacts on the urban poor. Some of the key urban hazards in Dhaka include, widespread flooding and waterlogging due to poor drainage; windstorms cause havoc in slum settlements because of the weak construction of houses; unplanned urbanisation and sub-standard building practices pose great risk in the event of a major earthquake; urban fires are common and are often believed to be ignited intentionally. This is high time that focus should get into the urban slums of the Metropolitan Cities. It is time to adopt a new paradigm and start to invest in human capital development in the slums of Dhaka city.

Rapid urbanisation and growth of slums in Bangladesh makes slum upgrading as an approach to address the problems of the urban poor. Dhaka is a rapidly urbanising megacity in one of the world's most densely populated and poorest countries, where almost 30 per cent of its more than 14 million population lives in slums and faces the impacts of a range of hazards. Hence, there is a need for building resilience. A move towards success needs a proper understanding of the urban context to identify the challenges and opportunities for building resilience in slums, which may then be followed by a sequence of inter-related activities.

Depending on specific circumstances, this could consist of provision of training on concepts and applications of urban resilience and toolkits for risk assessment and action planning. There could be a community based participatory risk assessment (CBPRA) to identify the inter-related hazards and vulnerabilities affecting the slum residents, supplemented by a survey of institutional actors; and a set of pilot activities guided by community action planning (CAP) workshops, together with community capacity building and developing community organisations.

There could be different kinds of risks for priority action—inadequate drainage, inadequate waste disposal and poor sanitation (e.g. focus on drainage, community toilets, water supply, and water purification), solid waste management (household and community level waste collection and disposal), housing improvement (plinth-raising above flood level) and awareness raising (cleaning event and billboards). The activities should also include extensive training and capacity building activities. A long-term community development plan (CDP) may also be developed.

No doubt, a number of challenges exist in terms of local expectations, capacity building, and working in a booming megacity. Therefore, there should be adequate preparation for community consultation and participation, and face the unpredictability of political circumstances.

7.5.7 Policy Priorities

Initiatives should be directed towards the development of prudent urban policies for both the short- and the long-term for which sound scientific knowledge and technical expertise in formulating the urban policy is important. In an increasingly urban Bangladesh, more than one-third of the country's total population now lives in the urban areas. While the country's urbanisation levels and trends closely mirror global patterns of industrialisation and development especially those in the developing world, this is still a remarkable transformation for Bangladesh. Rural–urban migration and the transformation of rural settlements into towns and cities have been important determinants of rapid urban growth in the country, but there has also been a general convergence in lifestyles between urban and rural areas as advances in transportation and telecommunications have caused distance and time to merge. Urban functions are being spread over larger and larger geographic areas so that the traditional distinction between urban and rural areas is becoming increasingly irrelevant for many purposes.

The broad patterns of spatial change highlight that virtually all of the country's population dynamics will occur in the urban areas in the foreseeable future. By 2030, almost 40 per cent of the population of Bangladesh will be living in the urban areas. To the extent that this reflects an expectation of further strong positive transformation of the economy, the changes will bring new dynamics towards more rapid development of the country. Nevertheless, many of the country's development programmes have yet to adequately recognise the anticipated rapid growth of small and medium cities or the deteriorating living conditions of the urban poor. The critical challenge over the next thirty years will be to take full advantage of the potential benefits of urbanisation in an inclusive way while lessening the obvious potential negatives. How well local authorities are able to respond to this challenge will shape patterns of the country's development in a major way, as well as the socioeconomic dynamics of the country.

Of particular concern for Bangladesh is the absolute scale of urban change that will occur in the country. Most of this growth will not occur in the largest cities but in smaller secondary cities and towns where poverty rates are higher and where existing coverage of basic public services is far from comprehensive, that brings to the forefront a different set of challenges and opportunities than if growth were to remain confined to a limited number of very large cities (e.g. Dhaka and Chittagong).

Thus managing urban growth has emerged as one of the most important challenges of the coming decades for Bangladesh. At the same time, the concept of urban governance has itself undergone a major transformation over the last few decades. Governance of cities has been affected by movements towards democratisation and political pluralism, an emphasis on decentralisation, and the rise of civil society. Numerous legal and institutional reforms have given shape to institutional reforms at the local and municipal levels. Consequently, solutions to urban problems are increasingly being sought at the local rather than at the national level. These trends underscore the urgent need to build and support the capacity of local governments to manage the environmental and social service problems that accompany rapid urban growth.

Policies therefore are necessary to promote scientific knowledge and help build and support the capacity of local governments in smaller cities to address their most serious urban challenges. Well-managed smaller cities are more likely to be able to cope with many of the challenges associated with rapid population growth and city expansion.

Good governance is a key concept for urban development and the term 'healthy urban governance' has often been used (Burris et al. 2007; KNUS 2008). The realisation of good governance can essentially be judged on the basis of how well the national and local governments and the cities perform in mobilising and empowering interest groups with no previous or only limited connection to the state. Burris et al. (2007: i159) concede that 'those with greater resources of experience, money or skill can game the local system as they can a national government'. Therefore, establishing good governance is not an easy process, but it may act as a strong ethic and political vision to follow.

To ease key congestion constraints, policymakers need to address three fundamental deficits of the local government—in empowerment, resources and accountability. Intergovernmental fiscal relations should be improved to address empowerment while practical ways should be identified to increase the resources available to the local governments to allow them to perform their mandated functions. Mechanisms must also be strengthened to hold the local governments accountable for their actions.

Three interrelated areas for policy action are instrumental to address the congestion constraints and help leverage urbanisation to improve prosperity and liveability: connectivity and planning; land and housing; and resilience to natural disasters and the effects of climate change. There should be more investments to strengthen intra- and inter-urban connectivity of the cities, adopt forward-looking planning approaches to guide expansion where it is most rapid on cities peripheries, invest in better quality public urban spaces to enhance pedestrian walkability and liveability, and utilise granular spatial planning approaches to permit greater variation in land uses.

There is a need for land and housing policy reforms and innovative housing finance to reduce the proliferation of slums. The first step in developing a resilience strategy for natural disasters and the effects of climate change is to accurately identify and quantify the risks at the national, subnational and city levels. The next step is to build a national georeferenced hazard exposure database, which includes public and private assets. Additionally, cities should revisit the design and enforcement of building codes and land use plans to avoid building further in risk-prone areas.

If urban governments are to play their potentially vital role as agents of local and national growth, countries must reduce the deficits in empowerment, resources, and accountability that hinder urban performance. As such, national and local governments need to take steps to, for instance, (1) expand and enhance urban empowerment, capacity, and incentives to plan and deliver services essential for economic and social development. These include services that urban governments can deliver on their own and those best shared with higher and peer levels of government and private and community partners; (2) reformulate flawed intergovernmental revenue systems. Transfers can support urban discretion and national priorities while promoting responsible fiscal behaviour. Urban governments should creatively strive to raise local revenues, including through borrowing, to enhance their credibility and effectiveness; (3) strengthen urban governments' accountability systems through better and more transparent financial management, workable coordination arrangements with key partners, enhanced citizen feedback channels, and stronger urban autonomy. Citizens and firms need information to back up their efforts to pressure urban governments to deliver; (4) strategically and pragmatically implement tailored reforms to ensure that new systems and processes will be feasible, productive, and enhance liveability and improve opportunities for prosperity, planners, government policy makers, and stakeholders need to better manage the spatial structure and intra- and interurban connectivity of the cities at different levels; (5) invest in the strengthening of transport links that improve connectivity between cities—between large and secondary cities, and between secondary cities and towns—to create more efficient systems of cities. Also invest in improved intra-city connectivity and traffic management to enhance mobility within urban areas and ease traffic congestion; (6) adopt forward-looking approaches to planning and guiding expansion where it is most rapid—on city peripheries. This approach will reduce the messiness of urbanisation, prevent undesirable spatial forms from being locked in, and facilitate future provision of infrastructure and basic urban services; (7) unlock the potential of city cores and carry out rejuvenation where cores have declined by investing in improvements such as better public urban spaces to enhance pedestrian walkability and liveability. Promote better management of developable land in city cores through effective land-assembly mechanisms; freeing up or making better use of publicly owned land; and reusing existing structures in an adaptive, appropriate, and innovative manner; and (8) facilitate the formation of more vibrant neighbourhoods through granular and contextual spatial planning approaches that permit greater variation in land uses and intensity of development. Such planning should be dynamic and flexible, allowing land uses to adapt to changes in market demand within a framework that takes a long-term view of a city's development. Strengthen city planners' and local governments' capacity to plan, coordinate, implement, and enforce development to deliver integrated, coordi nated, inclusive, and smarter planning policies.

As noted earlier, a sizeable proportion of the country's urban population lives in informal settlements (slums). Bangladesh needs quite a large number of housing units, mostly targeted to low-income households, to accommodate the projected urban population without further expanding the slum population. In order to meet the challenge, the government should: (1) enhance the quality of urban plans, development controls, and the efficiency of land markets (including informal markets); (2) provide and maintain sufficient infrastructure to meet the anticipated urban growth; (3) encourage the residential construction industry to produce affordable housing for all households; and (4) ensure that the capital markets channel more funding into housing construction and mortgage finance.

Many cities in Bangladesh are immensely vulnerable to natural disasters because economic activity and residents are highly concentrated in areas prone to natural risks. The risk is further exacerbated by high poverty rates and weak capacity to withstand the shocks of natural hazards, which result in a high human impact of disasters. To reduce hazard risks and plan for more resilient cities, policy makers need to: (1) identify risk by developing urban risk assessment frameworks and hazard maps; (2) mitigate risk by planning critical and multi-purpose infrastructure to be safe and resilient; (3) build management capacity in urban resilience among national and local institutions, and develop extensive risk data platforms and make them publicly available; and (4) establish a national catastrophe risk financing mechanism.

For Agenda 2030 and the SDGs, promoting sustainable cities is clearly featured in Goal 11: 'Make cities and human settlements inclusive, safe, resilient and sustainable'. Further, sustainable development in cities is critical to achieving goals like 'ending poverty' (Goal 1); 'reducing inequality' (Goal 10); promoting inclusive and sustainable growth, and full and productive employment (Goal 8); and taking urgent action to combat climate change and its impacts (Goal 13).

No doubt, in a country like Bangladesh, urbanisation pathways are interconnected in multiple ways. For example, whether cities develop in smart, compact ways or through suburban sprawl depends in part on the availability of efficient public transport infrastructure (which encourages compact development around public transportation hubs) or on whether transportation is car-dependent, which allows for and encourages sprawl. This is also linked to the issue of spatial inequality, liveability and hence potential to attract entrepreneurs and investments. Hence, decisions around infrastructure drive the degree to which inequality and pockets of poverty may arise, affecting in turn outcomes in urban development, social cohesion, and social conflict.

7.6 Social Protection in Bangladesh

Social protection is used as an important instrument of providing social security in development policy of Bangladesh. Social protection represents a fundamental paradigm shift in the country's policy framework as it is no longer perceived as a short-term means of ameliorating economic shocks, but rather as a major policy instrument of combining cash transfer programmes for extremely vulnerable populations, new programmes incorporating a social investment perspective into social transfer policies, and both public and private social insurance programmes for the people. One must, however, also recognise that social protection choices are not a simple technical matter, but require the gradual implementation of social learning in order to enable the creation of judicious policies (Barrientos and Hulme 2008). The discourse reflects a relatively coherent set of values and stable analytic framework through which social insecurity issues are evaluated and policy responses are devised.

Bangladesh's interest in social safety nets dates back to the period after independence. Historically, public safety net efforts in Bangladesh have clustered around the twin themes of food rations and post-disaster relief. The third cluster has been the informal safety nets at family and community levels to address issues of demographic and social shocks. There has also been pension scheme for the state employees. Over time, however, safety nets have transcended these historical pathways and have graduated to a mainstream social and developmental concern.

At the global level, the 1990 World Development Report (World Bank 1990) legitimised social safety net programmes, which were intended to protect people against two forms of economic adversity: the chronic inability to work/earn an income and/or a reduction of this ability during times of economic, political or environmental upheaval. Generally speaking, safety nets are based on monetary transfers or the provision of food supplies (Gentilini 2005). When possible, such initiatives endeavour to avoid the 'trap of dependency' by combining safety nets with recovery programmes (such as, public works programmes). In the 1990s, the term 'social safety net' has often been used to describe the concept of social protection which, the World Bank and other international organisations supported as a minimalist and pragmatic approach to protection (Devereux and Sabates-Wheeler, 2007a, b). However, the Asian crisis of 1997 highlighted the urgency of finding new means of protecting populations from adverse events. The 1995 World Summit for Social Development organised by the UN in Copenhagen, also lent new impetus to social protection.

A reformulation of the concept of social policy as 'social risk management' (SRM) emerged (Holzmann and Jørgensen 2000). The concept provides an expanded view of social protection; and the essence of SRM lies in reducing extreme poverty through better risk management. Significantly, the concept of risk is defined inclusively, in so far as it encompasses social, economic, political and environmental risks, including labour market-related risks, such as unemployment and non-employment (Holzmann and Jørgensen 2000). The SRM programme also targets those individuals who are 'most vulnerable'. The World Bank emphasised 'the double role of risk management instruments—protecting basic livelihood as well as promoting risk taking' (Holzmann and Jørgensen 2000). The SRM strategy is based on three key pillars: (1) risk reduction through labour market management; (2) risk mitigation through diversification of resources or the introduction of community and/or informal social protection mechanisms; and (3) risk coping, or the strengthening of capacity to respond to risk effectively, through the introduction of specific measures such as social transfers or public projects.[8] In effect, the approach neglects the key issue that social protection policies should extend beyond the economic aspects of risk and vulnerability to include legislative (i.e. the creation of status and rights) and institutional measures. The ILO also follows similar lines, advocating for recognition of the universal right to social security and corresponding creation of a social protection floor (ILO and WHO 2009a, b). At present, social protection is no longer seen as mere expenditure, but as a means of strengthening social and human capital; and is considered as a key element of development policies.

7.6.1 Conditional Cash Transfers (CCT) and Social Pension

The CCT programmes represent a form of social protection programme, typified by the narrow delineation of its target group—the poor or the poorest of the poor. Such programmes use a range of methods, such as demand, geographic targeting, means testing, proxy-means testing and community-based selection. In doing so, they combine financial assistance for poor families with a series of initiatives designed to strengthen their human capital. To receive benefits, recipient households must make quid pro quo commitments in the areas of health, education and nutrition.

[8] This World Bank model, however, came under heavy criticism for its failure to consider inequality and structural poverty (McKinnon 2004; Kabeer 2004a, b). Further, the adoption of social-rights centred approach was advocated with emphasis on (1) the universality of human rights; (2) their social dimension; and (3) the development of the means to improve the fulfillment of these universal social rights (DfID 2000a, b). This 'social rights for the poor' school of thought denounces extreme poverty and inequality as symptoms of social injustice and structural inequality. Generally, the approach seeks to institute a comprehensive approach incorporating social protection into development policy.

The CCT programmes are characterised by the specific targeting of recipient populations. By definition, targeting is intended to achieve greater efficiency in the fight against poverty by focusing efforts on poor households rather than the population at large (universality). In practice, however, identifying recipients is particularly difficult, due to the increased risk of two types of error: inclusion error—the incorporation of households that should not be eligible for the programme or policy and, conversely, exclusion error—which falsely deprives recipients of their rights. Bangladesh has used a variety of methods to effectively target recipient populations. Such methods may be divided into two main categories: (1) those that examine the validity of applicant requests based on existing data, which may then be supplemented by questionnaires and/or interviews; and (2) those that endeavour to classify individuals and households as poor or not poor. The first approach involves asking individuals and households to apply to local offices. Applications are then reviewed and sorted by administrative authorities on the basis of data collected and derived from other sources.

The second approach includes a series of varied methodologies. The most theoretically sound consist of conducting questionnaire-based surveys of populations to select households or individuals on the basis of their income or consumption level, a form of means testing. This can, however, be extremely difficult and prohibitively expensive to collect and accurately measure means-related data (e.g. income, transfers, donations and assistance). For the reason, another method, proxy-means testing, is sometimes used. This form of targeting involves the development of a numeric score derived from the addition and weighting of a limited number of variables related to household living conditions. These variables generally include housing quality and occupancy status; ownership of durable goods; household demographic structure; and the status, sector of activity or level of education of household members (Grosh 1994).

In any case, both traditional means testing and proxy-means testing have one major drawback: they require administrative capacities that are usually absent in Bangladesh. These methods are also very expensive, and may lead to the stigmatisation of recipients. Instead of targeting individuals or households on the basis of income per unit, it may be simpler and more effective to target geographic areas where poverty is most heavily concentrated. It has been shown, for instance, that place of residence, rather than other household traits, is often the most reliable indicator of poverty (Ravallion and Wodon 1997). The effectiveness of geographic targeting, however, is highly dependent upon the concentration of poor persons in the areas in question. If the population is fairly heterogeneous in terms of poverty, this form of targeting generates both inclusion errors (areas identified as poor but containing a large proportion of non-poor persons) and exclusion errors (poor persons living in areas identified as non-poor).

Alternatively, recipient targeting may also be aimed at particularly vulnerable segments of the population, defined on the basis of gender (women), age (children and the elderly) or ethnic background (minorities). Although it contains the drawback of making transfers available to individuals or households that may not actually be poor, the selection of recipients on the basis of vulnerability nevertheless offers significant advantages. Targeting by category is less costly and complex to implement than targeting systems based on strict income-related criteria, reduces stigmatisation, and enjoys greater public support. It also produces positive externalities (Duflo 2000).

The general philosophy underlying the provision of cash transfers conditional on recipients' participation in human capital strengthening programmes represents a departure from the safety net programmes, often issued in kind (i.e. food aid or subsidies for basic products) and relatively free of conditionality (Rawlings 2005). In short, CCTs simultaneously aim to relieve immediate poverty while also preparing for the future by breaking the intergenerational cycle of poverty.

Social pensions, on the other hand, entail the payment of old-age benefits at a standard (non-contributory) rate to all elderly persons below a given income level. The principle of 'universal' pensions, which have problems related to cost, administrative difficulty and potential negative effects are now re-evaluated in a positive light. It is recognised, for instance, that due to various crises affecting traditional solidarities, Bangladesh now witnesses a sharp increase in poverty among the elderly. It is now accepted that social pension programmes have a highly positive impact on poverty reduction and the maintenance of social solidarity. It is argued that under certain conditions, such as the existence of a minimal level of administrative and financial capacity and corresponding strength of political will, the creation of a universal old-age pension can emerge an appropriate option for Bangladesh.

7.6.2 Issues and Challenges

The importance of a more systematic and comprehensive framework for social protection programming is stressed in Bangladesh. An analytical inventory of social safety net programmes in operation in Bangladesh shows that annual outlay on safety net programmes amounts to BDT 114.70 billion (US$ 1.64 billion) which is approximately 1.5 per cent of the country's GDP. The portfolio of programmes include allowances for population groups with special needs, food security and disaster assistance programmes, public works/employment programmes, and, programmes focused on human development and empowerment. The highest allocation (44.3 per cent) is for Food Security and Disaster Assistance programmes. Those programmes with an urban focus as yet remain miniscule; at only 0.7 per cent of the total allocation.

The bulk of the safety net programmes are implemented through government channels. However, non-government channels play an important supportive role particularly in those programmes focused on sustainable graduation; 97 per cent of annual allocations are spent through 30 major programmes.

However, not all programmes listed in government budget documents can strictly be categorised as safety nets as many of these are more in the nature of sectoral development programmes. The inventory establishes that safety nets are a major policy focus. Questions, however, abound. Are all critical risks and vulnerabilities being addressed? Are there significant gaps and duplication? Is programme proliferation merely spreading tokenism? Are sustainable results being promoted? Do safety nets in poverty-dominated countries like Bangladesh need to embrace goals of promotion alongside the goals of protection?

The growth of safety net programmes in Bangladesh has seen a number of innovations over the years. Some innovations were a response to major crisis events while others were incremental unfolding of a policy agenda. The first round of innovations was in the 1970s when in response to the devastating famine of 1974, food-for-work was significantly scaled-up and the Grameen experiment with microcredit took off. The second round of innovations took place in the late 1980s. Here too the innovations were a response to consecutive floods of 1987 and 1988 when the need for all-weather infrastructure assumed high priority. Workfare innovations combining goals of road maintenance, social forestry and women empowerment were launched.

In the early 1990s, CCTs were launched in the form of food-for-education programme while in the late 1990s allowance programmes took off with focus on elderly and vulnerable women. In early 2000s, there was a broadening of programme focus with programmes increasingly combining protection and promotion goals. Finally, in the late 2000s, geographic targeting became a prominent focus. The future agenda too is pointing towards more innovations, particularly in the focus on a national data-base of the poor, as well as in the formulation of a comprehensive social protection strategy.

Three factors have driven the process of social protection in Bangladesh: (1) a political process whereby the welfare responsibilities of the state have come into sharper focus; (2) a social process of erosion of informal safety nets due to the decay of the extended family system; and (3) a developmental realisation that safety nets are crucial to a sustainable anti-poverty strategy. Consequent to these factors, Bangladesh has witnessed a proliferation of safety net programmes over time. Although many critics question social safety-nets as something politically expedient, stigmatising and highly inadequate to prime concerns of the poor, the necessity of such nets is never really discarded in practice. However, a new urgency is now visible in the discourse as safety nets and the broader issue of social protection is increasingly being seen as a mainstream development concern.

Originally, a narrow concept of public social safety nets operated amounting to noncontributing state transfers in cash or kind. These were sometimes universal, but more often targeted, to help the poor or those suffering from poverty to overcome their transient problems. More recent conceptualisation, particularly for developing countries, argues for a broader scope. There is a growing realisation that issues relating to the safety-nets and the broader issue of social protection needs to be discussed within the context of the relationship between risk management and the prospect of growth and the extent to which the growth process is pro-poor. In this sense, social protection impacts on poverty reduction through a series of direct and indirect channels.

A finding from early 1990s shows that an average rural household in Bangladesh loses 20 per cent of its annual income to crisis events. More recent data also confirms the significance of such shocks as a dimension of the poverty experience. Risks and vulnerability pose problems not only for those who are already below the poverty line but also for a segment of the non-poor who are above the poverty line but vulnerable to downward mobility due to shocks. Risks and vulnerability also exacerbate the problem of structural poverty. Newer risks are also emerging which demand priority attention. One of particular relevance is the rapid process of urbanisation and the attendant growth of slums and low income groups with very poor access to health and shelter. A second is climate change related vulnerabilities that pose formidable challenges for Bangladesh. A third is on youth unemployment.

There are other reasons too for according risk and vulnerability a high policy priority, reasons which tend to figure little at the margin within the economic discourse on poverty reduction. Although economists recognise the dangers posed by excessive risk aversion to entrepreneurship and investment decisions, they overlook the fact that the livelihood strategies of the poor are constructed within a psychological milieu. An endemic atmosphere of risk and vulnerability has concrete psychological consequences for a household's capacity to construct forward-looking graduation strategies. Addressing risk and vulnerability thus is also a way of improving the critically significant psychological atmosphere and assisting the poor in more robustly engagement on graduation aspirations.

Despite increased focus on social safety nets on the part of both government and non-government actors, independent and comprehensive assessments on results have been relatively limited. Most of these focus mainly on process issues that is coverage, benefit package, targeting and beneficiary profiles, rather than on outcomes. There are a number of conceptual and methodological challenges in assessing outcomes. The portfolio of safety net programmes address different dimensions of vulnerability and it is important for an assessment exercise not to fall into the trap of comparing apples and oranges. For example, programmes addressing transient food insecurity may not compare well with programmes focused on addressing structural poverty. The appropriate result to look for in the former is consumption smoothening and the prevention of a further slide in poverty status while in the latter, the appropriate result is graduation that is a process of upward rise in a broad range of household indicators leading to an escape from the ranks of the poor.

A second conceptual concern is about reversibility in outcomes. Assessment exercises often fall foul of over-optimistic conclusions when some of the reported gains prove to be reversible in the short-to-medium term. An appropriate time interval between programme participation and assessment is a key methodological concern.

A third concern is about attribution. How much of the observed changes in beneficiary welfare attributable to programme participation?

Use of control groups and the establishment of a sound counterfactual is the accepted methodological device to narrow down this problem. However, establishing a meaningful comparison on the basis of with and without control groups presents particular challenges when safety net type programmes have become multiple especially in poverty-prone localities.

Finally, assessment exercises need to be aware of the dual challenge of assessing individual programmes wherein the issues are adequacy, equity, cost-effectiveness, sustainability and assessing the overall system wherein the issues are appropriateness, balance between programme focus, and, process issues such as innovations and exit policy.

A key concern in assessing safety net programmes is coverage. Four factors are relevant to a meaningful conclusion regarding coverage: (1) establishing the size of the clientele, (2) planned coverage in terms of allocations, (3) actual coverage based on beneficiary survey, and (4) size of benefit package. The last is important to determine whether coverage is merely a token phenomenon or a meaningful one.

Data on actual coverage based on beneficiary surveys is limited. Even when such data are available, a common misperception is to view coverage with reference to the whole population rather than the population segment for which safety nets are relevant i.e. the poor and the vulnerable. Since risks and vulnerability may fall into analytically distinct types, a disaggregated view of coverage is often more significant than a summary statistic. The three broad risk categories safety net programmes address include: (1) transient food insecurity due to seasonality, disasters, crisis etc., (2) chronic or structural poverty, and (3) population groups with special needs such as elderly, widows, disabled.

For the first category (i.e. transient food insecurity), the size of the potential client group is usually determined by the upper poverty line. The 2010 data puts the estimate at 50.4 million. It is the second category of chronic or extreme poverty where the sensitivity of the measurement indicator becomes a more serious issue. For example, in the 2005 HIES data, Costs of Basic Needs (CBN) approach yields an extreme poor population of 34.8 million while direct calorie intake (DCI) method yields a comparable extreme poor population of 27 million. Other indicators such as self-assessed deficit status point towards a worse-off group within the statistically-defined extreme poor. A 2009 survey puts the size of this ultra-poor group at 8 million. The third category, relevant for allowances programmes, is easier to establish since the population categories are more well-defined.

Although broadly targeted at the extreme poor, safety net programmes utilise many eligibility criteria to identify their specific target groups. In practice, these are often vague and lack comprehensiveness. Study data have been culled to develop a generic profile of safety net target group. The typical safety net target household is:

- No land or land up to 10 decimals,
- Average income per person per day below Tk. 30 (43 US cents),
- A financial profile where debts exceed savings by an average of around Tk. 2500 (US$36).
- A greater presence of disadvantaged members such as vulnerable women.
- About a quarter of households have members participating in microfinance institutions (MFI).

A change from earlier times is that target households remain food-insecure but such insecurity is better understood as nutritional insecurity. Current target households are not characterised by large-scale hunger throughout the year. However, an overwhelming majority miss milk and meat in their weekly diet. Target households are regularly exposed to economic shocks. Most significant of these in terms of magnitude and recurrence are illness-related large expenditures, natural disasters and loss of livestock.

In the case of safety net programmes in operation in the country, three major questions are pertinent: How accurate is the selection of beneficiaries? Is the benefit package adequate? And are there leakages in the process? The study findings generally show inclusion error to be 16 per cent on average but varying considerably across programmes in the range 6–24 per cent. Two leakage issues are significant: informal entry fee for allowance type programmes and fraudulent muster rolls in the workfare programmes. Lesser leakage issues include lower value asset transfer and undefined deductions from stipend/cash grants.

Overall, programme support comes in eight forms: cash allowance, food support, asset, wage-employment, training, inputs, savings and community assets. Most programmes provide direct programme support per beneficiary (total for programme duration) in the BDT 15,000–18,000 range with only two programmes providing higher-value packages: Char Livelihood Programme (CLP) at BDT 28,300 and Rural Employment Opportunities for Public Assets (REOPA) at BDT 72,000. The question of programme duration is of course a factor in determining the overall size of benefit package. Programmes also differ in terms of proportion of project resources deployed on implementation costs.

Beneficiary perceptions on overall programme impact are generally positive but only half assess this impact as 'strong' as distinguished from 'moderate'. Such assessment vary across programmes and are determined both by the size of the benefit package and quality of the implementation process. Beneficiary perceptions are that most programmes have had an income impact. Other impacts have been on asset increase, increased employment, school attendance etc. However, to what extent such impacts are durable or are reversible in the short to medium term cannot be deduced from the perception data. A key issue therefore is to have insights into the dynamic aspects of the impact question. Supplementary insights from FGDs bring out some of these dynamics. For example, in the cases of Old Age and Widow allowance programmes, benefit package is small but for the beneficiaries the greater significance lay in the assured regularity of the benefits and the empowering opportunities these small benefits opened for these vulnerable members to be independent in some of their personalised expenditures such as medicine and leisure items. Perceptions data alone, however, cannot provide a basis for a robust assessment of programme impact. Two additional data source here is 'before and after' changes in key household indicators and 'with and without' comparison of beneficiary and control households.

'Before and after' data show clear improvement in the core 'protection' indicators of food security and self-assessed chronic deficit status for beneficiaries of all types of safety net programmes. Seasonal hunger was halved and chronic deficit status reduced from 30 per cent to 9 per cent. In comparison, there has been only modest average increase in per capita monthly income—14.5 per cent adjusted for inflation. Though some programmes have registered a higher rate of income change, this has been limited to 28 per cent.

In contrast to income, change in average savings has been positive and dramatic—an increase of 170 per cent with proportion of households saving also rising from 25 per cent to 61 per cent. There is however, considerable variation across the programmes. Average landownership size has shown a marginal decline but land access through the lease market has shown an increase. On the quality of life indicator of sanitation, proportion of households using sanitary latrines has doubled from 32 per cent to 69 per cent. Overall, there has been an improvement in poverty status in terms of the proportion of households who were self-assessed as chronic deficit declining from 30 per cent to 9 per cent.

To what extent were the observed changes due to programme participation? 'With and without' comparison of beneficiary and control households show that non-beneficiary households too improved their income situation but beneficiary households improved by 9 per cent and more. The three indicators on which difference has been more dramatic are on savings, land access through lease, and, self-assessed poverty status. Beneficiaries improved savings by 170 per cent while non-beneficiaries suffered a decline by 9 per cent. Landownership trend was similar but access through lease saw an 85 per cent increase for beneficiaries and 28 per cent decline for non-beneficiaries. On poverty status, beneficiary households saw a 72 per cent decline in chronic deficit status compared with a 13 per cent decline for the non-beneficiaries.

The scaled-up attention to issues of safety nets and social protection is not being driven only by the search for more effective anti-poverty strategies. It is also simultaneously an outcome of the deepening of welfare aspirations of citizens and the pressure on the state to respond to these aspirations. The nature of such responses is not a given but a better understanding of these political imperatives is often critical to a more effective assessment of ground-level outcomes and emerging policy directions.

While assessments demonstrate irrefutable short-term successes (school attendance, health of the monitored populations), there is little evidence of long-term effects. Social protection remains a component of the fight against poverty, but it constitutes neither an employment nor a growth policy. Bangladesh, with rapid progress and growing social inequality, needs to be more sensitive now to the need for social protection floors, rather than in the implementation of growth strategies or programmes with a more attractive electoral payoff (Hickey et al. 2009). In any event, social protection programme funding is an issue that requires deeper analysis in Bangladesh. Some studies estimate that the cost of social protection amounts to a small percentage (from 0.5 to 2.7 per cent) of GDP in low income countries (ILO 2006, 2008). Nevertheless, for Bangladesh, even this small proportion of GDP could be quite considerable, and the broader dissemination of social protection may not be possible unless the international community accepts its obligation to provide the long-term funding for a global universal social policy.

A key issue in understanding programme impact is graduation. Some policy proponents and programme implementers nurture an understanding of programme impact as one of a one-stop journey of 'graduation'—that is from being poor to becoming a member of the non-poor. Statistics belie such a neat conceptualisation pointing rather towards a multi-stage journey of change.

While there has been a significant decline in the worst-off category that is chronic deficit households, the improvement at the highest end of the poverty scale that is the surplus category, has been much more muted. The overall picture is one of cascading change—major decline in chronic deficit households, small change in the proportion of occasional deficit households, major increase in the proportion of break-even households, and finally, small increase in the proportion of surplus households. However, within this general picture, the multi-component programmes—SHOUHARDO, CLP, REOPA, TUP and VGDUP—have a comparatively higher rate of increase at the upper end of the scale that is in the 'surplus' category.

Analytically, the observed graduation path experienced by programme beneficiaries appears to be a two-stage journey—a relatively rapid journey within the poverty and vulnerability band that is from chronic deficit to break-even status, and a much slower journey to the 'surplus' category. The first is about a lessening of the intensity of the poverty experience while the second is about moving beyond vulnerability. The larger programme impact has been on the former while the impact on the latter has been a lesser one.

The complexity of this graduation path demands further exploration. Juxtaposing perceptions data with 'before and after' and 'with and without' data, it is possible to suggest an analytical framework to capture impact. Five impact types are identified: (1) reduction in the intensity of the poverty experience, (2) building of graduation platforms, (3) women's empowerment, (4) building community assets, and (5) building social capital. Impact has been noticeable on the first and third, uneven on the second and fourth, and relatively minor on the fifth. A noteworthy weakness has been on the usability and quality of training programmes to contribute to graduation.

Key policy lessons are about the disaggregated nature of the coverage gaps, multiple types of leakages, presence of some low value-for-money programme components, tendency to build parallel implementation structures which add to implementation costs but not to sustainability, need for micro-mapping, importance of exit strategy, and to ensure that eligibility criteria do not work at cross-purposes between programmes.

Clearly, there is a need for specific policy vehicles to take each of the policy issues up and anchor them within government and the results used for the development of a national social protection strategy, based on a menu of options dealing with different types of vulnerability faced by different social groups in different geographical settings.

Bangladesh has a reasonably good foundation on which social protection can be strategically scaled up to be a key component of poverty reduction and growth. Key issues in this challenge of strategic scaling up include: (1) need for a two-track approach: one component being consolidation of scalable models and the other component being design innovations on benefit package; (2) new vulnerabilities, sequencing and exit strategy; (3) data-base on extreme poor, (4) enhancing the focus on nutrition, (5) integration through actor-role synergy, and (6) broadening the focus on safety ladders to include issues of community assets and linkage to meso-economy.

7.7 Concluding Remarks

Social vulnerability and exclusion encompass a broad set of concerns. People may be excluded from many domains of life—social, economic, political, civil or spatial—and the relative importance of each domain depends on the country and local contexts. Exclusion is also a personal experience, and the views of those affected by it or at risk of being left behind cannot be disregarded. Measuring social vulnerability and exclusion and the impact of policy on either is therefore a challenging task.

Socioeconomic disadvantages play an important role in magnifying social vulnerability and hindering social protection coverage. In the labour market, members of ethnic minorities, persons with disabilities and young people are less likely than others to secure a decent job and, when they do, they often earn lower wages, as do women. These people often live in rural areas and in remote locations where access to public services and infrastructure is limited. Moreover, policy design and implementation play an important role in keeping social protection out of the reach of some; and giving those left behind opportunities to participate. The impact of social protection on poverty and inequality is greater in countries where more investments are made. However, its availability does not in itself guarantee that the needs of disadvantaged groups are addressed. The impact of social protection on social exclusion depends on the specific measures in place and on their implementation.

The human right to social security is recognised in the Universal Declaration on Human Rights and various human rights instruments, while International Labour Organisation (ILO) conventions and recommendations define the normative framework and set standards for the establishment and development of social protection systems.[9] The ILO Social Security (Minimum Standards) Convention, 1952 (No. 102), was the first international instrument to establish minimum standards applicable to all countries, regardless of their degree of economic development, for the following social security benefits: sickness, unemployment, old age, employment injury, family, maternity, invalidity and survivors, as well as medical care. In 1995, at the World Summit for Social Development, the governments agreed that social protection systems should be anchored in law and, as appropriate, strengthened and expanded 'in order to protect from poverty people who cannot find work; people who cannot work due to sickness, disability, old age or maternity, or to their caring for children and sick or older relatives; families that have lost a breadwinner through death or marital breakup; and people who have lost their livelihoods due to natural disasters or civil violence, wars or forced displacement'.[10]

There has been significant progress in Bangladesh, particularly since the early 2000s. However, legal coverage is limited to a few areas and only a minority of the population has access to social protection schemes anchored in national legislation. Often, only public sector workers or those in other types of formal employment are covered by contributory schemes, while tax-based schemes are fragmented and available only to a small percentage of the population.

Bangladesh has, however, tended to broaden its social protection systems sequentially, depending on national circumstances and development priorities. It began with stand-alone schemes to address employment issues, then introduced old-age pensions, disability and survivors' benefits, followed by sickness, health and maternity coverage for disadvantaged families. As systems become more comprehensive, steps have usually been

[9] See, the Universal Declaration of Human Rights (arts. 22 and 25), International Covenant on Economic, Social and Cultural Rights (arts. 9 and 11), the Convention on the Elimination of all Forms of Discrimination against Women (arts. 11 and 14), the Convention on the Rights of the Child (arts. 26 and 27), the Convention on the Rights of Persons with Disabilities (art. 28) and various ILO instruments. ILO has produced a compendium of social security standards and human rights instruments (see ILO 2017).

[10] Report of the International Conference on Population and Development (United Nations, Sales No. 95.XIII.18), chap. I, resolution I, annex, paras. 5.2 and 5.9.

taken to strengthen the links between different programmes. Most programmes in Bangladesh have improved the material well-being of disadvantaged groups and many have helped to break the intergenerational cycle of poverty. Solid evidence on the positive effects of social protection, combined with political support and financial capacity in Bangladesh, have led to its expansion. Further, with the adoption of the 2030 Agenda, Bangladesh has committed itself to working towards the realisation of the human right to social security. The challenge for the country is to put this commitment into practice.

References

Abdel-Rahman, H., and M. Fujita. 1990. Product Variety, Marshallian Externalities, and City Sizes. *Journal of Regional Science* 30 (2): 165–183.

Ali, Z., and M.K. Mujeri. 2016. *Revisiting Extreme Poverty and Marginality in Bangladesh: How Successful Are the Policies and Programs in Reaching the Extreme Poor?* Working Paper 30. Dhaka: EEP/Shiree.

Asaduzzaman, M., C. Ringler, J. Thurlow, and S. Alam. 2011. *Investing in Crop Agriculture in Bangladesh for Higher Growth and Productivity, and Adaptation to Climate Change*. Paper Presented at the Bangladesh Food Security Investment Forum, Dhaka, May 26–27.

Ayers, J., S. Huq, H. Wright, A.M. Faisal, and S.T. Hussain. 2014. Mainstreaming Climate Change Adaptation into Development in Bangladesh. *Climate and Development* 6 (4): 293–305.

Aysan, Y.F. 1993. Keynote Paper: Vulnerability Assessment. In *Natural Disasters: Protecting Vulnerable Communities*, ed. P. Merriman and C. Browitt, 1–14. London: Thomas Telford.

Bähr, J. 2004. *Bevölker ungsgeographie*. Stuttgart: Verlag Eugen Ulmer.

Barrientos, A., and D. Hulme. 2008. Social Protection for the Poor and Poorest in Developing Countries: Reflections on a Quiet Revolution. *Oxford Development Studies* 37 (4): 439–456.

BBS. 1984. *Bangladesh Population Census 1981*. National Series, Analytical Findings and National Tables, Bangladesh Bureau of Statistics, Statistics Division, Ministry of Planning, Government of the People's Republic of Bangladesh, Dhaka.

Becker, R., and V. Henderson. 2000. Effects of Air Quality Regulations on Polluting Industries. *Journal of Political Economy* 108: 379–421.

Black, D., and J.V. Henderson. 1999. A Theory of Urban Growth. *Journal of Political Economy* 107 (2): 252–284.

Black, P., C. Harrison, C. Lee, B. Marshall, and D. Wiliams. 2003. *Assessment for Learning. Putting it into Practice*. Maidenhead: Open University Press.

Blaikie, P., T. Cannon, I. Davis, and B. Wisner. 1994. *At Risk: Natural Hazards, People's Vulnerability, and Disasters.* London: Routledge.
Burris, S., T. Hancock, V. Lin, and A. Herzog Burris. 2007. Emerging Strategies for Healthy Urban Governance. *Journal of Urban Health: Bulletin of the New York Academy of Medicine* 84 (1): 154–163.
Caplin, A., and J. Leahy. 1998. Miracle on Sixth Avenue: Information Externalities and Search'. *Economic Journal* 108 (446): 60–74.
Devereux, S., and R. Sabates-Wheeler, eds. 2007a. Debating Social Protection. *IDS Bulletin* 38 (3): 23–28.
———. 2007b. Editorial Introduction: Debating Social Protection. *IDS Bulletin* 38 (3): 1–7. https://doi.org/10.1111/j.1759-5436.2007.tb00363.x.
DfID. 2000a. *Realising Human Rights for Poor People.* London: Department for International Development.
———. 2000b. *Sustainable Livelihoods Guidance Sheets.* Department for International Development. http://www.livelihoods.org/info/info_guidancesheets.html.
Dixit, A.K., and J.E. Stiglitz. 1977. Monopolistic Competition and Optimum Product Diversity. *American Economic Review* 67 (3): 297–308.
DMB. 2010. *National Plan for Disaster Management.* Dhaka: Disaster Management Bureau, Disaster Management & Relief Division. Government of the People's Republic of Bangladesh.
Duflo, E. 2000. Child Health and Household Resources in South Africa: Evidence from the Old Age Pension Program. *American Economic Review* 90 (2): 393–398., http://www.jstor.org/stable/117257. https://doi.org/10.1257/aer.90.2.393.
Ellis, P., and M. Roberts. 2016. *Leveraging Urbanization in South Asia: Managing Spatial Transformation for Prosperity and Livability.* Washington, DC: World Bank.
El-Shakhs, S. 1992. The Future of Mega-Cities: Planning Implications for a More Sustainable Development. In *Sustainable Development and the Future of Cities*, ed. B. Hamm et al. Trier, Germany: Universitiat Trier Press.
FAO. 2008. *The State of Food Insecurity in the World 2008.* Rome: Food and Agriculture Organization of the United Nations.
Ferreira, F.H.G., and J. Gignoux. 2008. The Measurement of Inequality of Opportunity: Theory and An Application to Latin America. *Review of Income and Wealth.* https://doi.org/10.1111/j.1475-4991.2011.00467.x.
Fujita, M., and H. Ogawa. 1982. Multiple Equilibria and Structural Transition of Non-Monocentric Urban Configurations. *Regional Science and Urban Economics* 12: 161–196.
Galea, S., C. Hadley, and S. Rudenstine. 2006. Social Context and the Health Consequences of Disasters. *American Journal of Disaster Medicine* 1 (1): 37–47.
Gentilini, U. 2005. Mainstreaming Safety Nets in the Social Protection Policy Agenda: A New Vision or the Same Old Perspective? *Journal of Agricultural*

and Development Economics 2 (2): 133–157. ftp://ftp.fao.org/docrep/fao/008/af137e/af137e00.pdf.

GOB. 2008. *Bangladesh Climate Change Strategy and Action Plan 2008*. Dhaka: Ministry of Environment and Forests, Government of the People's Republic of Bangladesh.

Grosh, M.E. 1994. *Administering Targeted Social Programs in Latin America: From Platitudes to Practice*. Washington, DC: The World Bank. https://doi.org/10.1596/0-8213-2620-1.

Hansen, N. 1990. Do Producer Services Induce Regional Economic Development? *Journal of Regional Science* 30 (4): 465–476.

Heineberg, H. 2000. *Grundriß Allgemeine Geographie: Stadtgeographie*. Paderborn: Schön-ingh.

Helsley, R.W., and W.C. Strange. 1990. Matching and Agglomeration Economies in a System of Cities. *Regional Science and Urban Economics* 20: 189–212. North-Holland.

Hewitt, K. 1977. *Regions of Risk: A Geographical Introduction to Disasters*. London: Longman.

Hickey, S., et al. 2009. The Politics of Protecting the Poorest: Moving Beyond the 'Anti-politics Machine'? *Political Geography* 29: 473–483.

Holzmann, R., and J. Jørgensen. 2000. *Social Risk Management: A New Conceptual Framework for Social Protection and Beyond*. Social Protection Discussion Paper Series No. 6. Washington, DC: World Bank.

Huq, S., A.U. Ahmed, and R. Koudstaal. 1996. Vulnerability of Bangladesh to Climate Change and Sea Level Rise. In *Climate Change and World Food Security*, ed. T.E. Downing, 347–379. NATO ASI Series, I 37. Berlin and Heidelberg: Springer-Verlag.

ILO. 2006. *Global Employment Trends for Youth 2006*. Geneva: International Labour Organization.

———. 2008. *World of Work Report 2008 – Income Inequalities in the Age of Financial Globalization*. Geneva: International Labour Organization.

———. 2017. *World Social Protection Report 2017/19*. Universal Social Protection to Achieve the Sustainable Development Goals. Geneva: International Labour Office.

ILO and WHO. 2009a. *Social Protection Floor Initiative*. Manual and Strategic Framework for Joint UN Country Operations. Geneva: International Labour Office and World Health Organization.

———. 2009b. *The Social Protection Floor: A Joint Crisis Initiative of the UN Chief Executives Board for Co-ordination on the Social Protection Floor*. Geneva: International Labour Office and World Health Organization.

IRIN & UN-Habitat. 2007. *Tomorrow's Crises Today: The Humanitarian Impact of Urbanisation*. Nairobi: Integrated Regional Information Networks and United Nations Human Settlements Programme.

IWM and CEGIS. 2007. *Preliminary Assessment of ASPS-II Components Vulnerability to Climate Change*. Dhaka: Institute of Water Modelling and Center for Environmental and Geographic Information Services.

Kabeer, N. 2004a. Globalization, Labor Standards, and Women's Rights: Dilemmas of Collective (In)action in an Interdependent World. *Feminist Economics* 10 (1): 3–35. https://doi.org/10.1080/1354570042000198227.

———. 2004b. *Re-visioning 'the Social': Towards a Citizen-centred Social Policy for the Poor in Poor Countries*. IDS Working Paper No. 191, Brighton: Institute of Development Studies.

———. 2005. Gender Equality and Women's Empowerment: A Critical Analysis of the Third Millennium Development Goal. *Gender and Development* 13 (1): 13–24.

Karim, S.M.R., T.M.T Iqbal, and N. Islam. 1998. Relative Yields of Crops and Crop Losses due to Weed Competition in Bangladesh. *Pakistan Journal of Scientific and Industrial Research* 41 (6): 318–324.

Karim, Z., S.G. Hussain, and M. Ahmed. 1996. Assessing Impacts of Climate Variations on Food grains Production in Bangladesh'. *Journal of Water, Air and Soil Pollution* 92: 53–62.

Klasen, S. 2001. Social Exclusion, Children and Education. Implications of a Rights-Based Approach. *European Societies* 3 (4): 413–445.

KNUS. 2008. *Our Cities, Our Health, Our Future: Acting on Social Determinants for Health Equity in Urban Settings, Report to the WHO Commission on Social Determinants of Health from the Knowledge Network on Urban Settings*. Geneva: World Health Organization.

Krugman, P. 1991. Increasing Returns and Economic Geography. *Journal of Political Economy* 99 (3): 483–499.

Leimgruber, W. 2004. *Between Global and Local: Marginality and Marginal Regions in the Context of Globalization and Deregulation*. Aldershot: Ashgate.

Malik, M.A., and J. Breckenkamp. 2007. *Links Between Urbanization and Chronic NCD Risk Factors, Morbidity and Mortality*. A Background Document. Unpublished.

Marshall, A. 1890. *Principles of Economics*. First Edition. London: Macmillan.

McKinnon, R. 2004. The East Asian Dollar Standard. *China Economic Review* 15 (3): 325–330.

Müller-Böker, U.D. Geiger, U. Geiser, V. Kansakar, M. Kollmair, K. Molesworth, and A. Suleri. 2004. Sustainable Development in Marginal Regions of South Asia. In *Marginal Regions of South Asia, Research for Mitigating Syndromes of Global Change. A Transdisciplinary Appraisal of Selected Regions of the World to Prepare Development-Oriented Research Partnerships*, ed. H. Hurni, U. Wiesmann, and R. Schertenleib, 225–261. Perspectives of the Swiss National Centre of Competence in Research (NCCR) North-South 8. Bern: Geographica Bernensia.

Nasir Uddin, M., W. Bokelmann, and J.S. Entsminger. 2014. 'Factors Affecting Farmers' Adaptation Strategies to Environmental Degradation and Climate Change Effects: A Farm Level Study in Bangladesh. *Climate* 2: 223–241.

Parr, J.B. 1985. A Population-Density Approach to Regional Spatial Structure. *Urban Studies* 22 (4): 289–303.

Piel, G. 1997. The Urbanization of Poverty Worldwide. *Challenge* 40 (1): 58–71.

Rauch, J. 1993. Productivity Gains from Geographic Concentration of Human Capital: Evidence from the Cities. *Journal of Urban Economics* 34: 380–400.

Ravallion, M. 2001. *Growth, Inequality, and Poverty: Looking Beyond Averages*. Policy Research Working Paper No. 2558. Washington, DC: World Bank.

Ravallion, M., and Q. Wodon. 1997. *Poor Areas, or Only Poor People?* Policy Research Working Paper No. 1798. Washington, DC: The World Bank. http://go.worldbank.org/61N7C0X1G0.

Ravallion, M., S. Chen, and P. Sangraula. 2007. *The Urbanization of Global Poverty*. Washington, DC: Development Research Group, World Bank.

Rawlings, L.B. 2005. A New Approach to Social Assistance: Latin America's Experience with Conditional Cash Transfer Programmes. *International Social Security Review* 58 (2–3): 133–161.

Road Safety Global Report. 2015. *WHO Global Status Report on Road Safety 2015*. Geneva: World Health Organization.

Romer, P.M. 1986. Increasing Returns and Long-Run Growth. *Journal of Political Economy* 94 (5): 1002–1037.

Sen, A. 2009. *The Idea of Justice*. Cambridge: Allen Lane and Harvard University Press.

Stephens, S., ed. 1995. *Children and the Politics of Culture*. Princeton: Princeton University Press.

Stephens, C., and P. Stair. 2007. Charting a New Course for Urban Public Health. In *2007 State of the World, Our Urban Future*. Earthscan, London: A Worldwatch Institute Report on Progress Toward a Sustainable Society.

UNFPA. 2007. *State of World Population 2007: Unleashing the Potential of Urban Growth*. New York: United Nations Population Fund.

UN-Habitat. 2006. *The State of the World's Cities Report 2006/2007*. London: United Nations Human Settlement Programme, Earthscan.

WCED. 1987. *Our Common Future*. New York: Report of the World Commission on Environment and Development.

Wheaton, W., and H. Shishido. 1981. Urban Concentration, Agglomeration Economies and Economic Development. *Economic Development and Cultural Change* 30: 17–30.

WHO. 2015. *Global Status Report on Road Safety 2015*. Geneva: World Health Organization.

———. 2015. World Report on Ageing and Health 2015, World Health Organization, Geneva.

Williamson, J.G. 1965. Regional Inequality and the Process of National Development: A Description of Patterns. *Economic Development and Cultural Change* 13: 3–47.

World Bank. 1990. *World Development Report 1990: Poverty.* Washington, DC: World Bank. https://doi.org/10.1596/0-1952-0851-X.

———. 2005a. *Maintaining Momentum? An Impact Evaluation of Interventions to Improve Maternal and Child Health and Nutrition in Bangladesh.* Washington, DC: Operations Evaluation Department, World Bank.

———. 2005b. *World Development Report 2006: Equity and Development.* Washington, DC: World Bank.

———. 2006. *World Development Report 2006: Equity and Development.* Washington, DC: World Bank.

———. 2012. *Bangladesh: Towards Accelerated, Inclusive and Sustainable Growth – Opportunities and Challenges.* Vol. 2. Main Report No. 67991. Washington, DC: World Bank.

CHAPTER 8

Institutions for Development

8.1 Introduction

The development literature has long recognised that economic growth and development is intimately linked to human and physical capital, technology and the quality of economic institutions. The role of human and physical capital and technology is well established by neoclassical growth models and their subsequent modifications (e.g. endogenous technical change). However, the role of institutions is of more recent origin and popularised more in the political economy debates. North (1990) suggests that 'Institutions are the rules of the game in a society or, more formally, are the humanly devised constraints that shape human interaction'.

Three important features of institutions can be identified from the above definition: (1) that they are 'humanly devised', which contrasts with other potential fundamental causes, like geographic factors, which are outside human control; (2) that they are 'the rules of the game' setting 'constraints' on human behaviour; and (3) that their major effect will be through incentives including development, inequality, and poverty (see North 1981). Reforming economic institutions for development, however, is a difficult task because these institutions are the outcomes of the political process in a country. Essentially, the economic institutions of the society depend on the nature of political institutions and the distribution of political power in society.

© The Author(s) 2020

M. K. Mujeri, N. Mujeri, *Bangladesh at Fifty*, Palgrave Studies in Economic History,
https://doi.org/10.1007/978-3-030-56791-0_8

It is now widely agreed that promoting democracy and accountability and checks and balances in the political system will certainly lead to better economic policies and institutions in Bangladesh. Yet this faces many challenges including: (1) defining institutions; (2) identifying core institutions for development; (3) identifying reform champions; (4) addressing the issue of trade-offs because, in most cases, major institutional reforms entail substantial losses for the beneficiaries of status quo; (5) ensuring the consistency of policies with institutional reforms; and (6) staying the course on reforms because institutional changes are long-term in nature and involve sustained progress without any reversals. Because of these challenges, institutional reforms typically require leadership from the top in the context of a stable government. But it is also clear that unless the core institutional constraints are addressed, Bangladesh will not be able to secure the long-term development targets of achieving upper middle income status and eliminate extreme poverty by 2030.

Institutions comprise, for example, contracts and contract enforcement, protection of property rights, the rule of law, government bureaucracies, and financial markets. They also include habits and beliefs, norms, social cleavages and traditions in education (the so-called informal institutions). Formal institutions typically tend to be the crystallisation of informal institutions (North 1990), as social norms in the realms of gender, class and caste, for example, determine rules of political participation and representation, methods of economic exchange, and inclusion of different groups in society (Pateman 1988).

8.2 Role of Institutions in Development

Institutions conducive to development reduce the costs of economic activity. The costs include transaction costs, such as search and information costs, bargaining and decision costs, policing and enforcement costs (Coase 1992; Dahlman 1979). They lower transaction costs by providing common legal frameworks (e.g. contracts and contract enforcement, commercial norms and rules), and they encourage trust by providing policing and justice systems for the adherence to common laws and regulations. These take the form of contracts, codes of conduct, standardised weights and measures, disclosure agreements, and enforcement through courts and policing. Where transaction costs are small, the private enforcement of contracts may still be preferred. But as economic relations develop and become increasingly impersonal, the role of a third party to enforce compliance to rules becomes increasingly necessary (Shirley 2003).

The protection of property rights requires an expanded role for state authority. Individuals and groups sacrifice a degree of freedom in order to ensure state protection; they accept levies and taxes to cover policing expenses, and state monopoly over the use of force for common security (Bates 2001). However, there is a risk that states which have the power to enforce property rights may use that power to expropriate property as well. Instead of reducing risk of economic transactions, this increases it. Thus property rights are by no means sufficient to spur economic growth, and must be balanced by institutions which limit the extractive capacity of the state power. These typically involve independent parliament and judiciary. Democratic institutions of political representation strongly contribute to this process (Rodrik 2000).

If economic institutions do not create the right incentives in society then a natural approach is to introduce reform in economic institutions. If security of property rights is the problem then measures are needed to introduce more secure property rights. However, the approach is likely to lead to pitfalls of institutional reform since any manipulation of economic institutions without thinking about the political forces that create or sustain them will not succeed. Making or imposing specific institutional reforms may have little impact on the general structure of economic institutions or performance if the underlying political structure remains unaltered.

Furthermore, directly reforming specific economic institutions (such as, the trade regime) may not be effective as there are many different ways and a multitude of instruments to achieve a specific goal. Using one instrument without altering the balance of power in society or the basic political balance may simply lead to the replacement of one instrument by another, a phenomenon known as the 'see-saw effect' (Acemoglu et al. 2003). Despite the Washington Consensus reforms in Bangladesh, for example, there was little change in the political structure creating policies that functioned as 'politics as usual'.

The political economy of income redistribution suggests that it is political incentives that lead income redistribution to take a socially inefficient form (Stigler 1971, 1982; Coate and Morris 2005). Although it might be better to redistribute to farmers by giving them lump-sum transfers, subsidising farm output might be more attractive politically because it is not perceived as income redistribution by other voters. Coate and Morris

(2005) argue that policy reform that aims not to use particular inefficient instruments might be counterproductive because rational politicians would be using the least-cost way of redistribution, given the political constraints and incentives they face. Nevertheless, it is possible to introduce successful reform in institutions and move to high growth. Growth can occur if the political equilibrium changes in a way that gives more power to those who want to push through reforms.

8.3 Institutional Reforms: Bangladesh Experience

There is a wide range of institutions that support Bangladesh society, incorporating structures that defend property rights and the legal framework, including the court system; the political system and the framework within which government operates; institutions which regulate economic and financial stability; and those that provides social safety nets and safeguard security (including the police and military). As such, these institutions make up the fabric within which citizens; businesses; political parties; and the economy operate; and provide a framework of rules, social norms and processes that are both explicit and implicit.

State institutions are the economy's primary facilitator of social and economic development. These institutions can be a major source of growth; effective institutions aid investment in physical and human capital, in research and development, and in technology. Institutions also have an important redistributive role to play in the economy—they ensure that resources are properly allocated, and the poor or those with fewer economic resources are protected. They also encourage trust by providing policing and justice systems which adhere to a common set of laws. Properly functioning institutions are a signal of a well-managed economy, enabling the government—and businesses—to borrow money at low costs. In turn, higher growth and lower borrowing costs give the government the resources to spend on social needs as well as on investment in infrastructure, health and education, and other priority sectors.

On the other hand, failed or ineffective institutions undermine trust, raise the cost of doing business and increase the cost of government borrowing, limiting the ability of the government to spend. If a government does not carefully manage its expenditure, rising borrowing costs can quickly lead to a debt spiral from which recovery is difficult, and where everyone suffers, but the poor the most.

One of the biggest challenges for the post-independence government of Bangladesh was to stabilise and reinvigorate the war ravaged economy. The government inherited an enormous stock of debt and a budget framework with persistently large deficits. Ongoing massive government spending fuelled a large external deficit as well, and the currency was vulnerable and prone to weakness. Inflation was rampant and interest rates volatile. Wealth and economic resources were highly concentrated with the rich, and for the majority of the people, the basic needs were not met. These issues reflected a vulnerability of the state and economic institutions.

However, the issue of institutions remained a neglected area in the 1970s and 1980s when the focus was mainly placed on planning, control and the policy environment. It was widely held that the distorted policy environment was the fundamental cause behind the slow economic progress; and 'good' policies were deemed necessary to ensure effective functioning of national institutions. In reality, this did not result in generating desired socioeconomic development and led to the dysfunctional institutions and poor governance which eventually emerged as the major bottlenecks in development. The political institutions as the major component of overall institutional arrangements of the country are closely linked with governance. As the World Governance Survey recognises, political institutions have the most critical link in the governance chain (Hyden et al. 2003). It also has significant economic and non-economic consequences.

Broadly speaking, institutions are component of governance along with traditions and processes that determine how power is exercised, how citizens are given voice, and how decisions are made on issues of public concern; the ways or types of using power in the process of management of national economic/social resources; and regimes of laws, rules, judicial decisions, and administrative practices that constrain, prescribe, and enable the provision of publicly supported goods and services. The 1994 World Bank Report holds that: 'Good governance is epitomized by predictable, open, and enlightened policymaking; a bureaucracy imbued with a professional ethos; an executive arm of government accountable for its actions; and a strong civil society participating in public affairs; and all behaving under the rule of law' (World Bank 1994).

From the good governance perspective, the existence of a network of institutions of government is important (UNDP 1997). There are three critical relationships among citizens and policymakers, policymakers and bureaucrats, and, bureaucrats and citizens. It is also a process involving the interactions of three key institutions: the state, the society and the market.

In Bangladesh, well-functioning institutions are more often referred to as 'good governance', signifying the reality that there is a failure of governance or mis-governance. Often, the scope of governance is extended with the argument that: 'the study of governance problem is, in essence, a search for ways and means of managing affairs of the state, taking into account the obstacles inherent in changes taking place in South Asian countries' (Sobhan 1992a, b).

The analysis on institutional reforms in Bangladesh in this section is divided into two phases: The first phase covers the period of 1971–1990; while the second phase covers 1991–2019. The structure and quality of institutions, especially the political ones, can affect whether the government facilitates or inhibits development. From the institutional perspective, Bangladesh is an amalgam of 'authoritarian and pseudo bureaucratic democracy' and centralised systems under which formal and informal sources of rules and norms have shaped the institutional arrangements at different times.

Enforcement of contract, the structure of incentives and organisational performance largely depend on the institutional arrangements of a country, which are manifested in rules, norms and policies in a particular social context. As in other developing countries, there are three distinct but interdependent spheres of institutional arrangements in Bangladesh—political, economic and societal. Political institutions help determine the limits on the exercise of power by politicians and bureaucrats. Institutions set the rules of game using diverse sources including formal legislations, rules and norms to informal traditions and customs. Likewise, the basis of the institutional arrangements in Bangladesh lies in both formal and informal sources of rules, norms and policies.

In Bangladesh, the formal political institutional arrangements are composed of several key institutions, which include the executive, legislature, judiciary, administrative system, local government, military and the political parties. After independence in 1971, Bangladesh emerged as a democratic country with a parliamentary system of government; and the government was set in motion to build the war-torn country. During the time, the public sector based economic system contributed to a further expansion of the role of the executive creating overwhelming dominance of public administration, which has more recently been termed as the 'development administration'.

After independence, the government took several tough decisions to rein in spending, to recapitalise the state enterprises, and create a transparent long-term budgeting process which anchored fiscal policy to a sustainable path. The constitution provided the framework for other institutions, and a commitment to growing, entrenching and protecting these institutions helped restore confidence and steered the economy onto a better growth path and a fiscally sound position. The state was able to spend on social sectors, to provide basic services to the poor, to reduce its debt and fund its spending at more reasonable levels.

During the period, policy uncertainty also played an important role in undermining the effective functioning of domestic institutions; ranging from delays in taking important decisions such as on addressing the ineffectiveness of state-owned enterprises. A range of challenges—from unemployment, poverty, inequality, low ability of the state to provide adequately for the victims of natural disasters—are reflective of institutions which were not functioning effectively.

During the time, the institutional reform process in the country demonstrated a clear dominance of international donor community perspectives. The fundamental concern of the donors involved restructuring the public institutions in order to facilitate wider role of markets in society. Generally, the public institutions took a central role in organising national activities in different sectors of the economy. The government used the available instruments to direct and control the national institutions through autarchy and state planning while it managed the socio-political system through a centralised and 'personalised' political regime. Although both formal and informal institutions existed, formal institutions were far more established and consolidated. However, both types of institutions were dominated by the state. The institutional mechanisms were exceedingly dominated by state regulations and agencies. The dominant rules and norms, however, were highly power and state-centric. Further, there was a lack of harmonisation of institutional mechanisms in various fields of national activities—political, economic and societal.

The beginning of the 1990s marked a significant political transition to democracy but the political transformation did not bring any fundamental changes in economic institutions, except some adjustments. An important change occurred in the role of bureaucracy. In 1991, a new business rule was adopted in which the minister was vested with more power and authority vis-à-vis the secretary in running the ministry. This has considerable significance for relations between the executive and the bureaucracy in dispensing services to the people.

Changes have also occurred towards strengthening legal institutions and the human rights regime in the country. Different initiatives were taken for ensuring the expeditious trial of legal cases in Bangladesh. Besides, necessary measures were adopted to establish the independence of the judiciary. In the case of human rights protection, an independent national human rights commission was established. In the case of combating corruption, the government established the Independent Anti-Corruption Commission (ACC) in 2004.

The devolution of power through transferring major functional responsibilities from the centre to sub-national level was also consolidated during the period. Although some changes were introduced during the 1980s, fundamental reorganisation took place in the mid-1990s, when the government revived the upazila parishad (UP) system. The local government in Bangladesh has three significant tiers—district, upazila and union parishad. Apart from this, there are other tiers such as the city corporations and pourashavas. All these tiers are now added to the electoral process. In addition, several initiatives are taken to expand representative power to the village level. The introduction of the village courts and reorganisation of the union parishads are significant attempts to strengthen the local government organisations. Another aspect of the process of decentralisation is the empowerment of women through creating opportunities to represent their interests from village to national level. Under the present structure of union parishads and upazila parishads, the provision for the election of female members has been incorporated. Thus, the level of decentralisation has now improved compared with earlier period, but proper decentralisation and devolution of financial and other powers to the local level needs further action.

It is clear that effective functioning of Bangladesh's institutions is a crucial precondition for economic growth especially in the long run. The vagaries of factors such as weather, global shocks and commodity prices cannot be avoided, but institutional strength is the key in a democratic system.

Institutions are no doubt powerful instruments with explicit orientation towards moving to a more efficient and growth friendly political and economic regimes. The role of economic institutions in a democratic polity, in essence, involves a process of steering through the development stream within the complexities of political institutions and governance structure. The period since the 1990s has no doubt been marked by more changes in the context of national policies, organisations and ideological orientation than the institutional settings and governance mechanisms in the country. On the other hand, the new trends of governance in development discourse exclusively refer to networking, interaction and institutional perspectives. But the institutional attributes of Bangladesh have remained largely unchanged although new institutions are being created. Similarly, efforts towards making more accountable and more effective economic institutions are mostly missing in the country's policy framework.

The presence of dynamic institutional arrangements based on both formal and informal rules and norms in the society is essential for effective harmonisation and coordination of economic, political and social policies in the country. The full-scale devolution with resources and meaningful power to democratic local institutions, an empowered complaint and regulatory mechanism, functional and coordinated programmes can create new development advantages and steer better performances in Bangladesh.

8.4 Land Reforms and Property Rights

Land tenure and property rights have significant impact on agricultural productivity and resource management especially in Bangladesh where agriculture is a major economic activity.[1] When property rights are secured, it gives significant incentives to the farmers to increase efficiency and productivity, invest in land development and ensure sustainability. Land tenure and property rights are closely interlinked. Secured property rights affect agricultural transformation through multiple channels, such as increasing incentives of farm households to invest in farm improvement, providing means to access credit and cushion against unexpected shocks, and creating diversified avenues for household asset ownership, productive development and better factor market functioning (Deininger 2003).

Land tenure is the relationship with respect to land which defines how property rights to land are to be allocated within the society. Land tenure plays a vital role in shaping farmers' land-use decisions (Feder et al. 1988).[2]

[1] One World Bank analysis of land policies in 73 countries between 1960 and 2000 shows that countries with more equitable initial land distribution achieved growth rates two to three times higher than those where land distribution was less equitable. See Deininger (2003).

[2] According to FAO, land tenure is the relationship, whether legally or customarily defined, among people, as individuals or groups, with respect to land. Land tenure is an institution, i.e., rules invented by societies to regulate behaviour. Rules of tenure define how access is granted to rights to use, control, and transfer land, as well as associated responsibilities and restraints. In simple terms, land tenure systems determine who can use what resources for

When land tenancy is insecure, farmers concentrate more on maximising short-term returns from land even at the cost of accelerating land degradation. Land tenure institutions have long been subjected to reforms considering agricultural and rural characteristics with differing objectives in specific countries or regions. In Bangladesh, land tenure reforms have been carried out at different times with multiple outcomes in view, such as food security, arresting social polarisation, increased farm investment, transparent production incentives, poverty reduction, increased employment and greater equity.

Property rights, on the other hand, are not directly concerned with who owns land; rather the issues of concern in this case are implications of formal and informal provisions that determine who has a right to enjoy benefit streams that emerge from the use of land (Bromley 1991; Eggertsson 1990; Libecap 1989). Thus, property rights involve a relationship between the right holder, other concerned parties, and a governance architecture to back up the claim. As such, property rights consist of two components—the rules and their enforcement mechanism (Schlager and Ostrom 1992). Property rights over land and other natural resources commonly use a classification in terms of several broad categories e.g. open access (no rights defined), public (held by the state), common (held by community or group of users), and private (held by individuals or 'legal individuals') property regimes.

In the context of Bangladesh, secured property rights are essential for increasing the demand for improvements of land and the supply of credit through the use of land as collateral. Better enforcement of property rights leads to greater long-term investments in productive and land conserving technologies and short-term investments in inputs leading to sustainable agricultural production. In practice, land tenure system is complex in Bangladesh, which originated with the British colonial land policies that overlaid the established patterns of land distribution.

The literature on land reforms is shrouded with significant controversies across different regions. While there are arguments (e.g. Griffin et al. 2002) that redistributive land reform is necessary to accelerate agrarian growth in developing countries, some studies (e.g. Faruqee and Carey 1997; World Bank 2000) maintain that the focus of reforms should be on improving property rights in agriculture and strengthening institutions

how long, and under what conditions. See FAO Corporate Document Repository: http://www.fao.org/DOCREP/005/Y4307E/y4307e05.htm.

that reduce transaction costs to allow the market to work for re-allocating land to more efficient users. In Bangladesh, the case for land reforms since the early days has rested on the comprehensive nature of such reforms that has the ability to improve not only asset distribution but also growth and efficiency. Some researchers argue that the issues of land transactions and productivity in Bangladesh require political economy approaches for understanding the dynamism and constraints facing agrarian transitions which cannot be easily accommodated within purely economic models of markets (see, e.g. Khan 2004).

The historical evolution of land tenure and property rights in Bangladesh shows that previously accepted concepts of property have changed with emerging conditions and passage of time. During the ancient periods, communities treated land and other natural resources mostly as a communal resource held in joint ownership. Under feudalism, status in the community was directly related to the rights a person held in land. Even though the distribution of rights has changed considerably over generations, understanding the history is important because it provides the basis for the present concept of property rights in Bangladesh.

8.4.1 *Land and Tenancy Reforms in Bangladesh*

After independence in 1971, the government promulgated a regulation in 1972 under which the ceiling to landholding was brought down to 13.4 hectares per family. This was relaxed in cases of cooperative farming and organised plantation. The *khas* (government) land was to be distributed among landless peasants and marginal farmers having not more than 0.61 hectare of land. The landless were to be especially encouraged to form cooperatives for settlement on large blocks of *khas* land. It was also decided that the recovered and accreted *char lands* by the rivers would not go back to original claimants, if there were any; rather, they would be vested with the government, who would settle them among poor landless peasants. The government, in addition, declared exemption from payment of the land revenue for agricultural households owning less than 3.3 hectares of land.

These measures, however, were not fully and effectively implemented. Very little could be acquired through the reduction of land ceilings. The landowners with excess land were very few in number and could find enough loopholes in land laws to help them hold on to their lands. Moreover, there were no concerted efforts to distribute the government land among the landless and marginal farmers. In addition, with more than 5 million households in the category of landless and marginal peasants, and the government having only about 182,000 hectares of land for distribution, it could not have created much impact, even if these were effectively distributed.

Under the 1984 Land Reforms Ordinance, the ceiling to ownership of agricultural land was reduced to 8 hectares for a family. It was maintained that a *bargadar* could cultivate up to 2 hectares of land and his/her contract for cultivation of *barga* land would remain valid for five years with provision for renewal. Further, it was stipulated that the owner and *bargadar* would each get one-third of the produce of the *barga* land. The remaining one-third was to be received by the owner or *bargadar* or both in proportion to the share of other cultivation costs borne by them. This shows that the land reforms in 1984 had in view both ceiling of land holdings and protection of rights of sharecroppers. However, as in the past, the provisions of the law were not fully implemented and agrarian relations changed significantly afterwards bringing in new complexities and challenges. These changes, however, led to the emergence of new tenure relationships in Bangladesh agriculture (see, Alamgir 1975; Abdullah 1976; Jannuzi and Peach 1977) (Table 8.1).

8.4.1.1 Existing Pattern of Land Tenure and Land Distribution

Under the existing system, farmers can be classified into four groups according to tenure arrangements:

1. Farmers cultivating own lands by themselves. They do not rent in or rent out any land (owner farmer).
2. Farmers cultivating own lands and renting out part of their lands (owner-cum-tenant farmer).
3. Farmers cultivating own lands and rented-in lands (owner-cum-tenant farmer).
4. Farmers cultivating lands of others either on sharecropping or cash annual/long-term rental contracts (tenant farmer).

As per the available statistics, 58 per cent of the land is operated by owners (i.e. who do not rent out any land), 40 per cent by owner-tenants, and only 2 per cent by pure tenants (APO 2000). About one-fifth of total operated area is under some kind of tenancy arrangements with sharecropping covering about one-half of the land. In Bangladesh, sharecropping is

Table 8.1 Major provisions of land related policies and acts in Bangladesh

Policy/Act	*Major provisions*
Transfer of Property Act 1882 and Registration Act 1908	Procedures for titling and registration of land ownership and updating of land records.
East Pakistan State Acquisition and Tenancy Act 1950	A 33-acre land ceiling on private landowners; excess taken over by the government on payment of compensation; surplus land to be transferred to landless; prohibition of use of agricultural land for other purposes without permission; permission required by indigenous community (except in CHT) to hand over their land to other communities; updating of land records according to hand over deed or land transfer deed; inheritance of land ownership following personal law.
Bangladesh Constitution 1972	All citizens shall have the right to hold, acquire, transfer and dispose of property.
Land Reforms Ordinance 1984	A 20-acre ceiling on holding of agricultural land and invalidation of *benami* transactions to evade land ceiling; greater tenure security to sharecroppers (*bargadars*) in sharecropping contracts with landowners; anti-eviction provision for agricultural households occupying farmlands.
National Land Use Policy 2001	Reduce high rate of conversion of agricultural land to non-agricultural uses; utilise agro-ecological zones to achieve maximum land use efficiency; discourage conversion of agricultural land for urban or development purposes; improve environmental sustainability of land use practices.

Source: Adapted from Uddin and Haque (2009)

the dominant form of tenancy arrangement but gradually other forms are becoming more prominent. In the case of large farms, sharecropping was lowest in 1997 and other forms of tenancy accounted for nearly as much area as in sharecropping. On the other hand, land tenure forms in Bangladesh may take several forms (Table 8.2). The changes in tenancy and related statistics since the 1980s can be seen in Table 8.3.

The concentration of landless or near landless peasants was nearly 17 per cent in 1951 and since then it has shown a continuous upward trend. According to the 1983–1984 Agriculture Census, the incidence of landlessness reached 56.5 per cent of rural households in 1983–1984. Of the landless, 8.7 per cent had ownership of no land, 19.6 per cent had

Table 8.2 Land tenure forms in Bangladesh

Tenure Form	*Major Characteristics*
Common law freehold	Exclusive ownership of land for an indefinite period, estimated to cover nearly 70 percent of agricultural lands.
Government land	Khas land and water bodies owned/managed by the Ministry of Land, waqf or trustee land under control of different ministries, forest land of the Ministry of Forests and Environment and land owned by railways and other ministries. The relevant ministries have their own Estate Officer to manage the land.
Khas land	Surplus land above landownership ceiling, land historically owned by the state, alluvial land, land without owner, auctioned land and similar other lands which could be distributed to landless families by the Ministry of Land.
Waqf land	Land held by the state and administered by the Department of Waqf for religious purposes. Usually personal property is endowed in waqf for religious, educational, or other benevolent purposes under specific terms and conditions under irrevocable legal contract.
Debottar land	Dedicated land and/or property for religious or charitable purposes by Hindu landowners usually by will or gift.
Leaseholder	The right to use land for a fixed period which is owned by another person.
Leases	Cash/temporary leases range from one to ten years for public or private land. Permanent lease covers a period of 99 years.

Source: Adapted from KIT (2012)

homestead land only, and another 28.2 per cent had at most 0.2 hectare of land in addition to homestead land. This shows that land reforms that emphasise on tenurial arrangements can hardly resolve the problem of access to land of these large groups of rural households. Meanwhile, tenurial arrangements are also undergoing significant changes.

In 1951, about 41 per cent of the land holding population were owner-cultivators, 47 per cent were owner-cum-tenants while the rest 12 per cent were pure tenants. Similar shares were reported as 65 per cent, 28 per cent and 7 per cent respectively in 1978. These trends continued in later years and the shares became 61 per cent for owners, 38 per cent for owner-cum-tenants and about 1 per cent for tenant farmers in 2008 (BBS 2014). The above shows that the share of owner farmers has significantly increased while the shares of both owner-cum-tenant and tenant farmers have declined over time. This has set in a process of transforming marginal

Table 8.3 Changes in tenancy and related indicators in Bangladesh agriculture

	1983–84	*1996*	*2008*
No. of all holdings, million	13.82	17.83	25.35
% of farm holdings	72.70	66.18	58.66
% of non-farm holdings	27.30	33.82	41.34
% of farm holdings			
Small farms (0.05–2.49 acres)	70.34	79.87	84.27
Medium farms (2.50–7.49 acres)	24.72	17.61	14.19
Large farms (7.50 acres and above)	4.94	2.52	1.54
% holdings owning no land	8.67	10.18	9.58
% of holdings			
Male-headed	…	96.52	95.67
Female-headed	…	3.48	4.33
Operated area			
All holdings, million acre	23.02	20.48	22.94
Per holding, acre	1.67	1.15	0.91
All farm holdings, million acre	22.68	19.96	21.95
Per farm holding, acre	2.26	1.69	1.48
Owned area of all holdings, million acre	22.60	20.33	21.99
Net cultivated area, million acre	20.16	17.77	18.26
No. of agriculture labour holdings, million	5.50	6.40	7.03
% of total holdings	39.77	35.91	28.64
% of holdings owning no land	8.67	10.18	10.65
No. of total farm holdings, million	10.05	11.80	14.87
Owner, % of total number	62.78	61.66	66.21
Owner-cum-tenant, % of total number	35.83	34.86	24.21
Tenants, % of total number	1.39	3.48	9.58
Total operated area of farm holdings, million acre	22.67	19.96	23.62
Owner, % of total area	58.76	58.51	55.97
Owner-cum-tenant, % of total area	40.69	39.59	41.93
Tenants, % of total area	0.55	1.90	2.10

Source: BBS, Agricultural Census, 2008

farmers (who used to rent-in land for cultivation from surplus landowners) into agricultural labourers in rural society.

The distribution of size of holdings has also undergone significant changes. The average size of holding which was around 3.6 acres in the early 1940s reduced to 3.0 acres in 1960. Afterwards, it declined at faster rates to 1.7 acres in 1983–1984 and further to 0.9 acre in 2008 (BBS 2014). In 2008, the number of holdings in rural areas of Bangladesh is estimated at 25.4 million, out of which 14.9 million are treated as farm households.[3] Farm households in Bangladesh are divided into three major categories in terms of their size of holdings: small (0.05 to 2.49 acres), medium (2.50 to 7.49 acres) and large (7.50 acres and above). According to Agricultural Census data, out of a total number of 10.1 million farm holdings in 1983–1984, small farmers constituted 70 per cent followed by 25 per cent for medium farmers and 5 per cent for large farmers. In 2008, the share of small farmers rose to 84 per cent and the shares of medium and large farmers declined to 14 per cent and less than 2 per cent respectively.[4]

The share of farm area under different farm sizes also changed along with changes in relative shares in numbers. The area under small farms went up from 16 per cent in 1960 to 29 per cent in 1983–1984 and further to nearly 50 per cent in 2008. On the other hand, area under large farms decreased from 38 per cent in 1960 to 26 percent in 1983–1984 and to 12 per cent in 2008. The share of medium farms changed very little. Medium farms accounted for about 45 per cent of the total cultivated area in 1983–1984 compared with 46 per cent in 1960. More importantly, the average size of farms in each of the three categories declined. For large and medium farms the shift is negligible, but for small farms it declined from about 0.45 hectare in 1960 to 0.38 hectare in 1983–1984, and further to 0.33 hectare in 2008.

The above changes point out to two important implications of agrarian changes in Bangladesh. First, Bangladesh agriculture is overwhelmingly dominated by small farmers. Second, the majority of the small farms are too small to generate enough returns to support even the subsistence needs of an average farm household. Disaggregated data show that about a quarter of the small farms are below 0.20 hectare and another 16 per cent are between 0.20 and 0.40 hectare. It is seen that farms below 0.60 hectare constitute nearly 54 per cent of the total number of farms but they account for only 15 per cent of total farm area. In addition, extreme disparity in land use is observed at the lowest size holdings which are below 0.60 hectare. Under this category, 25 per cent of the farms operate only 2.7 per cent of the cultivated area. At the other extreme, 0.17 per

[3] In Bangladesh, holdings having land of less than 0.05 acre are considered as non-farm households and the total number of such non-farm households is estimated at 10.5 million in 2008 in rural Bangladesh.

[4] In 1960, small farms represented about 52 per cent of total farms while medium and large farms constituted 38 per cent and 10 per cent respectively.

cent of the farms covering about 2.70 per cent of farm area are in the size category of 10 hectares and above. In addition, another 0.69 per cent in the 6–10 hectare farm size group operates only 5.47 per cent of the area under cultivation. All these figures indicate that land use pattern in Bangladesh is extremely unequal and on-going changes in the agrarian structure are making the pattern more unequal over time. At the same time, it should also be noted that large farms (defined as having about 3 hectares of land) in Bangladesh are not really large even by standards of major South Asian countries.

8.4.2 *Contract Farming: Implications for Small Farmers*

As the Bangladesh economy is changing fast, the organisation of agriculture and agricultural marketing practices along the supply chains are also undergoing rapid transformation. Enterprises dealing with agriculture and related outputs are introducing technology-driven and modern procurement and supply chain management practices to gain control over markets and improve efficiency of the value chains. Food processors and manufacturers, modern retailers, food service industry, and other participants in food supply chains presently face greater competition in the changing food markets in Bangladesh which now also have greater linkages with the global food industry. On the other hand, in view of the relatively high costs and technical and other requirements of accessing the modern market channels, small and land-poor farmers in Bangladesh face significant disadvantages and find it difficult to benefit from these changes.

One practice which is gaining rapidly rising applicability in Bangladesh agriculture is the use of contract farming for different crops and other non-crop agricultural outputs. The issue has also raised interests of policy makers in view of its potential as an institutional mechanism for including poor and small farmers in modern market channels. The interest in contract farming has also grown in other regions of the world especially with respect to its economic and social impact on smallholder farmers (see, for example, Smalley 2013; Barrett et al. 2012; Bellemare 2012; Miyata et al. 2009).

Contract farming involves agricultural production carried out under agreements between the buyers and farmers. In certain cases, the buyers may specify the quality of the produce and the price, with the farmers agreeing to deliver at future dates. The contracts may also outline the conditions for production of the farm products and the contract farmers agrees to supply pre-specified quantities of the crop based on quality standards and delivery requirements (FAO 2008). The buyer, often a company, may also agree to support the farmers through supplying inputs, assisting in land preparation, and providing production advice and post-harvest facilities.

Contract farming offers several potential advantages over independent farming. This refers to a situation under which private farms take over many of the responsibilities previously assumed by the state in the provision of information, inputs and credit (World Bank 2001a, b). There are several reasons for increased interest in contract farming in Bangladesh agriculture. Changes in farm size, risk-transfer mechanisms, agricultural technology inflows and rural labour markets are affected by factor- and product-market contracts which are not independent of one another. Structural changes that are occurring in agriculture (particularly food sector) in Bangladesh including rural-urban migration result in changes in the nature of food chains. Rapid urbanisation also increases the demand for transport, storage, processing and wholesale and retail distribution of food products. Migration also results in changes in the types of food that are demanded, in particular within a scenario when household incomes are rising steadily in the country.

In Bangladesh, contract farming has expanded rapidly in recent years due to several changes in the agriculture sector. With liberalisation of the agriculture sector since the 1990s, markets for private provisioning of agricultural inputs and services have expanded which has also increased the uncertainties that emanate from private supply channels. In many cases, contract farming has grown as a response to reduce the problems of accessing quality farm inputs by the farmers from the market, especially the small farmers who normally face difficulties in purchasing relatively small quantities of farm inputs required by them for cultivating small land areas. Under contract farming, the farmers can overcome many of these problems if the buyers supply the inputs under the terms of the contract.

Another important contributor to rapid growth in contract farming is the recent spectacular rise of supermarkets in food retailing in the country. Over the last decade, the number of supermarkets have increased rapidly especially in the urban areas. Supermarkets have procurement practices that favour centralised purchasing, specialised and dedicated wholesalers, preferred supplier systems and private quality standards (Shepherd 2005). These characteristics require more vertical coordination among the producers, wholesalers, and retailers which favour the growth of contract farming. In addition, the emergence of organised retailing using supermarkets has introduced a structural change in Bangladesh's retail market system under which the targets are the middle- and upper-income consumers through various store formats and own-store brands.

The government, NGOs, and other organisations have also played important roles in promoting contract farming as one of the instruments to strengthen access of small farmers to markets and link them to national and global markets. In particular, as contract farming arrangements often include provision of inputs and technical assistance, marginal and small farmers can benefit from these new market opportunities otherwise not available to them.[5]

Since there exist significant diversities across farmers and their socio-economic environments, several variant of contract farming models have evolved in Bangladesh.[6] Probably, the most common one is the centralised model under which the company (buyer) provides support to farmers (e.g. credit and inputs), purchases the produce and processes it, closely controlling the quality. The model is widely used for farm products, such as spices, vegetables, tobacco and other crops. At a lower level of sophistication, there exist intermediary models which involve subcontracting by companies to intermediaries who have their own (informal) arrangements with farmers. There are also examples of involvement of small and medium enterprises (SMEs) who enter into simple contracts with farmers on a seasonal basis, which may be repeated annually. These models mostly rely on the proximity of buyers and sellers for their success.

In response to ongoing market developments, prospects for further developing the contract farming practices for different agricultural products are wide. Such developments can bring significant benefits to the

[5] One study on contract poultry farming system in Bangladesh shows that (1) it is dominated by smallholders, (2) it provides a way of overcoming market imperfections, minimising transaction costs and gaining market access for smallholders; (3) it has benefits including access to credit and technology, better risk management and enhanced employment opportunities; and (4) it increases productivity, profitability and efficiency. See Begum et al. (2013).

[6] In broad terms, three types of contract between farmers and buyers may be distinguished: (1) market-specification (pre-harvest agreement on conditions governing the sale of crops/animals), (2) production management (farmers to follow precise production methods and input regimes in return for taking market risks by buyers), and (3) resource-providing (along with market outlet for produce, also provides key inputs which amounts to giving credit in kind for recovery upon product delivery) contracts. The contracts differ in objectives, in transfer of decision rights (from farmers to buyers), and in risk transfer. See Mighell and Jones (1963).

small farmers since food supply chains in Bangladesh are primarily fragmented. A practical approach which has traditionally been adopted by the market agents at each level of the supply chain is to establish alliances based on mutual trust with their immediate upstream and downstream chain partners in order to overcome the associated problems. But this has been an incomplete and imperfect solution which can be remedied by the adoption of appropriate models of contract farming.

The advantages of even the traditional attempts at developing contract farming models have encouraged the entry of corporate groups, multinational firms and other organisations into the agricultural sector in Bangladesh looking for different forms of vertical coordination modalities in their chains of interest. As a result, the agricultural sector has seen the emergence of integrated supply chains for several product lines. This has eased traceability and has helped to build up a competitive edge in the market, through product development and diversification as well as improved market penetration. There has also been some encouraging change on the export front which can be attributed, at least partly, to the World Trade Organization (WTO) agreement that has opened up global markets and brought about shifts in global food consumption patterns towards high value crops. Both these factors have created significant opportunities for Bangladesh agriculture to venture into new production lines. In practice, the models of integration have, however, varied across companies.

One group is the Programme for Rural Advancement Nationally (PRAN) which started its operation in 1980. Over time, PRAN has emerged as the largest processors of fruits, spices and vegetables in Bangladesh. Through using innovative contract farming models, PRAN procures raw materials directly from the farmers and processes through high-tech machinery in its factories into hygienically packed food and drink products. PRAN is now the country's largest contract manufacturer and promotes contract farmers through providing required assistance to produce quality crops with increased yields and obtain fair prices.

On the other hand, contract farming, as an institutional arrangement to facilitate market access for small farmers in high-value supply chains, has long been used as a means to strengthen supply chains in the livestock and poultry sector in Bangladesh. Contract arrangements are now widely used in the poultry sector having different types of contract arrangement, for example production–marketing contracts (agreement within a vertically integrated enterprise for supply of inputs and services, disposal of outputs, and sharing of risks and benefits), input-marketing contracts (contracts for supply of one or more inputs and services, generally to market agents who directly deal with producers), and output-marketing contracts (e.g. forward-purchase contracts in which buyers purchase outputs from producers).

Likewise, ACI Agribusiness implements a sustainable contract farming model that engages low-income farmers as producers and ensures a sustainable supply of high-quality, affordable crops for ACI. The business model involves three stakeholders—ACI, low income farmers, and an NGO facilitating low income agriculture initiatives with smallholders; and adopts a profit-sharing contract farming scheme. Similarly, a number of enterprises operate under different contract types in the poultry sector e.g. Aftab Bahumukhi Farms Limited (ABFL) established in 1992, Biman Poultry Complex (BPC) established in 1997, and BRAC which started its broiler farming contracts in 2002 (see Jabbar et al. 2007).

Contract farming practices have also expanded to seed production for different crops (including hybrid varieties of rice and maize) under public, private and NGO initiatives. Available evidence shows that with provision of required technical and financial support, contract growers could emerge as a sustainable source of supply of good quality seeds for the country's crop sector (Haque et al. 2012; Pingali and Pandey 2000). However, in the context of promoting contract farming in Bangladesh, it is important for the relevant companies to recognise that for availing potential export opportunities they need to adhere to the stringent quality parameters and standards related to good agricultural practices (Global GAP), good manufacturing practices (GMP), protocols developed by the British Retail Consortium or fair trade norms for exports, particularly to the European Union (EU) destinations.

It is also important to recognise that, in dealing with the corporate buyers, small farmers have their challenges since they may not understand the intricacies of emerging markets. They may lack capital for investments and other capacities required to build networks for developing linkages with export markets or organised retailers in the domestic markets, and they may not understand the need to change varieties and production practices in order to adapt to changing preferences of consumers. The availability of assured markets through contract farming for the disposal of specific crops provides them with an incentive to introduce shifts in cropping patterns towards high value crops.

In an era of marketing liberalisation and globalisation, one major concern in Bangladesh agriculture is how to integrate small farmers and entrepreneurs into modern markets as well as the global market economy. Contract farming in agriculture has been an important step to help small-scale producers gain access to resources and improve productivity and competitiveness in many countries including Bangladesh. To facilitate more effective and sustainable development of contract farming in Bangladesh, it is critical to pay attention to several areas.

First, more communication and mutual understanding are required between the farmers and buyers so that trusted relationships and long-term cooperation can be achieved. In Bangladesh agriculture, buyers are the leaders of the chain and farmers are in the weakest position. Better communication and trusted relationships would enable the farmers to obtain more information and resolve the problems emerging from existing power and information asymmetry. This will also improve the bargaining power of the farmers.

Second, there is a need to strengthen the farmer organisations. The major obstacles of keeping small farmers from contracting with buyers are unreliable supply, unstable quality and the difficulty of tracing when quality and safety problems arise. It is therefore important that small-scale farmers be better organised into cooperatives and farmer organisations that can help them to overcome individual problems and serve their collective interests. These organisations as wells as NGOs working for the benefit of small farmers can also take the lead and negotiate with the buyers on behalf of the small farmers.

Third, a better functioning macroeconomic policy environment is needed to promote healthy development of contract farming. The government has significantly changed its macroeconomic policy framework to remove anti-agriculture bias along with increased flows of trade, capital, technology and information. This has created a more conducive environment to fostering agricultural growth. However, government policies towards small farmers need further strengthening along with a longer-term view and employing sustainable policy tools, such as improving the micro and crop insurance system to protect the poor farmers during natural disasters and other factors causing crop losses. In addition, enforceability of legal frameworks should be strengthened to improve regulatory effectiveness and efficiency in favour of contract farming.

8.4.3 Policy Implications

Land is an extremely limited resource in Bangladesh; as such, its distribution and tenure structure are important determinants of land productivity and agricultural production in the country. The country's land distribution is highly unequal; about 52 per cent of the rural population are either landless or holds less than 0.5 acre of land. Ownership of land shows that 89 per cent of the landowners have less than 2.5 acre, 10 per cent own between 2.5 and 7.5 acre while only 1 per cent own more than 7.5 acre. Such inequalities in land distribution have been persisting despite implementation of a series of land reforms since the 1950s under which landownership ceilings were imposed, tenancy reforms were implemented, and public lands were distributed to the landless.

Land tenure systems affect agricultural production and productivity through a number of channels including efficiency in input use and adoption of modern technologies. Over the last decades, Bangladesh agriculture has undergone significant changes both in production level and production structure despite shrinking availability of land for crop production. As a result, average farm size has declined from 0.81 ha in 1996 to 0.49 ha in 2005 along with increasing fragmentation and subdivision of holdings.

While there are controversies regarding relative efficiencies of alternative tenure systems, one may argue that household farming or owner cultivation probably represents the optimal organisation of production in the context of Bangladesh. In contrast, tenant farming creates inefficiencies largely because of adverse consequences of tenure insecurity on long-term investments in farming and disincentive effects of output sharing arrangements on work efforts.

In Bangladesh, more than 60 per cent of the rural households are land-poor (having less than 1.5 acre of land) including the landless people. In addition to working in the non-farm rural sector, these people work as seasonal labourers and lease-in lands belonging to others. As a result, a range of tenancy arrangements, including sharecropping and term leases, have emerged offering the land-poor farmers a better access to land. Thus, while strengthening legislation is a necessary first step for ensuring access to land by the poor, policies and interventions should also recognise the complexities of the existing patterns of property rights which reduce the poor's security of tenure.

For land resources, secure ownership rights (including transfer rights) facilitate more efficient and equitable transactions of land rights through land rental and land sales markets and induce more investments in land improvement. The development of efficient land markets helps the poor farmers cope with increasing risks and uncertainties (including climate risks) through providing a coping response opportunity. This shows that strengthening the land rights of small farmers, particularly transfer rights, is a positive step towards providing a better exit option for those who want to leave farm-based livelihoods. Proper development of the rural land market can thus reduce transaction costs and enhance more efficient rural transformation. We must recognise that increasing landlessness is an inevitable consequence in a land-scarce country like Bangladesh, and the creation of alternative livelihood opportunities outside the farm sector is an integral component of the country's pro-poor development strategy. One must, however, recognise that the development of an efficient rural land market was never treated as an explicit objective of past land reforms in Bangladesh; and hence, the land market still remains in a stage which is probably in the most rudimentary stage across all markets in the country.

In order to be effective, land market operations and tenure laws should generally be responsive to local contexts and local demands. Moreover, pro-poor policies in this respect should emphasise the needs and rights of the poor in land laws and policy formulation. Currently, Bangladesh is undergoing rapid social transformation, driven by structural changes and social dynamics leading to accelerating rural–urban migration and the huge challenge of providing alternative livelihood opportunities, especially for the vast majority of the rural youth, who prefer not to continue with agricultural livelihoods of their parents. These youth are the key to future success of Bangladesh's development; hence land market and related policies in the rural areas must recognise these changing aspirations of the rural population explicitly in the policy contents.

There also exists evidence that capital market imperfections have important implications in determining the structure of rural land market (Ray 1998). One empirical evidence on the existence of these imperfections is the persistence of large landholdings (although declining in importance) despite the well-documented negative land size–productivity relationship in Bangladesh. The argument is also supported by the fact that the most land sales in the country are 'distress sale' in nature that inhibits the development of an efficient land market. These and other factors favour the potential buyers to undervalue the land, rendering the land market thin and less efficient.

One important lesson that emerges from experiences of different countries is the need to understand the details of responses to land reforms and changes in the land market and the way these responses create both gainers and losers. This requires a framework with a sufficiently long time horizon such that the full effects of reforms are visible. Moreover, one should also avoid the hazards of piecemeal reforms considering the land market alone in this second-best world keeping other important and related markets unchanged. For example, if tenancy persists partly due to a lack of credit market opportunities to become an owner-farmer, then increasing only the power of tenants may result in some tenants being forced to become landless labourers. The complexity of these general equilibrium and macro effects should be recognised; and the short-term political imperatives providing the impetus for reforms needs to be combined with the long-term economic impacts to draw policy guidelines for the rural land market which matters for future development of the Bangladesh economy.

8.5 Institutions and Quality of Governance

In Bangladesh, as elsewhere in the developing world, development is inextricably related to governance; unless the local and national governments perform their assigned tasks in a reasonably efficient manner, progress in development will be slow. It is widely acknowledged that development will occur only if a country has good institutions in place, and many of these institutions are either political or are political by extension. The establishment of effective property rights, for example, depends upon a structure of law and law enforcement; it does exist independently of government. Similarly, the development of a strong civil society is virtually impossible without the development of strong formal institutions of government.

An effective governance structure must be in place as a foundation for implementing the development policies. For example, leadership that is accountable and possesses a clear idea of development objectives is essential. In order to achieve these objectives while avoiding adverse trade-offs, policies are needed to be integrated into the governance structures and underlying institutions. Policy coherence and coordination are important aspects of development policies, especially when operating within a resource-constrained environment as in Bangladesh. Information and communications technologies (ICT) have become an important enabling factor for ensuring coordination and oversight.

Effective policy implementation and delivery of services require decentralisation, which can ensure proper provision to the differentiated segments of the population including the poor. Proper implementation of decentralisation requires that good governance structures are in place in order to ensure that local units can best target and serve those in need while operating responsively to both local populations and to the central government.

Globally, the lessons about the quality of governance and institutions suggest that effective, accountable and inclusive institutions at all levels are necessary to pursue sustainable development. In particular, the role of good governance and effective institutions is pivotal for: (1) ensuring a more adequate delivery of basic public services critical for making progress in development; (2) creating effective, responsive and responsible political leadership, with long-term strategic vision for development, needed for galvanising political will, transforming vision into national strategies, mobilising scarce resources, creating broad partnerships, coordinating actions, and motivating and ensuring accountability for the results; (3) ensuring effective coordination of policies and strategies at the national level and their coherent implementation at national, subnational and local levels, crucial for the integration of economic, social and environmental policies; (4) creating technical capacities at national and subnational levels—both for public financial management and the delivery of basic public services—by decentralising the delivery of public services through effective administrative and fiscal decentralisation; and (5) developing broad and multi-stakeholder partnerships at the national and local levels for robust engagement of NGOs, CSOs, the private sector, and other organisations (UN 2016). These efforts enhance the voice and participation of citizens, improve service delivery, enhance coordination and ensure better development outcomes.

In practice, the parameters of good governance may be categorised primarily into two types: (1) institutional such as independent election commission, effective parliament, efficient bureaucracy, independent judiciary, strong and autonomous local government, freedom of press and media, strong and vigorous civil society, independent and effective anti-corruption agencies; and (2) non-institutional which cover, for example, legitimacy of the political system, mass participation in the polity, dynamic and efficient leadership, responsiveness of government, accountability and transparency of government, efficient administrative system, respect for the rule of law, decentralisation, equitable distribution of the state's wealth and resources, respect for human rights, women empowerment, sound education system and combating corruption.

8.5.1 State of Governance in Bangladesh

The Bangladesh constitution provides the basic elements essential for good governance, although the country is yet to fully develop the right policies, institutions, capacity and practices of good governance. Democratic governance is also one of the missing elements that can safeguard the constitutional rights and interests of the common citizens and ensure better performance of the state institutions.

Further, proper accountability has not yet been fully institutionalised; and inadequate institutional capacity impedes development and the democratic process. The weak performance of state institutions fail to properly reform the state structures, make credible policy decisions, create an enabling environment, and provide leadership at different levels of government. The absence of effective accountability and transparency results in widespread corrupt practices. All these maladies, in a large number of instances, thwart justice and fairness, restrict outreach and quality of public service delivery and inhibit vibrancy of market forces. The Independent watchdog institutions such as the human rights commission and anti-corruption commission are also yet to be fully effective and institutionalised. As a result, there are missing links in the chain of accountability between the public, the legislature, the judiciary and the executive.

The World Bank's Worldwide Governance Indicator (WGI) provides aggregate and individual governance indicators for six dimensions of governance: voice and accountability; political stability and absence of violence; government effectiveness; regulatory quality; rule of law; and control of corruption (Kaufmann et al. 2010). These aggregate indicators combine the views of a large number of enterprise, citizen and survey respondents produced by a variety of survey institutes, think tanks, NGOs, international organisations, and private sector firms.

Voice and accountability: reflects perceptions of the extent to which a country's citizens are able to participate in selecting their government, as well as freedom of expression, freedom of association, and a free media.

Government effectiveness: reflects perceptions of the quality of public services, the quality of the civil service and the degree of its independence from political pressures, the quality of policy formulation and implementation, and the credibility of the government's commitment to such policies.

Control of corruption: reflects perceptions of the extent to which public power is exercised for private gain, including both petty and grand forms of corruption, as well as 'capture' of the state by elites and private interests.

Rule of law: reflects perceptions of the extent to which agents have confidence in and abide by the rules of society, and in particular the quality of contract enforcement, property rights, the police, and the courts, as well as the likelihood of crime and violence.

Regulatory quality: reflects perceptions of the ability of the government to formulate and implement sound policies and regulations that permit and promote private sector development.

Political stability and absence of violence/terrorism: measures perceptions of the likelihood of political instability and/or politically motivated violence, including terrorism.

In general, the figures in Table 8.4 show that the country has improved its internal efficiency and systems, but strategies must be strengthened to improve public perception on rule of law and the quality of governance.

For ensuring sustainable development, economic governance is of particular importance which consists of the processes that support and facilitate economic activities and economic transactions by securing property rights and enforcing contracts. It is also about taking and implementing collective action to provide the required level of physical and

Table 8.4 Bangladesh performance in worldwide governance indicators

Aggregate indicator	*1996*	*2000*	*2005*	*2010*	*2014*
Voice and accountability	47.6	40.9	29.3	37.4	32.5
Political stability and absence of Violence/terrorism	25.0	23.6	4.3	9.9	18.0
Government effectiveness	24.4	32.2	21.5	25.8	21.6
Regulatory quality	16.7	18.6	16.7	22.5	16.3
Rule of law	18.7	20.1	18.2	25.0	26.0
Control of corruption	27.3	15.6	4.9	14.8	16.8

Source: World Bank, Worldwide Governance Indicators, Country Data Report for Bangladesh, 1996–2014

Note: The numbers show Bangladesh's percentile rank on each of the six governance indicators. Percentile ranks indicate the percentage of countries worldwide that rank lower than Bangladesh, so that higher values indicate better governance scores

organisational infrastructure, so that private economic agents do not suffer from the under-provision of public goods.

Hence, it is concerned with the effectiveness of the government in delivering public services and related to the competence and the capacity of the public sector agencies to meet their mandates in development. The focus on the capacity of the state to deliver is important for Bangladesh along with other virtues such as the manner in which the authority is exercised and whether transparency and accountability is ensured within the operation of the public sector entities. The capacity of the state is critical for Bangladesh since there are examples of countries which have performed poorly in traditional good governance mandates (e.g. China, Vietnam) but have achieved impressive records in growth and development.

The governance discourse in Bangladesh should, therefore, highlight the importance of the state's capacity to deliver effectively the services that matter for efficient economic transactions across the economy. Along with institutions of accountability, the focus needs to be on institutions that deploy power, and it is important to formulate measures that can monitor the effectiveness of such power deploying institutions (Fukuyama 2013). Such power deploying institutions cover a wide range of government agencies such as the Bangladesh Bank, Bangladesh Power Development Board, Ministry of Finance, and other ministries and government institutions that are directly responsible for the level and quality of public goods available to society and their delivery.

The cross-cutting importance of governance in the overall development of Bangladesh suggests that it should be identified as the fourth pillar of priority along with effective measures to improve the quality of governance. The core governance system should be improved in areas such as public procurement, financial management, fiscal reporting, and watchdog institutions. The strategy should be to enhance accountability by strengthening 'core' governance institutions including the Comptroller and Auditor General, Public Accounts Committee, Bangladesh Bank, Public Service Commission, Securities and Exchange Commission and the courts. Efforts should be strengthened in supporting the public financial management reforms for introducing multi-year budgeting, strengthening financial management systems and improving auditing capacity. Greater support is needed to support union parishads, the lowest tier of elected local government in Bangladesh, in providing services that meet community priorities with focus on capacity building, particularly regarding financial management and procurement.

Efforts should also be initiated for giving citizens greater access to public documents, the Right to Information (RTI) Act was passed in 2009 in a bid to increase transparency and change the culture of government officials and their interaction with citizens. There should also be support for catalytic reforms including identifying the impact of governance issues in service delivery and improve the management of core public services. In the light of the low revenue base, strengthening domestic tax mobilisation is a priority objective as well as investments in the infrastructure sectors and private sector development efforts. These includes investments in health, education, sanitation, local government strengthening and safety net approaches, which are central to meeting the development goals and improving the quality and efficiency of social service provision to the poor.

8.6 Institutions for Middle-Income Bangladesh

The quality of the institutional framework and the degree of development of the financial system are two aspects that will explain how fast Bangladesh can move forward in future. Sound institutions, particularly a legal framework that can enforce contracts, support financial intermediation and reduce transactions costs, would contribute to economic growth, acting behind the classical determinants of growth (e.g. capital accumulation and technological innovations). Bangladesh also has significant gap in public budget to reduce poverty and achieve a more sustainable path to development. It is mostly related to poor revenue mobilisation and institutional problems. A middle income Bangladesh still faces considerable structural and institutional deficits and vulnerabilities that affect its development process.

Further, as a lower middle income country (MIC), Bangladesh continues to face significant development challenges. However, the nature of many these challenges varies substantially compared with the past. Bangladesh still has high level of poverty, with major concentrations in backward areas. On the policy front, Bangladesh has made great strides in reform, but the unfinished policy agenda is substantial. The country's institutional capacity to manage reform is limited. It has little access to international capital markets, and even with limited access, it must contend with volatility in private capital flows. Further, Bangladesh faces increased vulnerability to economic and financial openness as it exposes itself more to global flows of goods and capital. Without proper safeguards, the country runs the risk of being affected more by global crises.

Bangladesh needs to ensure that all banks (and non-bank financial institutions) are strong and healthy. It also needs to manage the pace of further liberalisation of the financial market and to balance it against the risk of interconnectivity of domestic financial market with global financial flows. As a lower MIC, Bangladesh also needs to implement a consistent macroeconomic policy framework with multiple instruments, including the traditional market based interest rate instruments and administrative measures, such as statutory reserves requirement, for absorbing the excess liquidity generated by the capital inflows (Anglingkusumo 2013).

One main challenge to growth and competitiveness for the lower middle income Bangladesh is industrialising while gaining in productivity. Traditionally, this is when a country in transition to industrial production experiences a sharp fall in the share of agriculture or primary production without experiencing a commensurate rise in secondary sector productivity. This is the central logic behind the 'middle-income trap' (Ohno 2011). The industrial upgrading is necessary, which tends to occur as a country enters the MIC stage, shifts the economy from labour-intensive to technology-intensive production, driving up wages and driving down competitiveness (World Bank 2012). The country becomes unable to properly mobilise technical skills to increase productivity for two major reasons. First, growth in industrial production is spurred in most cases by an influx of MSMEs which decrease overall productivity (Cervantes-Godoy and Brooks 2011). Second, the industrialising countries are often outpaced by regional powerhouses. China, for example, absorbs a large portion of cheap labour-intensive industry, creating a barrier to entry by its low wages and scale (Chandra et al. 2012), even though, in some cases, regional powerhouses pull up other neighbouring countries.

The challenge to competitiveness lies in establishing suitable institutions for industrial policy. At lower levels of industrialisation, gains in economic growth may be experienced by liberalising trade and safeguarding macroeconomic balances (Altenburg 2011). Less importance can be placed on institutions (e.g. in recent years, industrialisation in China and Vietnam has taken place in the absence of properly functioning institutions, see, Ohno 2009). However, institutions for industrial policy are important for Bangladesh for a number of reasons, such as for adjusting production across various sectors to identify what is profitable and feasible which requires support from the state; with expanding secondary sector production, Bangladesh will experience a lack of policy coordination among stakeholders in managing investment and growth agendas; and the government may not effectuate an efficient and equitable distribution of public inputs in the form of infrastructure, legislation, and research and development (Altenburg 2011).

The countries that have succeeded in putting in place the right industrial policy have also established effective institutions at the same time. For example, South Korea established 'insulated technocratic agencies' and strong private sector stakeholder dialogue along with economic liberalisation that contributed to gains in economic growth (Cheng et al. 1998). This suggests the importance of institutional alignment in tandem with economic liberalisation for the MICs (Altenburg 2011).

The ability of the state to effectively participate in coordinating economic activity presents another important challenge for Bangladesh. The MICs are especially prey to both falling into low equilibriums in sector productivity and being unable to mobilise investment and entrepreneurial enterprise (Rodriguez-Clare 2005). This is because MICs with a rising skilled labour force but insufficient capital endowments are not able to properly invest in and profit from modern sector production (Rodrik 1995). The state thus may have to play a central role in encouraging economic growth in Bangladesh. State intervention in some form is, therefore, desirable in negotiating market and coordination failures in Bangladesh. However, policies primarily aimed at correcting market failures should not be piece-meal, non-transparent and not well-coordinated. These should focus sufficiently on the accumulation of technological capabilities, which allows for broad-based structural change towards higher value added activities and is the driving force behind sustained productivity growth (Paus 2013).

Thus, Bangladesh needs to put in place the required institutions to address governance and institutional weaknesses, including prevalence of nepotism, corruption, crony and state capitalism. For example, South Korea ensured discipline that the state exercises over private firms using the model of 'Korea Inc.', implying better governance with focus on preventing rent-seeking opportunities (Amsden 1989). In this context, the new institutional economics (NIE) framework considers almost every aspect of institutional setting, including religion and culture. At the present stage, the key aspects for Bangladesh to focus are governance and institutional quality. These should be the institutions that can promote markets and ensure they function effectively by creating the right incentives to produce and by limiting transaction costs. This includes promoting competition, limiting rent-seeking activities, and enforcing property rights, creating incentives for the private sector to invest and trade, and fostering long-term efficiency and productivity. These institutional characteristics will help contribute to sustainable long-term growth needed to escape the middle income trap by Bangladesh.

Bangladesh can learn lessons from the experience of China which could generate impressive growth without high institutional quality (Kuncic 2014). In practice, Chinese growth has stemmed from a combination of government policies, state-led investments, structural change, including education and institutional reforms, such as significant market reforms. China's state-led growth and policies have indeed contributed to an increase in capital, labour, infrastructure, and high economic growth, helping the country to reach upper middle-income status. Institutions that enforce property rights, decrease corruption, increase incentives to produce, and limit transaction costs have a clear positive relationship to sustainable and long-term growth. While improving the level of governance and institutions is not easy, Bangladesh can benchmark its progress to those with experience and success in escaping the middle-income trap and ensure sustained high growth.

For Bangladesh, at its present level of development, institutions matter more for its future growth, indicating a significant shift from the 'Washington Consensus' which focuses mostly on sound policies: macroeconomic stabilisation, trade liberalisation, and privatisation. However, institutional quality takes a more central stage as the country develops covering diverse dimensions including aspects of physical infrastructure (telecoms, electricity, transport), access to skilled labour, stability of the macroeconomic environment, tax and customs administration, licensing, the legal system, labour regulation, and the impact of crime and corruption.

In the coming years, the policy focus towards getting institutions right has to be given more importance in Bangladesh. The process also needs to recognise that the pattern of change for economic institutions is different from the similar process for political institutions. Changes in economic institutions are fed more by global differences, and countries with weaker institutions experience greater institutional change.

Thus, economic institutions are more susceptible to change and more likely to converge than the political institutions. It is, therefore, more likely that political elites will undertake reforms in economic institutions, as such these changes may also directly benefit the ruling elites by increasing their rents and tax base, and possibly extending tenure (Andrews 2013; McGuire and Olson 1996). On the other hand, enhancing efficiency and improving political institutions is more path dependent, as it may not be in the interest of the political elites to change existing political institutions which are highly extractive. For economic institutions, it is therefore important to emphasise efforts to harmonise domestic institutions with global standards leading to institutional catch-up in the long run. In this respect, the emphasis should be on introducing context-specific reforms that consider domestic policy environment, social and economic contexts, and existing social norms.

8.7 Empowering Local Government Institutions

Fiscal decentralisation, as the public finance dimension of intergovernmental relations, specifically addresses the reform of the system of expenditure functions and revenue source transfers from the central to the local governments. Without appropriate fiscal empowerment, the autonomy of the local government institutions (LGIs) cannot be ensured and, hence, the full potential of decentralisation cannot be realised. Fiscal decentralisation is challenging for Bangladesh because it involves a wide number of dispersed actors across the central government and LGIs as well as agencies spread throughout the country. Decentralisation in Bangladesh involving a large number of actors also requires a carefully considered implementation strategy. More importantly, reforms are unlikely to be successful if implementation is driven by a fixed and comprehensive top-down blueprint approach decided by a few central actors who then rapidly impose it across the system.

For ensuring effective LGIs in the context of Bangladesh, three basic principles are important in performing their responsibilities:

- **Responsive governance:** The LGIs need to perform the right activities that is, to deliver services consistent with citizen preferences.
- **Responsible governance:** The LGIs should perform their responsibilities in the right way that is, manage their fiscal resources prudently. They should earn the trust of the residents by working better and costing less and by managing fiscal and social risks for the communities. They should strive to improve the quality and quantity of and access to public services.
- **Accountable governance:** The LGIs need to be accountable to their electorate. They should adhere to appropriate safeguards to ensure that they serve the public interest with integrity. Legal and institutional reforms may be needed to enable LGIs to deal effectively with accountability.

Despite the long history of local governance since the British colonial rule and post-independence decentralisation efforts, the LGIs in Bangladesh still play a limited role in delivering essential and mandated quality services to the citizens mainly due to inadequate decision making and financial authority; lack of resources and staff; and weak capacity. A key to Bangladesh's transition to an upper middle income country (UMIC) is to empower the country's LGIs through administrative and fiscal decentralisation, Further, the LGIs suffer from weak pubic financial management practices which hinder their service delivery capabilities.

Although the total spending of the LGIs in Bangladesh as a share of GDP increased from 0.67 per cent in 2001 to 1.1 per cent in 2013, it remains nearly five times lower than the developing country's average. In Bangladesh, spending by LGIs accounts for 7 per cent of total government expenditure, whereas on average it is 19 per cent in developing countries and 28 per cent in developed countries. The relatively low share of LGIs' spending in government's total expenditure indicates limited fiscal decentralisation in Bangladesh.

The LGIs are highly viable vehicles through which democratic processes and practices can be established and participatory development ensured in Bangladesh. These can create political leadership, ensure popular participation, develop accountable administration, and plan and implement people oriented development programmes. For emerging as vibrant and viable, the LGIs have to be participatory and empowered with political and financial authority. Accountability and transparency of all activities is a precondition for the viability of locally elected self-governing institutions. Further, recent emphasis on gender representation in the LGIs gives the issue more significance in the context of governance reform and development policies in Bangladesh. Gender participation is a vital key to a representative and responsive local government system. A local government system with devolved powers, functions, finances and gender participation is crucial to good governance and development in the country.

8.7.1 Decentralisation Dimensions

The process of decentralisation has at least three distinct dimensions: political, administrative and fiscal. The political dimension refers to the transfer of authority from central to local authorities; the administrative dimension is the transfer of functional responsibilities from central to local authorities; while the fiscal dimension is concerned with the financial relationship between all levels of government. The LGIs are more successful in promoting local participation and empowerment, democracy and development. In Bangladesh, all LGIs have the power to levy taxes and rates; and they are responsible to perform a range of functions and provide a range of services for which the mandate of each type of LGIs varies widely: from public health and hospitals, education and social welfare for city corporations and municipalities to the implementation of development projects, public libraries and roads for upazila and union parishads. Effective fiscal decentralisation, through earmarking revenue sources and providing revenue-earning power and authority to the LGIs, ensures that these institutions function effectively and efficiently and fulfil their mandates and service delivery responsibilities.

In Bangladesh, the central government's priorities emphasise the policy of decentralisation to bring the administration and services close to the doors of the local people. Currently, five LGIs function in the country. In the rural areas, zila parishads (ZPs), upazila parishads (UZPs) and union parishads (UPs) function while, in the urban areas, city corporations (CCs) and pourashavas operate. Within the local government tier in the rural areas, UZPs serve as the bridge between the central government and the roots level rural government and it can be a hub of people's participation, leadership building as well as the testing laboratory of democracy in the country.

8.7.2 Current State of Fiscal Decentralisation

The existing state of fiscal decentralisation in Bangladesh is far from satisfactory. The LGIs paved the way of buttressing associations between the centrally and locally dominant classes. The arrangement of local government finance also reveals the very nature of resources accretion in a societal foundation where the political framework plays a powerful role in production activities. In addition, the gap between the works to be implemented by the LGIs and the existing resources (both from own sources as well as transfers from the central government) is huge and thereby the LGIs in Bangladesh are not very effective mainly due to the negligence of the concerns of fiscal decentralisation.

The LGIs play only a limited role in delivering services to their citizens due to limited decision-making and financial authority; lack of resources and staff; and weak capacity. Consequently, the LGIs fail to meet citizens' needs. According to the World Bank Report 2019, to achieve upper-middle income status, Bangladesh must empower the LGIs through administrative and fiscal decentralisation. Moreover, the LGIs suffer from weak public financial management practices, hindering their service delivery capabilities (Table 8.5).

The LGIs are mostly dependent on intergovernmental fiscal transfers for financing their development interventions as their own revenues are too little to cover these costs. No doubt, this gives intergovernmental transfers substantial leverage for improving performance of the LGIs; however, over the longer term, local tax efforts would have to be stepped up given that this is critically important for efficiency and accountability objectives. Once the LGIs succeed in delivering effective public services, the tax-payers will be more willing to pay taxes and the trust relationship between citizens and LGIs will be strengthened.

In Bangladesh, the major fiscal transfer to the LGIs is channelled through the block grant mechanism of the annual development programme (ADP), which is a component of the development budget of the central government. The LGIs also receive central government assistance through other channels, such as UPs are given grants for TR, FFW, VGD, VGF, old age pensions, allowances for freedom fighters and widows, and other targeted and rural infrastructure maintenance programmes. However, the UPs have very little discretion or spending authority over

Table 8.5 Present structure of local government in Bangladesh

Level	*Unit*	*Number*	*Name*	*Headed by*	*Method of election*
Rural areas					
Upper most tier	District	61	Zila Parishad	Elected Chairman	Indirect election
Central tier	Upazila	492	Upazila Parishad	Elected Chairman	Direct election
Lowest tier	Union	4576	Union Parishad	Elected Chairman	Direct election
Urban areas					
Mega City	City Corporation	11	City Corporation	Elected Mayor	Direct election
Small Town/ City	Pourashava (Municipality)	329	Pourashava (Municipality)	Elected Mayor	Direct election

Source: LGD

these grants. Other tiers including pourashavas and city corporations also receive grants mainly for infrastructure development mostly earmarked for specific projects.

8.7.3 *Priority Areas for Fiscal Decentralisation*

Considering the overall structure and the actual performance of the local fiscal system in Bangladesh, seven priority areas are identified for fiscal decentralisation. These are: (1) persistence of a highly centralised system; (2) existing structure is complex and fluid; (3) LGIs have inadequate accountability; (4) expenditure assignments are imprecise in many cases; (5) LGIs suffer from limited access to own source revenues; (6) intergovernmental transfers are low in relation to global norms and unpredictable; and (7) monitoring of the central government is focused on quantity, not on quality service delivery.

8.7.4 *Road Map and Implementation Modalities for Fiscal Decentralisation*

Globally, no unique model for fiscal decentralisation exists as diverse historical incidents are mostly responsible for fiscal decentralisation. Different countries have different structures and therefore, fiscal decentralisation model of one country is not fully applicable to another. The study identifies twelve priority areas of reforms: (1) reduce dual taxation; (2) restructure resource allocations to LGIs; (3) enhance allocations to LGIs; (4) strengthen monitoring of LGIs' activities and audits; (5) strengthen taxation power and capacity of LGIs; (6) digitise land record keeping; (7) introduce budget planning and forecasting; (8) ensure regular dissemination of information; (9) improve understanding of financial matters by local government staffs; (10) ensure better performance and service delivery by LGIs; (11) motivate and strengthen supervisory committees; and (12) promote social responsibilities of LGIs.

In the decentralisation process, developing a road map and an appropriate work plan is very useful. With the existing challenges in the LGI's structures and actions, both short- and long-term reforms are necessary in Bangladesh.

The need is to identify the details of the appropriate fiscal decentralisation model and the implementation of the model through required reforms pursued in several steps with emphasis on right activities in each step. Bangladesh has reasonably satisfactory legal framework, institutional structures, and systems and procedures to carry out the fiscal decentralisation agenda. Also, it is reasonable to assume that the required political will in support of decentralisation would be forthcoming. In the case of central and sub-national capacity, sub-national capacity may be a constraint but the government has several on-going programmes to address the deficits. Similarly, strengthening central, sub-national and community oversight is a continuous process where both the government and the civil society organisations (CSOs) including the non-government organisations (NGOs) are active in the country.

The reform agenda should specifically address the reform of the system of expenditure functions and revenue source transfers from the central to sub-national governments in a comprehensive manner. The agenda should have the basic principles to follow, identify the challenges and strategies to follow in implementing each broad component of the reform agenda.

For effective fiscal decentralisation, the key responsibility of the central government is to design and supervise a system that works, while the LGIs face the challenge to use their often limited resources for delivering better local services. The implementation of fiscal decentralisation is much more than a mere technical adjustment of the division of responsibilities between different levels of government. It is more about power and politics in the country. Despite the holistic nature, in practice three issues need to be agreed clearly for implementing the reforms: (1) clarity of the roles and responsibilities among different levels of government, such as who provides what services; who taxes what; who is accountable to whom; (2) LGIs need a minimum degree of autonomy on the expenditure and revenue sides, staffing etc.; and (3) LGIs must have the required administrative and technical capacity to effectively carry out their assigned responsibilities.

Since fiscal dependency is likely to continue in Bangladesh in the near future, it is important to make the transfers more predictable and transparent. Improving the coordination between the central government and the LGIs is an important aspect of fiscal decentralisation reforms in the country. Further, there is good scope for enhancing own revenues of the LGIs especially for city corporations, municipalities, and upazila parishads by improving the cost effectiveness of collection and reducing losses through evasion and corruption. For the purpose, a multifaceted approach and strong political support from the central government is necessary to improve administration capacity, encourage compliance, and reduce the scope for corruption and political interference.

The need is to better understand the technical issues and the political and economic dynamics influencing specific subnational contexts and revenue sources. Fiscal decentralisation in Bangladesh should also be based on more in-depth knowledge on the links between taxation, improved service delivery and accountability; and political economy of different revenue sources and their implications for business development and taxpayer compliance. The Implementation of the reforms should also recognise the benefits and costs of fiscal decentralisation and the preconditions necessary for successful reforms. Improving the coordination between the central government and the LGIs is an important aspect of fiscal decentralisation reforms in the country.

8.8 New Institutions for Sustaining Growth Momentum

One of the key challenges facing Bangladesh today is how to acquire high-quality public sector institutions. In the coming decades, Bangladesh can rarely succeed in the absence of state institutions that can establish and enforce rules, collect revenue, and provide public services. It is true that the country has created anti-corruption commission (ACC), but there is no serious intention of identifying or recovering public funds that are stolen. Similarly, the One Stop Service (OSS) Centre has been launched to provide the investors with all necessary services from a single window but without addressing more significant challenges to operating a business. In the existing circumstances, Bangladesh with most in need of more effective public sector institutions is least likely to invest in the creation of such institutions. The performance targets that measure institutional forms rather than institutional functions are more applied to gauze success.

The present approach to 'institution building' is wide in the country that encompasses a variety of goals that have always been at the core of accelerating development. These goals include, for example, enhancing governance, that includes the framing and enforcing of rules and laws; improving public administration and regulations, which includes the provision of public services, such as electricity, water and sanitation; and more efficient and equitable provision of public goods and services, which range from defence to education and health. As such, the initial effort would have to focus on defining the nature of the task of strengthening and reforming institutions and define the parameters of their operations. This should cover the broad range of institutions that are critical to good governance and development.

Bangladesh can begin by identifying and concentrating on the institutions which are critical to the following: (1) implementing sound macroeconomic and social sector policies; (2) implementing and overseeing the development process; (3) better utilising development resources; (4) effectively implementing development administration and international trade negotiations; and (5) managing labour and employment, as well as vulnerability issues. The institutions must be made effective to spur development in the form of contracts and contract enforcement, common commercial codes, and increased availability of information, all of which will reduce the costs of transactions, risk, and uncertainty. For Bangladesh, institutions will also determine the degree to which the environment is conducive to cooperation and increased social capital; inclusive and participatory institutions increase the flow of information and the extent to which resources can be pooled to reduce risk and ensure sustained levels of livelihoods.

Further, the institutional reform process needs a more nuanced understanding of institutions and markets to identify types of institutional change needed by Bangladesh to sustain progress and ensure pragmatic, path-dependent and location-specific mixes of investment, in both standard institutional environment and non-standard institutional arrangements. The compulsion is to look for viable incremental changes that benefit the poor, which are 'politically viable' and consistent with longer term processes of pro-poor institutional and socioeconomic development.

8.9 Concluding Remarks

The future development path of Bangladesh will significantly depend upon the quality of its economic institutions. Though institutions often persist for long periods of time and create unintended consequences, the performance of economic institutions primarily reflects the nature of collective choices made by political institutions and the distribution of political power. Therefore, Bangladesh's future development would require an understanding of why political institutions create bad economic institutions and what instruments are available to push the society to move from the bad to a good political, and consequently good economic, institutions.

For Bangladesh, promoting democracy and accountability, and checks and balances, will no doubt lead to better economic policies and institutions. Although there have been successes of developmental authoritarian regimes in East Asia, this is not an option for Bangladesh from the point of view of both political freedom and economic growth. There are obvious pitfalls for Bangladesh in pursuing such growth options and improvements in accountability alone, for instance, can push Bangladesh to a much better growth path.

The above shows that Bangladesh has to be extremely cautious in promoting institutional reforms. For instance, the application of structural reforms emanating from the Washington Consensus did not produce good outcomes in Bangladesh, not because all of these reforms were necessarily bad given their underlying assumptions, but because these assumptions were not valid. Reform in one area leads other areas to remain unreformed. The challenging problem for institutional reform is to better the political realities underlying poverty and development in Bangladesh. Better institutional reforms and development policy will only come when these forces are recognised and understood. In China, for instance, dramatic shift to rapid growth occurred after 1978 when political shifts occurred in a manner that made the reformists more powerful. The consideration of institutional dimensions opens up new possibilities of understanding the determinants of political processes that can help design reforms in economic institutions that promote rapid development.

For ensuring credible reforms, institutional diagnostic tools may be used to identify weak institutional areas that restrict development, and indicate appropriate directions for reform. This is similar to growth diagnostic tools, but goes much beyond by focusing on the institutional weaknesses responsible for creating binding economic constraints. Obviously, these institutions in Bangladesh touch upon a variety of areas—political, administrative, judicial, economic, social, cultural, and so on and may be formal or informal. In such a circumstance, developing institutional diagnostics toolkit for use and identify reforms of binding institutional restrictions on development is no doubt a complicated challenge. The difficulties arise from a number of sources such as (1) multiplicity of institutions that affect development; (2) their close link with the structure and nature of political power, which needs to be considered as given; and (3) imperfect understanding of the functioning and evolution of institutions together with economic mechanisms and development.

Such institutional analysis needs to examine the rules that people develop to govern group behaviour and interaction in political, economic and social spheres of life. The analysis should be based on an understanding that these rules—whether formally constructed or informally embedded—mediate and could also distort the expected impacts of institutional reforms. The diagnosis should be participatory and systematic so as to understand the structural problems and opportunities. This is likely to develop the capacity to understand the current situations and empower to find and implement strategies which can bring sustainable changes in institutions.

It is well known that making institutions more inclusive is a time consuming and complex process. A first step in building inclusive institutions is to ensure that these are representative of and accountable to all segments in society, including the poor. To empower the poor, we require some key elements, such as respect for political and civil liberties, respect for individual rights of all citizens, and respect for their rights to participate in and contribute to social and economic decisions. This creates the pre-conditions for the emergence of pro-poor institutions and the poor's empowerment.

It must, however, be recognised that pluralistic and representative governments do not necessarily create the institutions that meet the needs of the poor and the disadvantaged sections of society for many reasons. The poor may not participate in these processes because they face constraints or they may feel that such participation is futile or irrelevant to their primary concerns and they have little ability to influence these institutions. The need is to strengthen the voices of the poor through such actions as disseminating information, promoting public debate, fostering community participation, and building a strong civil society and social capital in support of pro-poor institutions.

In Bangladesh, there exists enough scope to make institutions more inclusive. The existing institutions, by their very nature, mostly create polarisation in society creating a fundamental divide between the 'haves' with access to social, economic and political power, while the 'have-nots' remain mostly excluded from all these processes. For the purpose, actions are needed to re-structure institutions to bring down legal, social and economic barriers that act against the participation of the poor and disadvantaged groups in social life.

Of course, it is hard to change institutions; but building accountable and inclusive institutions at the local level can provide a useful first step towards a systematic change in the institutional structure of the country. Obviously, the issues of transforming and creating the right institutions for accelerating growth and lowering poverty in Bangladesh, as elsewhere in the developing world, is a complex process and no single model is available to create such institutional structures. But it is time for us to lay the essential foundations for the creation of inclusive and accountable institutions at the local and national levels—institutions that serve the broad interests of society, including those of the poor and the disadvantaged sections in society.

References

Abdullah, A.A. 1976. Land Reform and Agrarian Change in Bangladesh. *Bangladesh Development Studies* 4: 67–114.

Acemoglu, D., S. Johnson, and J.A. Robinson. 2003. An African Success: Botswana. In *In Search of Prosperity: Analytic Narratives on Economic Growth*, ed. D. Rodrik. Princeton: Princeton University Press.

Alamgir, M. 1975. Poverty, Inequality and Social Welfare: Measurement, Evidence and Policies. *Bangladesh Development Studies* 3 (2): 153–180.

———. 1978. *Bangladesh: A Case of Below Poverty Level Equilibrium Trap*. Dhaka: Bangladesh Institute of Development Studies.

Altenburg, T. 2011. *Industrial Policy in Developing Countries: Overview and Lessons from Seven Country Cases.* Berlin: German Development Institute.

Amsden, A. 1989. *Asia's Next Giant, South Korea and Late Industrialization.* New York: Oxford University Press.

Andrews, M. 2013. *The Limits of Institutional Reform in Development: Changing Rules for Realistic Solutions.* Cambridge: Cambridge University Press.

Anglingkusumo, R. 2013. Addressing the Complexity of Macroeconomic Management in Middle Income Countries. Paper Presented During the Experts Meeting on the Common Challenges of Middle-Income Countries, 13–15 May 2013, Seoul.

APO. 2000. *Impact of Land Utilization Systems on Agricultural Productivity.* Report of the APO Seminar on Impact of Land Utilization Systems on Agricultural Productivity, Islamic Republic of Iran, 4–9 November 2000, Tokyo.

Barrett, C.B., M.E. BachkeMarc, F. BellemareHope, C. Michelson, S. Narayanan, and T.F. Walker. 2012. Smallholder Participation in Contract Farming: Comparative Evidence from Five Countries. *World Development* 40 (4): 715–730.

Bates, R.H. 2001. *Prosperity and Violence: The Political Economy of Development*. New York: W.W. Norton & Company.

BBS. 2014. *Bangladesh Demographic and Health Survey 2014*. Bangladesh Bureau of Statistics, Ministry of Planning. Dhaka: Government of the People's Republic of Bangladesh.

Begum, B.A., P.K. Hopke, and A. Markwitz. 2013. Air Pollution by Fine Particulate Matter in Bangladesh. *Atmospheric Pollution Research* 4: 75–86.

Bellemare, M.F. 2012. As You Sow, So Shall You Reap: The Welfare Impacts of Contract Farming. *World Development* 40 (7): 1418–1434.

Bromley, D.W. 1991. *Environment and Economy: Property Rights and Public Policy*. Oxford: Basil Blackwell.

Cervantes-Godoy, D., and J. Brooks. 2011. *Smallholder Adjustment in Middle-Income Countries*. Food, Agriculture and Fisheries Working Papers No. 12. Paris: Organisation for Economic Cooperation and Development.

Chandra, V., J. Lin, and Y. Wang. 2012. *Leading Dragons Phenomenon: New Opportunities for Catch-Up in Low-Income Countries*. Policy Research Working Paper 6000. Washington, DC: World Bank.

Cheng, T., S. Haggard, and D. Kang. 1998. Institutions and Growth in Korea and Taiwan: the Bureaucracy. *Journal of Development Studies* 34 (6): 87.

Coase, R.H. 1992. The Economic Structure of Production. *American Economic Review* 82: 713–719.

Coate, S.T., and S.E. Morris. 2005. Policy Conditionality. In *Globalization and the Nation State: The Impact of the IMF and World Bank*, ed. G. Ranis and J.R. Vreeland. New York: Routledge.

Dahlman, C.J. 1979. The Problem of Externality. *The journal of Law and Economics* 22 (1): 141–162.

Deininger, K. 2003. *Land Policies for Growth and Poverty Reduction*. World Bank Policy Research Report. Washington, DC: World Bank and Oxford University Press.

Eggertsson, T. 1990. *Economic Behavior and Institutions*. Cambridge: Cambridge University Press.

FAO. 2008. *The State of Food Insecurity in the World 2008*. Rome: Food and Agriculture Organization of the United Nations.

Faruqee, R., and K. Carey. 1997. *Research on Land Markets in South Asia, What Have We Learned?* Policy Research Working Paper 1754. Washington, DC: World Bank.

Feder, G., O. Tongroj, C. Hongladarom, Y. Chalamwong, and C. Yongyuth. 1988. *Land Policies and Farm Productivity in Thailand*. Washington, DC: World Bank.

Fukuyama, F. 2013. *What Is Governance?* Working Paper 314. Washington, DC: Centre for Global Development.

Griffin, K., A.R. Khan, and A. Ickowitz. 2002. Poverty and the Distribution of Land. *Journal of Agrarian Change* 2 (3): 279–330.

Haque, M.A., S.S. Yamamoto, A.A. Malik, and R. Sauerborn. 2012. Households' Perception of Climate Change and Human Health Risks: A Community Perspective. *Environmental Health* 11 (1): 1–12. https://doi.org/10.1186/1476-069X-11-1.

Hyden, G., J. Court, and K. Mease. 2003. *Political Society and Governance in 16 Developing Countries.* World Governance Survey Discussion Paper 5. London: Overseas Development Institute.

Jabbar, M.A., M.H. Rahman, R.K.T. Talukder, and S.K. Raha. 2007. *Alternative Institutional Arrangements for Contract Farming in Poultry Production in Bangladesh and Their Impacts on Equity.* ILRI Research Report No. 7. Nairobi: International Livestock Research Institute.

Jannuzi, F.T., and J.T. Peach. 1977. *The Agrarian Structure of Bangladesh: An Impediment to Development.* London: Routledge.

Kaufmann, D., A. Kraay, and M. Mastruzzi. 2010. The Worldwide Governance Indicators: Methodology and Analytical Issues. *Hague Journal on the Rule of Law* 3 (2). https://doi.org/10.1017/S1876404511200046.

Khan, A.R. 2004. *Growth, Inequality and Poverty in China, A Comparative Study of the Experience in the Periods Before and After the Asian Crisis.* Geneva: International Labour Office.

KIT. 2012. *Bangladesh: Food Security and Land Governance Factsheet.* Amsterdam: Royal Tropical Institute.

Kuncic, A. 2014. Institutional Quality Dataset. *Journal of Institutional Economics* 10 (1): 135–161.

Libecap, G.D. 1989. *Contracting for Property Rights.* Cambridge, MA: National Bureau of Economic Research.

McGuire, M.C., and M. Olson. 1996. The Economics of Autocracy and Majority Rule: The Invisible Hand and the Use of Force. *Journal of Economic Literature* 34: 72–96.

Mighell, R.L., and L.A. Jones. 1963. *Vertical Coordination in Agriculture.* Agricultural Economic Report 19. Washington, DC: U.S. Department of Agriculture.

Miyata, S., N. Minot, and D. Hu. 2009. Impact of Contract Farming on Income: Linking Small Farmers, Packers, and Supermarkets in China. *World Development* 37 (11): 1781–1790.

North, D.C. 1981. *Structure and Change in Economic History.* New York: W. W. Norton & Co.

———. 1990. *Institutions, Institutional Change and Economic Performance.* New York: Cambridge University Press.

Ohno, K. 2009. Avoiding the Middle Income Trap: Industrial Policy in Vietnam. *Asean Economic Bulletin.*

———. 2011. Comment on "Revisiting Exports and Foreign Direct Investment in Vietnam". *Asian Economic Policy Review* 6: 134–135. Wiley Online Library.

Pateman, C. 1988. *The Sexual Contract (Sociology of Health and Illness Monographs)*. Oxford: Blackwell Publishers Limited.

Paus, E. 2013. Globalization and the Middle Income Trap: A Capabilities-Based Approach with a Focus on Latin America. Paper Presented During the Experts Meeting on the Common Challenges of Middle-Income Countries, 13–15 May 2013, Seoul.

Pingali, P.L., and S. Pandey. 2000. *World Maize Needs Meeting: Technological Opportunities and Priorities for the Public Sector*. Mexico: CIMMYT.

Ray, D. 1998. *Development Economics*. Princeton, NJ: Princeton University Press.

Rodriguez-Clare, A. 2005. *Coordination Failures, Clusters and Microeconomic Interventions*. Working Paper No. 544. Washington, DC: Inter-American Development Bank.

Rodrik, D. 1995. Getting Interventions Right: How Korea and Taiwan Grew Rich. *Economic Policy* 10: 55–107.

———. 2000. *Institutions for High-Quality Growth: What They Are and How to Acquire Them*. NBER Working Paper No. 7540. Cambridge, MA: National Bureau of Economic Research.

Schlager, E., and E. Ostrom. 1992. Property-Rights Regimes and Natural Resources: A Conceptual Analysis. *Land Economics* 68 (3): 249–262.

Shepherd, I.D.H. 2005. From Cattle and Coke to Charlie: Meeting the Challenge of Selfmarketing and Personal Branding. *Journal of Marketing Management* 21 (5–6): 589–606.

Shirley, M.M. 2003. Institutions and Development. In *Handbook of New Institutional Economics*, ed. C. Menard and M.M. Shirley. Springer.

Smalley, R. 2013. *Plantations, Contract Farming and Commercial Farming Areas in Africa: A Comparative Review*. LACA Working Paper 055. Land and Agricultural Commercialisation in Africa. www.future-agricultures.org.

Sobhan, R. 1992a. *Problems of Governance in Bangladesh*. Dhaka: University Press Limited.

———. 1992b. Rethinking the Market Reform Paradigm. *Economic and Political Weekly*, July 25.

Stigler, G. 1971. The Economic Theory of Regulation. *Bell Journal of Economics and Management Science* 2: 3–21.

———. 1982. Economist and Public Policy. *Regulation* 6: 13–17.

Uddin, M.F., and J. Haque. 2009. *Agrarian Transition and Livelihoods of the Rural Poor: Agricultural Land Market*. Dhaka: Unnayan Onneshan – The Innovators.

UN. 2016. *Sustainable Development Goals Report 2016*. New York: United Nations.

UNDP. 1997. *The Shrinking State: Governance and Sustainable Human Development – A UNDP Policy Document, Reconceptualising Governance –*

UNDP Discussion Paper 2. New York: United Nations Development Programme.

World Bank. 1994. *Governance: The World Bank's Experience*. Washington, DC: The World Bank.

———. 2000. *World Development Report 2000/2001: Attacking Poverty*. New York: Oxford University Press.

———. 2001a. *Social Protection Sector Strategy: From Safety Net to Springboard*. Washington, DC: The World Bank.

———. 2001b. *World Development Report 2000/2001: Attacking Poverty*. Oxford: World Bank and Oxford University Press. https://doi.org/10.1596/0-1952-1129-4.

———. 2012. *World Development Report 2012: Gender Equality and Development*. Washington, DC: World Bank.

CHAPTER 9

Financial-Real Sector Nexus

9.1 Introduction

Current development policy pays increasing attention to the importance of financial sector in economic and social development and on creating economically sound and stable financial institutions, especially in the middle income countries (MICs). Schumpeter argues that a developed financial system mobilises productive savings, allocates resources efficiently, improves risk management, and reduces information asymmetry, all of which facilitate innovation and entrepreneurship (Schumpeter 1952). The importance of innovation and its determinants is also a focal point of endogenous growth theory. Consequently, it comes as no surprise that recent work on the nexus between the financial and the real sector not only refers explicitly to Schumpeter (e.g. King and Levine 1993), but tries to base its models on endogenous growth theory (e.g. Levine 1997).

The models which focus on the growth-enhancing effects of the financial system derive their insights on importance of the financial system and financial institutions for growth from the theory of finance and through transplanting these insights into the growth model (see, e.g. Bencivenga and Smith 1991; Greenwood and Jovanovic 1990; King and Levine 1993). The positive correlation between economic growth and development of the financial system essentially results from higher marginal productivity of the invested capital. Moreover, higher economic growth from

© The Author(s) 2020

M. K. Mujeri, N. Mujeri, *Bangladesh at Fifty*, Palgrave Studies in Economic History,
https://doi.org/10.1007/978-3-030-56791-0_9

increased levels of financial asset formation occurs in countries where there is a low or medium per capita income, as in Bangladesh.

The relationships between the financial and the real sectors may be classified in terms of causality working through five possible hypotheses: (1) no causal relation; (2) demand-following relation; (3) supply-leading relation; (4) negative causal link from finance to growth; and (5) interdependence. In addition, a number of syntheses can be possible using the five hypotheses, basically with respect to evolutionary sequencing or different needs on the part of industries or types of enterprises.

The view of no significant relation between financial sector development and real growth is expressed most prominently by Lucas (1988). The assertion is consistent with a neoclassical world of zero transaction costs and perfect information. In such a world, the Modigliani-Miller theorem holds and institutions, in particular financial institutions, do not matter (Modigliani and Miller 1958). This 'irrelevance hypothesis' has been widely criticised on several counts: (1) economists increasingly deny the existence of frictionless markets, primarily based on informational and related arguments (such as, agency problems, transaction costs etc.); (2) the importance of institutions is now widely recognised; and (3) a large number of empirical studies show strong evidence for the relevance of finance for real growth. Robinson (1952: 86) argues that 'finance follows where enterprise leads' showing a causal relation from the real to the financial sector (demand-following finance). This hypothesis regards financial development as endogenously determined by the real economy or its needs. This view is consistent with the Coase theorem (Coase 1960) and the New Institutional Economics which argues that institutions adjust to market imperfections in a way that maximises individual utilities. The 'demand-following approach', on the other hand, is based on empirical evidence and regarded as a temporary situation that may persist only under special circumstances, such as transition to a market economy.

The recent supply-leading finance arguments begin with McKinnon (1973) and Shaw (1973), who consider finance as largely supply-leading, that is finance positively influences the real economy. There also exists a hypothesis that finance has a detrimental effect to the real development of an economy which refers to the danger of financial crises, often in relation with speculative bubbles (Bhatt 1995) or, more generally, hiding of the fundamentals of the real economy particularly through capital market speculation.

Empirical evidence, in general, suggests that both arguments in favour of supply-leading and demand-following finance are of relevance, that is the causal link between finance and real growth runs in both directions. The influence may be exerted at the same time, implying that financial depth (i.e. large financial markets) drives real growth, while the growing economy's demand for finance is met by the advancing financial sector. Alternatively, it may depend on an economy's general development stage whether its financial sector is supply-leading or demand-following. The most prominent hypothesis of such a sequential pattern of causation is put forward by Patrick (1966). Patrick argues that developing countries can gain significantly in real terms from developing their financial sectors (supply-leading finance), whereas, in the developed economies, finance becomes increasingly demand-following.

9.2 Bangladesh's Financial Architecture

The financial system of Bangladesh is comprised of three broad and somewhat fragmented sectors: (1) formal sector; (2) semi-formal sector; and (3) informal sector. The sectors are categorised in accordance with their degree of regulation. The formal sector includes all regulated institutions like banks, non-bank financial institutions (NBFIs), insurance companies, capital market intermediaries like brokerage houses, merchant banks etc., and microfinance institutions (MFIs). The semi-formal sector includes those institutions which are regulated otherwise but do not fall under the jurisdiction of the central bank, insurance authority, Securities and Exchange Commission (SEC), or any other enacted financial regulator. This sector is mainly represented by specialised financial institutions like House Building Finance Corporation (HBFC), Palli Karma Sahayak Foundation (PKSF), Samabaya Bank, Grameen Bank etc., non-government organisations (NGOs) and discrete government programmes. The informal sector includes private intermediaries which are completely unregulated.

The financial system is regulated primarily by the Bangladesh Bank (the central bank) which provides regulatory and supervisory oversight for banks and NBFIs. Two types of banks are recognised: scheduled banks (licensed under the Bank Company Act 1991, amended in 2013) which can perform all types of banking functions; and non-scheduled banks (specialised banks with restricted functions). The legal and regulatory framework for financial services is highly conducive to financial inclusion in which Bangladesh Bank plays a crucial role. The Bangladesh Post Office is also mandated to act as an agent, on behalf of the government, to mobilise savings and provide other financial services especially in rural and remote areas in the country.

9.2.1 *Overview of Current Landscape*

Bangladesh has a thriving financial sector with a robust infrastructure. In terms of numbers of providers, individuals and enterprises are served by 63 banks; 703 MFIs; 33 NBFIs; 78 insurance companies; 182,346 cooperatives; as well as the post office; savings groups; credit unions and a host of emerging digital financial service (DFS) providers. Large corporations and investors also make use of a range of service providers and play an important role; for example, capital markets and venture capital firms offer a source of funds for large-scale transformative investments in companies or infrastructure.

9.2.1.1 The Banking System

In 2016, the total number of branches of 56 scheduled banks stood at 9464 in the country showing significant growth in the physical network of banks and ATMs in recent years; but still there exists regional disparities in the distribution of access points reflecting the natural and economic tendency to concentrate in populous and urban locations. The distribution of deposits and loans is similarly skewed towards these locations. In recent years, the number of bank branches has risen rapidly in the rural areas and 5368 of the total number of 9464 bank branches are now located in the rural areas. Consequently, both bank-branch density per 1000 square kilometre and branch-density per 100,000 households have increased over time. Despite this, demographic concentration of branches is still low which is important for financial inclusion. Moreover, banks are mostly urban-biased; with the share of rural areas in total bank advances and bank deposits of only 10 per cent and 20 per cent respectively in 2016 (Table 9.1). Similarly, the ratio of rural advances to rural deposits has been 36 percent in 2016 showing that banks play a limited role in providing financial services to the rural households.

Under the financial inclusion initiatives and policy guidelines of Bangladesh Bank, the banking sector provides a number of services which include agent banking, mobile financial services (MFS), directed credit to small and medium enterprises (SMEs), refinancing scheme for SMEs,

Table 9.1 Outreach of banks in Bangladesh, 2015–2016

Bank outreach	*Year*	
	2015	*2016*
Number of branches: Total	9397	9654
Rural	5334	5466
Urban	4063	4188
Volume of advances (billion BDT): Total	5798.59	6686.57
Rural	571.26	680.00
Urban	5227.32	6006.57
Volume of deposits (billion BDT): Total	7939.81	8994.14
Rural	1575.09	1843.86
Urban	6364.72	7150.28
Rural branch/Total branch ratio	0.5676	0.5662
Rural advance/Total advance ratio	0.0985	0.1017
Rural deposit/Total deposit ratio	0.1983	0.2050
Rural advance/Rural deposit ratio	0.3627	0.3688

Source: Scheduled Bank Statistics, various issues, Bangladesh Bank

Note: Figures refer to end of December of respective years

school banking and no-frill accounts, and many other measures targeted towards financial inclusion.[1] Mobile financial services (MFS), under a bank-led model, deliver off branch digital financial services especially for the poor and unbanked population segments through mobile phone based solutions. Basic services delivered by MFS platforms include payment of inward foreign remittances; cash in/out into mobile accounts through agents/bank branches/ATMs/mobile network operator (MNO) outlets, P2B, B2P, G2P, P2G and P2P payments.[2]

[1] Other steps taken by Bangladesh Bank include opening of dedicated desks and service centres in banks for SMEs, special package for women entrepreneurs, yearly indicative targets for SME loan disbursement by banks, adopting strategic thrusts on cluster development, capacity building for entrepreneurs and staff, tiered monitoring system for SME sector growth, inclusion of share of SME loan in CAMELS rating of banks, and developing credit rating methodology for SMEs.

[2] Recognising the transforming role of digitisation, the Prime Minister's Office (PMO) is implementing the Access to Information (A2i) programme which has a focus on financial inclusion through its 5000+ digital centres established in all rural and urban local governance institutions around the country serving a monthly average of 4.5 million underserved citi-

One key issue, however, is to develop innovative financing models that go beyond traditional bank lending to provide comprehensive support services to MSMEs according to their needs and stages of business growth. This requires response to new financing modalities that include crowd funding, asset based finance and cluster financing. The need is also to develop an extensive knowledge base on access to finance by SMEs along with sharing best practices to promote evidence based policy making. In addition to credit, banks and FIs can internalise nonfinancial and business development services to develop successful MSME lending strategy. For providing effective credit guarantees, public credit guarantee schemes for small industry may be established which will provide overall portfolio credit guarantee rather than on a standalone basis.

Mobile and agent banking can significantly reduce the costs of delivering financial services, in particular in low-density and remote areas. In addition to explicit costs of providing financial services, policies for developing these low-cost technologies will reduce implicit costs as well such as the opportunity cost of travel time and waiting. The initiatives for bringing women into the financial inclusion framework should take into account significant differences that may exist between women and men in their access, needs and preferences of financial products and services.

Agent banking provides limited scale banking and financial services to the underserved population in branchless areas through engaged agents under valid agency agreement. Bangladesh Bank has identified some basic financial services, such as small value cash deposits and cash withdrawals, facilitating fund transfer and utility bill payment and so on that can be offered by the agent from designated business premises to the financially excluded population.

9.2.1.2 The Microfinance Sector

In Bangladesh, the existence of the quasi-formal market helps significantly in increasing the access to financial products and services by the unbanked population especially in the rural areas. There are 697 MFIs which are licensed under the Microcredit Regulatory Authority (MRA) in 2015. According to MRA statistics, the total loan outstanding in the microfinance sector (including NGOs, Grameen Bank, state-owned

zens with over 60 electronic services. The government is working to digitise all forms of G2P payments, P2G payments, P2P payments, and P2B payments for e-commerce countrywide with a particular focus on rural areas.

commercial banks, private commercial banks, and specialised programmes of several ministries) was BDT 504 billion in June 2015 and the volume of savings was BDT 321 billion. The total number of clients of the sector was 34.58 million including 6.72 million clients from the Grameen Bank. Credit services of the sector comprise of six broad groups: (1) general microcredit for small scale self-employment based activities; (2) microenterprise loans; (3) loans for the ultra-poor; (4) agricultural loans; (5) seasonal loans; and (6) loans for disaster management. Loan amounts up to BDT 50,000 are generally treated as microcredit, while loans above the amount are considered as microenterprise (ME) loans.

The MFIs in Bangladesh cover the Grameen Bank (established under the Grameen Bank Ordinance in 1983) and the non-government MFIs (NGO-MFIs) which are now licensed and regulated by MRA. Their geographical and demographic concentrations are high and these play a critical role in rural financial markets. During 2015, these institutions together have a network of 18,635 branches with 36.23 million active members (Table 9.2).

Available evidence shows that the poor and rural households have higher access to NGO-MFIs while the non-poor and the urban households enjoy higher access to formal financial institutions (Table 9.3). Around 37 per cent of the households have access to formal financial services (including insurance) while 43 per cent have access to microfinance services. The non-poor households (44 per cent) and urban households (54 per cent) have better access to formal financial services. Although 52 per cent of the poor households have access to microfinance, the non-poor's access is 40 per cent who mostly belong to the graduating members. Overall, nearly 57 per cent of the households have access to savings

Table 9.2 Microfinance sector in Bangladesh, 2015

	Grameen Bank	*NGO-MFIs*	*Total*
Number of branches (number)	2568	16,067	18,635
Number of members (million)	8.81	27.42	36.23
Number of net borrowers (million)	6.86	22.73	29.59
Loan disbursement (billion BDT)	149.23	679.54	828.77
Loan outstanding (billion BDT)	96.42	425.41	521.83
Borrowers per branch (number)	2670	1414	1587
Active borrowers per branch (number)	3429	1706	1944

Source: Credit and Development Forum, Bangladesh Microfinance Statistics 2015

Table 9.3 Access to financial services from different markets, 2014–2015

	Access to microfinance	*Access to formal financial services*	*Access to credit*	*Access to microcredit*	*Access to formal bank credit*	*Access to savings*
National	43.2	37.0	54.1	36.6	8.0	56.5
Rural	46.4	32.8	56.2	39.1	7.6	53.9
Urban	30.9	53.5	46.1	27.0	9.6	66.7
Non-poor	39.7	44.4	52.1	32.9	9.1	60.5
Poor	51.7	19.4	59.0	45.4	5.4	47.0

Source: Institute for Inclusive Finance and Development, 2015

while 54 per cent have access to credit in any financial market. The higher intensity of access to savings arises as the financial institutions mobilise savings from a larger number of savers and provide credit to a lesser number of borrowers.

Over the years, NGO-MFIs have contributed much towards expanding access of the poor and low-income households to microfinance services. However, it is also true that a significant number of vulnerable and low-income households including labour-headed and female-headed households still remain outside the network of financial services. The major reasons for exclusion are: inappropriate financial products, lack of information about microfinance services, and the negative attitude of microfinance staff regarding the extreme poor. The MFIs are not pure microfinance institutions and they normally provide a bundle of services including credit, savings, microinsurance, training and social services.[3] To further intensify the contributions of MFIs in financial inclusion, along with strengthening the existing processes and practices, there is a need for innovation and adoption pro-active approach to bolster financial inclusion through MFI interventions.

[3] Several studies suggest that microfinance programmes have positive impacts on poverty reduction and other economic outcomes. As financial inclusion by the MFIs is supply-driven, one estimate by InM shows that a 10 per cent increase in total supply of credit at the village level increases financial inclusion by 4 per cent. Similarly, another InM study shows that increase in financial literacy raises the intensity of financial inclusion. The effects of microfinance are also evident at the macro level and one InM study estimates that microfinance contributes by between 11 and 15 per cent to GDP under different assumption. See Raihan et al. (2017).

9.2.1.3 The Cooperatives

Cooperatives are social institutions in which members work together to promote socioeconomic development, sharing ownership and making decisions in a democratic manner. Cooperatives in Bangladesh are organised by the Department of Cooperatives under the Ministry of Local Government Rural Development and Cooperatives. There are more than 190,000 cooperatives in Bangladesh, among which 22 are at the national level and 1160 and 189,000 are in the form of central-level and primary-level cooperatives. The total membership is about 10 million. Cooperatives have the potential to play a significant role in promoting financial inclusion especially among the members through introducing financial inclusion plans along with their other functions, especially through developing appropriate business models for the cooperatives creating the scope for low-income communities to increase financial inclusion and acquire better livelihoods.

9.2.1.4 Insurance Sector

In addition to mainstream insurance sector, microinsurance is an important area which is given mostly to the low-income population. Basically, microinsurance is insurance that (1) operates by risk-pooling; (2) is financed through regular premiums; and (3) is tailored to the poor clients who otherwise would not be able to take out insurance. In Bangladesh, microinsurance is generally for those who are excluded from the traditional commercial insurance sector mostly because they belong to the informal sector, have irregular cash flows and large seasonal fluctuations in earning capacity.

Currently, 31 regulated life insurers (30 private and one public sector agency, Jiban Bima Corporation) and 46 regulated non-life insurers (45 private one public sector agency, Sadharan Bima Corporation) operate in Bangladesh.[4] Of these, 12 private life insurers and 5 private non-life insurers offer microinsurance services. The microinsurance products offered by the life insurance companies are life, micro-Takaful and endowment insurance. The microinsurance products offered by the non-life insurance companies include health, flood, crop and livestock. However, most of the non-life products are in piloting stage. The non-life companies have little experience in microinsurance. Both life and non-life insurers are struggling to upscale their products. The challenges are to transform insurance

[4] See, Annual Report 2015, Bangladesh Insurance Association, Dhaka.

regulations to make them conducive to microinsurance, enhance the knowledge and know-how of insurers on microinsurance, enhance product innovation, adopt new and innovative marketing methods, and create public confidence in the insurers.

The NGO-MFIs have been offering credit shielding microinsurance products for over 30 years. But these services were unregulated. The 2006 Microcredit Regulatory Act (MRA) and 2010 MRA Rules allowed NGO-MFIs, licensed by MRA, to offer insurance services to its borrowers and their family members. Although this provides a formal platform to microinsurance in the NGO-MFI market, but their microinsurance business remains unsupervised. Around 750 NGO-MFIs in Bangladesh offer mostly credit shielding insurance in various names. Some NGO-MFIs also offer life, health, livestock and asset/property insurance. The outreach of these products, however, remains insignificant.

9.2.2 *Digital Financial Services*

Digital financial services (DFS) refer to digital access to and use of formal financial services by the excluded and underserved populations. Moreover, such services should be suited to customers' needs, and delivered responsibly, at a cost both affordable to the customers and sustainable for the providers. There are three key components of DFS: (1) a digital transactional platform, (2) retail agents, and (3) use by customers and agents of a device—most commonly a mobile phone—to transact via the platform. The Strategy treats the government as the prime mover which will play the key role in supporting the evolution of a robust inclusive digital ecosystem and in moving the digital agenda towards financial inclusion.

Delivering financial services through technological innovations, including mobile money, can be a catalyst for the provision and use of a diverse set of other financial services—including credit, insurance, savings, and financial education. Those who are now excluded can enjoy expanded access to money-transfer, microfinance and microinsurance services. Digital finance also has an important role to play for small businesses. It not only provides them with access to finance but also to electronic payment systems, secure financial products and a chance to build a financial history. Innovations in electronic payment technology like mobile and prepaid enable people to live more secure, empowered and included lives.

For the small farmers, DFS can help to address specific challenges in the value chain—especially those challenges that need financial services solutions, and where the traditional financial sector is unable to fully address the demands in the rural market. This is often due to high infrastructure costs and a lack of incentives to adapt products to the unique needs of these farmers. Digital finance offers a way to expand access to the formal financial system (through a basic transaction account supervised by the banking regulator), taking advantage of the rapid growth of digital and mobile telephone infrastructure and the advent of branchless banking (which offers the ability to transact outside a traditional bank branch). These factors have a direct link to increasing farmers' income and enhancing food security.

Bangladesh Bank, the mobile money regulator, has adopted the bank-led model with significant scope of new investments in innovation and technology. The mobile operators have already introduced many social VAS, while MFS providers have adopted various VAS in the mobile money landscape. The digital initiatives have proceeded along two fronts in Bangladesh: (1) in the banking sector through introduction of internet, SMS, ATMs and POS based transactions; and (2) through MFS by the mobile bank account/mobile wallet. Bangladesh Bank has built a robust technology infrastructure with various enablement to support DFS such as, online credit and supervisory reporting; electronic fund transfer; Bangladesh automated clearing house; national payment switch and real-time gross settlement systems. Bangladesh Bank, in association with the NID authority, also plans to connect NID with the digital banking and MFS system to introduce e-KYC. Several initiatives have also been taken up such as NID linked G2P payments, union digital centres, agent banking; POS, rural branches and Rural Savings Bank.

9.3 Status of Monetary Transmissions in Bangladesh

9.3.1 Banking Governance and Rising Non-performing Loans

The ability of the monetary policy to influence credit and the real economy is a central concern for Bangladesh. Relevant channels are, however, weak; and changes in policy rates have only limited effect on other interest rates and on the economy. Since Bangladesh is a bank-dependent country, more liquid banks can enhance the impact of monetary policy on credit supply and the real economy. Similarly, financial development can strengthen the macroeconomic impact of monetary policy.

Banks in Bangladesh suffer from high levels of non-performing loans (NPLs) which reached 12.0 per cent in September 2019. Further, NPLs weigh on the supply of credit and thus on investment and growth via a number of channels, such as locking-in bank capital into unviable projects and unproductive activities, reducing bank profitability, and distorting capital allocation. High NPL levels also impair the monetary transmission mechanism to the real economy.

Further, high NPLs do not remain as problems for the banks alone. The government usually gets involved in a big way especially in the resolution process, such as injection of capital especially to the failing public sector banks, setting up of asset management companies (AMCs) or other measures. NPLs also have a significant implication on the fiscal sector through contingent fiscal liabilities; and the government, at times, ends up in bailing the financial institutions through recapitalisation.

Why do banks accumulate high NPLs in Bangladesh? Several factors contribute to the deterioration of the loan quality of banks. Some analysts point to macroeconomic factors such as financial mismanagement; others point to policy lending by the banks usually under the behest of the government; still others find links to weaknesses in bank regulations, poor bank management, corruption, and unscrupulous practices. The state-owned banks often act as if they are fiscal agencies, providing poor follow-ups once a loan is disbursed. Heavy bank losses usually result from poor quality of assets.

Some studies point to financial liberalisation, lax monetary policy and capital inflows as factors that contribute to increased liquidity in the economy; increased liquidity, in turn, affects the lending behaviour of banks and encourages them to engage in reckless lending, often leading to asset bubbles, particularly in equity and real estate prices. As a consequence, the bank's crucial role of financial intermediation is hampered.

Effective prudential regulation and supervision of banks are essential to financial stability and efficient operation of the economy because the banking system plays a central role in the payments system and in mobilisation and distribution of savings. In Bangladesh, although prudential regulations may appear adequate, the implementation is often inconsistent, leading to a moral hazard behaviour by the banking and corporate sectors.

In addition, lack of efficient and functioning insolvency laws or bankruptcy and foreclosure laws to support asset recovery and to deal with timely credit repayment not only accelerate the NPL accumulation process but also set a barrier in the efficient and swift disposition of NPLs. Besides the effects on bank intermediation, factors affecting NPL resolution vary considerably. There are important institutional factors or political will or inherent business cultures that are important determinants.

Several countries have used AMCs to rapidly clean up the books of banks of bad assets. The usual procedure is that banks unload nonperforming assets to an AMC, clean up their books, and continue with its primary role of financial intermediation. The AMCs, either government- or private-owned, then dispose the acquired assets through a variety of means such as public auctions, resale of assets to original borrowers, joint ventures, securitisation, or even running the acquired business themselves.

In terms of the institutional design, six criteria are considered important for an AMC's successful operation: (1) objectives (clear and non-conflicting); (2) management style (e.g. AMC is willing to consider new operational strategies such as joint ventures); (3) human resources (e.g. sufficient expertise and skills in associated areas); (4) funding availability (e.g. availability of government guarantees or adequate funds relative to the level of bad assets to be disposed); (5) relative portfolio size; and (6) political will (e.g. whether or not the AMC has extrajudicial power to accommodate rapid debt resolution). These are necessary for ensuring efficiency, flexibility and transparency of the AMC.

In general, empirical evidence from several countries suggests that AMCs help expedite the restructuring or resolution of huge stock of NPLs. They can also be instrumental in stopping the deterioration of banking sector profitability. However, the design of AMC has significant effect on its performance. There appears to be a trend towards establishing private, instead of public or government-funded, AMC that is strong in management and human resources. The private sector route may be followed through special purpose vehicles (SPVs), which may have less concern about political interference and funding. SPVs are private sector-owned AMCs that normally buy bad assets and dispose them for profit.

The varied performance of AMCs in different countries shows that the establishment of AMC is not, by itself, a panacea. There are preconditions and supportive institutional setups that facilitate its operation and render it more effective. AMC needs to have independence from political interference, sufficient financial resources, adequate pool of experts, and well-focused objectives. Successful AMCs may even be endowed with special legal powers to overcome the complex judicial procedures for asset recovery.

Since high GDP growth can reduce the cost, one policy to resolve NPLs is proper macroeconomic management that facilitates stability and growth. The government also needs to ensure the institutional and legal framework which is conducive to a speedy restructuring and resolution of the assets transferred to the AMCs from banks. The judicial and legal framework for insolvency should be efficient and least time-consuming.

Thus successful AMCs can help banks improve their balance sheet picture, thereby allowing banks to free up capital for lending. On the other hand, for successful restructuring of NPLs into high value uses, supportive institutional and legal framework of AMCs is crucial. The government may decide to set up special bankruptcy courts to attend to AMC-transferred assets cases only along with strict time-bound proceedings including the appeal process. These measures will help increase the price offered by AMCs to the banks as the residual value of restructured NPL assets will increase; thereby encouraging banks to release the better priced bad loans. The global experience points to one lesson: NPLs do not disappear with time; NPL problems only grow worse with time unless there is a political will to resolve them.

9.3.2 Monetary Transmissions

The financial system plays a growth-supporting role and takes on additional market functions. Financial institutions develop out of the need to deal with transaction costs and overcome information problems (Levine 1997). The real economy is influenced through enhanced capital accumulation and innovation. The development of endogenous growth theory focuses on innovation as a determinant of real growth and offers a more important role for finance as a driving force of the real economy (Thiel 2001).

Capital accumulation and factor productivity are the major channels through which real growth can be stimulated by the financial system. The financial system mobilises dispersed (hoarded) savings and pools them in order to make them available for investment. It also diversifies liquidity and more general risks. Furthermore, the financial system influences resource allocation with respect to investment productivity, both directly and indirectly. Banks and financial markets specialise in the acquisition and transformation of information on investment more efficiently than savers could, as duplication of efforts is avoided and transaction costs are reduced. In this respect the financial system also deals with agency problems which stem from asymmetric information between the borrower and the lender. This implies an investment evaluation function and an ex post monitoring function of the intermediaries and securities sectors.

For the Bangladesh Bank to achieve its mandate effectively, it is extremely important that monetary transmission works seamlessly, while any impediment to the monetary transmission process hampers the achievement of the central bank's mandate. Monetary transmission is essentially the process through which the policy action of the Bangladesh Bank is transmitted to the ultimate objective of stable inflation and sustainable high growth. The policy action consists typically of changing the interest rate at which it borrows or lends 'reserves' on an overnight basis with commercial banks.

In other words, monetary transmission is the entire process starting from the change in the policy rate by the Bangladesh Bank to various money market rates such as inter-bank lending rates, to bank deposit rates, to bank lending rates to households and enterprises, to government and corporate bond yields, and to asset prices such as stock prices and housing prices, culminating in its impact on inflation and growth. The transmission mechanism hinges crucially on how monetary policy changes influence households' and enterprises' behaviour. This change can take place through several channels. The primary channels are: (1) interest rate channel; (2) credit channel; (3) exchange rate channel; and (4) asset price channel.

The immediate impact of a change in the monetary policy rate is on the short-term money market rates (such as, call money rate, certificates of deposits, commercial papers, treasury bills), key financial markets (exchange rate, equity prices), and also on medium and long-term instruments (yields on dated government securities and corporate bonds). The impact is typically quick and broadly one-to-one from the policy rate to short-term money market rates such as the call money rate which is the unsecured or uncollateralised inter-bank lending rate. A bank will be willing to part with its reserves overnight to another bank only if it earns at least the rate that it could earn by keeping these funds with the central bank; and, if banks compete adequately for such lending, then the rate will in fact track closely the central bank's policy rate. The impact of the policy rate on other market rates varies across tenors and instruments depending upon the liquidity conditions and other factors such as how interest rates vary at different maturities.

In turn, Bangladesh Bank's changes in its policy rate are expected to impact the banks' cost of funds, both the rates they would pay to depositors and the rates they would demand for making loans. For example, when the central bank reduces the policy repo rate with the intention to support aggregate demand in the economy, the expectation is that there would be a reduction in the banks' cost of funds and lending rates, and in the spectrum of market interest rates (and vice versa when the policy rate is increased). Lower lending interest rates of banks provide a boost to the demand for bank credit from various segments of the society, for instance, from individuals and households for loans for consumer durables (such as automobiles) and for housing; and from entrepreneurs for new or increased investment in plant and machinery. An increased demand for automobiles, housing, and machinery generates increased demand for the inputs including labour in these industries, and hence, an increase in overall demands, incomes and output in the economy. As this process continues, it eventually puts upward pressure on wages of labour and prices of inputs, and this way, raises inflation. A central bank mandated to maintain stable prices while taking account of growth thus faces a trade-off while lowering or raising its policy rate.

The implicit assumption in the above is that bank balance sheets are strong and in a position to step-up quickly the supply of credit in response to lower funding cost and higher demand for credit—the bank lending or the credit channel of transmission. Cross-country evidence indicates that monetary transmission is greatly hindered if bank balance sheets are weak and they do not have much loss-absorption capacity to deal with their problem loans, resulting in accumulation of bad loans, resulting in misallocation of resources, productivity losses and slow growth. This way, attempts to stimulate growth with aggressive policy rate cuts when there are bank balance-sheet problems may not work and may lead to deeper balance sheet crisis.

Lower interest rates also boost asset prices such as housing and equity prices as these can be purchased at cheaper borrowing costs. The resulting boost to household/corporate wealth and improved cash flows due to lower interest rates also add to demand impulses. This is the asset price channel of monetary transmission. Higher asset prices can enhance the value of the collateral or net worth of the borrowers, interacting with the bank lending or credit channel, enhancing the capacity to borrow more and at competitive rates, reinforcing the impulses to aggregate demand.

Finally, lower domestic interest rates can lead to a depreciation of the domestic currency, on the one hand making exports more competitive in the global market and adding to domestic demand and economic activity. On the other hand, this may also have a direct upward impact on the domestic currency prices of imported inputs, making imports (e.g. crude oil) costlier. This is the exchange rate channel of transmission.

Further, all these channels do not work separately; rather, they work at the same time, and may reinforce or interact with each other, so that their individual impact is difficult to disentangle. It also needs to be recognised that the transmission mechanism is complex. The speed and strength at which the central bank's policy rate changes percolate to the rest of the economy could vary widely from country to country depending on the structure of the economy and the state of its financial system.

Although no empirical evidence is available on the lags with which monetary policy actions are felt on output and inflation in Bangladesh, these lags are likely to be substantial. Among the channels of transmission, the interest rate channel is the strongest. Given that the monetary policy impacts output and inflation with long (and often variable) lags, it is critical for monetary policy actions to be forward-looking, that is monetary policy should respond to expected output and inflation in future. Since expected output and inflation is more unpredictable in a country like Bangladesh, this renders the transmission analysis more challenging, adding to the complexity of the central bank's decision-making process. The key issue is that if the transmission mechanism is weak with low efficiency, then the monetary policy would be less effective.

Bangladesh's financial system still remains overwhelmingly bank-dominated. Hence, the overall efficacy of monetary transmission depends critically on the extent and the pace with which banks adjust their deposit and lending rates and meet adequately the economy's demand for credit due to changes in the policy repo rate. Overall, empirical evidence suggests that the pass-through from policy rate changes to bank lending rates is slow and subdued in Bangladesh. This lack of adequate monetary transmission remains a key policy concern for the Bangladesh Bank. Since the deregulation of interest rates in the early 1990s, Bangladesh Bank has been working to improve the speed and extent of the monetary pass-through by refining the process of setting lending interest rates by banks, while improving transparency to the borrowers and the flexibility in the process of interest rate setting.

In Bangladesh, a large proportion of the loans is at floating rates i.e., the interest rate charged to the borrower keeps changing depending on the reset periodicity. The floating rate is linked to some 'benchmark rate'. Banks also charge a spread over the benchmark to factor-in term premium and credit risk, among other factors. The actual lending rate is the benchmark plus the spread. The benchmark could be internal or external; an internal benchmark is based on elements which are in part under the control of the bank such as cost of funds, while an external benchmark is outside the control of the bank (e.g. it could be market determined rate such as certificate of deposit rate or treasury bill rate or inter-bank offer rate, or it could simply be the central bank's policy rate).

The virtue of an external benchmark is that it is transparent, common across banks, and borrowers can compare various loan offers by simply comparing spreads over the benchmark. As market rates normally move in line with the central bank's policy rate, an external benchmark is globally considered and adopted as more appropriate than an internal benchmark for transmitting monetary policy signals. In Bangladesh, banks enjoy the flexibility to use both the internal and external benchmarks, but the banks seem to prefer internal benchmarks on two counts: first, the internal benchmark reflects their cost of funds; and second, it is perceived that there do not exist any robust and vibrant external benchmarks.

In this context, what is important for Bangladesh Bank is to explore possibilities to reduce the weaknesses and rigidities in the transmission mechanism through effective measures. For example, the banks may determine their benchmark lending rates taking into account the marginal cost of funds, such that the lending rates could be more sensitive to changes in the policy rate. The actual lending rate may also include a spread for covering the costs of business strategy, credit risk premium and others. This will give better transparency, more flexibility and faster transmission.

The low pass-through from policy rate to bank lending rates is affected either by the banks not changing the benchmark rate or by adjusting the spread. The rate rigidity on the liability side of the banks may be caused by several factors in Bangladesh. In the country's banking sector, the overwhelming share of total liabilities of banks is in the form of deposits. Bank deposits are predominantly at fixed interest rates, thereby imparting rigidity to the transmission process. Further, more than one-third of the deposit accounts are fixed deposits, implying that their rates get reset infrequently and with significant lags to policy rate changes. While the banks' marginal cost of funds may drop quickly with a cut in fresh deposit rates, the average cost of deposits comes down rather slowly, which weakens the transmission.

Further, the banks in Bangladesh have a large access to low cost current and savings account funds. These funds constitute about 30 per cent of aggregate bank deposits with the share of saving deposits at around 20 per cent. More importantly, the banks are mostly free to decide saving deposit interest rates which do not necessarily follow the monetary policy signals. In addition, the deterioration in the banking sector health due to worsening of asset quality over the past several years and the expected loan losses in credit portfolios also induce large variability in spreads in the pricing of assets. Indeed, the weak banks aim to maintain profitability in the short-term even at the expense of long-term profits as well as deposits and lending shares. This also has significant impact on the transmission to the lending rates. These and other factors contribute towards rigidity in the liability side of banks' balance sheet with respect to policy rate changes, inducing a behaviour that makes the rates on the asset side of banks' balance sheet rigid as well.

Bangladesh Bank needs to take steps to enhance the transparency and transmission from monetary policy signals to the actual lending rates of the banks. In the long run, the need is to shift to an external benchmark based lending rate system as the internal benchmark based pricing regimes are not consistent with global practices on pricing of bank loans. The transformation should be pursued in a time-bound manner. While recognising that no external instrument in Bangladesh meets all the requirements of an ideal benchmark, the Treasury Bill rate or the Bangladesh Bank's policy repo rate may better serve as an external benchmark. Similarly, the periodicity of resetting the interest rates by banks on all floating rate loans, retail as well as corporate, may be reduced to once in a quarter to expedite the pass through from the monetary policy signal to the actual lending rates. To reduce rigidity on the liabilities side, the banks may be encouraged to accept deposits, especially bulk deposits, at floating rates linked directly to the selected external benchmark.

The efforts should be directed to improve the monetary transmission by ensuring that changes in the policy rate transmit quickly and adequately to banks' lending rates in a transparent manner. The aim is to make the banks' liability side more flexible so that the objectives of improving monetary transmission by the Bangladesh Bank and maintaining healthy net interest rate margins by the banks are effectively aligned.

Obviously, efficient monetary transmission is a pre-requisite for the successful pursuit of its objectives by any central bank. The transmission from the policy repo rate to bank lending rates, which is the dominant transmission channel in Bangladesh, remains an issue of concern. The key issue is to address: who should bear the interest rate risk in the economy—the borrower, or the depositor, or the bank? Retail depositors and borrowers are unlikely to have efficient tools to manage the interest rate risk. Banks, however, should have the ability to manage the interest rate risk. Similarly, large depositors and large corporate borrowers can also be expected to be in a position to manage the interest rate risk. Non-bank financial institutions with less exposure to interest rate risk, such as insurance and pension funds, could also be good repositories of this risk. A combination of interest-rate risk transfer mechanisms through market products such as interest rate derivatives (e.g. swaps) and securitised products such as collateralised loan obligations (CLOs) can also be good vehicles.

9.4 Financial Sector Challenges for Bangladesh

As a MIC, Bangladesh is likely to face increased vulnerability to economic and financial openness. The MICs which expose themselves to global flows of goods and capital without proper safeguards run the risk of being affected more by global crises. For avoiding financial vulnerability, Bangladesh needs reforms including the implementation of a strong and coordinated medium term macroeconomic framework so as to reduce the risks to financial and macroeconomic stability (World Bank 2010; Van Doorn et al. 2010). The important issues are a lack of flexibility in the exchange rate, high debt equity ratio, a lack of regional cooperation for volatility control, and weak institutional frameworks to deepen local currency markets (Gill and Kharas 2007; UN General Assembly 2011; Foxley 2009).

In addition, vulnerability may also emanate from the very economic integration which contributes to increased competitiveness. Rapid integration of the Bangladesh economy in the global market can have adverse effects when domestic industries are not sufficiently competitive and when there is an unplanned transfer from agricultural to industrial production. In the former case, domestic industries unable to keep up with global production fall behind, exposing the economy to volatile global commodity markets. In the latter case, a slow transfer of labour into industrial production increases unemployment and results in low wages of labour.

On the other hand, recovery in the face of a global financial crisis is facilitated by the capacity to attract large capital inflows, which allows reviving growth before undertaking restrictive monetary and fiscal policies. Furthermore, financial deregulation needs to be a long and gradual process especially in the context of large external account surpluses. There should also be monetary and fiscal policies to overcome weak economic fundamentals and the self-fulfilling nature of the crisis. The financial sector reforms should focus on quickly normalising the financial system through restructuring, and rebuilding a financial safety net to prevent future crises.

Further, Bangladesh needs to ensure that all banks (and also non-bank financial institutions) are strong and healthy. It also needs to manage the pace of further liberalisation of the financial markets and to balance it against the risk of interconnectivity of domestic financial markets with global financial flows. The country also needs to implement a consistent macroeconomic policy framework with multiple instruments, including the traditional market based interest rate instrument and administrative measures such as statutory reserves requirement, for absorbing the excess liquidity generated by capital inflows (Anglingkusumo 2013).

9.4.1 Financial Policies for Higher Income Transition

The analysis brings out a number of basic challenges that deserve well-articulated policies for ensuring a relatively smooth higher income transition of Bangladesh. One major challenge relates to economic and financial stability. In addition to domestic determinants, these are related to global and regional financial flows and the rising openness of the country's markets and trade regimes. Bangladesh needs to design specific macroeconomic mechanisms and tools to avoid crises, and recover from crises during its upper middle-income journey. There are also challenges to economic growth, in which the planning and implementing role of both the public and private sectors are important. Bangladesh needs to successfully navigate the relationship between the public and private sectors in overcoming the challenges to growth.

Also, challenges to social equity have particular dimensions in Bangladesh, and the country's approach to the problems of poverty and income inequality and access to social services needs to shape an effective social welfare regime. Environmental challenges are also keys to understanding and managing sustainable future growth for Bangladesh. Both environmental and social inclusiveness needs appropriate financing along with innovative strategies. These challenges should comprehend the crucial role of demography and urbanisation.

Further, adopting policies for Bangladesh's upper middle income journey is not a simple two-step matter of identifying the 'correct' policies and adapting these to Bangladesh context. More consideration needs to be given to the policy formulation process (the 'how') and to the fuller understanding of the direction that the country is taking for development (the 'why'). The policy agenda needs also to highlight the interconnectedness of the above issues and the importance of sequencing in tackling them. The traditional sequencing is to provide overriding priority to industrial growth, followed sequentially by efforts to rescue and prevent crises, promote equality and welfare, and finally alleviate climate change and environmental degradation. Also, the preference for addressing inequity is not by radical redistribution policies, but mainly by social protection measures. The real challenge for Bangladesh is to find a model that can tackle all the above issues within a short period of time without incurring serious adverse effects that fit with the country's multiple goals.

For an upper middle-income Bangladesh, one critical strategy for reducing inequalities is that of ensuring universal access to good quality basic goods and services. This can be seen as part of a 'social protection floor'—an integrated set of social policies designed to guarantee income security and access to essential social services for all, paying particular attention to the vulnerable groups and protecting and empowering people across the life cycle.

In the above context, it is important to recognise that the growth of social assistance has important implications for the working of the labour market and evolution of welfare institutions. Labour supply responses to social assistance transfers are broadly positive. Human development focused programmes targeting children's schooling mostly reduce child labour, while social pensions reduce the labour supply of elders. Social assistance programmes can facilitate a welfare improving re-allocation of household productive resources. A guaranteed minimum income can facilitate job search, labour migration, and improve labour earnings; but the effects are highly dependent on household conditions. The growth of social assistance will also shape in important ways the evolution of welfare institutions. Social assistance growth is effective in supporting the inclusion of informal and low income groups within social protection systems.

For the financial sector, an important priority is to ensure that all banks (and also non-bank financial institutions) are strong and healthy. It is well recognised that an economic crisis that includes a banking crisis usually have a more severe and prolonged impact on the real sector of the economy. An unhealthy banking industry also tends to weaken the determination of policy makers to implement a consistent macroeconomic policy when these policies are most needed. As a result, an unhealthy banking industry tends to exacerbate macroeconomic imbalances and solidify the foundations for a larger financial crisis.

Accordingly, the government needs to develop stronger regulatory and supervisory frameworks for the banking industry and continuously enhance the frameworks so as to make them in line with the international best practices. Another important financial policy is to implement a counter-cyclical capital buffer. This would reduce the pro-cyclicality of credit growth over the business cycles, hence promoting moderation of economic cycles. It is also necessary to ensure that the government's medium to long-term fiscal posture is solid. A weak fiscal posture projects inconsistency of macroeconomic policy and a credibility gap which severely lowers the government's ability to consolidate private supports for reform.

In addition, it is important to manage the pace of liberalisation of the financial markets. While introducing more financial innovations into the financial markets will add to the vibrancy of trading activities and improve liquidity, this course of action would also increase the interconnectivity of domestic financial markets with the global financial markets, particularly with markets in mature economies, and attract more speculative traders.

As such, macro-financial policy makers need to carefully weigh-in on the balance between advantages and disadvantages of such policy direction. Moreover, policy makers need to complement the implementation of stability oriented monetary policy with steps to further strengthen the regulatory, supervisory and monitoring frameworks of the financial system. The overriding aim should be to prevent excessive leveraging (risk taking behaviour) that may compromise the state of financial stability. The promotion of market discipline and injection of a reasonable dose of conservatism through strong regulations are key factors in ensuring that financial markets do not develop into a shock amplifying factor for the real side of the economy and hence a nullifying factor on the pace of poverty reduction.

Bangladesh's priority would be to implement a consistent macroeconomic policy framework with multiple instruments, including the traditional market based interest rate instrument and administrative measures such as statutory reserves requirement, for absorbing the excess liquidity generated by the capital inflows. This is particularly important at the initial stage of Bangladesh's financial development. Towards this end, the need is to accelerate the development of domestic capital markets, with a particular attention to the market for government bonds, by promoting a more liquid market for local currency government bonds and a well-functioning money market. These would help increase the effectiveness of the implementation of a market based monetary policy.

This may be followed by the use of fully sterilised foreign exchange market interventions, to limit the impact of real exchange rate appreciation on economic growth during episodes of large capital inflows. In other words, as Bangladesh wants to accumulate foreign exchange reserves, it needs to fortify itself with self-insurance against the adverse impact of volatile capital flows. But if this measure is taken, in addition to full sterilisation, Bangladesh needs also to expedite real sector reform, for real competitiveness is an outcome of value added and not of prices. In this context, Bangladesh needs to implement measures to strengthen the capacity of public institutions in planning, implementing and monitoring structural reforms. This would help remove a large portion of impediments to a more balanced and higher long run economic growth.

The hypothesis is strong that a key element in any strategy of development for higher income transition of a country like Bangladesh is to extend the 'frontier of finance'. In Bangladesh, the causality between finance and growth can have important differences due to institutional factors and the quality of finance, which are, in turn, determined by the quality of financial regulation and the rule of law. For example, an increase in financial deepening, as captured by standard indicators of financial development, may not result in increased growth because of corruption in the banking system or political interference, which may divert credit to unproductive or even wasteful activities or to feed speculative bubbles. Similarly, where it is used for consumption purposes as opposed to productive investment, the effect of financial depth on economic growth is limited (Beck et al. 2012).

9.4.1.1 The Monetary Policy

Although maintaining price stability is a predominant objective of Bangladesh's macroeconomic policy, Bangladesh refrains from the conservative stance of 'inflation targeting' (Hammond 2012), which has been widely adopted in many countries. The Monetary Policy Statement (MPS) of the Bangladesh Bank usually aligns with the overall macroeconomic objectives of the economy, and adopts '***monetary policy stance and monetary program.... with dual objective of maintaining price stability and supporting inclusive, equitable and environmentally sustainable job rich economic growth in tune with the government's strategies and goals for sustainable growth and development***' (Bangladesh Bank, Monetary Policy Statement, Fiscal Year 2019–20: 10).

For an upper middle income Bangladesh, the price stability challenge is complex and requires a careful review of what should be realistic short-run inflation, how low it should be, and how it is calibrated through potential inflation-growth trade-off. It is also important to trace the multiple causes of inflation, and the policy instruments that are traditionally applied to contain inflation. There are only few empirical studies on inflation-growth trade-offs in Bangladesh and monitoring of such trade-offs.

In Bangladesh, available evidence shows that the volatility in inflation comes from factors affecting both non-food inflation and food inflation. There are various factors behind food price fluctuations for example supply disruptions due to floods and other natural disasters, price distortions by market intermediaries, and rise in food import prices, among others. Clearly, controlling inflation in Bangladesh requires other interventions to complement the monetary instruments. Long-term public investments and other measures would be needed to address structural factors and food price volatility. It may be noted that, over the last two decades, the rate of inflation in Bangladesh has fluctuated, and the level of fluctuation was much higher in the 1990s than in the 2000s. Thus, volatility of inflation has not been a major concern during the past two decades in Bangladesh.

Furthermore, monetary policy seems to have limited power to control inflation in Bangladesh. The instruments at the disposal of Bangladesh Bank are often not effective to respond to inflationary tendencies. The Bank rate (the policy rate) has been held constant almost since FY2003–04 (Bangladesh Bank uses the repo rate as a proxy policy rate); instead, it addresses price stability largely through the credit/deposit channel, often by maintaining a closely monitored relationship between broad money

(M2) and reserve money (RM).[5] The use of control over money aggregates (credit channel) provides a pseudo control over the credit flow to the private sector. The credit channel, however, has its limitations, and may miss the inflation target. On the other hand, the policy rate channel cannot be made effective since the 'transmission mechanisms' are very weak, and financial infrastructure is underdeveloped.

For an upper middle income Bangladesh, reforms for greater market competition in the financial sector will have to be broadened and deepened. This will place increasing responsibility on the Bangladesh Bank's 'policy rate', the effectiveness of which will depend on, among others, greater financial deepening, strengthening of credit and debit markets and interbank transactions and integration—all within an efficient regulatory and accountability framework.

A major concern is to increase the efficiency of the existing monetary and financial system, along with its ability to control inflation and exchange rate stability in the near future, when the economy will be poised towards a higher growth pathway which may require greater external interaction. There are other potential threats to price stability that can trigger inflation uncertainties, such as fiscal dominance. Bangladesh's projected growth for transition to upper middle income status would require much higher public expenditure to meet infrastructural and social needs. Increased borrowing, especially from the banking sector, in case there is revenue shortfall will then likely to cause price instability.

Another potential source is the exchange rate volatility. Although in principle, Bangladesh maintains a market-based, free-floating exchange rate regime, Bangladesh Bank periodically intervenes to buy/sell foreign currency to reduce volatility and support international competitiveness of Bangladesh exports. In the growing Bangladesh economy, growth of export capacity to meet future import surge and sustained growth in remittance flows are important determinants of external stability.

In short, the working of the monetary policy at present remains constrained by serious shortcomings of several factors as reflected in the persistently unacceptable level of non-performing loans (NPLs) and capital adequacy ratios (CARs), high interest rate spreads, and the huge

[5] This reflects a calibration of inflation rate tracking and potential output growth, weighted by a money demand multiplier; usually taken as a sum up of projected inflation, GDP growth, plus a multiplier factor.

proportion of classified loans, especially in the state-owned commercial banks (SCBs).

Moreover, despite reforms and expansion of different types of institutions, a strong, competitive and efficient banking system has not as yet emerged. The banking system is mired in corruption, mismanagement, and direct interference from the government. The banks do not follow the practice of determining the interest rate under competitive conditions. Both lending and deposit rates are set under oligopolistic conditions, possibly following collusive or cartel type behaviours.

It may be noted that the banking sector is still the dominant financial intermediary in Bangladesh's financial system due to the underdeveloped money and capital markets, limited availability of financial instruments, and lack of confidence in the financial system as a whole. Bangladesh Bank faces significant limitations in following an independent monetary policy consistent with its objectives. The government still plays an important role in the financial sector as a major borrower from the banking system.

Further, overall stability and performance of the banking sector is not satisfactory due to high nonperforming loans (NPLs), lack of good governance and other factors. As Table 9.4 shows there exists a huge variation in CARs and the NPLs amongst various groups of commercial banks. The better performance in these indicators by the foreign banks allows them to maintain a higher interest rate spread. The interest rate spread is still high, and is often attributed to loan defaults (and scams), but also to alleged 'collusive, oligopolistic fixing of lending rates. Some of these factors are linked to political and vested interest groups. There also persist serious

Table 9.4 Banking sector indicators in Bangladesh

	2005			*2018*		
	CAR	*Gross NPL ratio*	*Interest rate spread*	*CAR*	*Gross NPL ratio*	*Interest rate spread*
SCBs	-0.84	24.37	5.14	2.0	28.24	3.57
SBs	9.20	34.90	5.13	-31.86	21.68	3.24
PCBs	9.45	7.76	5.25	12.24	6.01	4.33
FCBs	24.62	1.54	7.93	22.97	6.66	7.07
All banks	7.08	15.79	5.31	10.00	10.41	4.45

Source: Bangladesh Bank, *Annual Report*, different years

governance deficits, which constrain any move to bring the financial institutions towards the best-practice standards. The current turmoil in the banking and financial sector could increase rapid exposures to investment risks.

Further, proper assessment of risks and costs of alternative sources of funds are often acute in decision making by financial administrators. Lack of ethics in the banking sector is a part of a wider and persistent socioeconomic and political culture in the country (see, Mujeri and Islam 2008). Unhealthy competition among different banks displays lack of ethics in doing banking business.

9.4.1.2 Capital and Equity Market

For stimulating economic growth and development, Bangladesh requires long-term funding, far longer than the duration for which most savers are willing to commit their funds. In this regard, the capital market provides an avenue for mobilisation and utilisation of long-term funds for development and hence it is referred to as the long-term end of the financial system. An upsurge in capital market activity as a tool for fast-tracking economic progress is therefore extremely important for upper middle-income Bangladesh.

Bangladesh is still at a nascent stage of capital market development although a well-functioning capital market is of great significance for Bangladesh for channelling domestic saving to productive investments, attracting foreign investors to the market, and allocating the national savings most efficiently, among others. However, the Bangladesh equity market is small, it is thin and non-transparent, and it is inefficient as well.

Bangladesh has two major exchanges, the Dhaka Stock Exchange (DSE) and the Chittagong Stock Exchange (CSE). The DSE is the larger of the two stock exchanges in the country. Formal trading on the DSE began in 1956 while the CSE was established in 1995. In 1993, the Securities and Exchange Commission (SEC) was established under the Securities and Exchange Act 1993. The functions of the SEC include regulation of equity trading, protection of investors, ensure legislative and regulatory compliances, and promote a fair, transparent and efficient security market.

At present, the capital market intermediaries consist of the following:

- Stock Exchanges: DSE and CSE
- Central Depository: The depository system for the transaction and settlement of financial securities, Central Depository Bangladesh Ltd (CDBL) was formed in 2000 which conducts its operations under Depositories Act 1999, Depositories Regulations 2000, Depository (User) Regulations 2003, and the CDBL by-laws.
- Stock Dealer/Sock Broker: Under SEC (Stock Dealer, Stock Broker & Authorised Representative) Rules 2000, these entities are licensed and they are bound to be a member of any of the two stock exchanges. At present, DSE and CSE have 238 and 136 members respectively.
- Merchant Banker and Portfolio Manager: These institutions are licensed to operate under SEC (Merchant Banker and Portfolio Manager Rules) 1996 and 45 institutions have been licensed by SEC under this rules so far.
- Asset Management Companies (AMCs): AMCs are authorised to act as issue and portfolio manager of the mutual funds which are issued under SEC (Mutual Fund) Rules 2001. There are 15 AMCs in Bangladesh at present.
- Credit Rating Companies (CRCs): CRCs in Bangladesh are licensed under Credit Rating Companies Rules, 1996 and now, five CRCs have been accredited by SEC.
- Trustees/Custodians: According to rules, all asset backed securitisations and mutual funds must have an accredited trusty and security custodian. For the purpose, SEC has licensed nine institutions as Trustees and nine institutions as custodians.
- Investment Corporation of Bangladesh (ICB): ICB is a specialised capital market intermediary which was established in 1976 through the ordainment of The Investment Corporation of Bangladesh Ordinance 1976. This ordinance has empowered ICB to perform all types of capital market intermediation that fall under jurisdiction of SEC. ICB has three subsidiaries: ICB Capital Management Ltd., ICB Asset Management Company Ltd., and ICB Securities Trading Company Ltd.

However, the underdeveloped and non-transparent nature of the capital market in Bangladesh provides ample opportunities for unethical and even illegal manipulations resulting in several market crashes in recent decades. Such unwarranted crashes usually cause severe financial damages to investors, particularly the small investors and erode confidence in the market.

The role of capital markets in stimulating economic progress is less debatable as there are well established theoretical frameworks for a priori expectation to be in the affirmative. However, there are considerable challenges in developing the capital market in Bangladesh:

- Macroeconomic stability

A stable macroeconomic environment is crucial for the development of the capital market. Macroeconomic volatility worsens the problem of informational asymmetries and becomes a source of vulnerability to the financial system. Low and predictable rates of inflation are more likely to contribute to stock market development and economic growth. Both domestic and foreign investors will be unwilling to invest in the stock market where there are expectations of high inflation. Garcia and Liu (1999) argue that sound macroeconomic environments and high income levels, domestic savings, and domestic investments are important determinants of stock market development.

- Development of the banking sector

The development of the banking sector is important for stock market development. At the early stages, the capital market is a complement rather than substitute for the banking sector. Developing the financial intermediary sector can promote the development of the capital market. The conduct of macroeconomic policies not only affects but may also be affected by the condition of the financial system.

Support services from the banking system contribute significantly to the development of the stock market. Consequently, liquid inter-bank markets, largely supported by an efficient banking system, are important for the development of the stock market. Conversely, a weak-banking system can constrain the development of the stock market.

- Institutional quality

Institutional quality is important for stock market development because efficient and accountable institutions tend to broaden appeal and confidence in equity investment. The development of good quality institutions can affect the attractiveness of equity investment and lead to stock market development. Good quality institutions such as law and order, democratic accountability, bureaucratic quality are important determinants of stock market development as they reduce political risk and enhance the viability of external finance (Yartey 2007).

- Shareholder protection

Another key determinant of capital market development is the level of shareholder protection in publicly traded companies. Capital market development is more likely to take place in countries with strong shareholder protection because investors do not fear expropriation. In addition, ownership in such market can be relatively dispersed, which provides liquidity to the market.

No doubt, the stock market in Bangladesh is a complex institution imbued with inherent mechanism through which long-term funds of the major sectors of the economy comprising households, firms, and government can be mobilised, harnessed and made available to various sectors of the economy. The development of the capital market, and the stock market, provides opportunities for greater fund mobilisation and improved efficiency in resource allocation.

At present, Bangladesh's capital market does not have varied instruments/products in both equities and debt markets. The former are instruments or products that confer ownership rights on the investor, while the latter are interest-bearing obligations with fixed or floating interest-rates.

Moreover, the country's capital market problems are both endogenous and exogenous. The exogenous problems are those outside the direct control of the market but which are regulation-induced. The endogenous problems are those that are internal to the market but which are amenable to changes with improved operational procedures including the adoption of information technology. Some of these problems cover small size of the market, problem of illiquidity of the market, slow growth of the securities market, double taxation, lack of effective underwriting and macroeconomic instability.

9.4.1.3 Functioning of the Stock Market

According to orthodox theory, a stock market can contribute to development through a variety of channels: it could raise savings and investment by making it possible for individuals and households to purchase a fraction of an enterprise, thereby spreading the risk, without which investment may not occur. Similarly, the monitoring function is performed automatically by the stock market and, from the perspective of an entrepreneur, this helps raise investment. A well-functioning stock market allocates resources more efficiently through its normal pricing process, which would accord, other things being equal, higher share prices to efficient firms and lower prices to inefficient ones.

Further, the take-over mechanism ensures that not just the new investment resources but also the existing capital stock is efficiently utilised. Inefficient use of existing resources is penalised by the market for corporate control through disciplinary takeovers. In practice, how effectively the stock market can perform the above tasks depends on the efficiency of two critical market mechanisms, namely (1) the pricing mechanism; and (2) the take-over mechanism.

In the case of share prices, in the face of highly uncertain future, share prices are likely to be influenced by the so-called 'noise traders', and by whims, fads and contagion. In developing countries, apart from the normal mis-pricing, which is particularly likely to be severe as the firms are not likely to have a long track record, share prices are more volatile than in advanced countries. Share price volatility is a negative feature of stock markets for several reasons. First, it reduces the efficiency of the price signals in allocating investment resources. Secondly, it increases the riskiness of investments and may discourage risk-averse enterprises from financing their growth by equity issues, and indeed from seeking a stock market listing at all. Thirdly, at the macroeconomic level, a highly volatile stock market may lead to financial fragility for the whole economy (Singh 1999, 2000).

Bangladesh's stock markets are characterised by large volatility with recurrent periods of boom and bust that represent a destabilising force for the economy. For example, following a bull run during 2010, the Dhaka index fell by about a half from its December 2010 all-time high, corresponding to a loss of about 22 per cent of GDP by October 2012. The market correction wiped out $27 billion in market capitalisation and, with it, bankruptcies, savings, and jobs, triggering a wave of social discontent (Shah 2016). The ensuing liquidity crunch led to heightened solvency risks. Given the interconnectedness between banks and equity markets, such incidents can result in a negative feedback loop from the financial sector to the real economy.

The market for corporate control is often considered as the evolutionary endpoint of stock market development. An active market for corporate control presents a credible threat that inefficient managers will be replaced to maximise shareholder value and thereby raise corporate performance. This consideration is particularly important for developing countries like Bangladesh where there are large, potentially predatory, conglomerate groups. These could take over smaller, more efficient firms and thereby reduce potential competition to the detriment of the real economy.

At present, Bangladesh like most other developing countries does not have well-functioning stock markets. Not only is there inadequate government regulation, efficient private information gathering and disseminating firms are also absent. The markets suffer from significant regulatory and informational deficits: the markets remain 'immature' (i.e. riddled with insider trading and lack of transparency) and relatively illiquid. Most trading takes place in a few blue-chip shares. The regulator also finds it difficult to regulate the stock markets, as is indicated by frequent scams in the stock markets.

Volatility in the stock market may further accentuate if external portfolio capital inflows are allowed. This greatly increases the vulnerability of the economy not only to international shocks, but also to domestic shocks, substantially magnifying their effects. The main reason for this is that capital inflows lead to an interaction between two inherently unstable markets—the stock market and the currency market. In the event of a large shock (domestic or external), these interactions generate a negative feedback that may lead to, or greatly worsen, a financial crisis.

Therefore, along with developing the banking sector, Bangladesh needs to take appropriate measures and regulations to ensure that the stock markets do not become a source of instability or short-termism in the economy. For this reason, Bangladesh also needs to discourage the emergence of a market for corporate control. Bangladesh should find other institutional ways of replacing inefficient managements which are reliable and cheap compared with the takeover device on the stock markets.

For the middle income Bangladesh, regulation of the financial sector needs to be counter-cyclical—to prevent boom–bust cycles which can lead to developmentally costly crises—and comprehensive, to include all institutions that provide credit. Capital flows should also be prudently managed, and where appropriate, capital account regulations should complement domestic financial regulation. Furthermore, since borrowing on the international bond markets could lead to future problems; and needs careful monitoring.

The fact that Bangladesh's financial system is still relatively small in relation to the size of its economy allows more space for the policy-makers and regulators to try to shape the financial systems to serve well the needs of inclusive and sustainable growth (e.g. much needed lending to MSMEs), as well as desirable structural change. Furthermore, since the financial sector is smaller as proportion of GDP, it may imply it is less powerful politically; thus, potentially this gives more autonomy to the regulators to shape the financial sector to serve the real economy.

However, a key issue is not just the size, but also the structure of the financial sector. Because the financial sector is riddled with market imperfections and market gaps, it is important to have government intervention to correct these market imperfections (e.g. the pro-cyclical nature of private lending) and institutional arrangements to fill market gaps (e.g. sufficient long-term finance for helping finance private sector investment). In addition, it is useful for the government to have institutions and mechanisms to help finance development of particular sectors to implement the adopted vision and the strategy of development.

In this context, it is important to design instruments and institutions that can perform such functions. Public development banks have worked well in several countries (e.g. Japan, South Korea, and others) with appropriate regulations. Often it is argued that smaller, more decentralised banks may be more appropriate in developing countries, especially to lend to MSMEs, partly because they know their customers better, reducing both asymmetries of information and transaction and default costs.

Overall, a more diversified banking system, with large and small banks, as well as private and public development banks seems to offer benefits of diversification; and thus less systemic risk, complementarities in serving different sectors and functions, as well as providing competition for providing cheaper and appropriate financial services to the real economy.

However, capital markets are not without risks. In a country like Bangladesh, these may include the potential for asymmetric information between savers and users; non-transparency and lack of adequate regulation and monitoring of issuers; lack of adequate and efficient market infrastructure for issuing, trading, clearing and settlement; and the potential for increased volatility due to liquidity, interest rate and rollover risks. To reliably extract the benefits of well-functioning markets, adequate regulation for issuers, investors, and intermediaries in addition to robust supervisory arrangements to protect investors, promote deep and liquid markets, and manage systemic risk are critical. Such a framework in turn needs to be anchored in a good investment climate that includes a sound taxation and accounting framework, reliable and quality accountancy, creditor rights, property rights, and bankruptcy and competition law.

Finally, markets need an infrastructure—exchanges and trading platforms, clearing houses, and custodians. Typically, capital market offerings of debt securities start with the highest credit quality issuer which is typically the government, and government bond markets—beginning with short term money market instruments and extending to longer tenor bonds—form a basis for further market development by establishing price points along a yield curve and providing instruments for liquidity management. They also provide a critical mass of securities to support market infrastructure development.

Banks are often the next issuers able to come to the market. While banks may benefit from including capital market instruments in the funding mix to better match liabilities to assets, they tend to have a ready source of liquidity from deposits available to service their obligations. Utilities, which typically have long-term capital investment needs but steady and predictable cash flows, may follow and then follow the other corporates.

In parallel, it is critical that efforts be focused on developing the investor base. The most reliable and stable investor base is local. Nurturing domestic investible asset pools via pensions, insurance, and savings vehicles for individuals to deploy into the capital market is critical for local sustainable capital market development. Pension reform, development of the local insurance industry, and an increase in household savings are often part of a comprehensive capital market development programme.

Experience shows that the development of the local capital market and making greater use of it to fund private investment and strategic economic needs tends to happens in stages in a developing country like Bangladesh. Therefore, some sequencing of policies is essential. This is particularly true for debt markets, which require well-functioning money markets to create government bond markets, and they in turn are essential for corporate bond markets. Understanding the linkages between different segments of the market and their building blocks is critical to ensuring a proper sequencing of policy and regulatory reforms. Capital market development is a gradual process requiring strong leadership from the government as well as a significant commitment of time and resources. If done correctly, the payoffs can be substantial and long-term. The strategic imperative, however, is to develop strategies that fit the particular circumstances of Bangladesh.

9.5 Inflation and the Poor

In Bangladesh, it is important to recognise the costs of inflation for the poor in terms of both macroeconomic and distributive costs, such as level and distribution of income and the costs for the poor of inflation stabilisation policies in terms of growth and employment. The traditional claim is that inflation is especially costly for the poor, since their purchasing power is eroded especially for those groups whose earnings are fixed in nominal terms, their assets are devalued more as they hold a larger share of their assets in liquid form compared with the non-poor, and it is difficult for the poor to hedge against inflation due to their limited access to the financial system.

These losses are probably true in Bangladesh but this does not give the full picture. First, if the real wage falls due to inflation, employment should rise and employment effect of inflation could outweigh the real wage effect on poverty especially since the inflation (real wage) elasticity of poverty is likely to be less than the output (employment) elasticity of poverty (Garuda 2000). Second, many poor people, especially the extreme poor in rural areas, are relatively less exposed to the monetary economy than the urban population. Thus although inflation erodes the poor's wage income, the confiscation of their savings in not especially serious as they hold little cash. Third, the poor are often net debtors, and inflation possibly reduces their debt burden. Fourth, since the relative price of food generally increases through inflation in Bangladesh, at least some of the poor who are net food producers might be benefiting. However, inflation makes net purchasers of food among the poor as well as the middle class especially those having fixed incomes in monetary terms vulnerable because the middle class is highly dependent on monetary exchanges, has little surplus cash, and does not have much access to own produced basic goods.

One obvious consequence of inflation is the erosion of real income of the people resulting from the general increase in prices. The burden of income loss, however, differs across different income groups. No doubt, the household groups who are employed in the formal sector and whose salaries/wages are fixed in nominal terms and are re-fixed periodically are the worst sufferers. The same is true for those employees in the informal sector who have income fixed in nominal terms. In Bangladesh, a major concern, however, is the inflation-induced loss of real income of the poor.

While assessing the impact of inflation on the poor's income, it is important to keep in view that the poor is not a homogeneous group and they derive income from a variety of sources. The livelihood activities of the poor are diverse and their sources of household income are multiple, often involving subsistence and home-based production and participation in the low-remunerative activities in both formal and informal economy. The Household Income and Expenditure Survey (HIES) 2016 shows that, in the rural areas, the poor mostly consist of wage-labour based workers in agriculture and other nonfarm sectors, and other low-paid workers in production, services, and other activities. In the urban areas, the profile of the poor is very similar with daily wage labourers forming the majority. This shows that, since labour is the only major asset of the poor, the return to labour is the major source of their income. In the face of inflation, it is important therefore to examine whether the labourers are able to adjust the wage rate in order to make up, even if partially, for the loss in real income.

Available evidence shows that agricultural labourers, who constitute the largest poor group in the country, are usually successful in maintaining the level of their daily real wage almost unchanged through upward adjustment in the nominal wage rate without any substantial time lag (Mujeri 2008). One factor that seems to facilitate quick indexation of the nominal wage rate to inflation is the prevailing characteristics of the agricultural labour market that ensure flexibility and permit almost daily wage bargaining keeping in mind the reservation wage of a minimum quantity of the wage good (rice). A similar behaviour may also be noticed in the informal labour markets that set the daily wage rates in construction, services, and other low-paid activities in which the poor are the major participants. This shows that nearly half of the poor in the rural areas and more than one-third in the urban areas can negotiate an upward adjustment in their major source of earning, the wage component of household income, in the face of inflation. An analysis with group-specific consumer price indexes (CPIs) shows that relatively poorer households face higher inflation than non-poorer households and day labourers, and fixed income household groups face higher food inflation than non-food inflation (Hossain and Mujeri 2020).

The analysis of the dynamics of inflation and wage adjustments in Bangladesh's labour market shows that the daily wage labourers in both agriculture and non-agriculture sectors, who constitute the largest poor group in the country, are usually able to protect the level of their daily real wage in the face of rising inflation through upward adjustment in the nominal wage rate without any substantial time lag (see, Mujeri et al. 2020). A similar behaviour is also noticed in the informal labour markets that set the daily wage rates in construction, services, transport (including rickshaw pulling) and other low-paid activities in which the poor are the major participants. The poor day labourers in Bangladesh have some ability to at least partially revise their nominal wage income rather quickly to compensate for the loss in real income due to inflation. On the other hand, the self-employed category, salaried poor households, are more likely to be negatively affected since their real income is eroded by rising inflation while they pay higher prices for purchased goods. The remaining major poor group comprising nearly 10 per cent of the poor households in both rural and urban areas belongs to unemployed/not working category households and these households no doubt become extremely disadvantaged with rising inflation.

9.6 Concluding Remarks

Both theoretical reasoning and empirical evidence suggest that a well-developed financial system plays a positive growth-inducing role in development. For transiting towards an upper middle-income Bangladesh, a developmental approach to financial sector growth is necessary, while at the same time attending to prudent regulations. The country's progressive financial system must ensure a sound financial structure with varieties of financial products and services, including electronic trading system to trade derivatives in stock exchanges, a carefully outlined series of regulations that govern the market judiciously and allows market participants to contain systemic risks.

The key to financial sector development in Bangladesh is the reduction of fragmentation in financial markets, so that they gradually set more accurate (and therefore consistent) prices that reflect resource scarcity. The establishment of positive real interest rates is considered as a first step in this direction, providing a base from which the financial system can be developed to produce more refined prices. However, real returns may still experience significant dispersion unless issues such as information asymmetry and high transaction costs—a symptom of poor physical, technical, tax and regulatory infrastructure—are addressed.

The range of price dispersion decreases as the financial system develops. Development of mechanisms (like effective company and securities industry laws and regulations) to eliminate information asymmetry, creation of new institutions (like credit-rating agencies) to produce higher quality information, use of technology to improve the processing and dissemination of information (including prices), adoption of efficient business practices, and market organisation in the financial sector, together with deregulation, will facilitate further development over time. Markets for complex financial instruments, like derivatives, that require a sophisticated infrastructure base will emerge as the development process progresses.

Banks are the fulcrum of Bangladesh's financial system, but over time the relative importance of financial markets for instruments, like bonds, equity and commercial bills, will rise. Financial sector deregulation is an integral part of a wider set of economic reforms. Elimination of centralised controls over prices, resource distribution and trade flows and the freeing of nominal interest rates and exchange rates fundamentally alter the economic and financial risk exposures of financial institutions and companies, generating a demand for effective risk management products that cover liquidity and price risk. Only advanced financial systems have the infrastructure to provide them. These risk management products also reduce price dispersion by linking markets across space and time.

The development of the country's capital and equity markets will occur only as a part of a comprehensive endeavour that addresses all the factors that affect the profitability and attractiveness of private enterprises. The challenge is to ensure a delicate balance between a system that assures adequate protection of the investors and one that does not deter market growth.

However, for a successful journey, Bangladesh should not wait for the market to bring development. For example, since market outcomes of human capital are likely to be sub-optimal; a strong justification exists for state intervention. The need is to have 'smart' interventions. Instead of the top-down approach, the 'developmental state' approach is needed which uses 'market-following' policies, such as supporting the availability of skilled labour to attract enterprises towards greater productivity and value addition.

The developmental state paradigm holds that as an economy develops and its factor endowment becomes increasingly capital and skilled labour intensive, development demands a 'comparative advantage following' strategy of government support for structural transformation (Lin 2012). An economy's specific factor endowment determines its optimal industrial structure, and each industrial structure demands a particular level of tangible and intangible infrastructure, from transport to human capital.

Bangladesh needs to bring rapid structural transformation by emphasising human capital-focused strategies, skill development, and progressively higher value-added activities. The focus should be on upgrading the skills of the workforce and incentivising enterprises to invest in their own workers. A precondition for the above is to ensure strong public institutions so that the government can address 'government failure' before it can fix 'market failures'.

In the development process, one key issue for Bangladesh would be to introduce 'tripartism'—institutionalised cooperation of business, labour, and the government on economic issues—to help policymakers acquire the inputs for informed decision making and help build consensus. The strategy would be to advance in a planned way from labour-intensive industry to capital-intensive industry and finally to a knowledge-intensive economy that includes research, services, and high-end manufacturing.

In the Bangladesh context, investments in human capital can drive development for which the need is to ensure a combination of public investment, incentives for private investment, and close coordination with business and labour. This can rapidly upgrade skills and productivity; and ultimately the standard of living of the people.

However, rising inequality may pose a threat to Bangladesh's future development journey. The country's Gini coefficient of income and other measures of inequality are steadily creeping upwards. From a development perspective, the declining share of income going to wages might marginally benefit competitiveness, but this may face diminishing returns and threaten to undermine domestic demand. For ensuring equity, the need would be to recognise vulnerabilities, challenges, and opportunities; and build strong institutions for equitable development.

In this respect, a key challenge is to successfully change the culture and ethos of the education system, finding a balance between rigour and standards and innovation and creativity. The efforts towards skill training can only succeed if employers are able to fairly reward workers and can take advantage of the new skills. A close linking of education institutions to economic growth trends and skill requirements in the labour market is essential to keep training relevant.

Bangladesh, having successfully completed the journey from low income to lower middle income country, now faces the more perilous journey to upper middle income status and then to a high income country. While the first leg of the journey provides grounds for optimism, Bangladesh must become more innovative and productive in order to successfully complete the second and the third stages, a journey in which the financial sector needs to play a more supportive role to bring higher levels of prosperity.

References

Anglingkusumo, R. 2013. *Addressing the Complexity of Macroeconomic Management in Middle Income Countries.* Paper Presented During the Experts Meeting on the Common Challenges of Middle-Income Countries in Seoul, 13–15 May 2013.

Beck, T., B. Buyukkarabacak, F. Rioja, and N. Valev. 2012. Who Gets the Credit? And Does It Matter? Household vs. Firm Lending Across Countries. *B.E. Journal of Macroeconomics* 12: 1–46.

Bencivenga, V.R., and B.D. Smith. 1991. Financial Intermediation and Economic Growth. *Review of Economic Studies* 58: 195–209.

Bhatt, G.D. 1995. Enterprise Information Systems Integration and Business Process Improvement Initiative: An Empirical Study. *AMCIS 1995 Proceedings* 81. https://aisel.aisnet.org/amcis1995/81.

Coase, R. 1960. The Problem of Social Cost. *Journal of Law and Economics* 3: 1–44.

Foxley, A. 2009. *Recovery: The Global Financial Crisis and Middle Income Countries.* Washington, DC: Carnegie Endowment for International Peace.

Garcia, V.F., and L. Liu. 1999. Macroeconomic Determinants of Stock Market Development. *Journal of Applied Economics* 2 (1): 29–59.

Garuda, G. 2000. The Distributional Effects of IMF Programs: A Cross-Country Analysis. *World Development* 28: 1031–1051.

Gill, I., and H. Kharas. 2007. *An East Asian Renaissance: Ideas for Economic Growth.* Washington, DC: The World Bank.

Greenwood, J., and B. Jovanovic. 1990. Financial Development, Growth and the Distribution of Income. *Journal of Political Economy* 98: 1076–1107.

Hammond, L.D. 2012. *Creating a Comprehensive System for Evaluating and Supporting Effective Teaching.* Stanford, CA: Stanford Center for Opportunity Policy in Education.

Hossain, M., and M.K. Mujeri. 2020. Inflation and Household Welfare: Evidence from Bangladesh. In *Bangladesh's Macroeconomic Policy: Trends, Determinants and Impact*, ed. M. Hossain. Singapore: Palgrave Macmillan.

King, R.G., and R. Levine. 1993. Finance, Entrepreneurship and Growth. *Journal of Monetary Economics* 32: 1–30.

Levine, R. 1997. Financial Development and Economic Growth: Views and Agenda. *Journal of Economic Literature* 35: 688–726.

Lin, J. 2012. *New Structural Economics: A Framework for Rethinking Development and Policy.* Washington DC: World Bank. http://siteresources.worldbank.org/DEC/Resources/84797-1104785060319/598886-1104951889260/NSE-Book.pdf

Lucas, R.E., Jr. 1988. On the Mechanics of Economic Development. *Journal of Monetary Economics* 22: 3–42. North-Holland.

McKinnon, R. 1973. *Money and Capital in Economic Development.* Washington, DC: The Brookings Institution.

Modigliani, F., and M. Miller. 1958. The Cost of Capital, Corporation Finance and the Theory of Investment. *American Economic Review* 48: 261–297.

Mujeri, M.K. 2008. *Inflation and the Poor in Bangladesh*. Policy Paper 0801. Dhaka: Policy Analysis Unit, Bangladesh Bank.

Mujeri, M.K., and M.E. Islam. 2008. *Rationalizing Interest Rate Spread in the Banking Sector: Some Policy Suggestions*. Policy Paper No. PP 0804. Dhaka: Policy Analysis Unit, Bangladesh Bank.

Mujeri, M.K., M. Hossain, and T.T. Chowdhury. 2020. Labor Market Dynamics, Inflation and Wage Adjustments in Bangladesh. In *Bangladesh's Macroeconomic Policy: Trends, Determinants and Impact*, ed. M. Hossain. Singapore: Palgrave Macmillan.

Patrick, H.T. 1966. Financial Development and Economic Growth in Underdeveloped Countries. *Economic Development and Cultural Change* 14: 174–189.

Raihan, S., S.R. Osmani, and M.A.B. Khalily. 2017. The Macro Impact of Microfinance in Bangladesh: A CGE Analysis. *Economic Modelling* 62: 1–15.

Robinson, J. 1952. The Generalisation of the General Theory. In *The Rate of Interest and Other Essays*, 2nd ed. London: Macmillan.

Schumpeter, J. [1911] 1952. *Theorie der wirtschaftlichen Entwicklung*. Dunckerund Humblo, 5. Auflage Berlin.

Shah, N. 2016. *Honour and Violence: Gender, Power and Law in Southern Pakistan*. New York and Oxford: Berghahn.

Shaw, E.S. 1973. *Financial Deepening in Economic Development*. New York: Oxford University Press.

Singh, A. 1999. Review of *The Role of Government in East Asian Economic Development* by M.H. Aoki, K. Kim and M. Okuno-Fujiwara (eds.), Clarendon Press, Oxford, 1997. *Journal of Development Economics* 59: 565–572.

———. 2000. *Global Economic Trends and Social Development*. UNRISD Occasional Papers 9. Geneva: UNRISD.

Thiel, M. 2001. *Finance and Economic Growth – A Review of Theory and the Available Evidence*. Economic Paper No. 158. Directorate General for Economic and Financial Affairs, European Commission.

UN General Assembly. 2011. *Development Cooperation with Middle Income Countries*. New York: United Nations General Assembly, 66th Session. Report of the Secretary General.

Van Doorn, R., et al. 2010. *Can Middle Income Countries Deal with the Global Financial Crisis?* Washington, DC: World Bank.

World Bank. 2010. *World Development Report 2010: Development and Climate Change*. Washington, DC: World Bank.

Yartey, C.A. 2007. *The Institutional and Macroeconomic Determinants of Stock Market Development in Africa*. Washington, DC: International Monetary Fund.

CHAPTER 10

Future Perspectives

10.1 Achievements and Challenges

With 165 million people and the world's 35th largest economy in GDP purchasing power parity (PPP) terms, Bangladesh's recent growth performance is no doubt spectacular. The rapid progress achieved within the last fifty years is widely treated as a unique model of success on many counts.

In particular, the progress in social sectors has been noteworthy with several social indicators showing one of the fastest improvements in recent history. Bangladesh's social development has rested more on a premise where pro-active government initiatives supported by grassroots activism and social organisations have played key roles in bringing about innovative and low-cost solutions to social challenges. Another important achievement is Bangladesh's high degree of resilience to shocks and natural disasters that the people and the economy have achieved during the period. This resilience provides intrinsic economic and social strengths for quick recovery against any odds and allows the economy to grow in a sustainable manner.

In the case of economic transformation, the country's dominant agricultural economy has converted the nation from chronic dependence on food grain imports into an economy which is almost self-sufficient in food grains production. Life expectancy has nearly doubled, literacy rates have significantly multiplied, health conditions have improved, the country is on-track for most SDGs, and a sizeable middle class has emerged. Overall,

© The Author(s) 2020
M. K. Mujeri, N. Mujeri, *Bangladesh at Fifty*, Palgrave Studies in Economic History,
https://doi.org/10.1007/978-3-030-56791-0_10

the country has made tremendous progress in all aspects of economic and social development over a relatively short period despite insurmountable odds which has led many development observers to term Bangladesh's progress as a 'development puzzle'.

In recent years, the acceleration of structural reforms, move towards a rule-based policy framework and favourable global environment have provided a strong growth impetus to the domestic economy. Recent deregulation measures and efforts to improve the ease of doing business have also boosted foreign investment. However, quality job creation has been low, held back by educational deficiencies and the dominance of informal activities.

In a labour abundant economy like Bangladesh, employment is an important social concern and a useful yardstick to judge the nature of progress of economic activities. In Bangladesh, obviously open unemployment is not a meaningful measure of the level of employment as the poor cannot afford to remain unemployed. Essentially, the employment challenge needs to be interpreted in the context of movements in productivity and real wages. Available evidence shows that there has been a slow but steady improvement in average labour productivity including that in agriculture, where much of the 'surplus' labour exist. Over the years, the employment share of agriculture has fallen steadily and that of manufacturing and services have increased.

Improvements in productivity have led to increases in real wages across the entire economy including agriculture. The gender wage differential has narrowed down as well. This has also been true for geographical (e.g. district-wise) wage differential. In particular, wage increases in the *monga* affected districts (e.g. Kurigram) have played important roles in mitigating seasonal hunger and poverty. Overall, the country's economy has witnessed a significant tightening of the labour market.

With increasing labour productivity and rising real wages, poverty has also been declining sharply, in terms of both upper poverty (moderate poverty) and lower poverty lines (extreme poverty). Further, rapid rural transformation—leading to growth of CMSEs, nonfarm employment and remittance incomes—has led to significant increases in the incomes of the rural poor. Demographic dividends have also been creating positive impacts with sharp declines in total fertility rate and reduction in dependency ratios. The government's targeted programmes including safety nets for different disadvantaged groups and microfinance/microenterprise programmes of NGO-MFIs have led the poor's income to grow and contributed to their social and economic empowerment.

Bangladesh's progress in human development is also impressive; yet, the country has a long way to go in terms of educational quality, attainments in tertiary education and acquisition of productive skills in the context of the fourth industrial revolution. The country's aim is to expand the richness of human life, and focus on creating fair opportunities and choices for all people. The country's development agenda firmly holds that people must be given more freedom and opportunities through developing their abilities and giving them a chance to use them. Educating a girl would no doubt build her skills, but it will of little use to improve her welfare if she does not have access to quality jobs in the labour market. For the next decade, the key policy agenda for Bangladesh is to ensure a more rapid and comprehensive transition to more inclusive growth that systematically addresses:

(1) Problems of income inequality;
(2) Gaps in key social indicators including education, health and nutrition across different social groups; and
(3) Discriminatory institutions and norms including lack of empowerment of the disadvantaged groups.

Such a transition towards inclusive growth requires a shift in the country's development paradigm to bring changes in the growth pattern such that low-income households can have higher than average income growth; and the government can install effective redistribution policies favouring the poor and expand new avenues of economic and social opportunities for the poor and disadvantaged populations.

For closing social gaps, the focus has to be on provision of basic social services (e.g. education, health, and nutrition) to groups suffering from greatest disadvantages. Innovative and quality service delivery programmes and well-conceived modalities including early childhood interventions and integrated healthcare systems tailored to specific needs of disadvantaged groups deserve careful consideration. The 'leave no one behind' commitment under the 2030 Agenda for Sustainable Development aims to address critical interrelated concerns such as ending extreme poverty—in all its forms—and ensure that those who have been left behind (in either relative or absolute terms) can catch up with those who have experienced greater progress. The key to the implementation of Agenda 2030 is the prioritisation and fast-tracking of action for the furthest behind.

Successes in these efforts need frontal attack on social exclusion that reinforces existing inequalities of outcomes and opportunities. The priority would be to build multi-stakeholder coalition in support of crafting inequality-reducing ideologies and actions as well as for widening the policy space covering evidence-based agenda in support of the premise that reducing poverty and inequality would benefit all in Bangladesh society.

No doubt, economic growth is very critical to poverty reduction in Bangladesh. The poverty rate has declined substantially over the last fifty years, but the absolute number of people living in poverty still remains high. This calls for revisiting the growth–inequality–poverty nexus in Bangladesh to bring out new insights into their linkages.

Inequality matters for Bangladesh for a number of reasons. The concerns about inequality of both outcomes and opportunities are deeply embedded in the country's constitution and the value system that underpins the country's progress. Even though poverty reduction is the major concern for policy, the impact of growth on poverty is mediated through inequality. Bangladesh could have lifted more people out of poverty if the past growth could have been achieved without rising inequality. Further, inequality, in its different dimensions, may undermine the country's growth process itself through a number of channels and hence inequality is also a determinant of growth in Bangladesh.

With commitment to SDGs and strong desire to emerge as a high income country by 2041, Bangladesh's policy makers need to understand the role of inequality in the country's growth-poverty nexus and identify how and where inequality influences growth's transformation into poverty reduction. In the past, growth in per capita household income has been significantly lower than growth in per capita GDP in Bangladesh; and this partly reflects its relatively modest poverty reduction. Income inequality is another major mediating factor. Also the level of income (relative to the poverty line) is important; as this tends to increase the responsiveness of poverty reduction to both income and inequality changes.

Over the past years, nearly all of the success in poverty reduction of Bangladesh can be attributed to income growth rather than inequality changes. Different rounds of Household Income and Expenditure Survey (HIES) results show that changes in poverty since the 1990s are driven largely by changes in mean income rather than in inequality. These also show that the level of education, access to facilities and markets, and other institutional factors are significant drivers of both poverty and inequality.

Further, adopting appropriate inclusive growth strategies requires an understanding of idiosyncratic attributes as abilities to translate economic growth to poverty reduction and crafting effective polices crucially depend on inequality and income profiles in the country. There are several main drivers of inequality in Bangladesh such as increasing skill premiums in returns to human capital; falling labour income shares; and increasing spatial inequality especially between rural and urban areas. Overall, three key areas are important for inequality policies: efficient fiscal policy measures, interventions to address lagging regions, and more employment-friendly and inclusive growth. One must also take into account several broad conceptual issues including gender inequality, structural change and inequality, interactions between institutions and inequality, and redistribution and equity in fiscal policy.

A broad consensus seems to have emerged on the link between inequality and the quality of institutions. The negative impact of inequality on institutional quality is well established; ranging from political and institutional stability to property rights. At the same time, inequality also affects crime and violence and, through that, the investment climate. One must also realise that greater inequality may lead to a political backlash where pressure groups would plead for populist policy measures and the political process may favour short-term ad hoc policies for benefiting the poor but which, in the long term, could harm efficiency and growth.

Recent studies, moreover, provide convincing evidence on inequality–growth relationship. Often a key distinction is made between short- and long-term growth which corresponds to differences in issues between 'igniting' growth and 'sustaining' growth over the long term. Often countries can ignite growth in the short term, but may not be able to sustain it. Inequality is a key variable explaining long-term growth. Thus, rising inequality dents not only the poverty impact of growth, but it can also affect the sustainability of growth.

In addition, the following issues are likely to emerge as more pressing challenges in the coming decade:

(1) Rising capital flight and its implications;
(2) Global warming and environmental sustainability;

(3) Quality of primary and secondary education, and reforming higher education to meet development needs and creating remunerative jobs for the educated youth;
(4) Increasing inequality and ensuring social justice and long-term sustainability; and
(5) Managing challenges after graduation from LDC to a developing country.

One promising avenue for raising public resources for development by Bangladesh is through curbing illicit financial flows (capital flight) including various methods of tax evasion and avoidance. One popular and widely used mechanism for avoiding tax payments is through mispricing of trade (e.g. over-valuation of imports or under-valuation of exports). Through such manipulation, profits are transferred from one country to another, generally from countries with high- to countries with low-tax regimes. Estimates of such mispricing run into millions of dollars for Bangladesh. Similarly, multinational corporations (MNCs) often make price transactions between subsidiaries in different countries in such a manner that enables to divert profits to low-tax countries and thereby minimise their tax liabilities. In order to plug such loopholes, it is necessary to develop mechanisms for proper apportionment of costs between the domestic and foreign operations of firms operating within countries so that there is no loss of tax revenues, especially in the presence of treaties for avoidance of double taxation. Overall, the critical agenda for Bangladesh would be to make the existing pattern of public expenditure more effective and development oriented through reprioritising existing expenditure more towards development and making it more effective by reducing low priority and unproductive expenditures.

Poorly managed economic growth and the unsustainable patterns of production and consumption largely rely on unplanned exploitation of natural resources making a country increasingly vulnerable to adverse impacts of climate change and other unforeseen developments. In Bangladesh, ecological imbalances are mostly reflected in the degradation of key natural resources such as forests and freshwater, and in unsustainable use of energy.

Such imbalances pose formidable challenges to the sustainability of Bangladesh's development particularly in the long run. The production system, especially of the agriculture sector, and the livelihoods of a large majority of the people living especially in the rural and fragile areas are also adversely affected. Thus, measures are needed to protect the natural capital and address ecological imbalances. Along with expanding the 'new economy and green industries' through investments in renewable energy and in energy efficient technologies, addressing ecological imbalances of growth would also make substantial contribution to reducing poverty since the poor usually live in ecologically vulnerable areas and depend more on natural resources for their livelihood. A key to addressing the ecological imbalances will be the implementation of technological innovations to reduce the adverse impacts of production and consumption activities on the environment and unsustainable pressures on natural resources.

Another key area is to strengthen government initiatives to ensure a quality primary education and a transition into quality secondary education for all children, including the most marginalised groups. The priority is to improve access to education, quality of education and school governance. The schools must be considered as an entry point and the aim would be to ensure universal, quality, primary education for all children regardless of gender, ability, religion, location or their family's wealth. The policies should highlight training and supporting communities, schools and local authorities to identify, enrol and retain children at risk of exclusion from primary education as well as training and supporting teachers and supervisors so that they are able to provide an inclusive education that ensures all students can reach their potential.

Similarly, the policies must ensure that all children, especially girls, are able to attend and complete secondary school. The focus would be on supporting students to access technical and vocational training through their schools according to their needs and ability; providing life skills training to support children to reach their aspirations and become responsible citizens; and providing training for teachers and other school professionals to create a positive school environment, especially for girls.

The goal of higher education would be to produce adequate number of diploma graduates in professional, technical and technological disciplines to work as workforce and required number of bachelors as well as masters graduates in arts, science, technical and technological disciplines for academia and research who will ultimately lead, monitor and guide the huge workforce. The need is to review the current trends of higher education, both nationally and globally, and devise own higher education policies customised to our contexts, needs and goals.

Due to the existing economic, social and environmental disparities, the ambition of attaining inclusive growth in Bangladesh faces enormous challenges. At present, absence of and inadequate implementation of existing laws, corruption, and above all, various social stigma and negative mind-sets inhibit access to equal opportunities by all citizens of the country. The manifestations of this trend of disparity are observed not only in the case of consumption, income and asset ownership, but also in the areas of employment, human asset and regional development. Bangladesh needs to address rising inequality and ensure social justice and long-term sustainability in view of the compelling evidence that growing inequality is harmful for a country in many ways. The trend is harmful for the economy, for the environment, for the society, and for democracy as well.

In 2018, Bangladesh has achieved all the thresholds of three categories i.e. GNI (Gross National Income, $1272), HAI (Human Assets Index, 72.8) and EVI (Economic Vulnerability Index, 25) for graduating from the LDC. If Bangladesh can keep its momentum with this achievement for two consecutive triennial reviews by the UN Committee on Development Policy (CDP) of 2021 and 2024, it is expected that, Bangladesh would be graduated from LDC in 2024. After the graduation Bangladesh will get three more years (until 2027) to prepare itself for a smooth transition. In this context like any other LDC, Bangladesh will get nine years (2018–2027) to prepare it to face the new challenges of international trade and commerce, cooperation, technology and economy.

For being a member of LDC, Bangladesh currently enjoys several benefits, such as 12 per cent preferential margin on its export to the European Countries which provides a substantial price advantage over other countries; relaxation (one stage transformation) in provision of rules of origin in exporting commodities to EU countries; recipient of aid in absolute terms from the aid target of 0.15%–0.20% of donors' GNI; budget caps for LDCs' contribution to regular budget of UN, ILO and so on; technology transfer under article 66.2 of TRIPS (Trade Related Intellectual Property Rights.); assistance from LDC Fund constituted under UNFCC (United Nations Framework on Climate Change) to mitigate the effect of climate change; assistance under EIF (Enhance Integrated Framework) to strengthen the capacity of the Ministry of Commerce with a view to mainstreaming global trade with national development plan; enjoyment of transitional period up to 2033 regarding patent provisions especially for pharmaceutical sector under article 70.8 and 70.9 of TRIPS agreement; various types of scholarships and fellowships for its citizens; and travel incentives for the representatives participating in conference or summit organised by UN or its bodies.

Obviously, with the discontinuation of the above benefits, some loss will be incurred by Bangladesh after the graduation from the LDC. However, graduation is not the end of the development journey for Bangladesh. And, the journey is full of many challenges. One of the main challenges is to overcome the 'middle income trap'. To maintain steady growth, Bangladesh must manage the challenges properly. There is no alternative but to follow good and realistic policies, especially for removing the binding and strategic constraints and to promote inclusive development. Besides formulating the right policies, the need is to create efficient, corruption-free and accountable institutions, capable of facing the challenges of 2024 and beyond.

10.2 Market Systems Approach to Poverty Reduction

At present, around 20 million people live in extreme poverty. Bangladesh has committed itself to the SDGs under which the first goal is to end extreme poverty by 2030. The commitment to 'ending poverty in all of its forms everywhere' means that we need an explicit focus on multidimensional poverty. Extreme poverty reduction experiences in Bangladesh suggest that the right choice of entry points for extreme poverty reduction is critical. A proper choice of entry points is not only important for bringing changes in the lives of the extreme poor, but also for bringing spillover effects into other aspects of social relations.

Moreover, when reducing extreme poverty in a sustainable manner, it is not a case of either meeting practical needs or achieving strategic needs of the extreme poor. Rather, short-term gains including reduced insecurity can provide a platform for changing livelihood opportunities and bringing social changes over the longer term.

Hence, the approach to extreme poverty reduction at the household level can be more realistic if practical livelihood needs are met while also providing a material base which can contribute to achieving their strategic needs. Moreover, the right balance between interventions targeted at meeting practical and strategic needs, and the sequencing of these interventions, depends very much upon the operating contexts. For people living in extreme poverty an initial focus on practical needs, which acknowledges the daily imperatives of survival, is likely to be the most appropriate.

However, using an economic entry point alone is insufficient for ensuring strategic needs. In particular, the extreme poor need to expand their understanding of the choices which are available. Raising awareness through social development interventions is one way of doing this. Knowledge, however, is only a necessary, but not a sufficient condition of changing behaviours and social norms, especially over the short time period. Awareness-raising should be accompanied by other interventions which reduce economic and social risks associated with individuals making particular choices. This may mean different options in different contexts.

Successful approach to adopting such an approach needs ways to forge more dynamic and effective linkages between the interventions for the extremely poor and the market systems. Since most often a disconnect exists between the two in Bangladesh, market systems development means not only more competitive systems, but more inclusive and resilient systems as well.

There can be many ways of approaching the disconnect issue between extreme poverty interventions and market systems. The right choice has to depend on specific contexts. For example, the push/pull approach integrates the learning from graduation models, vulnerable livelihoods, behaviour and attitudinal change issues, business development services, market development, and inclusive market systems.

One major strength of the push/pull approach is its market-oriented pathway that seeks to strategically link efforts to support transitions out of poverty for the extreme poor and market development initiatives.[1] It uses both push strategies—which build capacities to engage in markets, and pull strategies—which expand the diversity and quality of accessible economic and social opportunities, to drive more beneficial and sustained inclusion of the extreme poor into market systems.

The core issue is to recognise that the extreme poor live in unique circumstances that often preclude them from being able to take advantage of economic opportunities created in evolving market systems. They have greater vulnerabilities to risk, limited or no resources to invest, fewer social relationships with people and a heavy reliance on marginal amounts of income from a diversity of sources. In addition, the extreme poor's voices are mostly unheard.

[1] For further elaboration of the approach, see Richards and Singh (2014). For a practical application of such a comprehensive approach, see PKSF (2017).

For sustained extreme poverty elimination, help must be provided to overcome these binding constraints. The approach must integrate a multitude of strategic efforts designed to incrementally build capacities and facilitate the emergence of accessible, quality opportunities in market systems that can reduce poverty for households. More than just one-off activities, a framework approach may be more useful to design, adopt, and implement actions that are rooted in pathways out of extreme poverty through markets. For example, push strategies can work best when they are market-oriented and demand-driven, designed with knowledge of local markets for goods and services that will play a central role for an extremely poor household and community's pathways out of poverty.

Pull strategies, on the other hand, will facilitate the development of market systems in a manner that expands the diversity and quality of opportunities accessible to the extreme poor to engage more successfully in economic transactions, as small producers, day labourers, cottage/micro business owners or as any other economic agents. The value chain development efforts are good ways to integrate these pull strategies provided the capacity-based constraints of the extreme poor are addressed and the opportunities are made inclusive to the extreme poor households.

Obviously, operationalising such integrated approaches is a big challenge; but Bangladesh needs to overcome these challenges to meet the SDGs. We need programmes which will explore the right types of push and pull strategies in specific local contexts in Bangladesh. Targeted research may be taken up to generate more information and analysis on adaptability and effectiveness of the approach on facilitating pathways out of extreme poverty. There are also best practices from other countries from which we can learn. These can provide useful insights to refine the approaches to extreme poverty alleviation in Bangladesh for the coming decade.

10.3 Employment Strategies for the Next Decade

Job creation is an immense challenge for Bangladesh. The inactivity rate (that is, the proportion of working age population that is not in the labour force) is high in Bangladesh: 41.8 per cent in total, which is 19.5 per cent for males and 63.7 per cent for females. In most countries, the male inactivity rate remains close to the low average of 7 per cent while, for the females, a high of above 50 per cent is reported only in North Africa and the Middle East.

The above shows that Bangladesh needs to create millions of new jobs over the next few years; and job creation will be the key factor to reduce poverty, improve people's lives, and reach the SDGs by 2030. The government's target is to create employment for more than 15 million people by 2023 as against 11 million new additions to the labour force during the period.

However, concerns exist relating to the outcome in the labour market which has not improved much for the large segment of the labour force. There has been slow growth of employment in the formal sector—where the 'good' jobs exist. The issue is of greater concern in the context of Bangladesh's potential of earning 'demographic dividends'—increase in the share of young adults in total population—which, if cannot be realised, may turn out to be a source of discontent rather than realising a potential.

One important challenge for Bangladesh is to deal with slow job creation in some sectors; along with meeting the shortage of skills in others. During the first ten years of the 2000s, the average GDP growth rate was about 6.2 per cent per year and, on average, 1.4 million new labourers were employed every year. On the other hand, yearly GDP growth rate rose to 6.6 per cent during 2010–2017, but employment creation declined to less than one million per year.

Creating more and better jobs requires two major economic transformations: moving workers from lower to higher productivity activities; and spatial transformation with urbanisation pulling villagers into secondary towns and cities. These shifts will have to be led by the private sector, the main engine of job growth in Bangladesh. For this to happen on a large enough scale, we need to look at what has worked best to create jobs, focusing on sectors that have the highest potential.

Agriculture still accounts for almost 41 per cent of total employment in Bangladesh. A central challenge for agriculture and the food system is to generate high value-added jobs across the value chain, especially for women and youth. For successful transition of Bangladesh, agriculture will have to play a major role as an engine for economic growth and employment. This will be through rising agricultural productivity and a shift to commercial crops which will be the dynamic engines for economic growth, job creation, higher incomes and rural purchasing power, wider markets for produce and the growth of downstream industries. The vast technology gap between the levels of agricultural productivity achieved by Bangladesh and the highest yields achieved globally represents an enormous untapped potential for stimulating economic growth and job creation. Bangladesh needs to focus strongly on an agriculture-led job creation strategy to generate productive jobs to eradicate poverty.

Excluding agriculture, there are more than 34 million own account and unpaid family workers in Bangladesh, representing 56 per cent of the workforce. Self-employed persons and the MSMEs that they establish have enormous potential for rapidly generating large numbers of new jobs and raising productivity to increase incomes, provided the right policy measures are in place to support them.

For example, China created 101 million jobs between 1985 and 1991, 70 per cent in 'township and village enterprises', of which nearly half were privately owned. A large proportion of MSMEs is established by women and employs predominately women in Bangladesh. An appropriate mix of policies focusing on access to technology, training, credit, marketing and distribution channels can substantially accelerate self-employment, particularly in the informal sector and rural areas, and among women.

Manufacturing, which has driven economic growth in the country, is changing with new technologies and shifting patterns of globalisation. While some industries remain feasible entry points for low-skill employment, technological innovations could cause substantial job losses in major sectors, such as the RMGs. We need to consider competitiveness, capabilities, and connectedness against shifting international trade patterns, market demands, and financial strengths of the Bangladesh economy for proper planning.

Beyond the traditional key sectors, we also need to harness the technological innovation and entrepreneurship that the digital age has unleashed. As start-ups and digital platforms mushroom across the world—from the Silicon Valley to Beijing's Zhongguancun—amazing examples can be found on how innovations are creating new and different jobs.

The service sector represents only 39 per cent of the employed labour force in Bangladesh compared with more than 67 per cent in many industrial nations. Contrary to common perception, services can be a major contributor to job growth even in countries at earlier stages of development such as Bangladesh. This sector is as amenable to stimulation by government policies as agriculture or manufacturing, and it also provides impetus for the growth of other sectors.

Supportive policies can enable trade, transport and other services to generate a sizeable share of all jobs. For example, services have produced more than half of all job growth in many Asian countries, including private day-care centres, nursery schools and computer training institutes, which are multiplying rapidly in many countries, but can be expanded much further. India, for example, has adopted an innovative, low-cost, self-employment strategy to expand availability of long-distance telecommunications services by setting up small private telephone and fax centres throughout the country. Informal private service enterprises in construction, commerce, food catering, repair and transport have vast growth potential. Rapid expansion of education, training and public health, especially rural health and education, can also serve as a conscious strategy for employment generation.

The government needs to consider new and innovative ideas for job creation, including labour law reforms. Several labour-intensive sectors, such as apparel, electronics, food processing, gems and jewellery, financial services and tourism may be targeted where employment will be encouraged. Furthermore, the policies should emphasise the role of exports in job creation and expedite the establishment of special economic zones (SEZs) and consider establishing coastal employment zones (CEZs), which need to be provided with relatively flexible regulatory schemes for land and labour.

The tariffs on entry-level labour-intensive products should be designed to grasp the natural comparative advantage of Bangladesh. The national labour-law reforms should allow workers to be employed on fixed-term contracts at wages and benefits similar to those of permanent workers, thereby providing formal employers the needed flexibility in responding to demand and technology shocks to compete with their foreign rivals.

Bangladesh faces job shortages in the aggregate, but not in every sector. There are some real imbalances across the economy, with some key sectors facing a shortage of skills and personnel. Such shortages are primarily in many social services and in highly skilled professions. The quality of these services, especially those available to low-income, remote and rural households, is shockingly low owing to the scarcity of quality doctors, nurses and teachers.

While robotisation may displace jobs in sectors facing adequate labour supply, it can be quite useful in filling the gap created by the shortage, if any, of skilled personnel. In this respect, Bangladesh may consider adopting a strategy based on the principle of filling up the skill gap. For example, specialised software can be used to diagnose diseases (and prescribing appropriate medications) or grading students' written work and providing feedback, thereby enabling large-scale online education.

So far, Bangladesh's information technology (IT) sector has not been able to create a large number of high-skilled jobs. In future, the support and maintenance services for AI, rather than IT, may be in demand, given that IT support itself is being robotised. For its future growth, the IT (and AI) sector needs to reinvent and position itself in a more innovative role, which will require considerable capacity building. Bangladesh should adopt a well-designed strategy in this respect which, among others, takes into consideration any job displacement threats from AI.

To expand gainful employment in the era of rising automation implies that not just IT but every sector, including manufacturing, trade, health care, and financial services, will have to prepare for massive retraining and skill building. As Internet penetration and data usage grow, there will be an explosion of digitally enabled ecosystems and growth in work opportunities across sectors such as retail, transport, financial services, and health care. Digital ecosystems are creating new opportunities for better quality work, and more remunerative work, for a segment of the workforce. For example, cab-hailing app-based companies such as Uber have a rapidly rising number of vehicles in operation which is estimated at 100,000 in Dhaka and Chattogram in 2018; and every week nearly 2500 drivers get registered with Uber. This means commensurate growth in work opportunities.

E-commerce players, including companies as well as a host of category specialists including furniture manufacturers, fashion retailers, and food delivery businesses, are creating new types of jobs in areas that have so far been less covered by the formal economy of Bangladesh. There are 8000 E-commerce pages in Facebook alone. In 2016, the government opened E-commerce sites for every district in the country. Since 2014, twenty companies have started as the nation's digital marketplace emerges. Unlike traditional marketing, digital marketing involves strategies designed to engage consumers and drive brand conversation on various digital platforms.

Digital financial services (DFS) in Bangladesh have been fuelled by the government's financial inclusion drive, and explosive growth of digital payments infrastructure which have contributed to create thousands of improved work opportunities. Banking correspondents (BCs) and agent banking networks acting as customer service points for basic banking services in underserved regions are good examples. Such growth translates into additional work and/or incremental income-earning opportunities for existing workers in other occupations. Similarly, microentrepreneurship is a rapidly spreading trend towards independent work which is being enabled by the government's small entrepreneur financing programmes.

The government needs to take policy actions to create an enabling environment. It needs to invest in education—from early childhood to adulthood; and build the human capital needed for a rapidly evolving global economy. It needs to build quality infrastructure to connect both domestically and globally. And it needs to set up the right ecosystem for private investments, especially for micro and small businesses and entrepreneurs.

No doubt there is a widening gap in technology between Bangladesh and developed and many other developing countries; but the gap in the technology of organisation is probably even greater. Creation of new types of systems and organisations can create markets and jobs in many ways. For example, the Dutch system of flower auction cooperatives is so successful that 68 per cent of the entire world's exports of cut flowers pass through markets in the Netherlands. The franchise system has led to a rapid proliferation of new businesses and new jobs in the West in such widely diverse fields as food services, home remodelling, dry cleaning and real estate.

Industrial estates, export processing zones, export promotion councils, export insurance, warehouse receipts, quality standards, and thousands of other organisational innovations have either been created or can be borrowed by Bangladesh to accelerate social progress. A comprehensive study of successful systems and institutions that can be transferred and adapted to local conditions in Bangladesh will document the enormous untapped potential for stimulating faster economic and job growth by inventing, imitating and further improving social systems.

Absorbing new technology, raising productivity, improving the quality and competitiveness of exports—all depend on the skills of the workforce. Training institutions and programmes in Bangladesh provide only a narrow range and low level of skill acquisition to a small portion of the labour force. The need is to raise skills to increase productivity by vastly expanding the lower tiers of the agricultural, craft, technical and vocational training systems at the local level to provide practical training in job-related skills. Imbalances between supply of and demand for skills exist at all levels. There is a need to make a careful assessment of present supply and demand for key skills. Bangladesh should compare the density of different types and levels of skill in countries at the next higher stage of development and evolve programmes to raise the quantity and quality of skills to at least that level.

At the present early stage of industrialisation in Bangladesh, there should be emphasis on primary and secondary education, especially in rural areas. This strategy increases the productivity of the workforce; helps promote income equality; raise consumer spending power; and provide broad support for high growth and pro-business policies. There should be particular emphasis on primary and secondary education, rural education, and education of young girls. The education system should help alleviate the problem of the educated unemployment through changing the type of knowledge and attitudes imparted. There should be reorientation of the educational curriculum at all levels, especially higher education, to impart the knowledge and attitudes needed to promote self-employment and entrepreneurship rather than salaried employment.

Conscious employment planning is an essential requirement for ensuring employment for all. The employment objectives should be high on the national agenda and a comprehensive plan is needed to identify the untapped growth potentials in agriculture, industry, exports and services. Bangladesh should adopt a combination of these strategies to generate 15 million new jobs within 2023, which will also have significant impact on the level of poverty. With a comprehensive approach, right mix of policies, good government, and a conducive international environment for trade, technology transfer and investment, Bangladesh should be able to meet the employment needs of its people within the next one decade.

In this respect, the experience of China is an example from which others can learn. In recent decades, China has succeeded in creating millions of employment opportunities and absorbing millions of new entrants into its labour market, while transforming its economy and society. China's path offers useful lessons. As it moves higher on the global value chain, China is also creating fresh opportunities for other developing countries. By looking closely at China's success stories, we can identify what the government can do to generate incomes and create jobs, by engaging the private sector and unleashing people's energy and creativity. What is important for Bangladesh is to unlock its own human and economic potential, through more and better jobs.

10.4 Future Transition: Medium-Term Policies

While Bangladesh has made a relatively rapid transition to lower middle income country status, even the most optimistic view would be to accept the proposition that the country would remain in this group for several years. As such, while exploring the policy options available to Bangladesh, it is important to take a relatively longer term view. One of the most important policy issues for the medium term probably is: how to raise the rate of aggregate growth in Bangladesh.

In the development literature, all growth models focus on capital as one of the central parameters in determining the rate of economic growth. An increase in the capital stock is needed to raise the growth of output. Therefore, GDP growth is generally higher in those countries which have relatively high investment-GDP ratios. An important pre-requisite for Bangladesh is therefore to increase the country's investment rate which is relatively low at present at around one-third of GDP.

Obviously, technology will be the key element for deriving maximum benefits from all development actions in future. To facilitate the process, Bangladesh should prepare itself to take full advantage from all global and regional efforts of technology facilitation and technology dissemination through regional and South–South cooperation mechanisms. Bangladesh needs to reassess its development path to identify the technologies that can reconcile economic growth with the country's social and environmental objectives without compromising with negative consequences. For effective technology transfer and dissemination, the priority for Bangladesh will be to build local capacity so that people and institutions can adopt and design technologies that can be diffused in society. The policy framework should also take into account informal technologies and transmission modalities including indigenous knowledge.

For Bangladesh, investment in infrastructure is especially important because infrastructure helps the producers to use modern technology which directly stimulates productive activities. Investment in education and training produces skilled and more productive labour force. Investment in agricultural research and extension services improves and facilitates the dissemination of the results of scientific research that increase production. Investment in human capital raises the value of parent time and cost of raising children. In turn, an increase in the cost of raising children decreases fertility and raises savings providing positive growth stimuli.

One critical concern for Bangladesh in the medium term is: how serious are the environmental impacts? For Bangladesh, two types of environmental issues are important. First, environmental degradation and water stress caused mostly by increasing population as well as rising growth and development. The second reflects the consequences of global warming, including an increase in climate-related disasters in the short-term, and changing levels of temperature, rainfall and sea level rise in the long term. No doubt, Bangladesh is one of the most vulnerable countries to climate change in the world and billions of dollars are needed to tackle its adverse effects. Obviously, this is by no means insignificant, but the country has to face many similar big challenges. It is likely that the problem of water stress will be made worse by climate change but it also needs to be recognised that increased water stress primarily comes from unsustainable withdrawals of water which need to be addressed as well. This is not to deny the gravity of the outcomes of climate change; rather to point out that the consequences of other unsustainable practices are equally urgent for Bangladesh in the medium term.

With the present level of per capita income, Bangladesh would have to grow by at least 8–9 per cent for more than a decade or so to graduate from the lower middle income category. Clearly, identifying what determines growth in Bangladesh is crucial to understanding how the country can become an upper middle income country. There would probably be a long list of factors which are important determinants of growth that cover diverse economic, social, institutional and other issues such as the quality of institutions and governance. We focus here on a few economic issues.

Among the economic factors, a key limitation on growth is the country's huge infrastructure deficit. Three major reasons can be seen behind this persistent deficit. First, due to resource constraint and compulsion to reduce fiscal deficits, public investments in infrastructure have suffered as it is much harder to reduce current expenditures than to reduce expenditure in sectors like infrastructure. Second, development partners now increasingly focus on social sector spending; and infrastructure has remained somewhat neglected in aid portfolios. Third, infrastructure is highly capital-intensive and, with low public revenues, even a relatively high allocation to infrastructure proves inadequate when seen against requirements.

For the medium term, there also seems to be a need for re-thinking about the adequacy and appropriateness of the current development strategies pursued by Bangladesh. For example, the explicit focus on economic growth and social sectors with little thinking on how economic growth and social sectors could be made more inclusive and pro-poor has produced significant biased outcomes in the past. On the other hand, investments in infrastructure, agriculture or other productive activities have been inadequate. Bangladesh would probably have to consider a broader approach to development with a right balance between investments in social sectors with strategies to promote inclusive growth of the real sector. This however is not simply a matter of re-formulating policies, but about a fundamental restructuring of the development paradigm adopted by the country.

As per capita income rises, it is typical that the country will experience structural changes in all respects. In particular, income growth would lead to a shift in the composition of production between agriculture, industry and services. For the government, two options are open when it faces a situation of structural change. First, it could continue to behave in a manner pre-occupying itself with core government functions and leaving it up to the private sector to determine the course of structural change. Second, the government can act as a pro-active driver of transition and structural change primarily keeping social benefits in view. For Bangladesh, the preference lies with the second option for obvious reasons.

One must also recognise that the country's future development constraints will increasingly be shaped by the new contexts of development where trade liberalisation brings both new challenges and new opportunities, technological revolution in ICT creates new dimensions of knowledge in development along with rapidly rising role of migration and remittances in domestic development. The challenge for Bangladesh will be to build and maintain a social compact under which the state will be committed to reduce the poor's risks through ensuring good governance at all levels, maintaining macroeconomic stability, providing basic services and institutions, and securing citizenship. Along with policies for enhancing inclusive growth and development, Bangladesh needs to boost intra-regional trade and investment flows along with more regional integration that benefits the country. The priorities will be to promote integrated markets, lower tariff and non-tariff barriers, ensure greater investments in physical infrastructure, create robust transportation networks and information platforms, and install better regulatory structures.

Bangladesh also needs to actively consider the issue of the size of the state. The state can either be 'too big' or 'too small' when it comes to assessing economic efficiency in performing public actions. For the purpose, two issues are important to consider: what social consensus exists regarding the size and functions of the state; and second, how sustainable are the present fiscal and institutional arrangements for achieving the stipulated functions. One also needs to take into account the scale and scope of government expenditure which changes over time and are affected by a wide variety of factors.

At present, Bangladesh has one of the lowest tax-to-GDP ratios in the world which is around 10 per cent. In raising tax revenues, one needs to consider two issues: (1) existence of a large informal sector; and (2) need to ascertain which factor primarily causes low tax revenue, is it low tax capacity or low tax effort. It is seen that tax efforts usually do not differ greatly between low- and high-income countries so that the low tax-to-GDP ratio in Bangladesh is more likely to have been caused by low tax capacity. If this is true, it would indicate that any dramatic increase in tax revenue is unlikely to happen within a short time.

Since remittance to the country is rising rapidly and it is emerging as a significant source of foreign exchange, its developmental role needs to be seen in the right perspective. Remittances are private financial flows and the primary objectives of these flows are to ensure economic security of the household members who are left behind by the migrant labourers. As such, remittances should be viewed and assessed, especially for the poor households, as a component of the strategy to smooth consumption over time, build up productive assets, and overcome the lack of opportunities of the remittance-receiving households. The flow of broader benefits of migration and remittances can only be realised if supportive conditions are created both at micro- and macro-levels.

10.5 Implementing the SDG Agenda

For Bangladesh, many of the SDGs present formidable challenges as these require a reversal of the past trends, such as reducing inequalities, or promoting sustainable patterns of consumption and production and meeting the climate change impacts. The key concern is to ensure that the country can identify the right direction and gather the required pace towards meeting the SDGs. Table 10.1 shows the progress of South Asian countries by individual goals. It can be seen that all South Asian countries are both at moderate or good level and on track in meeting SDG 1. For the SDGs for which the performance is moderate and shows some

Table 10.1 SDGs implementation: Bangladesh and South Asia

Levels and progress by goal

	Bhutan	*Sri Lanka*	*Nepal*	*Bangladesh*	*India*	*Pakistan*
1. No Poverty	Good, On track	Good, On track	Moderate, On track	Moderate, On track	Moderate, On track	Moderate, On track
2. Zero Hunger	Poor, improving	Poor, improving	Poor, improving	Moderately Poor, improving	Poor, improving	Poor, Improving
3. Good Health and Wellbeing	Poor, improving	Poor, improving	Poor, improving	Moderately Poor, Improving	Poor, improving	Poor, Stagnating
4. Quality Education	Moderate, maintaining	Poor, Improving	Insufficient data	Insufficient data	Insufficient data	Poor, Stagnating
5. Gender Equality	Poor, improving	Poor, Stagnating	Poor, improving	Moderately Poor, improving		Poor, Stagnating
6. Clean Water and Sanitation	Insufficient data	Good, On track	Insufficient data	Insufficient data	Poor, improving	Insufficient data
7. Affordable and Clean Energy	Insufficient data	Poor, Stagnating	Poor, Improving	Moderately Poor, improving		Poor, improving
8. Decent Work and Economic Growth	Insufficient data	Good, On track	Poor, improving	Poor, Stagnating	Moderate, On track	Poor, improving
9. Industry Innovation and Infrastructure	Insufficient data	Poor, improving	Poor, improving	Moderately Poor, improving	Poor, improving	Poor, improving
10. Reduced Inequalities	Insufficient data	Insufficient data	Insufficient data	Insufficient data	Insufficient data	Insufficient data

11. Sustainable Cities and Communities	Insufficient data	Poor, Stagnating	Poor, Stagnating	Poor, Stagnating	Poor, Stagnating	Poor, worsening
12. Responsible Consumption and Production	Insufficient data	Insufficient data	Insufficient data	Insufficient data	Insufficient data	Insufficient data
13. Climate Action	Good, Maintaining	Good, Maintaining	Moderate, stagnating	Poor, Stagnating	Poor, Stagnating	Moderate, stagnating
14. Life Below Water	Insufficient data	Poor, improving	Insufficient data	Poor, Stagnating	Poor, improving	Poor, Stagnating
IS life on Land	Poor, maintaining	Poor, improving	Poor, Stagnating	Very Poor, worsening	Poor, Stagnating	Poor, Worsening
16. Peace Justice and Strong Institutions	Insufficient data	Poor, Worsening	Poor, Stagnating	Poor, stagnating	Poor, Stagnating	Poor, Stagnating
17. Partnerships for Goals	Poor, maintaining	Poor, Worsening	Poor, improving	Poor, stagnating	Poor, Stagnating	Insufficient data

Source: SDG Index and Dashboards Report 2018

improvement, the current rate of progress needs to be accelerated to meet the goals. Bangladesh also shows stagnation or no progress for several SDGs.

Even with optimistic assessments for some indicators, the present status indicates that most of the 17 SDGs may be missed by Bangladesh at the current rate of progress. The key for Bangladesh is to address the constraints imposed by inequalities of income, power, access to services, and citizen's entitlements, which affect all SDGs in these countries. Despite the relatively low Gini coefficients of consumption inequality, Bangladesh suffers from high income and wealth inequalities and a complex and intersectional system of hierarchy and discrimination in which ethnic and gender discriminations are highly distinct. These significantly influence the opportunities for employment and income, affect access to housing, basic social services including health and education, and amenities like clean water and energy. Thus, reducing inequalities is a critical cross-cutting goal for Bangladesh; and right strategies of addressing this goal will significantly change the implementation outcomes of all SDGs towards achieving the 2030 Agenda.

No doubt, Bangladesh has made remarkable progress in terms of institutionalising the implementation mechanism and developing the integrated policy framework for the 2030 Agenda. For achieving Vision 2041 and emerging as a high income country by 2041, the country is currently preparing the Perspective Plan 2021–2041 and the 8th Five Year Plan (2021–2025) that aim to 'leave no one behind' (LNOB) and promote equitable and inclusive growth and development. Without quicker improvements among those who are lagging behind presently (e.g. the disadvantaged social groups and those living in the lagging regions), the existing disparities will not narrow down and these groups/regions will continue to be left behind; hence the policy priority is to focus on 'endeavour to reach the furthest behind first'.

Still, nearly 13 per cent of the population in Bangladesh live under extreme poverty and the top 10 per cent of the population hold around 38 per cent of total income; and several regions such as the north western, southern coastal, haor, and the CHT regions are lagging behind. There are also several marginalised and socioeconomically 'fallen behind' communities in the country including ethnic minority groups, tea garden workers, cleaners/sweepers, landless peasants, transgender community, commercial sex workers, environmental refugees, traditional fisher folk, traditional artisans, chronically ill poor people, rural extreme poor groups particularly older women, homeless and unemployed and their families, persons with physical and mental disabilities, and poor female-headed households.

The policy framework needs to focus on four pillars: (1) moderate income inequality; (2) reduce gaps in health, nutrition and education; (3) remove social and gender exclusion and discrimination; and (4) introduce explicit budgeting for the marginalised people and lagging behind regions. Further, action programmes should adopt an integrated strategy to develop a national database and strategic LNOB fund for the marginalised groups; develop and implement region- and community-specific strategic actions to combat marginalities; formulate target specific action plans to increase income levels and access to productive resources of the lagging behind communities; address limited access to education, health and nutrition services in the lagging regions and marginalised communities on a priority basis; increase socio-political participation of marginalised communities through adopting integrated approaches; and ensure special focus on lagging behind regions/communities in all national development plans and strategies.

These should be crafted within the broader national strategies that cover cross-cutting and national level issues, such as strengthening inclusive growth, ensuring financial inclusion, reducing income and social inequality, accessing quality education and health services, adopting appropriate macroeconomic policy, addressing pockets of lagging social groups/regions, and adopting initiatives at the local level for LNOB. Bangladesh should use both industrial and agricultural policies to facilitate employment-centred structural transformation. This requires greater public investment in infrastructure; adequate development finance to channel required credit to specific productive activities including MSMEs; and well-managed agricultural and industrial policies with focus on technology and productivity growth.

Bangladesh also needs to use effective governance capacity to transform the structure of employment, nurture mutual interdependence and symbiotic relationship between industry and agriculture through supporting expansion of agri-based industries and fostering demand and production linkages, generate remunerative employment and productive occupational opportunities, and social policies that improve health, nutrition, education, skill levels and well-being of the lagging population groups and regions. For practical reasons, the policies should put more emphasis on equality of opportunities relative to equality of outcomes. The policies should also strive to install fair processes and interventions to protect those who have fallen behind and emphasise on investments in equal opportunities to produce a more equitable society for the future.

Finally, LNOB has issues that are directly or indirectly related to the daily work of the local governments and local institutions. For implementing the LNOB agenda, one important element is to utilise the potential of local action to drive development and create appropriate legal and financial frameworks to support all local partners in playing their part in the achievement of the integrated and universal LNOB agenda. In this context, four areas may be highlighted: (1) Apply LNOB lens to the local strategies and policy/programme tools; (2) Leverage local institutions' ground-level data and information to help analyse progress in achieving LNOB; (3) Upgrade in-house capacity for integrated planning and policy-making at the grassroots level, and provide support to the local government to create a space for sharing mutual experiences on implementing the LNOB agenda; and (4) Raise awareness on LNOB among partners and the people.

Local government and other local institutions (e.g. NGO-MFIs) are the catalysts of change and are best placed to link the LNOB agenda with local communities in Bangladesh. Localising LNOB is a process to empower all local stakeholders especially the local government institutions (LGIs), aimed at making sustainable and inclusive development more responsive, and therefore, relevant to local needs and aspirations. The LNOB goals can be reached only if local actors fully participate, not only in the implementation, but also in agenda-setting and monitoring. Participation requires that all relevant actors are involved in the decision-making process, through consultative and participative mechanisms, at the local and national levels within the overall LNOB framework.

10.6 Concluding Remarks

It is true that Bangladesh has shown remarkable catching-up records in recent years through raising economic growth and fostering overall development. Presently, the main policy challenge for the country is to repeat and sustain the 'East Asian Miracle' performance during the coming decade. Further, for ensuring the best and most productive use of scarce resources, Bangladesh needs to take into account cross-sectoral synergies and emphasise thematic interventions covering economic, social, and environmental dimensions.

For the medium term, Bangladesh should also take appropriate measures to address four major concerns: First, design necessary domestic policies and institutions to ensure that the benefits of economic growth are more broadly and equitably shared within the society. Second, institutionalise deliberate efforts such that Bangladesh can derive greater benefits from the catching-up process. Third, put priority to move on technological—rather than factor-intensive mode of production—in order to close the development gaps. Fourth, provide more emphasis on policy coherence especially in agriculture.

It needs to be emphasised that as Bangladesh is currently undergoing transitions from largely an agriculture-based economy, it is more likely that investments in industry would create the most linkages. In this context, one important element would be to integrate the development corridors and special economic zones (SEZs) as components of growth poles to meet the needs of simultaneous and coordinated investments in many sectors focusing on, among others, infrastructure, regulation, capacity building and finance depending on perceived constraints to private investment and growth. The keys will be to find ways to develop specific areas of comparative advantage in industries, improve productivity, strengthen connections to and among markets and reap the benefits of the globalisation process.

Because huge infrastructure deficits remain and both the financial and implementation capacity is limited in the country, a critical issue is how best to use these scarce resources. For the purpose, Bangladesh needs to seriously explore a number of issues for example how best the infrastructure services be provided in a competitive manner; and what instruments (e.g. financial, regulatory, and participatory) can the government deploy to involve the private sector and other stakeholders most effectively and efficiently in the construction and maintenance of specific infrastructures.

Although Bangladesh faces a number of challenges towards becoming an upper middle income country, but one must also recognise that opportunities are plentiful as well, and Bangladesh is well positioned to take advantage of these opportunities. What is important for Bangladesh is to adopt a 'four I' approach covering income, infrastructure, inclusion, and institutions. The focus should also be on capacity building, knowledge management and networking along with support for improved development coordination.

References

PKSF. 2017. *Sustainable Transformation Out of Extreme Poverty: The PRIME Way*. Dhaka: Palli Karma-Sahayak Foundation.

Richards, M., and N. Singh. 2014. *Combining Push and Pull Strategies for Greater Scale and Poverty Outreach: Key Takeaways from the 2014 SEEP Annual Conference*. LEO Report No. 6, The SEEP Network for ACDI/VOC, U.S. Agency for International Development, Washington, DC.

Index[1]

A

Agricultural modernisation model, ix, 14, 95–101
Agricultural modernisation trajectory, 14, 96
Agriculture, 1, 35, 126, 238, 244, 300, 383, 453, 529, 536
Ambiguous, 117
Annual Development Programme (ADP), 67, 481
Asymmetric fiscal rules, 40, 43

B

Bad equilibrium, 9, 89n14
Biased technological change, 97
Bottleneck, 7, 86, 106, 272, 287, 297, 309, 449

C

Catch-up growth, 18, 20, 266
Central government, 38, 40, 43, 412, 470, 478, 480–484
Child mortality, 56, 174, 210, 215, 216, 220, 221, 224, 231, 298, 378, 406, 412
Circulars causation, 115
Civil society organization (CSO), 80, 470, 483
Climate change, 7, 8, 28, 67, 141, 146, 151, 152, 157, 243–248, 253n1, 290, 377–439, 514, 540, 542, 553, 555
Commodity boom, 72
Comparable economics, 36
Consumption cities, ix, 15, 102
Contraceptives, 56, 174, 199, 301
Corrective mechanisms, 85

[1] Note: Page numbers followed by 'n' refer to notes.

© The Author(s) 2020

M. K. Mujeri, N. Mujeri, *Bangladesh at Fifty*, Palgrave Studies in Economic History,
https://doi.org/10.1007/978-3-030-56791-0

Cost-of-basic-needs (CBN), 120, 432
Creative destruction, 91
Crisis-driven, 75–76
Crisis-driven economic reforms, 84, 85
Critical and complex development, 3
Crop failure, 3
Cumulative causation, 9

D
Delta, 1, 245, 387, 389
Democratic policy, 76
Democratic value, 76
Demographic dividend, 6, 54, 115, 149, 154, 175, 332, 352, 353, 355, 363, 536, 546
Dependency ratio, 6, 141, 297, 332, 352–354, 352n4, 536
Deprivation, 29, 38, 118, 129, 176, 177, 193, 217, 378, 379n3, 380, 407–409
Development challenges, 8, 9, 105, 317, 385, 474
Development economics, 9, 89n14, 90, 472
Development financial institution (DFI), 72
Development state, 88n13
Development strategy, 2, 29, 74, 141, 145, 178, 187, 249, 268, 341, 354, 358, 364, 468, 553
Deviant pattern, 53
Discrimination, 135, 144, 176, 214–219, 225, 228, 229, 232, 237, 317, 319, 322, 378, 379, 558, 559
Discriminatory, 1, 39, 42, 155, 156, 537
Disintegration, 2, 377
Dislocation, 2, 42
Disparity, 38–42, 100, 123, 131, 148, 174, 180, 184–185, 214–217, 226, 237, 254, 360, 401, 403, 418, 460, 496, 541, 542, 558
Diversified portfolio, 19
Domestic demand, 6, 101, 108, 284, 346, 509, 532
Domestic policies, 31, 58, 94, 478, 561
Donor community, 80, 451

E
Economic costs, 2, 280, 330, 382, 384
Economic disparities, 2, 39, 42
Economic growth, viii, 5, 6, 11, 13, 14, 16–19, 21, 23, 24, 29, 31, 35, 36, 46, 51–66, 68, 75, 76, 78, 80–84, 86–106, 108, 115–118, 121, 129, 130, 133, 136–137, 139, 142, 145, 149, 156, 159, 172, 175, 177, 187, 194, 231, 238, 243, 245, 251–253, 266, 268, 280, 282, 284, 285, 290, 297, 301, 309, 317, 334, 345, 346, 349, 352–354, 359, 364, 365, 369, 370, 380, 382, 403–404, 445, 447, 452, 474–477, 486, 493, 513, 516, 517, 520, 522, 532, 538–540, 546, 547, 552–554, 560, 561
Economic integration, 19, 20, 270, 512
Economic liberalisation, 93, 476
Economic parameters, 66
Economic policies, 19, 38–42, 57, 67, 72, 78, 88, 108, 156, 265, 383, 411, 446, 486
Economic reforms, 18, 54, 58, 67–70, 74, 76, 77, 280, 531
Economic system, 1, 74, 450

Economic transformation, viii, 10, 19, 535, 546
Empirical analysis, 116, 394
Empowerment, viii, 7, 8, 10, 26–28, 55, 69n2, 80, 134, 135, 172, 174, 175, 225, 228–238, 262, 339, 366, 402, 421, 422, 429, 436, 452, 471, 478, 480, 487, 537
Enterprises, 11, 19, 42, 49, 52, 67, 68, 71, 72, 74, 77, 86, 91, 93–95, 105–107, 143–145, 204, 250, 260–262, 264, 266, 267, 270, 272, 278, 314, 315, 318, 323, 337, 343, 346, 347, 394, 450, 451, 461, 464, 465, 471, 476, 494, 496, 507, 524, 531, 532, 547, 548
Equitable growth, 43, 152
Ethnicity barriers, 6
Exclusion, 30, 144, 176, 229, 317, 318, 379n1, 379n2, 380, 381, 409, 427, 428, 437, 500, 538, 541, 559
Executive Committee National Economic Council (ECNEC), 67
Exploitation, 2, 42, 86, 116, 335, 367, 540
Export, 6, 8, 19, 20, 26, 29, 35, 36, 38–41, 47, 50, 63, 64, 66, 69, 69n3, 75, 76n8, 78, 87, 89, 90, 93, 95, 102, 103, 266–270, 272, 279, 282, 284, 287, 342, 346, 348, 349, 403, 405, 464, 465, 509, 518, 540, 542, 548, 550, 551

F
Favourable initial state, 70, 75–76
Fertility, 23, 98, 141, 224, 298–301, 330, 371, 402, 552
Fertility behaviour, 55
First Five Year Plan, 41–43, 67, 72
Flood, 3, 72, 146, 151, 156, 246, 378, 386, 389, 392, 401, 409, 414, 419, 429, 501, 517
Foreign direct investment (FDI), 5, 19, 20, 68, 86, 265, 266
Foreign exchange, 5, 38–40, 69, 71, 74, 78, 364, 365, 377, 516, 555
Foreign exchange control, 38
Foreign trade, 53
Formal, 11, 28, 55, 66, 81n9, 147, 150, 153, 158, 187, 191, 201, 226, 230, 250, 262, 300, 304, 315–318, 327, 332, 334, 336, 337, 340–344, 350, 354, 356, 359, 360, 363, 396, 407, 416, 438, 446, 450, 451, 453, 454, 469, 486, 495, 499, 502, 503, 520, 528, 529, 546, 548, 549

G
Gangetic plain, 1
Gender parity, 4, 28, 134, 182, 233
Genocide, 2
Global economy, 19, 87, 153, 259, 270, 271, 550
Grassroots, viii, 7, 8, 10, 12, 13, 26, 27, 80, 86, 199, 233, 235, 395, 535, 560
Green Revolution technologies, 96
Grinding poverty, 3
Gross national product, 3
Gross regional product (GRP), 39
Growth acceleration, 36, 54, 59, 67, 86
Growth dynamics, ix, 15, 21–26, 29, 35, 54, 82–86, 85n12
Growth trajectory, 108, 363

H

Hidden urbanisation, 105, 397
Human capital, viii, 10, 26, 28, 29, 55, 76, 82, 83, 86, 88, 91, 95, 107, 144, 146, 148–151, 154–156, 158, 159, 175n2, 177, 194, 236, 238, 247, 276, 282, 283, 319, 335, 340, 352–354, 356, 356n5, 357, 361–363, 380, 397, 403, 419, 426, 428, 448, 531, 532, 539, 550, 552
Human capital availability, 54
Human development, 5, 7, 17, 26–28, 30, 35, 69n2, 108, 117–119, 141, 153, 155, 171, 174, 231, 280, 429, 514, 537
Human development index (HDI), 35, 119, 174, 255
Human resources, 18, 55, 135, 147, 158, 190, 222, 223, 230, 272, 369, 405, 505

I

Imports, 3, 18, 21, 29, 35, 38, 39, 41, 47, 50, 66, 69, 69n3, 71–75, 76n8, 77, 78, 268, 279, 287, 337, 365, 405, 509, 517, 518, 535, 540
Inclusion, 10, 30, 145, 155, 171–173, 176, 194, 231, 281, 291, 292, 301, 302, 344, 427, 428, 433, 446, 495–498, 497n1, 497n2, 500–502, 500n3, 515, 544, 549, 559, 561
Inclusiveness, 67, 108, 514
Income mediated, 5, 174
Induced innovation hypothesis, 97
Industrialisation, ix, 2, 15, 16, 18, 19, 21, 26, 40, 43, 65, 89–92, 102–105, 108, 247, 257, 266, 267, 334, 347, 393, 396, 397, 403, 420, 475, 551
Industrialisation-led urbanisation, 102
Inequality, 7, 16, 28, 29, 40, 43, 91, 98, 99, 107, 108, 115–159, 172, 176, 214, 218–220, 229, 230, 232, 236–238, 249, 250, 255, 280–282, 284, 285, 298, 319, 361, 377, 378, 379n1, 379n2, 380, 381, 407, 409, 417, 418, 424, 426n8, 435, 437, 445, 451, 467, 513, 514, 532, 537–540, 542, 555, 558, 559
Inequality-adjusted, 119
Infant mortality, 27, 141, 214–216, 298
Inflation, 5, 77, 78, 90, 149, 158, 287, 290, 434, 449, 507–509, 517, 518, 518n5, 522, 528–530
Informal, 11, 15, 26, 55, 61, 104, 140, 143, 148, 151, 201, 208, 222, 226, 259–261, 271, 284, 286, 289, 301, 312, 314–318, 324, 327, 328, 333, 336, 337, 339, 341–347, 355, 372, 407, 408, 410, 423, 425, 426, 430, 433, 446, 450, 451, 453, 454, 463, 486, 495, 501, 515, 528–530, 536, 547, 548, 552, 555
Innovation, 4–6, 56, 64, 90, 94, 95, 97, 98, 101, 105, 108, 143, 174, 227, 244, 248–260, 253n1, 269, 280, 346, 349, 351, 358, 359, 370, 373, 385, 394, 429, 430, 432, 437, 474, 493, 500, 502, 503, 506, 515, 532, 541, 547, 550
Invest, 93, 101, 107, 154, 252, 257, 267, 280, 342, 345, 348, 359, 362, 366, 403, 419, 422, 423, 453, 476, 484, 522, 532, 544, 550
Investment, 5, 35, 115, 175, 243, 318, 377, 448, 496, 536

J
Job creation, 30, 102, 105, 149–151, 159, 250, 260, 268, 333, 345, 346, 349, 370, 371, 397, 536, 545–548
Job opportunities, 66, 148, 149, 158, 232, 335, 336, 341, 372, 401
Job seeker, 258, 260, 336
Joint effort, 141
Joint-liability principles, 173
Jomtien Declaration, 177
Judicial decisions, 449
Juncture, 10, 106, 232
Jurisdiction, 396, 495, 521
Justice, 72, 118, 148, 158, 228, 235, 262, 279, 285, 414, 446, 448, 471, 540, 542
Juxtaposing, 436

K
Key partners, 422
Khas, 455
Knowledge, 52, 62, 63, 94, 103, 108, 172, 175n2, 177, 193, 228, 235–237, 244, 247, 251–255, 266, 267, 292, 318, 343–345, 348, 355–357, 356n5, 363, 377, 395–397, 403, 420, 421, 484, 498, 502, 544, 545, 551, 552, 554
Knowledge management, 395, 561
Kuznets curve, 90

L
Least developed country (LDC), 4, 7, 540, 542, 543
Liberalisation, 20, 25, 61, 64, 68, 69, 69n3, 72–77, 84, 85, 88, 271, 272, 286, 339, 349, 404, 462, 466, 475, 477, 504, 513, 515, 554
Liberation, vii, 2, 41, 42
Lower middle income country (LMIC), 4, 18, 109, 136, 152, 474, 532, 552
Low income countries, 5, 50, 73, 74, 218, 297, 353, 372, 398, 435
Low inflation, 38

M
Macro instability, 70, 73–75
Malnutrition, 2, 27, 77, 154, 195, 196, 212–214, 216, 221, 380, 412
Manifestations, 53, 187, 277, 542
Man-made calamity, vii, 3
Manufacturing, 6, 14–20, 24, 25, 47, 49, 53, 59–63, 65, 71, 92, 96, 102–104, 107, 140, 146, 147, 149, 151–153, 157, 159, 247, 250, 256n2, 259, 266, 268–270, 282, 287, 306, 308, 318, 319, 321, 322, 333, 334, 337, 347, 364, 367, 372, 397, 400, 405, 532, 536, 547, 549
Market failure, 89, 93, 107, 248, 476, 532
Maternal mortality, 4, 56, 130, 217–219
Messy urbanisation, 105
Micro Finance Institutions (MFIs), 7, 142, 495, 496, 498–500, 500n3
Micro-finance/microfinance, viii, 8, 10, 12, 13, 26, 27, 141–144, 173, 174, 235, 263, 301, 433, 498–500, 500n3, 502, 536
Microfinance revolution, 57
Micro, Small and Medium Enterprises (MSMEs), 6, 11, 55, 108, 145, 152, 244, 315, 316, 411, 475, 498, 526, 547, 559
Migrant worker, 6, 78, 276, 336, 364–369
Migration bonanza, 8

Millennium development goals (MDGs), 4, 171
Miracle, 7
Mobilise innovation, 95
Modernisation, 66, 95, 96, 98, 99, 101, 143, 238, 402
Money-metric poverty, 119, 135
Multidimensional, 88, 116–118, 124, 125, 127–129, 132, 134, 144, 148, 176, 247, 344, 378, 408, 543
Muslim conversion, 1

N

National economic council (NEC), 67
Natural disasters, vii, 3, 7, 18, 80, 141, 146–148, 151, 152, 157, 158, 245, 247, 386, 390, 401, 422, 424, 433, 438, 451, 466, 517, 535
Natural resources, 9, 63, 67, 102, 281, 282, 289, 378, 382–385, 454, 455, 540, 541
Neo-liberal development, 6–8
Non-agricultural economy, 57, 333
Non-tradable employment, 102
Nutritional norm, 119

O

Over time, 20, 23, 29, 41, 50, 65, 70n5, 95, 97, 117, 120, 129, 133, 135, 148, 156, 172, 173, 203, 210, 216–218, 220, 221, 237, 278, 282, 353, 397, 403, 425, 430, 458, 461, 464, 496, 531, 555
Overvalued, 38, 71

P

Palma ratio, 132, 133, 160–161
Paradox, 6, 325, 327
Periodisation, 70–81
Persian, 1
Pessimism, vii, 3, 10
Pessimistic assessments, 85
Planning Commission, 42, 67
Policies reform, viii, 12, 25, 81, 88, 146, 208, 281, 422, 448
Political democracy, 26
Political independence, 3
Political settlement, 7
Political turbulence, 70–73
Poverty decomposition analysis, 100
Poverty trap, 9, 50, 89n14
Privatisation, 72, 77, 279, 477
Production cities, ix, 15, 102–106
Public expenditure, 27, 38, 40, 46, 187–190, 205, 206, 289, 292, 362, 518, 540
Public policies, 6, 98, 135, 189, 233

Q

Quality-adjusted labour, 82, 83

R

Rapid urbanisation, 7, 28, 30, 94, 103, 137, 371, 397, 398, 402, 405, 419, 462
Rationalisation, 75, 77
Readymade garments (RMGs), ix, 6–8, 11, 15, 25, 55, 78, 104, 196, 233, 250, 269, 280, 303, 337, 372, 400, 402, 547
Refugees, 2, 387, 558
Relative poverty, 119
Remittances, viii, 5, 6, 10, 25, 26, 50, 78, 140, 144, 148, 151, 276, 335, 342, 364–366, 369, 497, 518, 536, 554, 555
Robust growth, 6
Rural, 2, 53, 115, 173, 244, 298, 381, 454, 496, 536

S

Secular trend, 53
Sequencing of chemicalisation and mechanisation, ix, 14, 95–101
Services sector, 6, 14, 15, 17, 19, 36, 49, 53, 54, 57, 59–66, 87, 96, 140, 152, 247, 259, 261, 269, 270, 304, 306, 313, 337, 347, 372
Settlement, 1, 55, 104, 148, 406, 408–410, 418–420, 423, 424, 455, 503, 521, 526
Shocks, 8, 73, 78, 87, 102, 103, 118, 143, 148, 149, 151, 154, 155, 159, 176, 271, 275, 285, 377, 378, 424, 425, 430, 433, 452, 453, 515, 525, 535, 548
Small and medium enterprises (SMEs), 92, 94, 143, 272, 347, 463, 496, 497n1, 498
Social development programme, 5, 12
Social indicators, 5, 19, 42–43, 77, 133, 134, 535, 537
Socioeconomics, viii, 9, 10, 28–30, 37, 43, 68, 75, 80, 101, 141, 154, 176, 186, 216, 227, 229, 231, 232, 237, 248, 249, 318, 325, 329, 371, 379, 394, 395, 400, 401, 407, 417, 420, 437, 449, 463, 485, 501, 520
Socioeconomic transformation, viii, 12
Southeast Asia, 5, 17–19, 21
Special economic zones (SEZs), 104, 105, 548, 561
Stable growth rate, 36
State intervention, 89, 107, 476, 531
Strategy of growth, 43
Structural changes, 21, 23, 51–66, 70, 92, 93, 140, 205, 333, 337, 370, 462, 463, 468, 476, 477, 526, 539, 554
Structural transformation, 8, 14–17, 24, 25, 30, 52, 57, 88, 89, 95, 107, 147, 149, 150, 152, 153, 157, 158, 247, 256, 397, 407, 531, 532, 559
Subsidies, 18, 19, 38, 70, 71, 74, 77, 95, 98, 181, 190, 256, 272, 292, 338, 343, 428
Support-led, 5, 174
Sustainable Development Goals (SDGs), 4, 8, 30, 105, 130, 171, 176, 243, 245, 286, 324, 424, 535, 538, 543, 545, 546, 555–560

T

Technological growth, 55
Technology transfer, 19, 56, 68, 94, 143, 252, 265, 282, 350, 394, 542, 551, 552
Theoretic approach, 117
Toiling masses, 116
Total factor productivity (TFP), 15, 29, 36, 54, 82–87, 84n11, 85n12, 91, 92
Trade, 14, 17–20, 25, 29, 35, 38 40, 49, 50, 60, 64, 68, 69, 73, 75, 76n8, 84, 86–88, 90, 92, 94, 96, 106, 108, 126, 140, 258, 265–272, 268n3, 279, 282, 286, 287, 289, 304, 306, 315, 316, 318, 321, 326, 339, 347, 349, 350, 365, 377, 403, 465, 466, 475–477, 485, 513, 530, 531, 540, 542, 547, 549, 551, 554
Trade fragmentation, 94
Trade policy, 38, 269
Traders, 1, 263, 415, 515, 524
Trajectory, 7, 8, 101
Transformative social change, 118

Transport system, 3, 413
Trap, vii, 4, 8–10, 28, 29, 31, 54, 89–95, 115, 149, 150, 159, 266, 278, 283, 425, 431, 475, 477, 543
Tripartism, 107, 532
Turning point, 53–58, 85, 90, 91
Two economy theory, 41

U
Unbalanced growth, 9
Upper middle income country (UMIC), 4, 245, 247, 479, 553, 561
Upper poverty, 122, 536
Upper poverty line, 120–122, 432
Urban, vii, 2, 53, 115, 137–139, 176, 247, 298, 379, 462, 496, 539
Urbanisation transition, 67

V
Vicious circle, 50, 89n14
Violence, 172, 218, 232–235, 365, 413–414, 438, 471, 472, 539
Voucher, 227
Vulnerability, 9, 16, 30, 108, 118, 143, 151, 154–155, 172, 228, 245, 247, 248, 285, 372, 377–439, 449, 474, 485, 512, 522, 525, 532, 544

W
Wages, 6, 16, 18, 81n9, 92, 94, 97, 98, 108, 140, 144, 147–151, 153, 157, 158, 250, 264, 271, 301, 302, 310, 312, 315, 317–322, 330, 333, 335, 336, 338, 342, 343, 354, 356, 361, 363, 367, 371, 372, 401, 404, 437, 475, 508, 513, 528–530, 532, 536, 548
War, vii, 1–4, 41–43, 67, 96, 172, 438, 449
Welfare-oriented programme, 55
Women-focused, 28

Z
Zero-tariffs, 6

The manufacturer's authorised representative in the EU is Springer Nature Customer Service Centre GmbH, Europaplatz 3, 69115 Heidelberg, Germany. If you have any concerns regarding our products, please contact ProductSafety@springernature.com

Printed and bound by CPI Group (UK) Ltd, Croydon, CR0 4YY
22/09/2026
02220984-0016